ENCYCLOPEDIA *of Impressionism*

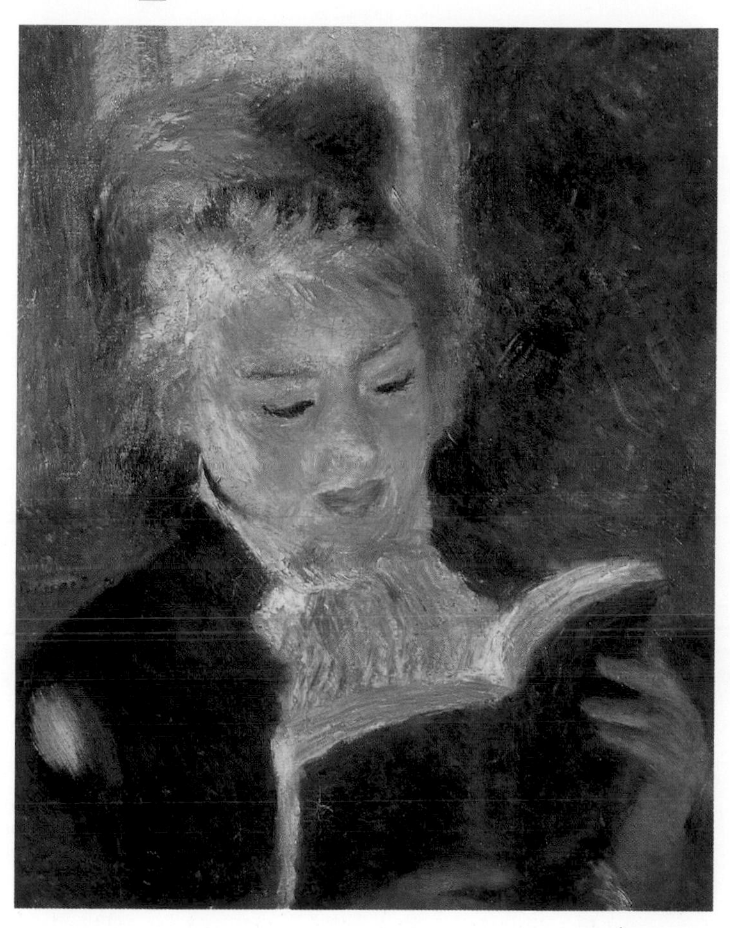

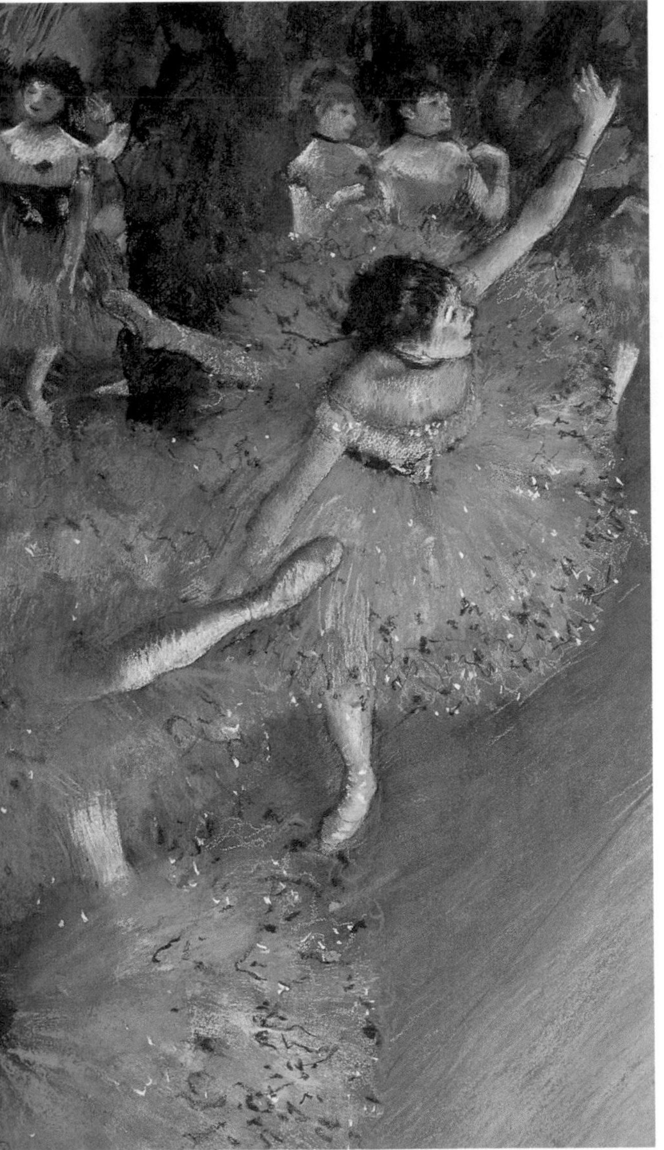

This page: Edgar Degas, *Green Dancers*; previous page: *Girl Reading*, Pierre-Auguste Renoir; opposite: *Camille Monet with a Child*, Claude Monet; overleaf: *The Walk to Argenteuil*, Claude Monet.

Dedication:

To my family,

Ghislaine, Max and Cordelia

First published in the USA by
Thunder Bay Press
5880 Oberlin Drive, Suite 400
San Diego, California 92121

THIS IS A CARLTON BOOK

This edition published by Carlton Books Limited 1997
20 St Anne's Court
Wardour Street
London
W1V 3AW

Library of Congress Cataloging-in-Publication Data available upon request.

Howard, Michael, 1954
The Encyclopedia of Impressionism,
ISBN: 1-57145-033-5 (hardcover)

Project Editor: *Sarah Larter*
Project Art Direction: *Paul Messam*
Design: *Jill Bennett*
Picture research: *Lorna Ainger*
Production: *Garry Lewis*

Printed in Dubai

ENCYCLOPEDIA *of* *Impressionism*

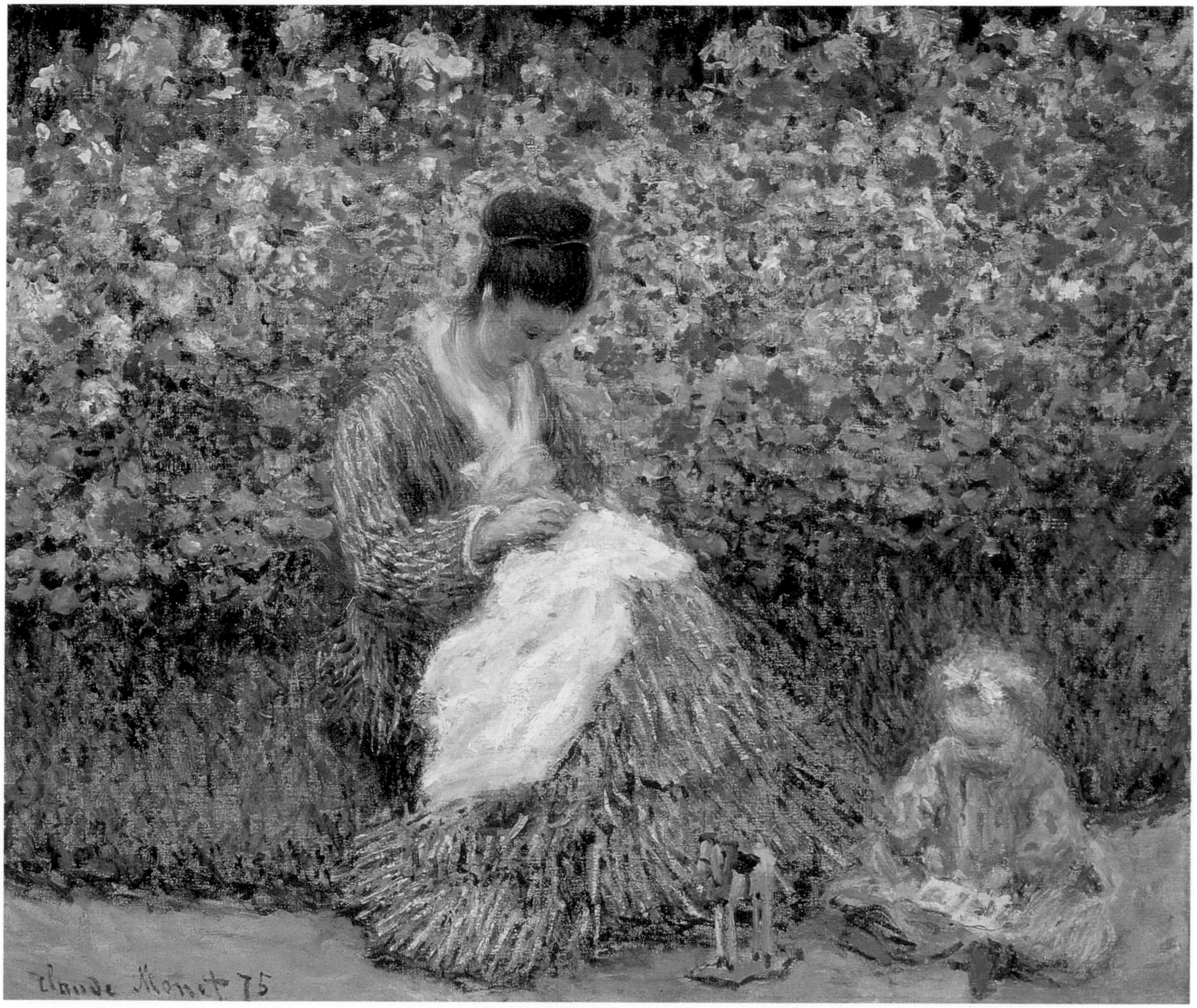

Michael Howard

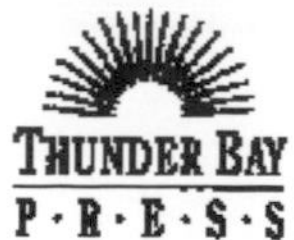

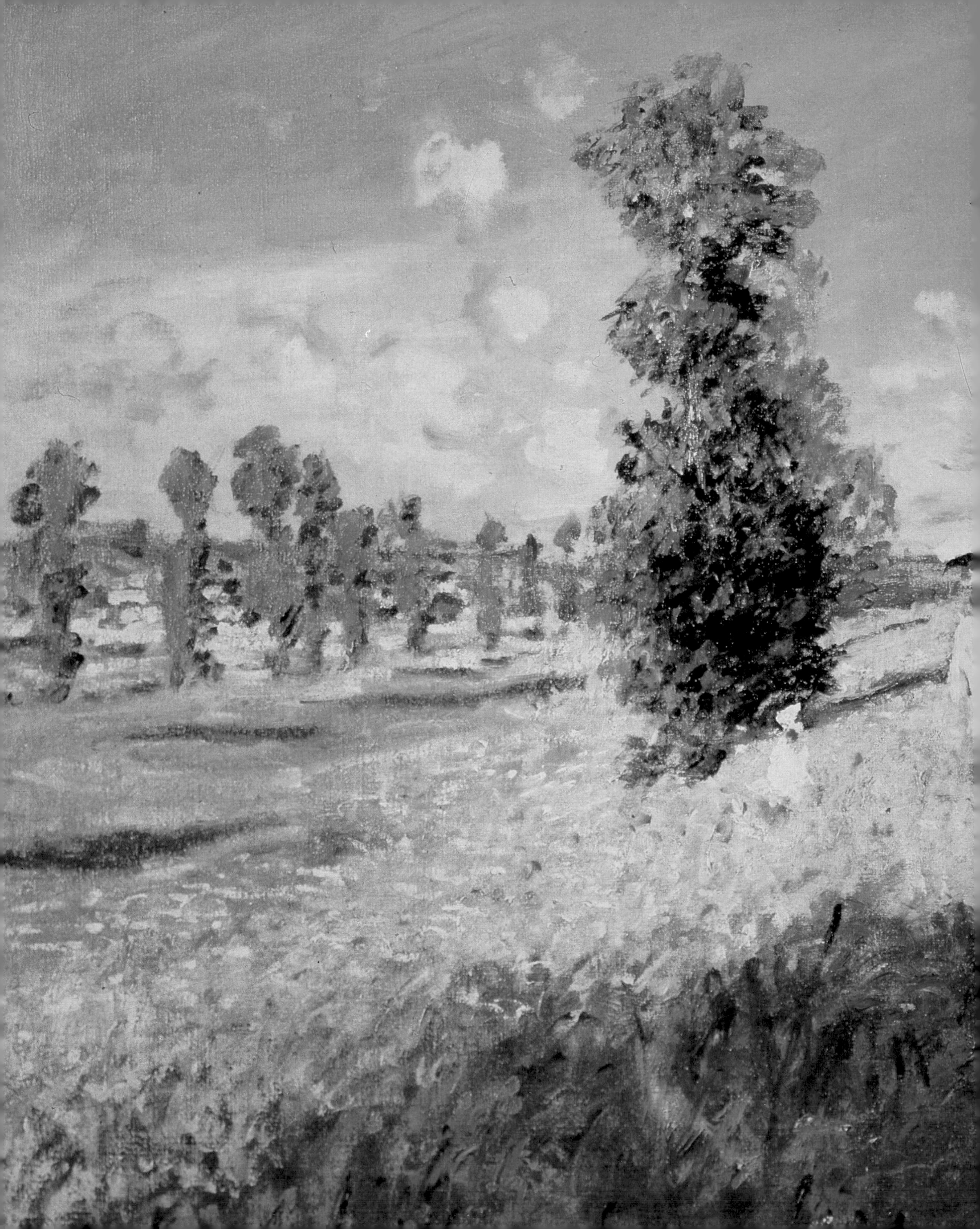

Contents

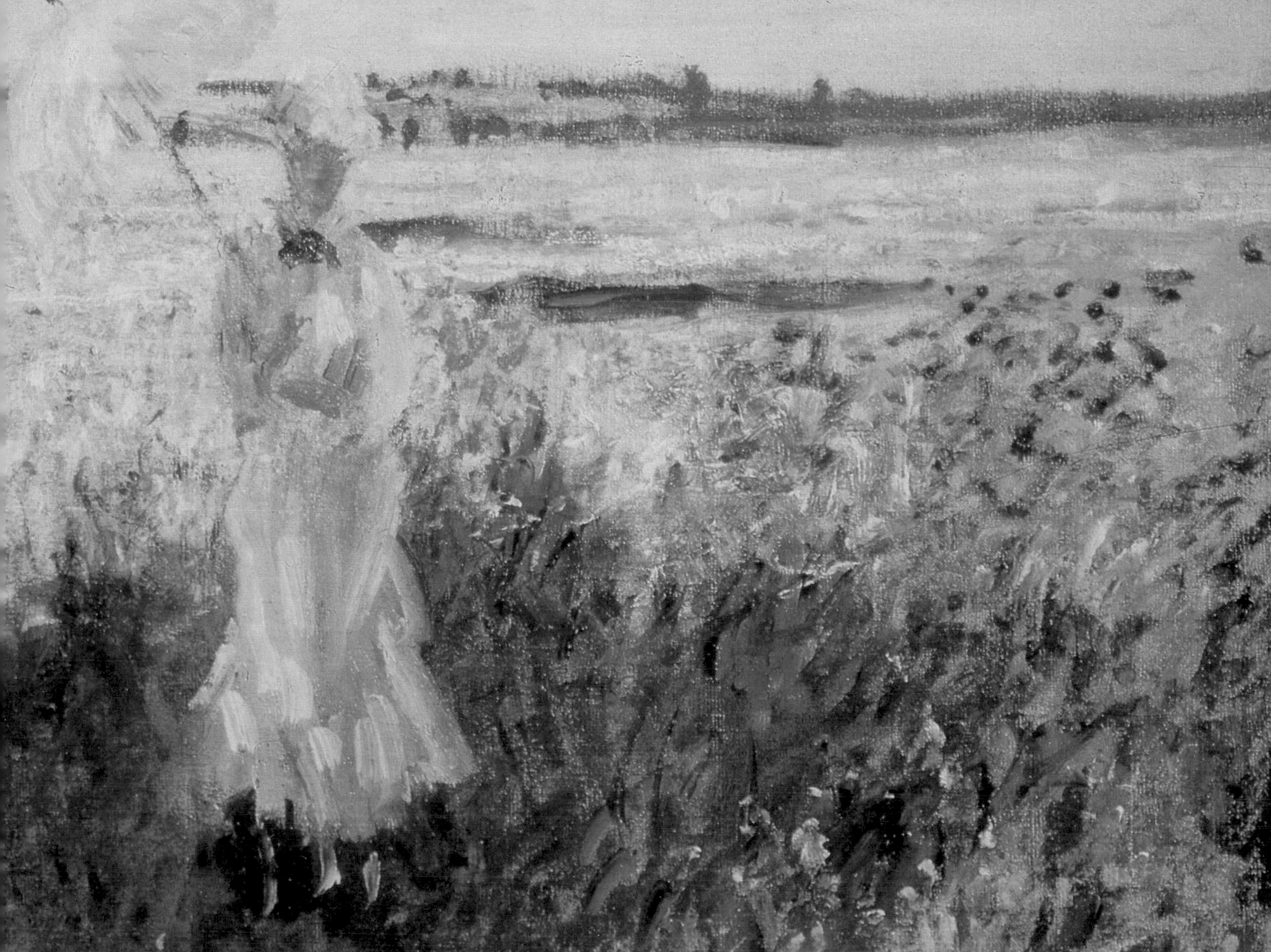

Introduction

The works reproduced in this book are among the best known and best loved paintings and sculptures in the world and our appetite for them is boundless. Impressionism is celebrated as a direct and intuitive response to the joys of living. Such is the apparent immediacy and naturalness of the Impressionist vision that the paintings of Monet, Manet, Degas, Renoir and their contemporaries seem to us to require little or no effort to understand and enjoy.

Impressionism seduces us with its sheer virtuosity, its vibrant color and dynamic brushwork and, not least, by the very nature of its subject matter. Impressionism abounds in depictions of the French landscape, seen in every aspect, in all kinds of weather and at all times of the day and night. People, as much as nature, were important to the Impressionists. They painted the inhabitants of the city and its suburbs, the villages and countryside, ordinary people going about their day-to-day activities. From ballet dancer to peasant, from the privileged world of the *beau monde* to the desperate world of the *demimonde*, each follows his or her daily round of work and leisure.

These familiar images have kept their power to enthrall, inviting us to take an imaginary journey to the Paris of the Second Empire and the Third Republic. They are kept before our eyes through a flood of advertising campaigns: images by Renoir, Degas and Monet are regularly used to sell us our dreams. Surely part of that recognition is due to the visual impact of Impressionist paintings and to our recognition of a shared image of the world. For all their chronological and geographical distance, these paintings appear to celebrate values that we still recognize and embrace today.

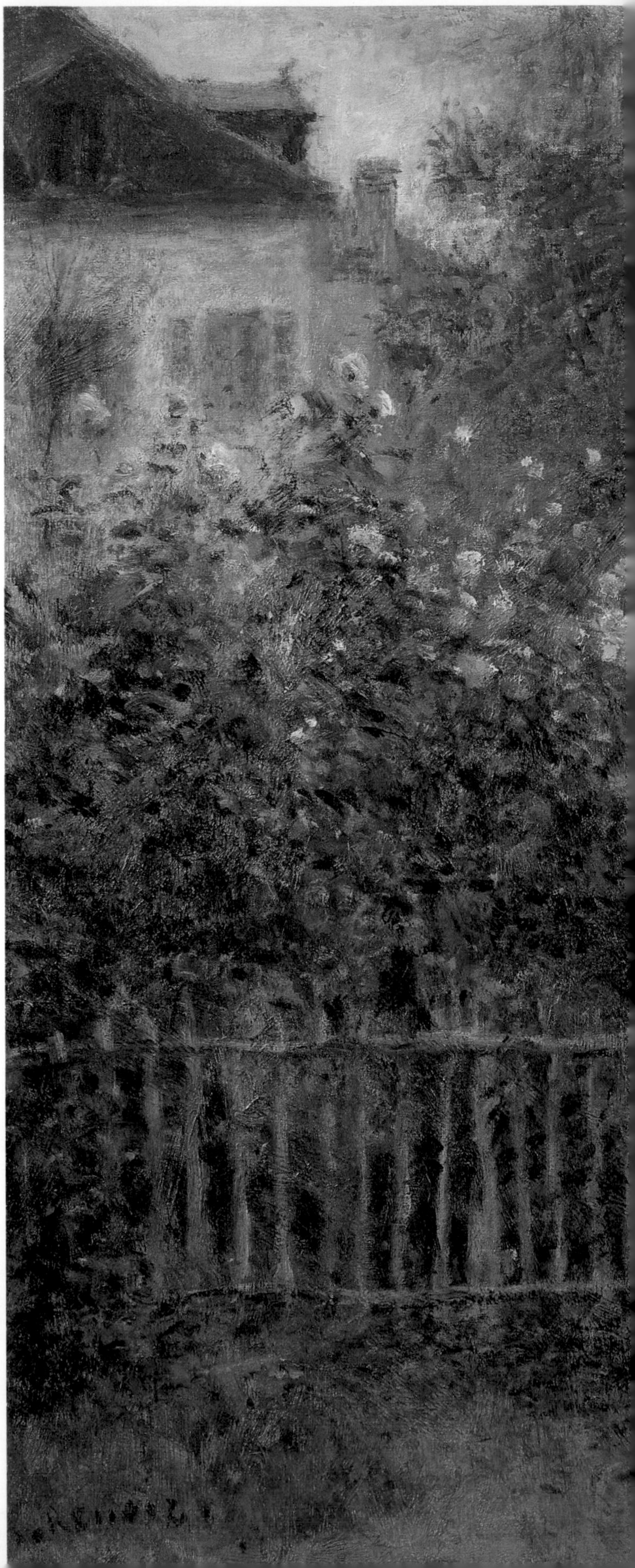

Pierre-Auguste Renoir,* Monet Painting in his Garden at Argenteuil, *1873. An intimate portrait of the artist, confirming the Impressionists' dedication to painting* en plein-air. *A parasol lies at the artist's feet to protect his eyes from the glare of the sun.

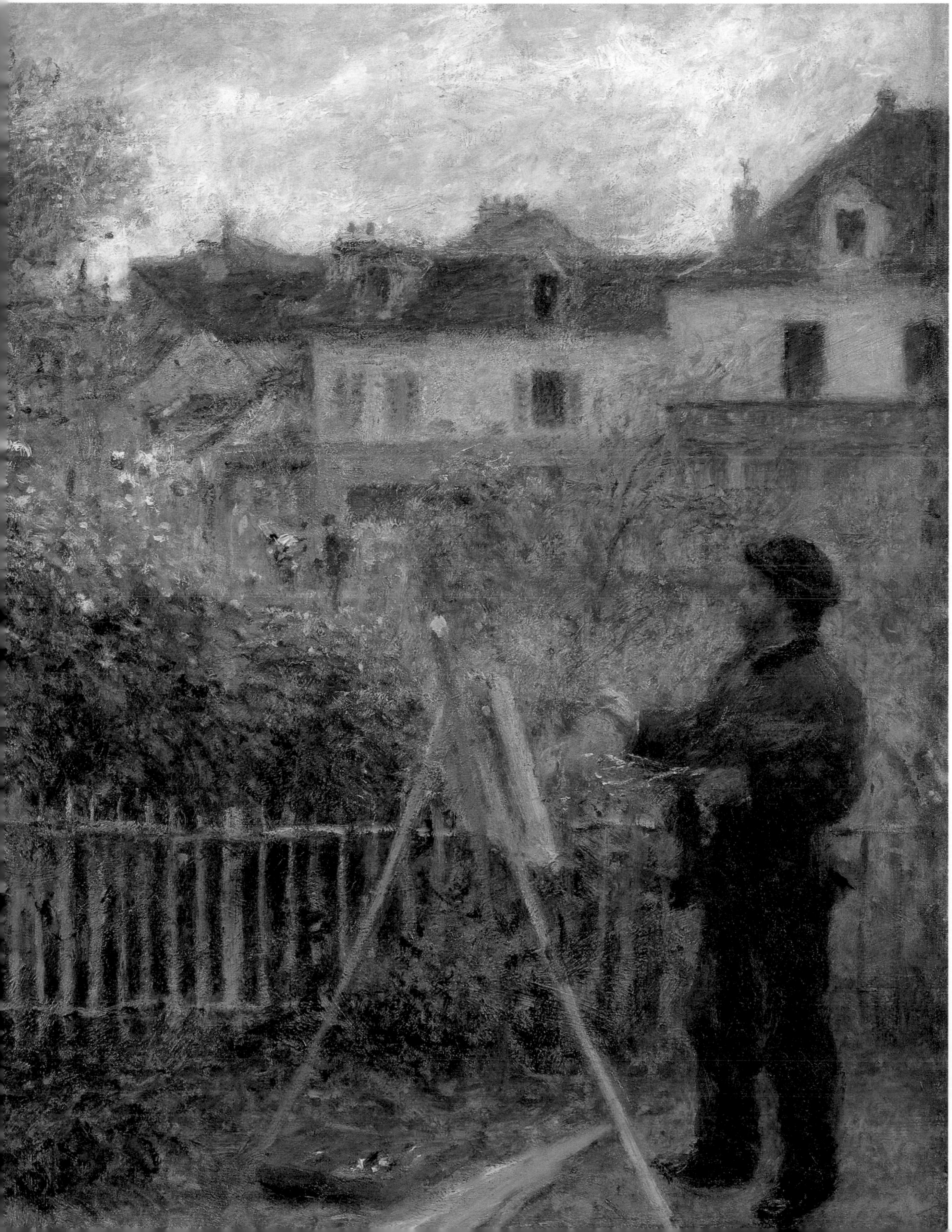

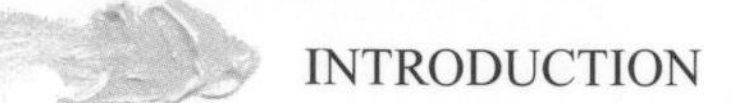

A Feast for the Senses

Gustave Moreau,* Salomé Carrying the Head of John the Baptist, *finished 1878, one of a number of paintings depicting the story of the biblical femme fatale.

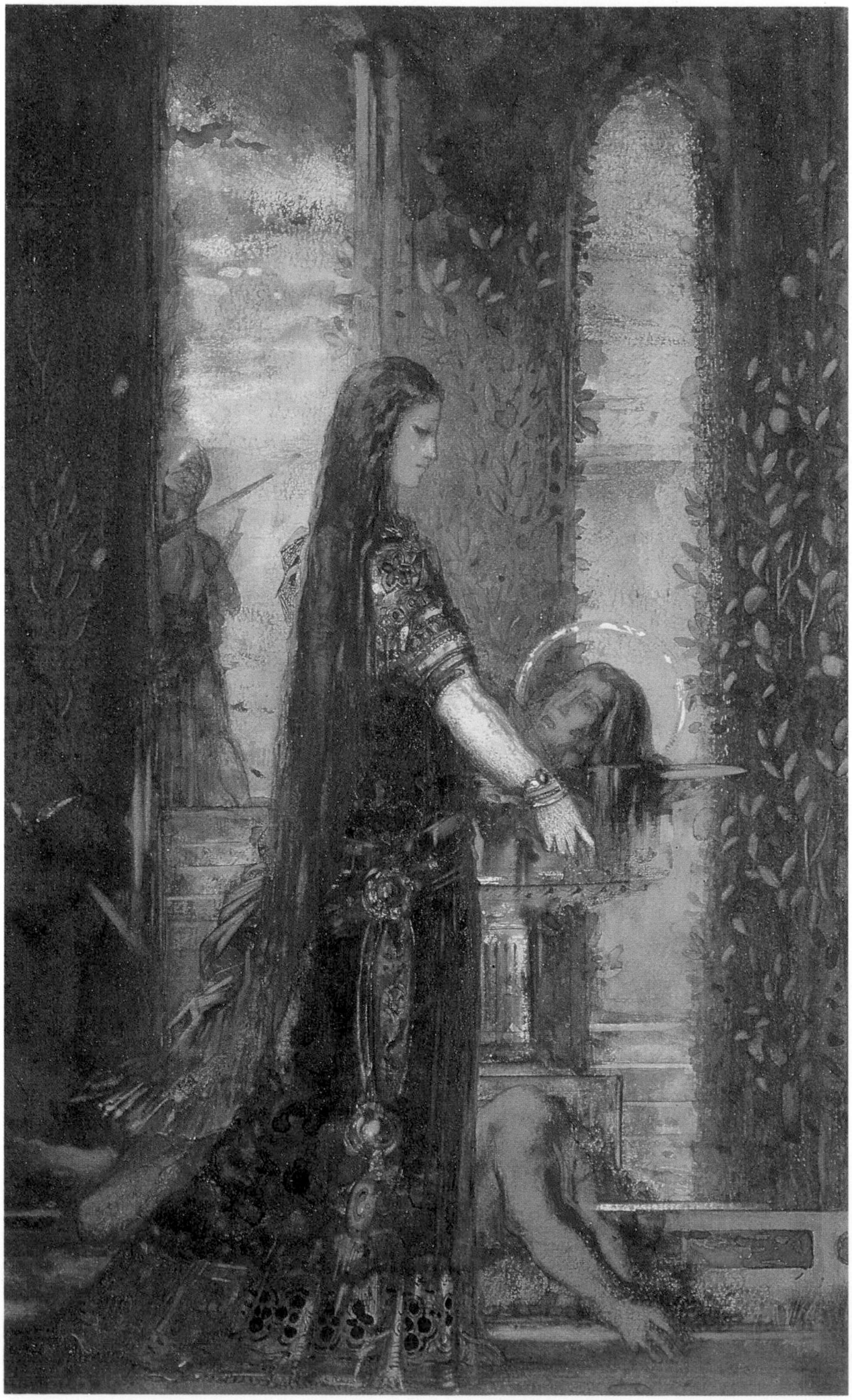

In 1878, Edouard Manet, often regarded as the "father of Impressionism," made a visit to the Fine Arts section of the Universal Exhibition being held in Paris. His response to the work of the many respected contemporary artists on show there was recorded by a friend:

> ***How can they laugh at the work of Degas, Monet and Pissarro, crack jokes about Berthe Morisot and Mary Cassatt, and double up with laughter in front of Caillebotte, Renoir, Gauguin and Cézanne, when they produce paintings like that! I do my best to find something I like. I simply can't. And there are things here that really annoy me. Look at Moreau. I've a great deal of sympathy for him, but he's going in the wrong direction ... [and] will have a deplorable influence upon our times. He favors a return to the incomprehensible whereas we want everything to be understood.***

Today, we take Manet's judgment very much for granted. The paintings of the Impressionists seem to us so fresh, spontaneous and natural in comparison with those of their contemporaries that it is astonishing to think that it has only been in the last fifty years or so that Impressionism has enjoyed its unassailable position as the most popular and instantly recognizable of all artistic styles.

Any gallery containing works by the Impressionists is alive with an appreciative hum, a murmur of recognition and a ready acceptance of the vision of the world they appear to offer. Their paintings sell for millions of dollars; countless books, exhibitions and television programs acclaim every aspect of their life and work, while thousands of greetings cards, prints and posters reproducing their works are given pride of place in our homes. Although it is now over a hundred and twenty years since the first Impressionist exhibition, the world recorded in their paintings seems not so very distant from our own.

An engaging art

One of the most obvious characteristics of Impressionism is its immediacy; these images are presented with an almost unparalleled directness, engaging the viewer in the most intimate and fleeting moments of everyday life. These paintings enter our consciousness as direct individual responses to the physical world, and offer a near-perfect remedy to the pressures of modern living.

However, these paintings are not the simple, direct and intuitive response to experience they may seem. Rather, as Degas observed, they are carefully planned and executed, "with all the deliberation it takes to perpetrate a crime." The artists adopted carefully chosen procedures to give the effect of spontaneity, an approach which gave them great difficulty and much anguish. Consequently, their images of contemporary life are not as simple and carefree as they may at first sight appear. Indeed, if their paintings were only superficial glosses on the more attractive aspects of a pleasure-filled life, then it is unlikely that they would remain so resonant in our consciousness.

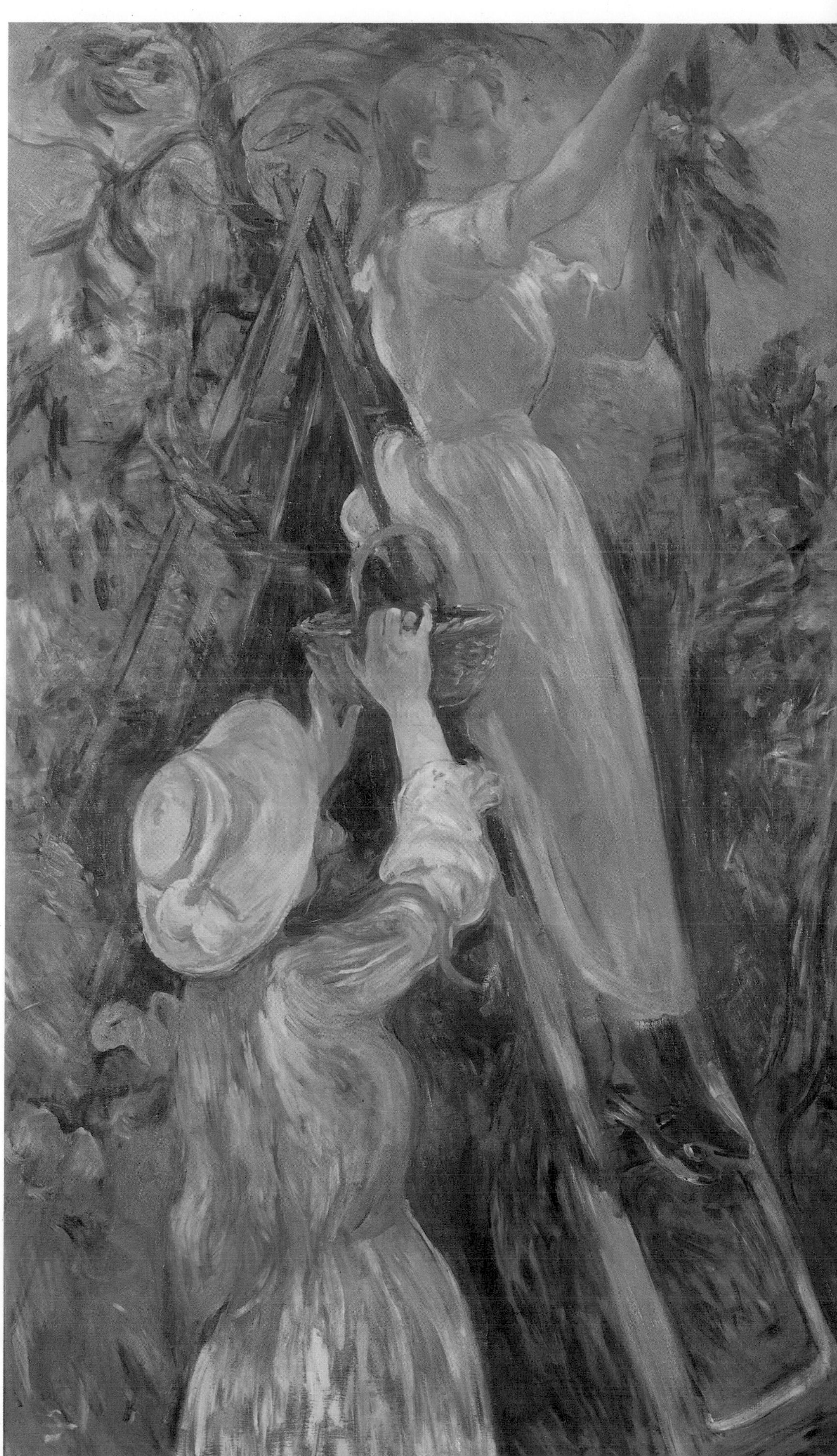

Berthe Morisot,* The Cherry Tree*, 1891.

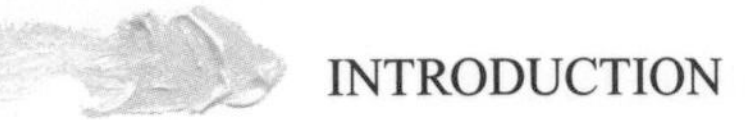

The Modern World in Formation

Surely one of the reasons why the work of the Impressionists is so popular today is because they took as their subject matter the modern world, a world in formation and one that, to judge from contemporary accounts, appeared problematic, confused, arbitrary and fragmented to the people who lived in it. Instead of hiding behind reassuring images that propagated an outmoded world view, writers such as Charles Baudelaire and Émile Zola attempted to articulate in their writings a creative response to what they recognized as the contemporary world. Like the painters they supported, they tried to give expression and thereby understanding to an age that to them was defined by a sense of unease and novelty. The Impressionist paintings created from this position of uncertainty are cogent images of this new world in formation, making coherent what appeared arbitrary and fragmented.

Instead of relying upon existing modes of representation, the Impressionists attempted to develop new ways of expressing their individual response to the world around them. Their works, for all their informality, suggest a sense of harmony and order, the uniqueness of their different styles being the result of their particular temperaments. As Manet's remark makes clear, this aspect of their work was not recognized by most of their contemporaries. It is one of the

Pierre-Auguste Renoir,* A Luncheon at Bougival, *now known as* Luncheon of the Boating Party, *1881.

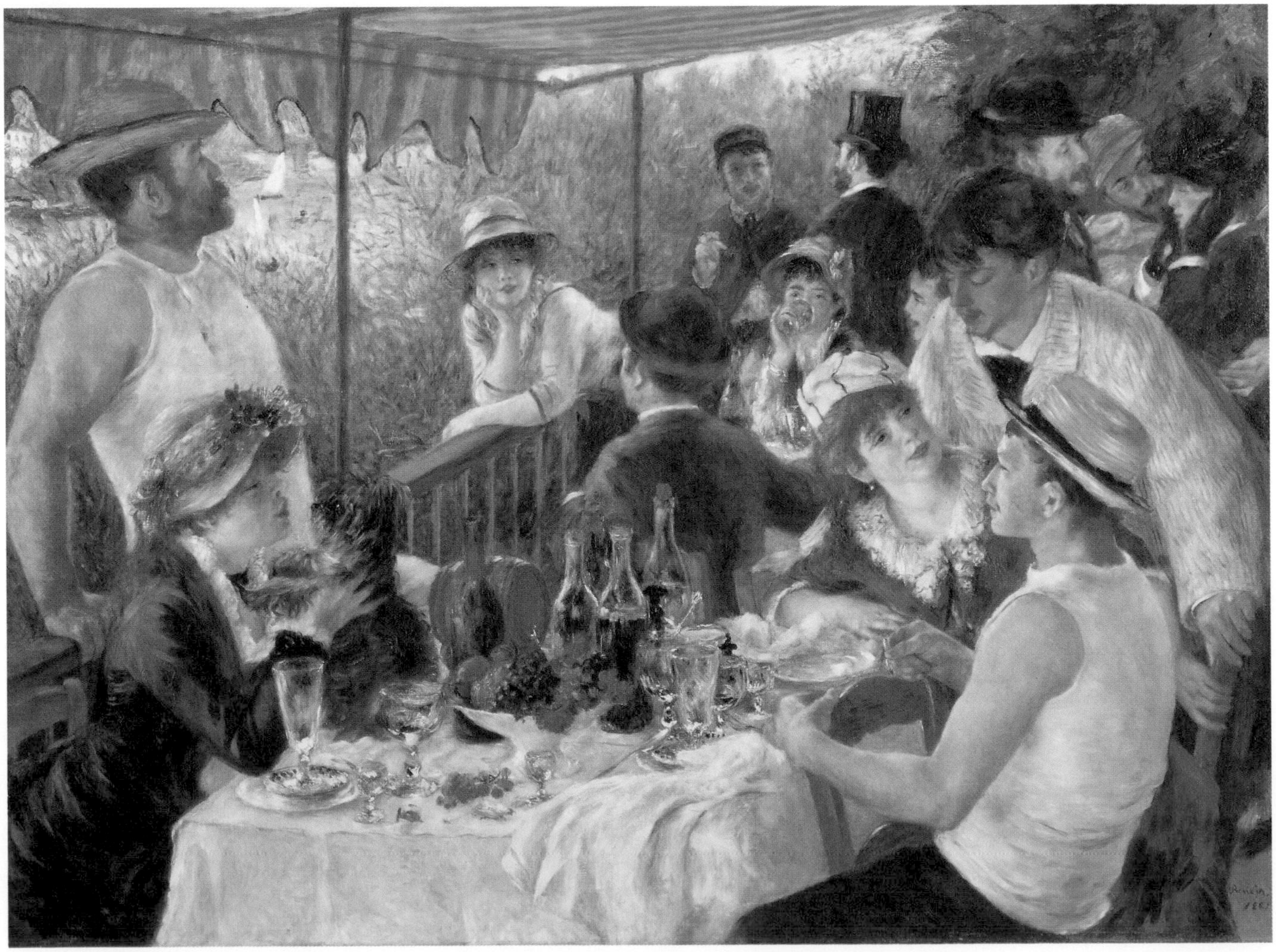

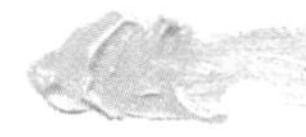

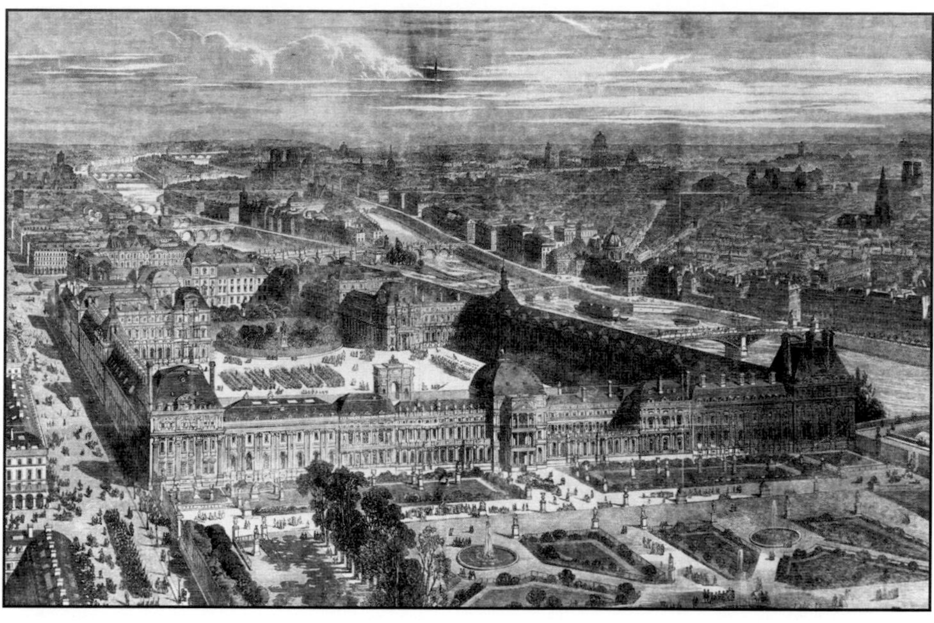

Anonymous wood engraving from **The Illustrated London News,** ***June 10, 1871. The slums that occupied this space were cleared to make way for Napoleon III's Tuileries Palace.***

ironies of history that these paintings were received with incomprehension and even derision by many of the same sort of people who today find them so appealing.

The shock of the new

It is only with a great effort of will that we are able to comprehend how original and shocking the now so-familiar work of these artists must have appeared to their contemporaries. From the beginning of the nineteenth century, painters had been struggling to break free from the confines of outworn traditions of representation condoned and sanctioned by the French Academy. There had been many attempts to create an art that would be better suited to interpreting the modern world. Despite many innovative attempts, the gallery-going public was not ready to accept direct challenges to accepted practices, a position supported and nurtured by the majority of critics and the establishment. The daring experiments of the romantics and realists of earlier generations had been greeted with cries of dismay and derision.

As the century progressed, the need to depict the ever-changing technological and sociological structures that characterized the age of capitalist expansion became ever more urgent. The 1830s saw the rapid development of public transport systems, the creation of the modern urban space and the growth of recognizably modern notions of habits of work and leisure with all the attendant anxieties that still occupy us today. The Impressionists and their writer friends unrepentantly gave themselves over to this emergent world, peopled by prostitutes and clerks, *modistes* and men about town who lived their lives in the new surroundings of a developing city, rich in public spaces and populated by men and women with the leisure time to enjoy them. The subjects they chose to paint were designed to symbolize the nature of this new society.

Nature vs. culture

The works of the Impressionists register not only the urban realities of modern life, but also the great shift in man's relationship with nature that took place during the nineteenth century. With the growth of the great urban centers, increased leisure time, and the availability of easy transport came the growth of popular travel. Many of the sites painted by the Impressionists were, in fact, places where people from the cities and towns went to relax and renew their contact with nature. Nature was marketed, managed, one could almost say packaged, to facilitate enjoyment and to restore the physical and spiritual health of the spectator/visitor. Villages and farms were equally subject to modern development, and the Impressionist landscapes of Monet, Pissarro and Cézanne mark a moment of transition from a non-industrial agriculture to one firmly rooted in the mechanical age. Impressionist landscapes enter into a complex relationship with such developments, sometimes making great play with the idea of including direct references to the "march of progress" and sometimes deliberately propagating the myth of nature as an unspoiled garden of Eden. No wonder then, that their paintings should seem to us at once so familiar and so distant. Impressionism is fully comprehensible and instantly recognizable.

Unlike the people of the Impressionists' own time, for whom these paintings were original and raw expressions of a contemporary consciousness, for us today they are shrouded in nostalgia. The passing years and the disturbing history of our own unsettled century have endowed these paintings with very different associations from those experienced by Impressionism's original audience: for them these works were shockingly new, for us they often suggest the innocence of a much simpler age.

A Modern Art

Impressionism might never have survived as a cohesive movement had it not been for the entrepreneurial drive of their most important dealer, Paul Durand-Ruel. Against Monet's better judgment, Durand-Ruel introduced their work to an American audience at a critical time, when the fortunes of the Impressionists were at a low ebb, and thereby secured their eventual commercial and artistic success.

This was consolidated during the twentieth century to such a degree that, in the 1980s, even relatively insignificant oil sketches by Renoir could reach astronomical sums at public auction. Although collectors and curators in the United States and Germany embraced Impressionism, the French were much slower in their appreciation, with the result that, in order to see the majority of Impressionist paintings, it is necessary to travel outside Impressionism's country of origin.

Such are just some of the fascinating aspects of Impressionist painting that will be covered in this book. In 1986 T. J. Clark, one of the most perceptive writers on the subject, wrote "We must unlearn our ease with Impressionism." Modern scholarship suggests that our very familiarity with Impressionism may sometimes blind us to a richer, more dynamic understanding of the qualities it possesses.

Impressionism has often been highlighted as the moment when painting becomes distinctively "modern." It appears to speak about our concerns more than previous art movements and allows us to ask some of the most basic and complex questions about the nature of art in our modern society. Why should these paintings, produced over a hundred years ago, still be relevant to us today and appear to say more, perhaps, about the way we experience the world than a good deal of more recent art?

Well before Impresssionism was defined as a "movement," Camille Corot had talked about the importance of Impression as a means of retaining the immediacy of the initial encounter with a visual experience on canvas as directly as possible. It was Monet's attempt to follow such advice in a sketch that he subsequently entitled *Impression, Sunrise* that was responsible to some degree for the group's name. It was only accepted by the group after much debate and with less than complete enthusiasm. Their original title, *Société Anonyme des peintres, sculpteurs et graveurs*, or as we would say, the limited company of painters, engravers and sculptors, indicates far better the concerns that united them. It was, in essence, a business operation – an open circle of artists interested in exhibiting independently of the Salon and in selling their own personally motivated works directly to the public without the intervention of either jury or dealer.

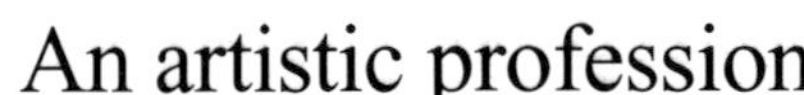

An artistic profession

Although this prosaic explanation of Impressionism ignores stylistic factors, it serves to remind us that these painters were, for the most part, professionals trying to earn a living in what was a very precarious profession: the production of luxury objects. Painters like Manet, Morisot,

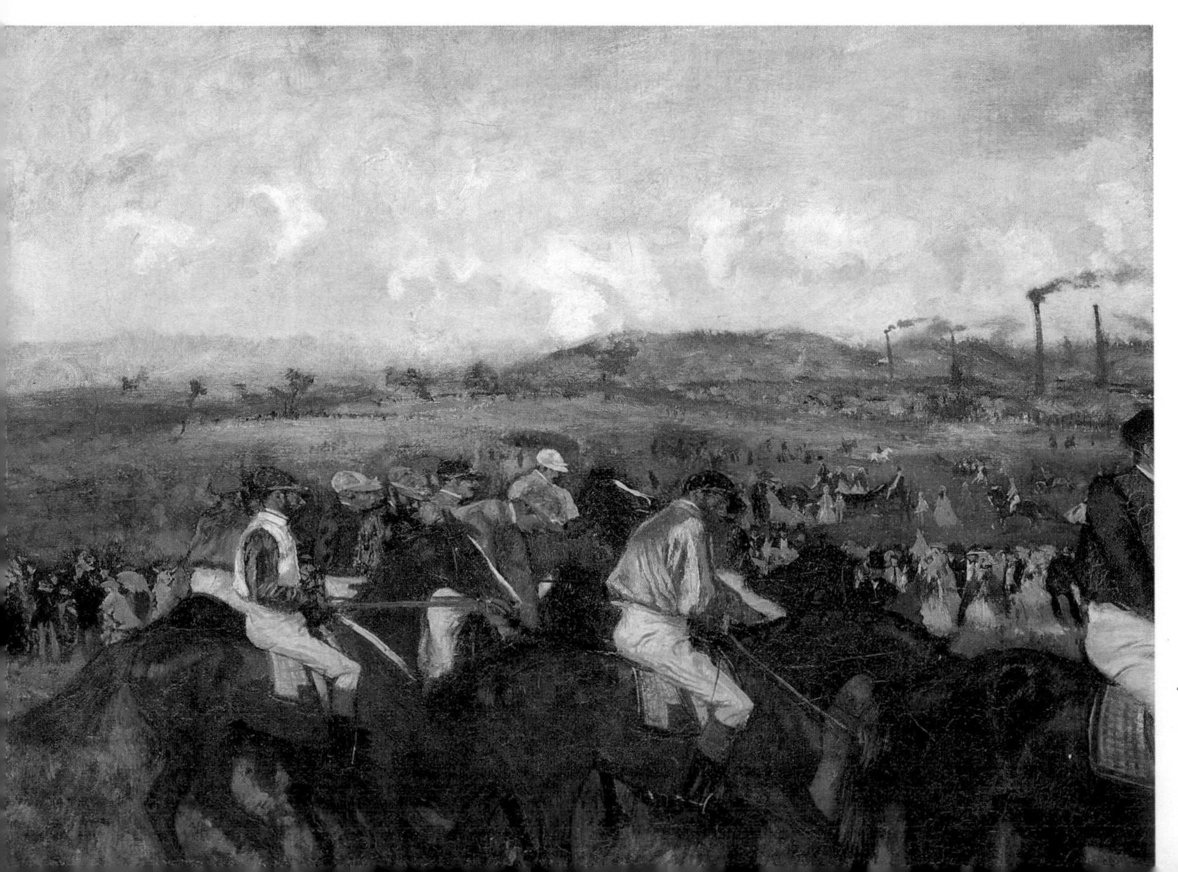

Edgar Degas,* Course de Gentlemen, *1862, reworked later, c. 1882. Amateur jockeys prepare themselves for the race. In the background, factory chimneys belch forth their smoke.

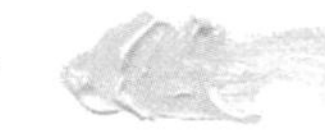

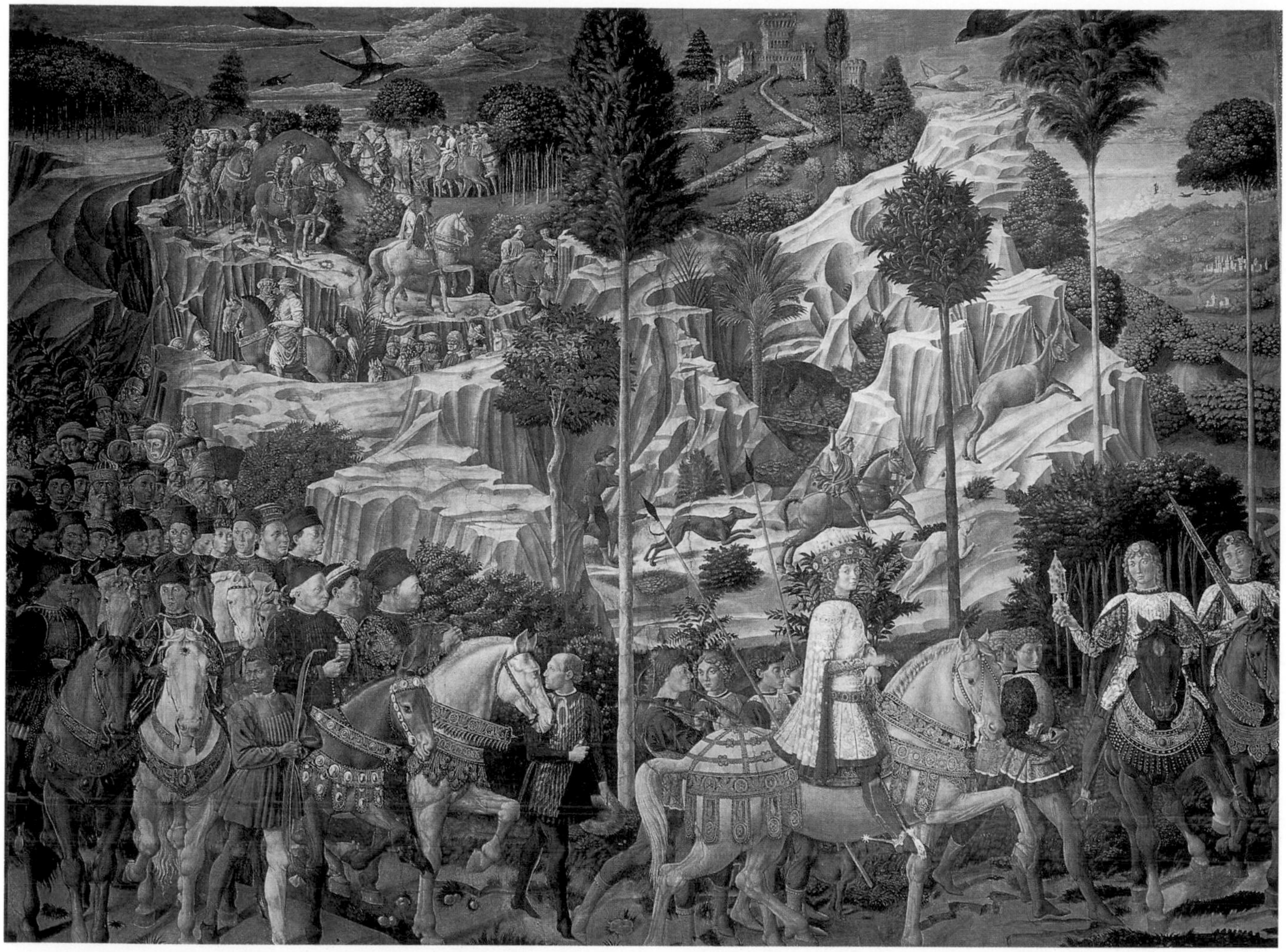

Benozzo Gozzoli, **Journey of the Magi,** ***fresco begun in 1459. One of many early Renaissance works that attracted Degas' attention.***

Degas and Cézanne, who had independent means, may well have had difficulties in their careers, but the pressing need to sell their work to feed themselves or their families was not one of them. The association allowed each of them the solidarity of a group of individuals working to support each other financially and emotionally in the very difficult business of organizing their independent exhibitions. They did not see themselves as rebels, more entrepreneurs in an age of high capitalism; the moment any of them felt they could leave the exhibiting group and gain success on their own, they did so.

These artists, after an number of abortive attempts, finally managed to organize an independent exhibition of their works in 1874. These shows continued in various forms for twelve years, until 1886, when with the eighth and final exhibition it was agreed that such events no longer served as the most effective means to further their careers. Only Pissarro exhibited in all eight exhibitions, Morisot and Degas participated in seven, while Monet and Caillebotte were represented in five, and Sisley and Renoir only in four. Nor were they the only artists to be involved in the exhibitions. Many of the other artists who were also involved have since disappeared from view. Some were friends or like-minded artists, some were technically inferior to the central group, while others were invited because they were well known. Relatively conservative artists could add a respectable air to the proceedings, and Gauguin, then a respectable and affluent stockbroker, was probably invited because he bought their work.

Just as their relationships with each other were complex and shifting, so was their relationship with the accepted face of the art world. They were not like artistic gunslingers fighting it out against the consolidated forces of reaction; rather, their relationship with the art milieu was more subtle and ambiguous than might be imagined. Many of the subjects they chose were treated by some of the most successful painters of the day and, for all the apparent radicalness of their techniques, many were adapted from traditional practices.

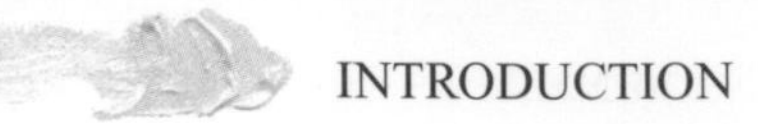

Different Sensibilities

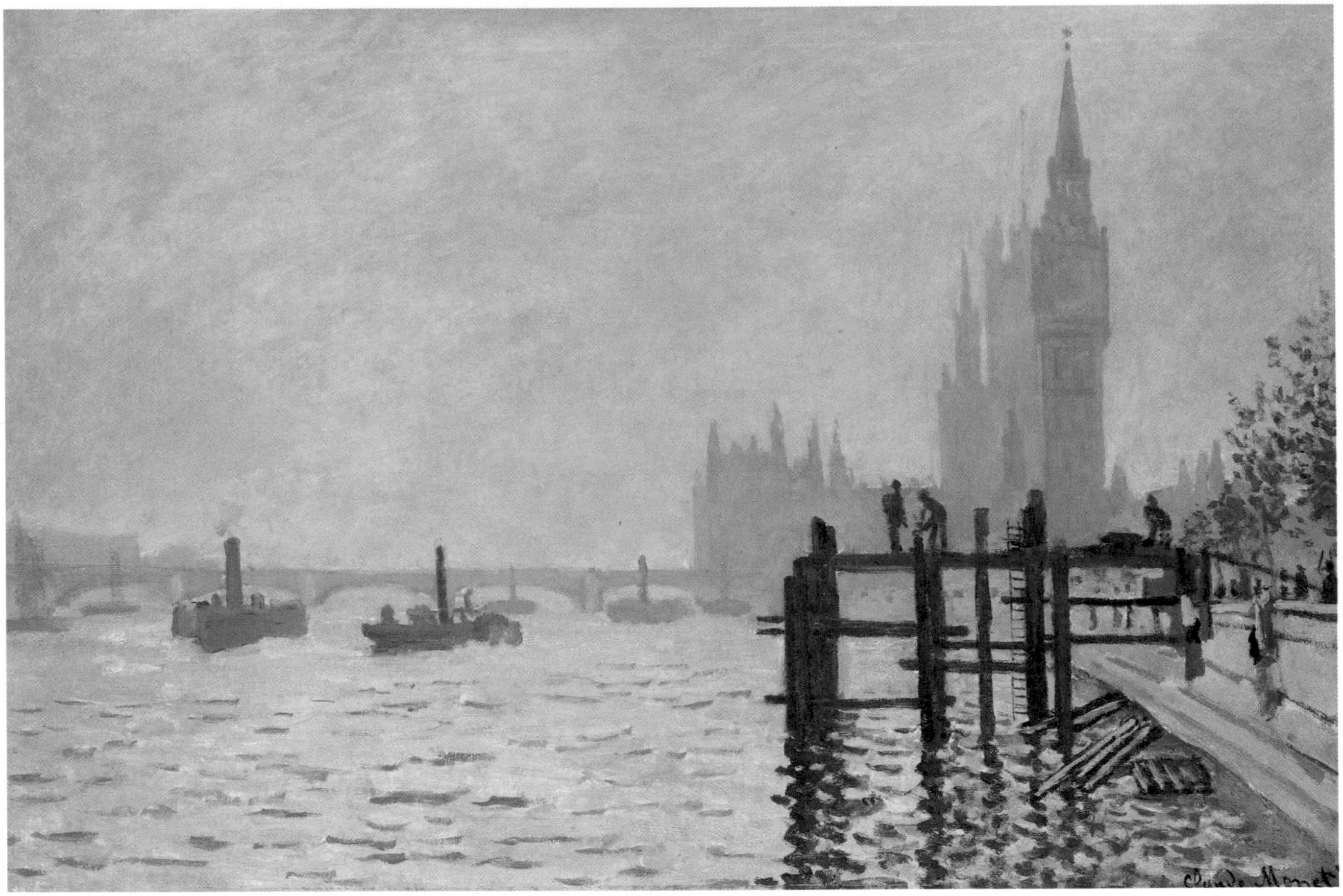

Claude Monet, **Thames Below Westminster,** *1871. Monet has composed his painting with great subtlety and art, ordering the scene before him to suit his own aesthetic desires.*

The merest glance through this book will reveal more differences between the artists' works than similarities; Degas' paintings and pastels could hardly be more different from those of Monet; Renoir's paintings, despite their superficial similarity to Monet's in the 1870s, are, in fact, the product of a very different sensibility. Even within the same artist's oeuvre we find extraordinary differences between the work produced in the early years of "High Impressionism," that is the late 1860s, and the decade of the 1870s, and that by the same artists in the later parts of their careers. Compare, for example, the early highly precisionist paintings of Degas with his work of exactly the same subjects produced later in life, or the photographically exact renderings of brilliant sunlight in Monet's paintings of the environs of Paris with his profound and deeply considered meditations on time, experience and the business of painting that occupied his later career.

Such observations raise interesting questions about the nature of reality and how it may be depicted. There was much discussion in the nineteenth century regarding the relationship of the individual to reality and of course, the thorny business of defining what is meant by reality. By trying to paint objectively and sincerely, these painters revealed the importance of individual temperament in interpreting phenomena. Set down any number of painters before the same motif, give them the same brushes and colors: ask them to paint what is before them as honestly as possible, and as many different treatments of the subject as there are painters will result.

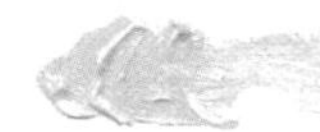

A new departure

For all this, the paintings of the Impressionists were seen by contemporaries as a new departure: and although the individual painting styles are idiosyncratic, nevertheless, it was recognized at the time, as it is today, that there were certain common themes that identified these artists as a group. Over the years, these qualities have come to define Impressionism. Such notions make it very clear that the paintings of the Impressionists may not be as straightforward as they may sometimes seem and that our enjoyment of them is not simply because of the subjects they represent but may be founded upon all kinds of complex issues: issues that will be examined in detail in this book.

The works seem so natural, so true to experience that it can easily be forgotten that they were created by men and women using materials pretty well identical to the oil paints and canvases that may be purchased today from any local art store. However real they may appear, they are, in fact, constructions, things made with bits of wood and canvas smeared and dabbed with pigment according to certain models of representation. These are dependent for their existence upon a complex weave of historical, personal, technical and cultural interactions. Equally, our appreciation and enjoyment of these works is not only dependent upon our personal histories and expectations but also is the result of a precise conjunction of the aforementioned elements; without mechanical reproduction, for example, which changes the physical aspect of a work of art and allows each of us to own a version of it at moderate cost, we would only be able to see these works in art galleries, which are in themselves a peculiar and complex social phenomenon.

Impressionism is a fascinating topic, its very accessibility and popularity allowing us to ask the most fundamental questions not only about what we expect art to deliver, but also how we expect the visible world to be represented. It is the intention of this book to provide an introduction to the work of the Impressionists and to spur readers to further their own research by seeking out exhibitions, reading the artists' letters and studying the many stimulating texts available on the subject.

Claude Monet, **Houses of Parliament,** *1904. A daring interpretation of the effect of London's mists and fog.*

CHAPTER ONE

The Early Years

The artists featured in this book totally transformed the business of painting into something that is recognized, even today, as being totally modern. In doing so, they changed the face of art forever.

Over a hundred years after they began to depict their pictures, we still to some extent see the world through Impressionist eyes. Their paintings, dedicated to the recording of their response to the world they saw around them, have acted as a challenge to the reality that went far beyond the notion of the artist as some kind of highly sophisticated recording machine.

In this chapter, we set the scene for the times and look at the origins and emergence of the Impressionist movement. The world from which Impressionism sprang was a world dominated by the Salon – to have your work exhibited here was a guarantee of success and acceptance by the artistic establishment. The works considered the most successful were those that gave a reassuring view of the world; that supported the beliefs of the majority of people.

The jury that selected the work shown at the annual Salon was a self-serving and self-perpetuating body. However, the ambitious young men and women, who were to become the Impressionists, were unable to accept the standards set down for them by their elders, and so committed themselves to finding a new form of art that would at once be a critique and a celebration of modern times.

Frédéric Bazille,* The Artist's Studio in the Rue de la Condamine, *1867. Bazille and Manet stand by the easel: the tall figure of the artist was probably painted by Manet. Zola is seen midway on the stairs looking down on either Renoir or Sisley. Behind Manet is Monet, while Edmond Maître, Renoir's musician friend, plays the piano.

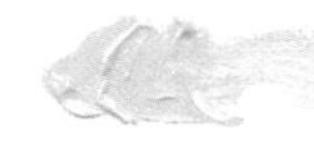

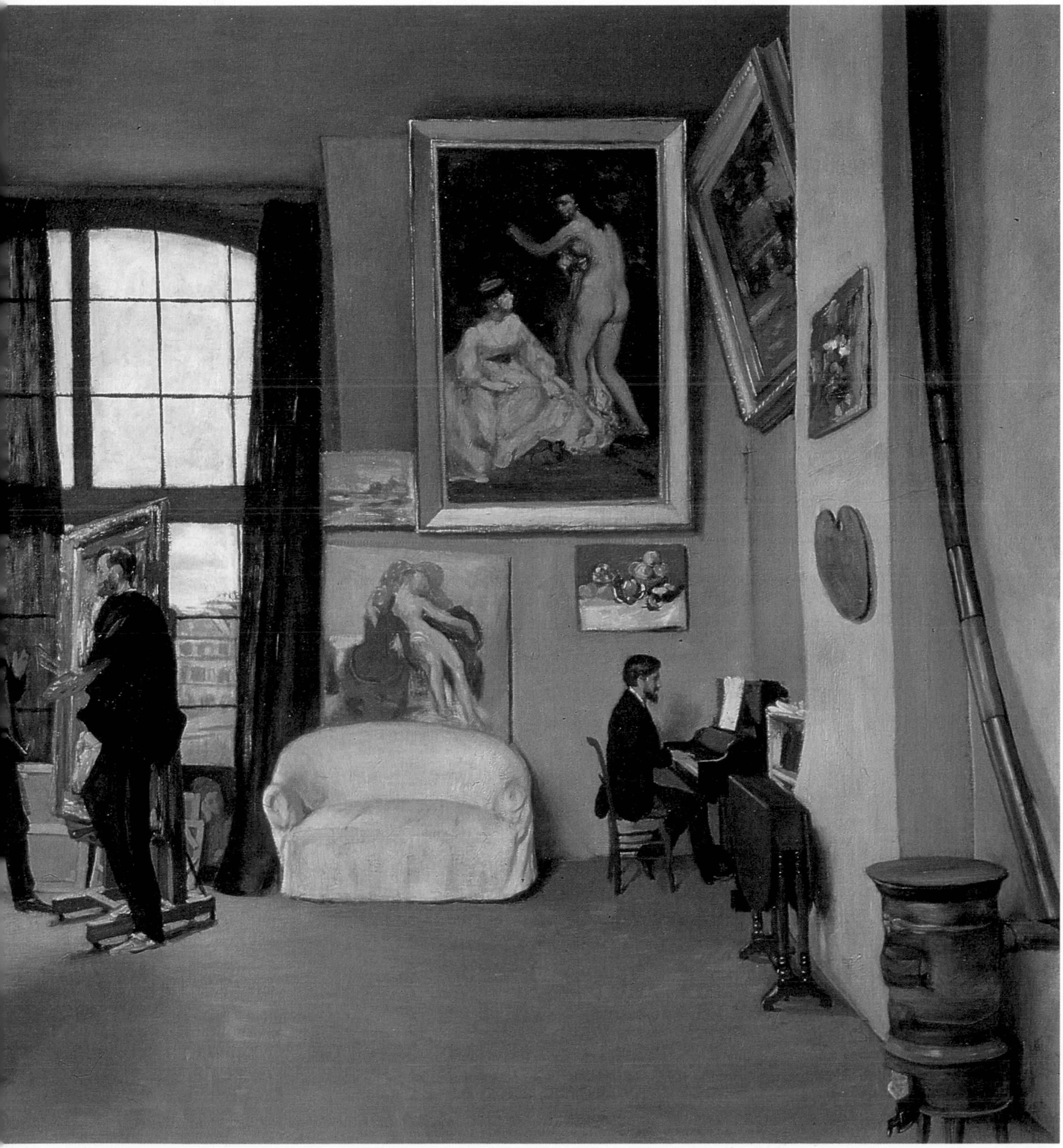

The Salon

In April 1866, the artist Jules Holtzappel committed suicide. Although his work had been accepted in previous years, his paintings intended for the Paris Salon of 1866 had been rejected. He left the following note: "The members of the Jury have rejected me, therefore I have no talent."

It is difficult today to realize how important the Salon was to artists in nineteenth-century France. There were few picture dealers until well into the middle of the century and, until Courbet's innovative independent exhibition of 1855, there was no tradition of one-man shows outside the jurisdiction of the Salon. The Salon was the only significant shop window where an artist could display his talent in order to win the esteem of the critics, attract potential clients and gain the approval of the crowd. Success at the Salon could result not only in the sale of the exhibited works but also could lead to lucrative government or church commissions. Held under the auspices of the Fine Arts section of the French Academy, the Salon was founded in 1667 by Louis XIV and his ministers, and was envisaged from the beginning as an extension in visual terms of government ideology. During the French Revolution the exclusive nature of the Academy was abolished, and in 1791 it was opened to artists of all nationalities and directed by a government-led committee. The nineteenth century saw a massive growth in the number of artists exhibiting, and visiting the Salon became a popular social event, attracting vast crowds. Art journalism occupied a significant place in the ever-increasing number of newspapers, magazines and art journals that sprang up at this time, which meant that reviews of the Salon were widely read throughout the country.

Establishment artists

Recruited from the ranks of artists who taught at the *Ecole des Beaux-Arts*, the members of the Salon were fully paid-up members of the establishment in whose interest it was to

Thomas Couture,* Romans of the Decadence, *1847. Rich in color and brushwork, Couture's painting was influenced by Veronese's* Marriage Feast at Cana, *1562–63. This academic painting was considered by some left-wing critics to be an attack upon corrupt government and a dissolute society through the evocation of the hedonism that heralded the collapse of ancient Rome.

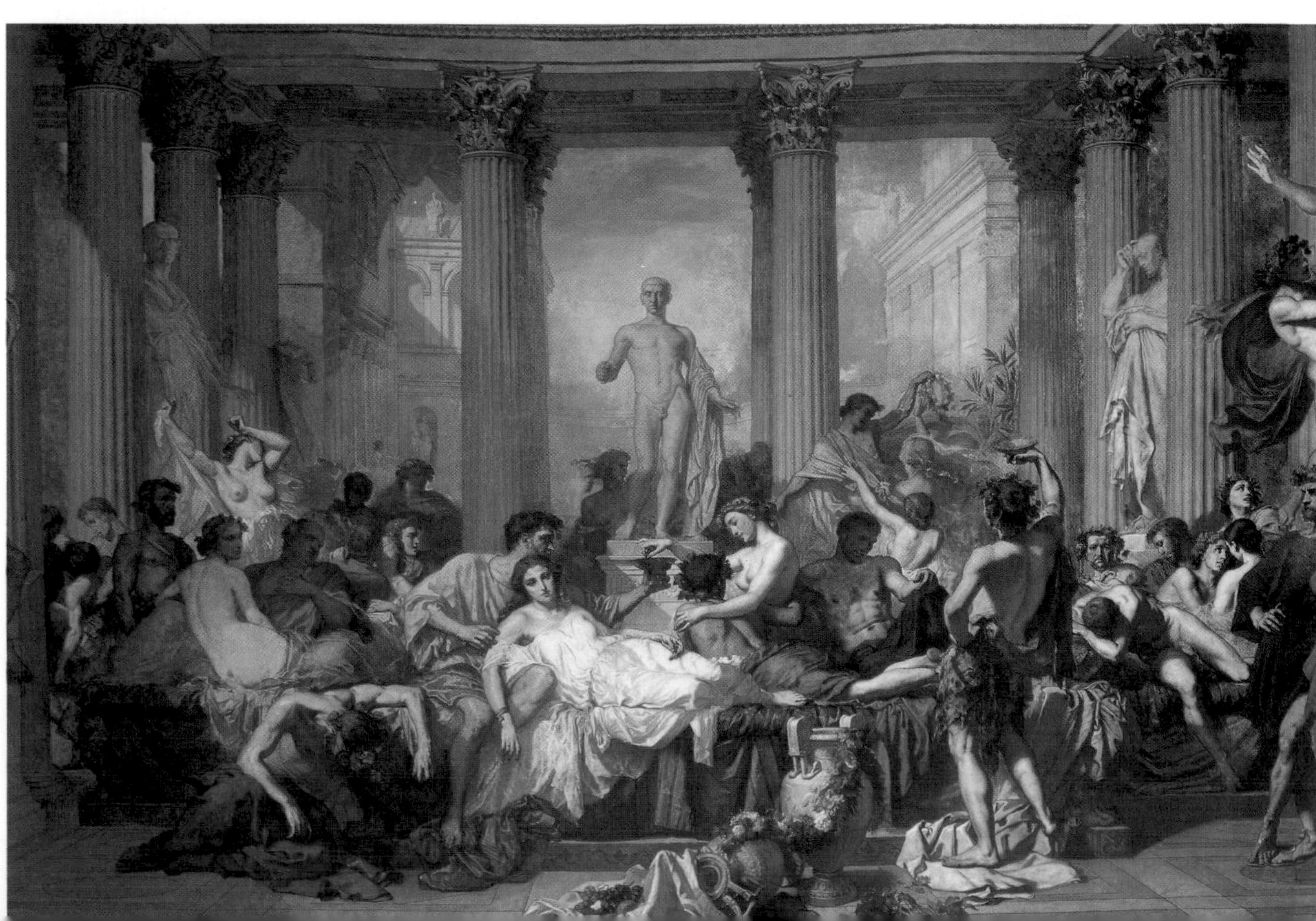

support the art that secured them their professional success. Artists who received major awards at the Salon not only won significant commissions but also were considered exempt from the formality of submitting works to the jury. In this way the jury could award prestigious honors to themselves and were in a powerful position to block anyone who threatened their positions.

After the revolution of 1848, the jury was abolished and an open Salon was instituted. Over 5,180 artists had their work exhibited, but the generally mediocre nature of much of what was on show ensured that this experiment in artistic democracy was never repeated. With the demise of the Republic, the administrators of the Second Empire were determined to keep tight control over the arts. The Fine Arts were kept under the watchful eye of the Comte de Nieuwerkerke, the *Intendant aux Beaux-Arts* and a favorite of the Imperial household as well as the lover of Princesse Mathilde Bonaparte. A subtle interplay of rewards and censorship gave the government the art it wanted. Major reforms instituted in 1863 led to the jury being elected in part by the government and partly by the artists themselves. Real control still lay with the government, however, a matter which caused innumerable problems for artists, as the frequent and disruptive shifts of government meant that no coherent policy could be followed for any prolonged length of time.

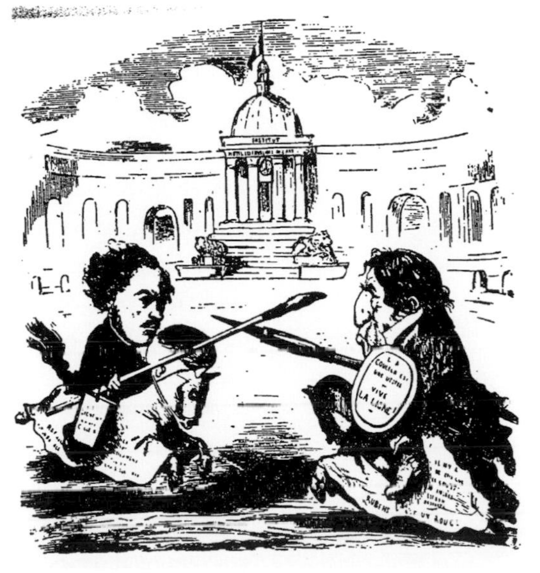

The conflict between line and color, identified as the prime elements of Classicism and Romanticism, are mocked in this caricature of Ingres and Delacroix clashing outside the august walls of the Academy. Ingres' shield says "Rubens is a red."

Even when some jury members were open to innovation, individual figures like the painters Cabanel and Bouguereau, who occupied key positions in the jury structure, were still stumbling blocks for the avant-garde. These painters, immensely popular in their day, felt it a matter of honor to safeguard the Salon from unworthy infiltrators.

As late as 1900, over twenty-five years after the first Impressionist show, the painter and sculptor Jean-Léon Gérôme, then a very old man, attempted to prevent the President of the Third Republic, M. Loubert, from seeing the Impressionist paintings hanging on the walls of the Universal Exhibition of that year, saying: "*Arretez, Monsieur le President, c'est ici le déshonneur de l'art français*."

The hierarchy of the genres

The work shown at the Salon was divided into a hierarchy of genres. Considered the most significant were *les grands machines*, large paintings dedicated to subjects taken from either the Bible, classical history or mythology. Such works were valued as the latest link in a chain that stretched back unbroken through French culture to the Italian Renaissance and beyond to classical antiquity. These paintings represented the moral high ground of art and justified the claim, often repeated through the century, sometimes arrogantly and sometimes with less than complete confidence, that France was the standard-bearer of European culture. In this context, it is easy to see why the genres of portraiture, landscape and scenes taken from everyday life were considered to be of lesser significance. Even though in 1817 a Prix de Rome was instituted for landscape, it specifically referred to "Historical Landscape" painting and not to topographical or atmospheric paintings of the French countryside. Although this system of classification was strictly adhered to, throughout the nineteenth century a wide variety of work was nevertheless available for view within the hallowed walls of the annual Salon.

The opening day of the Salon every year was a great social event in Paris. Its role as a public institution that could educate and reaffirm establishment values was reflected in the wide social spectrum of visitors, recorded in the many caricatures of the time, who flocked to admire, ogle and appraise. The cost of entry was kept to a minimum and on Sundays there was no charge at all. As many as 30,000 people would visit the crowded halls of the Salon Carré in the Louvre or the Palais de l'Industrie over the six weeks the works were on view. Armed with their Salon reviews and *livrets*, the public was able to judge for itself the worth of the works exhibited on the walls. Paintings were hung in alphabetical order and arranged in tiers, ranging from eye-level to just below the ceiling.

As the nineteenth century progressed, the authority of the Salon waned, but during the period of Impressionism it was still regarded as the centerpiece of French culture. For Manet and Corot it was the only place to exhibit, and neither artist showed their works in the independent exhibitions of their friends.

The Ecole des Beaux-Arts

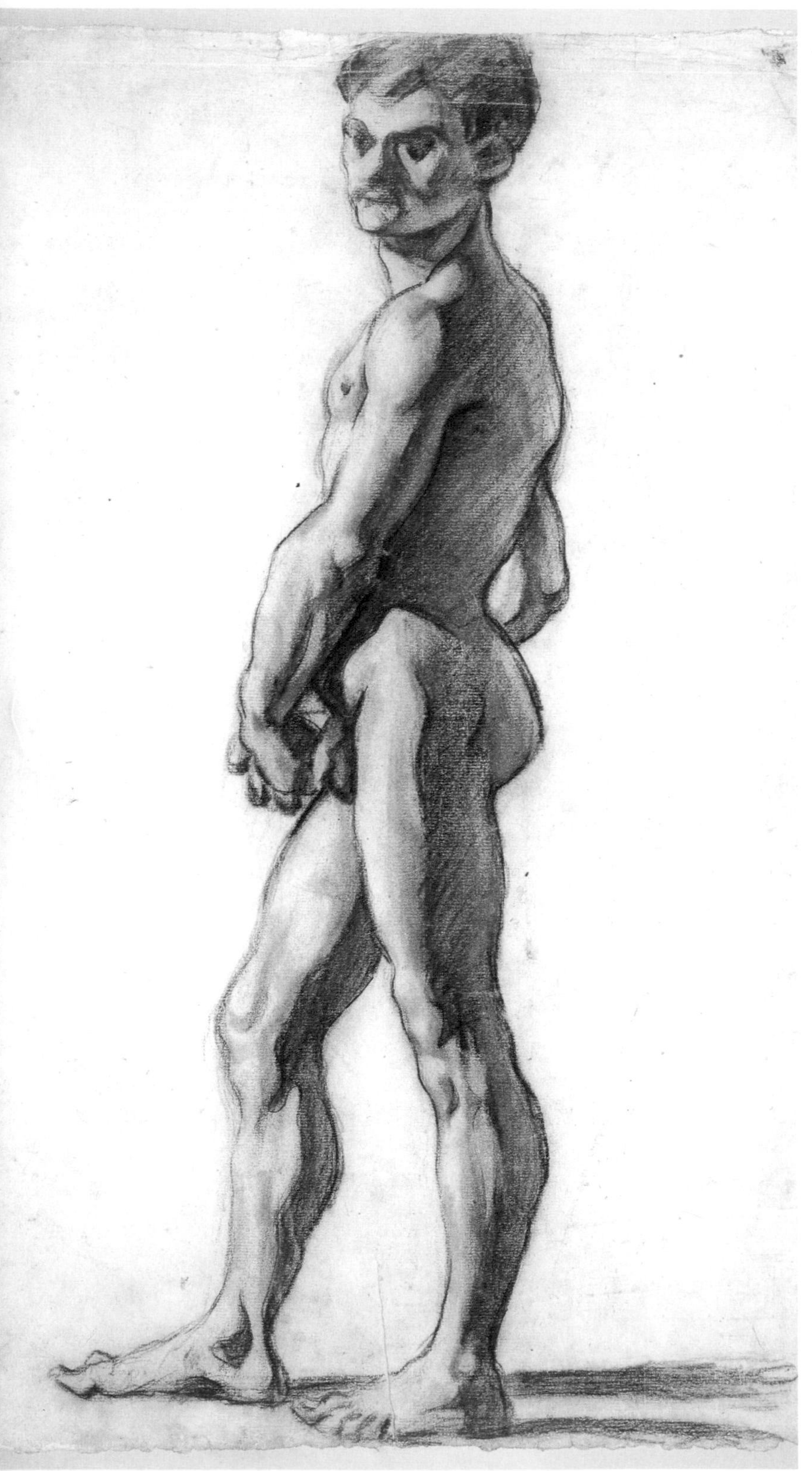

The surest way to become a successful artist in Paris was to enroll at the Ecole des Beaux-Arts. The Ecole was dedicated to the perpetuation of a certain kind of painting that was increasingly thought by many to be at odds with modern experience: tradition and not originality was the order of the day. Students began their studies by mastering the art of drawing, the "probity of art." Drawing was considered to be the intellectual and moral foundation of art, color and expressive brushwork being regarded with suspicion as appealing too frankly to the senses. "… Drawing is everything, the whole of art lies there," declaimed Ingres. "The material processes of painting are very easy and can be learnt in a week or so." Later, Ingres was to reduce the time needed to learn to paint, remarking that it had taken him seven years to learn to draw and three days to learn how to paint.

Students at the Beaux-Arts spent their time copying the work of the masters and making careful shaded drawings of classical casts and statues. An important element of their training was the production of *têtes d'expression*, a conventional series of facial expressions that were understood to represent particular emotional states. Only when drawing was mastered were students allowed to take up painting and pass on to the next stage of their training, the study of the naked male figure. Only then could he begin to combine his knowledge of ideal art with the visual reality represented by the model. Using the cool northern light falling on to the model at an angle of 45°, the student would make carefully observed tonal oil studies of the torso, keeping his work anatomically exact. "I do not know the exact names of all the bones in the body," said Ingres, "but they are all my friends."

The Prix de Rome

The main object of an ambitious student was to gain a Prix de Rome. This was a three-to-five-year scholarship, funded by the government, to be spent at the French Academy, housed in the Villa Medici, in Rome. To win this scholarship, it was necessary to undergo a prolonged series of elimination stages. Candidates had to be French, under the age of thirty and single. The culminating examination was the production of an oil sketch (*ésquisse-peinte*) of a subject taken from

Paul Cézanne,* Study of Male Nude, *1863–66. This painting reveals the artist's ability to draw with a passionate conviction.

classical history, mythology or literature. The chosen students, locked away in separate cubicles, their working space enclosed by a curtain, were expected to produce this sketch for *un peintre historique* within 72 hours. The most successful of these sketches ensured their creators a place at the Villa Medici and the expectation of eventual wealth and public esteem.

The fame of very few of the winners of this prestigious award outlasted their lifetimes and many of the most famous artists of the nineteenth century failed to achieve this sign of academic success. Of the Impressionists, only Renoir studied at the Ecole; though he remained there for only two years, it instilled within him a deep respect for traditional art practices.

Increasing numbers of artists looked for alternative ways of preparing themselves for their precarious profession. In 1862, despite his conviction that art could not be taught, Courbet was persuaded to open his studio to pupils, although the experiment did not last long.

A number of well-respected painters offered their services as mentors to aspirant artists. Manet studied for eight years at the studio of Thomas Couture, the painter of the famous *Romans of the Decadence*. The studio of Charles Gleyre provided the setting for the first meetings between Monet, Sisley and Renoir. The Swiss artist's liberal teaching techniques had a profound effect on their early artistic development, for he respected the uniqueness of individual temperaments and encouraged his pupils not only to study at the Louvre, but also to go out into the countryside to paint from nature.

Other establishments were the so-called "free" studios, which included the Atelier Suisse, founded in 1815 by a former pupil of Jacques-Louis David. Here, male and female models were available for study, but only to an exclusively male clientele. It was cheap, no formal teaching was offered and its convivial and informal atmosphere attracted independently minded artists as diverse as Ingres, Courbet, Corot, Diaz, Manet and Cézanne. The Académie Julian specialized in preparing students for entry into the Ecole des Beaux-Arts. It was known for its good teachers and was open every day except Sunday, and it accepted students of any age.

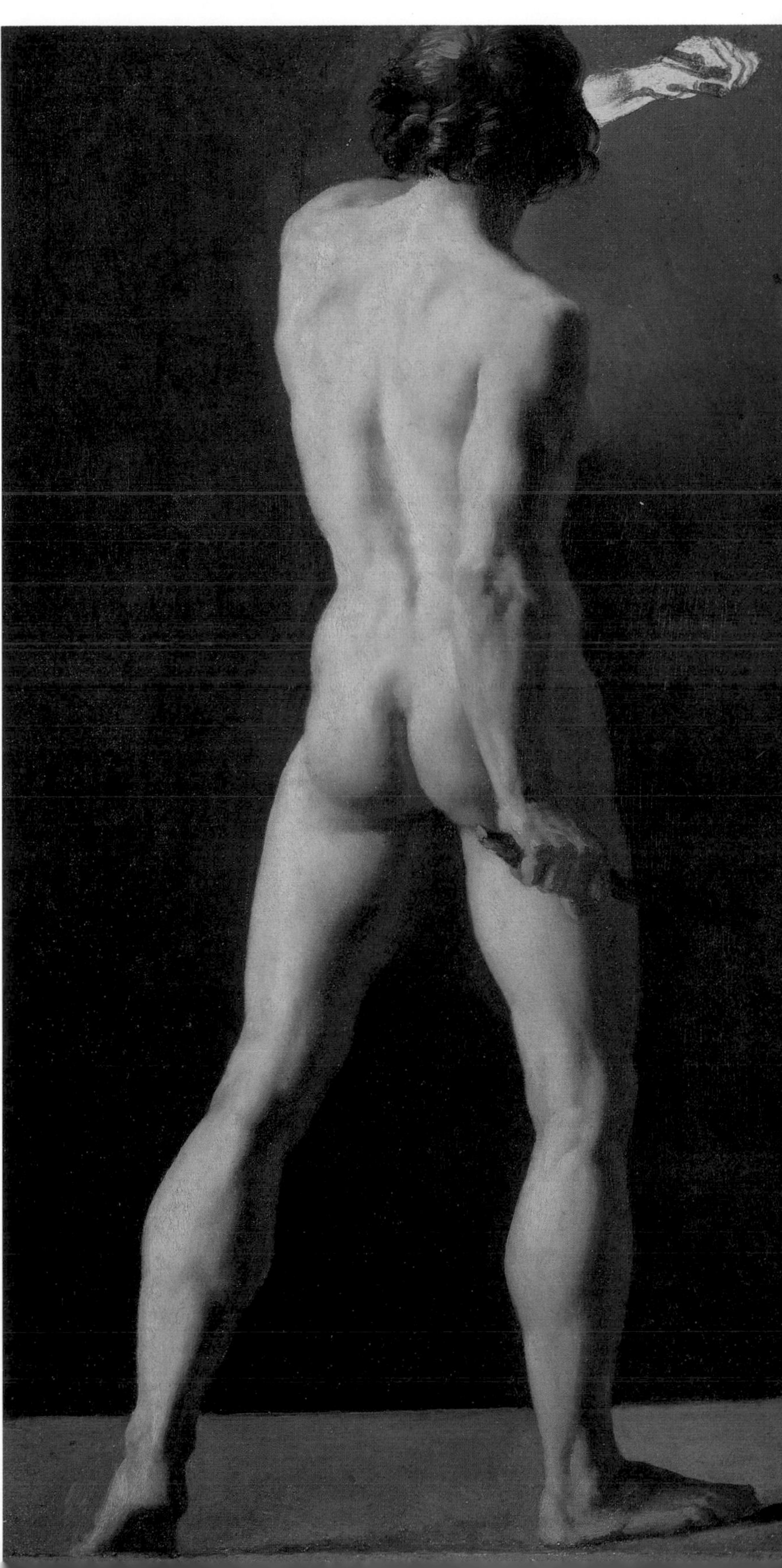

Anonymous,* Académie, *French, early nineteenth century. A carefully observed study of the male nude drawn and painted according to the academic requirements of the day.

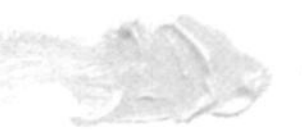

Gustave Courbet:
"... to create a living art"

Ebullient and controversial, Gustave Courbet (1819–1877), by the force of his art and personality, broke the stranglehold of academicism that had frustrated so many painters in the early part of the nineteenth century; in doing so he opened up for others the possibilities of a new art.

A committed individualist, his painting was founded upon an intense identification with the physical world and a refusal to take orders from anyone. Although he had studied the painters of seventeenth-century Spain and Holland with assiduous care, he promoted the illusion that his art was only dependent upon his own experience. His frank depiction of reality caused one of his friends to comment that he produced paintings as naturally as an apple tree bears fruit. He was the most radical artist of the 1850s, and it was his example that gave Manet, Monet, Renoir and their friends the framework on which to pursue their own radical programs.

Courbet demanded complete independence for the painter and the right to paint as he thought fit; he painted portraits, the nude, modern history paintings of a democratic nature and, most significantly for the younger painters, landscapes. His gift to the next generation of painters was his hungry appetite for the physical world and his total commitment to his own individual response to experience.

Born into a wealthy provincial family in the Franche-Comté district of France, Courbet adopted the bohemian persona of the rugged individualist who would brook no compromise with the establishment. He arrived in Paris in 1839 and spent the next decade trying to find a style of painting that would suit his personality and ensure success. He achieved this at the Salon of 1849 with a large genre scene showing himself, his grandfather and friend relaxing after lunch. The painting was bought by the State and it confirmed his association with the Realist school of artists and writers.

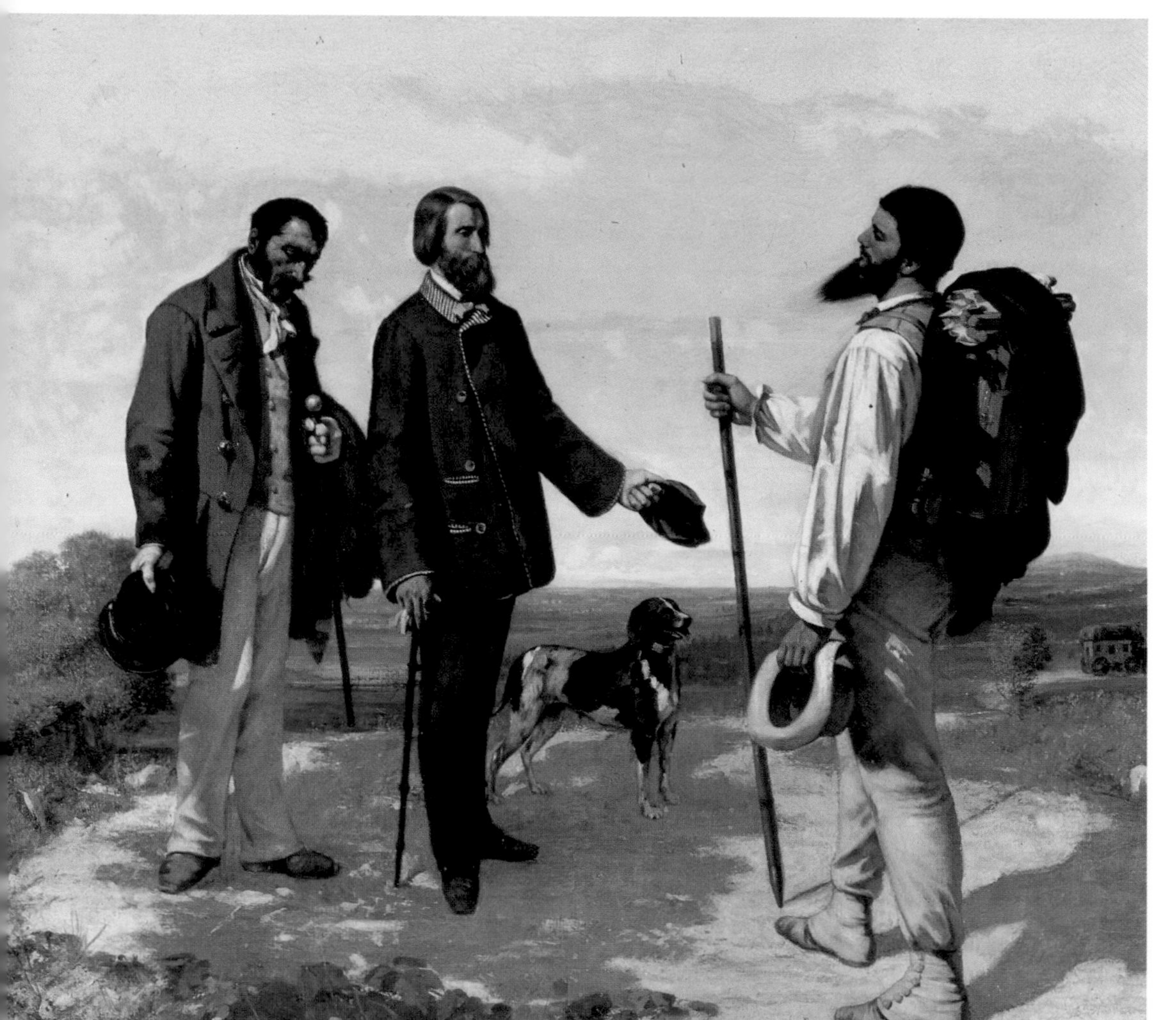

Gustave Courbet,* The Meeting, *1854. Courbet is greeted by his patron, his patron's dog, and his patron's manservant.

Friend of the truth

Courbet had very strong political sympathies with the socialist party that had come to power after the February Revolution of 1848, and canvases such as *The Stone Breakers* and the massive *The Burial at Ornans*, confirmed his standing as an heroic and controversial figure. His politics were deeply felt but non-specific: "Not only am I a socialist, but also a democrat and a republican," he once said. "In short I am in favor of the whole revolution and above all, I am a realist – a realist means a sincere friend of thc truth."

Like the Impressionists, he was sustained by a number of writers and critics, including Théophile Thoré and Jules Champfleury, whose championing of an unpretentious art for the people put them in conflict with the state-sanctioned hierarchy of genres. Courbet's paintings blew away the carefully orchestrated gradient of cultural significance that was accorded to different kinds of painting. His own sense of self-importance refused to allow him to subordinate his unique personality to any movement or organization. In 1855, he made a public declaration of his stance in the art periodical *L'Artiste*:

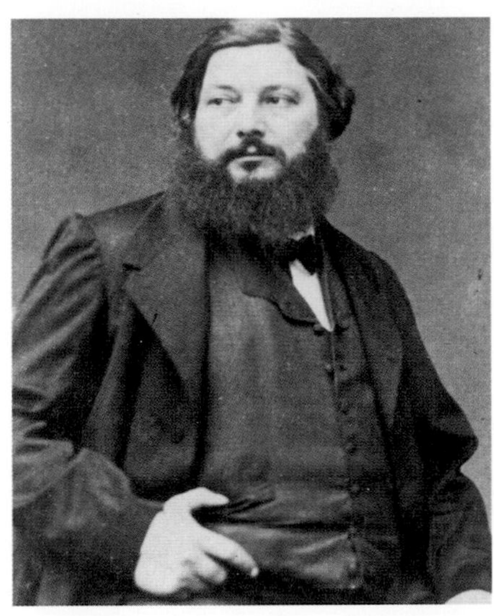

A photograph of an affluent and confident Courbet at the height of his renown.

> ***The title 'Realist' has been imposed upon me in the same way as the title 'Romantic' was imposed on the men of 1830 ... To derive a complete knowledge of tradition, a reasoned sense of my own independence and individuality, to achieve skill through knowledge – that has been my purpose; ... to create a living art – that is my aim.***

Politics and publicity

Courbet courted publicity and got it. He cultivated the identity of a bohemian, consuming vast quantities of beer in the student haunts of Paris, his favorite being the Brasserie Andler on the Left Bank, the same place in which Monet was later to regret wasting so much time as a young man. This bohemian identity, later also adopted by Cézanne, could be seen as a strategy to create an alternative to the sophisticated urbanity of the Parisian establishment as represented by Manet. The history of the French avant-garde is as much as anything a history of the meeting places where painters and writers gathered together to exchange ideas and support each other. As Courbet's friend, the socialist writer Castagnary, wrote, "the brasserie was merely an extension of the studio."

Courbet won the patronage of a wealthy young man from Montpellier named Alfred Bruyas who, while providing much-needed help, allowed the artist to follow his own direction. In 1855 Bruyas financed the independent show of Courbet's work that was erected against the very walls of the official Palais des Beaux-Arts and in which the artist revealed his gigantic painting, *The Artist's Studio*. He followed a program dedicated to the painting of modern life and, in the late 1850s and early 1860s, painted a succession of extraordinary works. Single-handedly, he showed how still life, traditionally a lowly ranked genre, could in his hands be the equal in significance of any other kind of painting.

Courbet's active involvement in politics almost cost him his life. During the period of the Commune, which followed the fall of the Second Empire in 1870, he was elected as a delegate with special responsibility for museums and works of art; he used the opportunity to abolish both the Academy and the Ecole des Beaux-Arts. It was with his approval that the Vendôme column, the most public symbol of the now unseated Bonaparte dynasty, was demolished. After the violent suppression of the Commune, Courbet narrowly escaped execution and spent seven months in prison. The government got its revenge by holding him personally responsible for the entire cost, assessed at 250,000 francs, of reconstructing the column. In 1873, bankrupt and ill, he fled to Switzerland. His alcoholism resulted in his death on the last day of 1877, still in exile in Switzerland.

The text of this caricature by Quillenbois reads:* "The Adoration of M. Courbet, *a realist imitation of* The Adoration of the Kings." *Even Calas the dog realizes the divine qualities of the artist and acts accordingly.

Caricature by Quillenbois

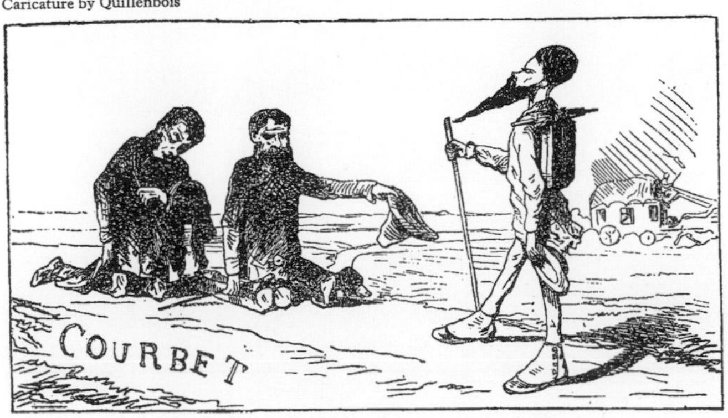

L'adoration de M. Courbet, imitation réaliste de l'adoration des Mages.

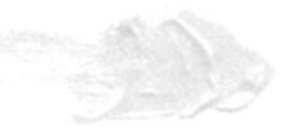

The Artist's Studio

1854–55, oil on canvas, 361 x 598 cm (142 x 235 in), Musée d'Orsay, Paris, France

A period that has failed to express itself through its own artists has no right to be expressed through later artists.
– Gustave Courbet

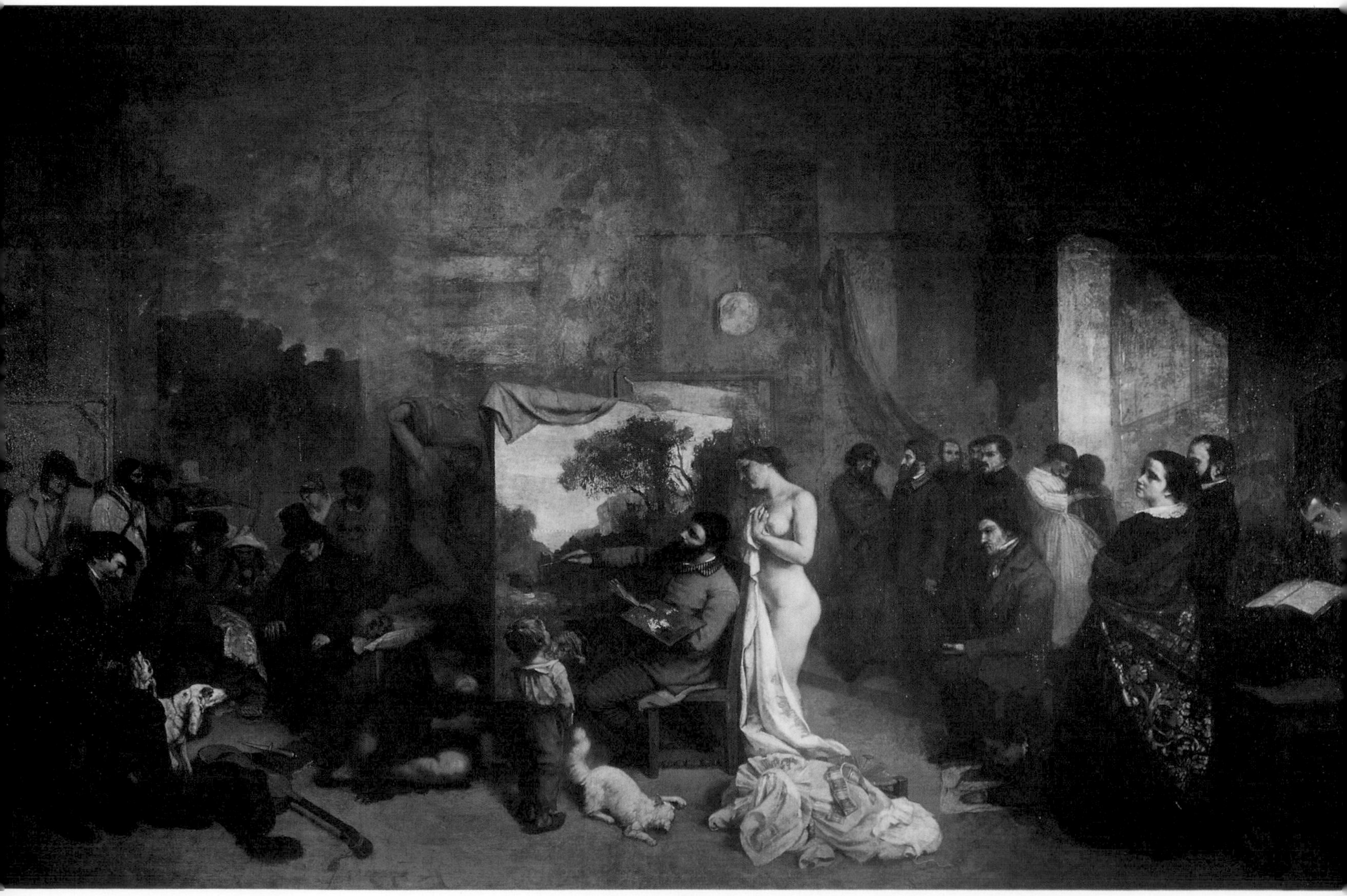

The clearest demonstration of Courbet's ambitions may be seen in his painting *The Artist's Studio* of 1855, the largest self-portrait in Western art. Its full title, *The Artist's Studio, A Real Allegory, A Summation of Seven Years of My Artistic and Moral Life,* is a declamation of his absolute faith in his own personality, profession and procedure. Painted with the knowledge gained from a study of Rembrandt (*The Night Watch*, 1642, and *The Hundred Guilder Print*, c.1643–49), Velásquez and Baron Gros, this painting is a unique tour de force and one of the masterpieces of the nineteenth century. It reveals Courbet's mastery of portraiture, still life, landscape and the nude, and his ability to create a modern history painting. Painted with broad brush and palette knife, the canvas has suffered some damage over the years as it was rolled, unrolled and re-rolled several times – once it was even used as a stage backdrop! Overall it is densely and rapidly worked – Courbet claimed in a letter to Bruyas that he could only spare two days to complete each

figure. His own portrait and the late addition of the standing child are freely and confidently painted, while others are more laboriously worked. The whole gives the impression of confidence, the figures are modeled convincingly and impetuously in an energetic handling of paint, freely handled with glazes laid on with a brush alternating with thick application of earth pigments, broadly applied with the knife.

The painting was not exhibited with his other works at the Universal Exhibition in Paris in 1855, but in an adjacent pavilion built at his patron's expense. Forty-two paintings and two drawings were exhibited inside this *pavillon du réalisme*, an act that declared his independence as clearly as the democratic subject matter of his works.

Two paintings dominated the rest, *The Meeting* and *The Artist's Studio (L'Atelier)*. In this painting, the seated figure of the artist shown in the very act of painting dominates the center of the composition. To the left are those who have inspired his work: beggars, acrobats, a Jewish money-lender and, among others, a weary-looking gamekeeper who bears an uncanny and probably deliberate resemblance to Napoleon III. On the other side of the artist are those who gave him critical and moral support. Courbet faces his canvas, in a pose suited to show his famous "Assyrian" profile to best advantage. He is in the very act of painting, putting the finishing touches not to some *peintre historique*, but to a landscape of his own provincial birthplace. The initialized life model seems very much at home in her professional place of work. She looks on, like some allegorical personification of "Realism," inspiring the artist to paint only the truth. A little boy, borrowed from Rembrandt's famous etching of Christ preaching before the people, draws a stick man, an act as natural and untutored as Courbet wished his own art to seem. An older boy stands before the canvas, at his feet a cat gambols playfully on the floor. The message is clear: Courbet's art is accessible to all, it breaks class boundaries and needs no university education for its comprehension. The poet and critic Baudelaire sits by a window, engrossed in his book, while behind him two lovers flirt. Dominating this side of the canvas are two wealthy amateurs who have come to the atelier to view the artist at work and, presumably, to buy one of his paintings.

Realist in style, but allegorical in content, the painting was characterized by Courbet, at the end of a long letter describing the work, as something that, in the end, it was up to each individual to make his own sense of. Courbet's disclaimer has remained in force, for the painting is one of the most enigmatic documents of the nineteenth century and much ink has been spilt attempting to give a definitive explanation of its mysteries. Whatever the complexities of its underlying themes, the painting's essential message is difficult to misinterpret: the full and frank independence for the artist to paint what he knows and what he believes, in a direct and straightforward style that relies on a full acceptance of the visual world for its effect.

The great photographer Nadar complimented the artist on having produced a page of social history. Until Manet's much smaller and more informal *Music in the Tuileries Gardens*, which in some ways is a reworking of the right-hand side of the painting, Courbet was *the* modern artist. His paintings became models for artists of the next two generations, many of their works being representations of Courbet's work.

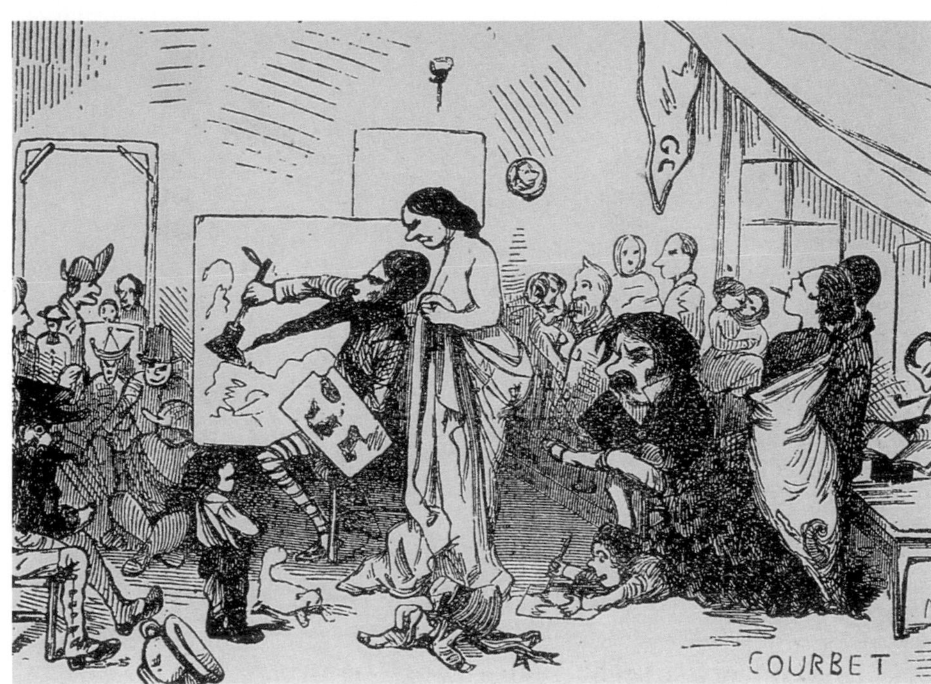

Quillenbois's caricature appeared in* L'Illustration, *July 21, 1855. Courbet's egoism and habit of out-flanking the artistic establishment made him a favorite target for caricaturists.

Painting the Landscape

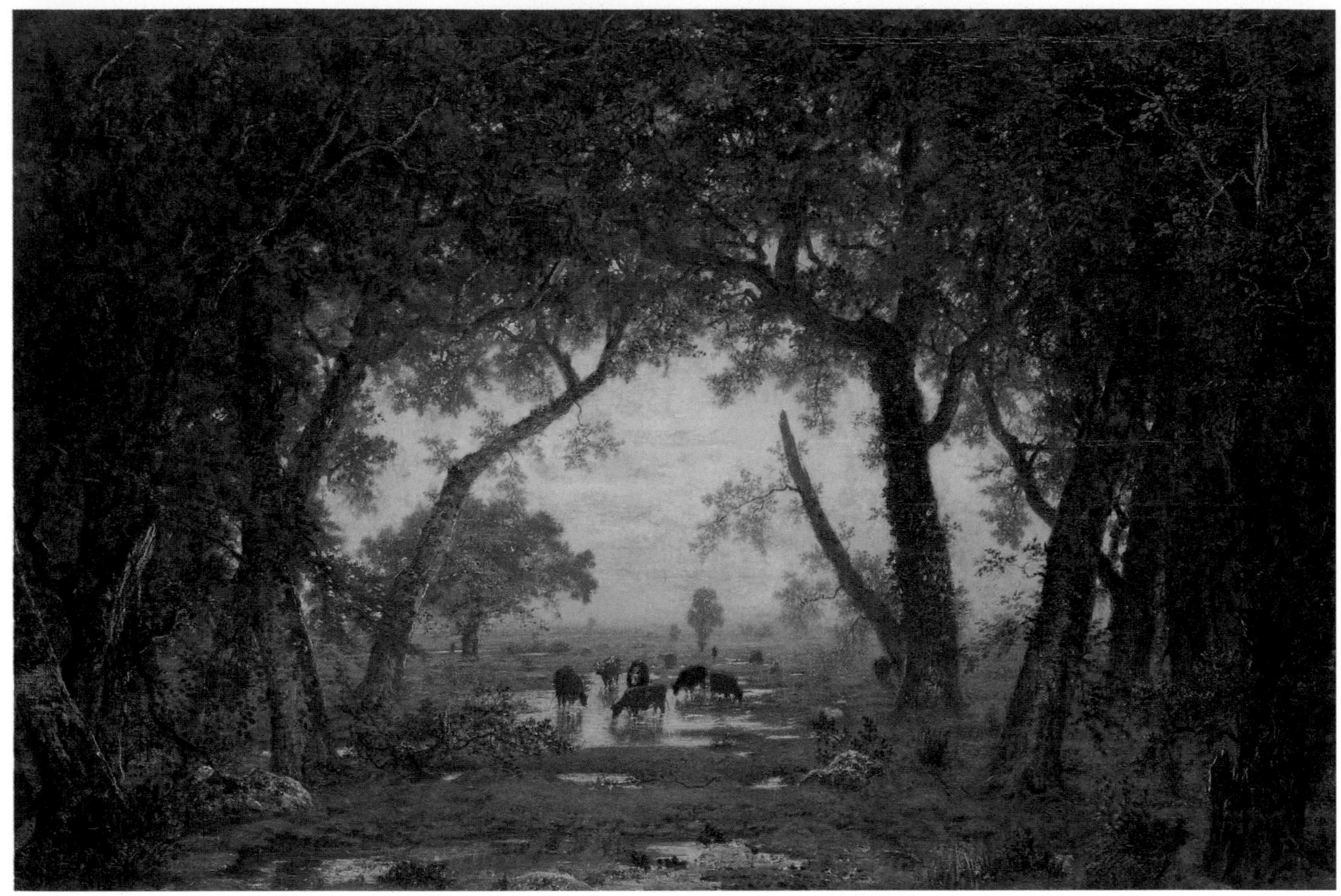

Théodore Rousseau,* The Forest of Fontainebleau, Morning, *c. 1850. A typical example of Rousseau's successful later style.

Although the Salon exerted a powerful influence on the contemporary art world in France, it could not hold back the irresistible rise in the popularity of landscape painting. The spectacular developments in the genre made by Monet and his friends in the 1860s did not happen without precedent; by the middle of the century the Salon itself was dominated by landscape painters and the rebels of the previous decade were enjoying official favor and financial success. In the 1820s, John Constable's paintings of the East Anglian landscape had been much admired by the French. In 1824 his *Haywain*, shown to universal acclaim at the Salon of that year, was almost bought for the nation. Delacroix, in particular, admired the English artist's handling of paint. Years later he recalled in his journal, "Constable says the superiority of the green of his meadows comes from its being composed of a multitude of different greens. The lack of intensity and life in the foliage of most landscape painting arises because they usually paint them in a uniform tone."

In the 1830s, landscape was proclaimed by *L'Artiste* as "truly the painting genre of our time." Despite such interest, officialdom was reluctant to encourage any additional prestige being granted to paintings of the rural landscape. Théodore Rousseau, the leading exponent of the Anglo-Dutch tradition of landscape, suffered continual rejection from the Salon from 1836 until 1841, when he gave up any further attempts to show there. For this reason, he was known as "*le Grand Refusé*," achieving success through independent exhibitions and private sales. He epitomized the notion of the avant-garde artist as an outsider, living and working away from Paris, producing works whose apparent "sincerity" was unacceptable to the sophisticated and decadent art establishment. Other painters of the landscape and simple life

– Millet, Dupré, Diaz and Daubigny, for instance – continued to produce their paintings in the face of official opposition. However, by the 1850s the state was acquiring their work in large numbers and though the Ecole des Beaux-Arts continued to emphasize the significance of historical landscape, they had to concede, their failure being marked by the abolition of the Prix de Rome for landscape in 1863. The reasons for this reversal of state policy are easy to explain. As more and more people moved into the capital, so the desire for images of the countryside increased. The artificiality and pressure of city living could be appeased by reference to the apparently slow-changing natural order of the countryside. Rural communities, which many urban dwellers had left only a few generations earlier, became symbols of continuity in a confused and anxious period of history, of national identity. In an increasingly secular society, nature was interpreted in countless books and paintings as a repository of truth. The century witnessed the beginnings of the development of tourism, and ease of travel and increased leisure time allowed urban dwellers to spend more time making excursions to the countryside outside Paris. Landscape painting became a viable profession: young artists like Monet, Renoir and Pissarro, in choosing to dedicate themselves to landscape painting, were making a shrewd career move.

The Barbizon School

Although there were many sites celebrated by landscape painters in the first half of the century, it was the paintings of the Barbizon school that exerted a special influence upon the young Impressionists. Barbizon was a small village tucked away on the edge of the forest of Fontainebleau, just a few kilometers from Paris. In 1848, Jean-François Millet had fled from the cholera epidemic that had swept through the capital and made his home there. In close contact with his friend Théodore Rousseau, who lived nearby, he painted the seasons of life and death, the continuity of the family and scenes of life within a non-industrial community. Rousseau was working within the seventeenth-century Dutch tradition of landscape painting. His pictures almost invariably showed the interior of the forest, while Millet essentially painted the plains around the village of Chailly, concentrating his interest on the human relationship with the landscape. Artists like Diaz and Dupré celebrated a more nostalgic view, peopling their paintings with gypsies and using a more delicate and showy manner of painting to make their works attractive to their Parisian audience. Although the work of Millet and Rousseau held tragic undertones, their paintings were normally viewed as affirmative images of a life closer to spiritual reality, obeying the laws of God and nature rather than of man.

Jean-François Millet,* Angelus, *1853–59. A powerful and reassuring image of peasants responding to the church bell.

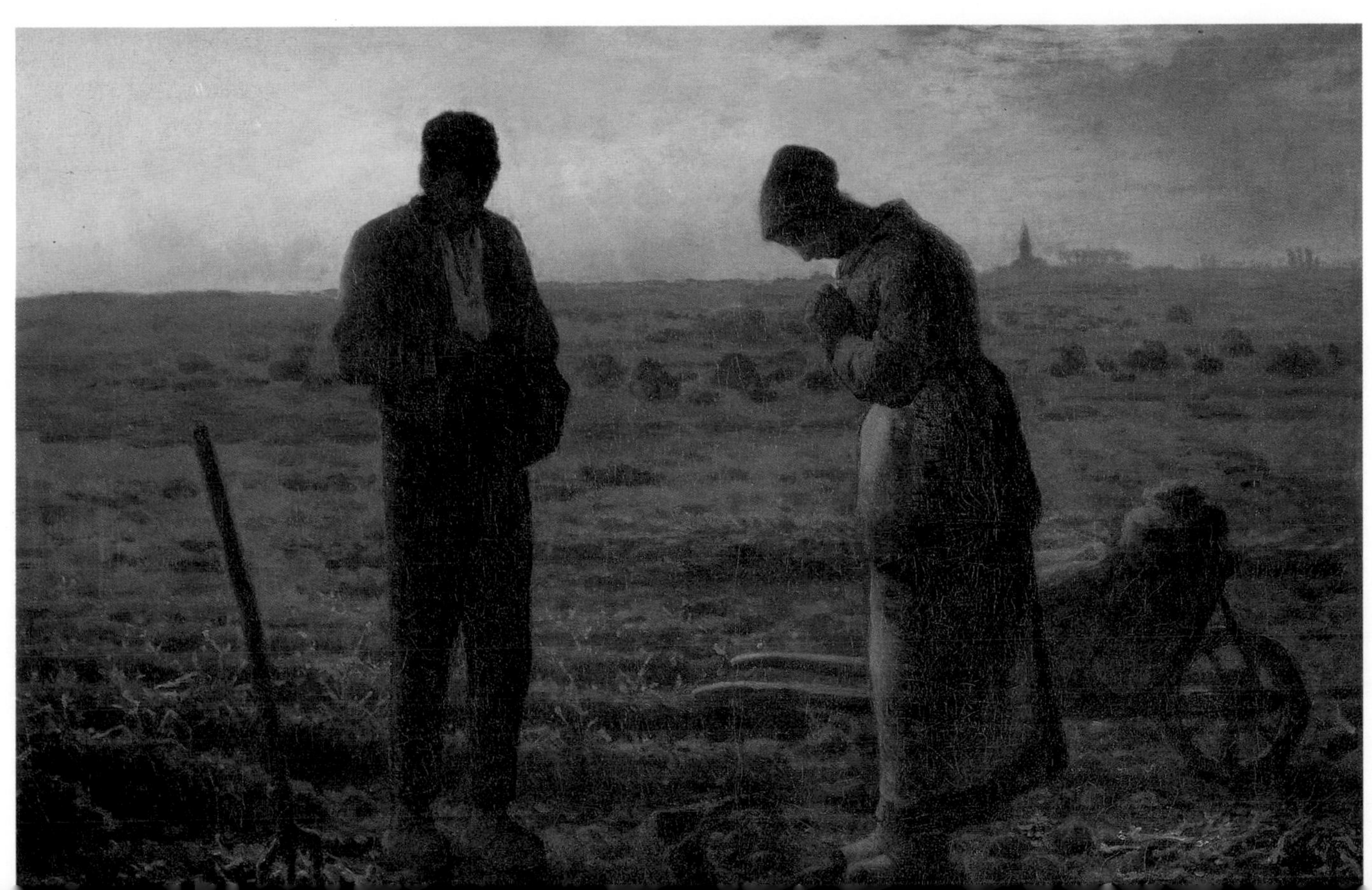

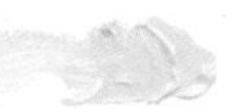

Painting "En Plein-Air"

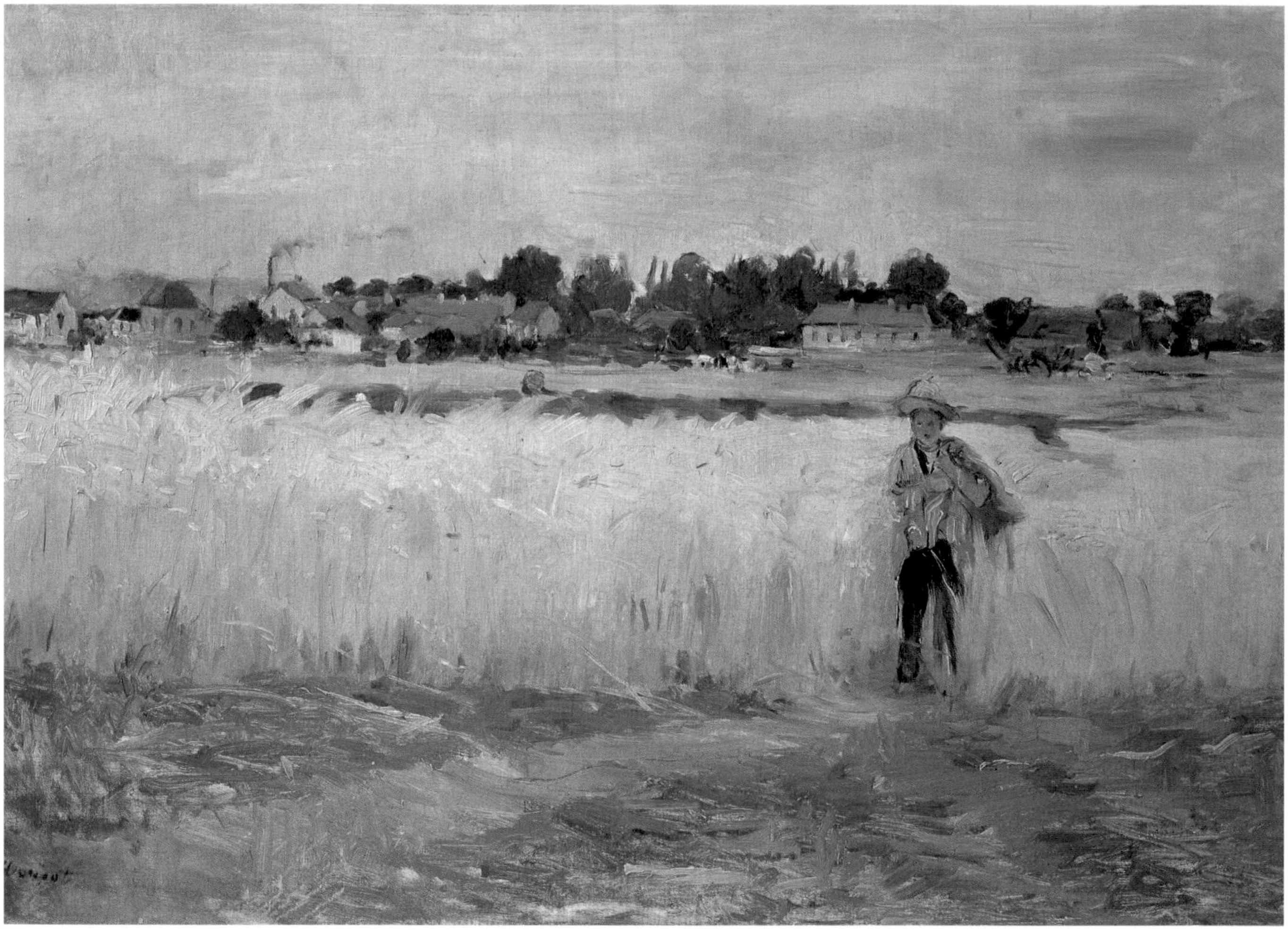

Berthe Morisot,* Amongst the Wheat, *1875. Painted during her summer vacation at Gennevilliers, a few miles east of Argenteuil. It shows the artist's acceptance of the presence of industrialization within the rural landscape.

One of the major characteristics of Impressionism is "*plein-air*" painting – the practice of painting in the open air, directly from the motif. In fact, the truth is somewhat different, Impressionism being more closely allied to traditional art practice than is often thought.

The practice of *plein-air* painting became popular with artists during the early part of the nineteenth century and was considered to be an essential element of the artist's craft, not as an end in itself, but as a means of studying the effects of nature. Nature was the raw material, to be transformed in the studio by the artist's intellectual and imaginative powers into the carrier of a moral message. Henri de Valenciennes (1750–1819), an influential teacher and landscape painter, had contributed to its popularity, suggesting working methods that later were recommended by Camille Pissarro to his son, Lucien, but in the finished works of the academicians there is little sign of the freshness and verve so apparent in the small notes made in the open air.

For later painters, the practice was made easier by the introduction of portable easels, collapsible tubes of paint and regular and affordable systems of transport, although with problems of portability and the wind, it is not surprising that most *plein-air* studies are of a modest scale. There is a well-known story of Monet, painting on rocks off the Normandy coast, being swept into the sea and nearly drowning, when a gust of wind caught his canvas.

Berthe Morisot has left the most sympathetic and amusing account of the tortures of painting *en plein-air*, writing to her sister Edma, from the Isle of Wight in 1875:

Everything sways, there is an infernal lapping of water; one has the sun and the wind to cope with, the boats change position every minute … The moment I set up my easel more than fifty boys and girls were swarming about me, shouting and gesticulating. All this ended in a pitched battle, and the owner of the field came to tell me rudely that I should have asked permission to work there …

Corot

"Papa" Camille Corot (1796–1875) was one of the most significant and innovative landscapists of the nineteenth century. His quiet, limpid and silvery-toned studies have a clarity and sureness of tone and composition unrivaled by any other painter. Although his sketches made in the open air were intended as aids to help the completion of his more finished Salon landscapes, they are complete in themselves.

Corot was ambivalent in his attitude to the Impressionists. He congratulated a friend saying that "he was lucky to escape from that gang." Nevertheless, they inherited many of his procedures and many of his recorded statements could have been said by the younger artists. For instance:

Beauty in art consists of truth imbued with the impression we received from the contemplation of nature … We must never forget to envelop reality in the atmosphere it first had when it burst upon our view. Whatever the site, whatever the object, the artist should submit to his first impression.

Corot's painting was based on a close and humble observation of the scene before him, set down as directly and simply as possible. It is important to note that he did not exhibit his exquisite sketches publicly and thought of them as an intermediary stage in the development of his more finished landscapes. In order to capture the pearly atmosphere of the light he mixed white with his colors, creating a distinctive luminosity or *peinture claire*, which gave his paintings a blondness and cleanness of light very different from the darker-toned paintings of his fellow exhibitors at the Salon.

It was this aspect of his work that particularly appealed to artists like Monet, Pissarro and Morisot who all mixed their pigments with white to gain a heightened luminosity. For the Impressionists, the capturing of transitory visual effects, without recourse to the example of past art or conventional studio methods, endowed their experiments with the authority of their own personal expression. In 1864, Monet wrote to his friend and mentor, Eugène Boudin:

Among these three canvases there is a simple étude which you have not seen begun, it is entirely made after nature, you will find in it a certain connection with Corot, but if so it is entirely without imitation of any sort. The motif and above all the calm and vaporous effect are the sole cause of this. I did it as conscientiously as possible.

In his later years, Corot produced more lyrical and imaginative canvases, often containing allegorical figures. These works, together with his paintings of statuesque women in softly lit interiors, became very popular the 1870s. As an influence on Monet and Pissarro and as the teacher of Morisot, he played a valuable role in the development of Impressionism, as well as being one of the most poetic painters of all time.

Camille Corot,* Ville d'Avray, *(1835–40).

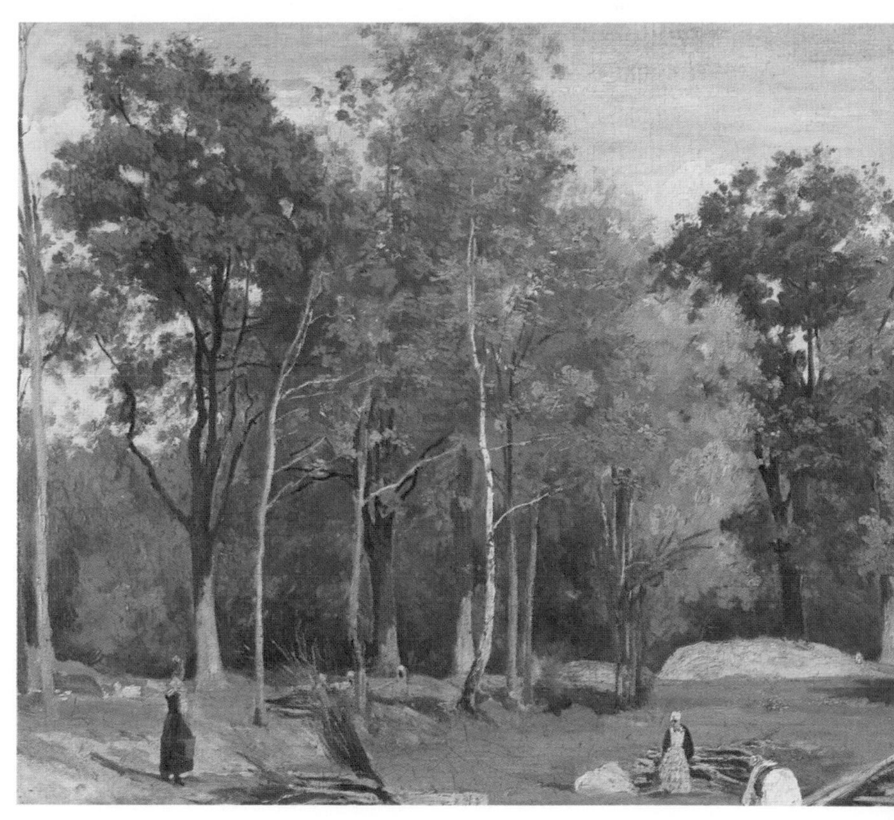

Monet's Revelation:
Boudin and Jongkind

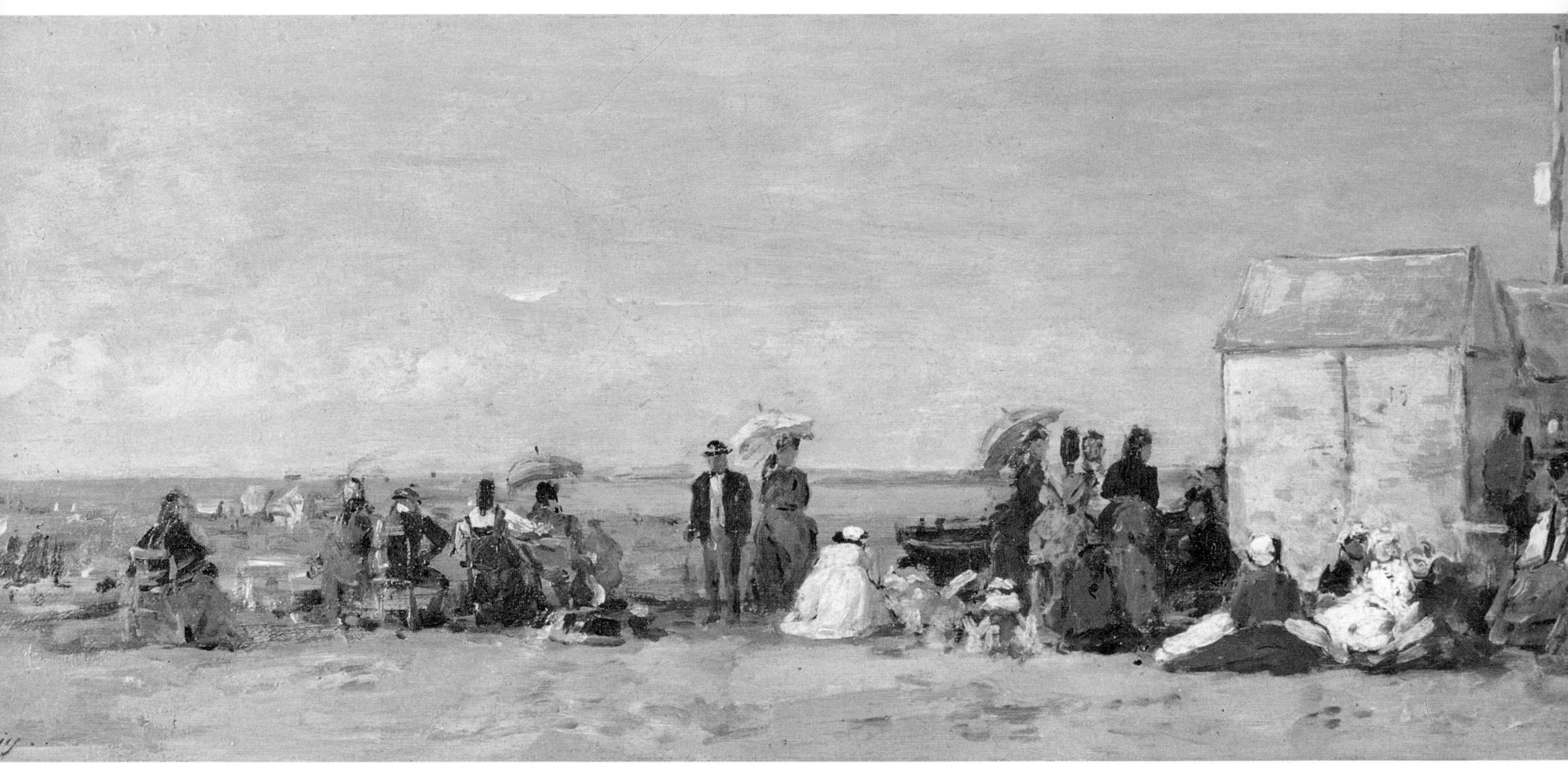

Eugène Boudin,* Beach at Trouville, *1863. These "prodigious enchantments of air and water," as Baudelaire called them, were painted at least in part in the open air. Such works were freely painted and were a great influence on the young Monet.

Prodigious enchantments of air and water.
– Baudelaire on Boudin
King of the Skies.
– Corot on Boudin

Late in life, Monet vividly recollected how, as a youth of seventeen in Normandy, he watched the artist Eugène Boudin (1824–98) set up his easel and begin to paint directly from nature. "… I must confess that I wasn't thrilled by the idea … I looked on with some apprehension, then more attentively, and suddenly it was as if a veil had been torn away; I had understood. I had grasped what painting could be." This was a decisive moment for Monet, transforming him from a callow youth with an aptitude for caricature into a determined, independent and ambitious painter. Born in Honfleur, Boudin made his living from producing exquisitely toned seascapes and lively informal paintings of the chic visitors who spent their summers in the fishing ports of the Normandy coast, which were then being rapidly developed for holiday and summer visitors. As Boudin said "The peasants have their painters ... that is as it should be, but those middle-class people strolling along the jetty at sunset, don't they also have the right to be portrayed?" Boudin's work was admired by the poet and writer, Baudelaire, who gave a brilliant, if idiosyncratic, evocation of his paintings:

All these clouds, with their fantastic and luminous forms; these ferments of gloom; these immensities of green and pink, suspended and added on to each other; these gaping furnaces; these firmaments of black and

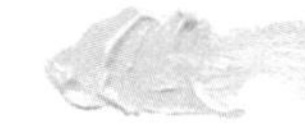

purple satin, crumpled, rolled or torn; these horizons in mourning, or streaming with molten metal – in short, all these depths and all these splendors rose to my brain like a heady drink or like the eloquence of opium. It is rather an odd thing, but never once, while examining these liquid or aerial enchantments, did I think to complain of the absence of man.

Baudelaire was one of Monet's favorite writers and it is fitting that his eloquent description of Boudin's achievement could equally well describe Monet's own work. Boudin's concern with sea and sky and the speed with which he jotted down his rapid notations, his reliance on instinct and his simple compositional structures left an indelible mark on Monet's future working practices. Boudin wrote in February 1863 that "... everything painted directly on the spot always has a strength, a power, a vividness of touch that one doesn't find in the studio." Advice like this remained with Monet all his life.

Through Boudin, Monet was introduced to the Dutch artist, Johann Barthold Jongkind (1819–91), whose seascapes were firmly situated within the Dutch seventeenth-century seascape tradition. "From that moment on, he was my master, and I owe to him the definitive education of my eye," Monet recalled. Jongkind was an eccentric, something of a nomad, who from the 1840s onward, wandered around the countryside of France collecting watercolor sketches of the sky and land, which he then worked up into finished oils in his studio. These paintings are brilliant, freely worked evocations of the effects of light, air and movement, the picture surface built in a series of small, interlaced calligraphic touches of paint, a practice that was to become the dominant feature of Monet's mature style and which was not without its influence upon the work of later artists like Jongkind's fellow Dutchman, van Gogh and the pointillist, Paul Signac.

A bohemian and an alcoholic, Jongkind's mental instability grew worse as his life progressed. Before he had even met Jongkind, Monet informed Boudin in 1860, "You know that Jongkind, the only marine landscape painter we have, is dead to art. He is completely insane." He suffered a crisis in 1879 and, after much suffering, died in 1891.

Jongkind, Large Sailing Boats at Honfleur ***(1865), his improvisatory technique perfectly suggests the freshness of this seaside scene.***

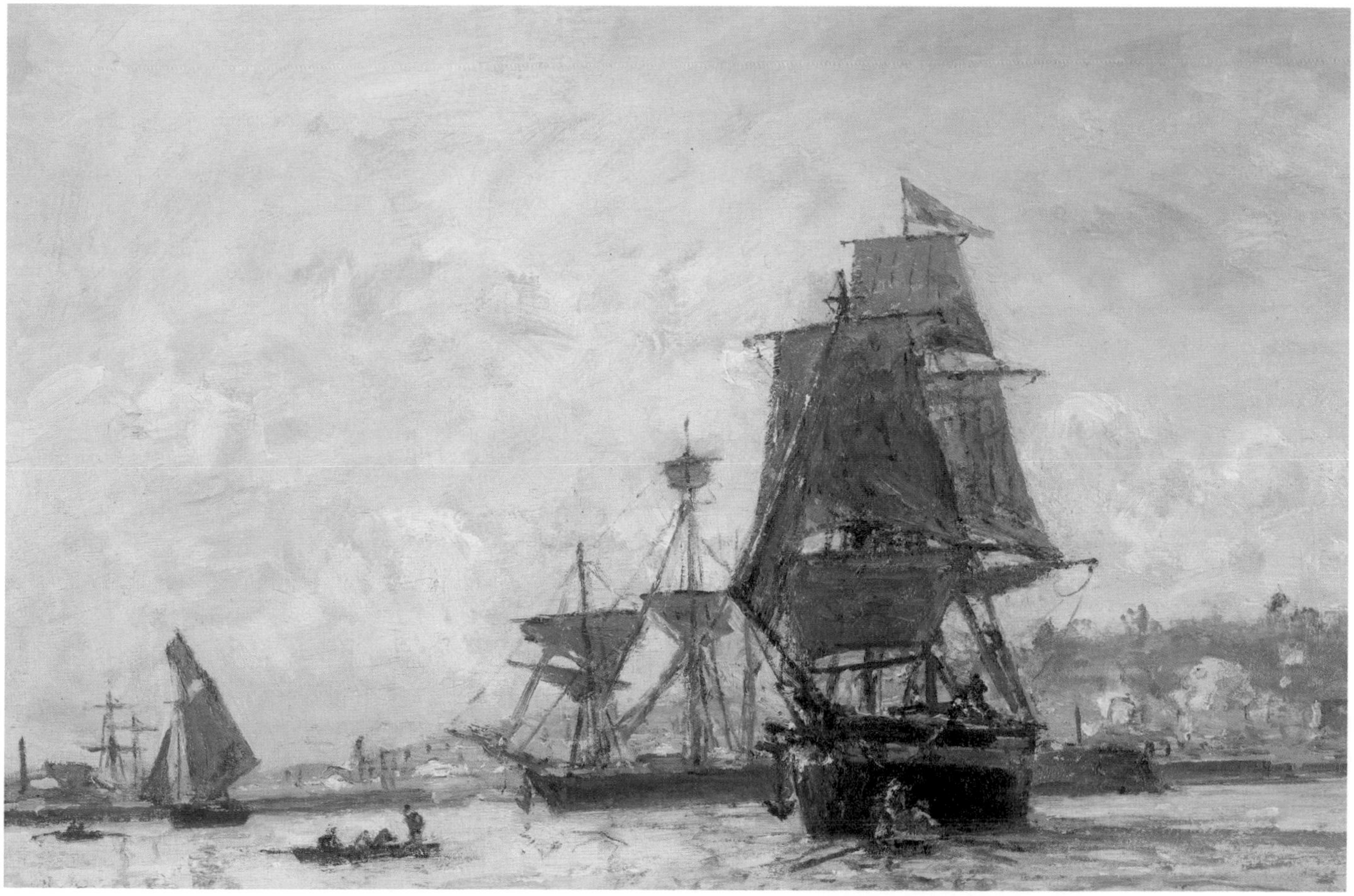

The Rebuilding of Paris

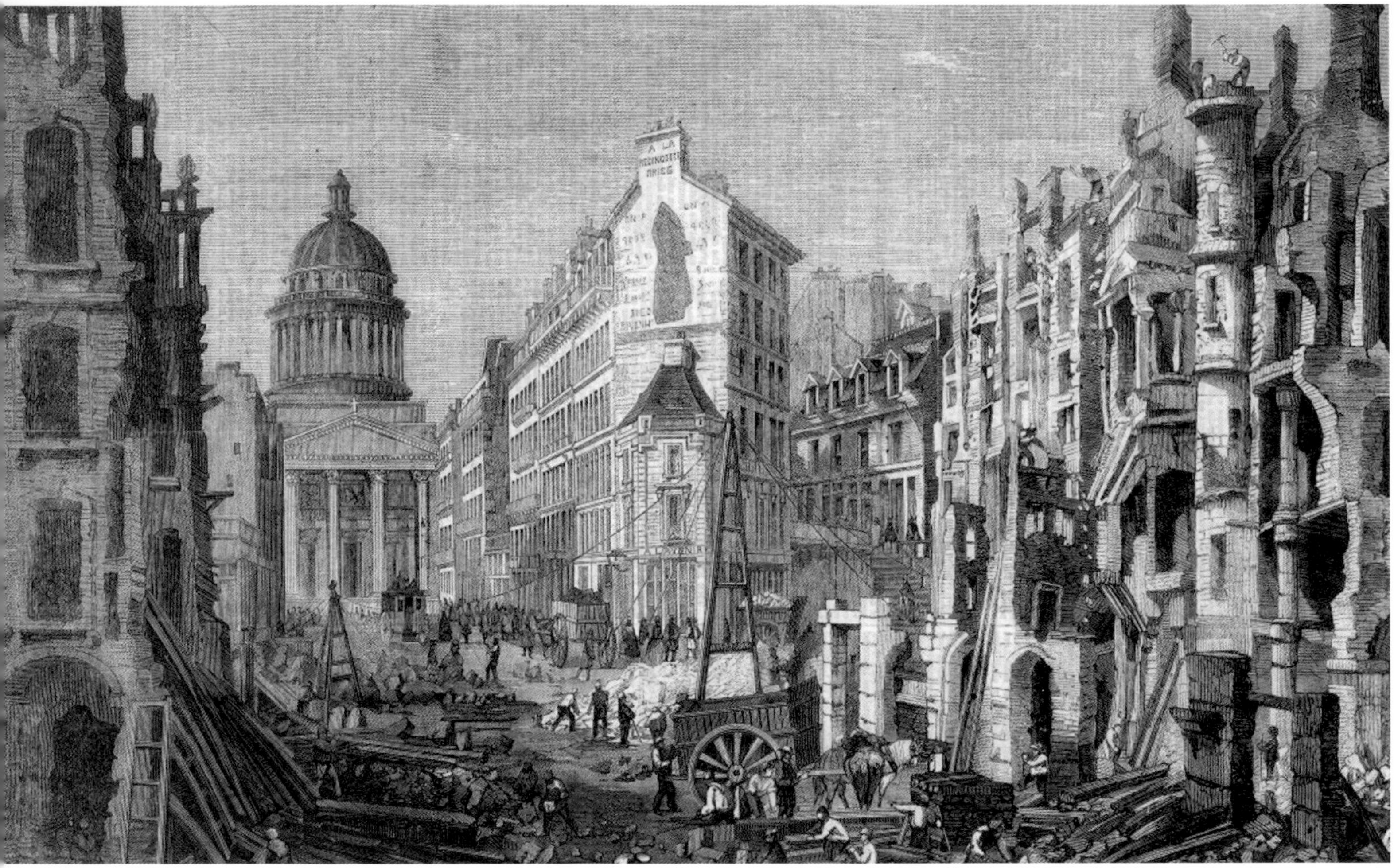

This print shows clearly the almost organic structures of the "old" Paris torn down to be replaced by a modern "Americanized" Paris.

Paris is becoming cleaner and brighter, but poetry is leaving her as fast as its wings can carry it.
– Henry Dabot, July 1854.

The Paris we experience today is substantially the Paris reconstructed under the autocratic supervision of Baron Haussmann, who was sanctioned by the Emperor Napoleon III to rebuild his capital as a suitable reflector of his regime. Paris was called by many *la ville illuminé*, a glittering visible celebration of modern capitalism. To others, the glitter was merely a facade which could not hide the sordid reality of this "modern Babylon," a hedonistic city dedicated to pleasure and the gratification of the senses. The tremendous changes endured by the city affected not only its physical structure, but also the hearts and minds of its inhabitants. Between 1831 and 1851 the city's population doubled, from 576,000 to 1,053,000, and by 1880 it had increased fourfold. Physically a small city, the sudden growth of Paris could only put intense pressures on established modes of living.

In 1848, Charles Louis Napoleon Bonaparte, the nephew of Emperor Napoleon I, had been elected President of France; three years later he organized a *coup d'état* and had himself declared Emperor, taking the title Napoleon III. This position gave him the opportunity to continue his illustrious uncle's project of making Paris a city worthy of being the hub of a new Empire: a new Rome. In the process, the heart of old Paris was ripped out and from the debris arose a new city, which to many contemporaries lacked the poetry and grace of the old capital, though not everyone thought so. "Like Augustus," Napoleon was told by one of his courtiers, "you found your city mud and left it marble." The Paris celebrated by the Impressionists was this new city, half building site, half spectacle.

Haussmann

The work was directed by Prefect of the Seine, Baron Georges-Eugène Haussmann, who was invested with complete authority over the project. Old narrow streets were demolished to make way for 85 miles of straight, tree-lined boulevards flanked by large anonymous apartment buildings. The indigenous population was flushed out; thousands were made homeless, their former world made anew for the affluent bourgeoisie who populated the new city. In the course of the redevelopment of the city over 27,500 houses were demolished and 102,000 new homes put in their place: smart, uniform apartment blocks that replaced the mix of architectural epochs that had been for centuries the hallmark of Paris.

There was more to Haussmann's plan than mere aesthetics. Paris was and still is a politically unpredictable city, and the straight avenues that made traffic communications so much easier also allowed troops access into the heart of the city to suppress any uprising. Beneath the boulevards ran a sophisticated sewer system, the cholera epidemics of 1848 and 1849 having taught the salutary lesson that disease is no respecter of class. The fetid courtyards and poor sanitation thought to be responsible for such outbreaks were eradicated and a large network of parks was created, often constructed in the very quarries that had supplied the raw materials for the new city. Paris was aglitter with illuminated cafés, their terraces spilling out onto the pavements along which "*le tout Paris*" glided, classes intermingling; identities confused. Paris was the first purpose-built city for the newly empowered bourgeois, its theaters, restaurants and monuments, its streets and apartments characterizing the new urban spectacle and laying down a challenge to the modern artist.

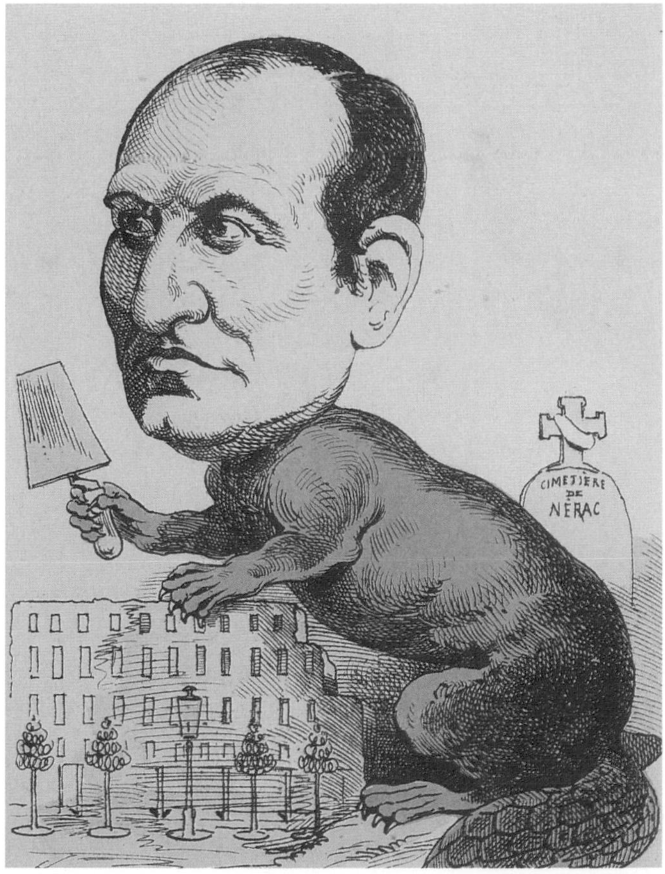

The two men most responsible for the transformation of Paris were Napoleon III and Baron Georges-Eugène Haussmann; the latter was accused by many of lining his own pockets in the process.

This was the Paris of Baudelaire, catching a glimpse of a woman he could love only to lose her to the crowd; where prostitutes could be confused with aristocratic ladies, and where blind beggars and rag-pickers rubbed shoulders with the aristocrat and the *flâneur*. In many ways the *flâneur* was the archetypal Parisian, cool, urbane and ironic.

The novelist Émile Zola made his fortune chronicling the epoch in a great cycle of novels (one of which was *Germinal*) based on the fortunes of the Rougon-Macquart families. These enthralled and disgusted a huge readership throughout the period. In his novels, the verbal counterpart to the paintings of Manet and the Impressionists, Paris is seen as a great hungry beast, devouring its prey.

Manet's attitude to this Paris was ambivalent. His early work was dedicated to both extremes of this society thrown together in the melee of reconstruction. His enthusiasm for this world and the opportunities that it offered cannot be missed in this letter to the minister of the Beaux-Arts, begging for a public commission to celebrate the public and commercial aspects of the new Paris: "I would have Paris-Markets, Paris-Railroads, Paris-Bridges, Paris-Underground, Paris-Racetracks and Gardens, Pont de l'Europe, the rebuilt Gare S. Lazare." His letter was ignored.

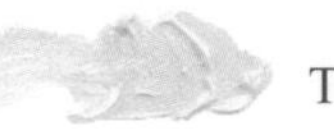

Inspiring Impressionism:
Charles Baudelaire

***Many people will attribute the present decadence in painting to our decadence in behavior … It is true that the great tradition has been lost, and that a new one has not yet been established.* – Baudelaire, 1846**

The Paris of the Impressionists has been repeatedly celebrated by poets, writers, artists and film-makers as one of the great romantic sites of the world. To those who witnessed its genesis, it presented a very different image. In his poem, *La Cygne (The Swan)*, Charles Pierre Baudelaire (1821–67) presents a world transfigured by a sense of alienation and loss, negative emotions which in being poetically expressed transform a prosaic reality into a series of dynamic images that burn in the consciousness like the poetry of Homer.

Le vieux Paris n'est plus
(la forme d'un ville
Change plus vite, hélas! que
le coeur d'un mortel).

Old Paris is no more (the townscape
changes faster, alas! than the human heart).

Théodore de Banville, standing at the poet's graveside, told those few gathered there, among whom was Manet, that Baudelaire "... accepted modern man in his entirety, with his weaknesses, his aspirations and his despair. He had thus been able to give beauty to sights that did not possess beauty in themselves, not by making them romantically picturesque, but by bringing to light the portion of human soul hidden in them; he had thus revealed the sad and often tragic heart of the modern city. That was why he haunted, and would always haunt, the minds of modern men, and move them when other artists left them cold." Baudelaire, more than anyone else, was the inspiration for the painters of modern life. Manet made Baudelaire's acquaintance in the early 1860s and was determined to use his writings as a program for his own artistic purposes. In his Salon review of 1846, Baudelaire included a section entitled "The Heroism of Modern Life," which was a plea to artists to turn away from outworn and outmoded forms of painting and to address modern life.

By "modernity" I mean the ephemeral, the contingent, the half of art whose other half is eternal and immutable. This painter of modern life will be he who concentrates upon its fashions, its morals, its emotions … on "the passing moment and all the suggestions of eternity it contains."

Although this describes Manet's painting perfectly, Baudelaire found his artistic commentator on modern life in the person of Constantin Guys, whose fleeting pen and ink sketches were also much admired by Manet. Baudelaire's hero, the man most suited to uncovering and giving form to the novelty of urban experience was the *flâneur*, a latter-day dandy whose ironical stance toward life put him in the ideal role as a detached observer of modern life.

Baudelaire and the flâneur

Impressionist paintings always give the impression that the viewer is a natural extension of the scene depicted or, to put it a different way, that it is the spectator's view that is being presented. You are quite literally in the picture. From this simple point another develops: who is this person, this viewer? In the twentieth century it would be fair to say that the expected audience of a picture could encompass all social types, but after the middle of the nineteenth century the view encompassed by most Impressionist paintings is that of the white, middle-class male. It is his view of the world that is presented for our appraisal. The viewpoint suggested by the paintings of Manet, Degas, Monet and Renoir is that of the *flâneur*, the detached ironic observer epitomized for Baudelaire in the figure of Constantin Guys, mobile, curious and detached, a wanderer in a world that no longer makes sense.

Baudelaire was the translator of American writer Edgar Allen Poe's stories and poems, including his short story, *The Man of the Crowd*, in which the man of the title watches the ceaselcss rush of humanity from the security of his coffee house and struggles to reach an understanding of their identities and characters. But such is the nature of modern existence that human relationships are now in crisis, no one knows their neighbors, identities are confused and the one who wishes to understand such things – like the detective heroes of Poe and, later, Conan Doyle – must do so in the reading of traits, and a search for clues hidden in people's physiognomies and bearing. Impressionist painting can be seen as an attempt to chart, order and interpret differing aspects of their world. Baudelaire wrote *The Painter of Modern Life* in the late 1850s and published it in 1863. It became the model for many other aspirant interpreters of "*la vie moderne*." For Baudelaire, the speed of the artists' execution had to match the transitory nature of the contemporary scene and Guys' rapid pen-and-ink sketches of high and low Parisian society did just that.

Manet meets Baudelaire

Manet was a young ambitious artist when he met Baudelaire, who was then reaching the end of his life and belonged to another generation. Baudelaire's real hero was Eugène Delacroix, admired by the young painters as a daring and rebellious artist, a great colorist and innovative technician, but who was, for the older poet, one of "*Les Phares*," a continuer of the great tradition stretching back past Goya and Watteau to Rubens. More than anything, Baudelaire wished for an artist who could interpret the tragedy of modern existence on the scale attempted by Delacroix. No wonder, then, that when he wrote to Manet, his words of encouragement were muted and enigmatic: "You are the first in the denigration of art." For all the perceptiveness of his writing, Baudelaire's vision of a great imaginative art remained indissolubly linked to the past.

Eugéne Delacroix,* Jacob Wrestling with the Angel, *1859–61. This large fresco is part of a cycle in the church of Saint-Sulpice, Paris, and was Delacroix's final masterpiece. In such works, Delacroix revealed his ability to create a heroic public art.

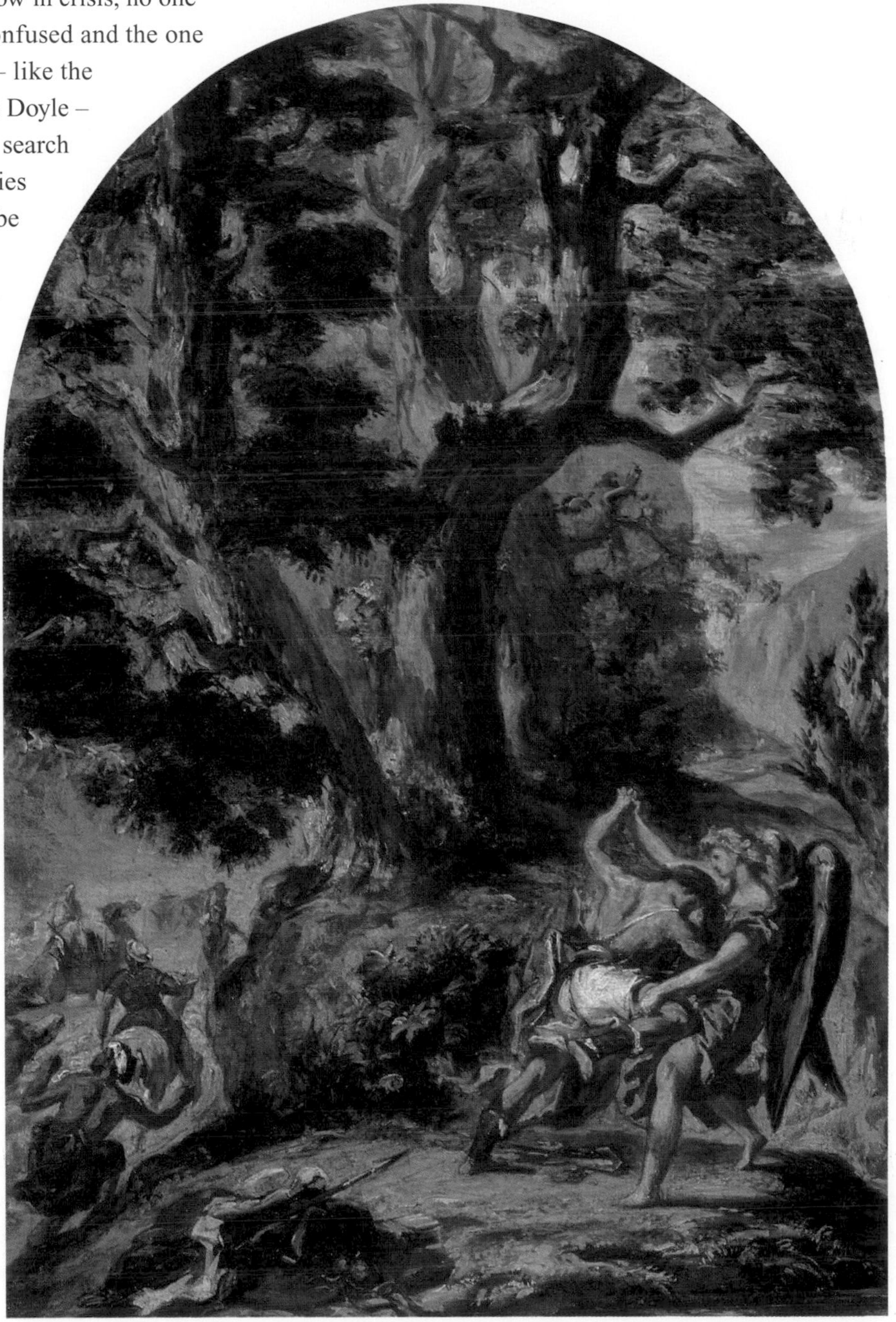

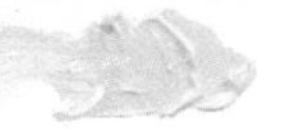

Edouard Manet:
the reluctant rebel

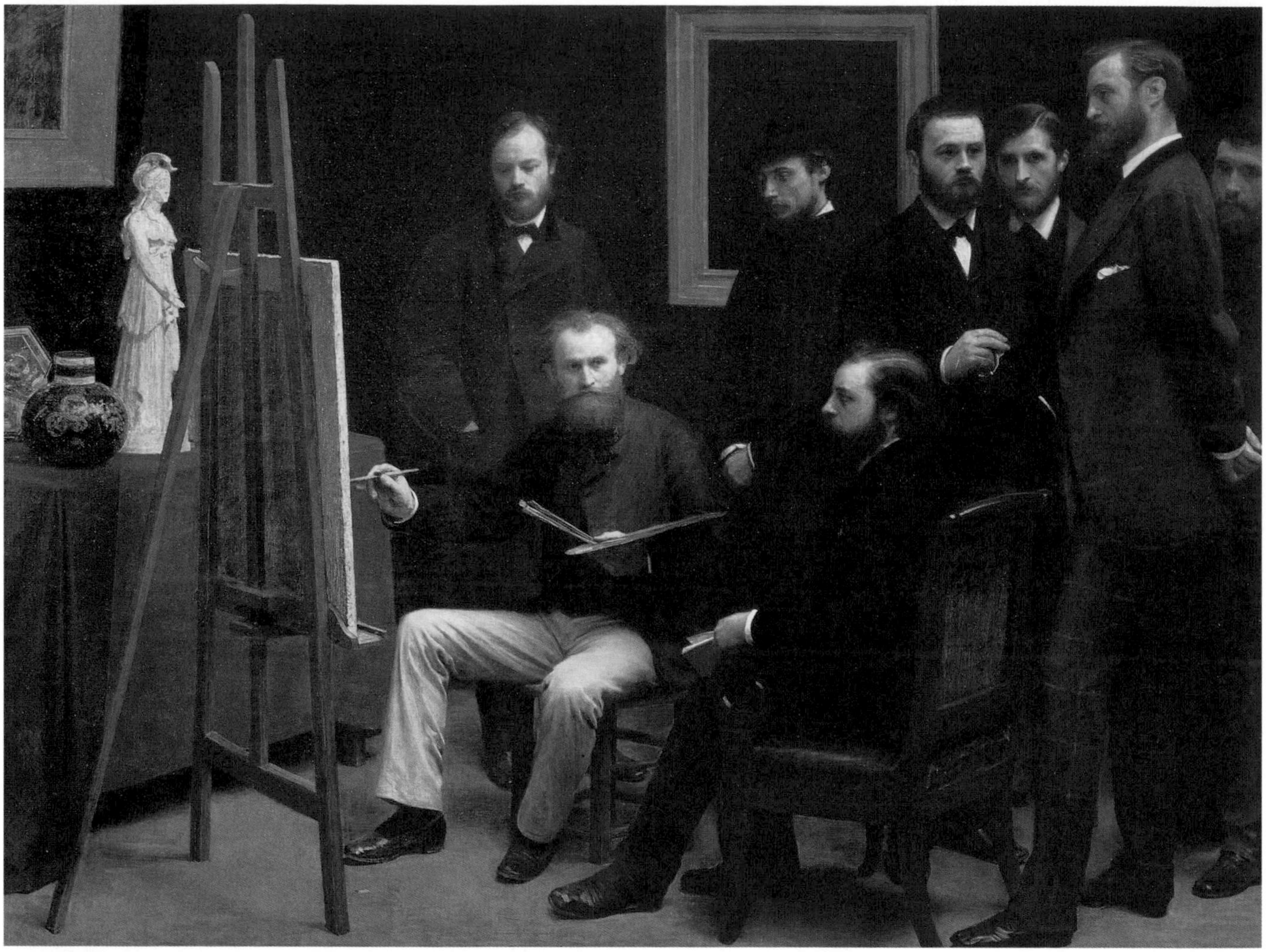

Henri Fantin-Latour, **A Studio in the Batignolles Quarter***, 1870. Manet is shown here surrounded by the realist cabal.*

> ***They're so boring these Italians, with their allegories, their characters from*** **Jerusalem Divided** ***or*** **Orlando Furioso*****, with all that showy bric-a-brac. An artist can say everything with fruit or flowers, or simply with clouds.*** **Monet speaking in Venice, 1874–75**

Edouard Manet (1832–83) was an immensely gifted painter from an upper middle-class family who, or so it seemed to most critics, was prepared to squander his talent in a series of inexplicably bizarre and subversive canvases that could only have a disruptive influence on the course of French art. A rebel *malgré lui*, he was regarded by friends as the epitome of the sophisticated boulevardier, handsome, immaculately attired, witty and urbane. Freedom from financial constraints gave him an independence not granted to some of his colleagues and his persistent refusal to show with the Impressionists may have been an indication of his middle-class attachment to officialdom. Although commonly held to be the leader of the Impressionists, he remained committed to his firm belief that the Salon was the only proper site for artistic disputes.

Abandoning plans to train as a naval officer, Manet entered the studio of the highly successful and well-respected academic history painter, Thomas Couture. Although in constant rebellion against the regime he found there, he remained on the studio's register for six years, absorbing a thorough grounding in academic practice and a healthy disdain for all that it implied. This did not stop him from adopting several of Couture's procedures, not the least of which included his rich encrusted surfaces, broad, expressive brushwork and the acquisition of a speedy improvisatory manner of painting. Manet's earliest paintings reveal his elusive and enigmatic character and show his allegiance to the romantic painting of Delacroix and the painterly schools of Rubens and seventeenth-century painters such as Frans Hals and Diego Velázquez.

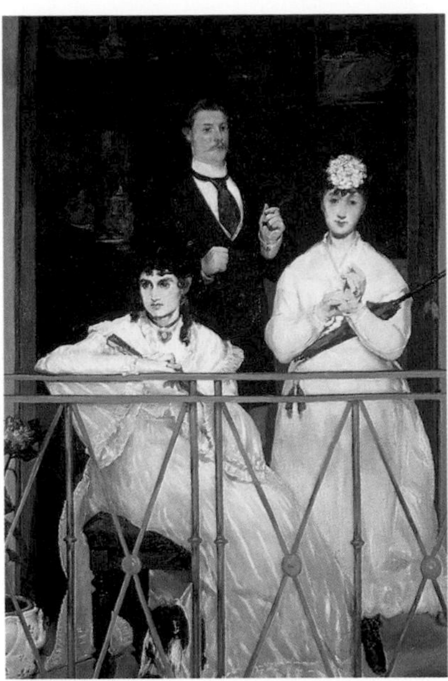

Edouard Manet, **The Balcony,** *1868–9.*

In the late 1850s he became infatuated with Baudelaire's writings and committed himself to the writer's program for the painting of modern life. The critic's profile appears in Manet's first masterly evocation of *la vie moderne*, *Music in the Tuileries Gardens*, completed in 1862, which shows a deliberate disregard for academic conventions. The artist's own features are visible at the far left of the canvas. Painted with verve and surety, the painting gives the impression of a frozen moment of time. For all its apparent spontaneity, close examination reveals the struggle necessary to give form to this informal gathering in the emperor's gardens.

Soon after, Manet completed *Luncheon on the Grass (Déjeuner sur l'herbe)* and *Olympia*, both of which were to meet with a chorus of critical disapproval. Shown at the Salon des Refusés of 1863, *Luncheon on the Grass* was seen as being morally and artistically provocative and ensured Manet's reputation as the leader of the avant-garde throughout the 1860s. This position was confirmed when *Olympia* was accepted at the Salon of 1865 and by the success of his one-man exhibition at Martinet's gallery in 1867.

Olympia suffered a critical fate identical to his *Luncheon on the Grass*. Its dependency upon Titian's *Venus of Urbino* could not sanction the model's obvious persona; she was clearly not some mythological goddess, which would have been perfectly acceptable, satisfactory, but a low-class prostitute reclining on a day bed, looking coolly out of the picture at her prospective client: the viewer.

In the 1870s Manet adopted many of the practices of his younger friends and companions. He turned away from reworking subjects from the past and paintings with overtly political implications for an art based upon a frank acceptance of the everyday. He adopted the younger artists' palette, with broken flecks of color, abandoning the beautiful "prune juice" for which he had been previously famed.

During this period he received a measure of official success. In 1873 his portrait of an engraver, Emile Bellot, *Le Bon Bock*, a homage to Frans Hals, was accepted at the Salon and gained considerable critical approval. Throughout the seventies his subjects continued his celebration of the leisure and low-life culture that had attracted him from the first and his paintings lost nothing of their subtle and enigmatic qualities. His late masterpiece *A Bar at the Folies-Bergère* (1881) combined all these elements.

Craving acceptance

Paradoxically, despite his continued ability to offend press and public alike, he craved official recognition, especially the prestigious *Legion d'honneur*, an accolade that eluded him until the year before his premature death at the age of 52.

The last two years of his life saw the production of some of his most exquisite works. Made during a period of dramatically declining health, his paintings of his garden, flower pieces and still lifes belie the suffering he was undergoing at the time. In 1882, Manet fell seriously ill with locomotor ataxia – an advanced complication of syphilis. In spite of the amputation of his leg, he died at his home at Versailles on April 30, 1883.

Manet's reputation remained in doubt until some years after his death. In February 1884 a public auction of his work was a failure. Eventually Monet, an ardent admirer of Manet, worked hard to raise funds to buy *Olympia*, one of the paintings that had failed to find a buyer at the auction, for the national collection of modern art at the Musée Luxembourg. After much publicity, and with the help of Zola, the painting was eventually acquired by the French state, and Manet's reputation as the leader of the avant-garde was confirmed.

The Salon des Refusés

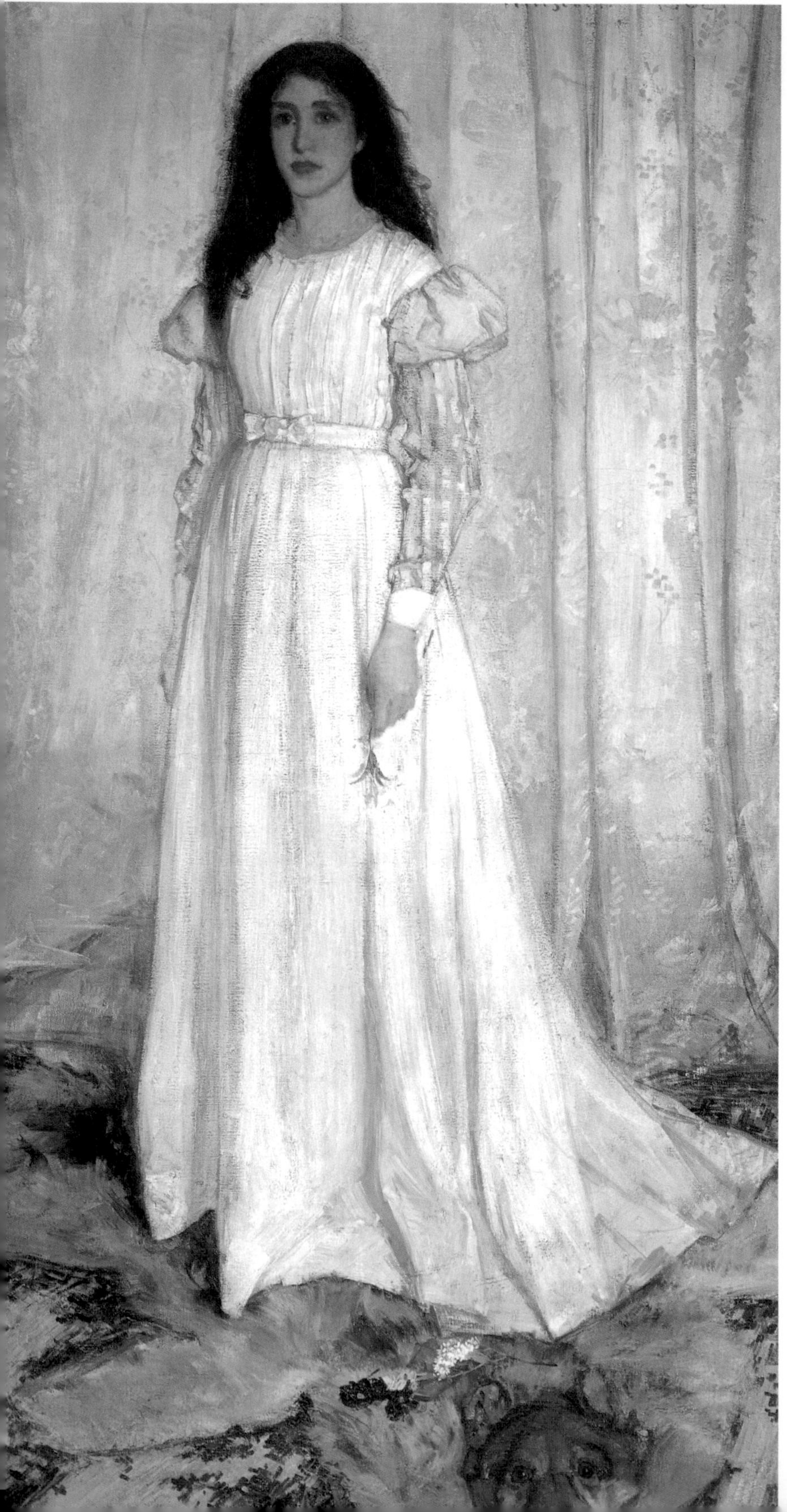

In 1863, 2,783 out of 5,000 works submitted for the annual Salon were rejected by the jury. This unwarranted severity was considered too much, even by the Emperor, and as a result, he initiated the Salon des Refusés. On April 24, *Le Moniteur Universelle*, the official newspaper of the regime, announced that those artists who wished to show their rejected works would be given the opportunity to do so, separately from the official Salon, in an annex of the Palais de l'Industrie. Entry was effected from the Salon by turnstile as if, as one commentator noted ominously "one was entering the chamber of horrors at Madame Tussaud's."

The Salon des Refusés might be seen as a cynical exercise in public relations on the Emperor's part, but it was also the first time that the public would be given the chance to assess the judgment of the jury. Any hope of a reversal in government policy was lost when the public took the opportunity to enjoy themselves at the artists' expense. The possibility that this might happen, as well as the fear of antagonizing the all-powerful jury, stopped many artists from accepting the Emperor's invitation. Those who were brave – or foolhardy – enough to exhibit, included Manet, Whistler, Pissarro, Jongkind and Cézanne. Cézanne's submission included a large female nude that was painted deliberately to provoke comment.

Over 7,000 visitors thronged the exhibition hall on the first day, among them Cézanne's friend the novelist, Émile Zola. An atmospheric account of the occasion is included in Zola's book, *L'Oeuvre*, published in 1886, in which he refers to a painting, *Plein Air*, which bears more than a passing resemblance to Manet's *Luncheon on the Grass*, which was originally titled *Le Bain (Bathing)*.

Although catastrophic for both Manet and Whistler, the Salon des Refusés delivered a crucial blow to the authority of the official Salon and set a precedent for further independent exhibitions, including, of course, the eight independent shows organized by the Impressionists. In 1881 the state renounced all control over the Salon, putting its affairs entirely in the hands of the artists themselves. By this time, many independent bodies were holding alternative exhibitions, effectively bringing the once near absolute authority of the Salon to an end.

James McNeill Whistler,* The White Girl, *1862. Rejected by the Royal Academy in London and the Paris Salon of 1863, the painting was exhibited at the Salon des Refusés.

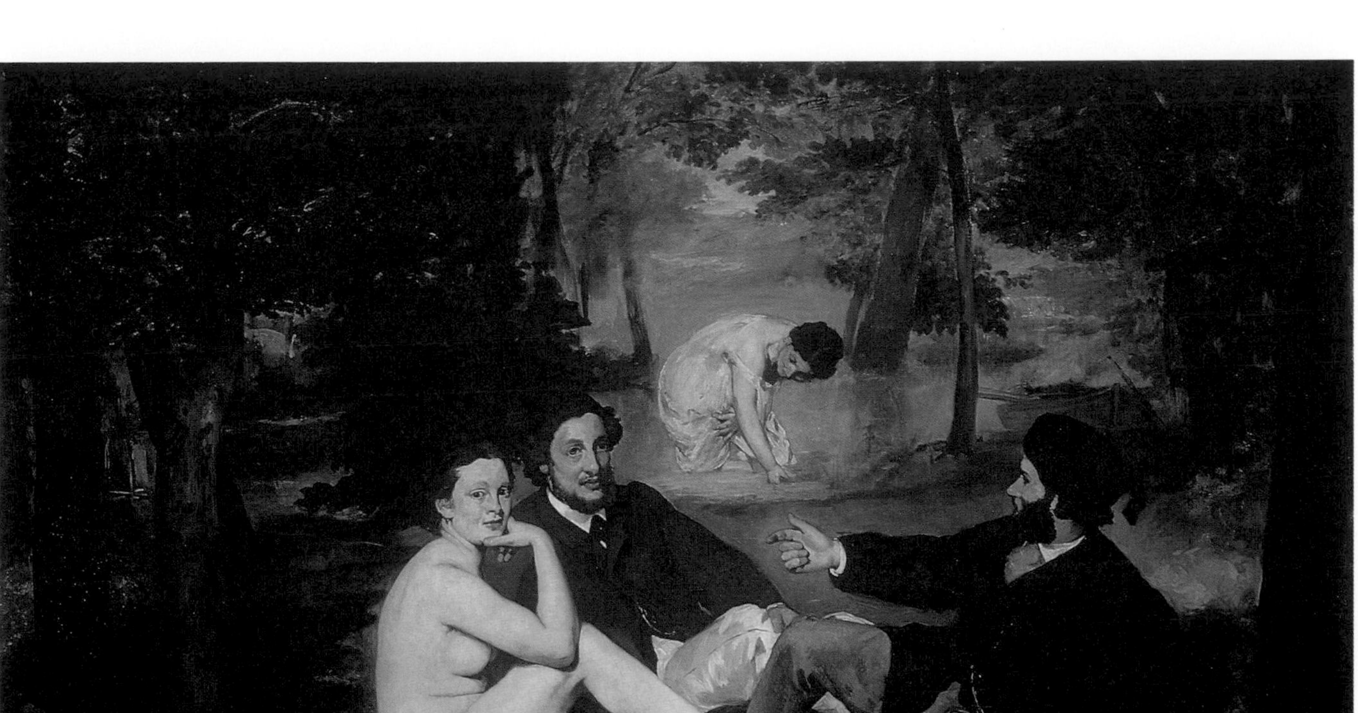

Edouard Manet, **Luncheon on the Grass (Le Déjeuner sur l'Herbe),** ***1863. Manet's favorite model, Victoire Meurent, looks out at the viewer in this modern reworking of Giorgione's*** **Fête Champêtre.**

The White Girl

Ridiculed at the Salon des Refusés, Whistler's *The White Girl*, painted in Paris in 1862, was a portrait of his mistress, the red-haired Irish model, Joanna Heffernan, who subsequently left Whistler for Courbet. With this work, the American artist hoped to carve a niche for himself in the Parisian art world. The critic Paul Mantz declared it a "Symphony in White," and this musical description was adopted by Whistler for many of his subsequent works.

Déjeuner sur l'Herbe

A calculated painting which takes the age-old theme of the female nude in the landscape, a familiar theme in Renaissance painting, here updated to make a statement on the liberated sexuality of bohemian life. The two young men were identifiable as modishly attired students, while the young women could well be milliners or laundresses, taking advantage of their leisure time and the lack of familial control to enjoy a trip upriver with their gentlemen friends. Manet, however, has refused to create a neat narrative which would allow the viewer to indulge in sensual reverie. The naked girl ignores her male companions and turns her face toward us as we intrude upon this scene of bucolic delight; we are no longer allowed to be passive observers of a sanctioned erotic scene, but instead are actively involved in the painting and what it depicts.

There they are, under the trees, the principal lady entirely undressed ... another female in a chemise, coming out of a little stream that was hard by, and two Frenchmen [Gustave Manet, Eugène's youngest brother and Ferdinand Leenhof, his brother-in-law] in wide-awakes sitting on the very green grass with a stupid look of bliss. There are other pictures of the same class which lead to the inference that the nude, when painted by vulgar men, is inevitably indecent. **PG Hamerton (critic), 1892**

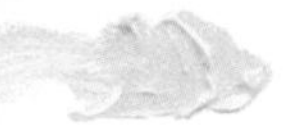

Modern Life:
Manet's Olympia

In his *Luncheon on the Grass*, Manet takes a theme that has occupied a central place in Western art for centuries, interpreting it in starkly modern terms. The idealized female nude has so often been painted by artists such as Botticelli, Poussin, Rubens, and others that it has become synonymous with art itself.

The nude enjoyed a special vogue during the nineteenth century; garbed with appropriate attributes, she could represent the highest of intellectual or moral values, while simultaneously allowing the male viewer to enjoy a piece of sanitized eroticism masquerading as high culture. Manet's painting, at a single blow, reveals this hypocritical practice by subverting the codes of representation that allowed such images to operate. In doing so, he posed questions that artists and writers on art have continued to wrestle with until the present day.

Birth of Venus

The Salon of 1863 was called the "Salon des Trois Vénus," a reference to the three classically inspired nudes that were on show there. All were highly praised by the press, but Alexandre Cabanel's *Birth of Venus* outshone them all. Made safe by its academic drawing, its careful modeling and the cosmeticized body of the goddess (unlike Manet's *Olympia*, she has no body hair) this voluptuous painting was the most successful of the year. The artist had confected a cunning mix of the theme of the captive slave (the Odalisque), the academic life study and classical mythology, with a reference to the revered seventeenth-century master of academic art, Nicolas Poussin, thrown in for good measure. Millet, who had begun his career as a painter of erotic subjects, recognized its appeal, noting that "I have never seen anything that seems to me to hold such an effective and direct appeal to the passion of bankers

Alexandre Cabanel,* Birth of Venus, *1863. A sensational trivialization of the Greek myth of the bloody birth of Venus, this sexy shocker was one of the great artistic successes of the year.

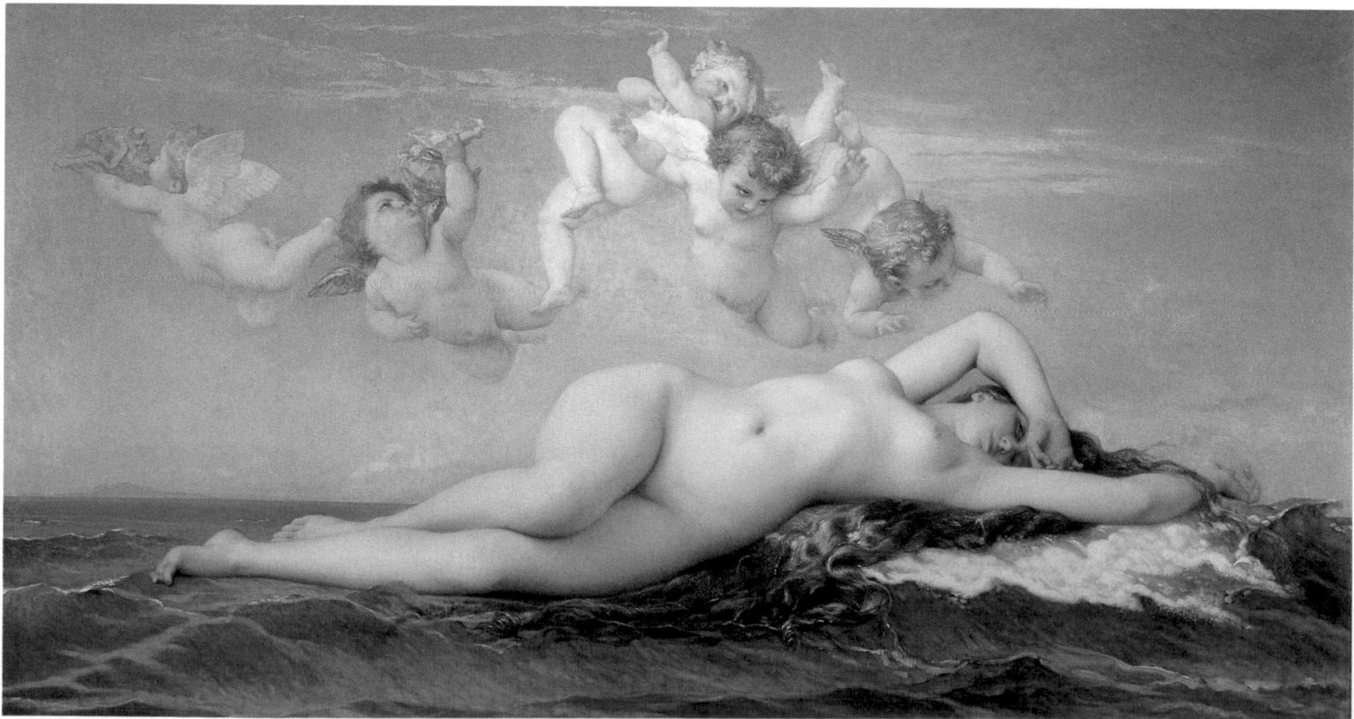

 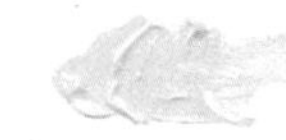

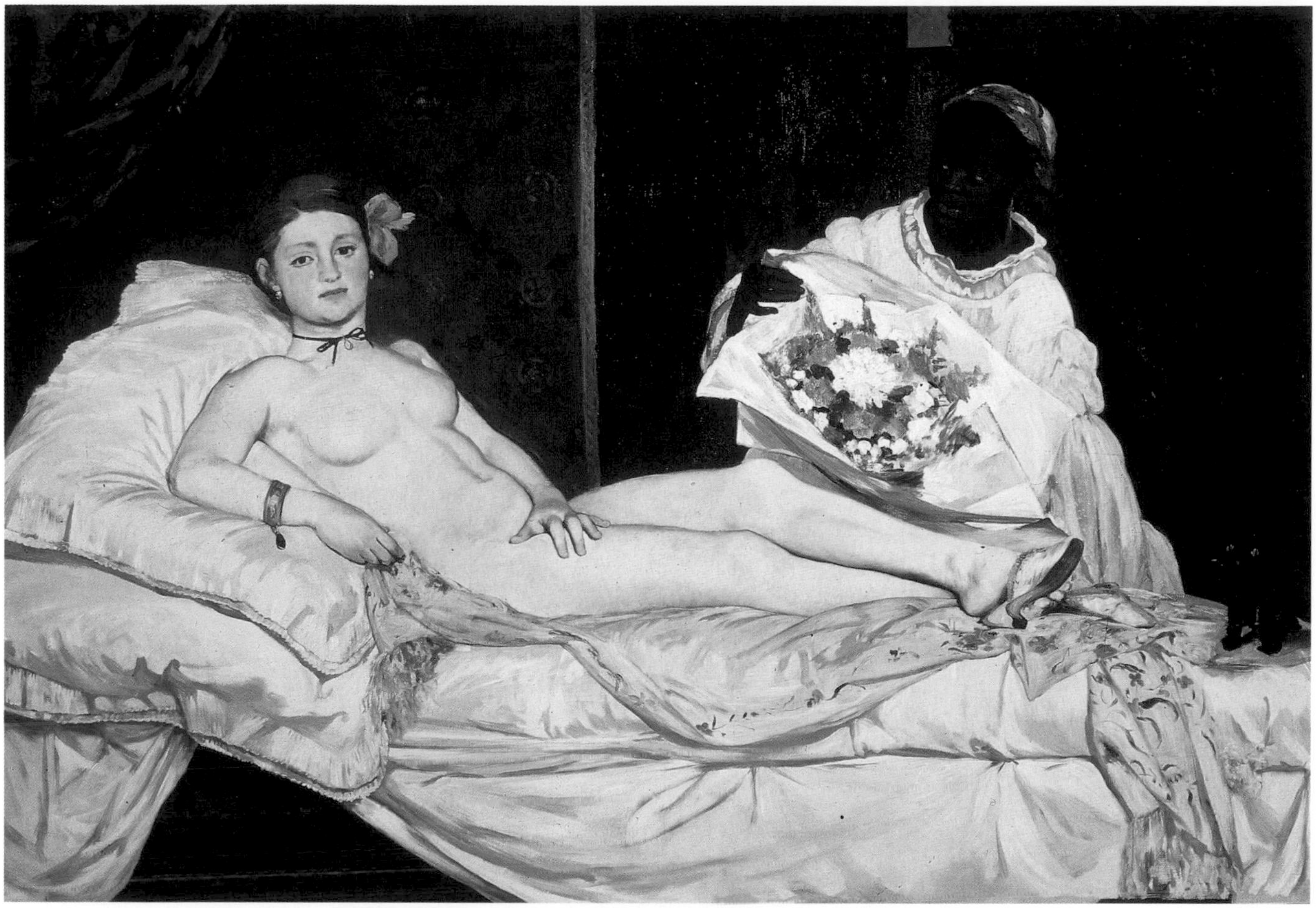

***Edouard Manet,* Olympia*, 1863. The title refers to the then well-known prostitute's name, which had featured in Alexandre Dumas' popular novel, adapted for the stage in 1855,* Les Dames aux Camelias.**

and agents of change." The sensual charge of the work was made even more evident by Zola's writing in *La Vie Parisienne, "la déese, noyée dans un fleuve de lait, en paté d'amande blanche et rose"* ("The goddess made of pink and white marzipan, drowning in a flood of milk"). The painting's official seal of approval came with its acquisition by the Elysée Palace, and its eventual arrival at the Musée du Luxembourg in 1881.

An act of homage

At once an act of homage to the past and a provocative gesture to the present, Manet's painting was a shock to the male audience for whom such works were primarily intended. The title is not a direct classical allusion, which might have given the painting a spurious respectability, but a reference to the main character in a recent novel about the life of a street prostitute. Her professional calling would have been abundantly clear to the contemporary viewer. *Olympia* makes reference not only to masterpieces of the past, but also to the stream of erotic or pornographic prints and photographs that flooded the Second Empire. The cat arches its back, the flowers proffered by the negro servant are ignored. The woman's cool gaze looks directly back at the viewer, incorporating him into the field of the painting and, by extension, identifying him as the client who has just entered the room and whose gift of flowers is being so assiduously ignored. She, unlike the cat, is not perturbed by this sudden arrival; she reclines, her breasts uncovered and her hand resting nonchalantly across her pelvis. This gesture does not invite access, but denies it. Here is a woman with a mind and, perhaps, a body, of her own. Manet has painted his model with a directness that parallels the frankness of her gaze.

Each aspect of the composition creates a dialogue with Titian's original. To our eyes, Manet's paintings have a distinctly self-conscious air, but to his contemporaries the paintings appeared supremely natural and, therefore, even more reprehensible. Such work, in an age that was concerned with the debilitation of "high art" and the corresponding popularity of realism, could only be regarded as the antithesis of art, and thereby, a threat to the fragile moral order of the day.

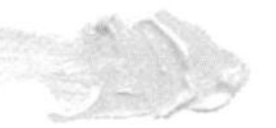

Edgar Degas: the paradoxical painter

Hilaire-Germain-Edgar de Gas (1834–1917) was born into an aristocratic family of Italian extraction. He received a strict classical education and inherited from his parents a passion for music. His father and mother encouraged their son in his artistic education, allowing him to travel to Italy between 1854 and 1859. There he followed a self-directed study of monuments and works of art. He was helped in his researches by the older artist Gustave Moreau, who remained committed to the high ideals of history painting.

On his return to Paris, Degas took the first steps toward becoming a painter in the manner of his hero, the arch academic painter Ingres, who by that time was an irascible old man. His advice to the young artist was never forgotten: "Draw lines, young man, many lines." Degas set about his canvases in the time-honored fashion, researching his sources and producing drawn and painted studies and sketches, a working procedure he never abandoned. None of these extraordinary early paintings was ever brought to completion, and many remained in his studio until his death, some retouched over the intervening years. While in Italy he had begun a portrait of his aunt and her family with whom he had stayed, the first of countless portraits of his family and friends. It was this practice that drew him inevitably away from history painting toward the painting of modern life, although he never forgot his allegiance to the art of the past. His relationship with the past is evident in his sometimes surprising and ingenious reinterpretations of previous works of art. His notebooks bear witness to this concern, for example: "O Giotto, let me see Paris, and you, Paris, let me see Giotto!"

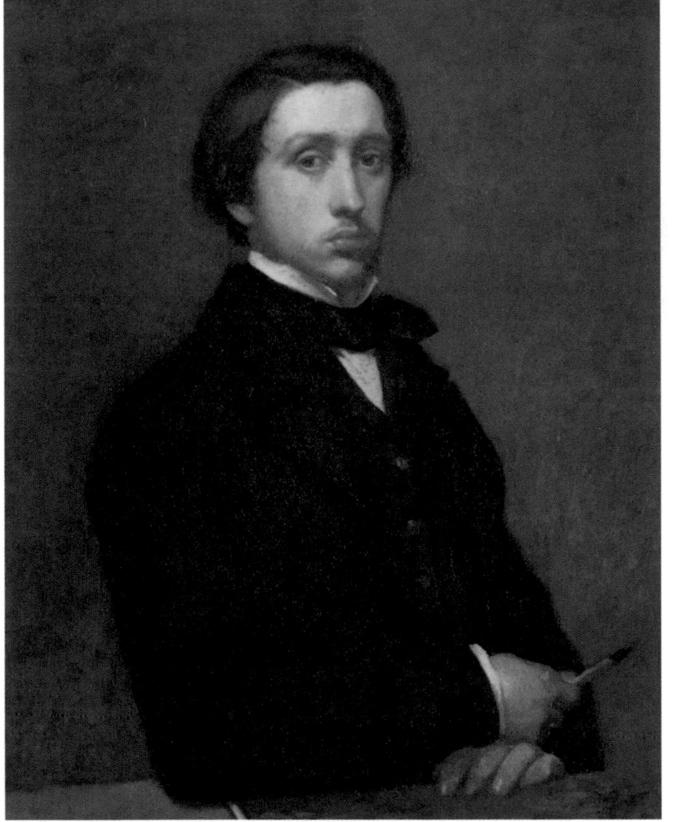

Edgar Degas,* Self-Portrait, *1857. The cool gaze, somber colors and careful drawing reveal the artist's association with the* Ingriste *tradition. The pose is reminiscent of Titian's portraits.

Extraordinary powers

Degas was an integral part of the sophisticated Parisian set. He remained close to Manet and, like him, stayed in Paris throughout the Commune and its aftermath. It was during this period that he developed the eyesight problems that were to plague him all his life. He was fiercely independent; paradoxically, it was he and not Manet who joined the Impressionists, although he remained somewhat apart from his landscape-orientated colleagues. He played an active part in organizing their exhibitions, but his caustic and idiosyncratic manner put a great strain on their personal relationships. After the failure of his family's bank in 1874, he undertook to honor the debts incurred by its collapse, which meant that he was obliged to consider the commercial aspects of his profession. His works, especially his early ones, were always in demand, and his reputation as an artist of extraordinary powers may well have been one of the reasons that his Impressionist colleagues put up with this increasingly cantankerous individual.

Paris fascinated Degas and he took full advantage of all the opportunities the city offered someone as visually voracious as himself. He painted and drew the opera, ballet dancers, jockeys and prostitutes, as well as the members of his own social circle. These were subjects shared by his social equal, Manet, but their resulting works were very different.

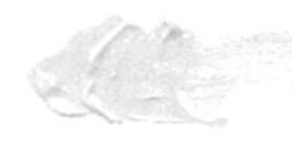

Degas remained a bachelor all his life. His obsession with the female form is evident in his countless depictions of women and young girls, in which the qualities of voyeurism and empathy intermingle. His wit and temper were much feared by his contemporaries. As he grew older and his eyesight deteriorated, he grew more and more intransigent, totally immersing himself in the processes of his profession: much of his late work remains unfinished. He practiced in every medium, pushing the aesthetic and physical possibilities of each to its extremes, whether it be charcoal, clay, wax, pastel or oil. His work rarely carries an overt narrative, but is pregnant with psychological tensions. Throughout, he maintained that his choice of subject matter was only a pretext for artistic concerns.

Degas continued to work well into the twentieth century, producing astonishing work right up to the eve of World War I. Degas died in 1917.

Edgar Degas,* Portrait of the Bellelli Family*, c. 1860. An incisive study of a dysfunctional family unit, startling in its psychological insight and innovative composition.

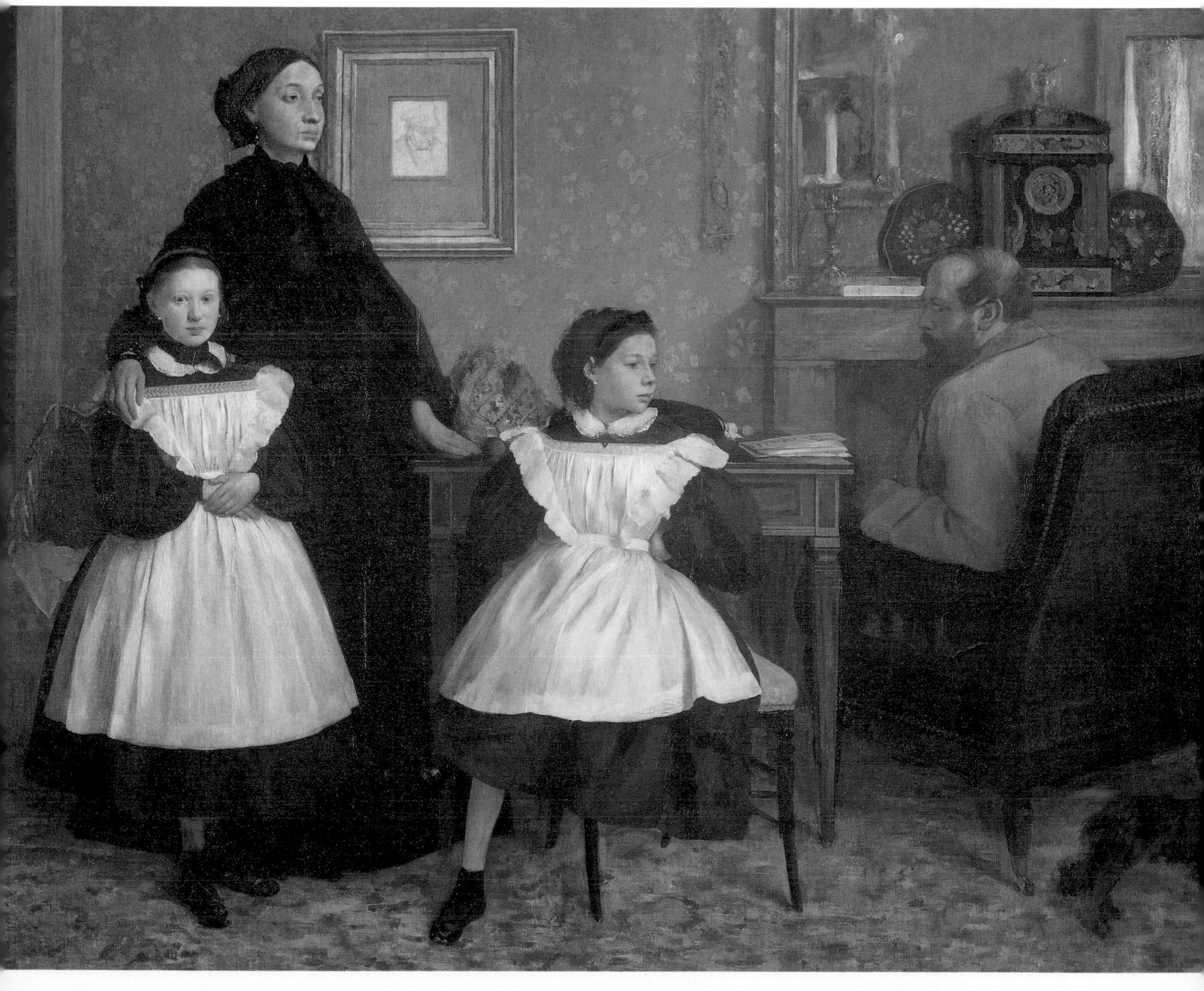

The Young Spartans

c.1860, oil on canvas, 109 x 154.3 cm (43 x 61 in), National Gallery, London, England

***They take me for a painter of the Ballet without realizing that it's only there I can discover the movement of the Greeks.* – Degas**

Manet's taunt "I was painting Paris when you were painting Semiramis," marks not only the rivalry that existed between these two friends, but also Degas' late conversion to modern-day subjects. Until the mid-1860s he struggled to bring his historical and Biblical paintings to completion; none ever was. All were left at various stages and many were subsequently reworked. *The Young Spartans* is almost a textbook example of this practice. Its surface is thick with repeated layers of pigment, scraped down in some areas and over-painted in others. A network of lines defines and redefines the shifting contours of the protagonists. The poses and attitudes seen in this work, its daring dynamics of color and line and the depiction of arrested movement, remain constant preoccupations in Degas' art. Degas was one of the most consummate draughtsmen in Western art. His obsession with the human form can be seen in the many preparatory studies that survive for this painting; a practice obsessionally followed throughout his working life.

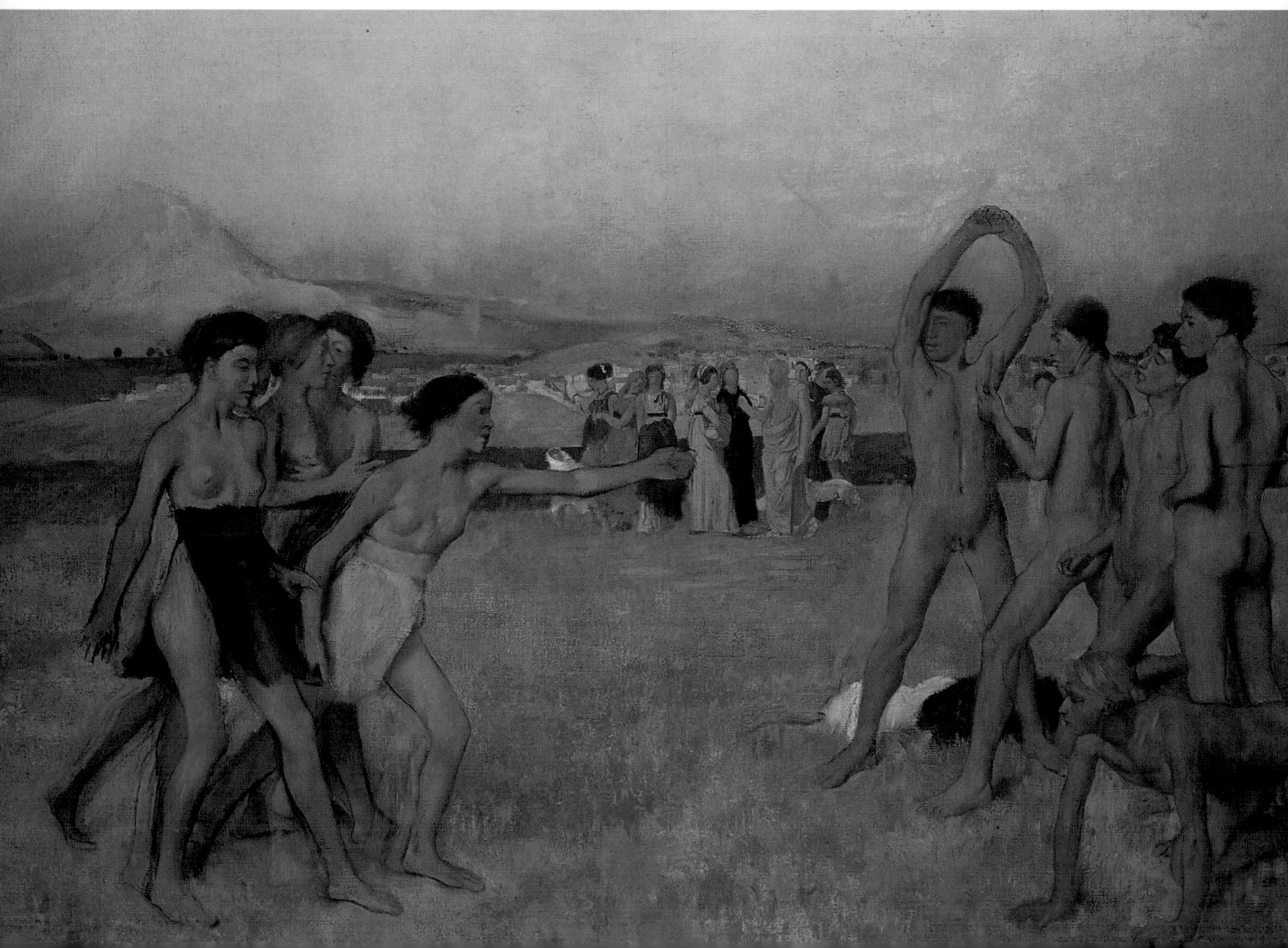

Like all males of his social class, Degas had been immersed in classical culture while at school and was taught that present-day culture had its roots in that of classical antiquity. An unusual subject, deriving from Plutarch, its full title is *The Young Spartan Girls Provoking the Boys*. In choosing to paint this scene of adolescent behavior Degas reveals his predilection for subjects that are founded on the subtle and occasionally not so subtle relationships between the sexes. The figures are set out as if on a stage, like ballet dancers or cabaret singers, and the overall composition could come from any number of sources; many have been cited, from Mantegna to Ingres, and including classical reliefs seen in the Louvre or in Naples, but no one source dominates any of the others. Degas' immense knowledge of past and present art has here been thoroughly assimilated with an authority nourished by direct experience.

As the young artist researched his sources, drew and painted his compositional sketches and made countless drawings from the model necessary for the preparation of an ambitious canvas, it is evident that he found it impossible to reproduce the banal idealized nudes favored by so many of his contemporaries. These "Spartan adolescents" are, in fact, young gamins and gamines from le Butte Montmartre, their proletarian features, snub noses and angular forms identifying them as unique individuals of the artist's own time. The painting has a vitality often missing from that of contemporary painters of mythological and classical scenes like Puvis de Chavannes, Gustave Moreau and Elié Delaunay. Degas was well aware of this, and later in life he referred to Moreau, his one-time artistic mentor, as an artist who painted "the Gods with watch chains."

A sense of heroic scale is suggested by the frieze-like nature of the painting. The two sexes are set on opposite sides of the canvas, a common characteristic of Degas' art. The girl's outstretched arm creates a dynamic link between the two groups and activates the empty space in the central portion of the canvas. Ochers and greens prevail throughout the canvas, relieved by occasional touches of bright color, most evident in the area of red paint in the lower left corner, scrubbed in at some later date. The passage describing the girls' legs show Degas' seemingly endless revisions, left apparently unresolved, but in effect giving an energetic power to the work. Degas' fineness of intellect and the influence of friends like Manet drew him away from the world of antiquity. Through painting portraits of his friends and family set in their immediate milieu and through his constant visits to the theater, opera and ballet, he began to depict the world of his social circle with all the high seriousness and creative insight evident in his history paintings.

Their archaic and often obscure subject matter, as much as their lack of completion, lends to these works an enigmatic character that is a feature of much of his later work.

The pictures of modern life he painted were conceived in the same way as his early biblical or historical works and his art may be considered as a sustained dialogue between the art of the past and the unavoidable necessity of painting pictures relevant to one's own time.

Degas once remarked "No art was less spontaneous than mine. What I do is the result of reflection and the study of great masters; of inspiration, spontaneity, temperament, I know nothing." In *The Young Spartans* the whole of Degas' art is here in embryo, his often underestimated interest in the landscape, his love of the art of the past, his concern for movement, color and drawing, and, in the transformation of the ancient Greeks into contemporary street urchins, his ambition to depict modern life. The painting was not shown at the Impressionist exhibition of 1880, despite the appearance of its title in the catalog.

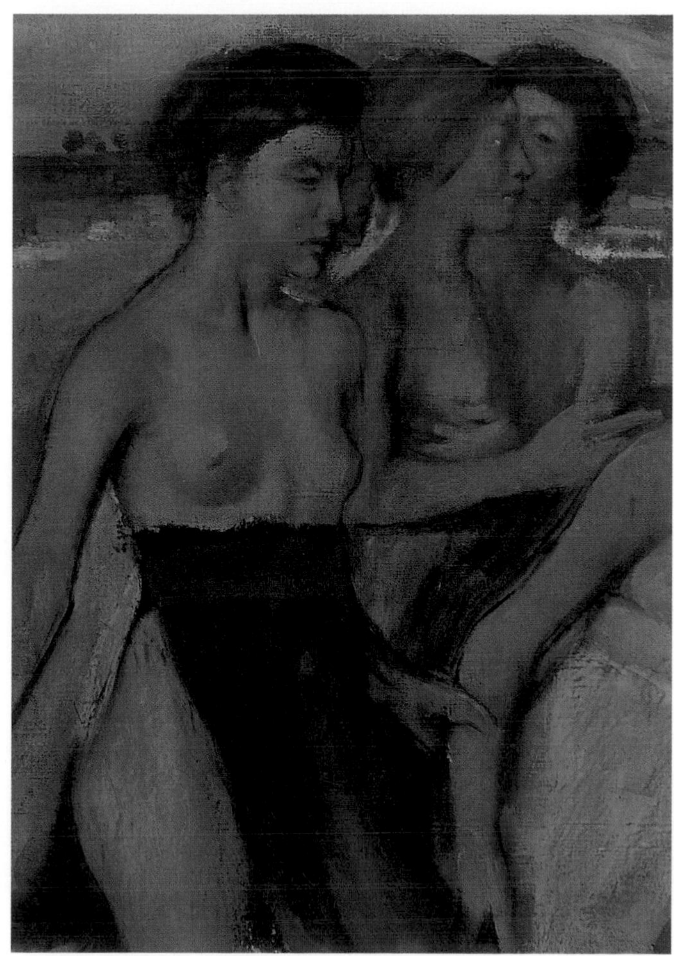

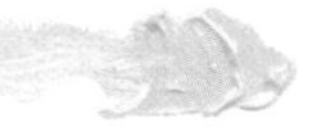

"La Vie Bohème": student days in Paris

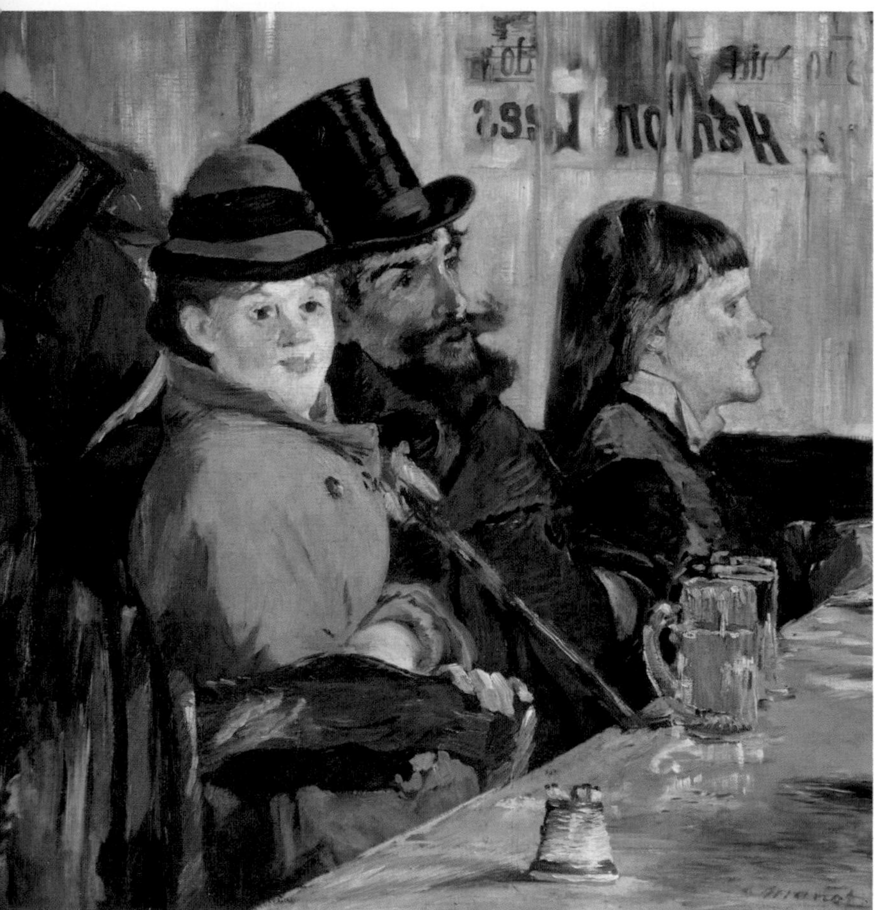

Manet, **At the Café,** *1878.*

In May 1867, Frédéric Bazille, writing to his parents, told them of a "document" that was being "signed at this moment demanding an exhibition of the Refusés. This petition is being supported by all the painters of Paris who are of any value." Although the plans referred to by Bazille came to nothing, they sowed the seeds for future events.

During the 1860s the artists referred to by Bazille had met and become acquainted with each other in the various studios and bars of the city. At the end of the working day they would gather in haunts such as the Café Guerbois and, in later years, the Café de la Nouvelle-Athènes, both situated conveniently in the newly developed Batignolles district of Paris. Avant-garde groups of writers and artists were gaining confidence and solidarity by forming cabals of like-minded friends. The Irish writer George Moore, then an aspirant artist and general hanger-on, left this vivid description of the Café de la Nouvelle-Athènes:

> ***I can hear the glass door of the café grate on the sand as I open it. I can recall the smell of every hour. In the morning that of eggs frizzling in butter, the pungent cigarette, coffee and bad cognac; at five o'clock the fragrant odor of absinthe; ... the usual marble tables are there, and it is there we sat and aestheticized till two o'clock in the morning.***

Such places were male preserves and out of bounds to respectable women, which meant that artists such as Berthe Morisot, friend of Manet and pupil of Corot and Fantin-Latour, and, later, Mary Cassatt were deprived of the privilege of sharing the lively and not infrequently acrimonious exchanges of ideas and opinions. Their knowledge of such intimate and important goings-on could only have reached them secondhand.

At the Académie Suisse

Although Impressionism had such a spectacular birth in 1874, its gestation was a long and anxious one. On his arrival in Paris, Monet sought out the Académie Suisse, where he met Camille Pissarro, the "only one landscapist" there. Pissarro was Monet's elder by eleven years, and the meeting would have strengthened their mutual concern with *plein-air* painting. Paul Cézanne, encouraged by his childhood friend, Émile Zola, a Paris resident of three years' standing and a habitué of its literary cafés, had followed his example and had arrived in the capital in 1861. Determined to be an artist, he also attended the Académie Suisse, making powerfully realized studies from the life model and, like Monet, benefiting from the example and character of the kindly Pissarro.

Monet frequented the bohemian world of Courbet, centred on the Brasserie Andler, known to many as the "Temple of Realism," and the Brasserie des Martyrs. The drinking and

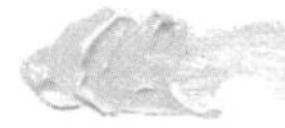

womanizing, as well as the artistic and political discussions that took place in such establishments were celebrated in Henri Mürger's novel *Scènes de la Vie Bohème*, first published in 1851. Such an existence was a far cry from the bourgeois order of Monet's family home in Le Havre and would have contributed to his already considerable sense of independence.

All this came to an abrupt, if temporary, halt for Monet in 1862, when he was conscripted and found himself shipped to North Africa. His stay there was brief, but the experience of Africa's intense color and light, shared with his hero Delacroix who had visited North Africa in 1832, was crucial to the development of his art.

Charles Gleyre's studio

On his return to Paris later in 1862, Monet enrolled at Charles Gleyre's studio, where he remained until it closed eighteen months later. Gleyre was an isolated and independent artist who accepted landscape as an important genre in its own right. He was generous with his advice and encouraged the development of individual talent. How often Monet actually attended the studio is open to question, but it was here that he met two wealthy art students who immediately became his close friends, Frédéric Bazille and Alfred Sisley. Bazille was the son of indulgent parents with a flourishing wine-growing business in Montpellier; while Sisley, British-born but raised in Paris, belonged to a prosperous textile-importing family.

The fourth member of Monet's "gang" was Pierre-Auguste Renoir, who enjoyed none of the financial security of his three friends. Precociously talented, Renoir's early apprenticeship with a firm of porcelain painters had left him with a lifelong respect for the well-crafted art of the eighteenth century and an acute sense of the loss of traditional skills and values. His attitude to his art was as individual as he was and remained a constant throughout his life. When asked by Gleyre, "Doubtless you paint to amuse yourself?" Renoir replied "Certainly, if it didn't amuse me, I wouldn't do it!" Unlike Monet, Renoir publicly acknowledged the Swiss painter's influence, and long after Gleyre's studio closed down in 1864 he continued to refer to himself as "*élève de Gleyre*."

Close by, another group of young artists, influenced by the example of Courbet, was looking toward the artistic traditions of Holland and Spain in the hope of finding there a style of painting relevant to the modern age. The American artist James McNeill Whistler, who abandoned both France and realism in the early 1860s, was at this time a significant member of the Parisian avant-garde. Degas would later recall

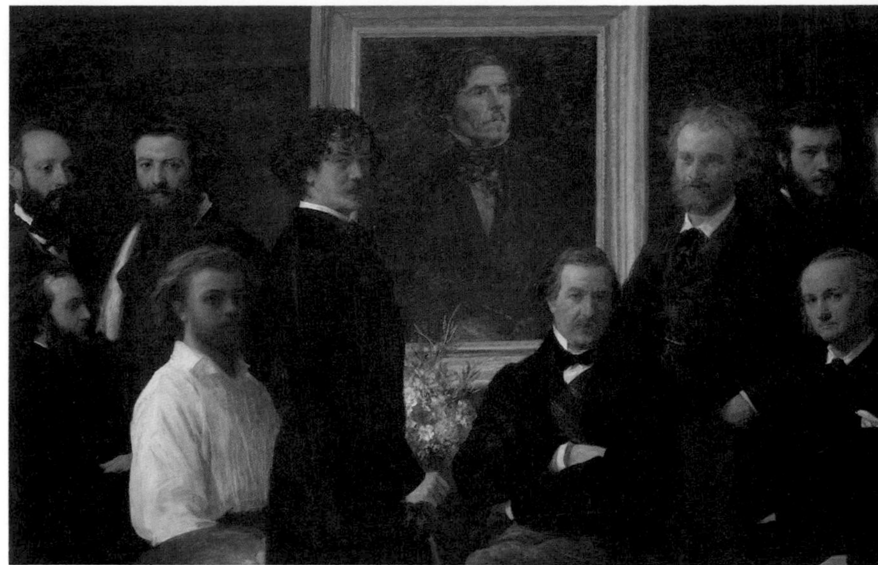

Henri Fantin-Latour,* Homage to Delacroix*, 1864. Fantin-Latour, in his white blouse, sits before the portrait of Delacroix.

"In our beginnings, Fantin, Whistler and I were all on the same road, the road from Holland." Whistler's ambition to create a perfect harmonious abstract beauty based on the prolonged study of natural phenomena seems very different from the ideals of his friends: nevertheless, he had a significant impact upon their work. He remained friendly with Monet and in uneasy rivalry with Degas throughout their lives.

Henri Fantin-Latour's *Studio in the Batignolles*, painted in 1869, records the activities of the realist group centred on the Café Guerbois and makes a clear reference to Courbet's famous painting *The Artist's Studio* of fourteen years earlier. Fantin-Latour's painting is, in effect, a homage to Manet, whose dapper figure is seen seated before a canvas surrounded by representatives of the Naturalist school, including the tall Bazille, Renoir, his close friend, the musician Edmond Maître and Monet and perhaps even Sisley, who appears on the extreme right. Degas, present in the original sketches for the work, fails to make it into the final composition and is replaced by a bust of Pallas-Athène. A contemporary caricature mocked the high seriousness of the work by redrawing it as Christ surrounded by his disciples. The so-called Naturalist writers were characterized by an almost scientific relationship to art, attempting to dissect the world as a surgeon might dissect the human body, with little regard for the romantic notions of the soul. Their emphasis upon empirical investigation was crucial for the young painters depicted in Fantin's canvas.

Degas and Manet were the twin stars of the Café Guerbois set, although in the seventies they preferred the more sophisticated ambience of the Café de la Nouvelle-Athènes.

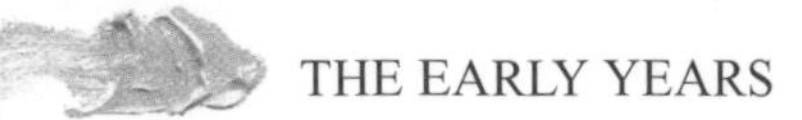

Experiments in Landscape

In the spring of 1863, Renoir, Bazille, Monet and Sisley traveled to the forest of Fontainebleau to begin a concerted campaign of *plein-air* painting. The forest was originally a wild place, partly cultivated in earlier times to facilitate hunting. By the 1840s its proximity to the capital – only ninety minutes away by train once the railway line had opened in 1849 – had transformed it into a thoroughly commercialized tourist site. The nearby Palace of Fontainebleau had been developed over the years from a mere hunting lodge into one of the most sumptuous of the royal palaces. Favored by Emperor Napoleon I, his nephew, Napoleon III, continued the Bonaparte association, and this added to the forest's romantic appeal.

Gustave Flaubert's first and, to many, greatest novel *A Sentimental Education*, completed in 1869, includes a vivid account of a couple, a young man and his mistress, enjoying a brief escape from the pressures of city living:

> ***It conjured up thoughts of hermits of old ... The warm air was full of the smell of resin; tree roots interlaced on the ground like veins. Rosamund stumbled over them, felt miserable and wanted to cry ... A painter in a blue smock was working at the foot of an oak, with a paint-box on his knees. He looked up and watched them pass.***

Like many other academic painters, Gleyre had encouraged his pupils to make studies after nature, and the forest of Fontainebleau was a favourite haunt for artists of all persuasions. Even the popular Meissonier was glimpsed there, although the painting he was working on was not a *plein-air* work but one of his meticulously painted eighteenth-century genre scenes!

As early as 1864 Monet had mentioned having made a sketch "painted entirely after nature ... without having any painter in mind." Such reliance upon the direct experience of the landscape without intermediate models to compromise one's sensations was to usher in a decade of experimentation in which the young artist aimed to unite his interest in painting in the open air with his need to produce work for the Salon. He was determined to make a spectacular painting dedicated to contemporary life which would make his reputation and secure his future.

Monet at Chailly

In May 1865, after Gleyre had been forced to shut down his studio because of his failing eyesight, Monet settled for the summer at an inn called *Le Lion d'Or* (the Golden Lion) at Chailly-en-Bière. His plan was to produce an updated version of Manet's notorious *Déjeuner sur l'Herbe* for the Salon of 1866. The work would be painted on a large scale, using the freedom of brushwork and coloration he admired in Manet's *Music in the Tuileries Gardens*. Instead of the older artist's studio-centered art, however, his would be informed by the *plein-air* tradition practiced by his friends Boudin and Jongkind.

Following what would become a life-long preference, Monet used, as far as possible, his friends as models. One professional model involved in the project, Camille Doncieux, was soon to become his mistress and later his wife. Monet suffered several setbacks, not the

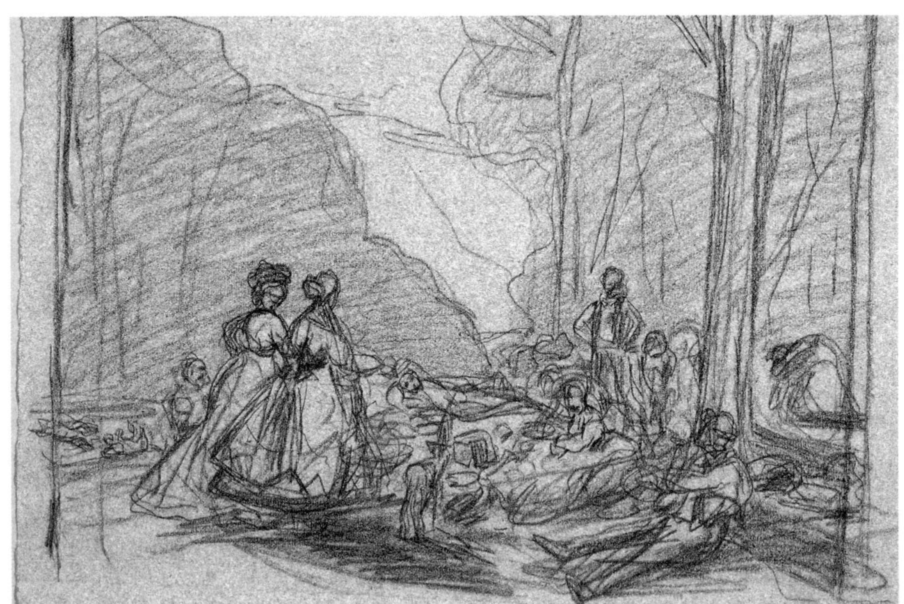

Claude Monet, pencil study for* Le Déjeuner sur l'Herbe (Luncheon on the Grass), *1865.

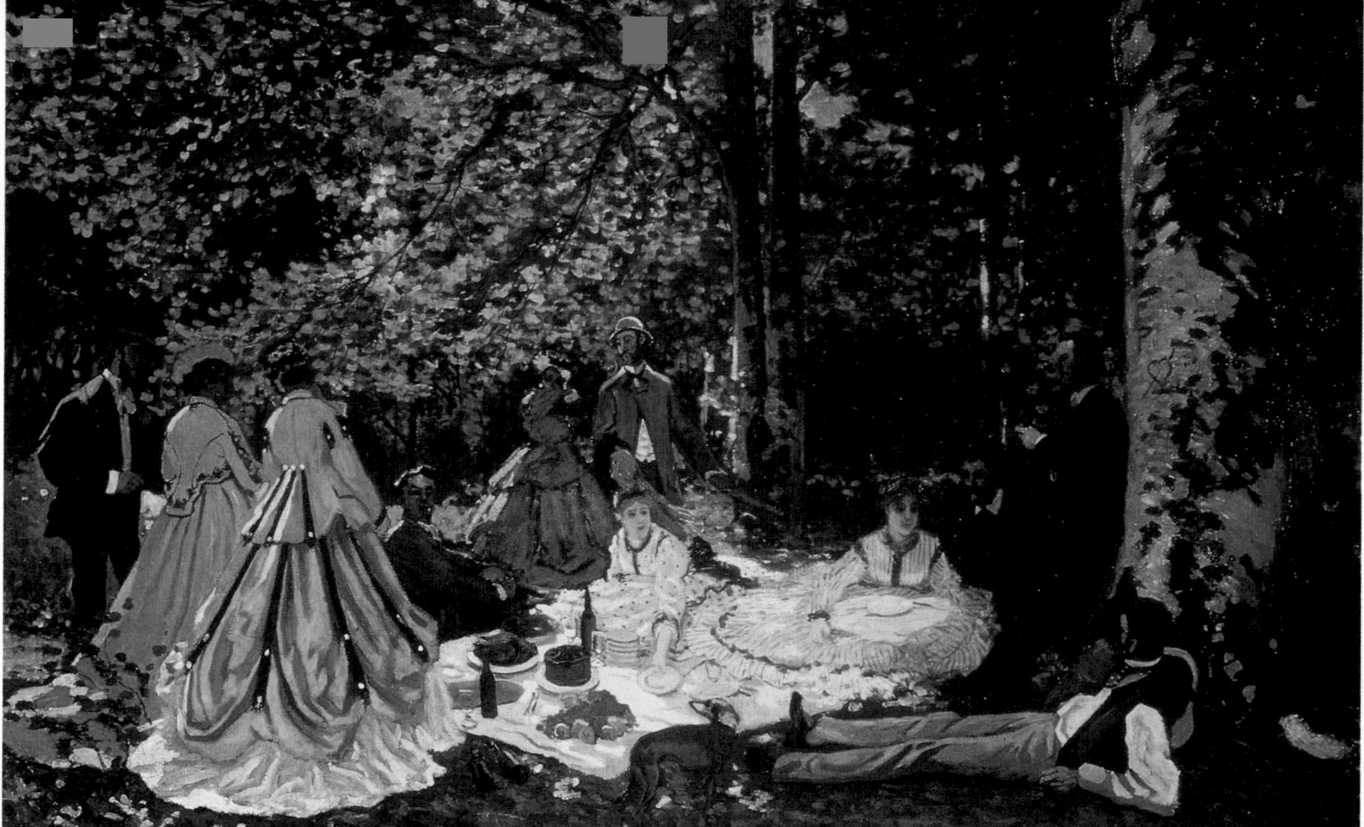

Claude Monet, sketch for* Le Déjeuner sur l'Herbe, *1865–66. Note the heart and initials carved into the tree and the discreet manservant preparing the victuals.

least of which were the many delays caused by Bazille's non-arrival on the scene. He had agreed to model, but was finding it difficult to escape his family. At the end of July, an exasperated Monet wrote to him in the South of France, "All I can think of is my painting and if I thought it was going to fail, I believe I should go mad." A further delay was caused by an accident which kept him inactive for a number of weeks.

Monet worked on his painting, *The Picnic*, from April 1865 to April 1866. Most of the problems he encountered may have stemmed from his inadequate knowledge of traditional practices or – perhaps more likely – from his deliberate avoidance of those academic techniques which would have allowed him to move smoothly from his initial sketches, made on a large scale *en plein-air,* to the completed canvas. The painting was never completed, the surviving fragments revealing the problems this relatively inexperienced painter had set himself.

The major sketch, begun in September 1865, was dependent upon studies made over the spring and summer. It catches perfectly the distribution of the dappled light as it falls through the branches and foliage of beech and oak trees on to the figures beneath. The study, which measures 130 x 181 cms (52 x 74½ in), has an ease and fluency that one associates more with Renoir than Monet, qualities that are clearly absent from the fragments that remain of the final version, which was itself left incomplete. The original canvas measured a staggering 4 x 6 m (13 x 19 ft 9 in). The traditional reason given for its present fragmented state is that the artist, being unable to pay the bill for his board and lodging at the inn, left the work as collateral, returning to collect it a number of years later only to find it had been partially devoured by rats and severely damaged by the damp.

Looking at those pieces that have survived, we see clearly Monet's difficulties and ambitions. He has rejected traditional *chiaroscuro* effects (the careful modeling from dark to light that was so much part of normal studio practice) and has imitated the small clean single brushmarks of Boudin on a larger scale, the light color superimposed on top of the local color signifying the fall of light on the figures. In September he had come back to Paris to complete his painting in time for the Salon of 1866, working on the final version in Bazille's studio which overlooked the studio of the recently deceased Delacroix.

By mid-March, the enormous canvas had begun to take shape, Monet having broadly brushed in the fashionable clothing of his friends over which he superimposed broad slab-like strokes to denote the fall of the light across the figures. This technique, while successful in small-scale work, such as Manet's *Tuileries Gardens* and Boudin's open-air sketches, is impossibly difficult to sustain on a large-scale canvas. Courbet's presence in the sketch is intriguing and suggests amongst other things that Monet was consciously claiming a traditionally aristocratic subject matter for a wider audience, particularly the *arriviste* bourgeoisie. Such an action was not that of anti-establishment artists, but the maneuvering of artistic entrepreneurs trying to take advantage of a new market.

In the Forest of Fontainebleau

In the spring of 1865, Sisley and Renoir joined their friends Monet and Bazille in the forest of Fontainebleau, a place they had first visited in 1863. They settled themselves at nearby Marlotte, where Renoir's friend, Jules Le Coeur, the son of a wealthy contractor, had a house. Marlotte was popular with students from the Ecole des Beaux-Arts as a site for painting; they could make forays into the woods and fields carrying their lightweight painting equipment: portable easels, parasols to guard them from the glare of the sun, and, for those who could afford them, easily manageable collapsible tubes of oil paint. While not explaining the popularity of open-air painting, such technological developments certainly made the whole process much easier.

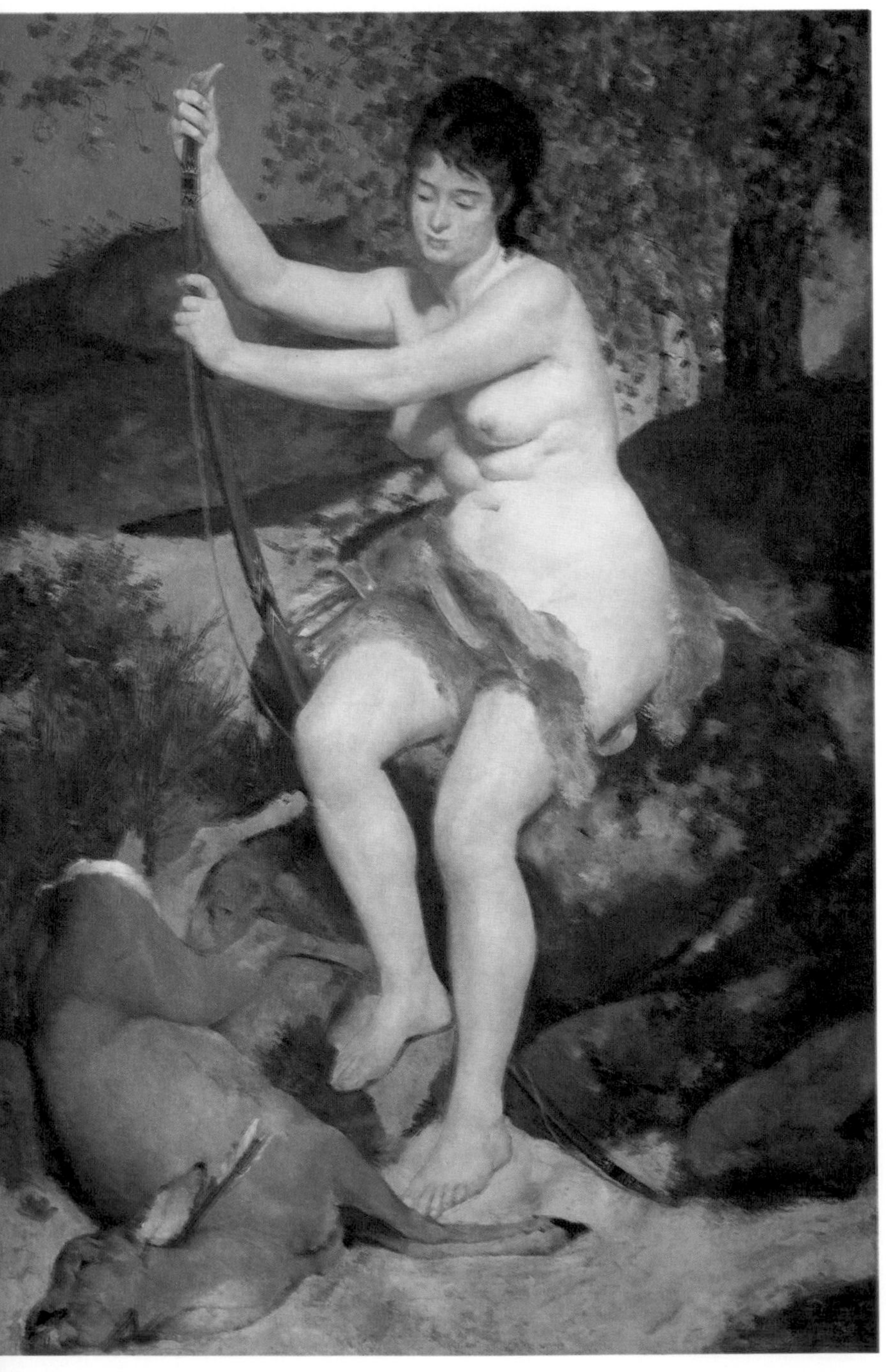

Following the practice recommended by the early nineteenth-century painter and theoretician, Henri de Valenciennes, the friends would set out early to capture the particular properties of the morning light. It was while Renoir was working in the forest that he met the Barbizon School painter Narcisse-Virgile Diaz de la Peña. Renoir later took great pride in retelling the story of how Diaz, whose rococo-inspired interpretations of the forest were very popular, persuaded him to abandon bitumen and to lighten his palette. Sisley, whose work up to that point had been relatively somber, followed suit.

Monet was the most experienced *plein-air* painter of the group, and one can imagine his friends looking on and learning from his example. Renoir, who was not to become totally committed to landscape painting until the next decade, concentrated instead on combining his love of eighteenth-century art with the bold painting style of the realist Courbet. Hoping that such a compromise would win him much-needed success at the Salon, Renoir chose the subject of the classical goddess, Diana the huntress. He had tried the subject once before, in 1864, with no success. This time, Renoir's model is shown in *contrapposto* – posed with one part of the body twisted in the opposite direction from the other; she is solidly modeled and carefully drawn. Nothing could be further from Monet's bravura experimentation.

Fortunately for the development of Impressionism, Renoir's calculated attempt to win recognition at the Salon was unsuccessful as *Diana* was rejected by the jury of 1867. During this time, Renoir experimented widely and eclectically,

Pierre-Auguste Renoir,* Diana, *1867. Despite its open-air setting, Renoir's mistress, Lise, has been painted in the studio.

 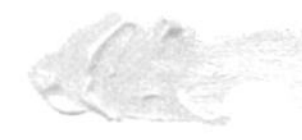

negotiating his way between various alternative traditions to create an exciting and unusual dialogue with the art of the past and the most radical areas of contemporary painting.

Mother Anthony's Inn

At the same time as Monet was struggling with his experiment in ambitious *plein-air* painting, *The Picnic*, Renoir was working on a group portrait of his friends set at their lodgings at Marlotte, known as Mother Anthony's Inn. His task was less technically demanding than his friend's, the painting being essentially a genre scene writ large, probably influenced by Courbet's first great success, *After Dinner at Ornans*, (1847).

Unlike an open-air subject, Renoir's interior in *At Mother Anthony's Inn* is unaffected by fluctuating levels of light and shadow; the range of color the scene offers is also limited and therefore more easily controllable. An indoor subject also minimizes any problems raised by perspective. Renoir's realization of form follows the traditionally accepted manner of smoothly gradated brushwork and is a far cry from his friend's courageous experimentation with broken surfaces of high-colored slablike strokes. Mother Anthony's Inn features in *Manette Salomon*, a novel of artistic life by Jules and Edmond Goncourt. Their notes for August 1863 record their personal experience of the place, describing a different atmosphere from that suggested by Renoir's cozy image:

> ***Anthony, who harbors wretched painters, along with Mürger's disgraceful phalanstery and licensed harem. There are paintings scrawled all over the house; the window sills are like palettes and the walls look as though house-painters had cleaned their hands on them. We ventured out of the billiard room into the dining room, which is daubed with guard-room caricatures and cartoons of Mürger. There were three or four men there, wearing rough jackets and looking like thuggish workmen, but they could have either been boaters, barbers or daubers. It was three in the afternoon and there they were having lunch with the disreputable women of the house, who come from the Latin Quarter and go back the way they came, in their slippers with no hats on … It seems that Anthony's is like Closerie de Lilas, a rough house that goes on day and night with people playing guitars and breaking plates, with the occasional stabbing. They have exhausted the forest and it is deserted. I saw only two artists' umbrellas at the Mare des Fées, this majestically robust landscape of granite, green grass and purple heather that used to be like one large open air studio, with the artists' mistresses sewing and mending in the shade of the easels.***

There is no telling whether this version is any "truer" than Renoir's, but such commentaries make evident the selective eye of artist and writer. Renoir held a sentimental attachment to the painting, a reminder of what was a happy time for him, whatever the state of his bank balance.

Pierre-Auguste Renoir,* At Mother Anthony's Inn, *1866. This group portrait of his friends remained one of his favorites.

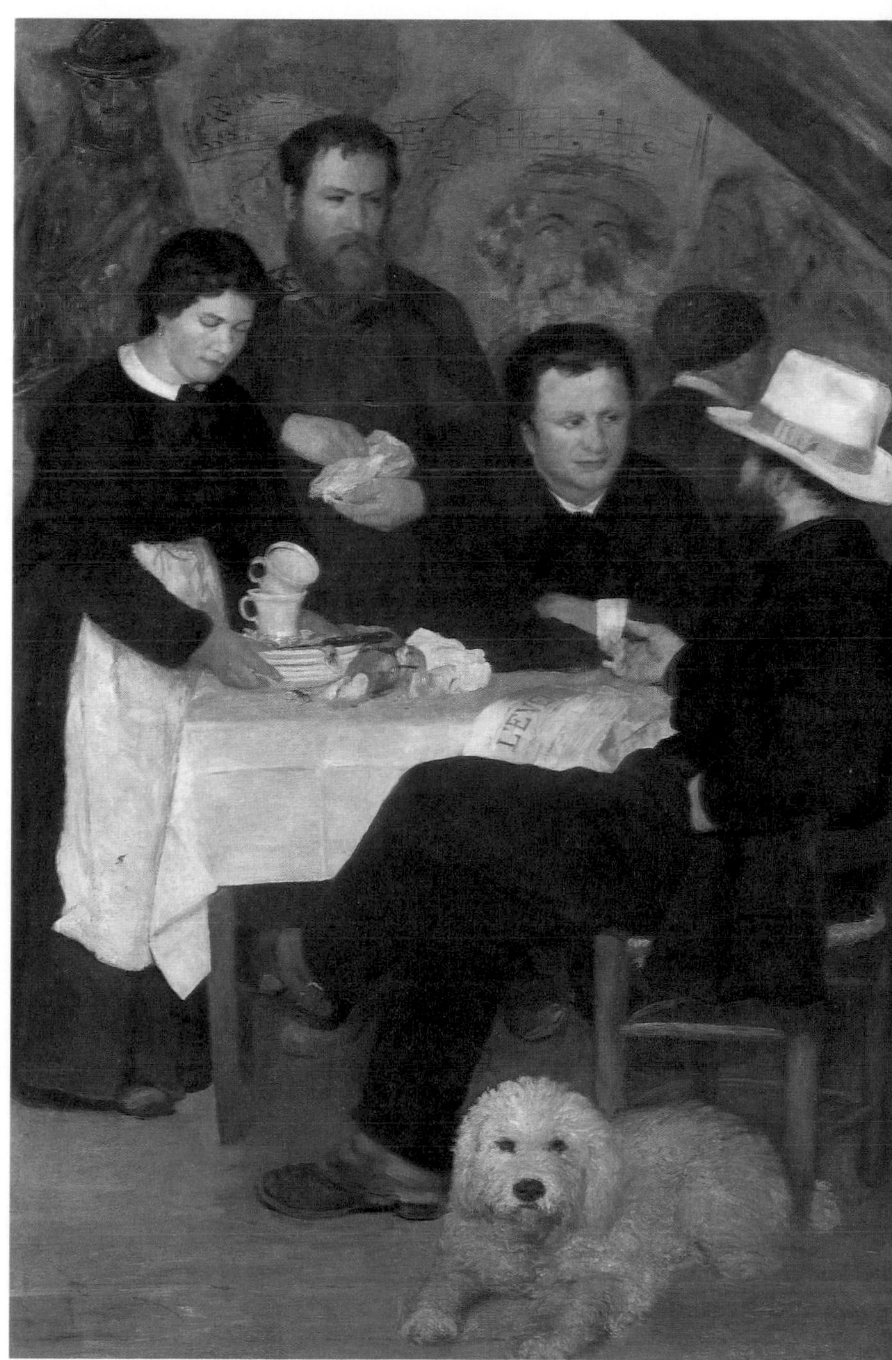

Women in the Garden

1866–67, oil on canvas, 255 x 205 cm (102 x 82 in), Musée d'Orsay, Paris, France

Monet dedicated the summer of 1866 to working on a canvas even more ambitious than the recently abandoned *Luncheon on the Grass*. He moved to Ville d'Avray, a suburb of Paris, with his companion Camille and began work on what was to become his *Women in the Garden.*

This time, the entire canvas would be painted in the open air with direct and continual reference to the model. In order to draw maximum attention to the work, and to signal it as a challenge to both Courbet and Manet, Monet decided to make it as large as possible. The artist even had to construct a trench in his garden in order to reach the upper half of his canvas. No wonder that Courbet, when he came to see Monet, was bemused at such self-imposed difficulties.

The subject is once again figures in an outdoor setting, though this time the setting is not the royal forest of Fontainebleau, but a domestic garden in the Parisian suburbs. The four women are all based on Camille, wearing a variety of modish dresses and with different hair colors. Given the extreme naturalism of the painting, its subject matter is distinctly odd: this is not a scene of everyday domestic life, but an artificially conceived *tableau-vivant* organized specifically to act as a means to pursue certain artistic ends. Unlike the smaller, highly finished paintings of similar subjects by artists like his friends Alfred Stevens or Auguste Toulemouche, who was related to Monet through marriage, the artist has refused to allow any hint of narrative to intrude on the scene. Like a contemporary fashion plate, it suggests no story and is merely a pretext to study the fall of afternoon sunlight on four pretty, fashionably dressed women parading their up-to-the-minute crinolines for the viewer's delectation. By limiting his figures to four, and by using only Camille – he never used professional models at any time of his life – Monet cut down on some of the potential problems that beset him with his ill-fated *Luncheon*. The subject matter of *Women in the Garden* relates not just to Courbet, Manet and the whole *fête champêtre* tradition, but also to the fashion-conscious paintings of his mentor, Boudin. The radical nature of the painting can clearly be seen when it is compared with Renoir's academically inspired goddess, *Diana*, or Winterhalter's court portrait of 1855 featuring the Empress Eugènie and her ladies in waiting.

Monet's ambition to start and finish the painting outdoors proved impossible to fulfill and the work was completed away from Camille at the parental home in Le Havre. He had returned home, not out of choice, but because he had run out of time and money and needed calm and security if he was to complete the painting for the forthcoming Salon. The painting is, nevertheless, extraordinary. Large weighty brushstrokes laden with opaque pigment chart the fall of light from the triangle of sky in the top right-hand corner down on to the women below. The most spectacular part of the painting is the seated figure holding a parasol to shield herself from the glare of the sun. Her face, seen in shadow, is described solely in terms of the light reflected from cut flowers – possibly a reference to *Olympia*'s bouquet – strewn across her lap. Drawing is kept to an absolute minimum and no conventional aids have been used; instead, the figures are given their solidity by the use of contrasting warm and cool colors: black is nowhere to be seen. Virtuoso passages, such as the flesh seen through the diaphanous green-striped sleeve, again mark Monet as an artist fighting to paint without recourse to accepted conventions of picture making.

The painting was rejected by the Salon jury of 1867, although it was bought by Bazille for 2,500 francs, payable in monthly instalments of 50 francs. Such support was vital to the artist, for Camille was pregnant and his family, learning about this liaison, withdrew their financial support in the time-honored fashion of parents hoping to bring their young son to heel. The initial Salon successes that Monet and his friends had enjoyed were now a thing of the past. Such rejections as Monet had just suffered only strengthened their determination to find alternative venues for their work. Maybe his experience also convinced Monet of the foolhardiness of painting large Salon "machines": for the next decade he concentrated on much smaller canvases that would appeal more to the consumerist bourgeoisie.

In his 1868 article, *Les Actualistes,* Émile Zola praised the innovative nature of Monet's painting:

> ***I have seen canvases by Claude Monet that are indeed his flesh and blood ... No effect could be more strange. An unusual love for our times is required to risk such a*** **tour de force,** ***with the fabrics divided into sunny and shady halves and these ladies placed on a garden path well groomed by a gardener's rake.***

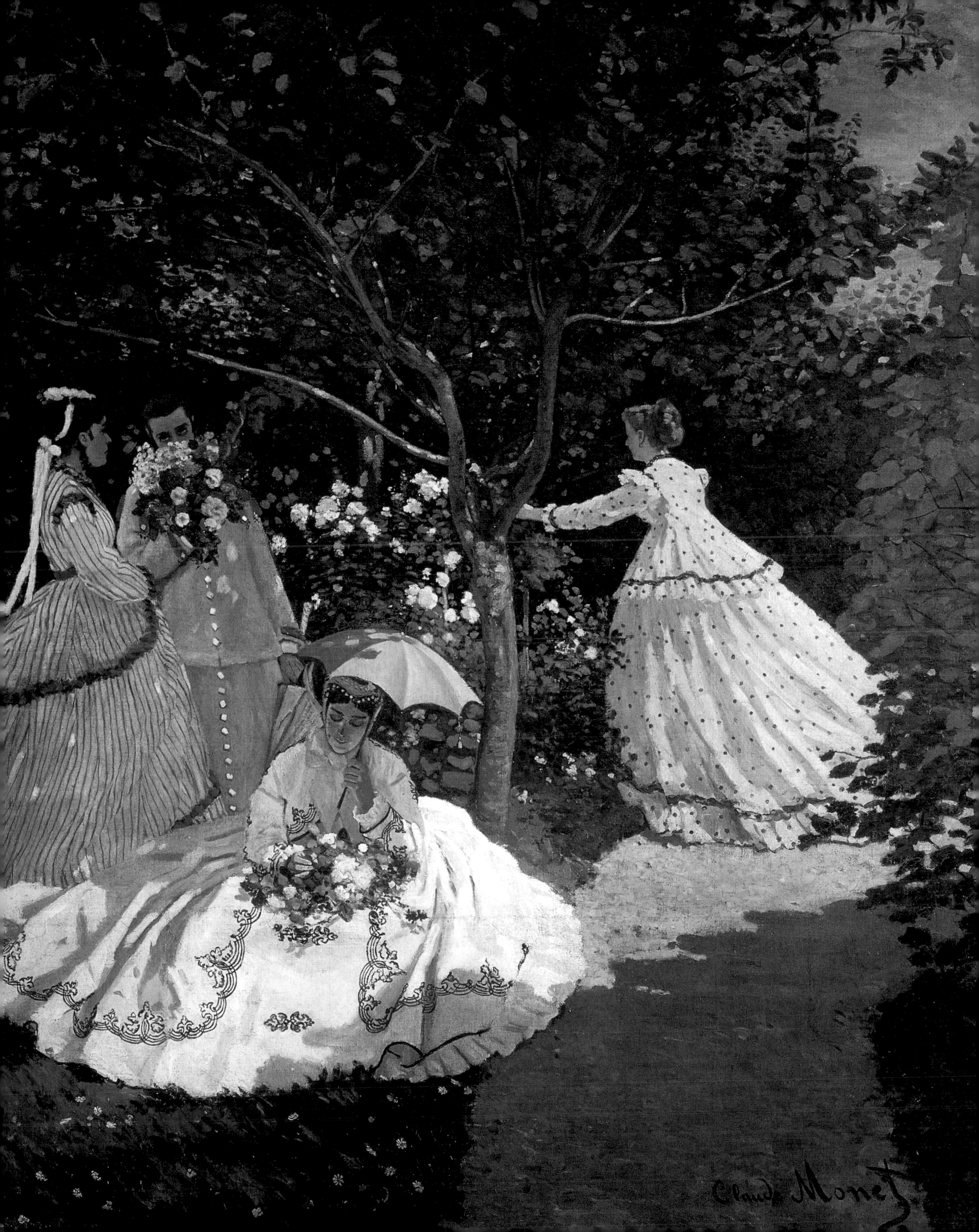
Claude Monet

The Urban Paintings of Monet and Renoir

The urban paintings of the Impressionists are contemporary with countless photographs that record the development of the modern city of Paris, and it is evident that the artists were much influenced by the qualities they found in such images. However, it is equally true that their early attempts to paint the urban scene owed as much to traditional cityscapes or *vedute*, such as those painted by Corot and others, as they did to the technical developments of the age, including photography.

In spring 1867, Renoir, following Monet's example, produced a number of *plein-air* cityscapes. Monet's were more deliberately ambitious; Renoir's more traditional, as may be seen in his choice of a low viewpoint for his *Pont des Arts*. His ordering of the architecture and the people is reminiscent of Corot and Canaletto, and incidental details, such as the people, were probably added after the initial painting was dry: ridges of paint corresponding to the architectural structures can be made out beneath their vividly sketched-in forms.

Following Monet's example and the procedures of Boudin and Manet, Renoir has distributed touches of pure color across the canvas. Dabs of emerald green and vermilion are set against the cool mauvish shadows. The painting is given a distinctive character by the inclusion of the quirky shadow pattern cast by the building situated behind the artist. At some stage after the initial lay-in, Renoir has over-painted the sky, perhaps to lighten the overall coloration of the canvas and to enhance its decorative character. The figures, despite their summary visualization, are intensely alive, each distinct in attitude and action. It is almost as if a Boudin beach scene has been transposed to the capital.

In fact, the Impressionists were hardly unique in choosing such subjects. Books and magazines of the period were filled with such images, and artists as diverse as Jongkind and Stanislas Lépine, whose airy urban scenes featured in several Impressionist exhibitions, also made the city the focus of their attention. The sunlight that drenches Renoir's scene falls upon an institution, the Académie, that must have been the object of much derision amongst the young painters of the day, although, ironically, in time Renoir would receive its highest award: the coveted *Legion d'honneur.*

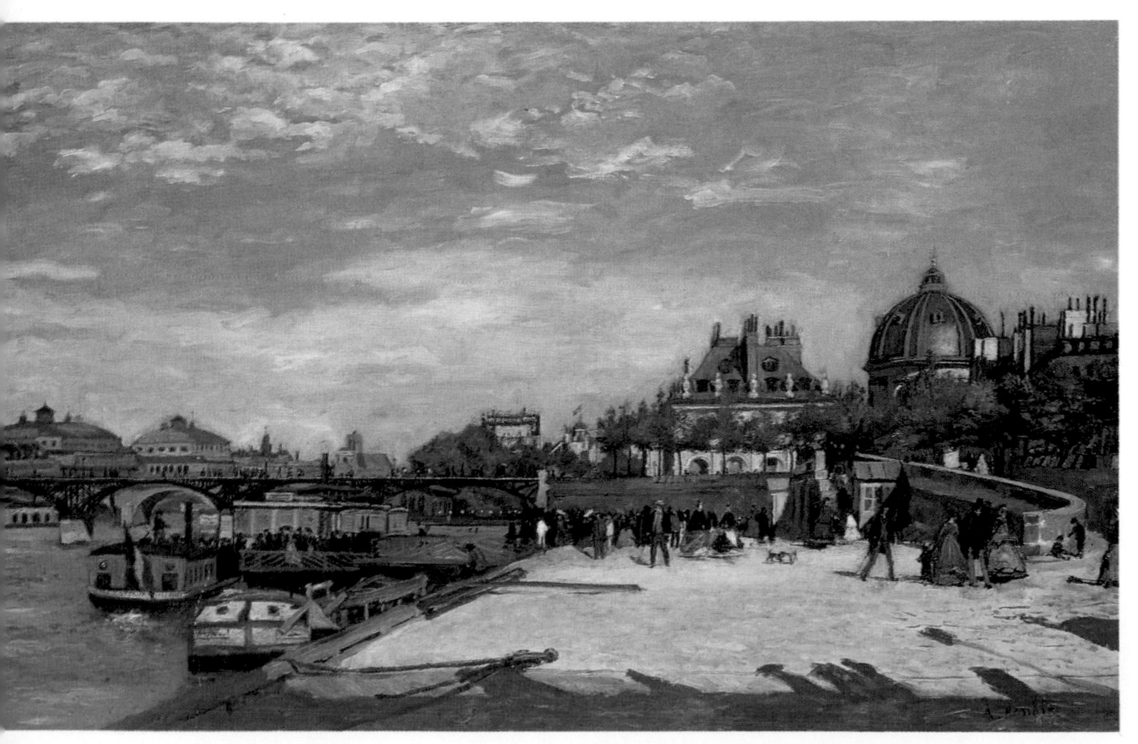

Pierre-Auguste Renoir,* Pont des Arts, *Paris, c. 1867. Renoir's relatively traditional composition may be compared with Monet's more innovative aerial viewpoints of his cityscapes.

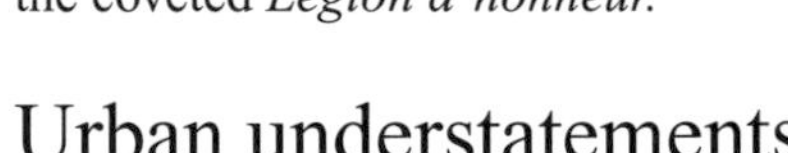

Urban understatements

Monet and Renoir organized their compositions by choice of viewpoint. Their color balance was based upon the artists' close observation and their awakening interest in color theory, as is evident in the ways both artists chart the changing effects of light and shade upon the colors of the urban environment. The overall effect of city views by Monet and Renoir is understatement; they are hardly official celebrations of Haussmann's splendid urban creation,

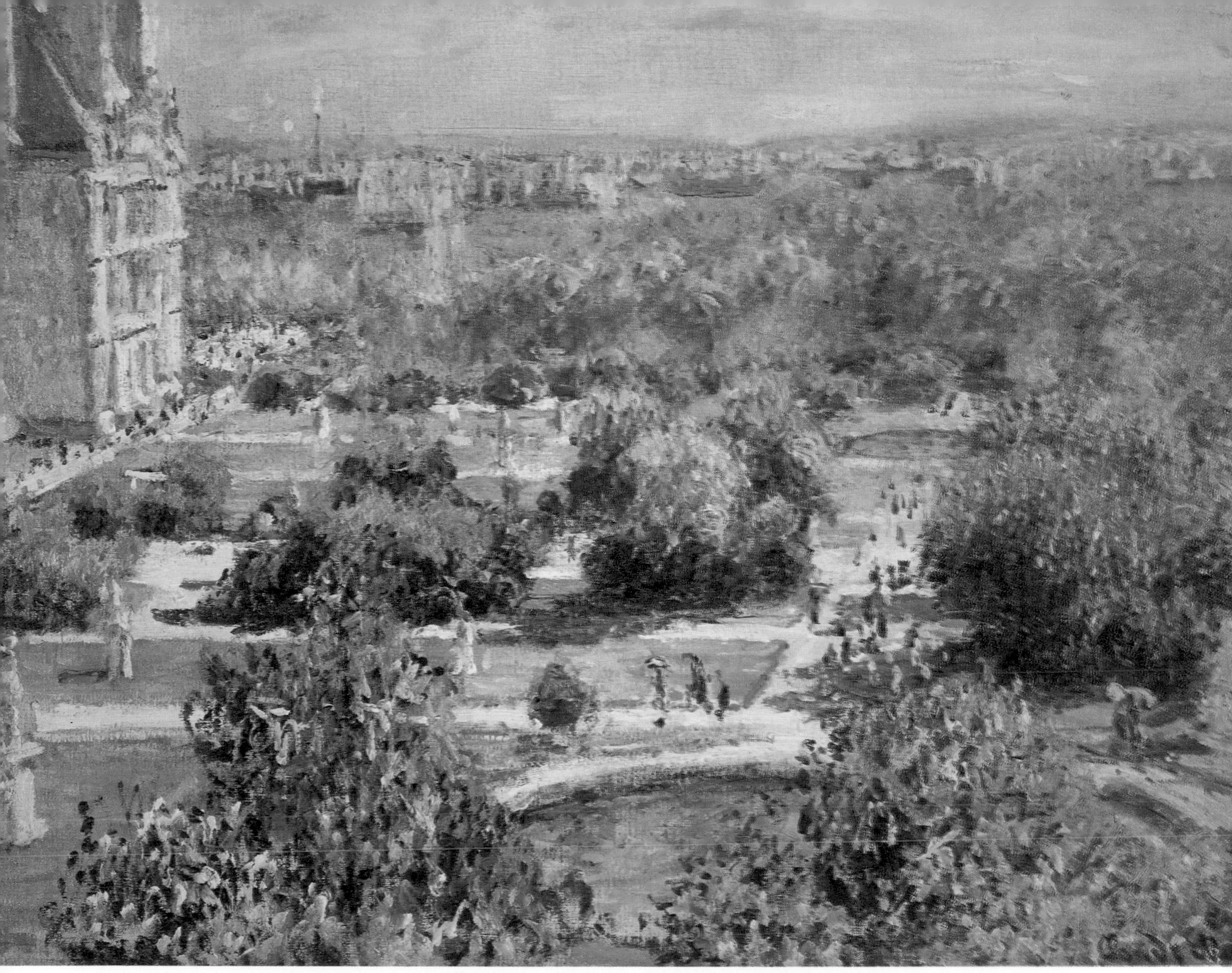

Claude Monet,* The Tuileries, *c. 1876. Painted just five years after the destruction of the Tuileries Palace, this painting is carefully edited to omit the scarred ruins that lay immediately to the left of the canvas edge.

but nor are they the caustic critical investigations we associate with Manet. Rather, they appear as disarmingly frank acceptances of an almost mechanical mode of vision. This leads us to one of the most startling aspects of these paintings, the way in which they parallel the thousands of photographic images of the time. The effects of photography on the work of the Impressionists will be dealt with later in the book, but it should be pointed out here that many of the peculiarities to be found in the photographs of the period may also be found not only in much Impressionist art, but also in paintings of previous epochs.

Aaron Sharff mentions a collection of 197 stereoscopic photographs published as *Vues Instantanées de Paris*, taken around 1860–66 and put on sale by Hippolyte Jouvin. Such images, with their figures frozen in time, the apparently arbitrary compositions, which cut off figures in the most unexpected ways, and the simplification of tonal values would have had the effect of confirming the Impressionist innovations in painting as being in tune with recent technological developments.

Certainly, no critical or even ironical edge can be easily discerned in these paintings; rather, they – Renoir's in particular – exude a sense of well-being and confidence in the prosperous world of the Second Empire, one that their exclusions from the Salon would effectively bar them from enjoying for some time. It is a salutary reminder of the perseverance of the artists and the corresponding difficulty of associating these pictures, in all their apparent gaiety and optimism, with the often difficult private lives of the artists who painted them.

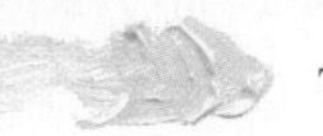
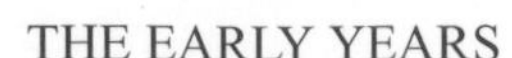

Monet at Sainte-Adresse

The tensions in Monet's personal life are evident in *Terrace at Sainte-Adresse*, his famous picture, painted in 1867, of his father and aunt on the terrace of her home in Sainte-Adresse, an affluent outreach of Le Havre. In the distance can be seen the sailing boats and steamships from which Monet's father, a wholesale grocer, derived his income. Two figures standing at the terrace overlooking the sea may signify the artist and his pregnant mistress, in reality left back home in Ville d'Avray, here reconciled beneath the paternal gaze of his father. As is usual with Monet, the scene is forthright, with the directness and high color of a popular print or fashion plate. Many commentators have pointed out the painting's similarity to Japanese prints that had been popular with artists and collectors since the mid-1850s. Monet

Monet,* The Seine at Bennecourt, *1868. The perfect evocation of a still summer's day, a masterpiece of early Impressionism.

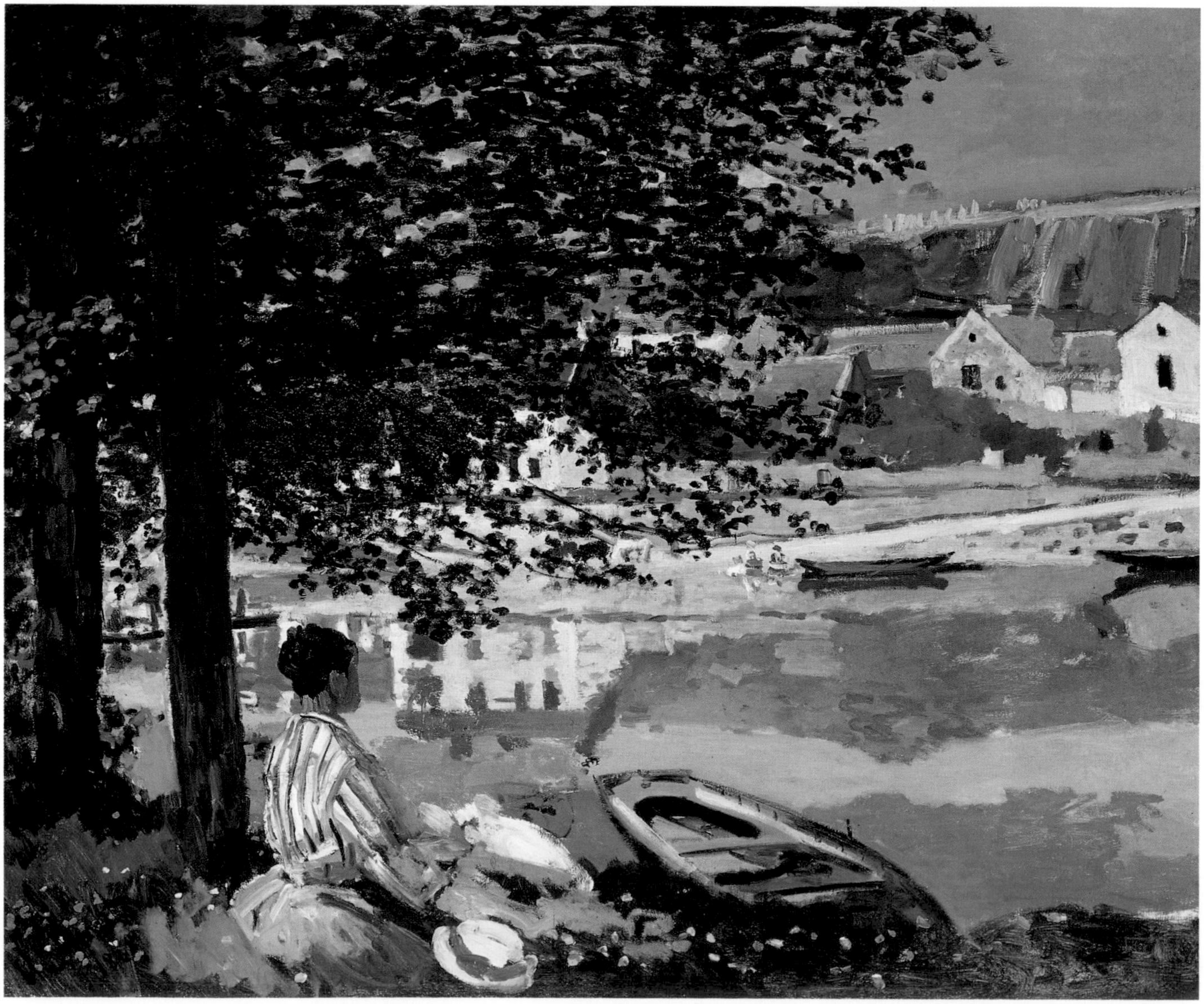

himself called the painting his "Chinese painting with flags in it," "China" and "Japan" being generic terms for the exotic and bizarre. The statement makes clear the artist's deliberate avoidance of the traditional structuring of Western pictures, in which perspective and composition draw the viewer's eye to the most significant aspects of the image in a regulated way.

Painted a year after *Terrace at Sainte-Adresse*, *The Seine at Bennecourt*, a relatively small painting, is a perfect realization of Monet's aims up to that time: the painting has been started and completed in the open air, although some areas of selective over-painting are apparent. The figure, sky, water and land are perfectly integrated through the unified treatment of light and the bonding structure of an open weave of highly colored brushwork. With this painting, Monet's future concerns are announced.

The myth of Monet's total commitment to *plein-air* painting has long been exploded, even though it was one the artist and his supporters took care to propagate. As late as 1880 Monet told a journalist, "My studio! But I have never had a studio ..." Such comments served to enhance the notion that *plein-air* painting was the defining feature of the Impressionist movement and that it was based upon painting *au premier coup*, that is, at a single sitting before the motif.

Monet had little interest in suggesting his model's state of mind, a characteristic that separates this work from similar pieces by Courbet and Manet in which the psychological aspect is paramount; unlike theirs, this painting has no overt erotic content, either. The head of the child once cradled in Camille's arms has been painted out, possibly to make the work more saleable. The arms and body can still be seen as the area of white paint above Camille's dress. The addition of the signature shows that Monet regarded this painting not as an *étude*, but as a "finished" work of art.

In the painting, Monet's companion looks across the Seine toward the village of Le Gloton, near Bennecourt, just south of Giverny, where he was to settle much later in life. Camille is dressed in the summer clothes of a sophisticated Parisienne, enjoying a beautiful summer's day away from the bustle of the city. It is a reminder that Monet's commitment to visual truth once caused the now notorious Zola to call him *"un actualiste"*:

> ***A true Parisian, he brings Paris to the countryside, he is unable to paint a landscape without placing in it ladies and gentlemen who are all dressed up. Nature would seem to lose interest for him if it did not bear the mark of our manners and customs.***

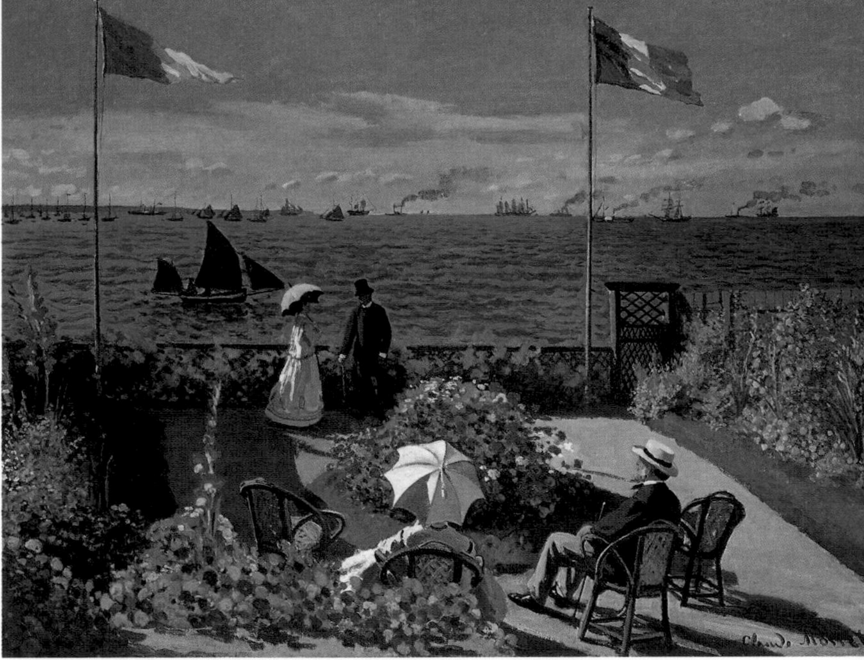

Monet,* Terrace at Sainte-Adresse, *1867. Monet has utilized lessons learned from his study of Japanese prints to create this stunning work.

The painting owes much to Boudin and Corot. Camille is seen with her back to us, like the main figures in *Terrace at Sainte-Adresse*. The painting is free of narrative, the artist giving the viewer little opportunity to imagine a supposed relationship with the woman, who is no classical nymph or private bather but a fully clothed tourist enjoying the tranquility of a well-known beauty spot.

The psychological tension and split composition evident in *Terrace at Sainte-Adresse,* where each figure remains isolated and distinct, have been replaced by a relaxed, genuinely informal atmosphere. Camille's personality is reduced to that of a referent – someone who, like the viewer, enjoys the view that the skill of the artist has enabled us to share as directly as possible.

In the process, Monet has left the means by which the image is achieved evident on the canvas. The pigment has been rapidly applied in short opaque strokes, which describe in a brilliant visual shorthand both the still and the fast-moving areas of the river. The sky is visible to the viewer only by its reflection in the water: signified by a patch of blue applied later when the rest of the paint was dry.

Camille and Claude stayed at the inn seen reflected in the water; the boat visible by the shore is simply there as the couple's means of transport to and from the painting site. Unlike so many other works that contain such details, it does not carry with it the suggestion of a clandestine trip down the river.

In Zola's novel, *L'Oeuvre*, published in 1886, the fictional painter-hero Claude Lantier and his mistress Christine spend the happiest moments of their lives in the self-same village. Perhaps Zola knew something of Monet's life that we do not.

La Grenouillère

Winter is ahead of us, a season very appropriate to unhappiness. And after that comes the Salon. I haven't considered that, since I won't have anything ready. I have a dream of a picture [tableau], the bathing area of La Grenouillère, for which I have done some bad sketches [pochades], but it is a dream. Renoir, who is spending two months here, also wants to do this picture.

So wrote Monet to his wealthy artist friend Bazille, on September 25, 1869.

Monet's letter reveals both the comradeship shared by the young painters and his artistic insecurity. The "bad sketches" he refers to have become some of his most popular paintings and are regarded by most commentators as marking the moment when the Impressionist style is defined.

Monet has used the same technical resources he developed in his 1868 painting, *On the Seine at Bennecourt,* to create a convincing painterly equivalent for his visual

Claude Monet,* The Bathing Place at La Grenouillère, *1869. Affectionately known as "the camembert," or "the flower pot," the little island has become the center of Monet's composition.

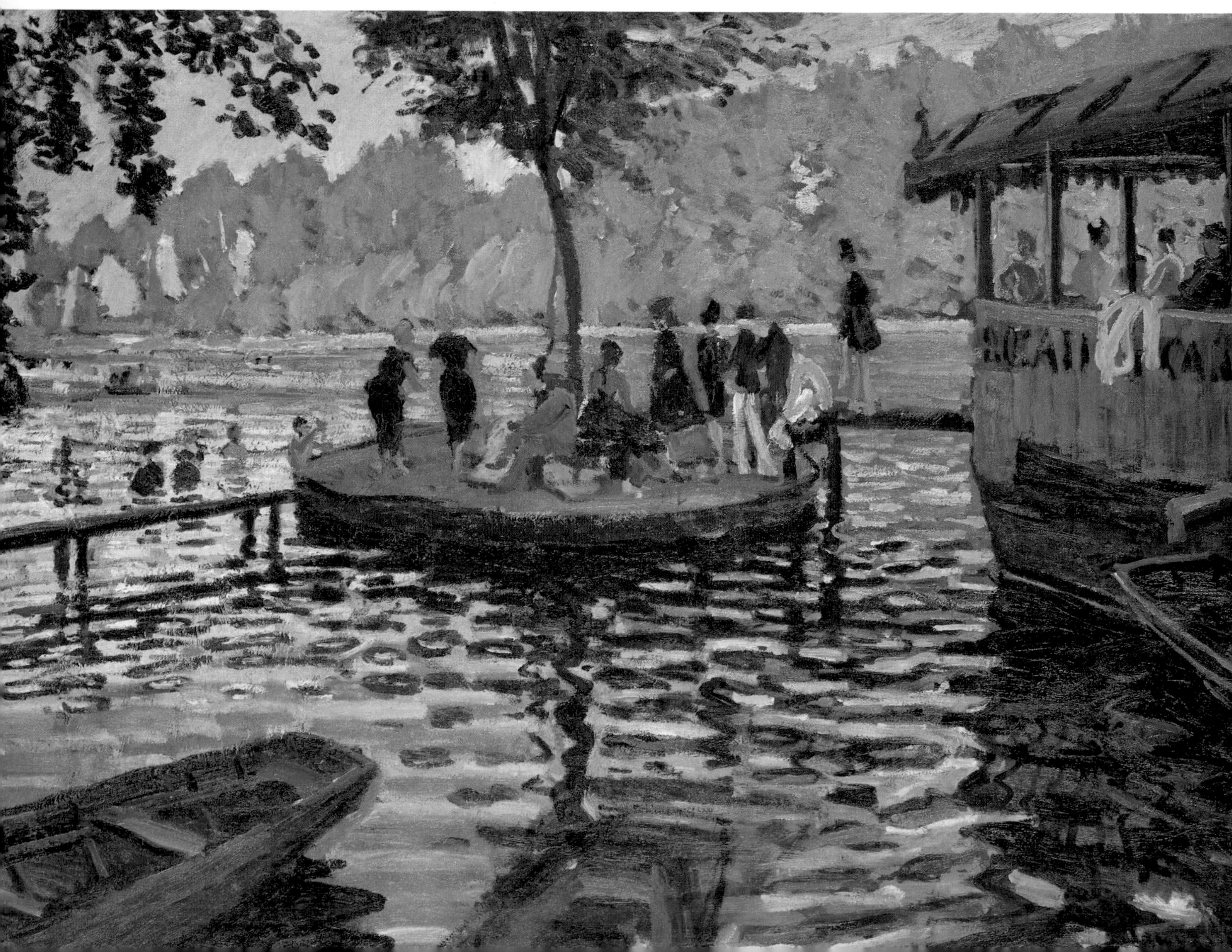

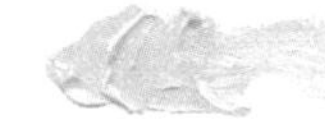

experience as he looked out from the bank across the river. The brightness of the sun reflected on the rippling surface of the water is almost blinding. Broken brushwork and rapid notational drawing suggest the animated movement of boats and people.

This was an anxious time for the artist. His plans to succeed at the Salon with large attractive pictures of modern subjects painted entirely in the open air had gone awry. In the hope of realizing these ambitions, he had chosen the popular bathing and boating establishment known as La Grenouillère as a suitable subject. Only twenty minutes by train from the Gare Saint-Lazare and close to the village of Bougival where Monet was living in the summer of 1869, it was an ideal choice of subject for Monet and his friends Renoir and Pissarro. Its proximity to Paris and the inevitable mingling of class and sex gave it a rather licentious reputation. Here was a subject guaranteed to create an impact; if only it could be pulled off in time for the submission date.

Renoir had hitched his wagon to Monet's star and was watching every move he made. Nearby was Pissarro, also focusing his attention on this fashionable site, much illustrated in the popular journals of the time; his surviving paintings of the scene are much more traditional than those of his colleagues.

Monet and Renoir – the same but different

Three interpretations of the scene by both Monet and Renoir survive. Although superficially similar, close examination reveals just how different the paintings by Monet and Renoir are from each other. Renoir, who was never fully committed to the idea of being a landscape painter, has given emphasis to the human aspect of the scene before him. His versions are essentially modern reworkings of aristocratic *fêtes-galantes* from his beloved eighteenth century. Feathery glazes of translucent pastel-toned paint bear some relation to Monet's choppy, opaque, brick-like slabs of color but the effect is entirely different.

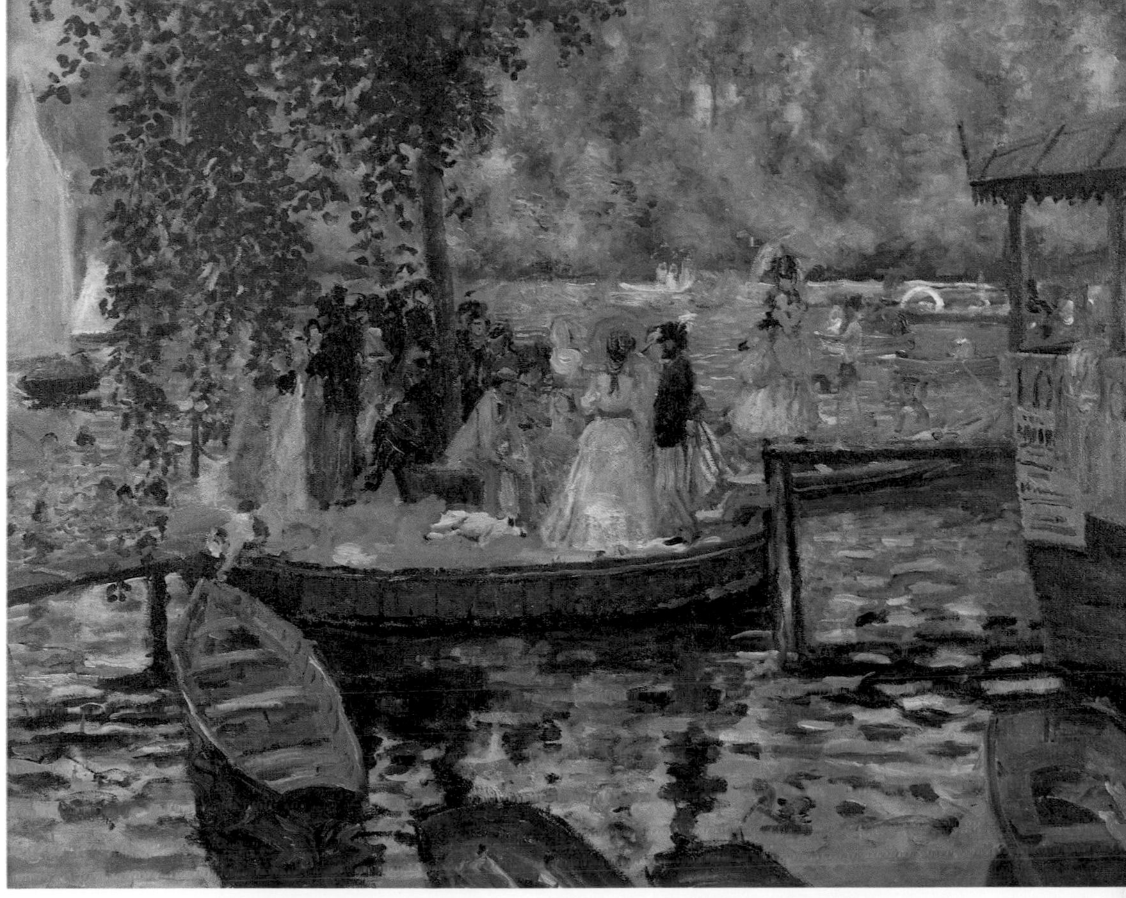

Pierre-August Renoir,* La Grenouillère, *1869. The artist has taken the subject from almost exactly the same viewpoint as his friend, but with a very different result.

Monet is much more objective and distances himself and the viewer from the spectacle of human affairs that this racy scene suggests. Instead, he concentrates upon the painterly problem of transcribing visual experience as directly as possible, using lessons learned from Manet's *Music in the Tuileries Gardens,* which he had seen in 1867 at Manet's one-man show, and also from the experience of working with Boudin and Jongkind.

For all their apparent casualness, the pictures illustrated here are carefully composed and reveal a certain degree of over-painting, presumably away from the motif. Traditional art practice would have only used such sketches as *aide-memoires* for a much more elaborate and finished painting. It is possible that Monet followed this tradition; if he did, the resulting painting no longer exists.

Monet later realized that these *plein-air* sketches were complete in themselves, equivalents in paint to the artist's experience "before the motif." The problems and challenges revealed in the studies he made at La Grenouillere would continue to preoccupy Monet's artistic imagination throughout his very long life.

Frédéric Bazille:
the forgotten Impressionist

Frédéric Bazille (1841–1870) is still very much the forgotten Impressionist; even after the work of Berthe Morisot and Gustave Caillebotte have been revaluated, Bazille's achievement in the early years of Impressionism remains relatively unknown.

His father was a wealthy wine producer from the Languedoc in the South of France, and his family were indulgent of his ambitions to become an artist. He went to Paris, ostensibly to study medicine, but in November 1862 he entered Gleyre's studio and became friendly with Monet, Renoir and Sisley, who had joined the *atelier* at about the same time. Bazille recounted his introduction to the studio in a letter to his parents, writing that "I started at the *atelier* without too many problems; I had to sing; I was forced to stand on one leg, etc., etc., all tedious incidents, but I am left in peace now; I have started in a drawing class, and I have observed with satisfaction that there are many pupils as good, or rather as bad, as I am." The pranks he described were a traditional and normal aspect of studio life.

Frédéric Bazille,* Self-Portrait at Saint-Saveur, *1868. Seen* contre-jour, *this rapidly brushed-in self-portrait was probably made with the aid of two mirrors.

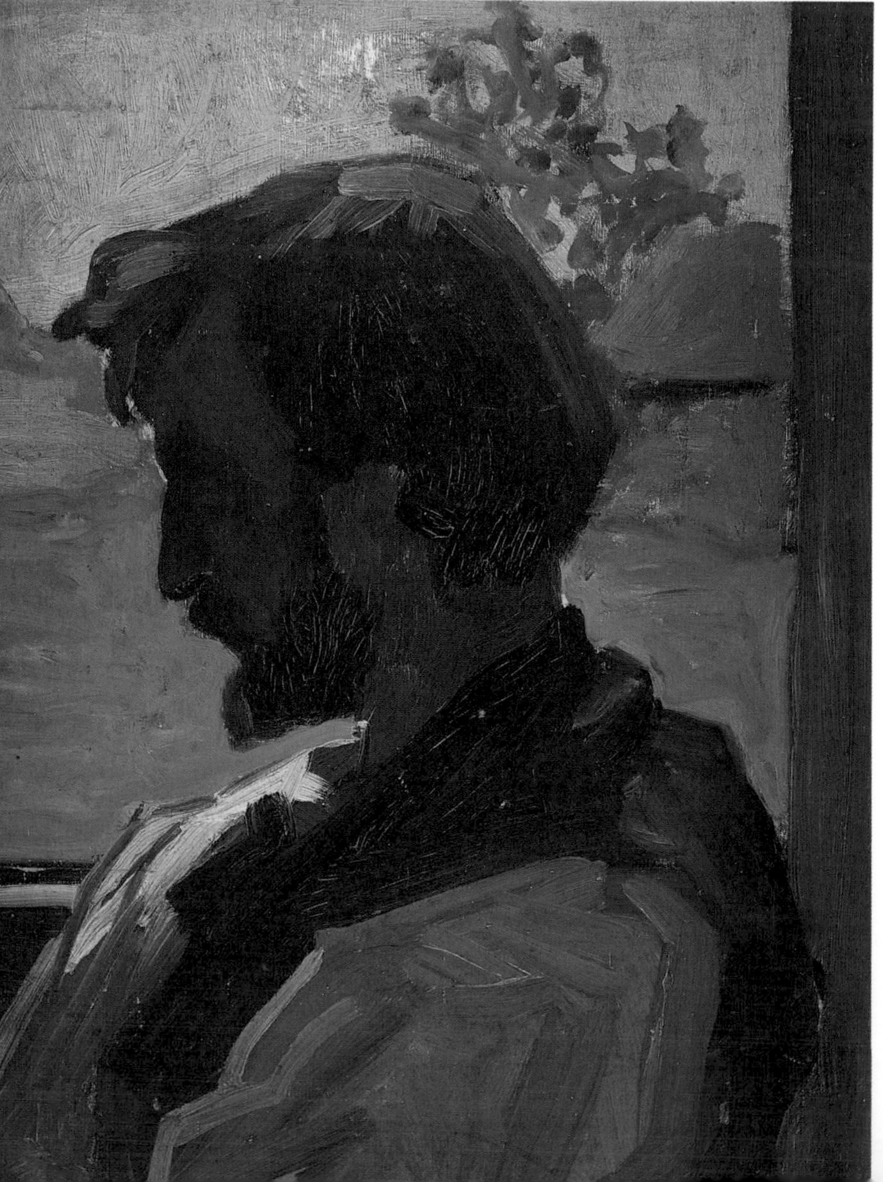

Bazille enjoyed the privileges that came with his social position; he loved the theater and opera and had no urgent need to earn a living with his brush. As a result, his art did not follow the single concerted program of action that shaped the early work of, for example, Courbet or Monet. Shortly after the closure of Gleyre's studio, and after failing his medical exams, in the summer of 1865 Bazille joined his friends in Fontainebleau, where they had first gone to work in the open air in 1863. He never took up the broken brushwork that characterized Monet's work and while his work follows no single direction, it is notable for its experimental qualities. Bazille's painting is diverse in subject and technique and, in spite of his friendship with Monet and Renoir, his work is closer in spirit to the painting of Manet and Corot.

He was a generous friend and supported Renoir and Monet during their periods of hardship. He was besieged by letters from Monet in the mid-1860s, asking either for money or demanding his presence in the forest of Fontainebleau in 1865, where he had agreed to act as a model for his friend's ambitious canvas *Luncheon on the Grass*.

In Bazille's studio

Bazille's painting of his own studio, *The Artist's Studio in the Rue de la Condamine,* painted at the end of the 1860s, is one of the most precious documents of those early days of friendship and struggle. The tall figure of Bazille is instantly recognizable, looking on, palette in hand, as his friend Manet appraises the canvas on the easel. His friends Renoir, possibly Sisley and Edmond Maître, their musician friend, are shown casually dispersed about the studio space. The painting

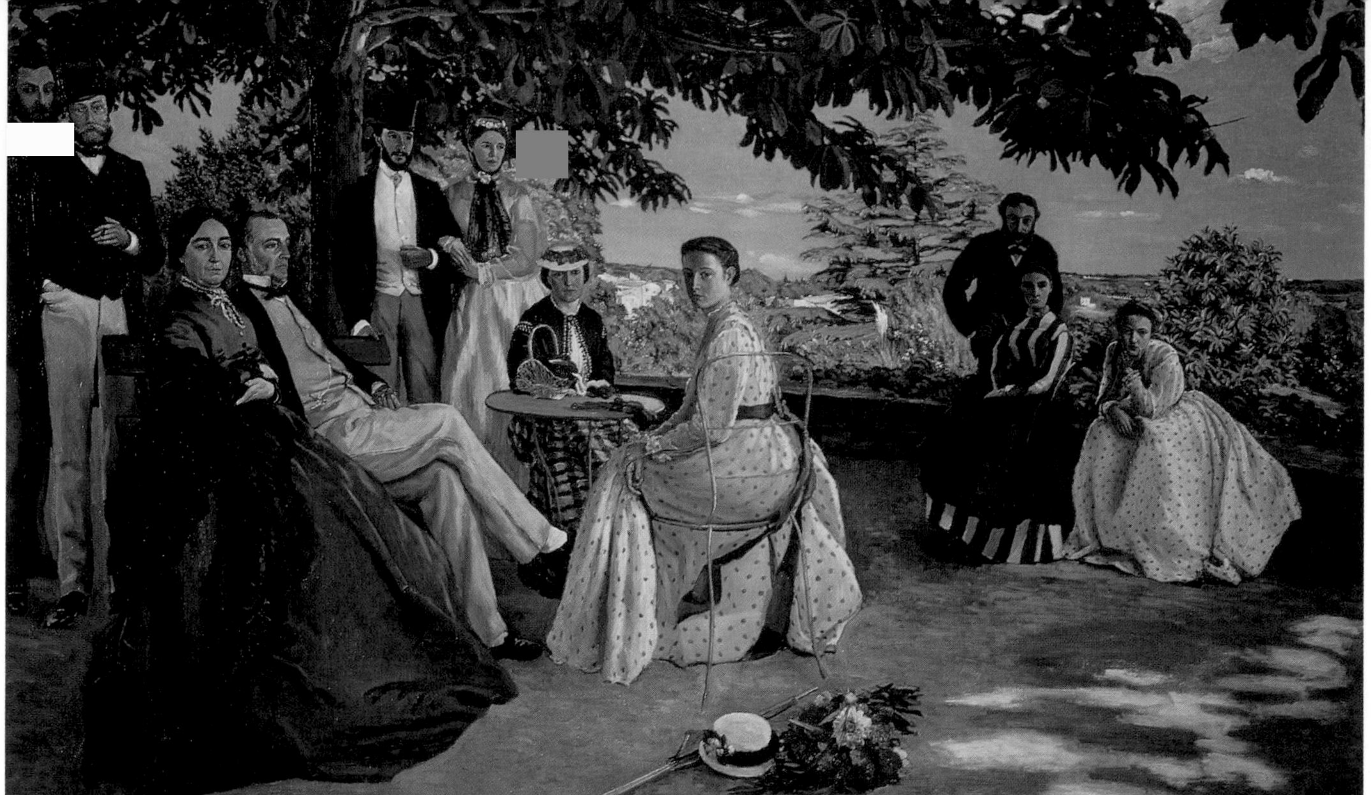

Frédéric Bazille, **The Family Reunion,** ***(also known as*** **The Artist's Family on a Terrace Near Montpellier*).*** ***This painting was exhibited at the Salon of 1868 before being retouched and dated 1869. The artist may be seen standing on the extreme left.***

celebrates this easy comradeship not just in terms of its imagery, but in its very facture: Bazille's figure was painted in by Manet himself. This is not a "realist" studio like Courbet's, full of cast-off romantic imagery, but a so-called naturalist canvas, accepting physical reality at face value; attempting to present life as it is, with no deliberate allegorical implications. On the walls hang a number of canvases, some of them by Bazille. His *La Toilette* of 1868 can be identified hanging close to the large studio window. A number of what appear to be large *plein-air* studies of women in a landscape setting *à la* Monet may also be seen.

The Admissions Jury for the 1867 Salon was exceptionally severe. As Zola wrote to his friend Valabrègue, "... the jury, irritated by my Salon, has thrown out all those who are taking the new road." Those affected by Zola's review included Monet, Cézanne, Sisley, Pissarro and Bazille. It was Bazille who organized their response – a direct letter to the comte de Nieuwerkerke, signed by 125 artists asking for another Salon des Refusés. Although unsuccessful in securing its immediate aims, this informal alliance would be the precursor to the events of the 1870s and it is apparent that Bazille was one of the mainsprings of this direct-action group.

As the Intendant des Beaux-Arts, Nieuwerkerke agreed to make the following year's Salon less restrictive. In spite of this, the 1867 Salon was a disaster for the young Naturalist painters, Bazille showing his generosity by purchasing Monet's rejected *Women in the Garden*. The next Salon, that of 1868, was a major turning point for the friends, however, for Manet, Renoir, Monet and Bazille all had their work accepted, if poorly exhibited. After his meeting with Nieuwerkerke, Bazille wrote a prophetic letter to his parents.

> ***A dozen talented people feel as I do. So we have resolved to rent a big studio each year where we will show our works, as many as we please … Courbet, Corot, Diaz, Daubigny and many others whom you may not know have promised to send pictures … With these people and Monet, the strongest of all, we are certain to succeed.***

They eventually did, but, sadly, Bazille did not live to share their success. In 1868, his painting *The Family Reunion* was accepted at the Salon. This impressive group portrait of his relatives is rather stiff and formal and it has none of Monet's or Renoir's fluency and ease. Encouraged by this success, he set about the Monet-inspired *View from a Village*. Bazille's freedom from financial concerns and his lively social life meant that he produced few large canvases a year; like Caillebotte, who succeeded him after his death in the role of "artist with money," his painting always seems laborious.

During the late 1860s he was the recipient of tragic letters from Renoir and Monet, his life of ease painfully at odds with their privations. When the Franco-Prussian war broke out in 1870, Bazille volunteered, enlisting in the crack regiment, the Zouaves. Renoir and Monet were horrified, but their pleas made no impression upon their friend. He wrote to his parents, "As for me, I am quite certain I shall not be killed; I have too many things to do in my life." The following day, November 28, 1870, he was killed just a few days before his twenty-ninth birthday.

View of a Village

1868, oil on canvas, 147 x 110 cm (59 x 44 in), Musée d'Orsay, Paris, France

I have tried to paint, as well as I can, the simplest possible subjects. In my opinion the subject matters little provided what I do is interesting as a painting. I have chosen to paint our own age, because this is what I understand best and because it is more alive, and because I am painting for living people. So, of course my pictures will be rejected.
– Bazille, 1866.

Early in their friendship, Monet wrote, perhaps rather resentfully, to his wealthy young friend, then enjoying the benefits of a caring and indulgent family life at Méric in the south of France, "What I'm certain of is that you don't work hard enough, and not in the right way. It's not with playboys … that you can work. It would be better to be alone."

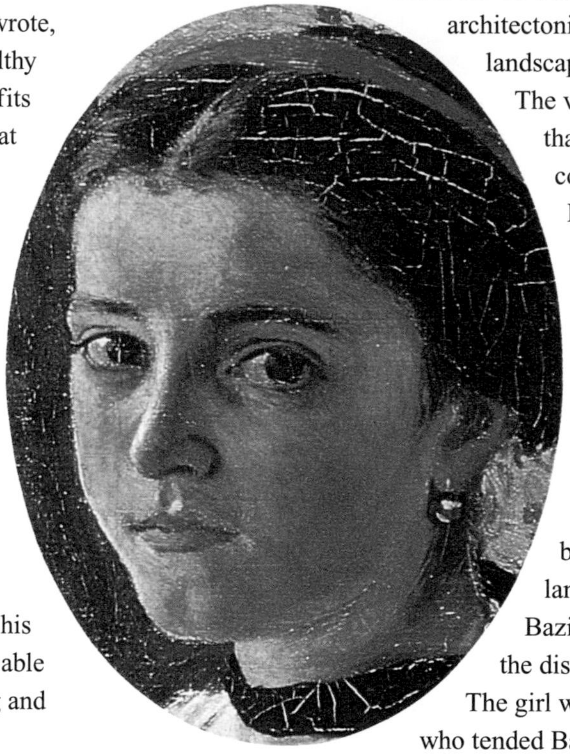

Monet, already burdened with a wife and child and all the responsibilities such things bring, may be forgiven for the rather pompous tone he adopted in addressing his 22-year-old bachelor friend. But away from the shadow of his immensely gifted friend, Bazille was able to reap the rewards of a warm, loving and supportive family.

At a time when Monet was agonizing over his bold experiments in *plein-air* painting, Bazille produced *View of a Village*. Writing to her sister, Edma in May 1869, Berthe Morisot described Bazille's painting, which she saw at the Salon:

Our good Bazille has done something which I admire very much. It is a portrait of a little girl in a very light colored dress, in the shadow of a tree beyond which is a small town. There is much light, sunshine. He is seeking what we all have sought: how to place a figure in outdoor surroundings; this time I think he has really succeeded.

The vivid pink of her sash and ribbon, together with the more delicate tracery of the pattern of her dress, balance the warm ochers and terracottas of the distant village. The careful modeling of the face, so much more cautiously handled than Monet's *bravura* re-creation of Camille's face in the garden of his house at Ville d'Avray just a few years earlier, is set against a ragged area of lilac representing the reflected sky. The handling of the distant landscape is totally confident and looks forward in its generalization and solid architectonic forms to the Provençal landscapes of Cézanne.

The view is not dissimilar to those that Cézanne, years later, would commemorate in his canvases of Mont Saint-Victoire. The young girl looks out rather as Victorine Meurent does in so many of Manet's canvases, only instead of that famously cool appraising and ironical stare, Bazille's model behaves much more sedately. She sits, rather as Camille did at Bennecourt, sheltered from the brilliant sunlight that illuminates the landscape beyond the confines of the Bazille family estate. Clearly visible in the distance is the small town of Castelnau. The girl was the daughter of the gardener who tended Bazille's parent's estate at Méric near Montpellier.

A comparison with Monet's work reveals Bazille's more conservative nature. The drawing of the face is the result of prolonged and attentive study and the strain of posing for what must have been considerable periods of time for her father's employer's son may also have contributed to the rather drawn expression evident on the girl's face.

Despite Morisot's praise, Bazille has not wished or perhaps not been able to engage in the radical procedures of Monet, but has remained faithful to a modified form of previously accepted practices. In this too, he is similar to Gustave Caillebotte, with whom his art and personality shares many interesting parallels.

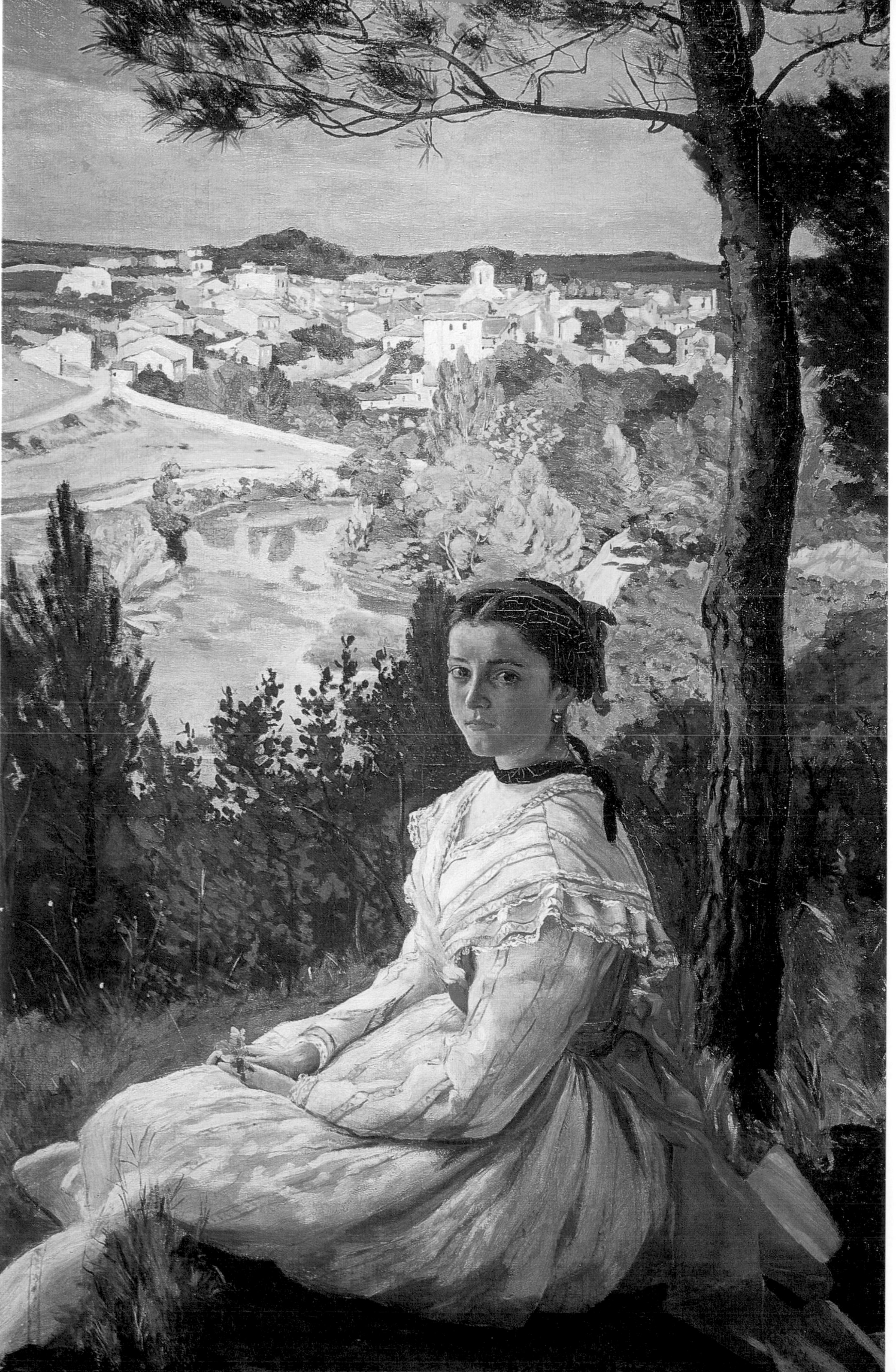

Claude Monet: "…what an eye"

Cézanne's famous statement about Claude Monet (1840–1926) – "Only an eye, but my God, what an eye!" – does the artist a disservice, suggesting that he was merely a recording agent of perceptual reality.

Though born in Paris, Monet was raised in Le Havre where his father developed a successful business as wholesale grocer to the shipping trade. His father recognized his young son's talent and persuaded the municipality to award Claude a scholarship to study in Paris. Supported by his aunt, Mlle. Lacadre, and about 2,000 francs earned from the sales of caricatures, Monet left for Paris in May 1859. At the Salon he singled out Daubigny, Corot and Rousseau and an animal painter called Monginot as worthy of his attention.

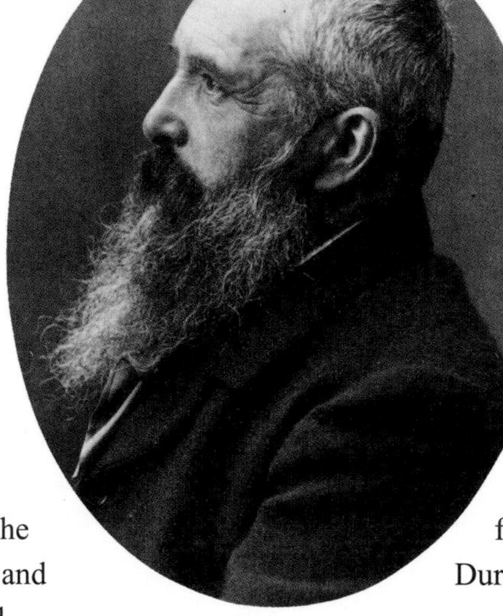

Probably the most popular painter of all the Impressionists, Monet's struggle to achieve his art is often overlooked.

He made use of an introduction to visit the studio of the painter, Constant Troyon. He had already met Boudin and Jongkind and been influenced by their atmospheric paintings of the northern coast. Monet was as interested in fashion plates and Japanese art as he was in the art of his friends; above all, however, it was the excitement of painting as directly as possible the visible world that fired his imagination.

His liaison with Camille Doncieux and his refusal to consider enrolling at the Ecole des Beaux-Arts resulted in the allowance he received from his family being withdrawn. Throughout the 1860s he was to know real hardship. In 1862, Monet entered Gleyre's studio, where he met Bazille, Renoir and Sisley; the following year, the four friends began working together in the forest of Fontainebleau. Monet also worked with Boudin and Jongkind along the Normandy coast before returning to Paris in 1865, where he renewed contact with Pissarro and Cézanne.

In April 1865, Monet returned to Chailly, near Barbizon in the forest of Fontainebleau, to paint, entirely in the open air, a large-scale major work that would be self-consciously modern, owing much to the examples of Courbet and Manet and little to the art traditions of the Ecole des Beaux-Arts or the past. This initiated a series of bold experimental canvases none of which met with the painter's total approval. The difficulties of carrying out this ambitious program in the face of a largely unresponsive public should not be underestimated; in 1868, lost in despair, Monet claimed to have contemplated suicide. At about that time he abandoned the notion of figure painting on a large scale and concentrated on the production of more intimate studies of modern subjects, highly colored and animated by broken rhythmical brushwork.

The year after Camille gave birth to their son Jean in 1869, Monet moved to London in order to escape the Franco-Prussian War, leaving his family behind. There he met the dealer Paul Durand-Ruel, whose support was to be of crucial significance to him and his colleagues in the years ahead.

On his return to France in 1871, Monet lived at Argenteuil and later Vétheuil, in the countryside of the Seine valley northwest of the capital, before finally settling in 1883 at Giverny, further down the valley of the Seine. During the period of the 1870s and early 1880s, Monet painted in Paris, Argenteuil, Le Havre and London. He painted cityscapes, landscapes and seascapes, and many views of the Seine made from a converted studio boat he had had built in the early 1870s. His work, and that of Caillebotte, Renoir, Sisley and Manet during this decade, represents the high point of Impressionism.

Although the title of one of Monet's paintings, *Impression, Sunrise*, exhibited at the first independent exhibition of Impressionist artists in 1874, gave the movement its name, Monet's involvement with the Impressionist exhibitions was idiosyncratic and provisional; at the 1877 exhibition he exhibited thirty canvases, including seven of the Gare Saint-Lazare, but in 1880 he organized his own one-man show at "La Vie Moderne." Two years later, he participated in the seventh Impressionist show with thirty-two canvases in what was basically a mini-retrospective exhibition. In 1876 Monet took his family to stay at Mongeron, the home of a wealthy collector, Ernest Hoschedé, and developed a liaison with his patron's wife Alice. Hoschedé was bankrupted in 1877 and the Hoschedé family moved in with Monet's at Vétheuil. Monet thus became head of a household that included his wife Camille, Alice Hoschedé and eight children. On September 5, 1879, Camille died of cancer and Alice took her place, eventually marrying Monet in 1892, after the death of Ernest Hoschedé in 1890. Monet had always been a shrewd businessman, which was just as well, for from 1879 his art had to sustain an increasingly affluent lifestyle and his newly expanded domestic base.

After the death of his wife, Monet's interest shifted to more elemental aspects of the natural world. His paintings of the severe winter of 1879–80 are the beginnings of a program of work that represents a more complex and deeply romantic relationship with the world. He painted a wide variety of climatic conditions, from the snowy landscapes of Norway, the melancholy bleak landscape of the Creuse Valley, and the dawn breaking over the River Seine to the heat haze of the Mediterranean coast. He revisited the fashionable sites of his childhood home, painting not the modish life on the promenades of Trouville as Boudin had done but the rugged grandeur of the cliffs and sea. Although he frequented tourist sites, including Belle-Ile, Menton, and elsewhere, he always stressed their naturally romantic aspects.

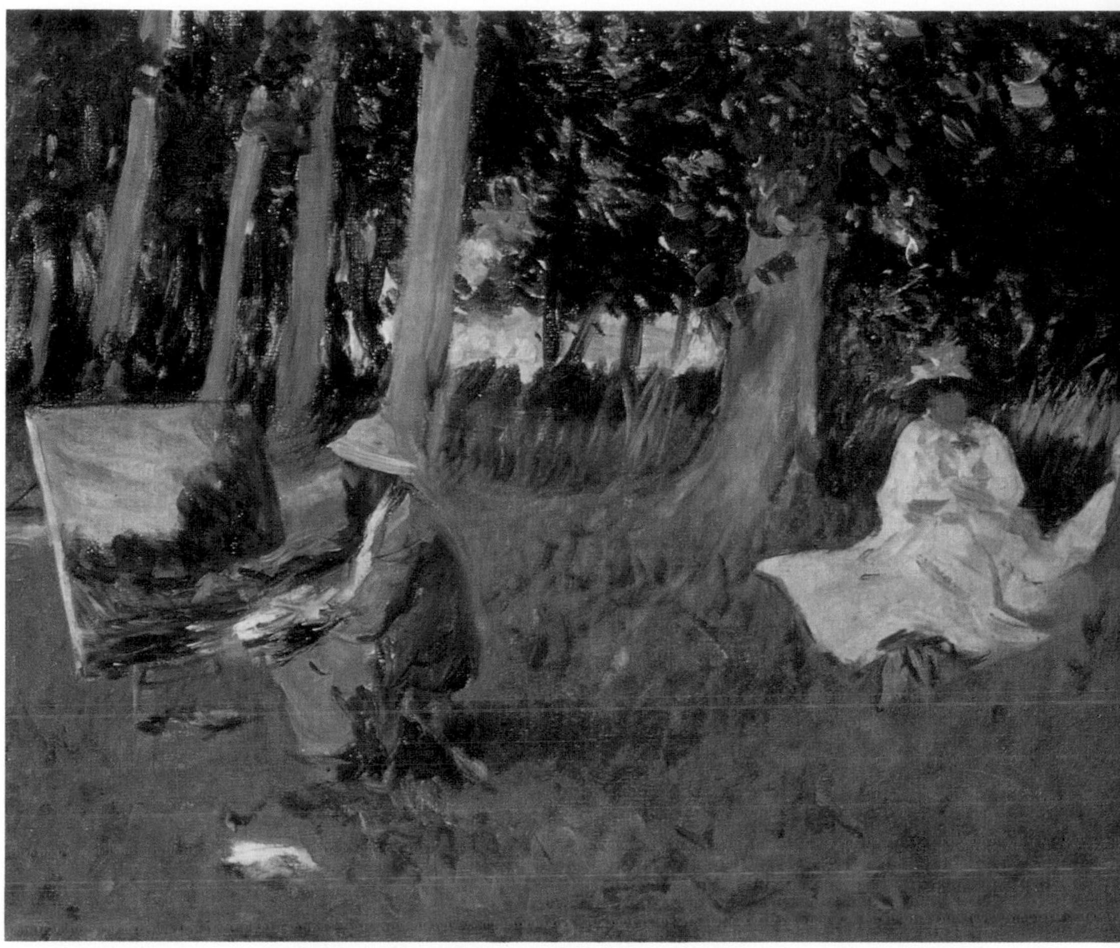

John Singer Sargent,* Claude Monet Painting at the Edge of a Wood, *c. 1887.

Fame and financial success

In the 1880s Monet began to achieve real success, financial and critical. In 1889 after a joint exhibition at the Galerie Georges Petit in Paris, shared with the sculptor Auguste Rodin, he enjoyed a national and international reputation of high standing. A shrewd businessman, Monet would play his dealers off against each other to achieve the best price for his paintings. During this period Monet grew closer to his former colleagues, enjoying café life again, especially between 1890 and 1894 when he often joined his friends at the Café Riche in Paris.

Monet had bought his house at Giverny in 1890, and in 1898 he began to paint the gardens he had developed there. His waterlily ponds became the central point of his concerns; in his meditations upon their surfaces and reflective qualities, the artist was continuing a journey begun in his youth when he painted the beaches and rivers of northern France.

The paintings of his final years reveal the increasing profundity of Monet's thought. The paintings became meditations on time, memory, experience and the business of painting. Begun in earnest in 1914, many of the mural-size paintings of Monet's last decade were donated to the nation as a memorial to those fallen in the First World War. Their installation in the Orangerie in Paris was completed just before his death on December 5, 1926. On May 17, 1927, the decorative cycle was unveiled to the public. Despite problems with his eyesight, Monet was able to work on paintings of his gardens until well into the 1920s. Some of these remained unseen until the 1950s and when they were exhibited they became highly influential with a new generation of painters.

The Beach at Trouville

1870, oil on canvas, 38 x 45.8 cm (15 x 17¾ in), National Gallery, London, England

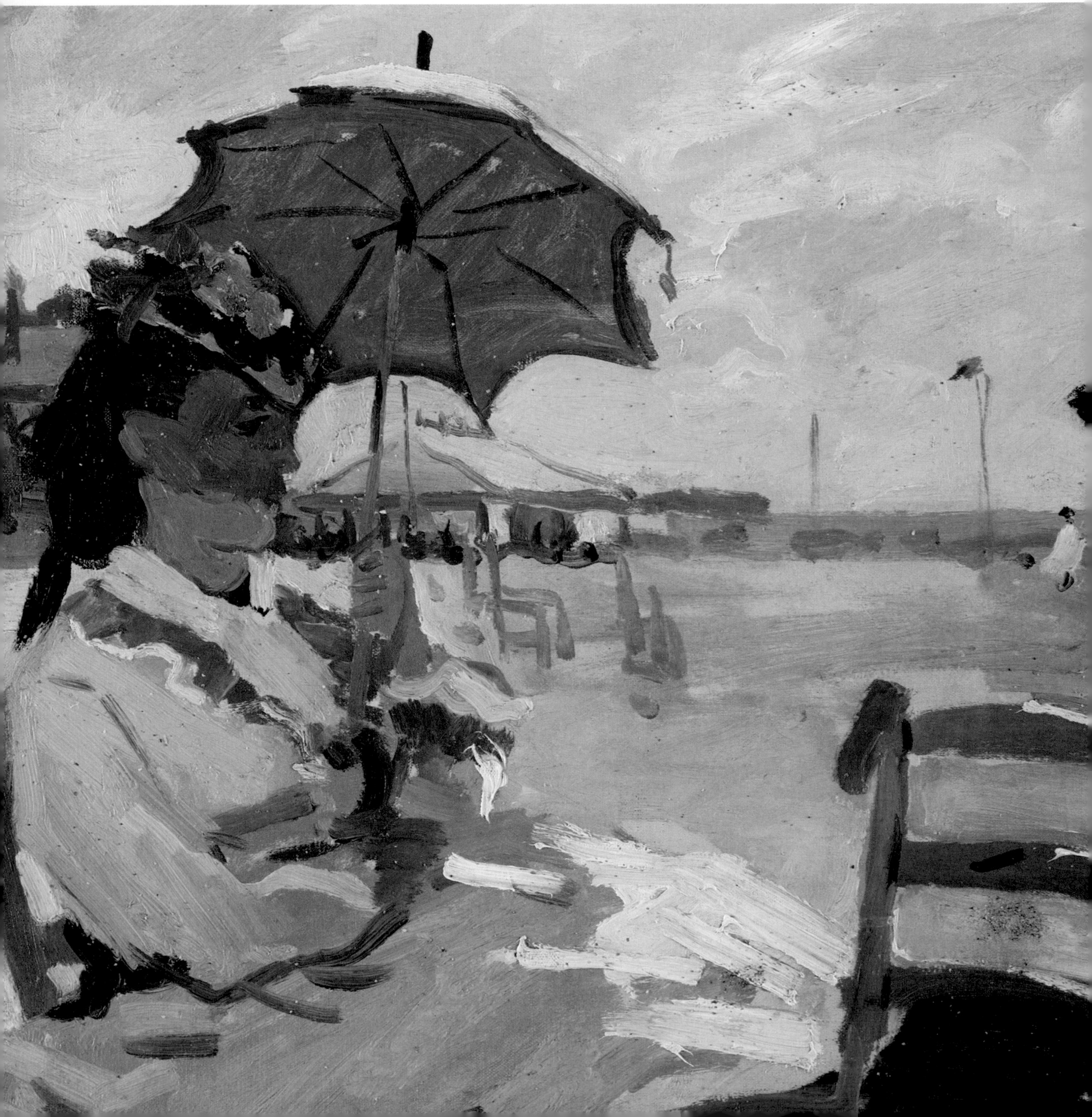

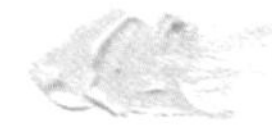

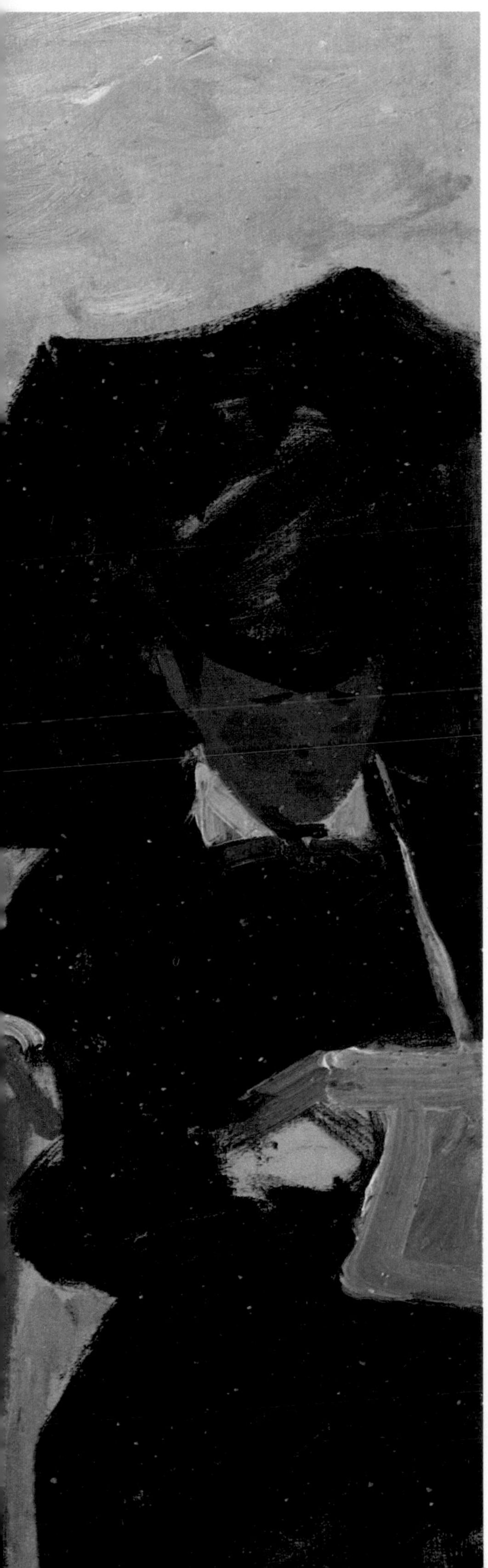

The Beach at Trouville is dependent upon the precedent of Boudin's jewel-like improvisations. Painted entirely in the open air, Monet's painting presents the viewer with a close-up of two women, one of whom is Camille, who he had married on June 28, 1870, and the other is possibly Madame Boudin. Monet's baby son, Jean, is touchingly indicated by the two little shoes drying in the brilliant sunshine on the back of the chair that separates the two women, each locked in her own world.

In September, Monet would have to leave his wife and child behind in France as he fled to England from Le Havre to avoid the Franco-Prussian War. None of these pressures are foreshadowed in this sunny painting. Boudin, who was painting with him at the time, recalled these times in a letter to Monet in 1897: "I can still see you with that poor Camille at the Hotel de Tivoli … little Jean plays on the sand and his papa is seated on the ground, sketchbook in his hand."

The painting is one of a number of surviving studies made on the beach. This particular one is supremely confident, rapidly worked, the decisions governing its form founded upon his experience and upon his intuitive responses to the subject before him, given shape by his manipulation of the materials available.

On a cream-colored canvas, Monet first sketched in the figures in a thin dark diluted paint, working in areas of thin blue pigment mixed with black to establish the basic elements of the composition. It is possible to follow the genesis of the painting in detail: the figure in black reading the newspaper is realized in a single skin of lightly worked thin paint, while the figure of Camille is more robustly formed by working wet on wet, a practice common to the Impressionists and which consists of dragging further layers of paint over paint that is still wet. Using square-tipped stiff brushes loaded with white pigment, Monet has laid down, just as he had done in his *Women in the Garden*, single separate blocks of clean white pigment to suggest not only the fall of light on the white dress but also its thick folds. Camille holds a parasol that Monet has rapidly sketched in the most minimal manner; it casts a shadow over her face, an inconsistency with the fall of the light in the rest of the painting, which has led some commentators to see it as a veil. Her hat is enlivened by a number of dabs of pure pigment and the rich impasto contrasts with those areas of the sky, around the back of the chair and the reading figure's hand, that are left uncovered, the color of the untouched creamy ground being used as a positive element in the realization of the image. The speed and assurance of these improvisations ensure a sense of informality and immediacy.

The painting is renowned for bearing physical traces of its having been painted in the open air: numerous grains of sand have embedded themselves into the still wet paint, remaining there to stand as evidence of the immediacy with which Monet captured a single moment of time, on a beach over one-hundred-and-thirty years ago in an image that is as fresh and resonant as if it were painted yesterday.

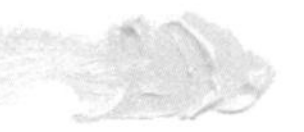

Exile in London

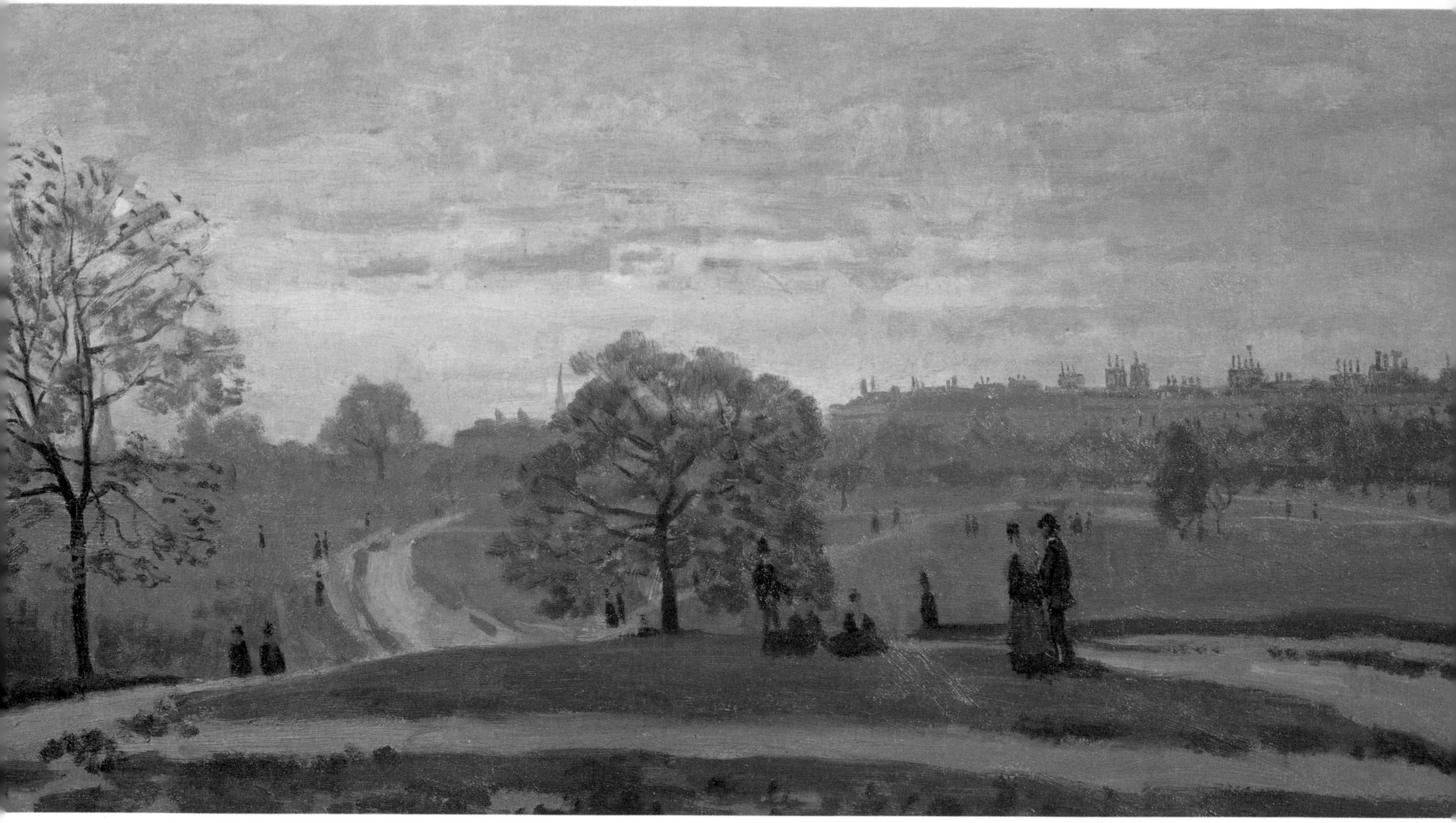

Claude Monet, **Green Park,** *London, 1871. The treatment of this urban scene brings to mind the sketches of Constable and Turner. No English painter of Monet's time would have treated this urban landscape in so summary a manner.*

Claude Monet and Camille Pissarro both escaped the Franco-Prussian War and possible conscription by exiling themselves to London. They made their ways independently to London, Pissarro living south of the Thames at Lower Norwood, where he had relations, and Monet staying in the center of the city, living first at 11 Arundel Street, The Strand, and later in Bath Place, Kensington.

Monet was nearly 30, desperate for money and, save for his friend, alone in London, having left his family in France. Through the agency of Daubigny, who had spent part of 1870 painting views of the Thames, he made the acquaintance of the dealer Paul Durand-Ruel, who was nurturing the English taste for the Barbizon painters and whose support for the impoverished painters was to be crucial throughout their lives.

Pissarro arrived in London during December 1870. Two months earlier his home in Louveciennes had been ransacked by the Prussians and hundreds of his canvases had been mindlessly destroyed, or used as duckboards. Unlike Monet, Pissarro had found time to arrange for his family to come with him to share his exile.

Pissarro was soon disillusioned, having found no buyers in England. Even so, he felt that the city offered many opportunities for painting, particularly enthusing over the effects of fog, snow and later the impact of springtime on the city. Pissarro carefully planned and modified his pictures, slowly developing his paintings from a direct response to the scene before him. He began with muted colors that were overworked later to achieve a densely worked and textured surface.

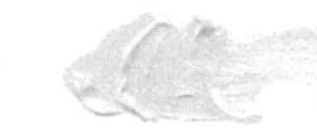

A London showing

Paul Durand-Ruel showed Monet's and Pissarro's works in his galleries in New Bond Street in the winter of 1870. Ironically, the gallery had previously been the premises of something called the "German Gallery." Durand-Ruel's father had built up a reputation with his marketing of the Barbizon painters; now, Paul Durand-Ruel decided to update their portfolio of artists, holding eleven shows of contemporary French art in London between 1870 and 1875.

Monet and Pissarro would have had a professional interest in the state of recent British art. It is often said that the development of Impressionism owed a lot to the example of the English painters Turner and Constable, and Monet said on occasion that he admired Turner. At this time, however, there were few of the great painter's works on public show, although *Rain, Steam and Speed* (1844) was on view in the National Gallery. In 1870 there was little by Constable on exhibition in the National Gallery, apart from *The Cornfield* (1826) and *The Valley Farm,* (1815). It seems more likely that Monet's and Pissarro's admiration for these artists matured over the years and had more effect on their later paintings than on the ones done at this time.

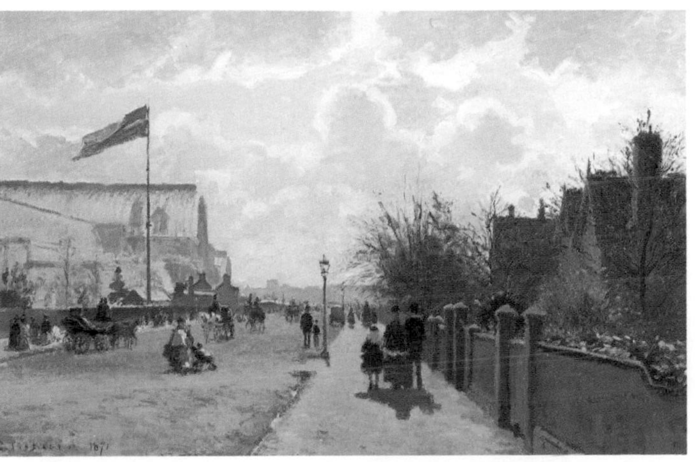

Camille Pissaro,* Crystal Palace, *London, 1871. This was the first work by the artist to be purchased by Durand-Ruel.

Things were not easy for French artists in England at this time. The French were widely regarded as the transgressors in the conflict between their country and Prussia; worse, from Pissarro's point of view, was the fact that the English seemed to have little interest in their painting. A despondent Pissarro wrote to the critic and journalist, and great supporter of the Impressionists, Théodore Duret,

> ***I shan't stay here and it is only abroad that one feels how beautiful, great and hospitable France is. What a difference here. One gathers only contempt, indifference, even rudeness; among colleagues there is the most egotistical jealousy and resentment. Here there is no art; everything is a question of business ... My painting doesn't catch on, not at all. This follows me more or less everywhere.***

His pessimism was confirmed by an article in *The Times* of April 27, 1870, which said

> ***In the work of the school we are now considering, we find a harshness in the juxtaposition of tints, a crudeness of local coloring, a heaviness of hand, what seems to be a deliberate avoidance of delicate workmanship, and in short, what in France would be called a franchise naive et brutale, we should suppose the very antipodes of anything suggested or sought by Corot ... One seems to see in such work evidence of as wild a spirit of anarchy at work in French painting as in French politics.***

Such a reaction to Pissaro's work becomes almost understandable when one sees a work such as his painting of the Crystal Palace, which had been built for the Great Exhibition of 1851 and to which he gives the same level of significance as the row of brick-built suburban dwellings that flank its iron and glass exterior. Both Monet and Pissarro continued their practice of working in the open air while in London, and both were rejected by the Royal Academy in 1870. To us, their London paintings are marked by a freshness and informality, Pissarro concentrating upon the suburbs where he lived and Monet painting the Thames and London's parks. Their casual and understated interpretations of national institutions like the Crystal Palace and the Houses of Parliament and their sketchy and prosaic depictions of the great parks and recent suburban developments would have looked extremely daring, not to say distinctly odd, to a British audience of the time, especially when seen in the context of contemporary British art.

Although both artists left London in 1871, both were to return several times to paint some of their most-admired works, inspired by the particular atmospheric effects of the frequently fog-bound city. Pissarro, in particular, had a strong link with London in the person of his son Lucien, who came over to England to live; Pissarro's letters to him are some of the most precious documents of Impressionism.

The Franco-Prussian War

The image of the Second Empire as a glamorous regime is sustainable as long as our eyes are fixed firmly on the highly visible life of the Imperial court and the relatively few who were able to take advantage of all the opportunities it had to offer. The reality behind the facade was more complex. Just before the outbreak of the Franco-Prussian War, Mr. Washbourne, the newly installed American Ambassador, noticed, as he recalled later in his *Recollections of a Minister to France*,

> ***There were certain appearances of prosperity, happiness and content; but they were like the fruit of the Dead Sea, and to the last degree deceptive. Beneath all this outward show there was to be heard rumbling popular discontent. The people were dissatisfied, restless and uneasy. They considered that their rights had been trampled upon, and their discontent was often made manifest in Paris by their turbulent gatherings on the boulevards … Night after night large numbers would be arrested as rioters and revolutionists, and locked up in the prison of Mazas, or sent to the casemates of Fort Bicêtre.***

On September 1, 1870, the Franco-Prussian War, which Napoleon III had

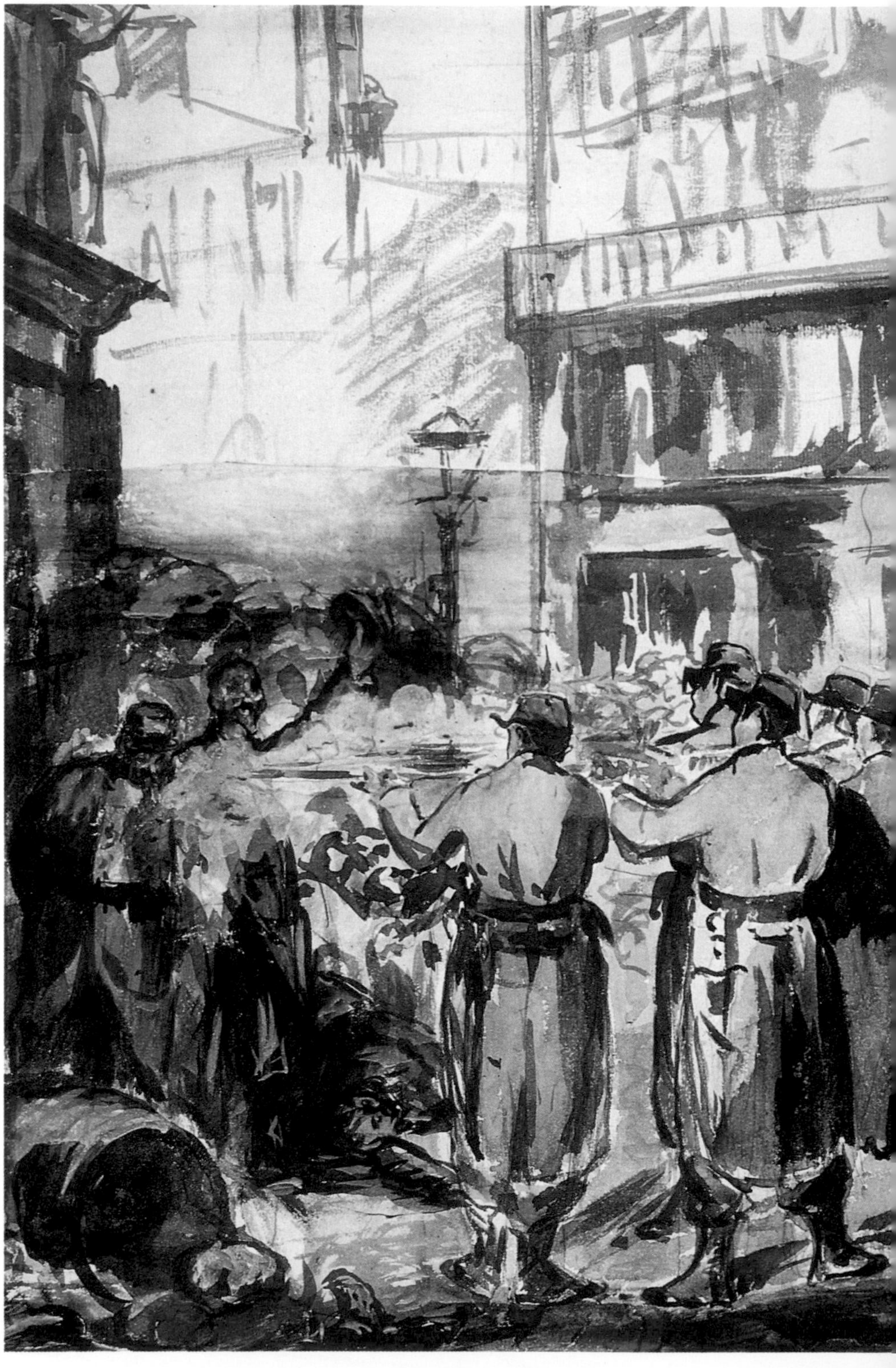

Edouard Manet,* The Barricade, *1871. Manet based this scene of execution on Goya's* Third of May, 1808 *and* The Execution of the Defenders of Madrid, *which was produced in 1867–68.

declared in July, reached a nadir for the French at the fortress of Sedan, where the Emperor was defeated and held prisoner. It was the end of the Second Empire, though the war would not be over until May 1871.

"It may not have been much of an Empire," remarked one diplomat, "but by God, we had a good time." The war, declared by the French though largely engineered by the Prussians, had disastrous consequences for France and in the long term, for all of Europe. Three days after, Sedan France declared itself a republic once again. Two days later, amid scenes of great rejoicing in Paris, the Third Republic was proclaimed and France had to come to terms with yet another shift of government.

The bloodshed and turmoil did not end with the surrender at Sedan, but dragged on into 1871. By the end of September, Paris was besieged by the Prussian army. As the siege continued, two million people living in Paris found themselves facing famine and sickness. As meat became more difficult to obtain, dogs, cats, rats and even the animals at the zoo fell victim to the butcher's axe. By January 1871, the Prussians were bombarding Paris, and shells fell on the cemetery of Montparnasse and in the Latin Quarter. An armistice was finally negotiated at the end of January.

Degas, Manet and Berthe Morisot, despite Manet's exhortations for her to leave, had remained in Paris. For them and for others who had stayed, life did not yet return to normal. France elected a new General Assembly in February, and the Prussians finally evacuated Paris in March. Then more revolutionary elements in the capital, including a section of the National Guard, refused to accept the new conditions and declared Paris to be a commune. The result was civil war. This extraordinary state of affairs lasted for three months. There was killing and savagery on both sides as the city was laid siege to by the troops of the French Government at Versailles. Berthe Morisot's house was commandeered by troops, and it was said that her mother's hair turned white overnight.

The effects upon the Impressionists were incalculable. Bazille, who had volunteered for active service, was shot dead in the closing days of 1870. Both Pissarro and Monet had fled to England to escape involvement, and in Paris, Manet and Degas served in the artillery of the National Guard under the command of the highly successful painter of precisionist military and eighteenth-century scenes, Jean-Louis-Ernest Meissonier. Manet left Paris in February 1871, returning immediately after the *semaine sanglante*. His sketch of the barricade was an initial idea for a major painting to commemorate the massacre. Also in the regiment was the portraitist Carolus Durand, a good friend of Monet and one of the most fashionable portraitists of the time. Through the action of influential friends, Renoir had joined the *cuirassiers*, escaping the privations of the siege but nearly dying of dysentery. Cézanne had been bought out of active service by his uncle and spent the war in hiding at L'Estaque. Courbet's public involvement in the government of the Commune and the role he played in the destruction of the Vendôme Column effectively ruined his life.

After the fall of the Commune, a period of restoration was looked for, and culture was allotted a very significant role in the reconstruction of France and the reinstituting of national pride after the country's humiliating defeat and the shame and stigma of civil war.

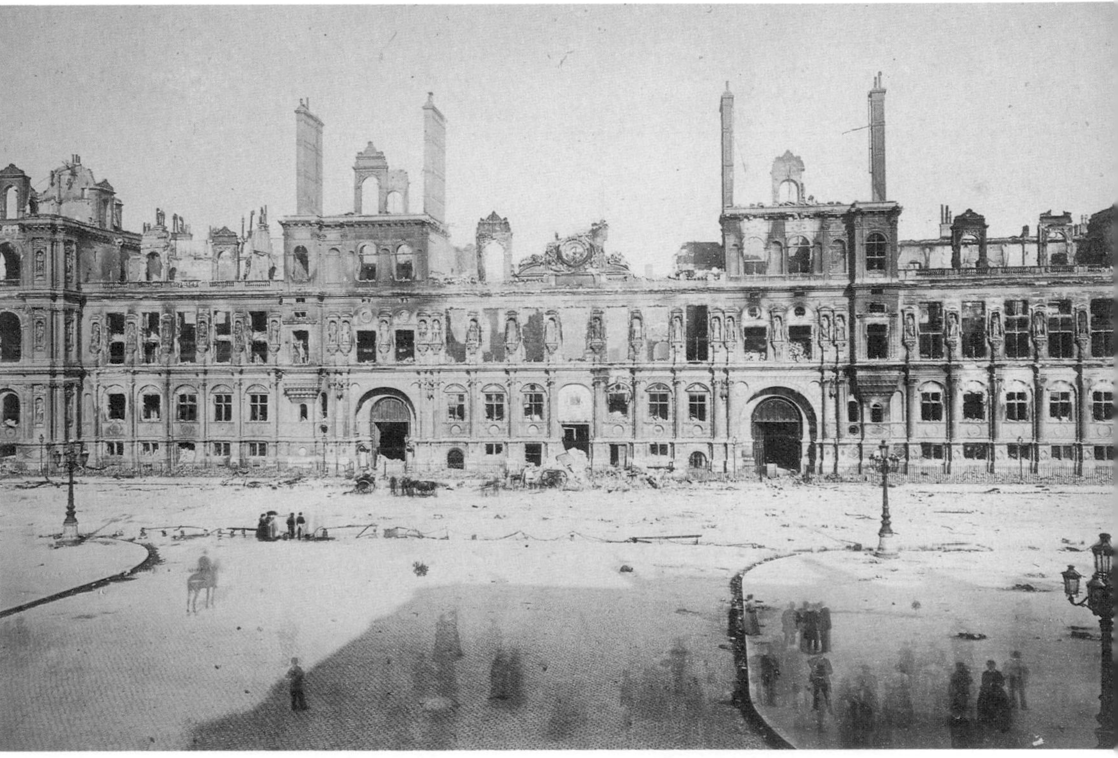

***Ghostly figures make an eerie presence in this contemporary photograph of the burnt-out remains of the Tuileries Palace taken from the Place du Carousel, the very spot Baudelaire chose as the setting for his poem,* The Swan (La Cygne).**

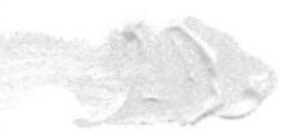

Post-War Paris

Despite the spectacular fall of the Empire and the humiliation and shame of the events that followed it, the mass of the bourgeoisie of France were able, despite periodic financial and political crises, to continue to consolidate the gains they had made throughout the century, marking their affluence by their conspicuous consumption of the luxuries of life.

On a public and private level, those who could afford the luxury of thinking about the arts considered that this should be a period of consolidation, a time to heal the wounds left by the terrible recent events. It was no time for experimentation in the arts, but a time to pull together to rekindle traditional values. In such a climate, any artist who based his work upon radical individualism was bound to find it difficult not only to

The Great Boulevards, ***1875. Renoir's painting presents a warm, soft-focused, romantic interpretation of the city.***

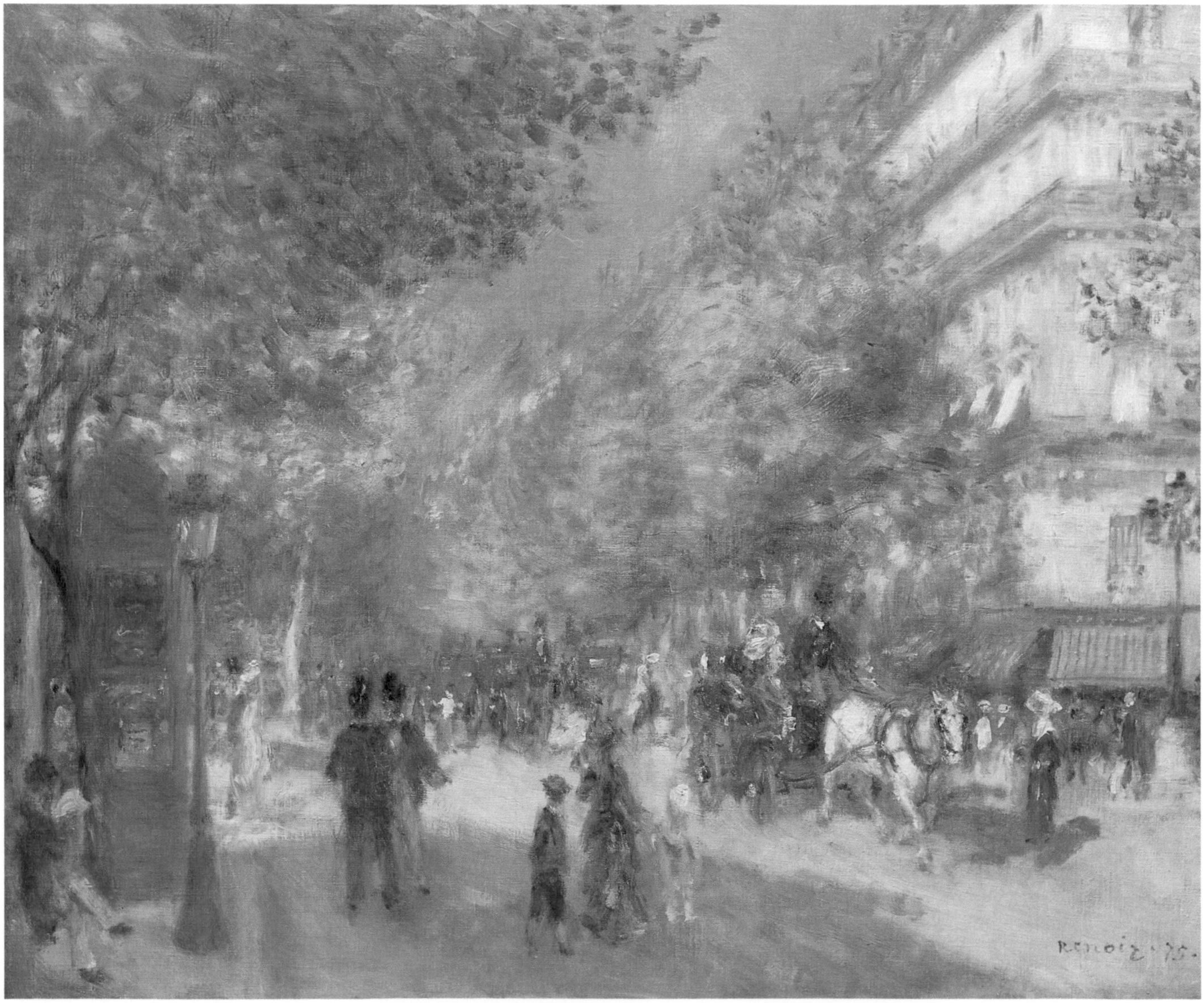

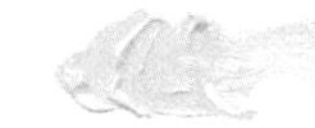

find an audience, but also to find a site where his work could be seen. Landscape painting in any form was not favorably regarded; instead, a return to heroic art that could stir the nation and aid the moral regeneration of the country was encouraged. The only forms of landscape painting that could be tolerated were those that consciously or otherwise followed this agenda. Favored paintings were those that evoked a sense of continuity with past traditions and presented an image of France that could instill a sense of harmony and pride in national and provincial identity and unity.

The Search for outlets

There was a conscious attempt to reform the Salon. The liberal days of the Empire being deemed to be over, the Salon should be promoted as a sanctuary of art, with artists being encouraged, through stricter admission policies, to paint elevated subjects. At the same time, fewer works should be admitted.

The reaction of those artists dedicated to the landscape and other so-classed "lesser" genres was predictable. They demanded the right to be able to show their works. On the rejection of their works from the Salon, petitions flooded into the administration from older and established artists such as Daubigny and Corot and also from younger artists such as Renoir, Pissarro and Cézanne. Since Salons des Refusés were not longer to be tolerated, artists began to renew the search for other means of exhibiting their works.

Durand-Ruel was a major outlet, but he, too, was finding it difficult to sell works, although there were individual buyers who, for speculative or aesthetic reasons, were interested in collecting the works of the young avant-garde painters.

Monet returned to Paris via Holland late in 1871 and, reunited with his family, moved to Argenteuil, nine kilometers (5½ miles) from the center of Paris and already developed as a fashionable resort for yachting and boating. During the years he lived there, he used delicately tinted grounds and carefully chosen pigments, repeating them across the canvas and thereby securing harmony. Works painted specially for dealers were more conventionally finished, their colors more muted.

Edouard Manet had been away from the capital during the Commune but had returned in time to witness the bloody reprisals and summary executions; Renoir was nearly shot as a spy, whilst Degas stayed with friends at Valpinçon, well away from the immediate troubles. Berthe Morisot was in Saint-Germain with the well-respected academic painter Pierre Puvis de Chavannes. Paul Durand-Ruel, returned from London, began signing up the friends of Monet and Pissarro and made contracts with Sisley and Degas. Outwardly, he was an unlikely supporter of avant-garde art; Renoir, whom he first met in 1872, remembering him as "a respectable middle-class man, a good husband, an ardent royalist and a practicing Catholic." Obviously, Durand-Ruel was concerned with making a profitable business career out of his artists, but it should never be forgotten that he was prepared to take what must have seemed very considerable professional risks in the backing of these painters and that, unlike some other dealers, he was not driven by speculation alone. Durand-Ruel's buying from the Impressionists during the early 1870s meant that they did not have to suffer the indignity of submitting to the Salon. Through Alfred Stevens, the extremely popular painter of modishly dressed beautiful women in fashionable interiors, Durand-Ruel bought twenty-five pictures by Manet, worth 35,000 francs.

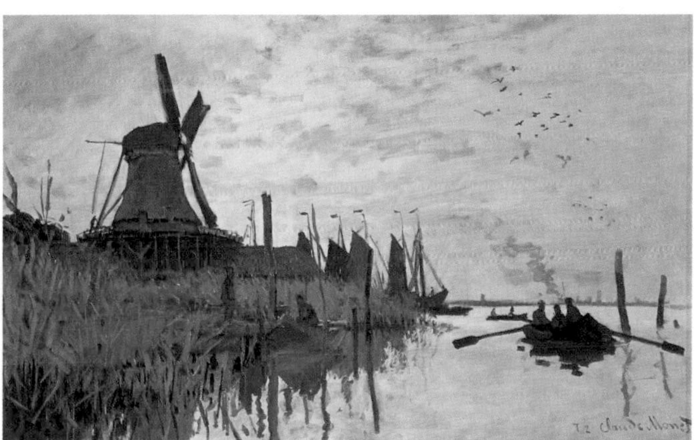

Monet,* Windmills at Zaandam, Amsterdam, *1871. Monet made his way back to France via Holland.

Post-war artists

The painters who soon would come together to form their own independent exhibiting society were a disparate group of individuals. Degas had begun to paint the theater and ballet in the early 1870s and, after visiting New Orleans where he had family and business interests, came back determined more than ever to dedicate himself to the painting of what he saw as the distinctive features of modern Parisian life.

Degas' art was predominantly studio-based, whereas the experiments of Pissarro and Cézanne took them out of the city to the market town of Pontoise. Pissarro lived in the town or the neighboring hamlet of L'Hermitage for the next ten years painting, almost cataloging, the humble buildings and domesticated landscape of the neighborhood. Meanwhile, Renoir remained in Paris, working close to Monet, almost as if the war and Commune had never happened.

CHAPTER TWO

The Exhibitions

During the years from 1874 to 1886 many artists at one time or another showed their work together in what were soon termed the "Impressionist" Exhibitions. The exhibiting core of this group included artists who have since become among the most famous in the world. Their cooperation for this short period of time, despite various fallings out and disagreements has meant that the achievements of these very different artists have been grouped together as "Impressionist." As is apparent in this book, this term is inadequate to represent the variety of work produced by these remarkable artists, thrown together by the force of circumstance.

All too often, we forget that for most artists, painting is a professional practice and selling work is a prerequisite of feeding oneself and one's family. This section gives an account of the different exhibitions that took place and how the artists and their dealers attempted to create a market for their work outside the state-dominated Salon system. Each had his or her own reasons for participating, and each had his or her own following, although all essentially supported each other's activities.

Berthe Morisot's letter, written to her aunt after the second Impressionist exhibition of 1876, sets their activities into context:

> ***If you read any Paris newspapers among others* Le Figaro*, which is so popular with the respectable public, you must know that I am one of a group of artists who are holding a show of their own and you must also have seen how little favor this exhibition enjoys in the eyes of the gentlemen of the press. On the other hand we have been prides in the radical papers but these you do not read. Anyway we are being discussed and we are so proud of it that we are all very happy.***

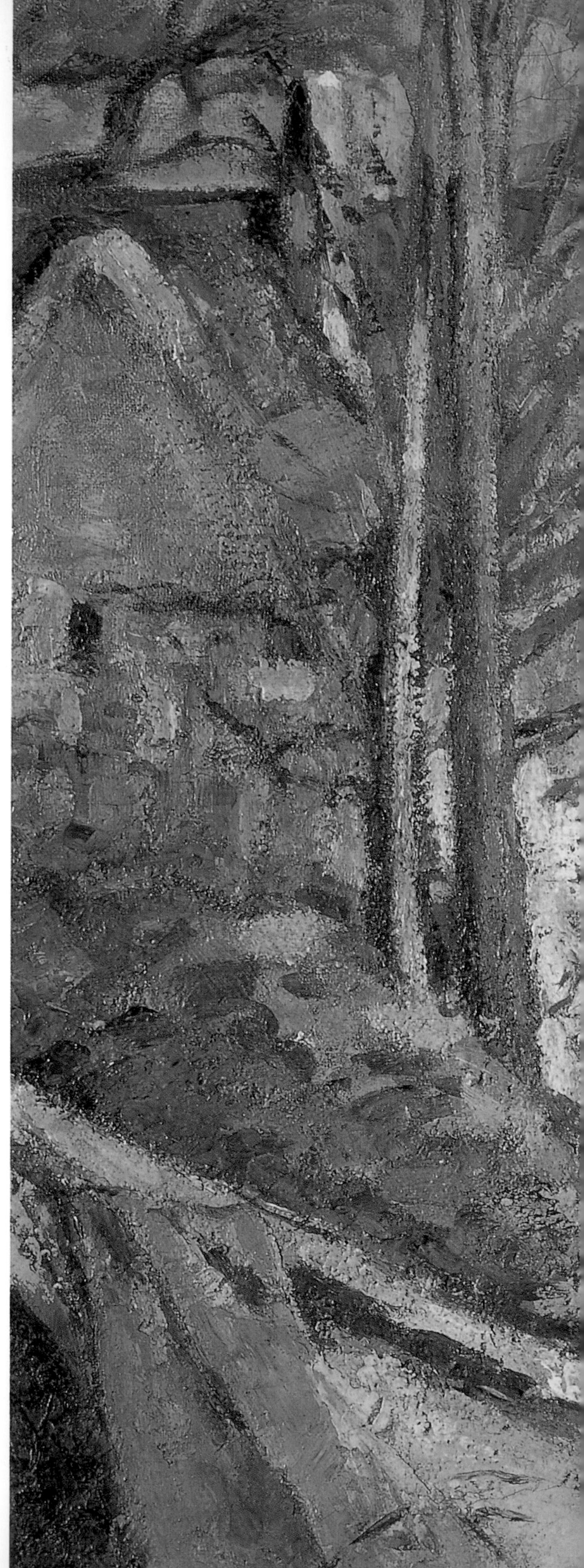

Cézanne's painting,* House of the Hanged Man*, 1873, was on show at the first exhibition of independent artists.

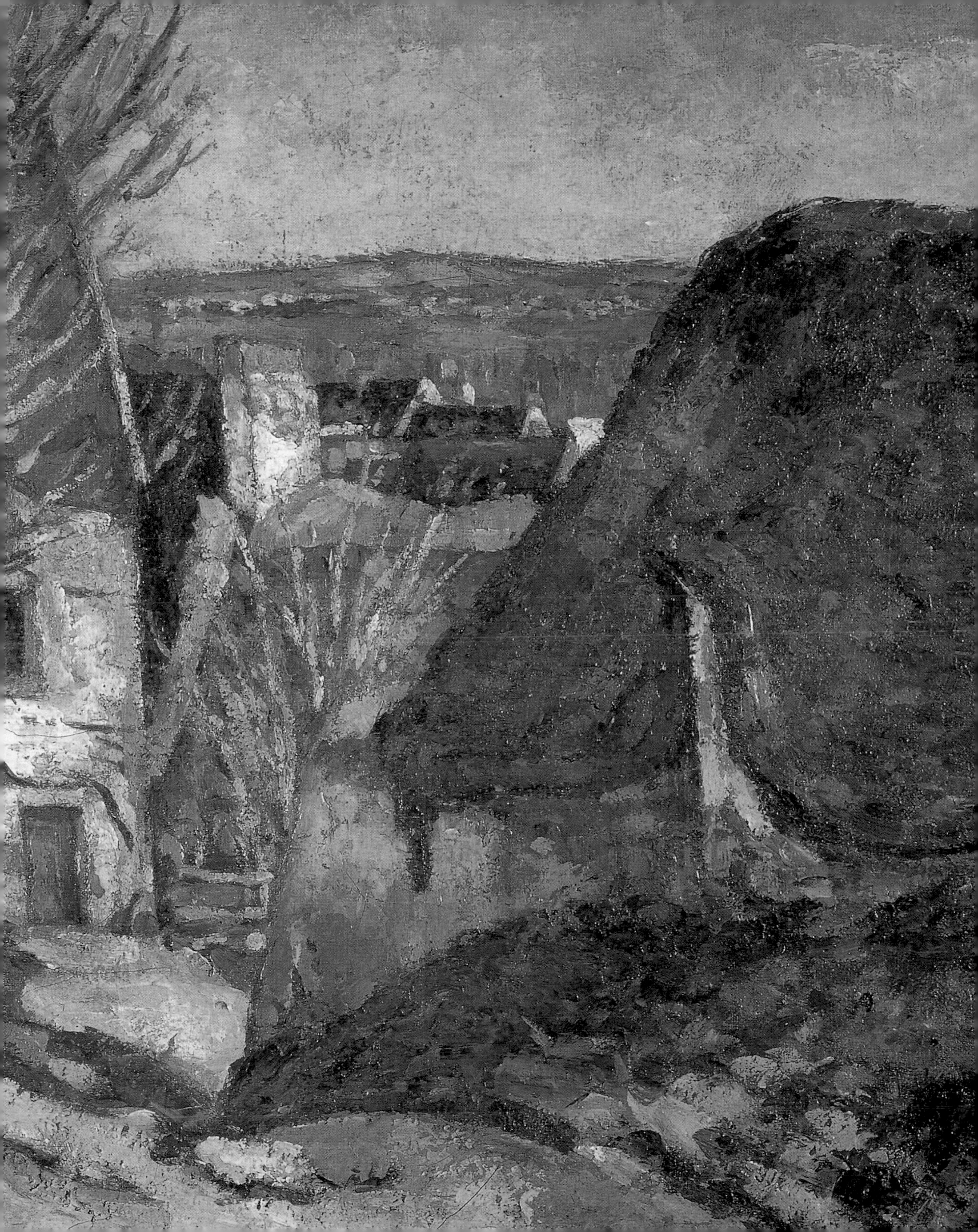

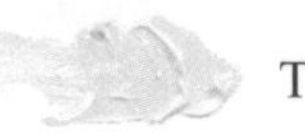

The First Impressionist Exhibition, 1874

The project which Bazille had first outlined in a letter to his parents in 1867, for "a dozen talented people … to rent a big studio each year where we will show our works," finally came into being in 1874. On April 15 that year, at 10 o'clock in the morning, the doors opened into the former premises of the famous photographer Nadar, on the second floor of number 35 Boulevard des Capucines. Inside were on view paintings and pastels by a group of artists exhibiting under the title *Société Anonyme des artistes, peintres, sculpteurs, graveurs, etc.,* the French equivalent of a joint stock company or limited company.

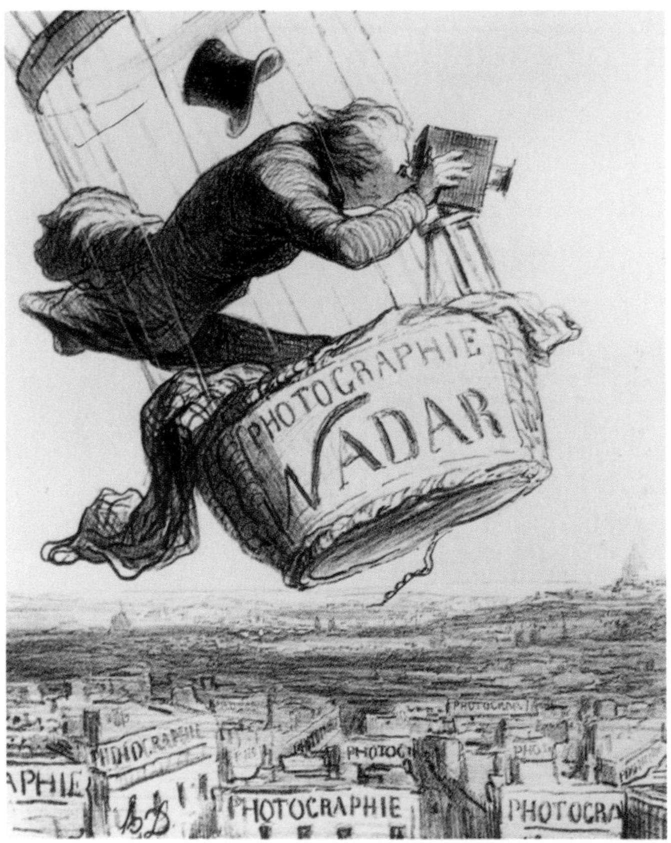

Honoré Daumier's lithograph, **Nadar Elevating Photography to the Level of Art,** *published 1862.*

The artists who had chosen to set up their own exhibition outside the officially sanctioned system had the support of the dealer Paul Durand-Ruel. The recent relatively successful sale of their paintings from the collection of Ernest Hoschedé had further raised their hopes that the moment was right for such a venture. But the economic recovery that followed the debacle of the Franco-Prussian War and the Commune was short-lived and by 1874 Durand-Ruel was finding it difficult to promote and sell their works and had been forced to stop purchasing works.

A defining moment

The exhibition at Nadar's former studio remained open for only a month, but by the time it had closed history had been made. It became known in time as the first Impressionist show, even though those artists – Monet, Renoir, Sisley, Morisot, Degas, Pissarro and Cézanne – who were to become known as Impressionists were in the minority. The founding members included Armand Guillaumin, Edouard Béliard, sculptor Auguste Ottin, Auguste de Molins and Ludovic-Napoléon Lepic. There were thirty participants in all, and the more than 200 works on view had been seen by 4,000 people by the time the exhibition closed on May 15.

The range of work on view was extremely diverse in subject and technique: there was even a sculpted bust representing the arch-academic artist Ingres. Pissarro had based the constitution of the event on a baker's cooperative he knew of in Pontoise, and there was no coherent strategy or shared vision beyond the most immediate of pressing concerns, which was to find a space where individuals not favored by the regime could sell their works.

Dissension was in the air from the first, Degas arguing for the inclusion of successful artists including those who exhibited at the Salon in order to make clear the unradical nature of the enterprise. Pissarro argued the opposite and this time his view prevailed. With the backing of Durand-Ruel and with five months careful planning, the event was from the first an experiment in selling. There was no jury, no awards, and the work exhibited was for sale. The subversive effect of holding an independent exhibition could not be avoided, and Manet and Fantin-Latour, possibly aware of how participation might be detrimental to their careers, refused to join. Manet also found it hard to stomach the deliberately boorish Cézanne and, like his friend Duret, felt that to show independently of the Salon was, in effect, to flee the battlefield. Nor could he bring himself to jeopardize his craving for official recognition and honors.

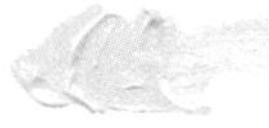

The intimate space of Nadar's studios must have contrasted markedly with the overcrowded massive spaces of the Salon. Unlike in the Salon, the paintings were sympathetically arranged, no more than two deep. The subject matter, with a few exceptions, celebrated the experiences of those who came to see them; scenes from contemporary life and landscapes, these were paintings not destined for great galleries but for the modern domestic interior.

A hostile press

However, the reaction of the press was not favorable and the exhibition received a lot of adverse publicity and hostile criticism. Sales were few, and the press as a body took the opportunity offered them to mock the exhibition and the whole enterprise. Others art critics remained silent. Predictably, Cézanne and Monet were singled out for most of the attacks.

Louis Leroy, a painter and art critic, presented his critical account of the exhibition in the periodical *Charivari* as seen through the eyes of an imaginary cantankerous academic painter whom he called Monsieur Vincent. He used his invention as a foil for the critic's own ideas and the oft-quoted passages should not be read as being representative of the critic's personal opinions:

M. Vincent is standing by one of Pissarro's landscapes and he pontificates to his friend who is accompanying him around the exhibition,
'...They are just scrapings from a palette arranged upon a muddy canvas. The work has no head nor tail, no top nor bottom, no front or back.'
'Maybe, but the impression is there.'
'Well, it's a funny impression! And this?'
'An Orchard by M. Sisley. I'd like to point out the small tree on the right. It's sparkling, but the impression!'
A catastrophe seemed to me imminent, and it was reserved for M. Monet to contribute the last straw.
'Ah, there he is, there he is!' he shouted in front of number 98. 'I recognize him: papa Vincent's favorite! What does it depict; have a look at the catalog.'
'Impression, Sunrise.'
'Impression; I was certain of it. I was just thinking that as I was impressed, there had to be some impression in it. And what freedom! What ease of handling! A preliminary drawing for a wallpaper pattern is more highly finished than this seascape.'

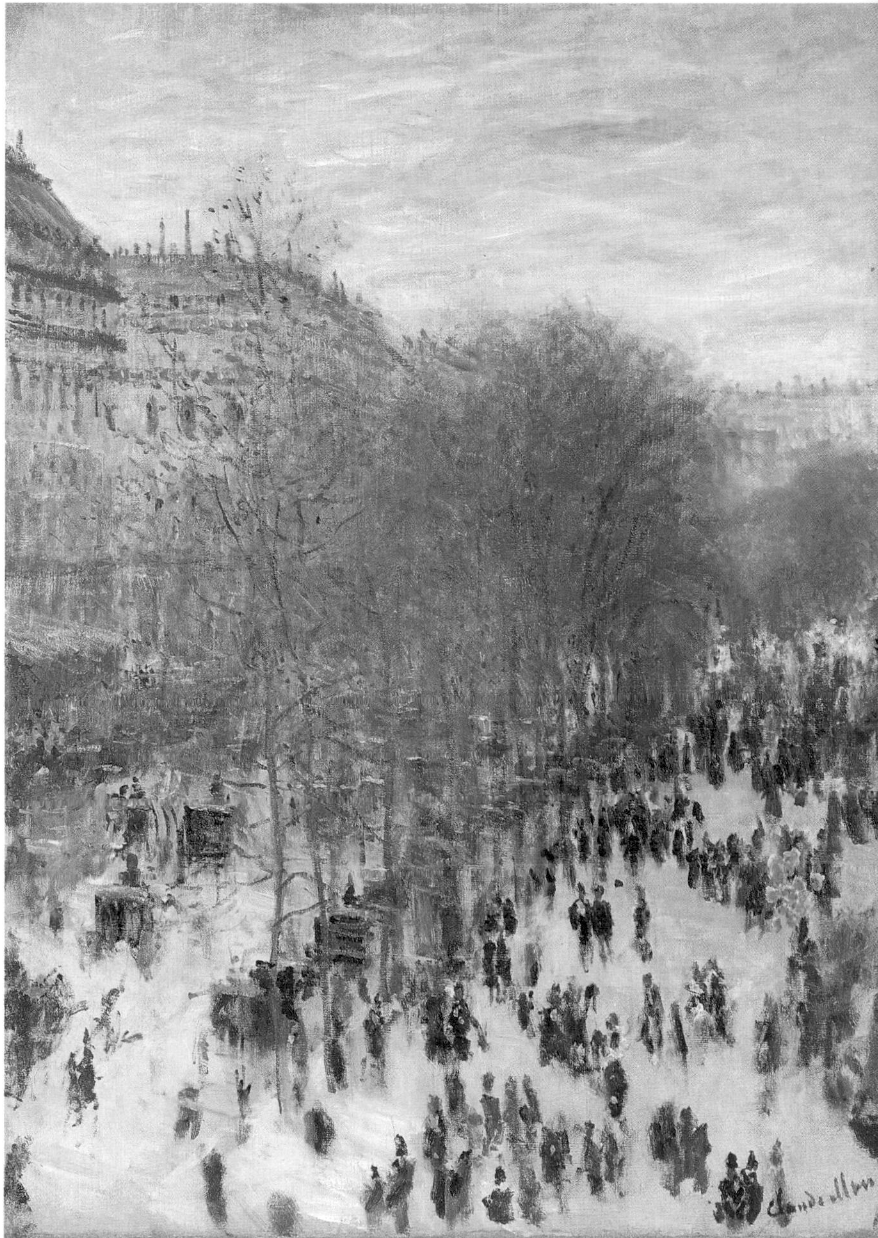

Claude Monet, **Boulevard des Capucines,** *1873–74. Two top-hatted Parisian men-about-town look down on their fellow human beings.*

Berthe Morisot had nine works on show at this first exhibition. For better or worse, one of her paintings was exhibited next to a Cézanne. Morisot's former teacher wrote to her mother,

If Mlle. Berthe must do something violent, she should, rather than burn everything she has done so far, pour some petrol on the new tendencies. How could she exhibit a work of art so exquisitely delicate as hers side by side with **Le Rêve du Celibataire [The Bachelor's Dream*****: in fact, Cézanne's*** **A Modern Olympia]** ***?... to negate all efforts, all the aspirations, all past dreams that have filled one's life, is madness. Worse, it is almost a sacrilege.***

Impression, Sunrise

1872, oil on canvas, 48 x 63 cm (19 x 25 in), Musée d'Orsay, Paris, France

Monet produced a number of canvases of Le Havre in the 1860s, but he could never have guessed that this rapidly painted sketch of the inner harbor would become one of the best-known paintings in the world. Exhibited as number 98 in the first exhibition of 1874, it was probably considered by the artist to be one of the least important of his works on show. Its title, chosen in haste for insertion in the catalog, precisely indicates its status as an "Impression," Monet himself later remarking that he had called it "Impression" as "it could not pass for a view of Le Havre." As we have seen, the painting was singled out by a critic who dismissed it as "an Impression, nothing more" and therefore, by implication, not worthy of its status as a finished painting. This judgment was then applied to the whole show and the word "Impressionism" became forever associated with the work of Monet and his friends.

When Monet was painting his views of Le Havre, the town was the busiest port in France and the source of his family's income. With minimum means, the artist suggests the soft misty atmosphere of the harbor, pierced by the rays of the vermilion sun. Monet has lightly brushed the entire canvas surface with a thin, diluted wash of variegated color to establish the enveloping atmosphere and then with thicker paint he has cursorily established the main features of the scene. The sun and its vibrant reflections have been set down in a series of short strokes that are one of the main features of his work at this time. The spiky dock architecture and the funnels and masts of the steamships are silhouetted against the early morning sky. Three rowing boats add a human dimension to the painting.

Although only a sketch, the composition owes a good deal to the more formal paintings of the ports of France produced by artists such as Joseph Vernet (1714–89) and others, whose work, in turn, owed much to the paintings of the seventeenth-century artist, Claude Lorraine. The subdued tonality and thinly laid on paint also suggest an affinity with the paintings of Monet's friend Whistler, while the heavily painted sun in the center of the canvas recalls the English master of sunlight, Turner. Like Turner, Monet was an obsessive artist and the concerns revealed in this sketch would continue to occupy his mind and art for the next fifty years.

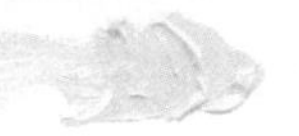

Auction Disaster

The world of art is intimately connected to that of finance: artists need money to carry on working. Despite – or perhaps, because of – the Impressionists' first exhibition in Paris, Paul Durand-Ruel had not been able to interest anyone other than a small circle of collectors in their work; in agreement with Monet, Sisley, Renoir and Morisot, he organized a public sale of their works at the Hôtel Drouot, Paris' premier auction house, early in 1875. A total of 73 paintings – around twenty each from Monet, Renoir and Sisley and a dozen from Morisot – were included in the sale, which took place on March 24, 1875. Durand-Ruel left nothing to chance, gracing each painting with what he termed a "superb" frame. He might as well have saved his time, for the sale was an unmitigated disaster.

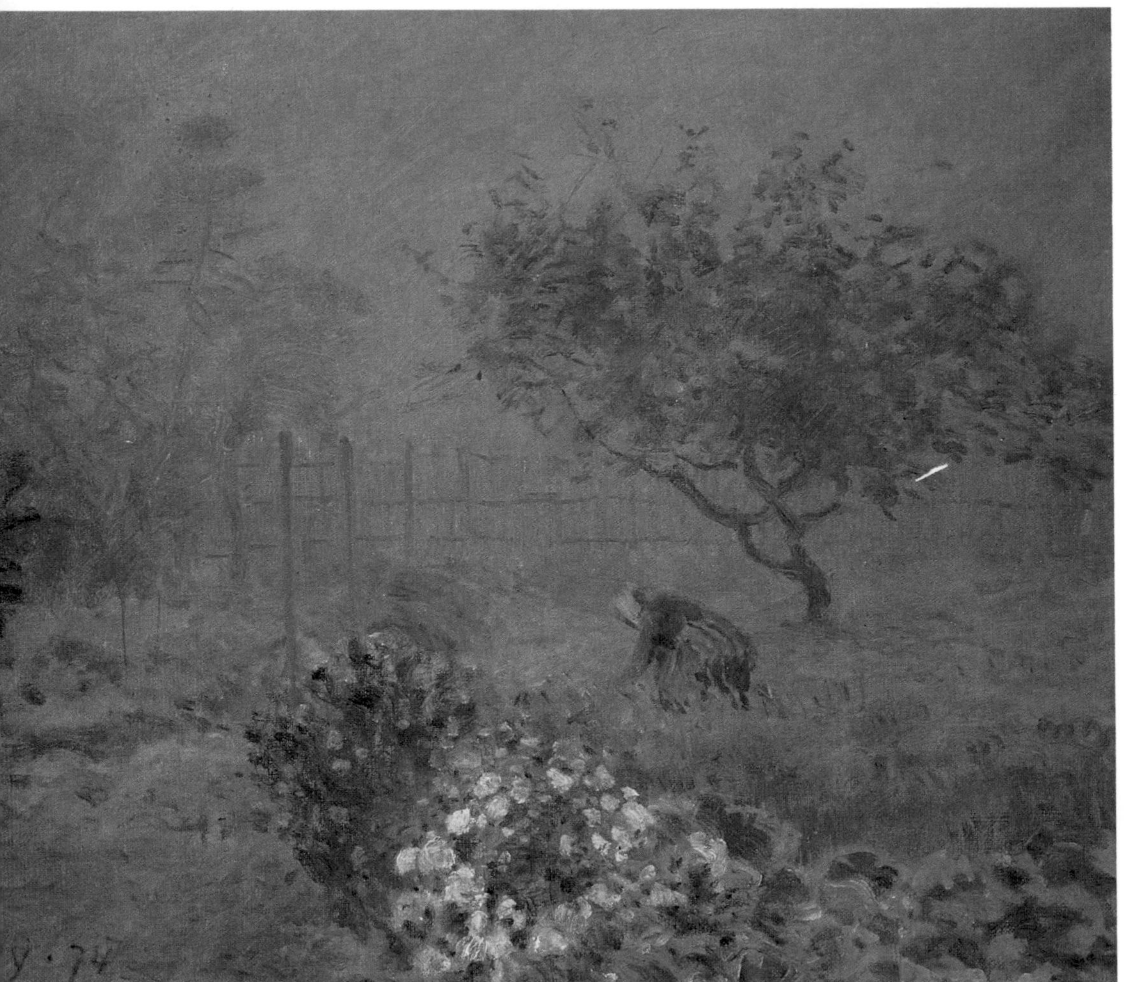

Sisley, **Misty Morning,** *1874. It is difficult to realize how refined, delicate and sensitive works like this could fail to win the approbation of the crowd.*

These were troubled times in France; the years following the debacle of the Franco-Prussian War were marked by political and social tension. Being labeled as politically intransigent by the press meant the artists could be considered to represent a potential threat not only to artistic standards, but also to the whole political, moral and social order. The auction had been widely publicized and opposing factions made use of the occasion to display their aesthetic prejudices. Paul Durand-Ruel recalled the auction later in life:

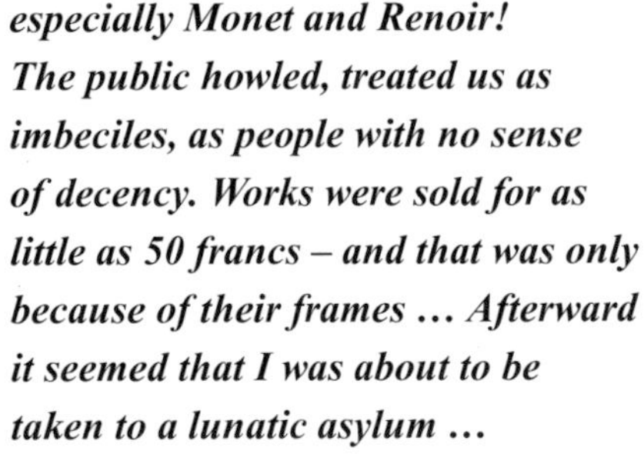

The insults they hurled at us – especially Monet and Renoir! The public howled, treated us as imbeciles, as people with no sense of decency. Works were sold for as little as 50 francs – and that was only because of their frames … Afterward it seemed that I was about to be taken to a lunatic asylum …

A press conspiracy

An article in the conservative newspaper *L'Art* reveals the dismissive attitude shared by many at the time.

… one could not see without smiling several worthy chaps well set up in matters concerning colonial goods, calico and flannel, decked in borrowed plumes as connoisseurs, in front of the most formless scribbles; we heard one of them speak of the genius of M. Claude Monet and pronounce the great name of Turner in the same breath as the ignorant aberrations of this painter.

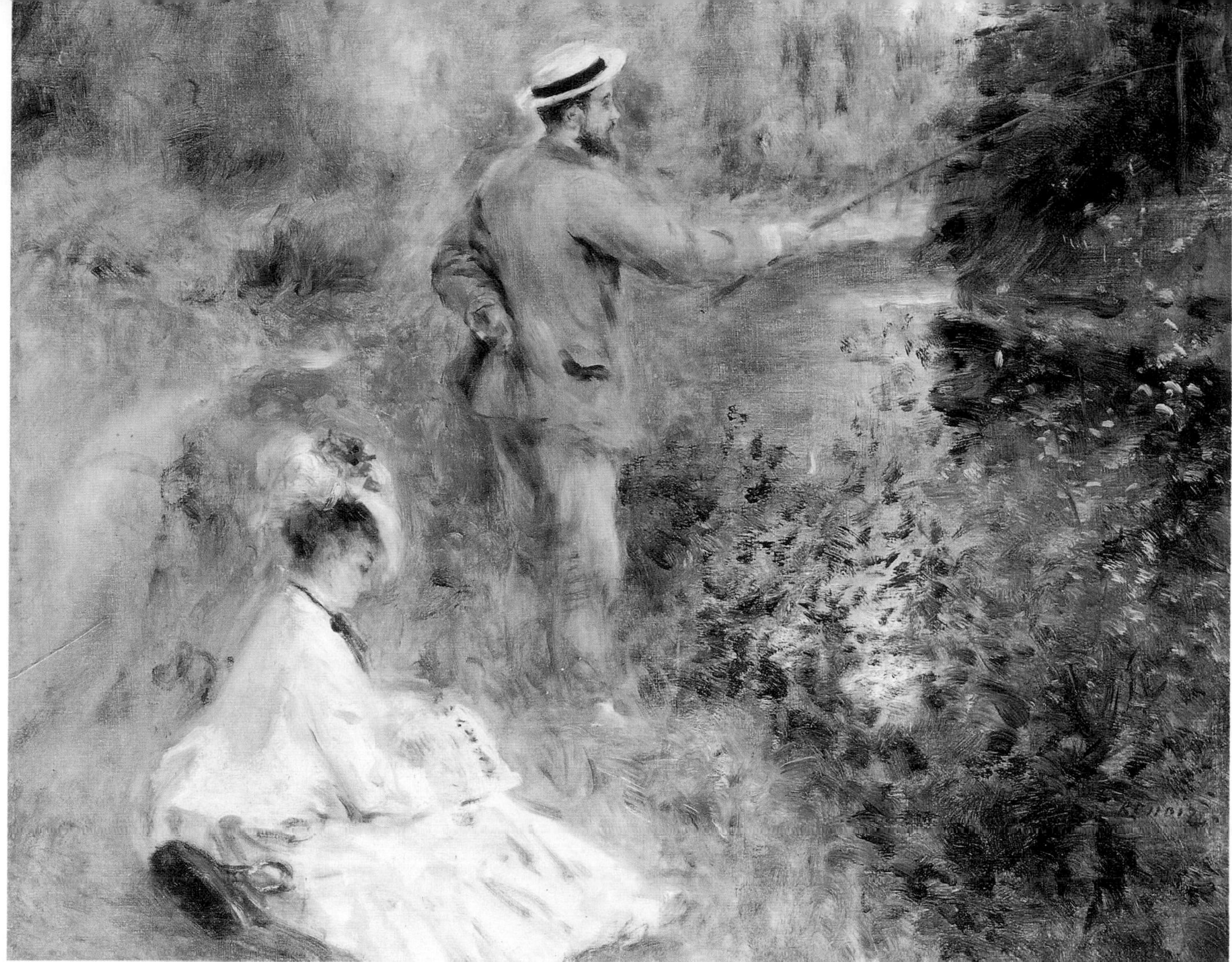

Renoir,* The Angler*, c. 1874. Renoir has rendered this informal and delightful scene with light and fluid brushwork. Transparent washes of color are floated on to the canvas to create a sparkling vision of relaxation.

It would seem that there had been a concerted attempt to discredit both the dealer (and organizer of the sale) and his painters. Philippe Burty, who had written the preface to the catalog of the auction, claimed in an article for *Le République Française* that "… peevish connoisseurs and idlers who had taken their orders from well-known studios had tried to interrupt the bidding which was gallantly sustained by a group of serious collectors." Durand-Ruel later confirmed the existence of a deliberate conspiracy to discredit himself and his painters. He recalled how they had to intervene "to stop disagreements degenerating into serious fights. The public were exasperated by the few supporters of the unfortunate exhibitors and tried to prevent the sale, uttering howls of rage at every bid."

In his lively memoirs of his father, Jean Renoir recorded that one so-called gentleman was so outraged by the works on view, especially those by Berthe Morisot, that he called her *une gourgandine* – a streetwalker. The involvement of Morisot in the event is something of an enigma. Unlike her colleagues, she enjoyed financial independence and had no need to sell her works to survive. She had recently married Manet's younger brother, Eugène, who was tireless in the promotion of her works and those of her friends. She may have seen the event as a means to declaring her allegiance to her colleagues and the world of avant-garde art. Like many of her friends, she was uncertain of the worth of her paintings and it is possible that her husband may have wished to use this opportunity to raise the profile of her work in her own eyes and that of the public.

Needless to say, in such an atmosphere the prices achieved were ridiculously low, especially for Renoir and Sisley: Georges Charpentier bought Renoir's exquisite *Angler* for 180 francs. The dealer and the artists were obliged to buy in a number of their own works. Sisley managed to sell twenty paintings, although their average price was a mere 120 francs per canvas, and even Monet's personal best for the day was only 165 francs. A measure of the interest Berthe Morisot attracted was that she achieved the best price of the day – 480 francs. However, as Durand-Ruel recalled, "… My revenge was complete. A painting which I bought in at 110 francs, later made 70,000 francs at a public auction." Perhaps the only positive aspect of the affair was that it introduced new collectors to the circle though, if Renoir's memory is to be trusted, their main motivation was not so much a matter of aesthetics as a matter of compassion.

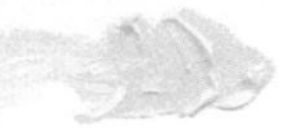

Collectors

The Impressionists were fortunate in having a number of committed supporters who patronized them throughout the difficult years of the 1870s. These critics and collectors seemed to work on a personal basis; they were a distinctly diverse set of individuals, some eccentric, some speculators and others friends whose main motivation may have been kindness.

Hyacinthe-Eugène Mürer (1845–1906)

Mürer was a restaurateur and pâtissier, poet and novelist who lived with his half-sister Marie at their shop and restaurant at 95 Quai Voltaire in Paris. During the 1870s, Monet, Renoir, Pissarro and Sisley attended his weekly *soirées* at his *Crèmerie.* He was an assiduous buyer of the Impressionists' work and gathered a formidable collection, including 21 Sisleys (whom he rated above Monet), 24 Pissarros and 21 canvases by his old school friend, Armand Guillaumin. Although he gave the Impressionists a sense of their own worth, he was a canny collector and a driver of hard bargains, often offering hospitality in return for work.

He could be rather unscrupulous in his actions, often "forgetting" to return works lent him on approval, and was frequently late in settling his accounts. In 1877 he organized a lottery, the prize for which was a painting by Pissarro; a servant won the main prize, but opted to accept one of Mürer's cream cakes instead. In the late 1870s, Mürer sold up, moved to Rouen and opened a restaurant, where he frequently entertained Pissarro. He sold his collection at a considerable profit and retired to the Auvergne, where he took up painting and held two exhibitions of his works.

Victor Chocquet (1821–1891)

A high-ranking civil servant in the French customs service, Chocquet was passionately involved with Impressionism. He began as a collector of Delacroix, then moved to Renoir, who introduced him to the work of Cézanne. Chocquet's collection, when it was sold in July 1899 at the Hôtel Drouot, included 32 Cézannes, 11 Monets, 11 Renoirs, and works by Courbet, Corot and Manet. During the Impressionist exhibitions of 1876 and 1877 he haunted the exhibition rooms; Renoir's friend, Georges Rivière, later recalled the kindly connoisseur:

... dragging a perverse art lover almost by force before the canvases of Renoir, Monet or Cézanne and trying to make the other share his admiration for these disgraced painters ... Persuasive, vehement, domineering in turn, he devoted himself tirelessly, without losing the urbanity which made him the most charming and formidable of opponents.

Cézanne,* Portrait of Victor Chocquet in an Armchair, *1877. One of Cézanne's many intimate portraits of his friend set within his collection. The interlocking fingers, which feature prominently in this picture, were to become, for the artist, an analogy for a successful composition.

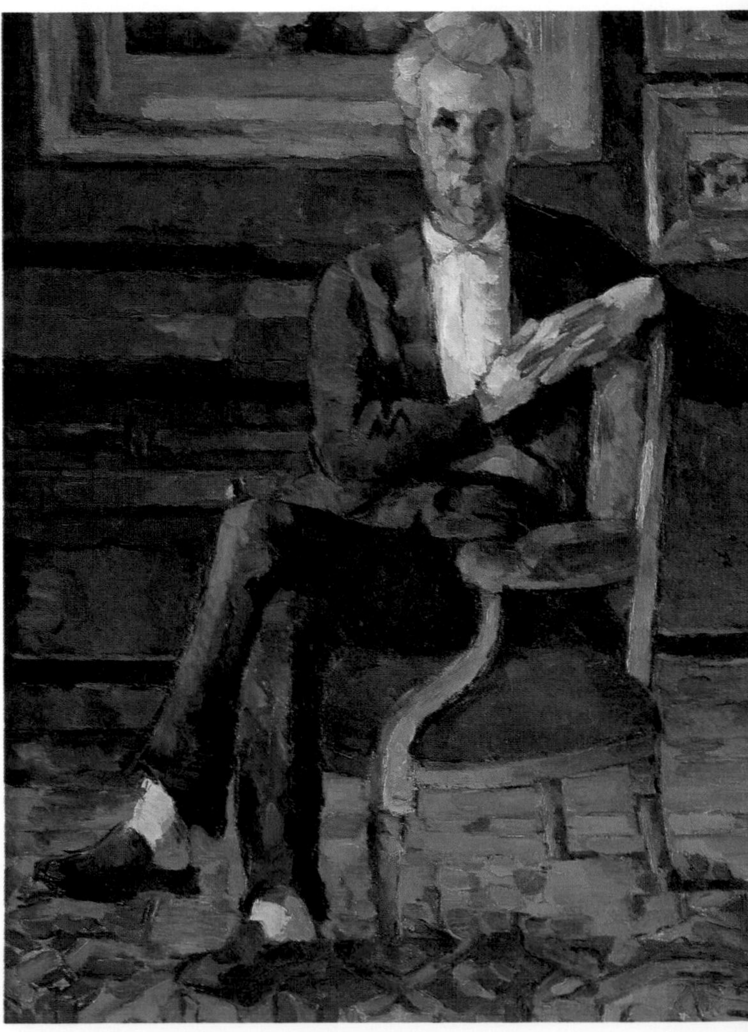

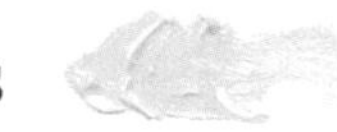

Georges de Bellio (1835–1894)

A confirmed bachelor who had lived in Paris since 1851, de Bellio was a successful Romanian homeopathic doctor who attended Manet in his last days. A mark of his friendship with the Impressionists was that, like Caillebotte, he tended to acquire work that otherwise would not easily find a buyer. He bought Monet's *Impression, Sunrise* from Hoschedé and also owned Sisley's *Spring Near Paris – Apple Trees*.

Ernest Hoschedé (1837–1890)

Hoschedé was a director of a large Parisian department store, *Au Gagne Petit*. From 1871 he was buying from all the Impressionists. Manet, Carolus-Duran, Monet and Sisley all visited his country estate, Mongeron, near Paris. In January 1874 he sold his collection, which included three Monets, three Sisleys, six Pissarros and two by Degas in a sale that served to introduce the public to Impressionism. The sale took place just before the famous group exhibition at Nadar's studio and the works attracted unexpectedly high prices, one of Sisley's landscapes fetching 375 francs. Hoschedé had a close friendship with Monet, inviting him to spend long periods at Mongeron, where he painted a series of decorative panels. The estate features in a number of Monet's major paintings of 1877. In that year, however, the entrepreneur was declared bankrupt and on June 5 and 6, 1878, the rest of his collection was sold, with disastrous results. His thirteen Sisley's sold for an average of 112 francs each. This was a catastrophic event, not only for his creditors, but also for the reputations and financial credibility of the artists. During his time at Mongeron, Monet became intimate with Madame Alice Hoschedé, Ernest's wife. Alice eventually married Monet after Ernest Hoschedé's death.

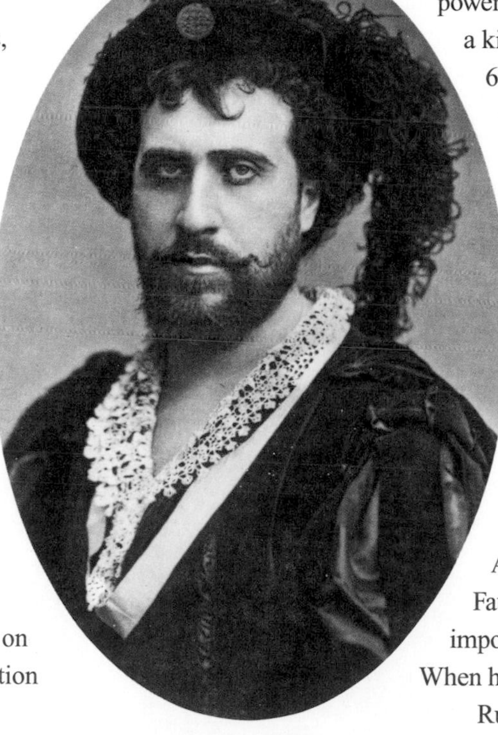

Faure, dressed as Hamlet and painted by Manet in 1877.

Georges Charpentier (1846–1905)

An innovative publisher, Charpentier was a champion of the Naturalist novelists Zola and Daudet and an early collector of Impressionist paintings. In spring 1879 he founded his influential magazine, *La Vie Moderne*, which allied itself to the Impressionist cause, and to which Renoir's brother Edmond was a frequent contributor. The office was used as an exhibition space and Monet's first one-man show was held there in 1880. Before this, Renoir had been commissioned to paint a portrait of Madame Charpentier and the two Charpentier children, Paul and Georgette, with their large Pyrenean Mountain Dog. The painting took over fifty sittings and Renoir received 10,000 francs payment for it. The painting was exhibited to great acclaim at the 1878 Salon and was a major turning point in the artist's career. Renoir was the Charpentiers' favored artist, but they also supported Sisley. Madame Charpentier held a regular salon where the painters could mingle with such influential personalities as the writers Zola, the Goncourt brothers, Maupassant, Daudet and any number of powerful politicians. Georges Charpentier was a kind and generous patron; he sent Sisley 600 francs in March 1879 in response to a desperate plea for aid. It was at the Charpentiers' house that Renoir met Paul Bérard, who became an important friend and patron. Pissarro remained outside this chic circle, where Renoir and Manet remained frequent guests, although Degas, Caillebotte, Monet and Sisley were seen there less often.

Jean-Baptiste Faure (1830–1914)

A famous baritone at the Paris Opéra, Faure was one of the earliest and most important supporters of Impressionism. When he was living in London, Paul Durand-Ruel introduced him to the works of Manet, Degas, Sisley and Pissarro. In 1873 Faure sold off most of his Barbizon paintings and, advised by the dealer, concentrated on collecting the works of his friends. He played a full part in the social life of the group and bought widely, although his frequent reselling of various elements of his collection suggests that he collected for the purposes of investment as much as from aesthetic delight. He particularly admired Sisley, and collected his work throughout the artist's life, eventually owning nearly sixty of his works. In 1874, Faure paid for Sisley to accompany him on a singing engagement in England, the costs of his trip being set against paintings. The visit resulted in some of Sisley's most innovative paintings.

The Second Impressionist Exhibition, 1876

After the Opera fire, here is a new disaster overwhelming the district. At Durand-Ruel's there has just opened an exhibition of so-called painting … a ruthless spectacle is offered … five or six lunatics – among them a woman – a group of unfortunate creatures stricken with the mania of ambition …* – Albert Wolff, *Le Figaro

After the Impressionist artists' first exhibition, the purpose of which was to make the picture-buying public aware of their existence, the second exhibition of these independent painters can be seen as a calculated attempt to prove their respectability and their professional status. In the aftermath of the disastrous auction of 1875, such a program was not merely an option but a necessity. The second exhibition was, in effect, a commitment to their independent route, confirming their status as a recognizable group of artists with a particular agenda operating outside the official circus of the Salon.

The Salon jury continuing their restrictive policies, the artists were facing the possibility of a return to the hardships they had endured in the previous decade. After an initial post-war boom, the economy had slowed down and hence the luxury goods market, of which painting and especially Impressionist painting was a part, suffered correspondingly. The auction at the Hôtel Drouot had made real their worst fears. They had to find a way to stimulate sales and protect their reputation and, in doing so, boost the monetary value of their wares.

The second exhibition took place at Paul Durand-Ruel's gallery, 11 Rue Le Peletier, the dealer thus confirming his position as a major player in their operations. The show itself was probably organized by Renoir and Degas and his friend, the wealthy engineer, collector and amateur painter, Ernest Rouart.

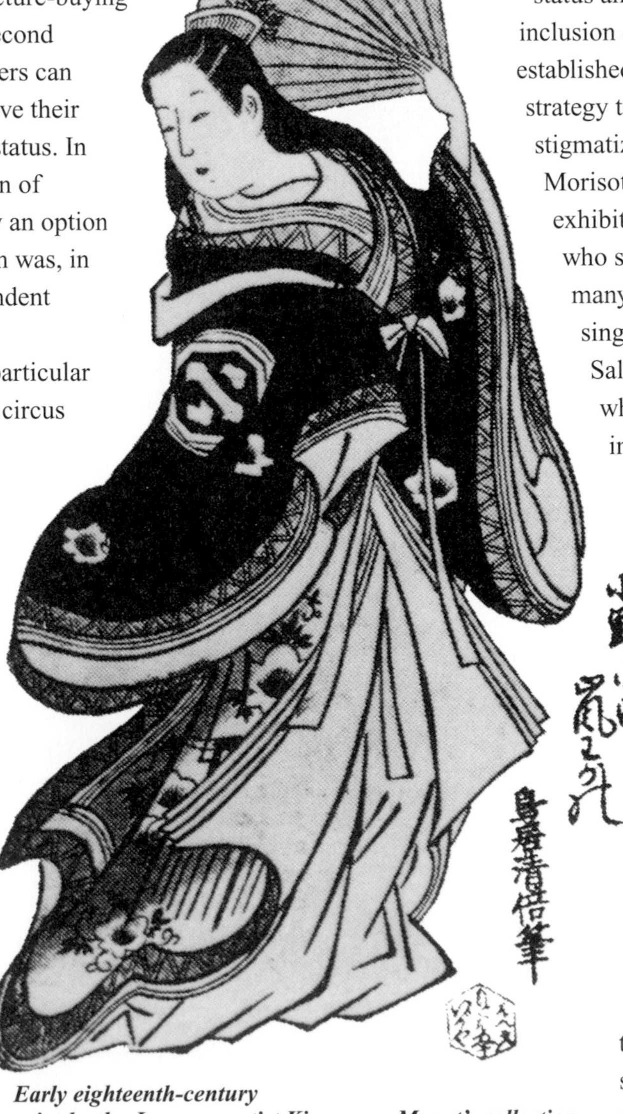

Early eighteenth-century print by the Japanese artist Kiyomasu, Monet's collection.

The exhibition was open during April 1876; on show were at least 252 works by twenty artists. The use of Durand-Ruel's premises gave their work a certain status and this, together with the inclusion of artists with already established reputations, was a deliberate strategy to avoid the show's being stigmatized as a Salon des Refusés. Morisot's paintings and pastels were exhibited in the first rooms; Monet, who showed eighteen paintings, many of which were lent by the singer Faure, shared the Grand Salon with Renoir and Sisley, while Degas and Pissarro showed in the final room.

The exhibition received a good deal of critical attention: it was the subject of reviews by writers as diverse as Henry James, Stéphane Mallarmé, Émile Zola and Auguste Strindberg. The painters had managed to consolidate their position as operators outside the Salon, although there were considerable differences of opinion within the group; not all of the artists participating were convinced that their actions would create a sustainable and permanent alternative to the official arena.

The exhibition was billed as *The Second Exhibition of Paintings by MM …*, a title that revealed little of their aims. By this time the terms "Impressionists" or "Intransigents" were being applied to the group, not least by Stéphane Mallarmé whose famous essay on the painters was published in the London magazine, *Art Monthly Review*, in September 1876. Ironically, given Manet's nonparticipation in their events, the essay was entitled "The Impressionists and Edouard Manet."

> ***Now Manet and his school use simple color, fresh or lightly laid on, and their results appear to have been attained at the first stroke, that the ever-present light blends with and enlivens all things. As to the details of the picture, nothing should be absolutely fixed, in order that we may feel that the bright gleam that lights the picture, or the diaphanous shadow which veils it, are only seen in passing, and just when the spectator beholds the represented subject. This was part of their conscious campaign which, being composed of a harmony of reflected and ever-changing lights, cannot be supposed always to look the same, but palpitates with movement, light and life …***

The term "Impressionism" was not necessarily a pejorative one, although the use of the epithet "Intransigents" was seen by some of the more conservative members of the group of artists as a cause for concern because it was a political term with left-wing connotations. Indeed, most of the favorable reviews of the exhibition had, as Berthe Morisot pointed out in a letter to one of her aunts, appeared in radical as opposed to establishment newspapers. Importantly for the inner core of artists this year, a wealthy collector and artist, Gustave Caillebotte, joined their number, taking the place of the late Bazille as a friend, organizer, benefactor and collector of their work. Another friend, the collector Victor Chocquet, lent work from his own collection and visited the exhibition on a regular basis. "He turned into a kind of apostle," wrote Duret. "One by one he took hold of the visitors he knew and insinuated himself with many others in order to persuade them of his convictions … It was a thankless task."

The exhibition closed showing a profit: after all expenses were paid, each exhibitor not only got back his or her initial contribution, but also a dividend of 3 francs! Although critical voices differed, as Berthe Morisot noted, depending in which paper they appeared, an ominous note was sounded even by some of the supportive critics. It was generally felt that the works exhibited did not as yet show evidence of maturing into substantial statements on modern life; their earlier promise had not yet been fulfilled and much of their work still seemed merely sketches for works that were yet to be painted. One of the foremost to voice such concerns was their former defendant, Zola, who gave form to his disillusion in his subsequent criticism and, spectacularly, in his novel of 1886, *L'Oeuvre*, which caused great upset among the Impressionist circle.

Claude Monet,* La Japonaise (Japonnerie), *(also known as* Madame Monet in the Red Kimono*), 1876.

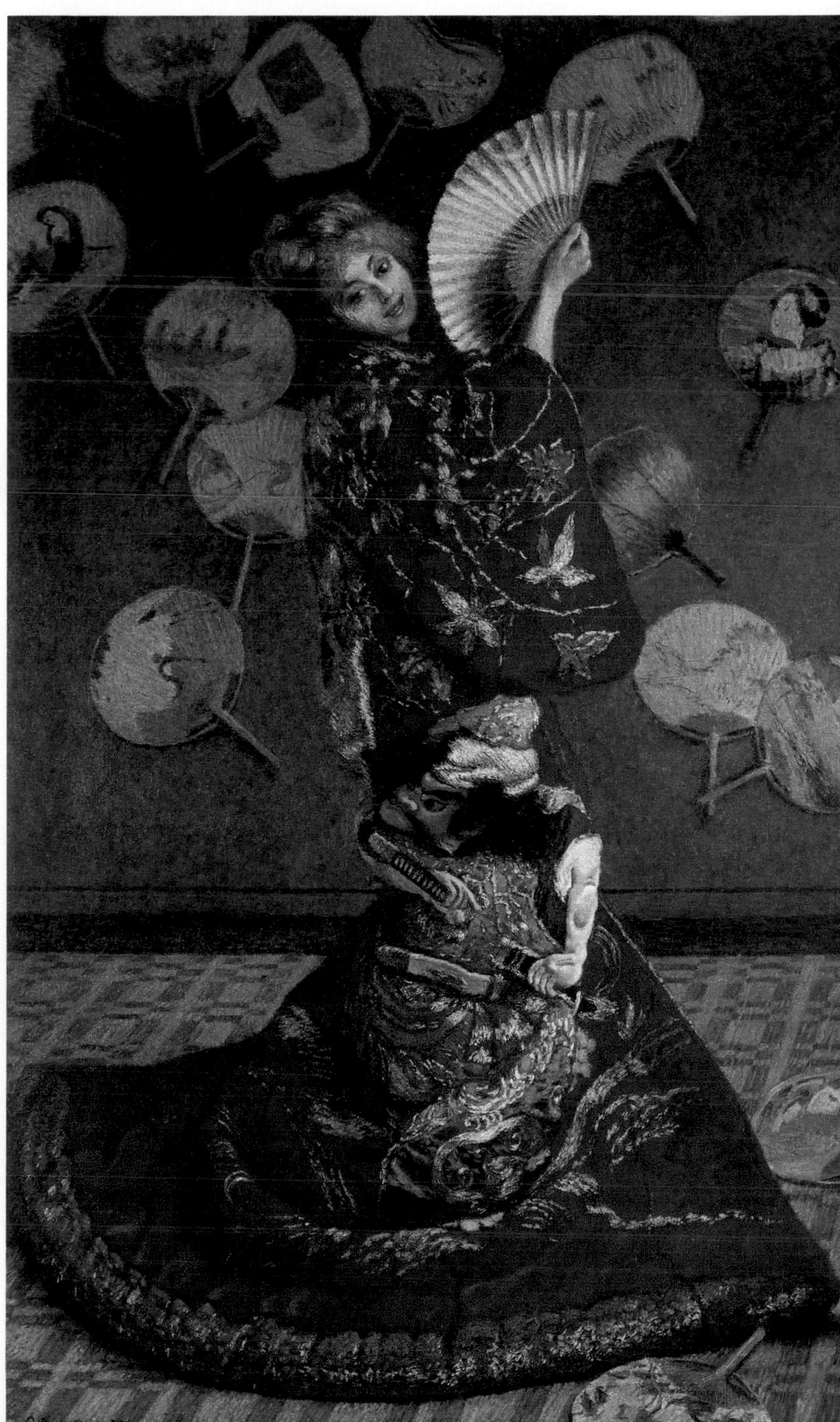

Alfred Sisley:
the undervalued Impressionist

Alfred Sisley (1839–1899) is perhaps the most undervalued of the Impressionist painters. Unlike his friends, he showed no interest in painting the human figure and dedicated his life to painting the modest landscape of the Ile-de-France. His work is quiet and undemonstrative in technique and subject matter. His paintings of the floods that inundated Marly-le-Roi convey a sense of implacable calm, even nonchalance. His reticence was apparent in his life as much as in his art.

He was born in 1839 in Paris, into a British family, his father William Sisley being a wealthy importer of gloves and fancy goods. Although he spent almost all his life in France, Sisley made only inconsequential attempts to acquire French citizenship, the last being made only two years before his death, and so remained until his death a British subject.

He made three trips to Britain during his life, including one to London lasting three years when he was in his teens, when he was unsuccessfully involved in his father's business. He dressed impeccably, but, despite his beautifully starched white collars "*à la manière Anglais*," his "habits, attitudes and tastes" remained indisputably French.

Sisley showed no aptitude for business, preferring to follow an interest in art. His family grudgingly supported him in his chosen career and in 1862 he entered the studio of Charles Gleyre where he met Renoir, Bazille and, a few weeks after his arrival, Monet. Like Bazille, Sisley's comfortable circumstances allowed him to pursue his chosen *métier* with something less than the total conviction shown by his other two less well-off friends. Biographical information concerning Sisley is scant, and it is difficult to build up a convincing picture of his life and attitude to art at this time. It is known, however, that throughout the early 1860s, he and his friends painted *en plein-air* together in the forest of Fontainebleau.

An exquisite sense of tone

Sisley's limpid studies of light and foliage recall the work of the Dutch landscapists of the seventeenth century, although his work finds its closest parallels with that of Corot. He shares with that artist not only the former's retiring character, but also his exquisite sense of tone and his dedication to clear, harmonious compositions. Sisley's paintings, like those of Corot, reveal their subtle qualities slowly. Once revealed, the true quality of Sisley's achievement is made abundantly clear. Until the late 1870s, when his work does get somewhat repetitive and overworked, his paintings are the equal in quality and invention of those produced by any of his colleagues.

A direct result of the Franco-Prussian War was the collapse of the luxury goods market, and William Sisley found himself a ruined man. His son was left without parental support and thrown upon his own devices. Until recently it was believed that this was the catastrophe that shaped the artist's subsequent life. Richard Shone has discovered, however, that Sisley's fall into relative poverty was more likely the result of his family's disapproval of his liaison with a model, the stopping of his allowance by his family coinciding with the birth of his first child, Pierre, in 1867. Sisley's companion was Marie-Eugénie Lescouezec, his elder by five years. Monet also became a father at roughly

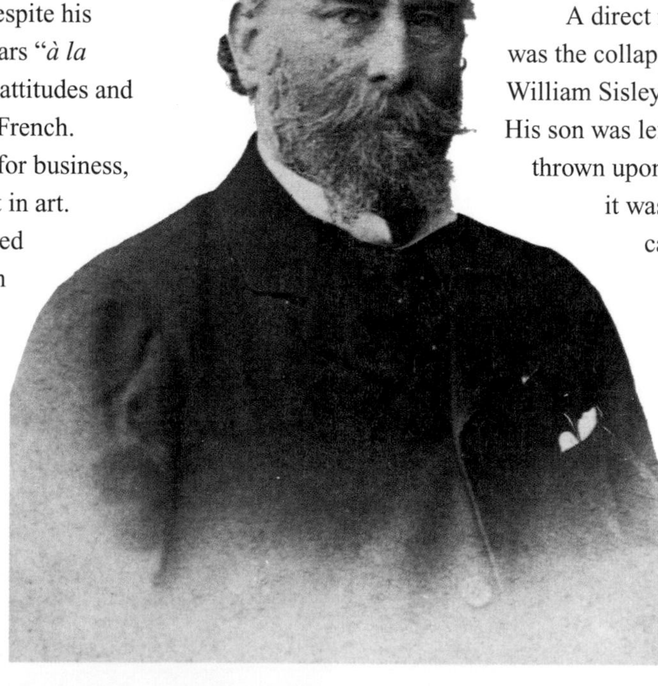

"To give life to the work of art is certainly one of the most necessary tasks of the true artist." Alfred Sisley, c. 1880.

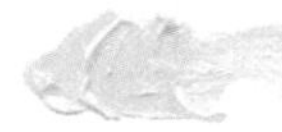

the same time and it is interesting that Pissarro, Cézanne, Monet, Renoir and, later, Seurat all formed lifelong attachments with artist's models. Although Alfred Sisley and Marie Eugénie were devoted to each other all their lives, recent research has suggested that they never married, despite her being called "Madame Sisley" all her life – one of Renoir's most celebrated portraits, painted in 1868, is *Portrait of Alfred Sisley and his Wife*.

Our image of Monet and Renoir as the main protagonists of Impressionism is colored by the destruction of much of Sisley's early work. Like Pissarro, he lost a considerable part of his output during the occupation of his home in Bougival by Prussian troops. This terrible event, together with the artist's own reticence, goes some way to explaining the difficulty of allotting him a place in the heroic early stages of the development of Impressionism.

In late 1872 Sisley moved from Paris to nearby Louveciennes. He had close ties with the dealer Paul Durand-Ruel and showed at his gallery in Rue Lafitte and in his London gallery at 168 New Bond Street. The artist possessed neither the dogged determination of Pissarro, the business acumen of Monet, nor the networking skills of Renoir and he remained relatively impecunious all his life, sometimes having to endure periods of real poverty. He was never ideologically committed to their independent stance, his involvement with the Impressionist exhibitions being motivated very much by the need to make a living. Despite his connection with Durand-Ruel, his wife continued her occupation as a florist and it is a measure of their financial instability that the couple lived all their lives in rented accommodation.

After the first Impressionist show Sisley dedicated himself to painting the effects of the weather on the villages and countryside immediately outside Paris, living in Louveciennes and later at Marly-le-Roi. "I am tired of vegetating for so long," he wrote to Duret in 1879. "We are still far from the moment when we shall be able to do without the prestige attached to the official exhibitions. I am therefore determined to submit to the Salon."

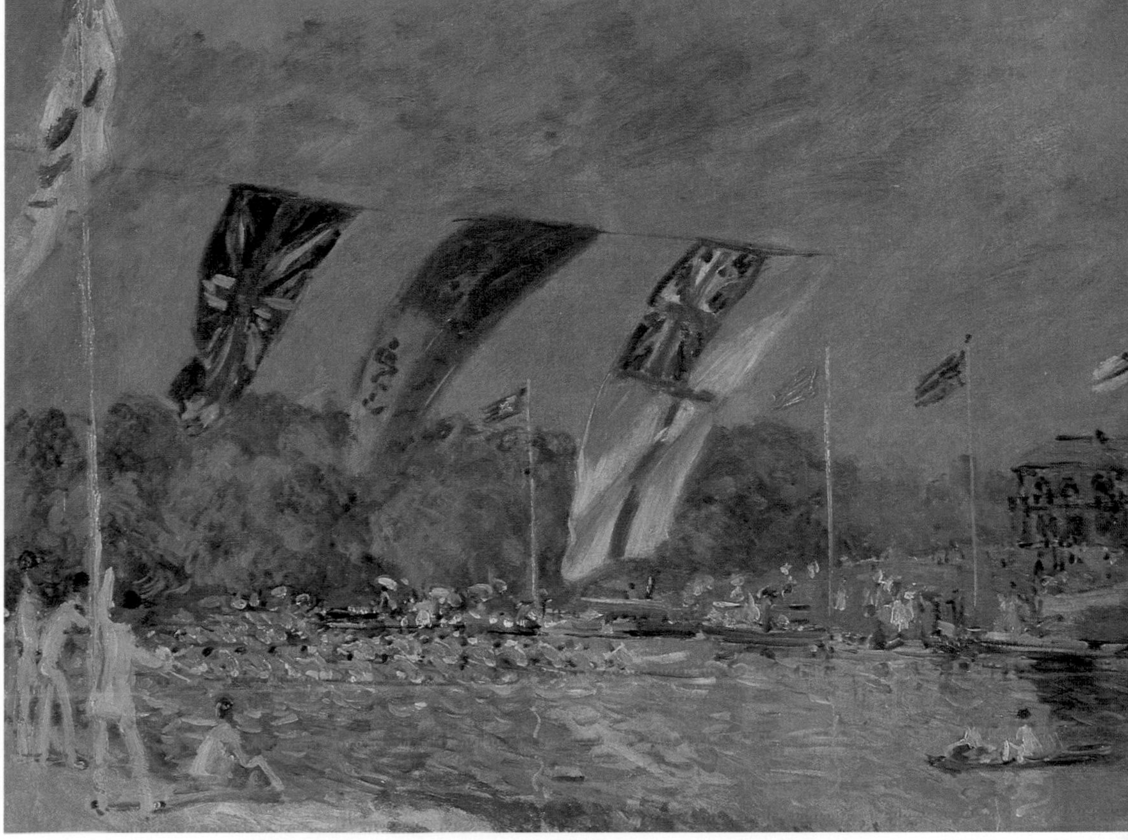

Alfred Sisley,* The Regatta at Molesey, Near Hampton Court, *1874, (part of the Gustave Caillebotte bequest, 1894). Some of the artist's most vigorous and exhilarating canvases were painted on his trip to England. "These effects of light," he wrote, "which have an almost material expression in nature, must be rendered in material fashion on the canvas."

In 1880 Sisley and his family moved to Moret-sur-Loing, bordering on the forest of Fontainebleau, where he lived until his death from throat cancer in 1899. His major achievement of these years is his series of paintings, influenced by the example of Monet, of the picturesque church at Moret in which he recaptured the promise of his earlier career.

Sisley had a one-man exhibition at Durand-Ruel's in 1883 and another at Georges Petit's in 1897, but neither was very successful. He was a painter attuned to delicate shifts of color, nuances of tone and the harmonics of composition. His work did become somewhat repetitive and unexciting in the 1880s and 1890s, although ironically, having suffered relative neglect during his lifetime, soon after his death his reputation increased – as did his prices – and his work was chosen to represent France at the 1900 Exposition Universelle. Pissarro wrote to his son Lucien only a week before Sisley's demise in 1899, " He is a great and beautiful artist, in my opinion he is a master equal to the greatest." Like Monet and Cézanne, Sisley had the gift of reaffirming the beauty and wonder of experience.

The Watering Place at Marly-le-Roi

1875, oil on canvas, 49.5 x 65.4 cm (19½ x 26 in), National Gallery, London, England

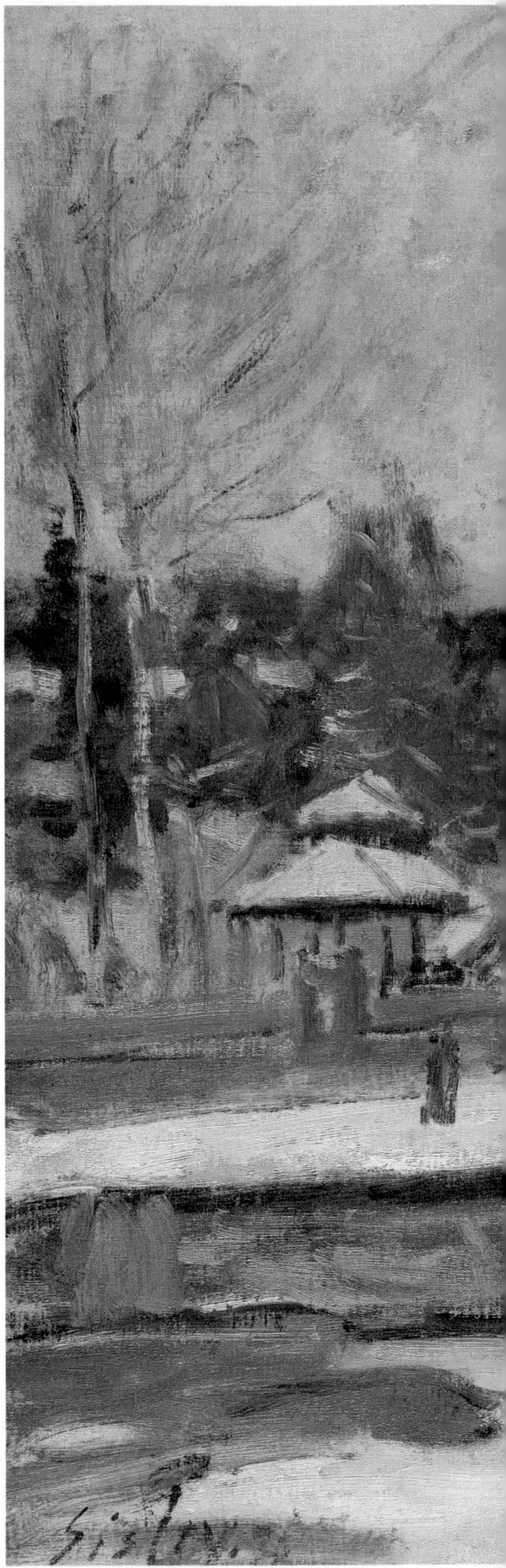

For him, the interest in a canvas is multiple. The subject, the motif, must always be rendered in a simple way, easily understood and grasped by the spectator. By the elimination of superfluous detail, the spectator should be led along the road indicated by the painter, and from the first, should be made to recognize what the artist has felt.
– Adolphe Tavernier, *L'Art Français*, March 18, 1893

Sisley's eye was remarkably attuned to the subtle changes that mark the different times of the year. Habitually he painted the most prosaic of scenes, but in this case he chose the watering place at Marly, one of the great monuments from the age of Louis XIV. Although the chateau had been sacked during the French Revolution, traces of the gardens still remained and Sisley has painted the *abreuvoir*, or watering place which served to contain the overspill from the water gardens of the park. In the hands of Turner or even Monet, one might expect some reference to the frailty of man's creations in the face of omnipotent nature. But such ambitions are not part of Sisley's character, instead, he has used the site as a means to record the delicate nuances of a winter's day.

Like Pissarro and so many of the other Impressionists, Sisley has used a roadway, enlivened by a few figures, as the central feature of his composition, which gives a sense of recession to the scene. The roadway makes a startling white triangle; at it's apex, the dying embers of a winter's sun add a hint of warmth that is echoed by the touches of orange ocher that enliven the middle ground of the canvas. This underlying warmth is in part due to Sisley's use of a tinted ground that can be clearly discerned through the painting and particularly in the thinly painted area of the trees and sky. One of the most charming aspects of the painting is the simplicity with which Sisley has perfectly described the snow lying on the ice that has formed over the pool, broken only in the area at the right where the running water enters the stillness of the pool. Within the blanketed silence of the scene one can almost hear the sound of its fall.

Like Monet's *Beach at Trouville*, the painting is the product of a single session, with only the minimum of subsequent retouching. Here, instead of the brilliant sunlight and warmth of high summer, one can imagine the bitter cold and oncoming gloom of dusk and the effect these would have had on the painter, rushing to finish his work, his haste adding a sense of urgency and improvisation to the painting. The forms were initially laid in fairly vigorously with dark paint which Sisley has gradually worked over with lighter tones to create a variegated surface, rich in invention. An economy of means, almost Japanese in sensibility, has been used to create a subtle, delicate meditation on the scene before the artist. Sisley signed and dated the painting, marking it as a finished piece, and it formed part of his submission for the Second Impressionist Exhibition of 1876.

The Third Impressionist Exhibition, 1877

The 1877 exhibition was the first to be labeled by the participants themselves as "Impressionist." The friends who had shown together on the two previous occasions had now split into two definite factions. On the one hand there were those artists identifiable by their allegiance to the landscape and broken brushwork who centered around Monet; on the other, was a group based around Degas, who were more realist and urban in their aims and who did not adopt obvious "Impressionist" techniques. Degas wrote to his friends, urging them to participate in the organization of the show and saying that "A big question is to be debated: whether or not one can show at the Salon and also with us. Very Important!"

Degas had always been against the term "Impressionist," and at one stage had even suggested that the group call themselves *capucines* (cornflowers), a presumably flippant reference to the Rue des Capucines, the site of their first exhibition.

Gustave Caillebotte, the organizer of the third exhibition, had to expend a great deal of energy, tact, diplomacy and flattery to bring the various factions together. He rented a luxurious five-room apartment in 6 Rue Le Peletier for the exhibition. It was just across the street from Durand-Ruel's premises where the 1876 show had been held. This was the heart of the new capital, fashionable and exclusive, and reveals yet again the relationship between the Impressionists and the bourgeois market they were trying to attract. The entrance was off the exclusive boulevard Haussmann where it crossed the Boulevard des Italiens, just down from Garnier's opulent masterpiece and quintessential symbol of the Second Empire,

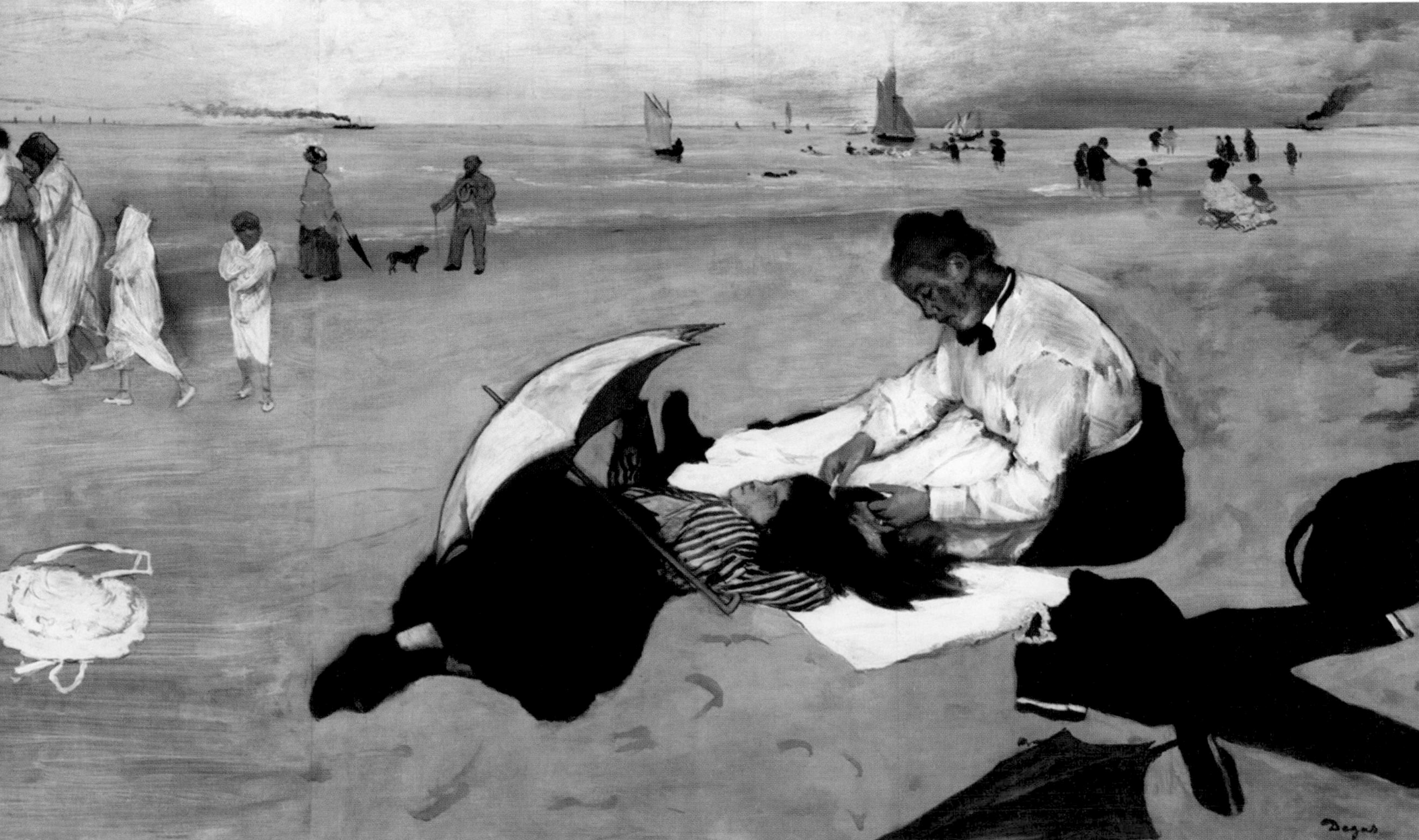

Degas,* Combing the Hair on the Beach, *1876–77. Painted on three separate pieces of paper, the joins of which can just about be made out, one touching the girl's right boot; the other runs through her companion's body.

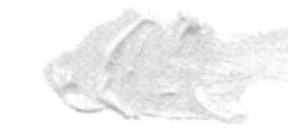

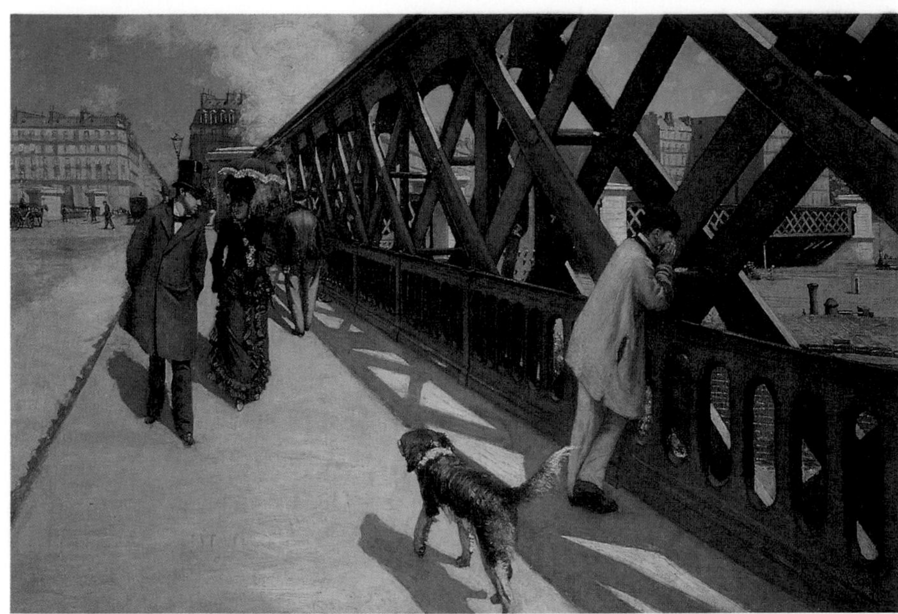

Gustave Caillebotte, Pont de l'Europe, 1876. All the strangeness and newness of the city is caught in this powerful evocation of urban life.

the Paris Opéra, inaugurated only two years previously. Caillebotte was not only the major exhibitor, but also sent out invitations and paid for all the publicity. Included in his display were two of his most important works, *Pont de l'Europe* of 1876 and *Paris Street: Rainy Day* of 1877. He also lent generously from his own collection of Impressionist works. *Pont de l'Europe* is an intriguing and enigmatic composition; the rushing diagonals that describe the structure of the bridge, its shadows, the edge of the pavement and the humorously observed streetwise dog lead the eye inevitably to a young man who turns to respond to a smartly dressed woman who appears to have attracted his attention. The workman in his blouse looks down upon the very space that was painted so memorably by Monet in his various versions of the Gare Sainte-Lazare.

As Richard Brettel and others have demonstrated, this exhibition was the tightest and best-informed of all the Impressionist shows: only eighteen artists participated, showing two hundred and thirty works. Among the eighteen were, as well as Caillebotte, Cézanne, Degas, Guillaumin, Monet, Morisot, Pissarro, Renoir and Sisley. The prevailing atmosphere within the luxuriously appointed rooms of the exhibition was one of professionalism. The canvases were ambitious, many, like Renoir's *The Moulin de la Galette* and Caillebotte's exquisitely worked and carefully drawn canvases, showing as much attention to detail and composition as might be found in the official Salon. The size and subject matter of some of the works revealed how in the mid-1870s some of the Impressionists returned to their ambitious notions of large-scale modern-life paintings.

Dissension within the Impressionist ranks might explain the fact that Degas's work was hung separately from the others. Among the twenty-five works by Degas was his extraordinary *Combing the Hair on the Beach*; his other pastels and paintings continued his exploration of urban types, ballet dancers and his endless fascination with the female form.

Manet was still the *eminence grise* of Impressionism, Caillebotte having been unable to persuade him to exhibit with the group, even though his 1876 Salon entry, *The Railway*, had obviously influenced Caillebotte and Monet. The latter was represented by thirty works, including his interpretations of the interior of the steam-filled *Gare Saint-Lazare*.

Taken as a whole, the exhibition was very successful. The advance publicity had worked well, and attendance figures suggest that as many as 500 people visited the show each day. The exhibition opened in early April and closed at the end of that month. The critical reaction was, on the whole, positive and even the bad publicity helped to establish Impressionism as a recognizable phenomenon.

The artist who gathered most adverse comment was, predictably, Cézanne, who, surprisingly, shared his space with Berthe Morisot, she having contributed an exquisite collection of oils, watercolors, pastels and drawings. Cézanne's contribution was stoutly defended by the collector Victor Chocquet, now retired from the civil service, who attended the exhibition every day in order to explain and defend his friend's paintings to a largely uncomprehending public, which according to Duret were convinced of Chocquet's "mild insanity."

Zola's criticism was notable for the support he gave his friend Cézanne, "… the greatest colorist of the group. There are, in the exhibition, some Provençal landscapes of his which have a splendid character. The canvases of this painter, so strong and so deeply felt, may cause the bourgeois to smile, but nevertheless contain the making of a great artist …"

There is a prophetic note to this piece of writing, for Zola was to continue to develop his notion of Impressionism as a movement of promise which in the end failed to deliver what had been expected of it.

Gustave Caillebotte:
the silent partner of Impressionism

His signature is attached to some of the most arresting images of the nineteenth century and yet despite the fierceness with which Impressionism has been marketed over the last half century, his name has remained overshadowed by those of his more illustrious friends and associates.

From 1877 Caillebotte played a crucial role in the organization of the eight Impressionist exhibitions and his paintings featured in all but the last two. He provided financial support in times of need, buying paintings such as Renoir's large *The Moulin de la Galette*. An unusual and distinctive artist, Caillebotte's work is a curious mixture of the conventional and the avant-garde; he developed a synthesis of the Impressionist notions of broken brushwork and high coloration with a style of painting learned from the academic painter Léon Bonnat based on careful drawing and exact tonal values. Degas' work followed a similar development with very different results.

Caillebotte's paintings were seen by contemporary critics as being among the most significant and ambitious of the Impressionist canvases, and his paintings are characterized by an agenda shared with many of the artists and writers of the

Gustave Caillebotte,* View of the Rooftops (Snow Effect)*, now known as* Rooftop in the Snow, Paris*, 1878. The snow defines and regularizes the sprawling haphazard structures of the Parisian skyline in this impeccable study of winter chill.

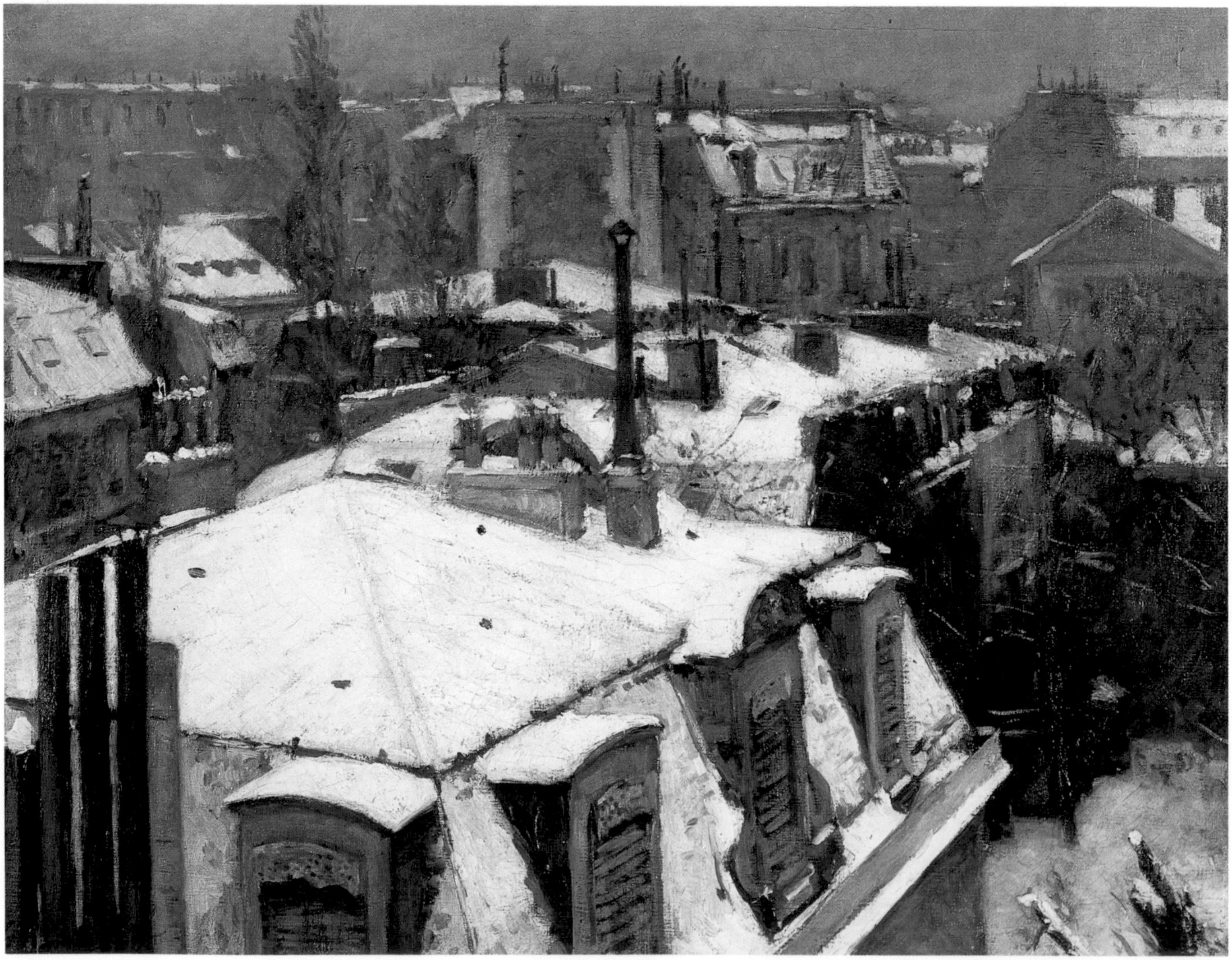

period who were attempting to find a suitable means of expressing the experience of modern life. His themes are those found in Émile Zola's novels and in the painting of the Impressionists themselves: the reality of living in modern Paris, images of work and leisure, the city and the countryside, and interpretations of public and private life. Caillebotte's interpretations of such subjects have fascinated recent historians in his constructions of images of class and gender.

A man of many interests

He was born into a wealthy family on August 19, 1848, and lived a life of leisure; he began a career in law, but abandoned the profession after a year and with the approval of his family he entered the atelier of the respected academic artist, Léon Bonnat. It was probably through his master's friend, Degas, that he came to know the Impressionists. His highly finished painting of a working-class subject, *Floor Scrapers,* was rejected from the Salon. This effectively put the young independent artist in the same camp as Monet, Renoir and the others. He showed with them for the first time in their next exhibition– *Floor Scrapers* became one of the sensations of the show. Caillebotte was a man of many interests and his work may be seen as a celebration of modern consumer culture by an individual whose sympathies lay not only with those who could enjoy this culture, but also with those who served it.

With his brother, Martial, he was one of the most significant philatelists of the age and his interest in yachting and horticulture equaled his love of painting. He never married and after the death of his parents he lived with his brother in a large apartment at the corner of the Rue Miromesnil, facing on to the Boulevard Haussmann, at the very center of "*le nouveau Paris*," the chic new quarter of the wealthy bourgeoisie. His wealth allowed him to pursue his own idiosyncratic concerns unaffected by the commercial constraints that dogged so many of his friends, a fact not lost on his contemporaries, one of whom referred to him as a "millionaire who paints in his free time".

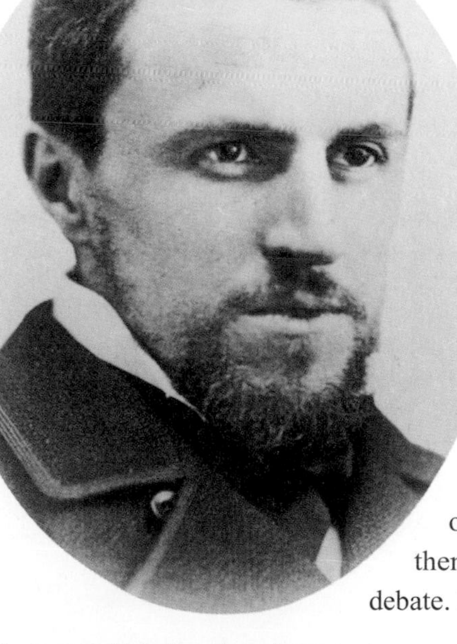

Gustave Caillebotte, whose important collection of Impressionist works was bequeathed to the museums of Paris.

Caillebotte's paintings, developed from the dry, beautifully toned work of Bonnat, bear the signs of hard work and the careful application of an applied talent that is very different from the apparently easy virtuosity of Manet, Degas, Monet and Renoir. The stigma of amateurism could be one of the major reasons why he has not been taken seriously by earlier commentators on Impressionism.

Due perhaps to the accessibility of Caillebotte's style of painting at this time, his work was in general well received by the critics; but after 1877 Caillebotte adopted a rather self-conscious and mannered Monet-esque facture and a somewhat crude heightening of his color range replaced his former carefully considered tones. His later paintings are marked by the rather clumsy use of impasto and an uneasy mix of two very different ways of constructing analogies for visual reality. His work defies traditional notion of aesthetics. They may be striking and impressive, but they are rarely beautiful, indeed one is tempted to think in terms of an anti-aesthetic at work.

In 1876, after the death of his younger brother Réné, Caillebotte made an extraordinary will that would have repercussions far beyond anything the young benefactor could have intended. Not only did he leave money for the running of the next group exhibition, but he offered his collection to the French nation, on the condition that it be shown in the Musée du Luxembourg, the Paris museum dedicated to living artists, and on their deaths to enter the Louvre. His collection contained 67 Impressionist paintings and pastels: only 38 were grudgingly accepted, and then only after a petition and much public debate. In 1897 they were put on view in the Musée du Luxembourg. Today, the collection, which includes works such as Manet's *The Balcony (Le Balcon)*, Renoir's *The Moulin de la Galette* and one of Cézanne's most important views of L'Estaque, forms the core of the Impressionist galleries of the Musée d'Orsay.

Caillebotte died at the early age of 45, on February 21, 1894, his interest in horticulture and yachting having for some time displaced his once passionate involvement in avant-garde painting.

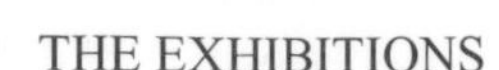

Paris Street: Rainy Day

1877, oil on canvas, 212.2 x 276.2 cm (83½ x 108¾ in), Art Institute of Chicago, USA

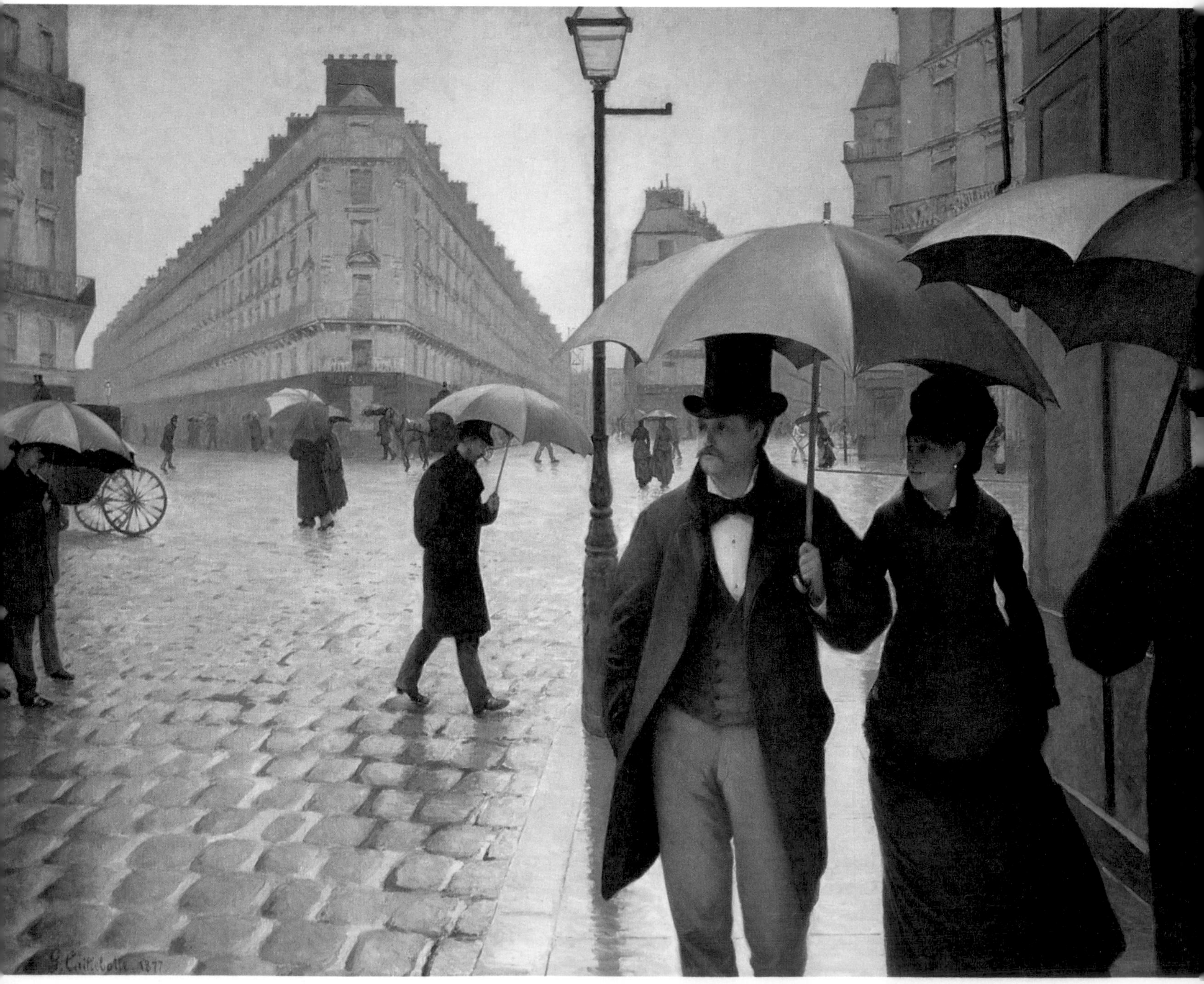

Painted when the artist was only 28 years of age, *Paris Street: Rainy Day* (*Rue de Paris: Temps de Pluie*) is one of the most memorable of the Impressionist canvases and is surely Caillebotte's masterpiece. Its reputation is such that in recent years it has come to be considered as one of the most significant paintings of the nineteenth century. This is partly because historians have moved from an aesthetic appreciation of Impressionist paintings to an approach that is more concerned with modes of representation and the ways in which paintings can be used to interpret social history. Caillebotte's work fits this agenda perfectly and, in doing so, allows for a reassessment of our understanding of Impressionism.

During the 1870s, Caillebotte lived with his parents and brothers in the heart of the new Paris in an area called the "Quartier de l'Europe." This was close to both Manet's home and to Degas' studio. The scene depicted by Caillebotte in *Paris Street: Rainy Day* is still easily identifiable today as being the Rue Leningrad, which was then called Rue St. Petersburg, between the railway lines of the Gare Sainte-Lazare and the Place Clichy. It is possible to stand at this precise spot and experience the almost vertiginous pull of the perspective as the converging streets disappear into the distance.

For all its casual atmosphere, every detail of the painting has been planned with meticulous care through numerous preparatory sketches, figure studies and perspectival diagrams. The lamppost that occupies the exact center line of the composition, breaks the composition into two halves. Its severe verticality is modified by the tilted angle of the umbrella held by the main male figure, who advances toward us with his companion, each occupied with their own thoughts and both supremely unaware of our presence before them. Caillebotte has caught the archetypal *flâneur*, confident, blasé even, this is his territory, one in which he is in control.

Caillebotte's originality does not lie in the sensuous manipulation of paint across the canvas surface, nor in the dissolution of tangible form into the enveloping atmosphere, qualities so often associated with Impressionism. Rather, through his innovative compositions he is able to suggest the physical realities of the modern world.

The painting contains none of the broken brushwork or heightened hues that are normally associated with Impressionism. The overall tones of the work are silvery; perfectly catching the atmosphere of a dull rainy day, subdued grey blues dominate the composition punctuated by subtle touches of orangey ocher in the building on the right and the chimney stacks.

The line made by their interlocked arms is repeated in reverse by the silhouetted building creating a strong surface rhythm that serves as a dynamic foil to the dazzling perspective of the buildings. It is quite extraordinary that all

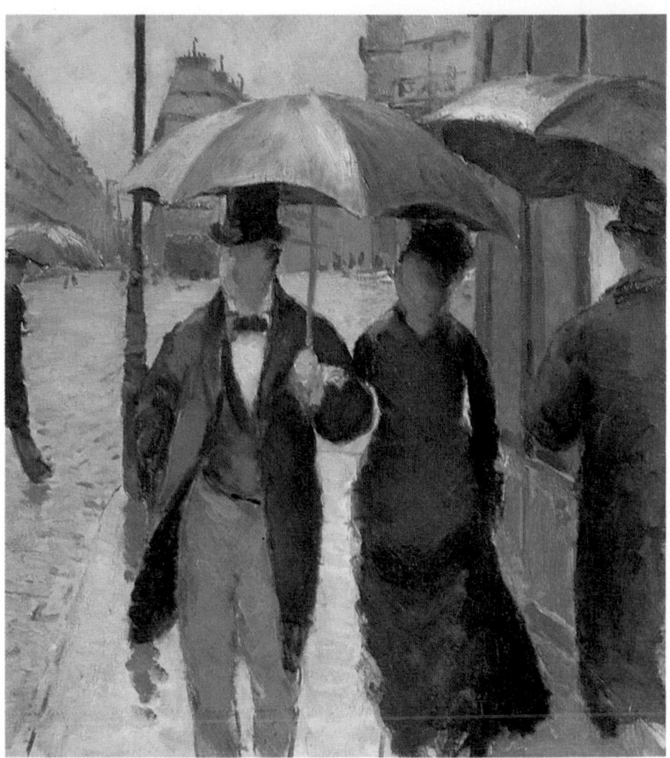

The immaculate finish and carefully organized tonal and color harmonies are brought into relief by the single fleck of white paint that describes the woman's earring.

the careful preparation that has gone into the picture has not produced a deadpan image of urban life, but one that has re-created the equivalent for the unpredictability of visual experience.

Like Degas, Caillebotte had a fondness for situating his figures asymmetrically across the canvas, creating an empty center that implies movement from the scene depicted in the painting out into the world beyond. Perhaps he was inspired by his friend Duranty's 1876 text, *The New Painting*, which laid out the foundations for a realist painting. In the essay the writer proposed that "sometimes, the figure is not always represented as a whole: Sometimes it may appear cut off at mid-leg, half-length or longitudinally."

Caillebotte has in his picture cropped close in on the two figures to give the impression that they could quite literally step out of the painting into the viewer's space. The effect is disarming and allows us to read into the image our own presence and our own narrative. The alienation and anonymity common to urban experience, effectively analyzed by Baudelaire and presented so authoratively in this painting, would be reassessed later in the work of Seurat, who knew this painting, and more expressionistically in the Norwegian painter, Edvard Munch, who worked in Paris in the last decades of the century.

The Fourth Impressionist Exhibition, 1879

***This designation seems to me an unhappy one, but it is undeniable that these Impressionists – since they insist on that name – are at the head of the modern movement.* – Émile Zola, 1879**

The deeply conservative policies of the Director of Fine Arts in France, the Marquis de Chennevières-Pointel, had ruthlessly dominated the arts since the late 1860s. Chennevières-Pointel had instituted a series of restrictive measures that favored a monarchist, religious and aristocratic art, and he had restored to the Salon jury much of the power it had lost in the 1860s. In 1878, as a result of his alleged mishandling of the Universal Exhibition of that year, Chennevières-Pointel resigned. This event was echoed in the larger sphere of politics as the government lurched to the left. In this new climate, landscape artists found themselves back in favor. Taking advantage of the situation, a number of the Impressionists felt that the moment had arrived for a renewed attempt to gain official recognition at the Salon. Renoir achieved success with his submissions, two portraits, one of Madame Charpentier and the other of Jeanne Samary, and some pastels, but submissions by Sisley and Cézanne were rejected. Indeed, Cézanne, in spite of his continual lack of success, seems to have taken a perverse delight in sending work to the Salon, only to have it rejected.

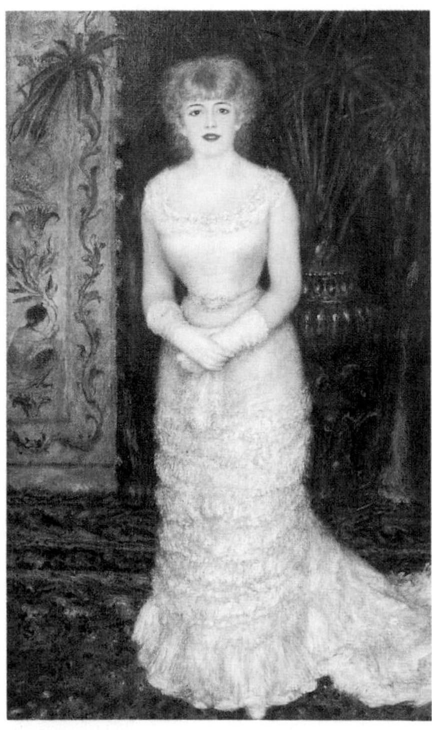

Pierre-Auguste Renoir,* Portrait of the Singer Jeanne Samary, *1878.

Such actions highlight the lack of a coherent program among the so-called Impressionist painters. Caillebotte worked hard to get the group to work together for an exhibition in 1878, but to no avail. Aided and abetted by Degas, Pissarro and Mary Cassatt, the opportunity of holding an exhibition of their work in the full glare of publicity that shone on the arts in the year of the Universal Exhibition was lost.

Things were growing difficult for the Impressionists. Durand-Ruel, who had recently bought in a large number of canvases by the Barbizon masters, was experiencing financial difficulties. This was in part due to the fact that a number of the Barbizon painters, including Millet, Diaz, Corot and Daubigny, had died recently. Subsequent studio sales had caused a glut in the market, making it impossible for Durand-Ruel to make a large profit. To add to his problems his main rival, Georges Petit, was making a concerted effort to take over his territory.

The fourth Impressionist exhibition eventually opened on April 10, 1879, at 28 Avenue de l'Opéra. At Degas' insistence, the exhibition was not billed as "Impressionist." The show included paintings, pastels, drawings and decorated fans, hung in rooms that were lavishly decorated.

As the American artist, Mary Cassatt, who had been encouraged to participate by Degas, explained, the exhibition had not been an easy thing to organize.

There are so few of us that we are each required to contribute all that we have. You know how difficult it is to inaugurate anything like independent action among French artists, and we are carrying on a despairing fight and we need all our forces, as every year there are new deserters.

The rooms contained over 260 works from sixteen artists. For the first time, Paul Gauguin was among their number. But there were, as Cassatt had suggested, major absences in the ranks. Renoir, Cézanne, Sisley and Morisot had all failed to participate. Their absence called into question the credibility of the group as a coherent exhibiting body. Morisot, who had made a big contribution to the third exhibition, was in poor health after the birth of her daughter, Julie, and Monet had only agreed to exhibit after much persuasion, eventually delegating

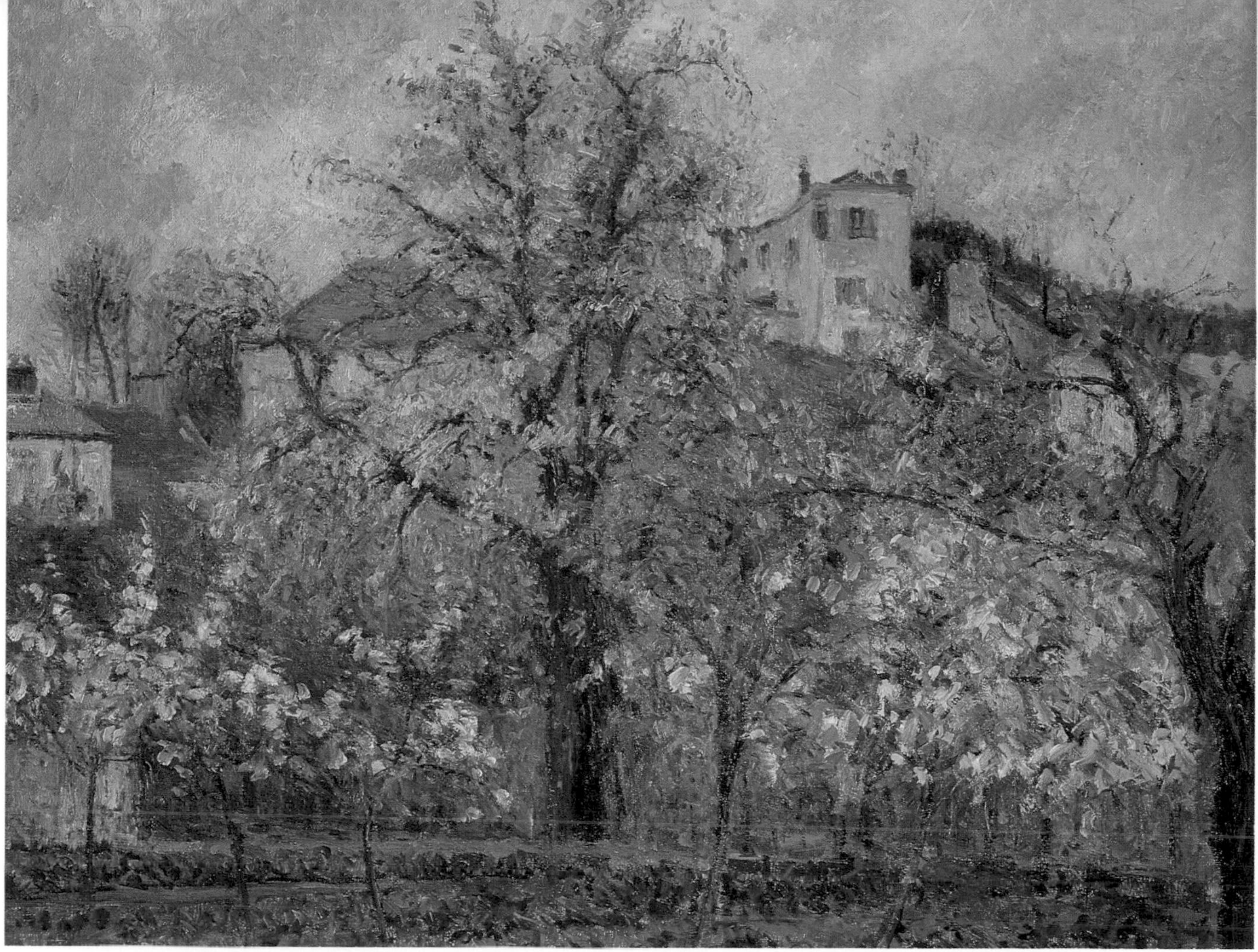

Camille Pissaro, **Kitchen Garden and Trees in Blossom, Spring, Pontoise,** *1877. A masterful evocation of spring.*

the selection of his work to Caillebotte, who chose twenty-nine works to represent the artist – almost a mini-retrospective.

Monet was suffering from one of his periodic bouts of depression. He had never really seen the exhibitions as anything other than a temporary measure and he believed that group activities weakened his independent status and undermined the originality of his work. He was also experiencing heavy domestic pressures, which mitigated against his total involvement in the project. His wife, Camille, was ill after the birth of their second son in 1878 and was to die tragically a few months later, in September 1879.

Caillebotte showed a number of canvases, including boating and bathing scenes, that revealed his move toward the high color and variegated brushwork of Monet. In doing so, he lost much of his earlier critical support, one critic writing of Caillebotte's work that, "It is he, more than all the others, who provokes the public outrage …" Cézanne was happy to submit work to the exhibition but also wanted to be able to send work to the official Salon. Such an attitude did not please Degas, ever an abrasive factor in the equation, and he insisted on a new proviso: that only artists who did not submit work to the Salon could be accepted amongst their number. Degas contributed to the 1879 exhibition, and to the one that followed in 1880, sending in oils, pastels and painted fans. It was Degas, continuing his push for power, who at the last moment invited the amateur painter, collector and stockbroker, Paul Gauguin, to join their ranks. It also proved difficult to get Degas to keep to his promises regarding the number and nature of his submissions. Exasperated, Caillebotte wrote to Monet, "He is very trying, but we have to admit he has great talent." Degas' unassailable artistic genius and consummate draughtsmanship made him too valuable an asset to lose.

Degas' friend, Mary Cassatt, showed for the first time in 1879, exhibiting a number of portraits in oil and pastel. They were presented in an unusual and distinctive way that reveals the Impressionists' concern for the presentation of their works. At least two of Cassatt's paintings were presented in frames colored to enhance their particular qualities, her *Woman with a Fan* in a vermilion frame and her *Box at the Opera* in a green one.

The show was, despite all the dissent, a success; at the close of the exhibition on May 11, it was realized that in financial terms, it had been the most successful ever mounted by the group, with over 16,000 visitors coming to see their works. After all the accounts had been dealt with, each participant received 439 francs: with her dividend Cassatt bought a Degas and a Monet.

The Fifth Impressionist Exhibition, 1880

I am still and always intend to be an Impressionist ... but I see only very rarely the men and women who are my colleagues. The little clique has become a great club which opens its doors to the first-come dauber.
– Claude Monet, quoted by E. Tabouréux in *La Vie Moderne*, June 12, 1880.

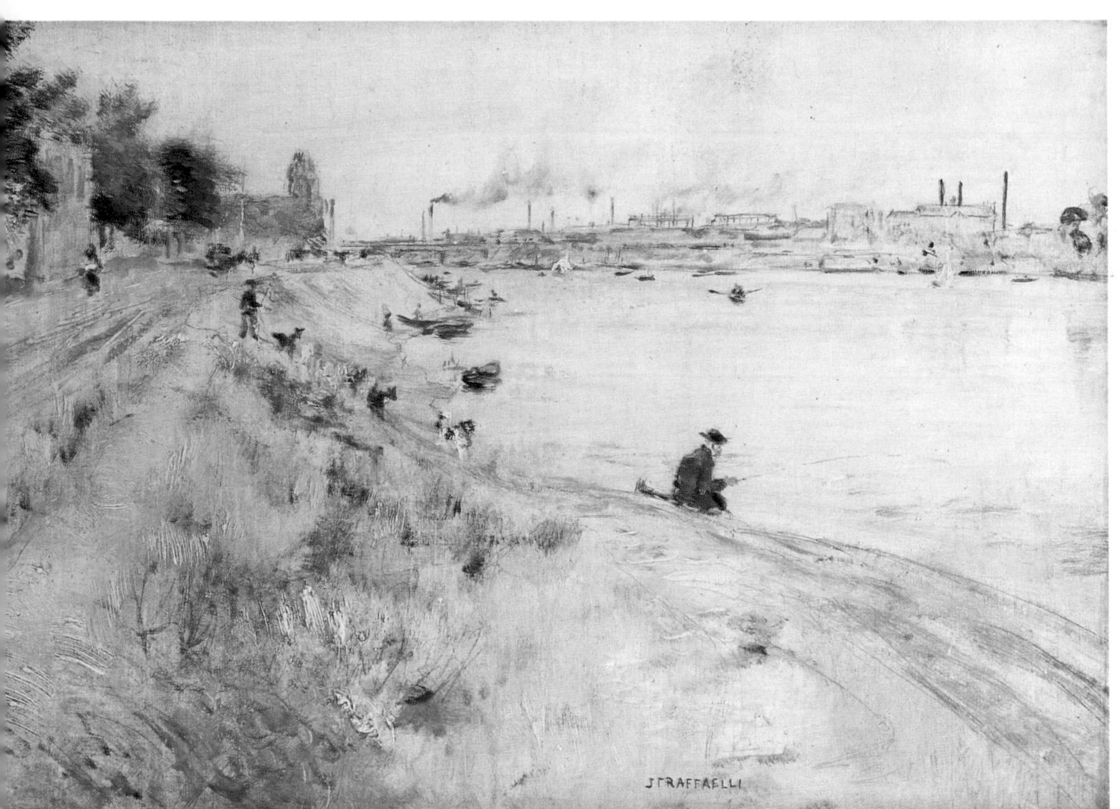

Raffaëlli's* Pêcheur sur la Rive de la Seine. *Raffaëlli's popularity irked the Impressionists.

This 1880 exhibition was the least comprehensive of all the Impressionist shows. Monet, Renoir, Sisley and Cézanne were not represented. It opened on April 1 at 10 Rue des Pyramids, just off Rue de Rivoli, in the mezzanine of a badly lit building still in the process of construction, so that the pictures had to vie with the noise of workmen to gain the attention of the visitors.

Degas, as the promoter of the show, had publicized the exhibition as "A Group of Independent Artists," once again avoiding the term "Impressionism," which he so disliked. Quarrels over every aspect of the show seem to have broken out between Caillebotte and Degas, a division which was revealed in the organization of the exhibition itself. The work of eighteen diverse artists was arranged on walls and screens. This lack of visual coherence was reflected in the comments of such respected critics as Armand Silvestre and Joris-Karl Huysmans, who noted the spirit of compromise and commented upon the apparent weakness of the work exhibited, characterizing the show as one with a general lack of ambition; unfavorable comparisons with the Salon were made.

Monet, affected by his economic hardship and envious of Renoir's success at the Salon the year before, submitted work to the Salon of 1880. One of these works, a rather fussily-worked *Seine at Lavacourt*, was accepted, and a more loosely worked *Floating Ice on the Seine* was rejected. In June, following the example of Renoir and Manet, Monet held a solo exhibition at the offices of Georges Charpentier's *La Vie Moderne*. Degas treated such compromises with contempt, and relations between him and Monet were never the same again.

Renoir's success at the Salon of 1879 with his *Portrait of Madame Charpentier and Her Children* had also inspired Sisley and Cézanne to try to seek success at the Salon of 1880, attempts which, once again, were doomed to failure. Sisley wrote rather pathetically to Charpentier in March 1879, "Since I decided to exhibit at the Salon I find myself more isolated than ever." He had been driven as much by poverty as anything else to submit an entry for the 1879 Salon; even though his entry was rejected, his action had put him out of bounds for joining the fourth Impressionist exhibition that year. Now, he did not exhibit at the fifth exhibition either.

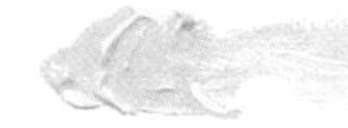

Pissarro remained firmly committed to the ideal of independent shows in spite of his own financial hardships, a fact that separated him from the others who exhibited in 1880, all of whom enjoyed differing degrees of financial security.

Market forces at work

Such diffusion of energy suggests that the avant-garde had lost its identity as an independent body and shows the influence of overpowering market forces. The most successful artist at the 1880 show was Jean-François Raffaëlli, who showed over thirty-five works. Pissarro, who had exhibited numerous oils in the previous exhibition to little effect, now exhibited a number of prints mounted on yellow paper and with purple frames, but once again failed to attract any significant critical notice or sales.

Gauguin exhibited an accomplished bust of his wife and a number of more amateurish still lifes and landscapes. Apparently, he also expelled the young Signac, the future neo-Impressionist and colleague of Seurat, from the exhibition for daring to copy the works on show.

Such problems of identity and originality were highlighted in the pages of the powerful and influential newspaper *Le Figaro*, whose much-feared art critic Albert Wolff dared to ask the question "Why does a man like Degas dally with these incompetents? Why doesn't he follow the example of M. Manet who long ago deserted the Impressionists?"

Paradoxically, times were catching up with the Impressionists, their work no longer seeming as radical as it once had. The Salon jury of this year, more liberal than in previous years, had come close to awarding the already seriously ill Manet a Second Class medal. In spring of the next year, Manet finally received due recognition from what had once been seen as the enemy camp, he was awarded a Second Class medal from the Salon for his portrait of Henry Rochefort, and in September he was awarded the Legion of Honor.

Claude Monet,* On the Seine at Lavacourt, *1880. It was accepted by the Salon jury of 1880.

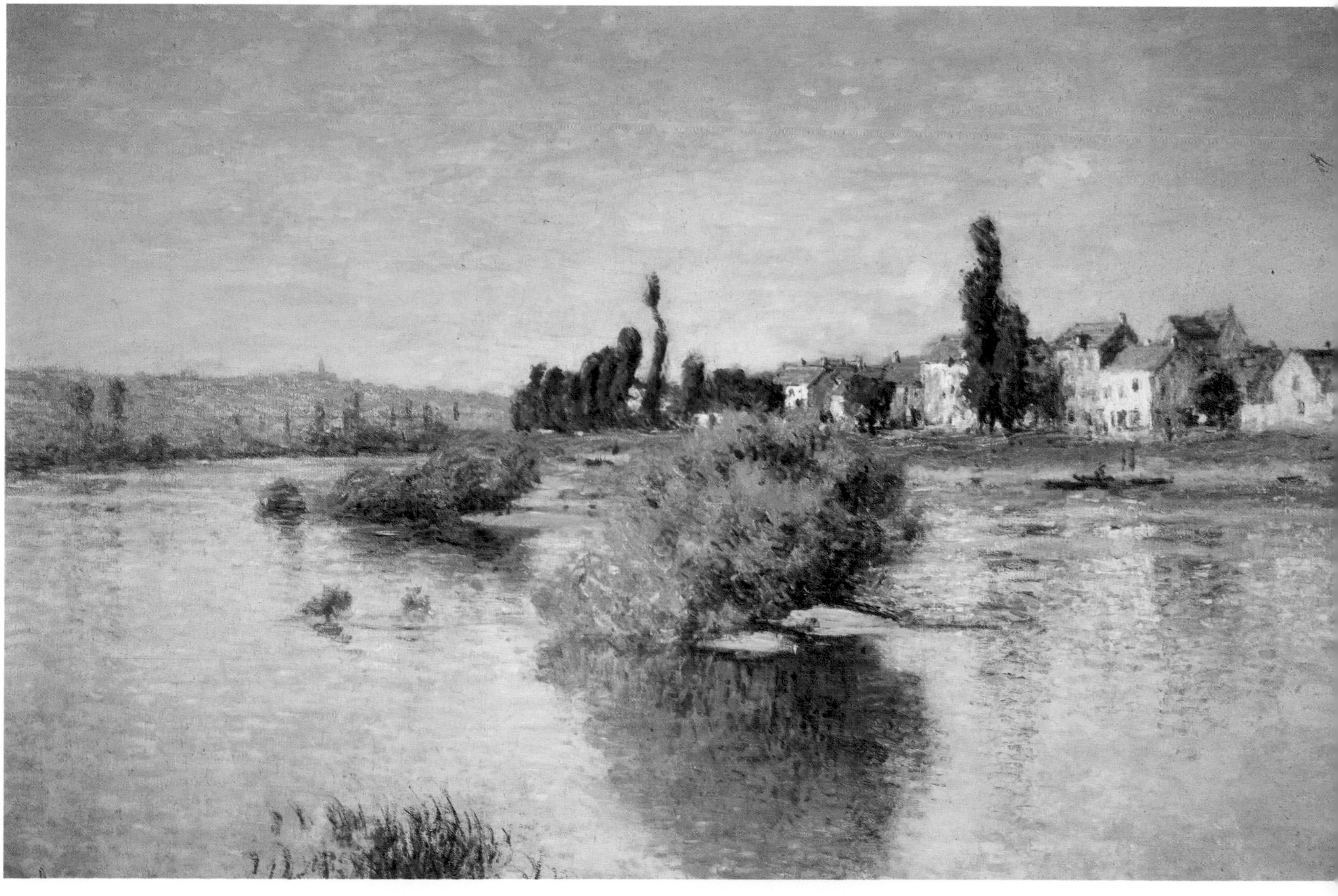

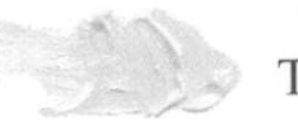

The Sixth Impressionist Exhibition, 1881

Caillebotte, Pissarro and Morisot were the only artists who, by the 1880s, remained committed to the ideal of independent exhibitions based upon the tenets developed in early 1870s. "What is to become of our exhibitions?" wrote Caillebotte to Pissarro,

> ***This is my well considered opinion: we ought to continue, and continue only in an artistic direction, the sole direction – in the final sense – that is of interest to us all. I ask, therefore, that a show should be composed of all those who have contributed real interest to the subject, that is, you, Monet, Renoir, Sisley, Mme. Morisot, Mme. Cassatt, Cézanne, Guillaumin, and if you wish, Gauguin, perhaps Corday and myself. That's all, since Degas refuses a show on such a basis.***

The 1881 exhibition took place in the cramped annex of 35 Boulevard des Capucines, connected to the building that had been the setting for the first of their exhibitions. Caillebotte had refused to show with the others, due to a quarrel with Degas concerning the inclusion of Raffaëlli, while Monet, Renoir and Sisley exhibited at the Salon. Cézanne, who was refused by the Salon in 1881, did not take part either.

Berthe Morisot showed seven works. Those shown by Mary Cassatt were singled out for praise by Huysmans, who had previously noted not only the influence of Degas in her work but also, more oddly, the impact of English painters such as Millais. This year, however, he wrote the following account of her work in *L'Art Moderne*: "… There has arisen an artist who owes nothing to anybody, an artist who at first attempt has established her personality." One critic went so far as to suggest that she and Morisot were the only interesting artists exhibiting.

Viewing of the 170 works was uncomfortable. In the absence of Caillebotte, the disruptive Degas was probably mainly responsible for the organization of the exhibition and he made it very much his own. At the center of the display was his wax statue of the *The Little Dancer, Aged 14 Years*, promised from the previous year. This, together with his pastel study of two criminals, revealed once again the realist base of his ambitions. Pissarro once again used colored frames on his canvases and was the largest exhibitor; it was not in his character to desert Degas: "He's a terrible man," he wrote, "but frank and loyal."

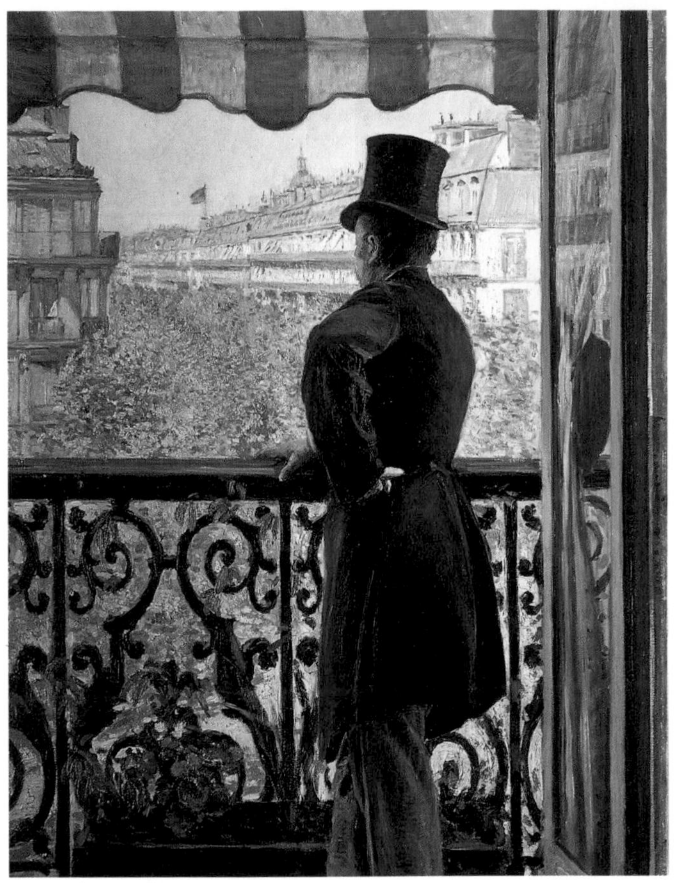

Caillebotte,* Man at a Balcony, *1880. The image reveals the artist's concern with inventive formal compositions.

Gauguin, inspired by Degas, exhibited some sculptures and a rather finicky study of a nude model occupied in needlework. The painting was enthusiastically taken up by the critic Huysmans, which may well have strengthened Gauguin's desire to take up modern art as a full-time career.

This year was a critical one for the Salon: the state formally abandoned its supervision of that institution, and Renoir and Manet enjoyed critical and popular success there. The disagreements among the Impressionist circle now hardened as the divisions that had once separated the avant-garde from the official world of art became increasingly difficult to discern.

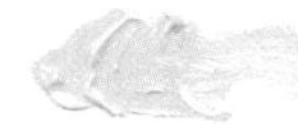

The Seventh Impressionist Exhibition, 1882

At the beginning of the decade it appeared that the economic depression that had affected the Impressionists' careers was finally lifting. The banker Feder invested in Durand-Ruel's business, and the Impressionists, working with the dealer, began to enjoy a measure of financial stability. In this optimistic atmosphere, Caillebotte once again attempted to organize an exhibition of his friends' work. Things proved difficult. Degas refused to give up Raffaëlli and, therefore, refused to participate; Gauguin followed suit, leaving Pissarro in a difficult position, caught between the two camps.

Caillebotte could get nowhere amid such intrigue; things were looking bad and Paul Durand-Ruel, who had invested so heavily in their affairs, was deeply concerned. This concern became more critical when his associate Feder was declared bankrupt during the economic crash of 1882, which was precipitated by the collapse of the Union-Générale Bank.

By now, Durand-Ruel was losing confidence in the economic sense of large exhibitions and was beginning to concentrate instead upon smaller ventures based upon the marketing of individual artists. Sisley and Pissarro both disagreed, the latter considering a group exhibition a "necessity" for dealer and artists alike; somewhat reluctantly, one imagines, Durand-Ruel organized the 1882 show, which opened at Salons du Panorama de Reichshoffen, 251 Rue Saint-Honoré, in March.

Pissarro, as always, was present, but a sign of Durand-Ruel's influence over the painters is evident in the dealer's refusal to allow him to exhibit his works in white frames. Durand-Ruel had persuaded Monet to cooperate in the venture and Renoir was also represented, although he was absent from the capital, painting in the south of France. Renoir had been initially unenthusiastic about exhibiting with "that old Jew Pissarro" – a remark for which he subsequently apologized. Nine of Morisot's works were on view, chosen on her behalf by her husband, Eugène Manet. Caillebotte and Sisley also showed, although Degas and Cassatt, Raffaëlli, Gauguin and the painter and caricaturist Forain, remained apart. Cézanne was also absent.

The growing appreciation of Cézanne's intense dedication and experimentation is evident in a letter written by Pissarro to the critic Huysmans in 1883, "Why is it that you do not say a word about Cézanne, whom all of us recognize as one of the most astounding and curious temperaments of our time and who has had a very great influence on modern art?" Huysman's excuse was that the artist so described was in his opinion, "an incomplete Impressionist."

At long last, thanks to the intervention of his friend Antoine Guillemet, Cézanne had a painting accepted, on charity, for display at the Salon of 1882. Predictably, his *Portrait of M. L. A.* went unnoticed and Cézanne did not exhibit again in Paris until 1895.

Caricature by Draner (Jules Renard 1833–c. 1900) of 1882 exhibition, caricaturing Caillbotte's two paintings.

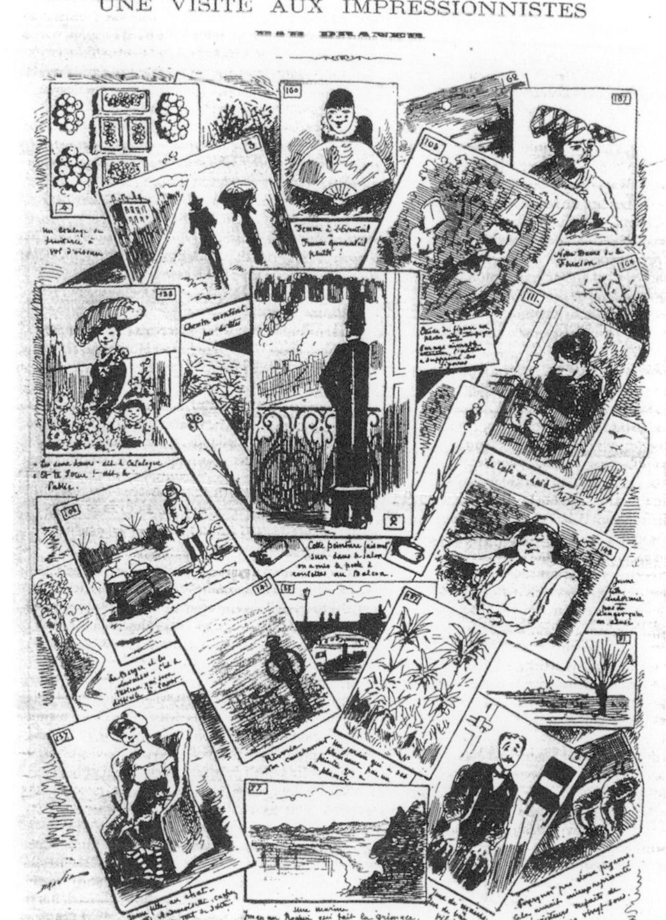

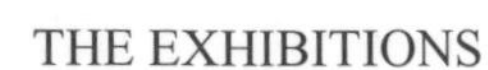

Impressionism in Crisis

Edgar Degas, **Portrait of Duranty,** *1879, tempera and pastel on canvas. A powerful study of the artist's friend and supporter, in a characteristically informal pose, surrounded by the tools of his trade.*

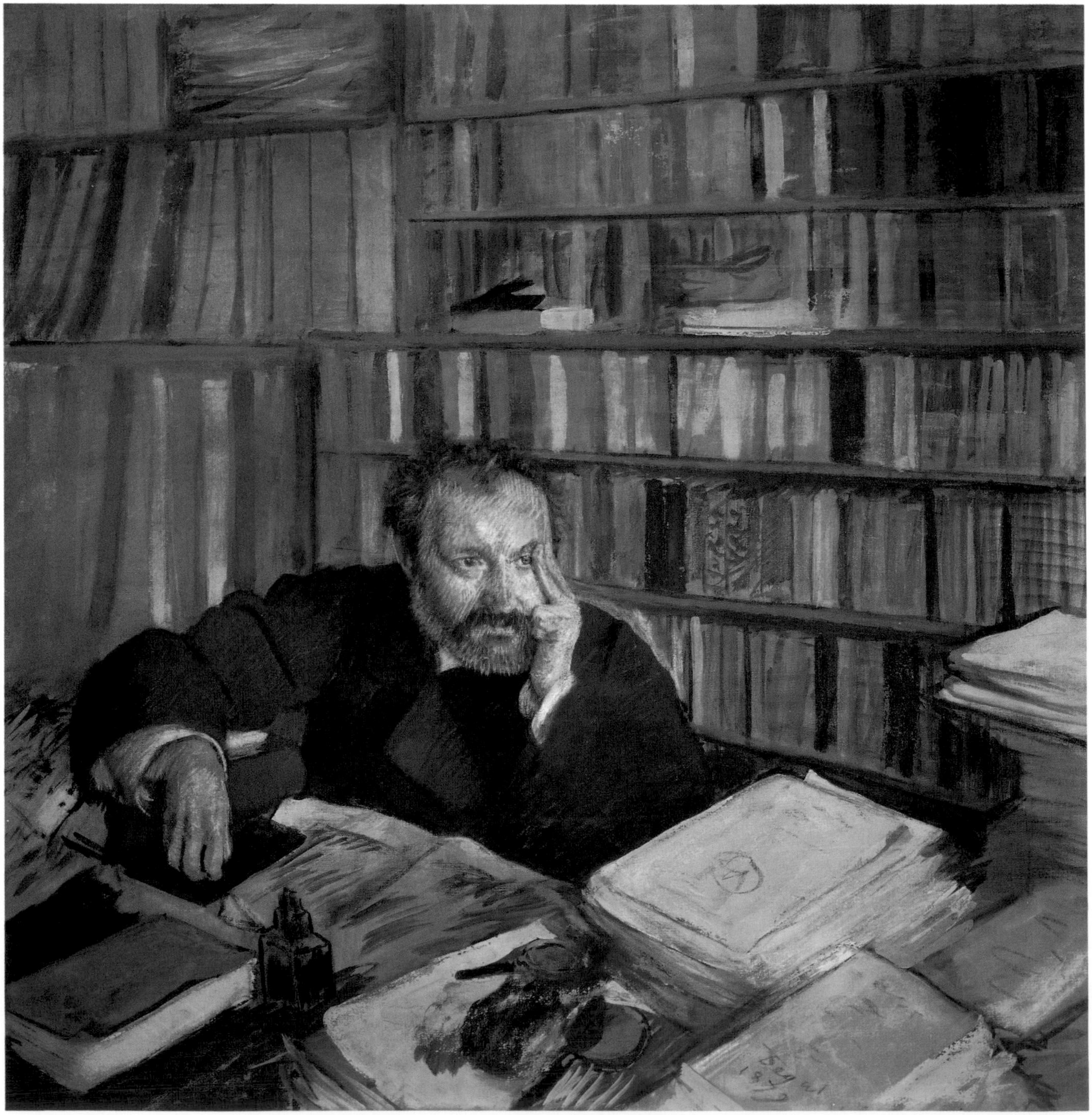

Around 1883 it became apparent that a shift or change of emphasis had taken place in the work of all the major protagonists of Impressionism. This had not happened overnight, and the reasons for what is often referred to as the "crisis of Impressionism" were many and affected each artist differently. The tensions within the group were the result of numerous factors, all of which played a part in their dispersal and in the collapse of the notion of jointly organized group exhibitions. Most of the artists involved realized that the exhibitions had not been able to counter the prevailing economic depression that continued through the early 1880s. There was pressure to attempt once again the traditional routes to artistic and financial success. In 1880 even Emile Zola was arguing that the Impressionists should send work to the Salon: "one joins the battle in the open air ... a simple question of opportunism, as our politicians say these days," he remarked.

The time had come for the Impressionists, by this time mature artists, to take stock of their careers. Many felt that Monet's *plein-air*-derived technique, based upon notions of spontaneity and improvisation, had proved unequal to its task of creating a significant art. Their friend and erstwhile supporter Émile Zola, having come to this conclusion, remained faithful to it until the end; as late as 1896 he could refer to Cézanne as "*un grand peintre avorté*" – that is, an artist who had failed to develop his greatness.

Officialdom loosens its grip

Outside their immediate circle other factors were at play. There was a perceptible relaxation in the government's control over the arts. Although the hopes that had been originally harbored for a more progressive and liberal attitude to the arts had not come to fruition, new possibilities were now available to artists and writers wanting to voice their opinions. In more radical circles especially, there was a continuing and deepening sense of frustration. Impressionism, once considered a new and dynamic alternative to the forces of convention, had, in its turn, become conventionalized; it was only to be expected that alternatives would present themselves and that a new avant-garde would emerge.

1883 was marked by the entry into the Impressionist milieu of Georges Petit, a dealer who courted an aristocratic and upper-middle class clientele, putting himself in direct competition with Durand-Ruel. As the influence of the official Salon waned, so dealers came to occupy an ever-more-significant place within the contemporary art world generally and for the Impressionists in particular. Successful artists were now paid on a regular basis by dealers who were thereby able to exert a greater influence upon the nature and quality of their output. Artists were encouraged, directly or indirectly, to paint works specifically for wealthy clients who were in turn courted by entrepreneurial dealers. This was not without its benefits. For instance, artists no longer had to struggle to produce the single "great painting" that would impress the Salon jury and capture the fickle attention of the visitors to the Salon.

The history of Impressionism parallels the development of this new commercial world – a world that was supported by a network of critics who, writing for the journals and magazines of the day, had the potential power to make or break an artist's career. The mid-to-late nineteenth century saw the publication of many books and articles extolling romantic interpretations of the artist's life and work. Such publications sustained the myth of the artist as a unique creator, whose works were the result of an individual temperament expressed in a recognizably personal style that was regarded as the touchstone of artistic value.

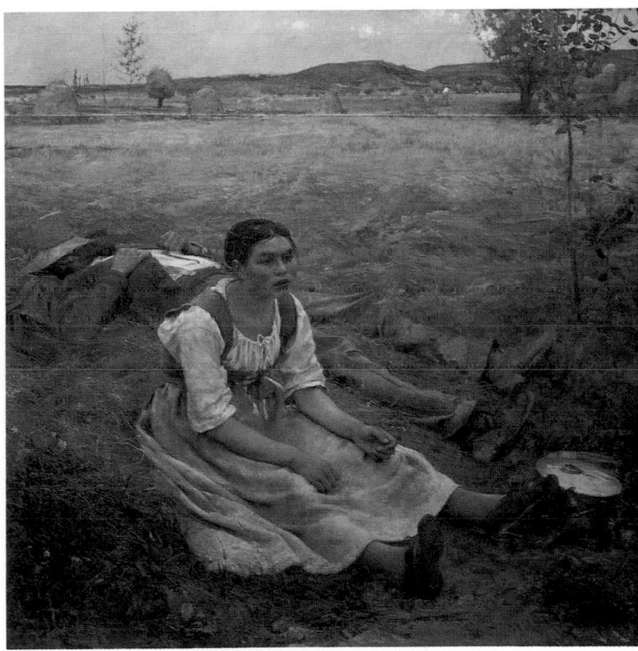

Jules Bastien-Lepage,* Les Foins *(*The Haymakers*), 1877.

Despite the new opportunities outside its sphere of influence, the Salon was still the social and artistic event of the year and many artists within the Impressionist group hankered after the opportunities that were offered by the possibility of painting on a large scale. Few artists were happy ignoring "*la grand tradition*" and almost all the Impressionists during the previous decade had pursued an active engagement with the art of the past, trying to produce works on a scale normally reserved for museum pieces. Artists sanctioned by popular and official success may have trivialized the category of history painting, but they could not destroy it. Impressionism has become such a popular movement that its popularity can obscure the fact that, in reality, it was a small loose association of individuals working in very different ways: there were many other alternative ways of working that were being developed by different artistic groups and individuals.

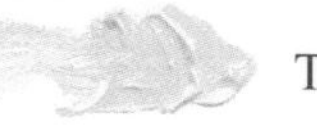

The Final Show, 1886

There was prolonged gap in independent exhibitions by the Impressionists after the seventh in 1882, Durand-Ruel having in the meantime developed his strategy of holding one-man shows. Eventually, it was Berthe Morisot and her husband who managed to convince all the interested parties that another "Impressionist" show would be a worthwhile venture.

On May 15, 1886, what was to be the final Impressionist exhibition opened. It was held on the second floor of Maison Dorée, the famous restaurant close to the fashionable café, Tortoni's, at 1 Rue Laffitte, the well-known "street of picture-dealers." The work of seventeen artists was on view, including newcomers Odilon Redon, Georges Seurat and Paul Signac.

The artists had traveled a long way in the twelve years since the original exhibition on the Boulevard du Capucines. Both Monet and Renoir had distanced themselves from the group and were absent from the show. They were busy establishing links with other dealers, such as Georges Petit – a calculated plan to weaken their dependency upon Durand-Ruel.

"Scientific" Impressionism

Over the years, Pissarro had allied himself with the more "scientific" version of Impressionism that had been developed by Seurat and Signac. He considered their work to be a logical and rational development from the now outmoded "romantic Impressionism" of his former colleagues and had been for some time producing works in the Pointillist manner. Pissarro was still dedicated to the idea of group exhibitions, but the artistic and personal differences of the individuals made any concerted action impossible. His commitment to the younger artists and their vision was total and uncompromising. As he had once championed Cézanne, so now Pissarro was doing the same for the younger artists. He wrote to his son Lucien in March 1886, telling him of one such piece of championing:

Degas,* The Two Milliners, *1885–86. The pastel reveals his acute awareness of the professional at work.

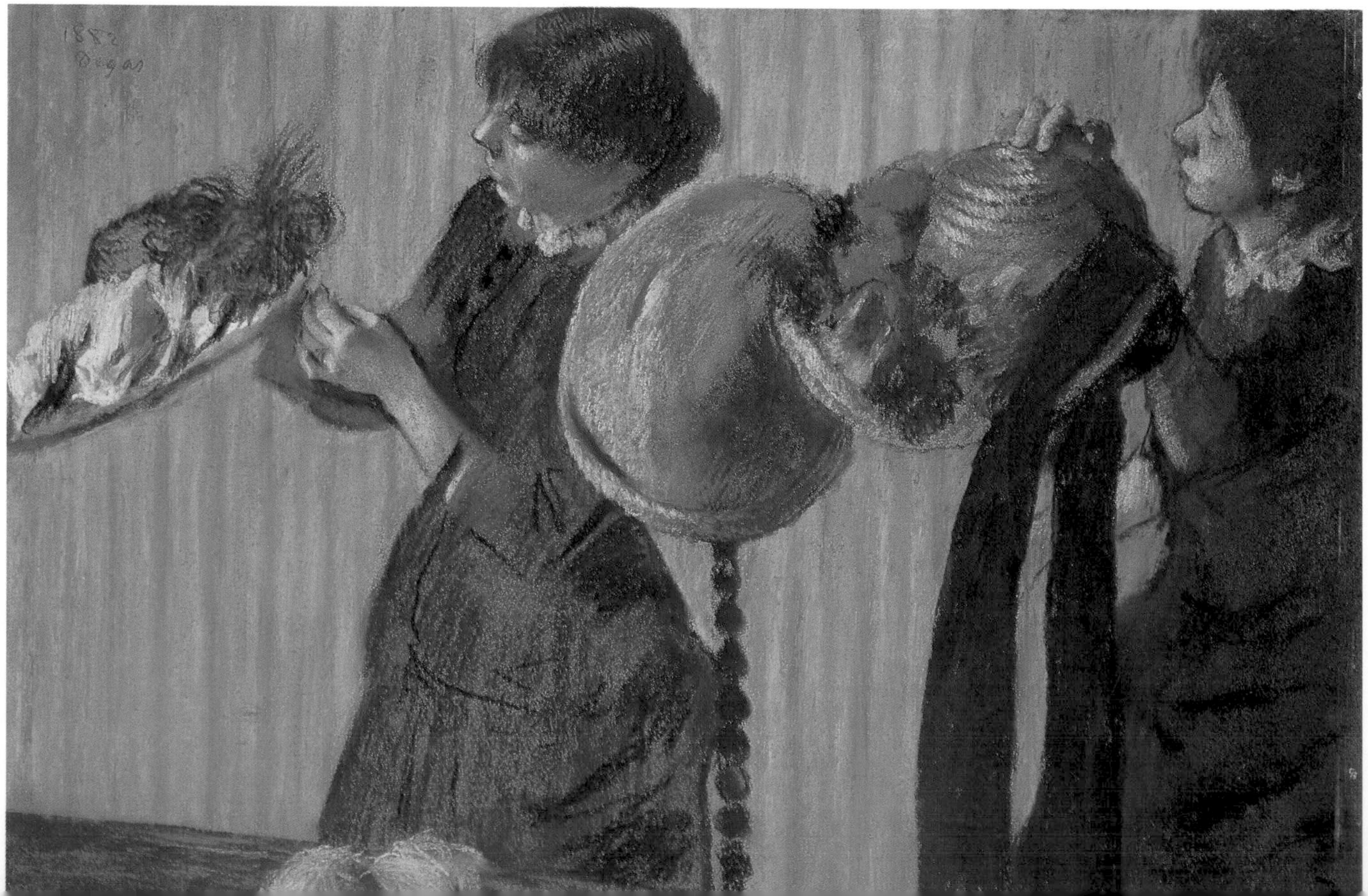

Yesterday, I had a violent run in with M. Eugène Manet on the subject of Seurat and Signac. The latter was present as was Guillaumin. You may be sure I rated Manet roundly; which will not please Renoir … I explained to M. Manet … that Seurat has something new to contribute, which these gentlemen, despite their talent, are unable to appreciate, that I am personally convinced of the progressive character of his art, and certain that in time it will yield extraordinary results.

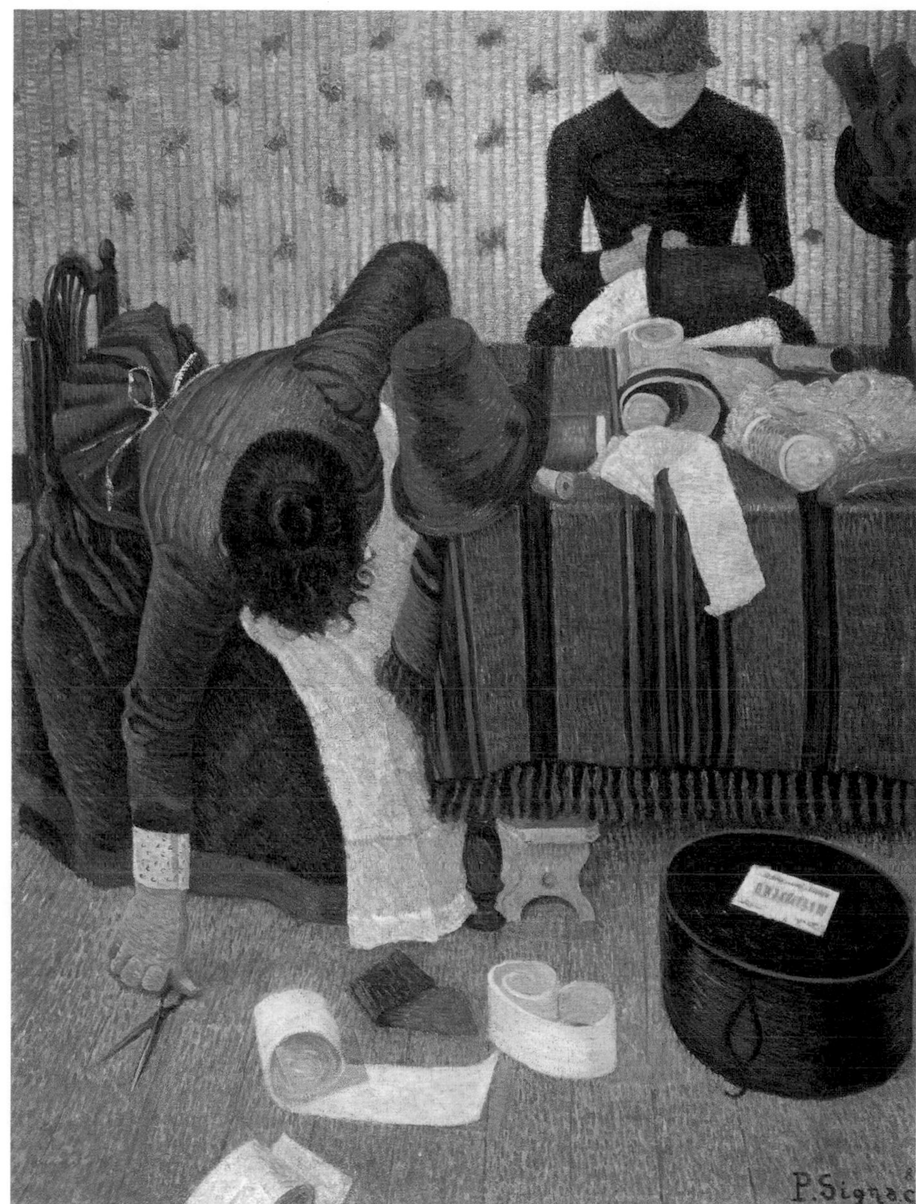

Paul Signac, **The Two Milliners,** *1885–86. Despite the informality of the leaning figure, the highly organized nature of the painting is as apparent as it is disguised in the Degas.*

Georges Seurat, then aged 27, who had on exhibition his large and ambitious painting, *A Sunday Afternoon at the Island of Grand Jatte*, which he had completed after much effort the previous year. This massive undertaking with its complex hierachic composition and unquestionable authority revealed itself as the strongest challenge yet to the intuitive painting typified by Monet, Renoir, Sisley and Morisot. The difference was manifested physically at the exhibition in the grouping together of the work of Seurat, Signac and Pissarro in a room apart from the others.

Caillebotte, Sisley and Renoir, for various reasons, decided not to show; Monet had initially refused, although a number of his works were exhibited, chosen by Durand-Ruel apparently without the artist's permission. Monet was, for the second time, showing with, among others, Renoir and Raffaëlli, at Georges Petit's Exposition Universelle of that year.

Problems continued into the run of the show. Morisot was represented by a varied selection of works, but, as if to confirm Pissarro's support of the younger painters, her work was considered by at least one commentator to be "… Impressionism as it was shown in previous manifestations." Although Seurat's painting was the major attraction, Degas' pastels of women bathing and at their toilette caused a scandal. The works were seen as deliberate provocations, as subversive challenges to the accepted ideal of womanhood. The Irish writer, George Moore, who was present at the opening of the exhibition, recalled the "boisterous laughter" that rang through the galleries, "exaggerated in the hope of giving as much pain as possible," and Berthe Morisot's conclusion was that the show as a whole had been "a complete fiasco."

There would be no more "Impressionist" exhibitions. The circle had fragmented and broken, and the once publicly orientated program of their exhibiting policy had come to an end, leaving Impressionism firmly in the hands of the dealers and, as a consequence, in the private sphere of their exclusive galleries.

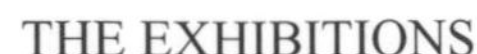

Seurat and Pointillism

Georges Seurat's two major works of the Impressionist epoch are *Bathing at Asnières*, painted in 1884, retouched in the Pointillist style in 1887, and *Sunday Afternoon on the Island of La Grande Jatte*, exhibited in 1886 at the eighth Impressionist Exhibition, where it caused a sensation.

The subject of both paintings is familiar. It is an outing on the banks of the River Seine, but the informality of the older artists' paintings has been transformed by the younger artist into massive hierarchical images. Seurat's Parisians enjoying their Sunday wandering on the island, just outside the city's boundaries, have their apparently casual attitudes caught forever in a scrupulously orchestrated charade characterized in their postures and gestures in a manner more reminiscent of the low reliefs of ancient Egypt or the great wall paintings of the Italian Renaissance.

Historians have argued over Seurat's intentions just as they have been endlessly troubled by those of Manet. The young artist's ambition is self-evident; Seurat was only 27 when he completed *Sunday Afternoon on the Island of La Grande Jatte* (he was to die in 1891 at the age of thirty-two). He was a mysterious individual, born into a well-to-do family and with an eccentric father, and he had a predilection for silence that has further added to the aura of uncertainty surrounding his personality and work.

Georges Seurat,* Sunday Afternoon on the Island of La Grande Jatte, *1884–86. This is the final sketch for the finished work seen opposite.

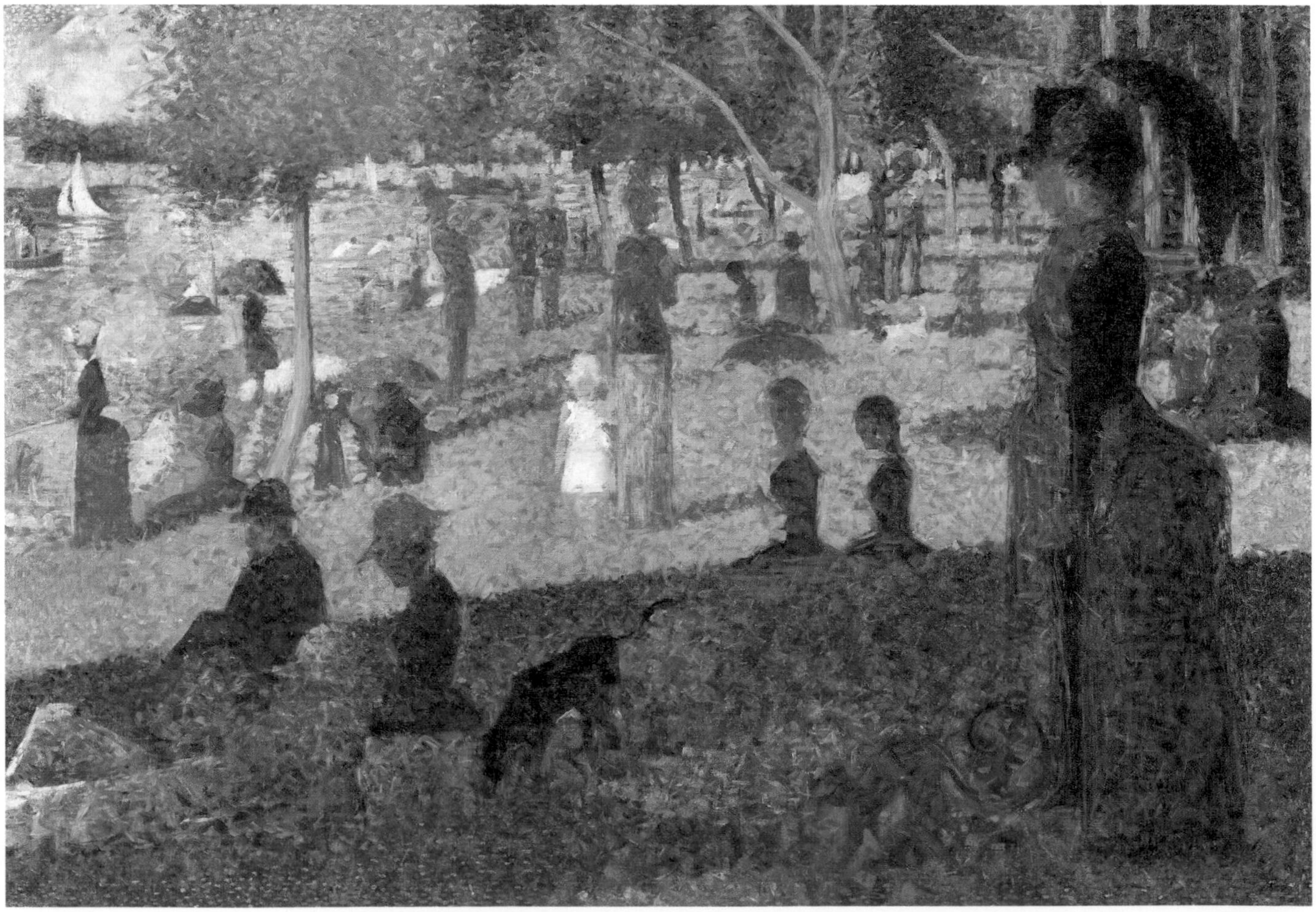

Trained at the Ecole des Beaux-Arts, Seurat worked assiduously to master the art of drawing and composition, which formed the basis of a period of self-imposed study that he undertook on leaving the institution.

Seurat has constructed in his two great works contemporary history paintings conceived on a grand scale. His figures are not dressed in the borrowed garb of other epochs or cultures, nor unconvincingly stripped naked to represent some supposed utopia. Instead he has accepted, as Caillebotte did, the manners and customs of his own age, and from them forged an art that is unique.

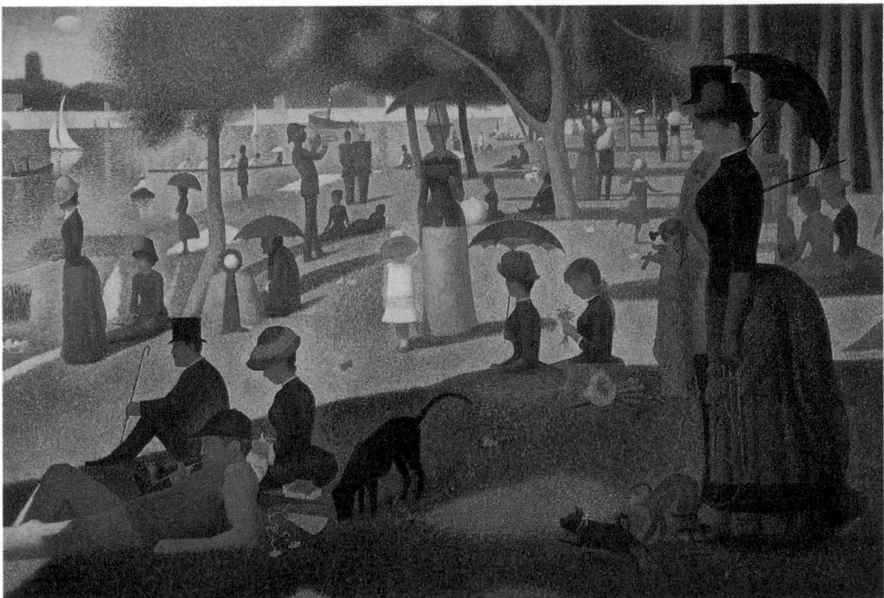

Georges Seurat,* Sunday Afternoon on the Island of La Grande Jatte, *1884–86. The large final version measures over 205 x 305 cm (81 x 120 in). Only a few changes are evident between the two versions.

No one faced the reality of contemporary life quite like Seurat. His paintings are composed of real people, transposed on to a heroic scale with disturbing results. In *Sunday Afternoon on the Island of La Grande Jatte*, a boatman, lost in reverie, surveys the river, a wet nurse looks after her charge and, on the right of the composition, a wealthy man-about-town walks toward the river bank with his female companion, who leads a monkey on a leash. But not everything is as it may seem: an initial reading of the man and the woman as a married couple is contradicted by the presence of the monkey, a symbol of licentiousness. There appears to be little or no communication between the figures, who are locked within their own private worlds. The painting has been read as a disturbing vision of a dysfunctional society made up of arbitrary groups of individuals who can no longer act as a coherent unit. In the face of such a magnificent achievement, the role of Pointillist color technique in the painting seems almost irrelevant; it is not, but it is only one element of a larger whole. Most contemporary commentators found the formalized rigidity of the painting, rather than its painting technique, its salient feature.

In Seurat's paintings the apparently intuitive brushwork and spontaneous response to nature that had come to characterize Impressionism has been called to order and developed into something much more considered. His style of painting was so removed from that of the older artists that it was given the label "*neo-Impressionism*." It was a manner of painting founded upon the principle of optical mixing, in which small separate dabs of pure color were set adjacent to each other to allow the eye of the viewer to create the desired color effect, rather than the traditional practice of placing ready mixed dabs of color on the canvas. This elaborate and time-consuming process was partly a reaction to what Seurat considered to be a failing in Impressionist painting and was nourished by his awareness of scientific color theories prevalent at the time.

Historians have pointed out how Seurat's adoption of the famous Pointillist dot or dab, which was developed through modifying Monet's separated and gestural brushwork into something more mechanistic and impersonal, would have seemed to many to be a style of painting more suited to the age. It has also been suggested that Seurat may well have been consciously emulating technological developments in contemporary color printing, thereby allying his art practice not to "high art" but to those of the world of commerce.

Seurat was involved with the anarchist circles of his day and such possibilities were in keeping with his highly analytical turn of thought. Equally important to the artist were the notions of a scientist, Charles Henry, concerning the correlation of certain expressive lines and curves to the psychological and emotional states of the viewer. Such complex ideas were assimilated into the final version of the painting through a process of countless drawings and oil sketches, at first based upon close observation of reality, which over time were corresponded to his particular vision. Despite the attempts of his followers to continue the artificial style of Pointillism, in the hands of others it became an attractive but stolid technique. Only with Matisse, a generation later, did this bizarre style find renewed life and vigor.

Camille Pissarro: the father figure

Camille Pissarro (1830–1903) was born into a bourgeois French-Jewish family on the island of Saint Thomas in the Virgin Islands. The island was a Dutch trading colony, and the artist remained a Dutch citizen until his death. He was sent to France to be educated in Paris in 1842, but returned home in 1847 to work in his father's business, only to run away in 1853 to Venezuela where he worked with a Danish artist, Fritz Melbye.

By 1855, Pissarro was back in France, settling initially with relations in Passy, and was determined to follow his artistic vocation. At the Universal Exhibition in Paris, he was profoundly impressed by the work of Delacroix and, above all, by that of Courbet and the Barbizon painters; shortly after he also met Corot, who was to be a big influence on him. His early work is firmly rooted in the then modern art of the Barbizon School. In 1859, the year in which he met Monet at the Académie Suisse, he exhibited at the Salon. He met Cézanne and Guillaumin the following year. Also at this time he began a lifelong relationship with his mother's maid, Julie Vellay. In 1863 their first son, Lucien, also destined to be an artist, was born.

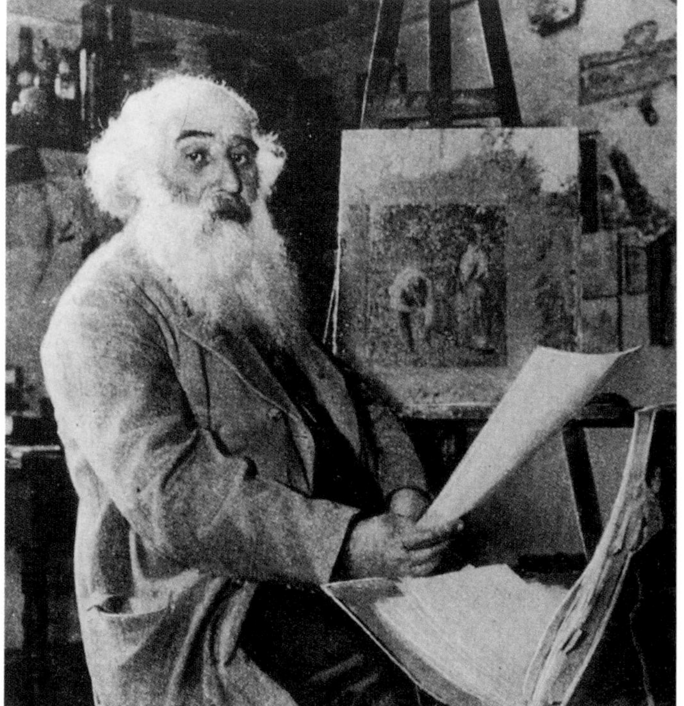

An engaging portrait of the artist in his studio, with a characteristic painting half-finished on his easel.

Pissarro enjoyed a certain success at the Salon, showing eleven works there throughout the period that Manet and Whistler were having theirs rejected; in the Salon *livret* he referred to himself as a "pupil of Corot." His work was rejected only in 1867 and in 1863, when he showed three works at the Salon des Refusés, marking his allegiance to the younger avant-garde and to Manet, who was of his own generation. Although he received some allowance from his father, Pissarro was continually in difficult financial straits; in 1865, things were so bad he found it necessary to take a job as a lawyer's messenger.

In 1866 he moved out of Paris to Pontoise, then, in 1869, to Louveciennes, but always remained in touch with his friends through his regular attendance at the Café Guerbois discussions. With the outbreak of the Franco-Prussian War he fled initially to Montfoucault, where his good friend Ludovic Piette had a country house, only to move on to London in December 1870.

In London, Pissarro associated with Monet and began to exhibit with Durand-Ruel. Unlike Monet, who had left his family in France, Pissarro had brought his with him to London, and they all stayed with relatives in the south London suburbs around Lower Norwood; he and Julie were married at this time.

Post-War France

On his return to his old home in Louveciennes in June 1871, Pissarro discovered that in his absence the occupying Prussian troops had used his house as a butcher's shop and in the process, so Pissarro claimed, they had destroyed some 1,500 canvases, using some of them as duckboards; only 40 were salvaged. The number of paintings destroyed may have been closer to between two and three hundred. He stayed only briefly at Louveciennes, moving back to Pontoise, where he worked in the company of Cézanne, selling his work to a small group of collectors.

From the start, Pissarro was involved in all the discussions and organizing that went into the independent exhibitions. He exhibited in the first show in 1874 and was

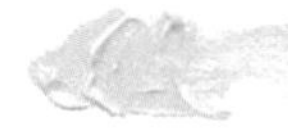

the only one of the group to exhibit in each of the seven subsequent shows. Pissarro insisted on the inclusion of Cézanne and Guillaumin in the first exhibition and Gauguin in the 1879 one, and was responsible for the inclusion of Seurat and Signac in the final exhibition of 1886.

Although Degas was so different in character and outlook from himself, Pissarro was sustained artistically throughout the 1880s by this trenchantly conservative artist. With Mary Cassatt, he was involved in Degas' ill-fated printmaking venture of 1879. Not long after this, Pissarro began to be troubled by the eyesight problems that were to plague him until his death.

After a modestly successful exhibition of his work at Durand-Ruel's in 1884, Pissarro bought a house at Eragny, where he lived for the rest of his life. By the mid-1880s he had met Signac and, more significantly, Seurat, and he fell under the younger artists' influence, adopting their Pointillist manner, even to the extent of reworking some of his earlier canvases.

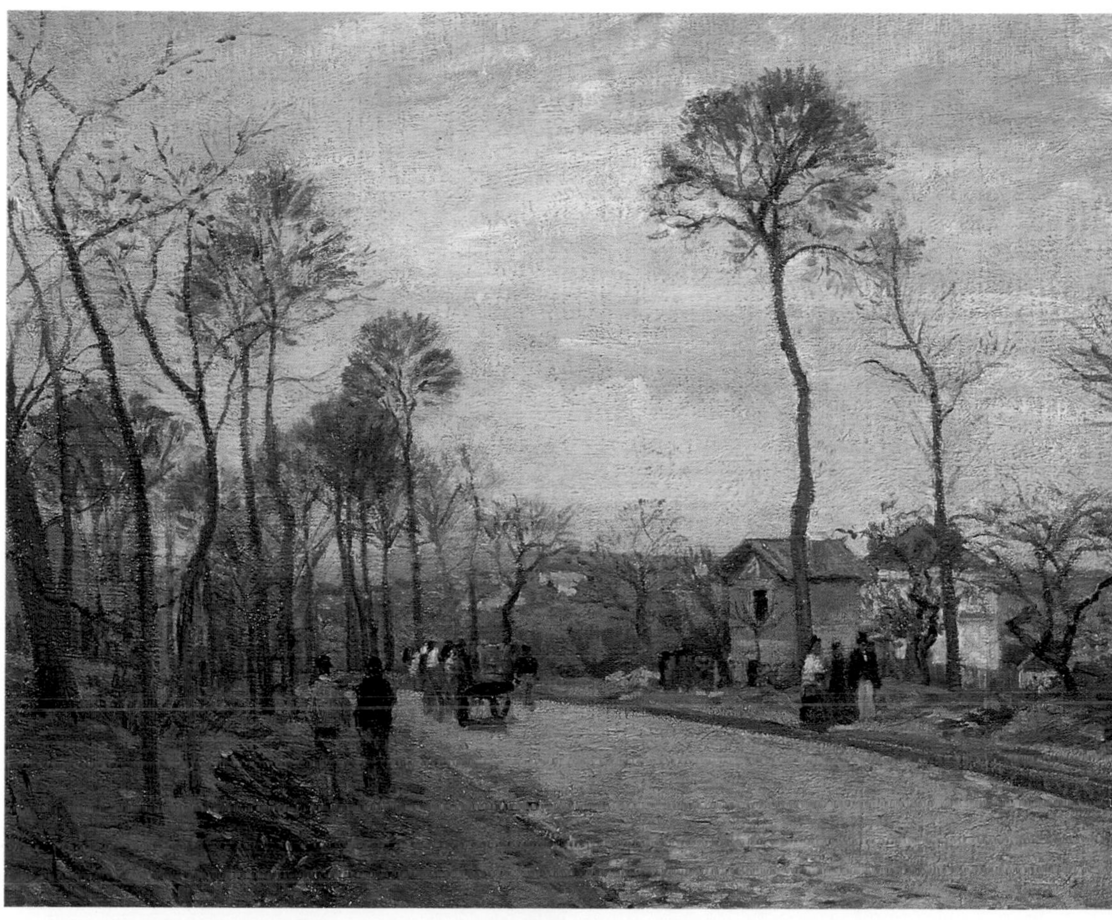

Pissarro,* The Road to Louveciennes, *1870. An archetypal Impressionist scene, its limpid tones and simple composition reveal the debt to seventeenth-century landscape painting.

Recognition came slowly to Pissarro. He continued working in the neo-Impressionist style until the early 1890s, when he returned to a modified form of traditional Impressionist practice. The tide began to turn in 1892, when he held a successful exhibition at Durand-Ruel's and began to paint an impressive series of paintings of Dieppe, Rouen, London and Paris. Finally, official recognition was granted to him and the other Impressionists, when in 1900, three years before his death, a room was dedicated to their works at the Universal Exhibition.

Political and moral influences

Always something of a radical, as Pissarro grew older he became increasingly politically aware and was particularly affected by the writings of Prince Kropotkin, the anarchist writer. Although he thought of himself as an Impressionist, he was always somewhat set apart from the group. Intensely self-critical, he kept himself open to a variety of influences. Consequently, his work followed a number of clearly differentiated shifts as he reappraised his technical and moral procedures in the light of his experience. This tendency has meant that his innovations have been somewhat undervalued.

He was of the same generation as Degas and Manet and was thus viewed by the younger members of the group as an almost paternal figure. A deeply moral man, Pissarro was intensely loyal and had a great gift for friendship. His art was an integral part of his life and although his earlier work may not have the same consciously critical interaction with modern life as say, Monet's, it became as he grew older a moral extension of his own being and, as he saw it, a force for good in the world.

His letters reflect his kindly nature and his own vulnerability and concerns. "What I have suffered is beyond words. What I suffer at the actual moment is terrible, much more than when I was young, full of enthusiasm and ardor, convinced as I now am of being lost for the future," he wrote toward the end of his life. His letters to his son Lucien are some of the most precious documents of nineteenth-century art. Both Gauguin and Cézanne were indebted to him – and acknowledged their debt, Cézanne referring to himself late in his career as a "pupil of Pissarro."

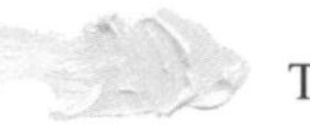

Pissarro and Cézanne at Pontoise

Pissarro's work throughout the 1860s and 1870s was centered upon his relationship with the town of Pontoise, in the Oise valley about 32 kilometers (20 miles) northwest of Paris, to which he moved in 1866. This relationship has been studied to great effect by Richard Brettel in his magisterial study *Pissarro at Pontoise,* which reveals the complexity of his art and the individual way that he interpreted the town and its neighboring landscape. Pissarro's paintings might appear to be quite literal representations of a prosaic landscape; however, their solid workmanlike approach masks the inventiveness of the artist's mind and the innovatory nature of his achievement.

Pissarro's paintings are organized with a care and subtlety learned from his mentor, Corot. They combine the immediacy and visual veracity associated with *plein-air* painting with the tough tactility and solidity that he admired in Courbet's work. From these artists Pissarro inherited the identity of painter as artisan, which separated him distinctly from his younger friends Monet, Renoir and Sisley. His working method was built upon contrasts of tone, and while color was integral to this process, it was the surety of what Corot called "*les valeurs*" (tonal values) together with a nature attuned to the humbler aspects of French rural life that gave Pissarro's paintings their particular quality.

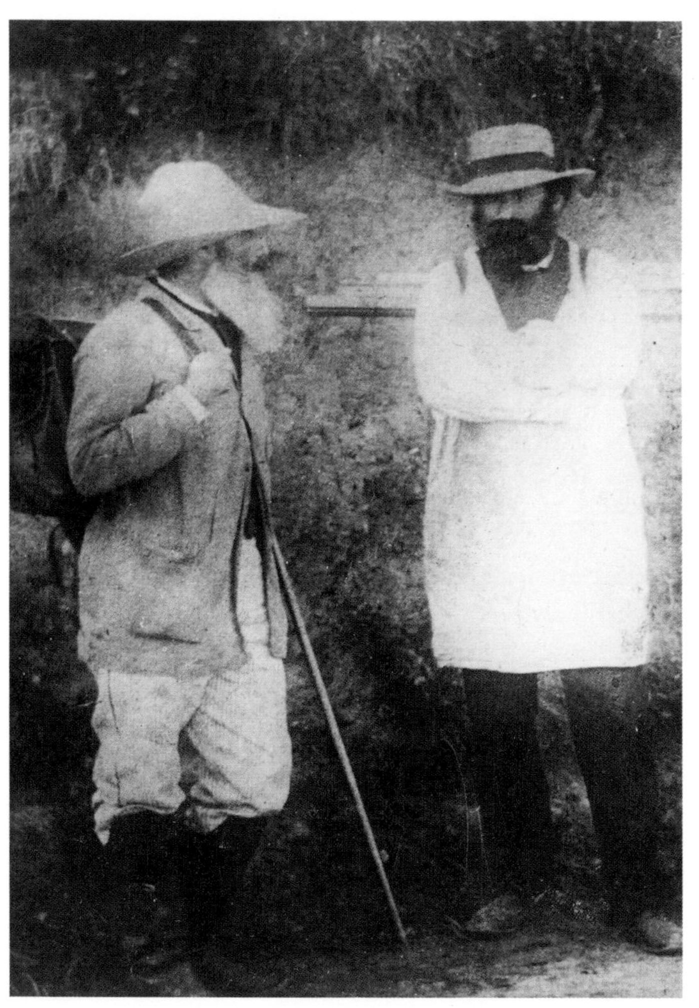

An informal photograph commemorating a period of great friendship and artistic communion: Pissarro and Cézanne seen together dressed ready for work **en plein-air.**

Zola greatly admired his integrity and declared publicly in his Salon review of 1866:

> ***You should realize that you will please no one … and that your picture will be found too bare, too bleak. Then why the devil do you have the arrogance to paint so solidly and to study nature frankly? Yours is an austere and serious kind of painting, an extreme concern for truth and accuracy, a rugged and strong will. You are a great blunderer, sir – you are an artist I like.***

Zola believed that it was such qualities that should characterize modern painting rather than the picturesque beauties offered by the Salon artists. Zola's ideas would not be lost on his friend Cézanne, who first visited Pissarro at Pontoise in 1872. Cézanne shared Pissarro's feeling for the region. As a native of the south of France, he felt the attraction of novelty in the lush northern landscape. He learned from Pissarro how to organize a dynamic coloristic and tonal balance using the rich greens of the trees and foliage set against the high-toned yellow ochers of the simple houses. Like Monet and Sisley, he used individual brushstrokes to register changes in light and structure, but he imposed on them a more disciplined regime that created a unified sense of pictorial architecture.

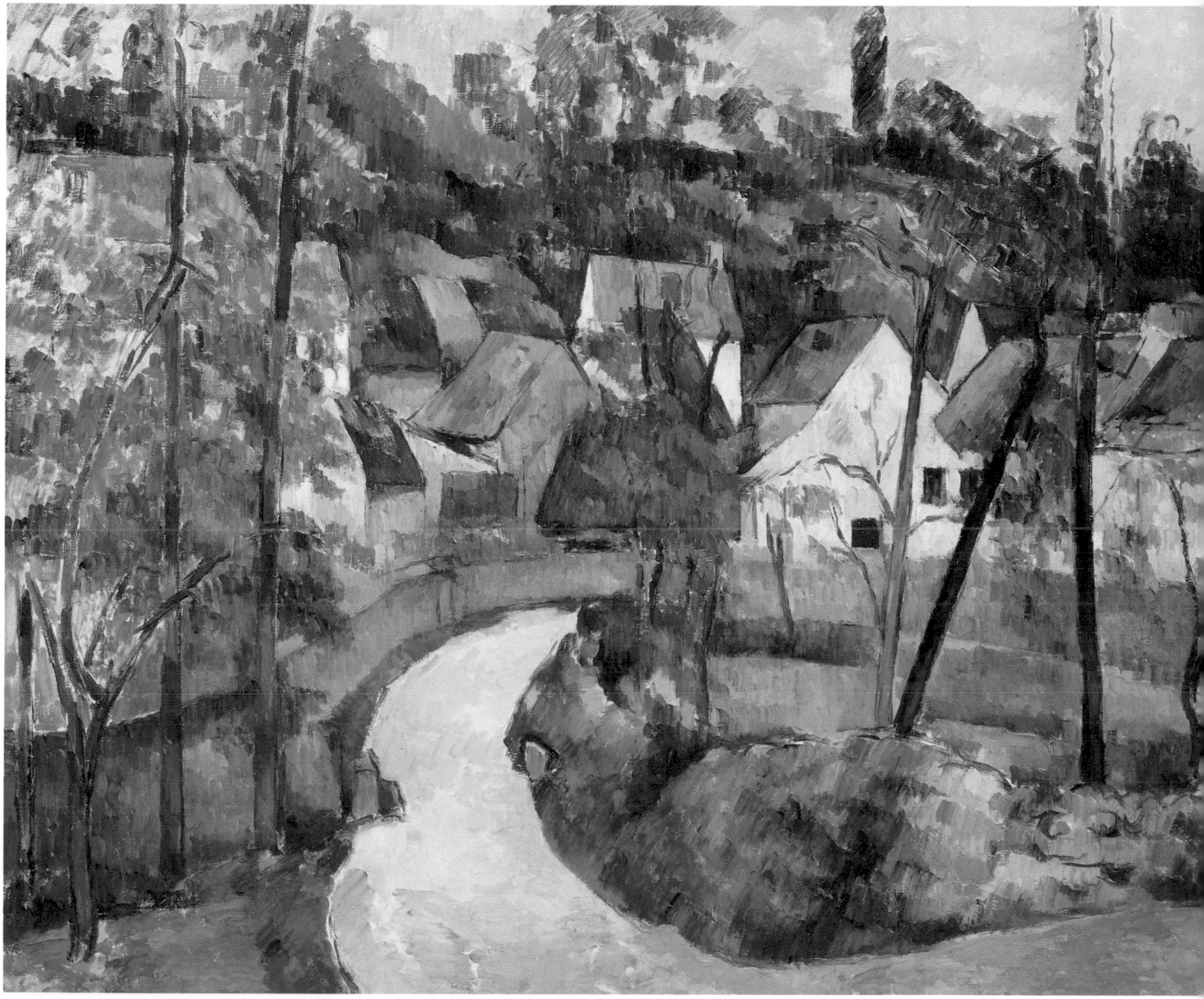

Cézanne, **Bend in the Road,** *1879–82. This painting shows Cézanne's innovative and complex compositional constructions. His masterly handling of paint and subtle use of color reveals a much more confident approach that his earlier canvas* **House of the Hanged Man.**

Both Pissarro and Cézanne made frequent use of a palette knife to create the solid, mural-like effect noticeable in their works of this time. Gradually, both artists abandoned the practice; Cézanne, in particular, used small, bricklike dabs of thick paint, regulating his brushmarks to create an ordered surface that tied architectural and natural elements into a single unified structure. Cézanne later said, "I wanted to make of Impressionism something durable, like the art of the museums," and in his landscapes as much as his figure paintings we can see him striving to achieve just that end. Despite the similarities of their working methods, there is a great difference between the paintings of Cézanne and those of Pissarro. The elder artist's landscapes always have the feeling that they are inhabited, that people, real people walk the roads, live in the houses and dig the fields. In Cézanne's paintings there is a distance from such immediate concerns, which contrasts markedly with the geographical and socially particularized world presented by Pissarro.

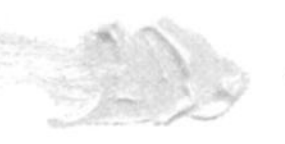

View From My Window, Overcast Weather

1886, reworked 1888, oil on canvas, 65 x 81 cm (26 x 32½ in)
Ashmolean Museum, University of Oxford, England.

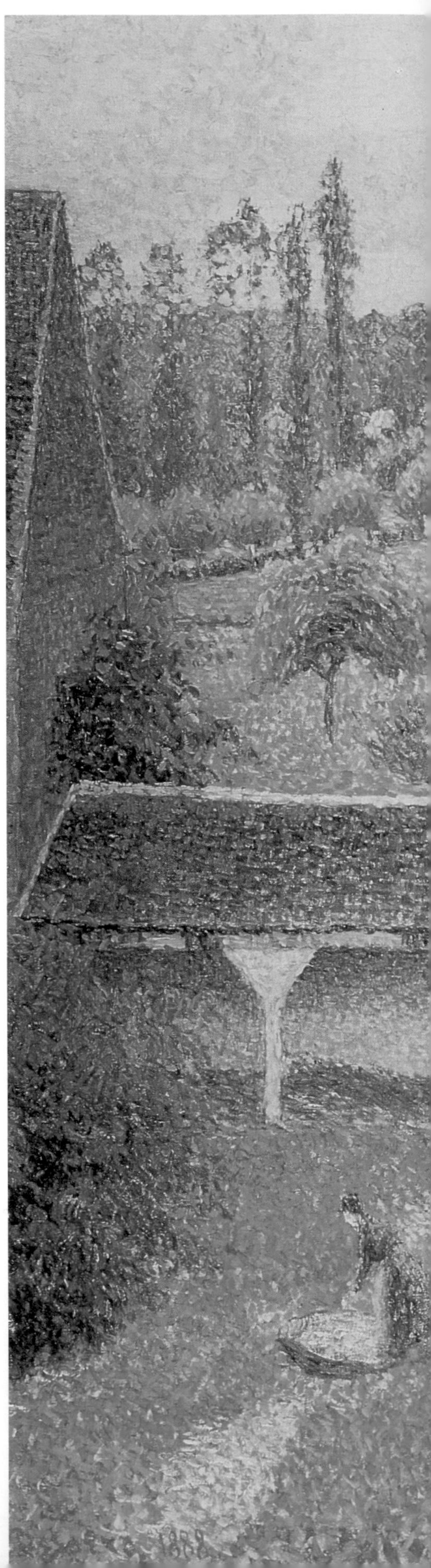

This rural idyll was the view from Pissarro's bedroom at Eragny, a village on the River Epte, south of Dieppe, where he had come to live in 1884. The picture is a consequence of his initial bout of enthusiasm for neo-Impressionist techniques. A network of small dabs of complementary colors gives a shimmering effect to the canvas. Pissarro has built up the surface with very small touches of paint that give the canvas a curious gray cast perfectly suited to its title.

This was a transitional work for the artist and was shown with Seurat's *Sunday Afternoon on the Island of La Grande Jatte* and other canvases by Signac and his own son, Lucien, at the eighth Impressionist show in 1886. Durand-Ruel was unhappy about Pissarro's change of style, telling the artist that the prominence allotted to the red-tiled roof and the poultry would make it difficult to sell. Possibly as a result of Durand-Ruel's unease, Pissarro reworked the canvas, although the deep thrust into space represented by the strong diagonal line of the roof that passes under the nearby tree does create a tension within the composition.

The viewer is looking across the meadows toward Bazincourt. The weather in 1886 was cold and, as he would do later in his career, Pissarro has set up his easel within the comfort of his own home protected from the extremes of the weather. The canvas has a homely atmosphere, as do many of the artist's works. Like an early Mirò, everything is arranged with an almost inventorylike precision: we can make out the barn, poultry yard, cottage garden, orchard and cattle, all cozily enclosed by a neat brick wall. There is a charming toy-town atmosphere to the painting that adds to its appeal. By 1888, however, when Pissarro reworked the canvas, he was aware that in comparison to his previous manner of painting, the Pointillist style was deeply time-consuming and somewhat mechanical and resulted in a loss of the sense of immediacy he experienced before the motif. In a letter at this time, he wrote, "How can one combine the purity and simplicity of the dot with the fullness, spontaneity, and fullness of sensation postulated by our Impressionist art? … the dot is meager, lacking in body …". He resolved this problem by making numerous studies in watercolor. Pissarro later wrote,

I do not paint my pictures [tableaux] directly from nature: I only do that with my studies [études], but the unity that the human spirit gives to vision can only be re-created in the studio. It is there that our impressions, previously scattered, are coordinated and enhance each other's value to create the true poem of the countryside.

For the artist, a painting should never be a direct transcription of the artist's feelings before nature, but something more – a deep humanity and with a quality of innocence.

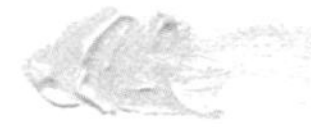

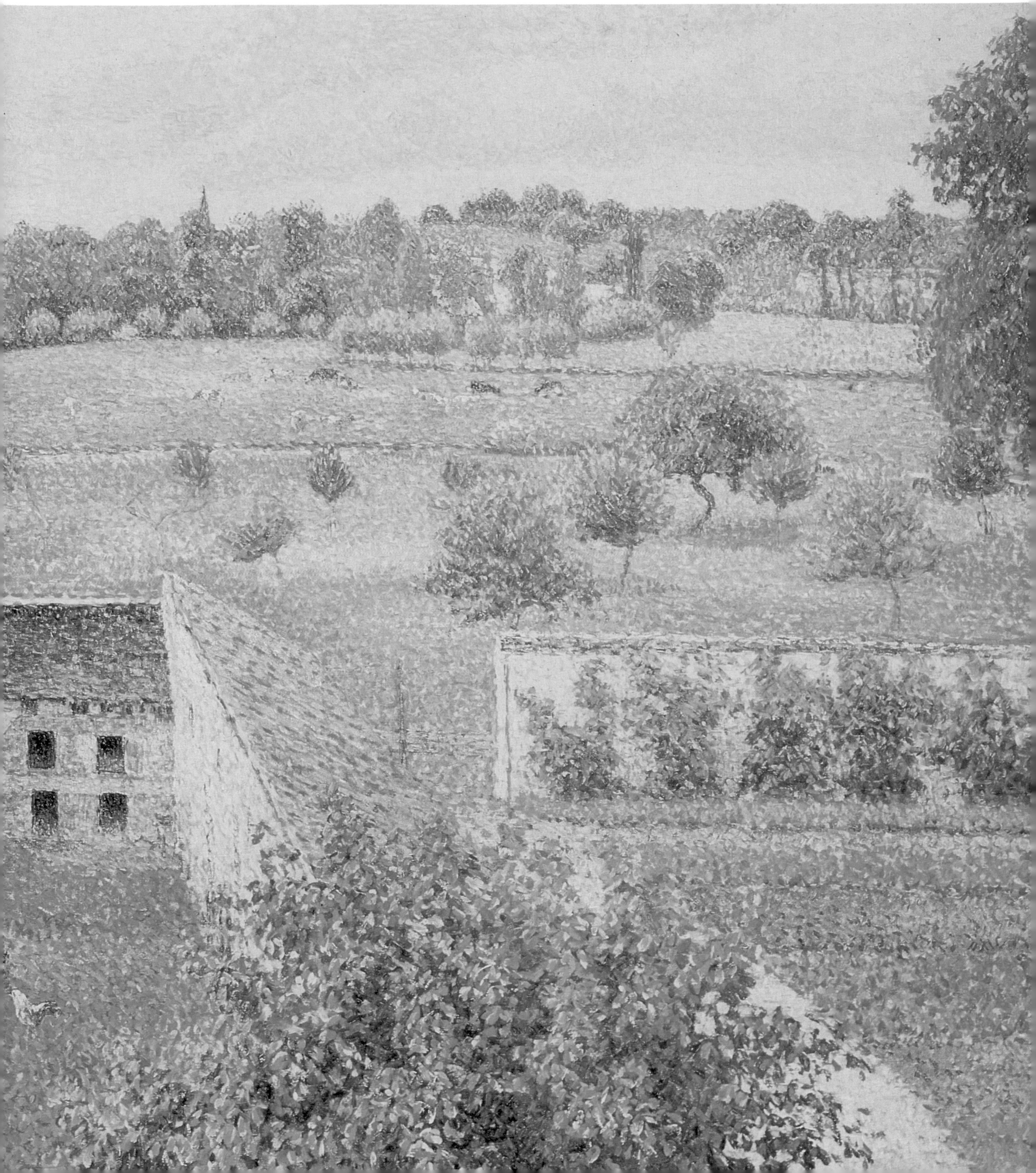

Paul Cézanne:
"The Hermit of Aix"

Paul Cézanne (1839–1906) was the son of Louis-Auguste Cézanne, a self-made man who had begun life as a laborer and a hatter and had gone on to become one of the most successful bankers in Aix-en-Provence. Paul Cézanne was relatively successful at his school, winning a prize for painting and passing, at the second attempt, his baccalaureate. He was never to forget the idyllic days of his youth when he and his two friends, Baptistin Baille and the future novelist Emile Zola, tramped the countryside around Aix, swimming, picnicking and writing poetry.

In 1861, after much encouragement from Zola and after a brief period studying law at the University of Aix, he followed his friend to Paris, to become an artist. He enrolled at the Académie Suisse, where he became acquainted with Monet and Pissarro. This was a difficult time for Cézanne, so difficult that, discouraged, he returned home to Aix to work at his father's bank. The urge to paint was overwhelming, however, and he returned to Paris in November 1862.

For the next seven years he moved between Paris and Aix, embracing the world of avant-garde painters and producing robustly painted pictures in the tradition of Rubens, Delacroix and Courbet. It was the example of Courbet, perhaps, that encouraged him to adopt the pose of the untutored provincial to protect himself from some of his more sophisticated associates.

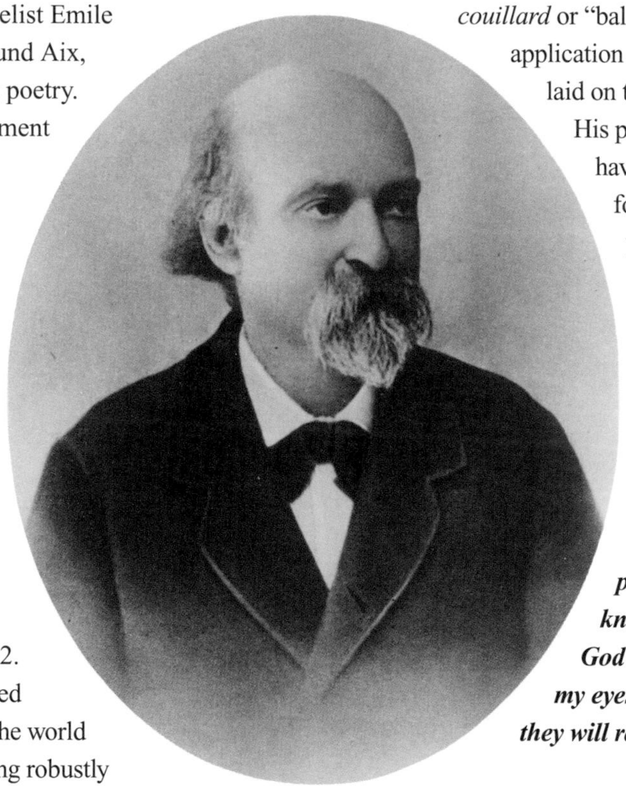

A contemporary photograph of Cézanne, which gives a much more conventional image of the volatile and difficult man than is found in his many painted self-portraits.

A passionate nonconformist

Cézanne's determination not to conform to social mores was matched by his provocative paintings that echoed his early encounters with the often dark and violent baroque paintings found in the churches and museums at Aix. The subject matter of his paintings not only responded to his own passionate nature but also to the subjects painted by those artists he most admired, the tradition that incorporated the sixteenth-century Venetians, Rubens, and the recently deceased (1863) Delacroix.

Images of rape and murder vie with scenes of seduction and excess. His attitude may be summed up by his own later and possibly disparaging description of his distinctive manner as *couillard* or "ballsy": an apt term for his vigorous application of thick tonal slabs of color often laid on to the canvas with a palette knife. His portraits and still lifes of this period have a monumental power that foreshadows the work of his future years. His powerful style may well have been influenced by Zola's contemporary art criticism:

> ***It is not the tree, the countenance, the scene offered to me in a picture that touches me; it is the man whom I find in the work, the powerful individual who has known how to create alongside God's world a personal world which my eyes will never forget and which they will recognize everywhere.***

Toward the end of the 1860s, his palette lightened and he began to paint a remarkable series of landscapes. His work was continually rejected from the Salon; only once, in 1882, did he have a work accepted. In order to avoid any possible involvement in the Franco-Prussian War, he retreated to L'Estaque, near Marseilles, where he painted a number of startling and dramatic landscapes. After a brief period in Paris, staying opposite the Halle aux Vins, he moved out to Pontoise in 1872 with Hortense Fiquet, his mistress and the

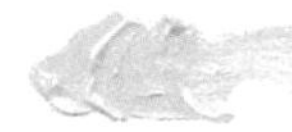

mother of his new son, Paul. Soon, he moved on to Auvers-sur-Oise, where he worked in the company of Pissarro, whose work and personality had a considerable effect on him.

His work became more collected and analytical, he brushed in creamy taches of paint, building up the image in a weave of thickly applied pigment that described the tones and simple structures of the landscape around his chosen home. As the decade wore on, his sense of color lightened and his paintings became more light-filled.

With Manet and Whistler, he had shown at the Salon des Refusés of 1863 and, in 1874, at the invitation of Pissarro, he took part in the first Impressionist exhibition. He was represented at the 1877 show by sixteen canvases. Throughout the decade he continued, with complete lack of success, to submit to the Salon, only in 1882 having one of his works accepted on charity. Affected by the adverse publicity, he decided to withdraw from the public arena.

Cézanne's difficult personality as much as his art made him an outsider. Even his father seemed less than supportive, cutting off his allowance, perhaps because of his relationship with Hortense Fiquet. He was supported by his friendships with Zola, with Dr. Paul Gachet (later to befriend van Gogh at Auvers-sur-Oise), Guillaumin, and Pissarro. In 1886, deeply hurt by the publication of the novel *L'Oeuvre*, in which he felt himself to have been wrongly portrayed as an artistic failure, Cézanne broke with Zola, his oldest friend, and never spoke to him again. In the same year he married Hortense and inherited a considerable fortune from his father, who died in October. Cézanne now had the freedom to paint and live to his own standards.

A growing reputation

Toward the end of the 1880s, Cézanne's reputation developed and he became an artist of interest among the Symbolist circle of writers and painters. In 1889 his *House of the Hanged Man* was squeezed into the Universal Exhibition and he was invited to exhibit with the Symbolist group, Les Vingt, in Brussels, which he did the following year. In November 1895 he sent approximately 150 of his works for an exhibition at Ambroise Vollard's gallery in Paris; two years later the dealer attempted to buy the entire contents of Cézanne's studio near Corbeil.

Soon after the death of his mother, Cézanne's family home, the Jas de Bouffan, which featured in a number of his paintings, was sold and Cézanne moved into the center of Aix. Now he began to paint the landscape to the east of the town, dominated by the profile of Mont Sainte-Victoire. In 1897, two works by Cézanne were shown at the Berlin National Gallery, but were banned by the Kaiser. Two years later, Vollard held a one-man show of his work and the reputation of the "Hermit of Aix" grew ever more significant among the young avant-garde in Paris.

Young artists like Emile Bernard and the Marseilles-born Charles Camoin made the pilgrimage to see him, as did the dealers Vollard and Gaston Bernheim-Jeune. His work was exhibited widely, including at the Salon des Indépendants in 1901, and given full recognition at the 1903 Salon d'Automne. He continued on his determined quest to realize his sensations before nature right up to his death, caused when he developed a chill after being caught in rain while painting. He died on October 22, 1906. In 1907, fifty-seven of his works were exhibited at the Salon d'Automne, where they became a catalyst for the work of young avant-garde artists such as Picasso, Braque, and Matisse.

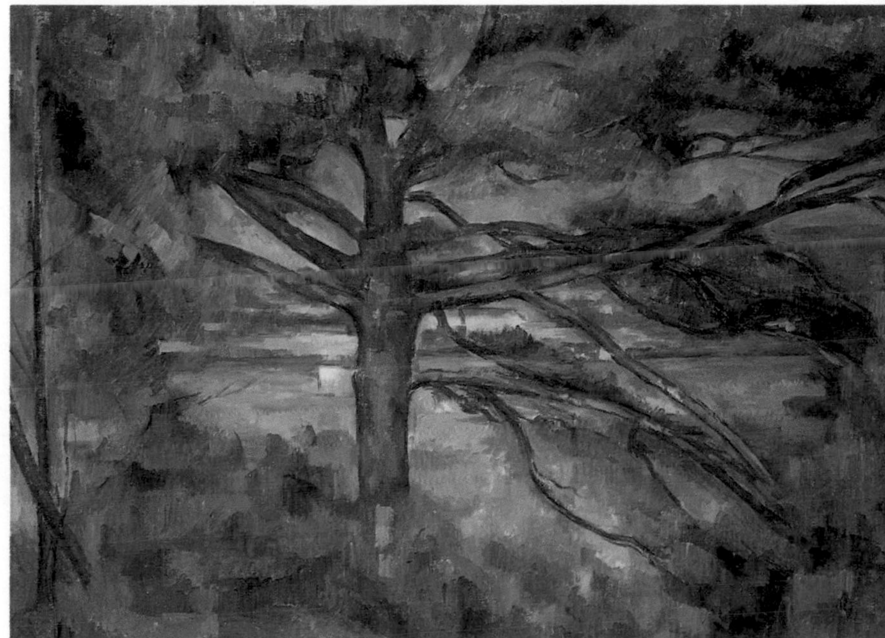

Cézanne,* The Great Pine, Red Earth, *1890. A good example of the artist's ability to find painterly equivalents for the strength, dynamism and variety of nature.

His lifetime's achievement, his total dedication to his art, and the sheer beauty of his paintings of whatever period, together with his determination "to progress" make his art unique. His images of landscapes, figure paintings, and still lifes at once reveal the anxieties and high delight of the act of seeing and painting. Never content with merely capturing the ephemerality of the passing scene, he wished to create from the variousness of experience what he called "something solid, like the art of the museums." In doing so, Paul Cézanne became one of the great models for twentieth-century artists of all persuasions.

The Temptation of Saint Anthony

c. 1874–75, oil on canvas, 47 x 56 cm (22½ x 22$\frac{1}{16}$ in), Musée d'Orsay, Paris, France

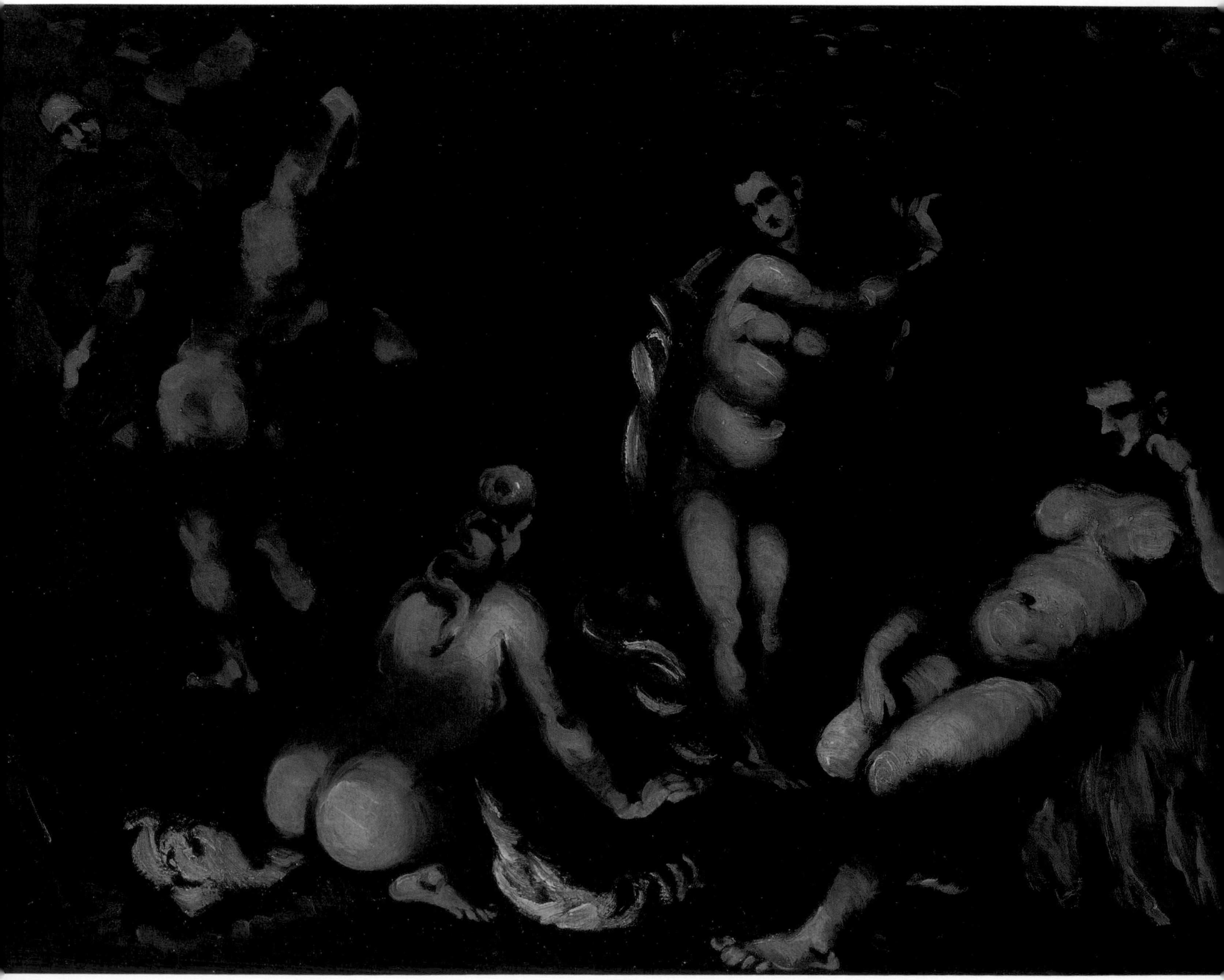

 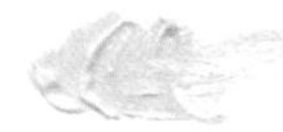

The great paintings of the Renaissance haunted artists of the nineteenth century, including the Impressionists. We have already seen how Manet at once extended and subverted the great traditions of painting represented by such masters as Raphael, Giorgione, and Titian, a concern that also affected Degas, Renoir, and even Pissarro. Perhaps only Monet, Sisley, Morisot and Cassatt remained untouched by this need to assess their work by its relationship to the great artists of the past.

Cézanne's burden

No-one felt the burden more keenly than Cézanne. In a questionnaire he completed as young man, he revealed that the literary or theatrical figure with whom he most identified was "Frenhoffer," an imaginary seventeenth-century painter invented by Balzac, and made the tragic hero of a short story entitled *The Unknown Masterpiece*. It was Cézanne's ambition to paint honestly, to break away from accepted conventions of representation, and yet to remain a part of the chain of great artists that Baudelaire called "*Les Phares*" – the beacons of past art. In Baudelaire's poem of that name, the last great representative of that tradition was Delacroix:

Delacroix, lac de sang, hanté des mauvais anges
Ombragé par un bois de sapins toujours vert,
Ou à, sous un ciel chagrin, des fanfares étranges
Passent, comme un soupir étouffé de Weber.

(Delacorix, lake of blood, haunted by bad angels,
Shaded by a forest of evergreen trees,
Where, under a glowering sky, strange fanfares,
Pass by like a smothered sigh by Weber.)

The poem's doom-laden imagery celebrates the musical and coloristic aspects of Delacroix's art that appealed to much in Cézanne. Cézanne had grown up with paintings of martyrdoms, which were constructed in the gloomy *tenebriste* baroque style of Caravaggio and such violent, dramatic, and erotically charged art remained very important to him throughout his life.

A man of strong feelings, Cézanne took time to distill that passion into his landscapes, still-life paintings, and later figurative works. Despite his passionate nature, Cézanne was a shy man, nervous in front of women and most of his figure painting was done from old life drawings or studies after the great masters.

Cézanne's temptation

The Temptation of Saint Anthony was a common subject for paintings in nineteenth-century art and was very much in vogue during the Second Empire. It fascinated Cézanne throughout his middle age, and he produced at least three canvases on the subject and numerous studies which, together with similar works, reflect to some extent his troubling and often violent fantasies concerning the female sex.

The painting is hardly a religious painting: the saint appears more like the reluctant hero–victim of a seduction scene in fancy dress. Its immediate model was the novel, *La Tentation de Sainte-Antoine* by Gustave Flaubert. Extracts from the novel first appeared in *L'Artiste* in 1856–67 and Cézanne's version, while not depicting any one scene in the narrative of the saint's ordeal, is forceful in terms of his renunciation of the dubious pleasures of the material world. Many artists and writers of the time were afraid that their artistic creativity would be sapped by sexual and marital commitment to the opposite sex.

The artist as saint

The painting suggests vividly the worldly temptations that assail a young man, the saint clearly stands for the artist's figure, who has to struggle to remain true to his vocation. The subject is an apt model for Cézanne's career, which traveled, over a prolonged period of time, away from such frankly licentious scenes to a calmer more meditative vision of reality as represented by his physical relationship with the visible world.

In Flaubert's notes for his novel is the following passage, quoted from Kitty Mrosovsky's 1980 introduction to the work, which could be applied to Cézanne's own journey.

Toward the end. He is too far, in an abstract land, having looked at everything, having no longer any consciousness of himself and being just a looking machine, a living contemplation.

The richly colored image would reappear, purged of its romantic and melodramatic overtones, in the many depictions of bathers that preoccupied Cézanne in his final years.

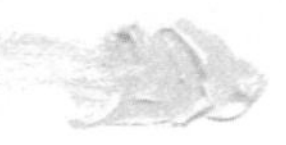

CHAPTER THREE

Themes and Variations

The vividness of individual experience is ever-present in Impressionist painting. Degas kept a series of private notebooks in which he jotted down his ideas for paintings, records of colors and effects he had witnessed, important addresses and lists and, of course, countless studies, sketches and caricatures. In one of his notebooks of the period 1877–83 may be found the following passage in which the artist set down current observations "... houses and monuments from below, close in; as one sees them in passing by on the street ..." Another note records different kinds of smoke: "... smoke from smokers, pipes, cigarettes, cigars, the smoke of locomotives, from high chimneys, factories, steamboats etc., the piling up of smoke under bridges, steam."

In this section we will visit, through the paintings of the Impressionists, the sights and sounds of the city they celebrated – Paris. Through the eyes of these artists we explore the public and private lives of those who lived there.

Although many of the Impressionist canvases of the city can be read as a critique of city life, Renoir's paintings are very much celebrations of the ease and leisure that the city offered. Renoir's brother, Edmond, told the art historian John Rewald how this canvas, *Le Pont Neuf*, came to be painted. Renoir stood at the second floor window of a café opposite the bridge, while his brother engaged the passers-by below in casual conversation in order that his brother would have time to sketch them into his work. The old and the new mingle together as the equestrian stature of Henri IV is all but lost among the detail that fills this high-colored and delightful image of modern life.

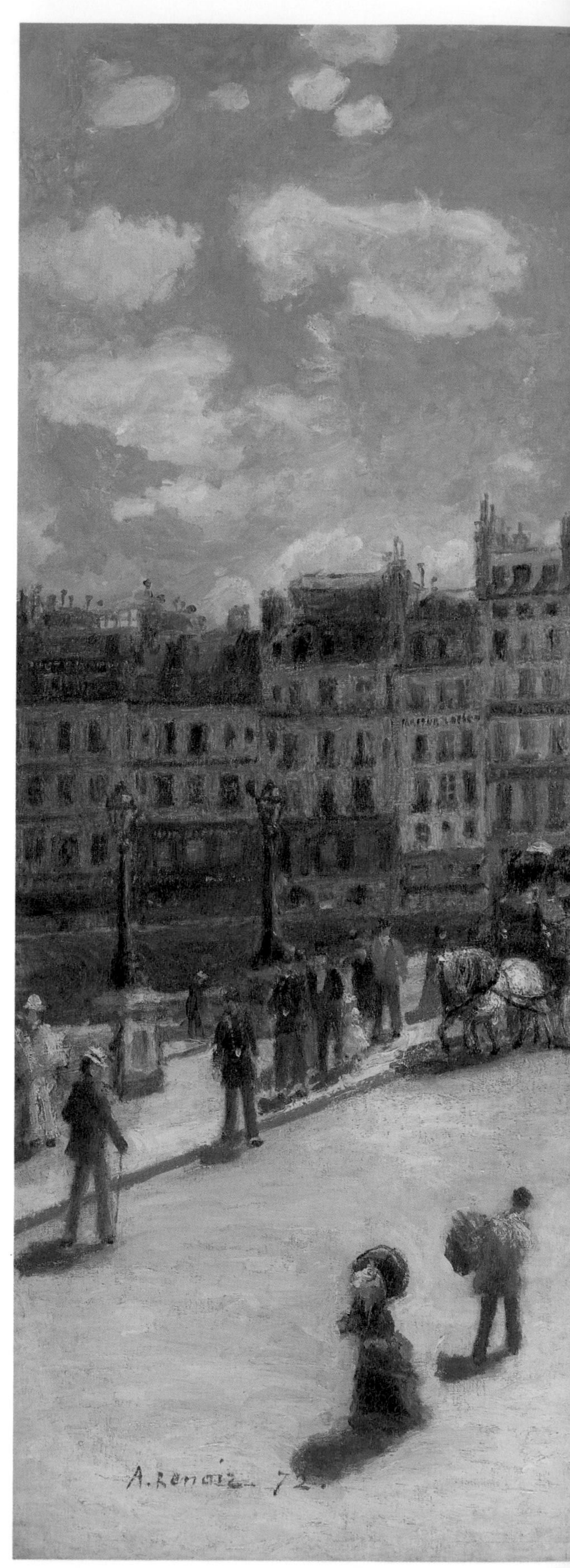

Pierre-Auguste Renoir,* The Pont Neuf, *1872. This brilliantly sun-filled scene perfectly captures the animation of humans and dogs enjoying their leisure on the oldest bridge in Paris.

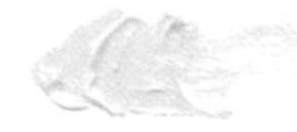

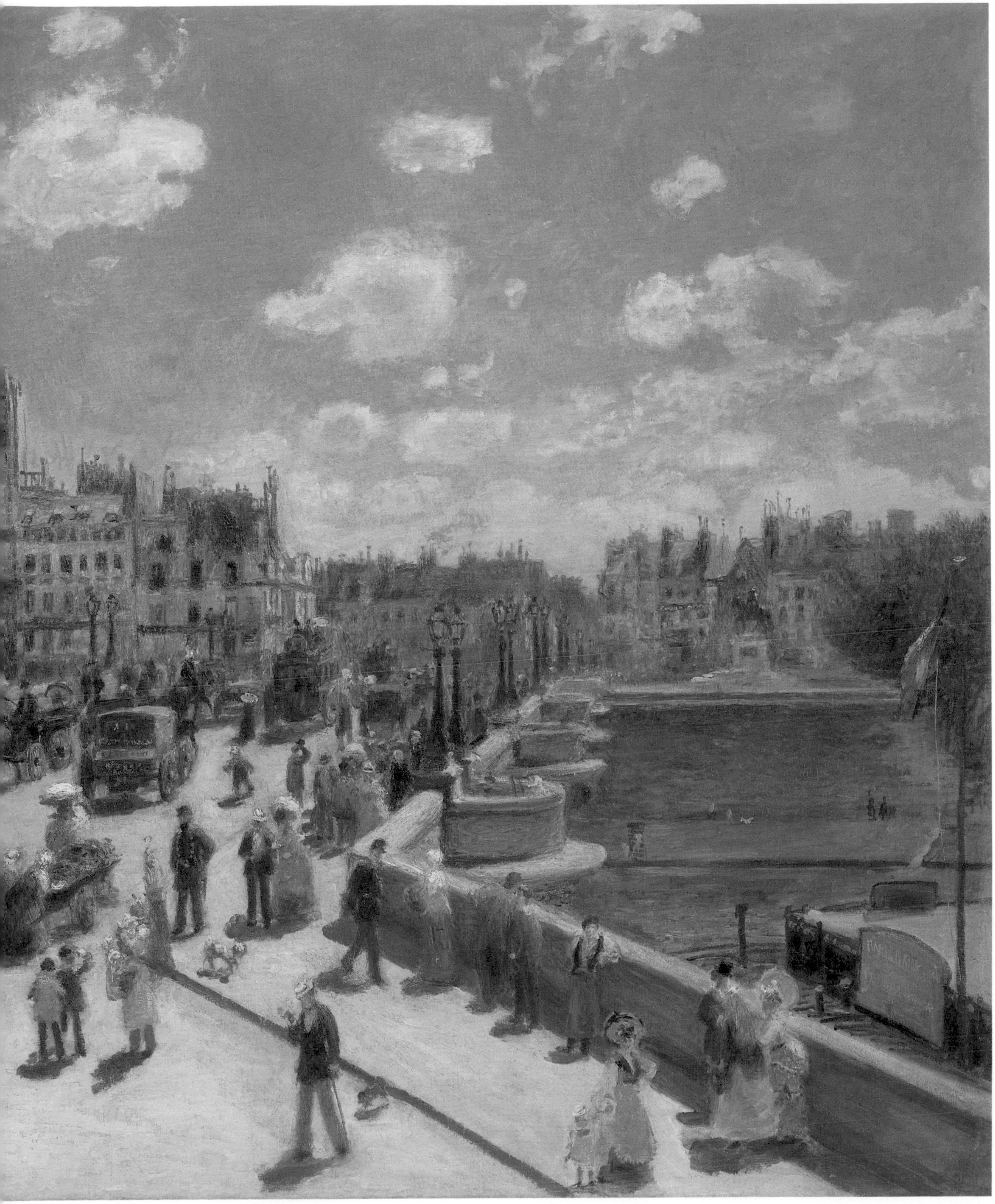

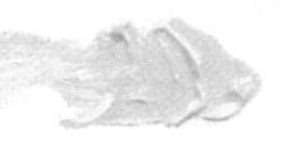

The Painting of Modern Paris

Although not undertaken as a consciously structured program of work, the paintings of Degas and Manet constitute a record of modern Paris. Excited by the novelty of living in a brand-new city, both artists nurtured an ambition, never fulfilled, to develop their work on a large scale suitable for public display in the new buildings of the capital. The evidence for this in Degas' art was his lifelong relationship with the great masters of the past and his constant desire to emulate their achievements: "It's been my lifelong dream to paint walls," he had once remarked, thinking, perhaps enviously, of the opportunities that artists such as Giotto, Masaccio and Michelangelo had enjoyed.

Degas,* Women in Front of a Café, Evening, *1877. Pastel over monotype. A group of prostitutes relax within the shelter of a café.

Frustrated plans for epic works

An incident in Manet's life reveals that, for a time at least, he too considered working on the epic scale that mural painting can offer. His dreams were frustrated and we can only imagine the extraordinary works that may have resulted had the artists of the Impressionist circle been awarded some of the major commissions that went to more academically inclined artists.

In 1879, Manet sent a letter to the President of the Seine Department and the President of the Municipal Council in which he set out his ideas for a program of paintings for the interior of the recently rebuilt Hôtel de Ville, one of the most important buildings in Paris, which had been burnt down during the Commune. Manet offered to produce,

> ***A series of painted compositions representing* the Belly of Paris, *... the various corporations would be shown in their appropriate settings, representing the public and commercial life of our times. I would show the Paris markets, railways, the river port, subterranean systems, parks and race courses.***

Unfortunately, his offer was refused, the artist telling his friend Antonin Proust that he had been treated by the officials in question "as if I were a dog about to lift its leg against a municipal wall."

Manet had intended to paint on the main ceiling of the building, "a gallery and, walking around it in appropriate groupings and poses, all those eminent citizens who have contributed, or are contributing to the grandeur and wealth of Paris."

Contemporary events as history

Many modern commentators have been struck by the fact that Manet's paintings are profoundly ambivalent toward the very culture that he apparently wished to commemorate. His submission to Paris's Municipal Council reveals how far Manet had moved from his earlier work with its calculated and barely disguised borrowings from past art. Now his art was much more concerned with using the manners and behavior of contemporary life in a more direct way. His idiosyncratic use of allegory, subversive or otherwise, is evident in his notion of representing the "wines of France, for example: Burgundy wine symbolized by a brunette, Bordeaux by a redhead, Champagne by a blonde." Although never to be presented on such epic scale as he had wished, Manet, like his friends, Tissot and Stevens, would later use images of fashionably dressed women as allegories of the four seasons.

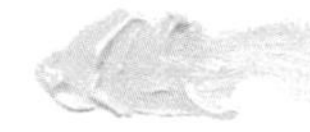

Manet's ambition to paint on a heroic scale was evident throughout his life. He had painted two major religious paintings in the mid-1860s, *The Dead Christ with Angels*, which was exhibited at the Salon of 1864, and *The Mocking of Christ,* which was accepted along with his notorious *Olympia* at the Salon of 1865. Such open acts of homage to the art of the past, subversive or otherwise, had become more muted by the 1870s, although paintings such as *The Execution of the Emperor Maximilian* (1867–68) and his *Sea Battle of the Alabama and the Kearsage* (1864), as well as his portraits of politicians, reveal his ambitions to interpret contemporary historical events on a major scale.

Baudelaire, who had been absent from Paris for most of the 1860s and who was to die at the age of 46 in 1867, had written to Manet in 1865, saying, "You are the first in the decrepitude of your art." The exact meaning of this statement is ambiguous and elusive. Baudelaire may have been suggesting that in an age without ideals and the qualities necessary to engender an epic art, the only intelligent response to such a situation would be to use painting as an ironic commentary on such a state of affairs. In this way, painting could, by allusion, critically represent an age characterized in Baudelaire's writings as one lacking moral certainties, one that had mistaken mechanical and technological progress for spiritual progress. It is in the light of such ideas that the work of the Impressionists was produced, creating an art that admirably conveys the surface pleasures and inner tensions that characterize urban life.

One of the versions of Manet's* Execution of Emperor Maximilian, *1867–68. This modern-day history painting, influenced by Goya, is a searing indictment of a humiliating and tragic moment for the French Imperial Family.

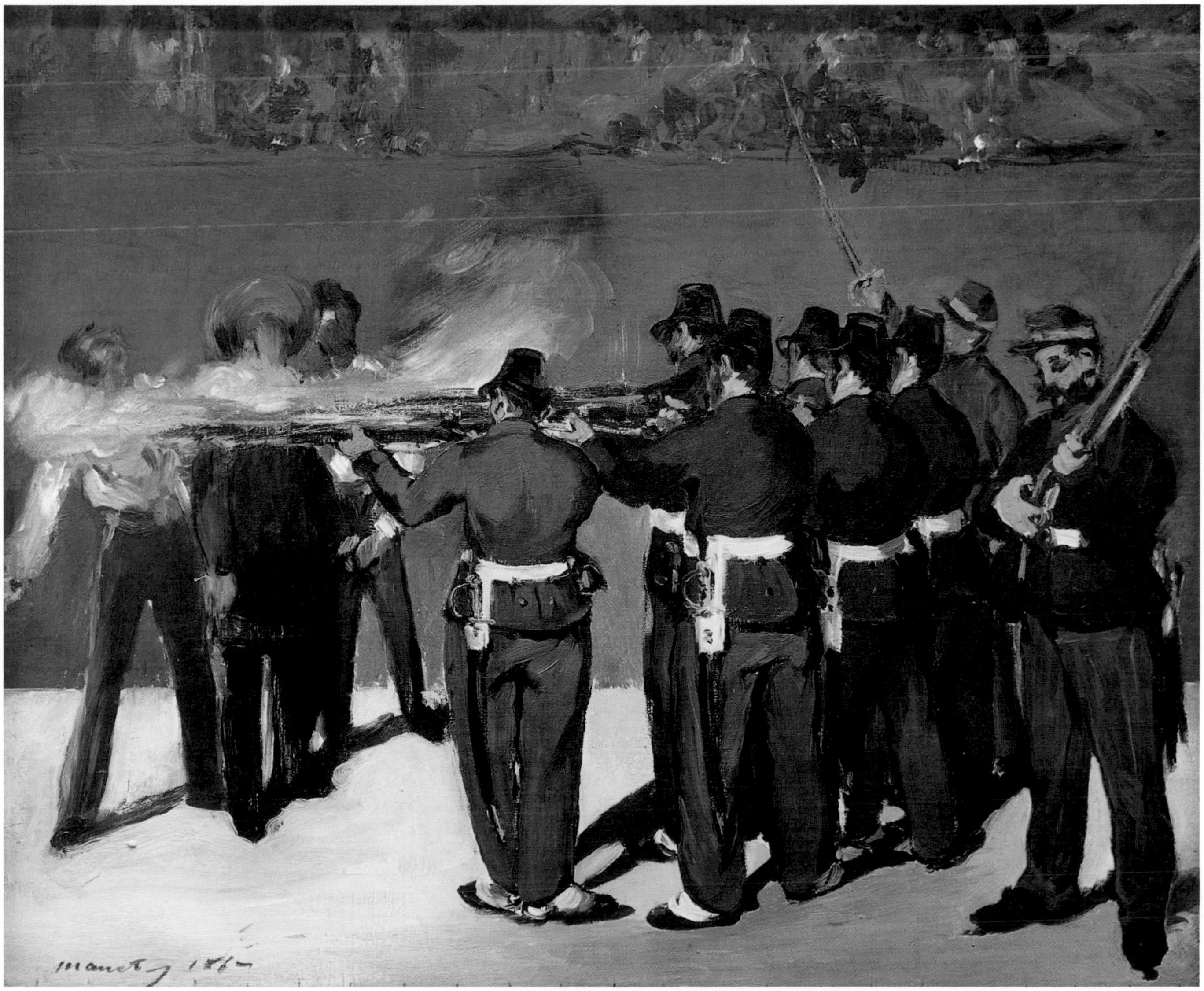

The City Street

Paris was a public theater. Outside the cafés on the Champs-Elysées, chairs were placed to allow the customers to view the crowd hustling past: Haussmann's Paris was, and still is, a wonderful place for watching people.

Well before the development of the "new" Paris, writers had noticed that the size and anonymity of the city, the huge increases of population and the breakdown of old, established ways of behaving had created a place that was mysterious and unknown. Town planners, lawmakers, writers, photographers and artists, all in their different ways, worked together toward making this sprawling, living entity into something comprehensible.

The Impressionists had many precedents to help them produce their images of the urban scene: the example of Manet cannot be overestimated, but illustrations in popular books, guide books and journals were also important. Photographs, Japanese prints and the caricatures of Daumier, Gavarni, Cham and others were also part of the rich diet of images that the Impressionists drew upon, consciously or otherwise. Such books and images created a body of knowledge on which to base an understanding of the city and its inhabitants.

The prime target for such images was the male viewer; the figure of the *flâneur*, who, prowling the streets like the detectives of Arsène Lupin or Edgar Allan Poe, could unravel the scattered clues that pointed to the truths that lay

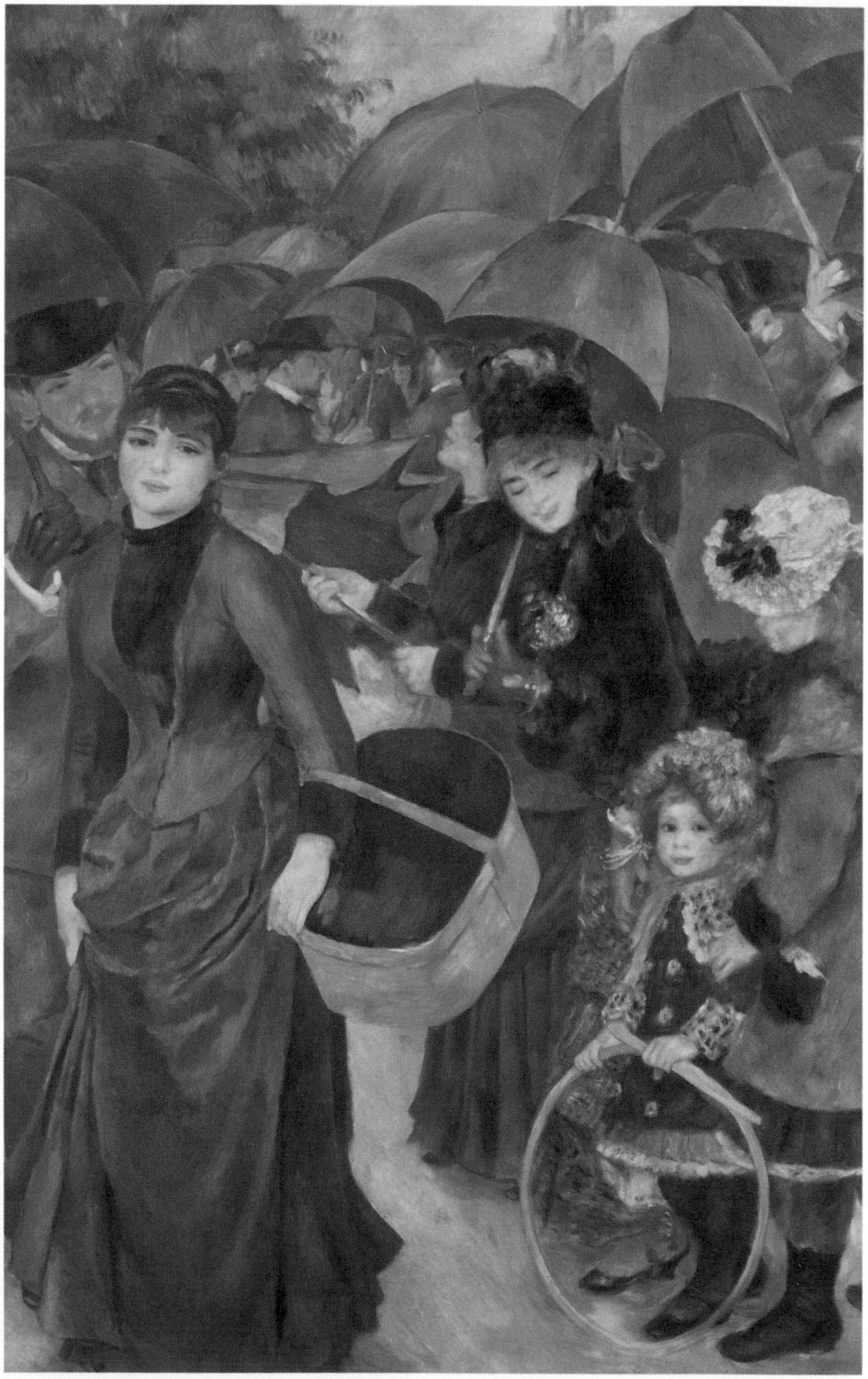

The Umbrellas, ***1881–85. Renoir's crowded, constructed cityscape.***

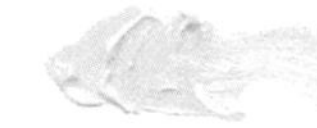

behind the superficial activity of the urban populace. In English and French novels of the period there is a sense of pride of ownership in the urban space, a truly democratic sense of sharing the city, whether it be with the high-class courtesan, the shop girl, the aristocrat or the self-made man. This quality of curiosity and empirical investigation of what was a new phenomenon was what fueled the Impressionists' painting of the city: the desire to find a novel way of giving shape to a novel experience.

Woman's adornment

> ***Everything that adorns woman, everything that serves to show off her beauty, is part of herself; and those artists who have made a particular study of this enigmatic being dote no less on all the details of the* mundis muliebris *than on woman herself … what poet, in sitting down to paint the pleasure caused by the sight of a beautiful woman, would venture to separate her from her costume?***

Baudelaire's insights, expounded at length in his essay *The Painter of Modern Life*, published in 1863, are visualized in paint in the work of the Impressionists. The theatricalization of Paris, the city as stage set where everyone plays their part, is their subject. For Renoir, the city, its streets, parks and ballrooms, are presented as opportunities to act and to engage in romantic badinage. As suggested by Baudelaire's text, Renoir has moved far from his reworkings of classical models, to present woman as the type known as "*La Parisienne*," not naked but dressed in the costume of her own times, moving confidently through the cityscape.

The composition of Renoir's painting *Place Clichy* (1880) is fluid and informal, the girl's head and bonnet that fills most of the canvas is boldly cropped to draw her closer to the viewer, almost intimately close, though she is as yet unaware of our gaze. Despite this, it is clear that she is being presented to a viewer and in Renoir's own time, and – a point probably still valid even today – that the imagined viewer is assumed to be male. Further, he would be the figure so well-described by the poet – the liberated man about town, the *boulevardier*, a man like Manet, free to make his way through the crowds and to enjoy all the city has to offer, including perhaps the young woman.

The *Parisienne* has been presented to us as an object of male desire, despite her modest dress. She is open-faced and preoccupied with her own business, but our closeness and her momentary hesitation – she is about to cross the busy street – offers us the chance to make her acquaintance. Beyond her, in soft-focus, the activity of the street continues and, as a supporting mechanism to the interpretation offered above, just above the young woman's head another shopgirl or milliner is about to be accosted by a well-dressed man, a projection of the imagined male viewer.

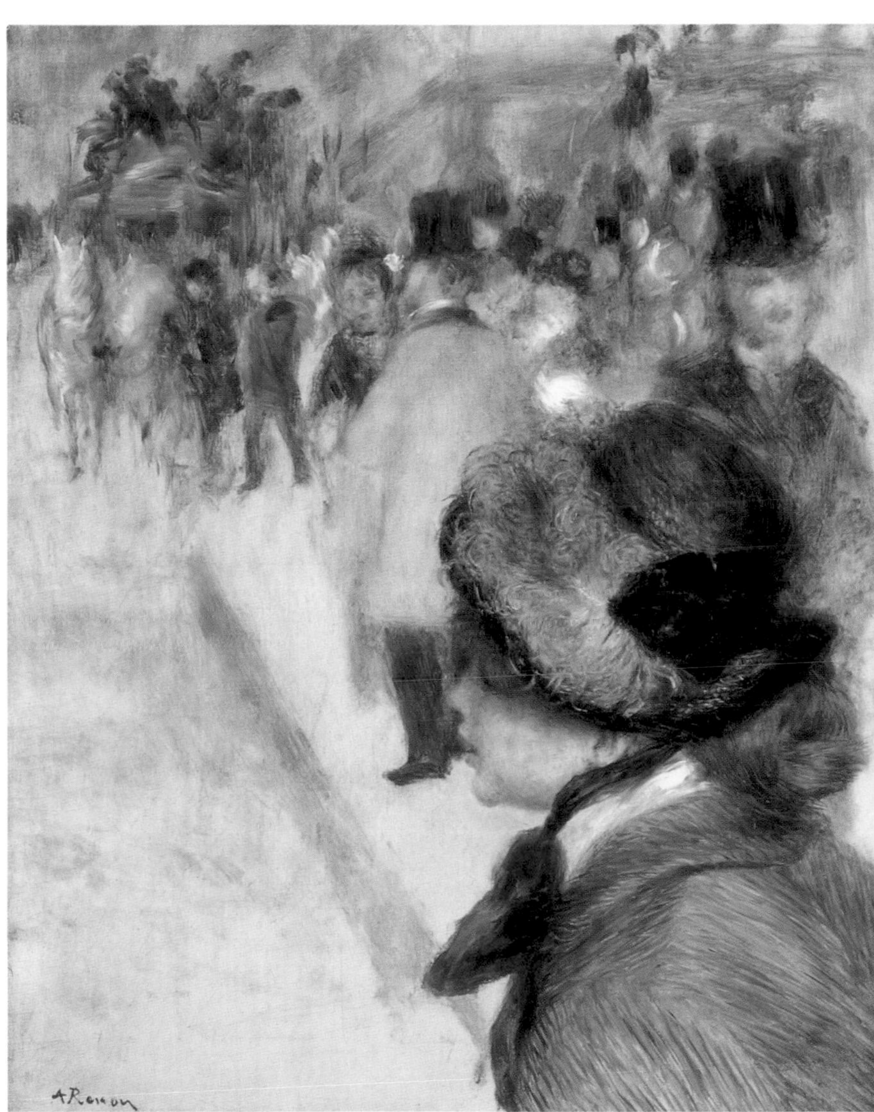

Renoir,* Place Clichy, *c.1880. Few artists have been able to suggest with such apparent ease and fluency the effect of a momentary experience, glimpsed for an instant and then lost forever.

In many ways, despite its delightful informality, the painting anticipates and acts as a foil for Manet's masterpiece of 1882, *A Bar at the Folies-Bergère*. In that painting, the vulnerability of the female sex in a "*Babylone Américaine,*" as the Goncourts termed modern Paris, is projected with an ambiguity and certain critical discernment that is completely absent in Renoir's painting.

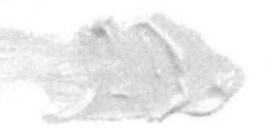

The World of Work

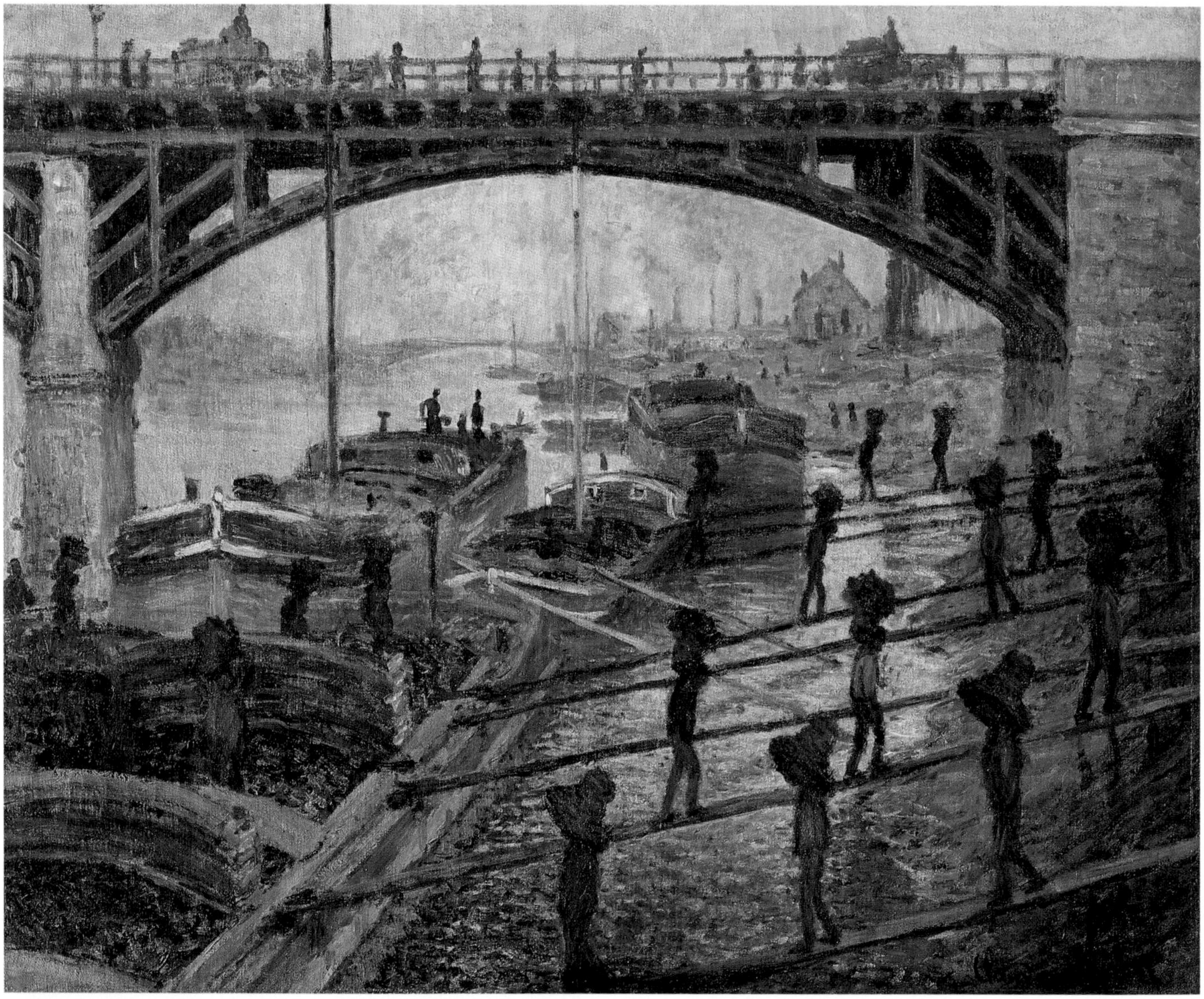

Claude Monet, **Unloading Coal,** *1875. A very different interpretation of Paris life from Renoir's upbeat images.*

Impressionism is so frequently associated with the world of leisure that it is surprising to find just how many images of work exist in Impressionist art. In viewing their works, one is seduced into forgetting that one person's leisure is the result of many other people's labor. Manet's *A Bar at the Folies-Bergère* is just one such image, and could be seen as the most intriguing and enigmatic of the many studies the Impressionists constructed of the intimate relationship between these two essential apects of modern urban life.

Images of work appear most openly in the work of Degas, Caillebotte and Pissarro. Although Pissarro's images of work tend to be rural rather than urban, there are exceptions; during 1872–73, he painted four pictures that center upon the prosaic appearance of a factory near Pontoise, although any sense of the place as a site of physical labor is absent.

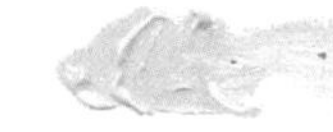

Unusual in Monet's work is the painting *Unloading Coal* of 1875, which deals directly with the spectacle of urban labor. As so often with the Impressionists, it is the visual spectacle the scene offers that has attracted the artist, rather than any analysis of the social realities it may represent. Its composition is simple and powerful, informed by Monet's awareness of Japanese prints. The arduous labor of hauling coal from the laden barges on to the quayside has been seen through the screen of the artist's aesthetic sensibilities; tones, flickering brushwork, repeated forms set against the diagonals of the planks, all minimize the harsh realities Monet is surveying. Or do they?

The bent silhouettes of the *déschargeurs* trudge back and forth from the long line of barges that stretches in an uneven diagonal from the lower edge of the composition far into the murky distance. Each of the burdened men is painted as an elegant shape, each identical to his neighbor, suggesting the reduction of the individual to a cog in some gigantic, almost medieval, scene of numbing physical labor.

T. J. Clark has identified the scene as being the Seine at Asnières, situated between Argenteuil, the site of leisure and pleasure, and the city of Paris. A few years later, the area would be the focus of Seurat's first major painting, *Bathers at Asnières* , depicting the inhabitants of the working class area just outside Paris relaxing on the banks of the river. The same writer also draws attention to the fact that Monet referred to *Unloading Coal* as *une note à part,* which suggests that in the artist's mind, at least, this painting was indeed a one-off, a unique and not to be repeated foray into the harsh realities of existence.

The use of repetition, seen again in a different context, in Caillebotte's *Floor Scrapers* of 1875, is a feature of Impressionist art, one possibly influenced by the multiple-pose photographic *cartes de visites* of the period.

Caillebotte's painting, together with a variant on the same subject, was exhibited at the Second Impressionist show of 1876. Both works directly transposed into contemporary terms the academic painting style of his master, Léon Bonnat. Instead of the martyred saints and freed prisoners familiar in the dramatically lit paintings of that artist, Caillebotte has used the same technical and theatrical means to create a memorable image of craftsmen at work. The low viewpoint, the artificially enhanced perspective and the filigree pattern of the balcony seen against the pale sky afford the viewer a glimpse of the rooftops of Paris. They also remind us that we are situated in the artist's home and secure these semi-naked workmen into their working environment.

Degas' fascination with work

Of all those artists connected with Impressionism, it is Degas who reveals the most consistent and even obsessive fascination with the world of work. His depictions of musicians, jockeys, laundresses, dancers and his many images of bather–prostitute figures reveal a profound concern with the mechanics of work and leisure. These are only the obvious professionals: all too often the labor of the artists' models of the period is overlooked as being a profession indispensable to the production of art.

Degas' images of work are extremely ambiguous and things are rarely as they seem at first glance. His countless depictions of laundresses, for example, while they do frequently reveal the effort and skill necessary for the job, are fundamentally a result of his obsession with particular visual effects and his interest in finding motifs that might typify "modern Paris." They are not deliberately structured investigations into the back-breaking realities of any particular profession and the below-subsistence wages that were the lot of many.

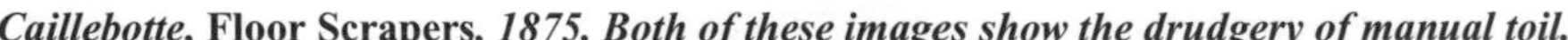

Caillebotte, **Floor Scrapers,** *1875. Both of these images show the drudgery of manual toil.*

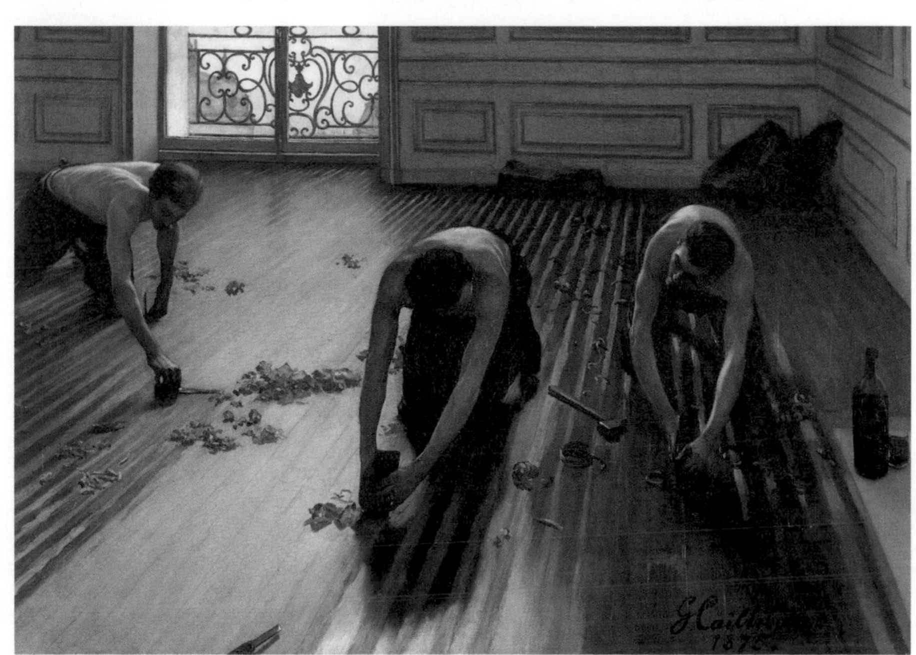

Pierre-Auguste Renoir:
"Why shouldn't art be pretty?"

The hedonistic world conjured up by Renoir's delightful images has led to his work being overvalued financially and under-valued critically. Renoir has been the victim of his own myth, though recent attempts to revise our understanding of his achievement have not succeeded in demeaning his achievement. Rather, it has allowed his work to become the focus of debate as much as celebration, and he has emerged the greater artist because of it.

Pierre-Auguste Renoir,* Boating on the Seine, *1879-80. The flecks of pure color are the epitome of Impressionist painting. Complementary colors orange/yellow and blue add a shimmering realism to this scene of two girls dressed in white rowing on the river.

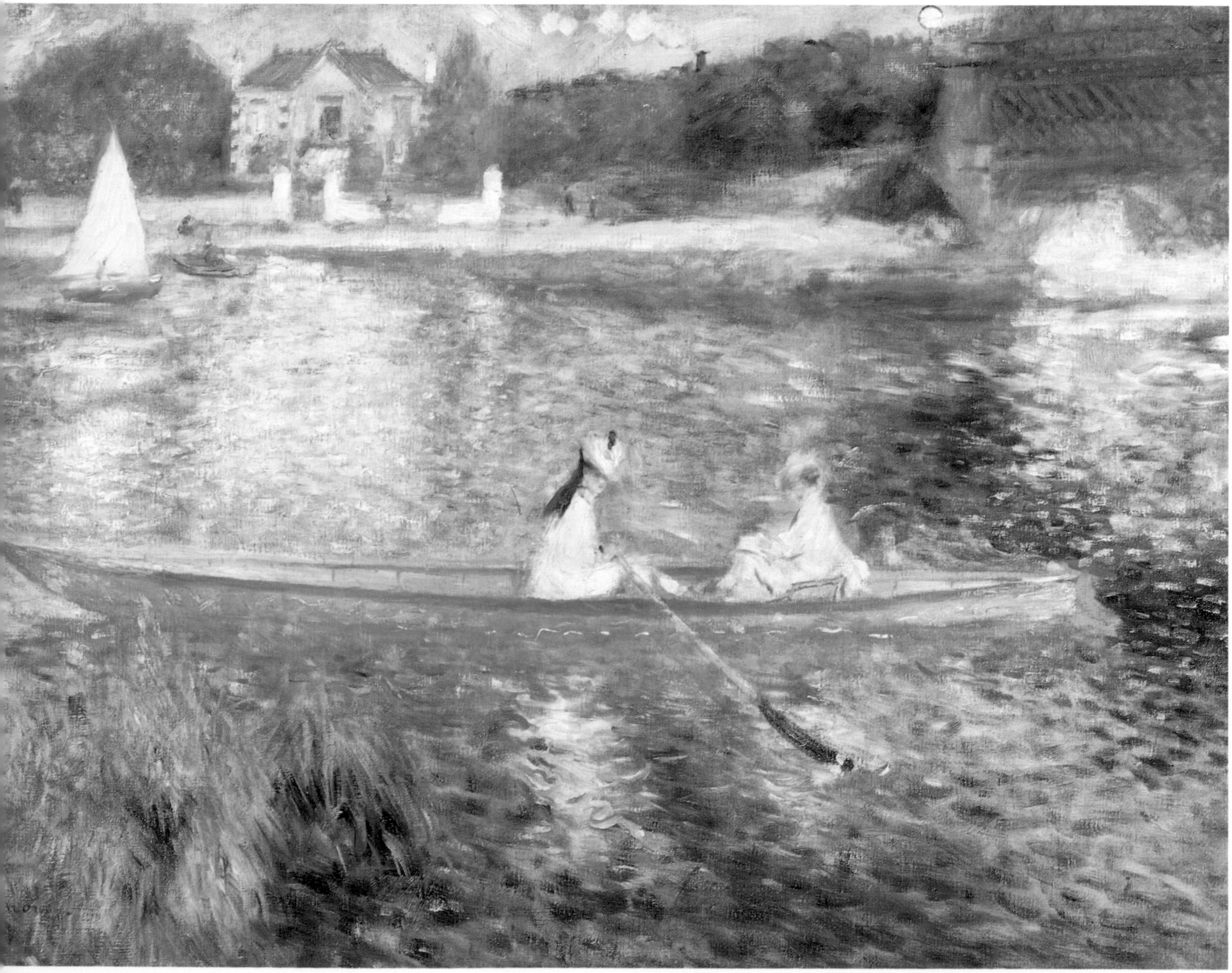

Renoir must bear some of the blame for his bad press, not least because delightful art is always difficult to evaluate critically and because it has the illusory air of being made without any of the struggle that we associate with great art.

Pierre-Auguste Renoir (1841–1919) was born in Limoges, but brought up in Paris. He had none of the security that family wealth brings and, in spite of his modesty, he was adept at finding wealthy friends and patrons to support him throughout his life. At the age of fifteen he was apprenticed to a firm of porcelain painters. Nicknamed "M. Rubens" by his colleagues, Renoir stayed there for four years. At the age of twenty-one he passed the entrance exams for the Ecole des Beaux-Arts, entering Gleyre's studio in 1861, where he met Monet, Bazille and Sisley. With his friends from Gleyre's studio, Renoir was soon engaged on an ambitious campaign of figure painting in the forest of Fontainebleau. It was there that he encountered the painter Diaz, who advised him to lighten his palette. Renoir's art reveals a more conciliatory attitude to officially condoned art than that of his friends, his continuing dialogue with the art practices of the past a feature that reemerged as one of the major elements of his *oeuvre*. He took no part in the Salon des Refusés of 1863 and, in spite of the intervention of Daubigny, he had a major work rejected by the Salon of 1866.

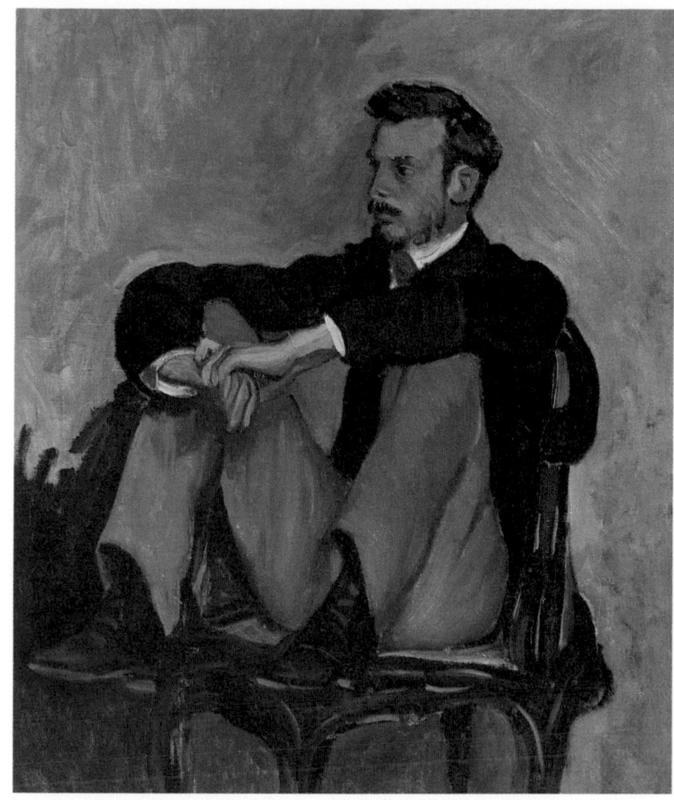

Frédéric Bazille,* Portrait of Renoir, *1867. While Renoir's pose is typical of Impressionist portraiture, its informality is not.

Renoir painted in many styles in this early period, but his shared visits to La Grenouillère with Monet in the late 1860s saw the development of a painting style that would become characterized as one of the major elements of Impressionism. After the Franco-Prussian War, Renoir was rejected from the next two Salons and participated in the Salon des Refusés of 1873. He took an active part in the first group exhibition of independent artists in 1874, where his work was well received by those critics who deigned to review the exhibition. This may have encouraged him to take a leading part in the disastrous Hôtel Drouot auction of 1875 in which his work fetched in the lowest prices. He exhibited at the Impressionist exhibitions of 1876 and 1877, but in 1878 he submitted to the Salon once more and was accepted. He took no part in the 1879 group exhibition, his work growing steadily more popular with collectors. At the 1879 Salon, his portrait, *Madame Charpentier and Her Children*, was critically acclaimed, and his reputation soared.

In 1883 Durand-Ruel held an exhibition of seventy of his works and in 1884 Renoir even stopped submitting to the Salon. Throughout this period, Renoir was seeking to return to painting based upon the solid foundation of drawing and surety of technique. He traveled to North Africa, following the example of his idol Delacroix, and then to Italy where he could study the work of the great masters of the Renaissance and classical antiquity. In the early 1880s he worked first with Cézanne and then with Monet in the south of France, but on his return to Paris he suffered such intense despair that he destroyed a number of his canvases. As he later told Vollard, he "had reached the end of Impressionism, and had reached the conclusion that he could neither paint or draw." Slowly he began to forge an art based upon his domestic scene transformed by the museum-oriented ambitions he held so dear. The culmination of this prolonged and painful investigation was his major figure painting, *Bathers* (1884–87), which revealed his new linear style and provoked unease and even hostility in many.

By now, Renoir had a family, his first son, Pierre, being born in 1885. He had kept his attachment and eventual marriage (in 1890) to his model Aline Charigot a secret from his friends until well into that decade: possibly her humble origins, she had been a laundress, doing work for both Renoir and Monet when he met her in 1879, were an embarrassment to him. As he grew older, suffering from arthritis, Renoir's subject matter remained rooted in celebrations of the female nude, the luscious landscape of the south of France near Cagnes, where he moved in 1903, still lifes and paintings of his children. His work became more improvisatory, exuding radiance, color and light. But the female figure in its full amplitude remained his favorite motif.

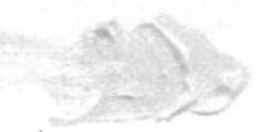

La Loge

1874, oil on canvas, 80 x 63.5cm (32 x 24½ in), Courtauld Institute Galleries, London, England

Paris in the second half of the nineteenth century was the theater capital of the world: a perfect place to savor, celebrate and question what Baudelaire called the "pageant of modern life." The theater and its audience were favorite subjects of the Impressionists and they found the image of the *loge*, or theater box, particularly fascinating.

The theaters that attracted the painters were the ones patronized by the middle-class. The sumptuous richness of theatrical decor, the dresses, the evening clothes, the coiffure and jewelry and all the other fashionable embellishments necessary for a successful night out made the subject a natural one for a middle-class audience to enjoy. For the artist, all these elements, illuminated by the brilliant artificial light of the theater, created their own challenge.

A theater box was, and still is, a place where one expects and is expected to be on display. Just as those occupying this privileged space are consciously and artfully displaying themselves to the rest of the audience, so the subject offers a chance for the artist to display his or her skills in an equally conscious and flamboyant manner. There are many other reasons why the subject might attract an artist: for instance, the architectural features of the theater box itself form a marvelous framing device, whether looking into the enclosed space of the interior, or looking out toward the open space of the audience and stage.

Allied to the notion of display is the idea of the gaze. The theater box is a place for looking, the viewer of the picture, and those inside the picture are all engaged in the action of either seeing or being seen. Some of the images, and especially Renoir's *La Loge*, play a flirtatious game well within the areas of social acceptability. In others, including those by Morisot and particularly Cassatt, the role taken by the women depicted in their paintings is more problematic.

Renoir's *La Loge* is the most striking indictment of the notion that the Impressionists banished black from their palette. Here, black is used not as a means to create dark tones, but as a color in its own right. It is a magnificent juxtaposition of white, black and blue-black passages of paint that weave the voluptuous figure of the woman and her partner, the artist's brother, Edmond Renoir, into a single unit. The woman was a professional model called Nini "*Guele-de-Raie*" or fish-face. Like so many of Renoir's paintings, this one is a technical tour-de-force, an immensely complex mix of intuitive painterly decisions forming an image brimming over with the vitality of life.

This, the first of a number of paintings of the same subject, is built up in a series of feathery brushstrokes of thin, translucent paint, licked across the surface and then overlaid with glazes and semi-glazes to achieve the final effect. The rhythmical passages of black create a pattern that leads the viewer's eyes inevitably to the woman's face, which looks out as enigmatically as a latter-day Mona Lisa. She controls our gaze, her partner's face is obscured by the opera glasses with which he scrutinizes not the stage but the occupants in the cheaper seats high up in the auditorium. His concern for his own visual pleasure allows us to indulge ours, and his partner accepts our regard, without committing herself to any course of action.

As was Renoir's custom, he has used different techniques in different parts of the painting, Nini's face being more finished than the rest of the composition. The painting is executed on a warm white ground, which is apparent in various parts of the canvas, as in the area above the glove on her right hand. In other areas, the paint is laid on more thickly to describe her corsage and opera glasses, which are modeled with a wet-on-wet technique – fresh paint dragged across a surface of paint already laid down but not yet dry. This allows the colors to intermingle and leave a dynamic trace where the brush has disturbed the pigment. In order to gain a sense of shadow and solidity, Renoir has used cobalt blue, sometimes diluted, as in the structure of the face, and sometimes mixed directly with black, as in the gloves and the the model's dress.

This painting was one of the highlights of the first Impressionist show, where it was well received, but not sold. It was exhibited again in London but once again it did not find a buyer. Eventually, desperate for money, Renoir sold it to a dealer, Père Martin, for 425 francs. Later, in 1899, Durand-Ruel bought it back for 7,500 francs and it was finally sold to Samuel Courtauld so that it now hangs alongside Manet's *A Bar at the Folies-Bergère* in the Courtauld Institute Galleries in London.

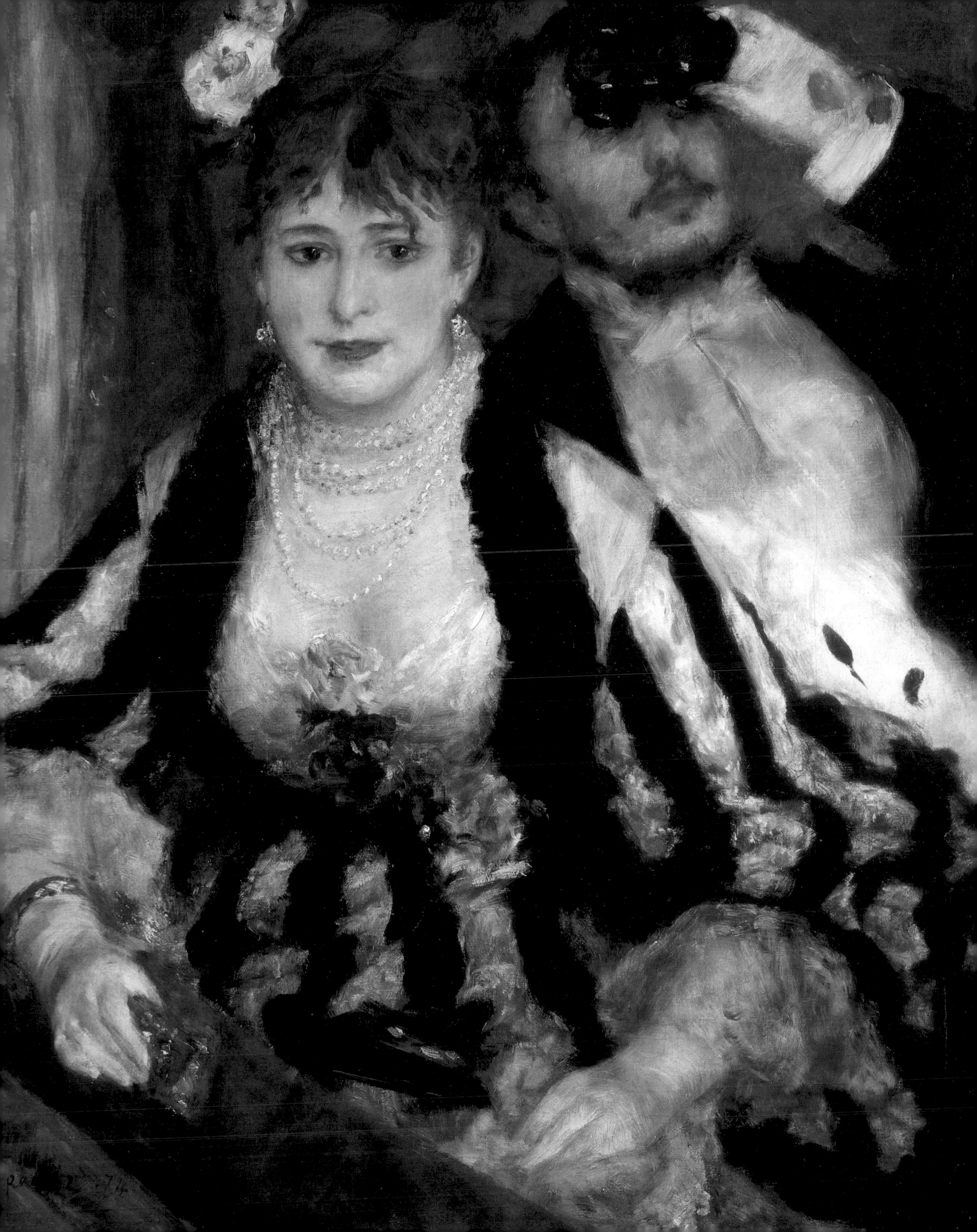

Concert at the Café des Ambassadeurs

c. 1875–77, pastel over monotype, 37 x 27 cm (14½ x 10⅝ in), Musée des Beaux-Arts, Lyons, France

The Café des Ambassadeurs was a glamorous establishment attracting a well-heeled international clientele. Situated on the Champs Elysées in a classical revival building, it had an outdoor performance area framed by a fluted proscenium arch. The café-concert was a particularly Parisian phenomenon and one used by commentators to illustrate the degree to which that "frivolous" nation, France, had lost its essential moral values. English writers, in particular, were keen to differentiate between the essentially home-oriented and thereby more responsible Englishman and the publicly oriented and correspondingly irresponsible Frenchman.

Café-concerts ranged from the most basic of establishments to the most opulent. Degas, like others of his class, enjoyed the vulgarity of the performances at them. In 1872 he noted the "idiotic songs ... and other stupid absurdities" that were sung by the personalities who were "stars" in the modern sense of the word. Ian Dunlop's biography of Degas quotes this passage from *Paris by Sunlight and Gaslight*, written by an American, in 1870.

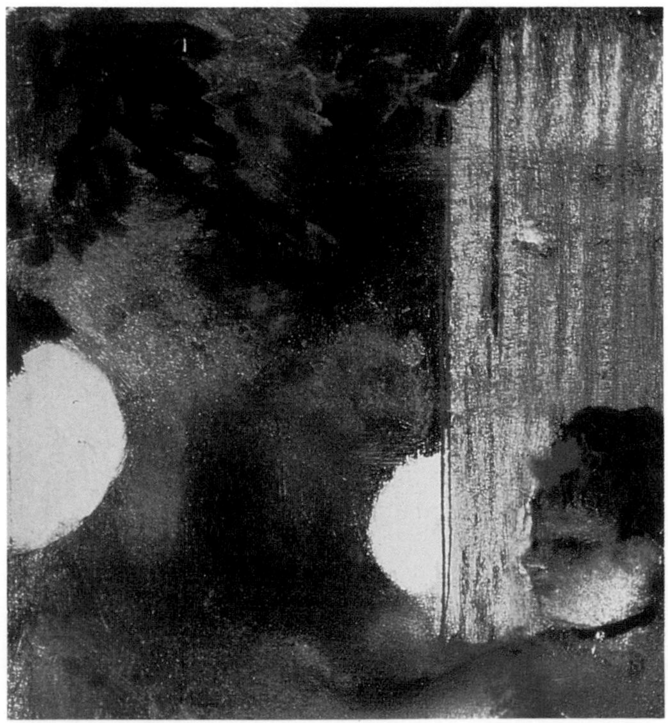

Joris-Karl Huysmans made the point somewhat pungently in his description of the Ambassadeurs as "the only place in Paris which smells deliciously of both the powder of bought caresses and the weariness of corruption."

There were countless café-concerts in the capital, catering to a wide variety of social types. Here could be found a casual mingling of the sexes, all decked out in their finery and enjoying the spectacle of entertainers seen from below and artificially lit by gas globes, barracking or cajoling their audience. The subject was ideal for painters like Degas and Manet, for it allowed them to produce works of a quintessentially modern aspect. Degas' pastel, *Concert at the Café des Ambassadeurs*, is a case in point. Its vitality and presence belie the complex means by which it was made: from 1872, Degas made frequent visits to the concerts held at the venue where he could make rapid sketches and commit to memory the gestures and idiosyncrasies that made the performers unique. Degas adored women; as Richard Kendall has pointed out, images of the female sex account for approximately three-quarters of his output. He was also intrigued by professional activities of all kinds, especially those that included repetition of gesture and involved skill in delivery. His favored subject matter – laundresses, jockeys, dancers and performers – all shared these characteristics. Degas, himself so preoccupied by professional practices, appreciated the skill and effect of a job well done. He said of Theresa, who features in this print, "She opens her rather large mouth and out comes one of the roughest yet most spiritually tender voices in existence."

Images of the café-concert may be found in a variety of media, including paintings, lithographs, and monotypes. This image is a monotype, an image drawn into the wet ink using a pointed implement, rags or fingers to remove a greater or lesser amount of ink from the surface of the plate; the plate is then passed through a press, producing one or two unique proofs. It was often Degas' practice, as is evident here, to work over the image with rich swaths of pastel; the dark tones of the ink giving the luminous tones of the pastel an added richness and depth. Much of the vividness of the image comes from the fact that it is the viewer and not the artist who has been left to supply the performer's outstretched hand.

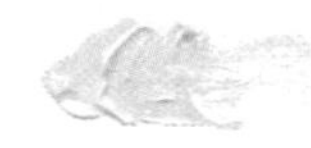

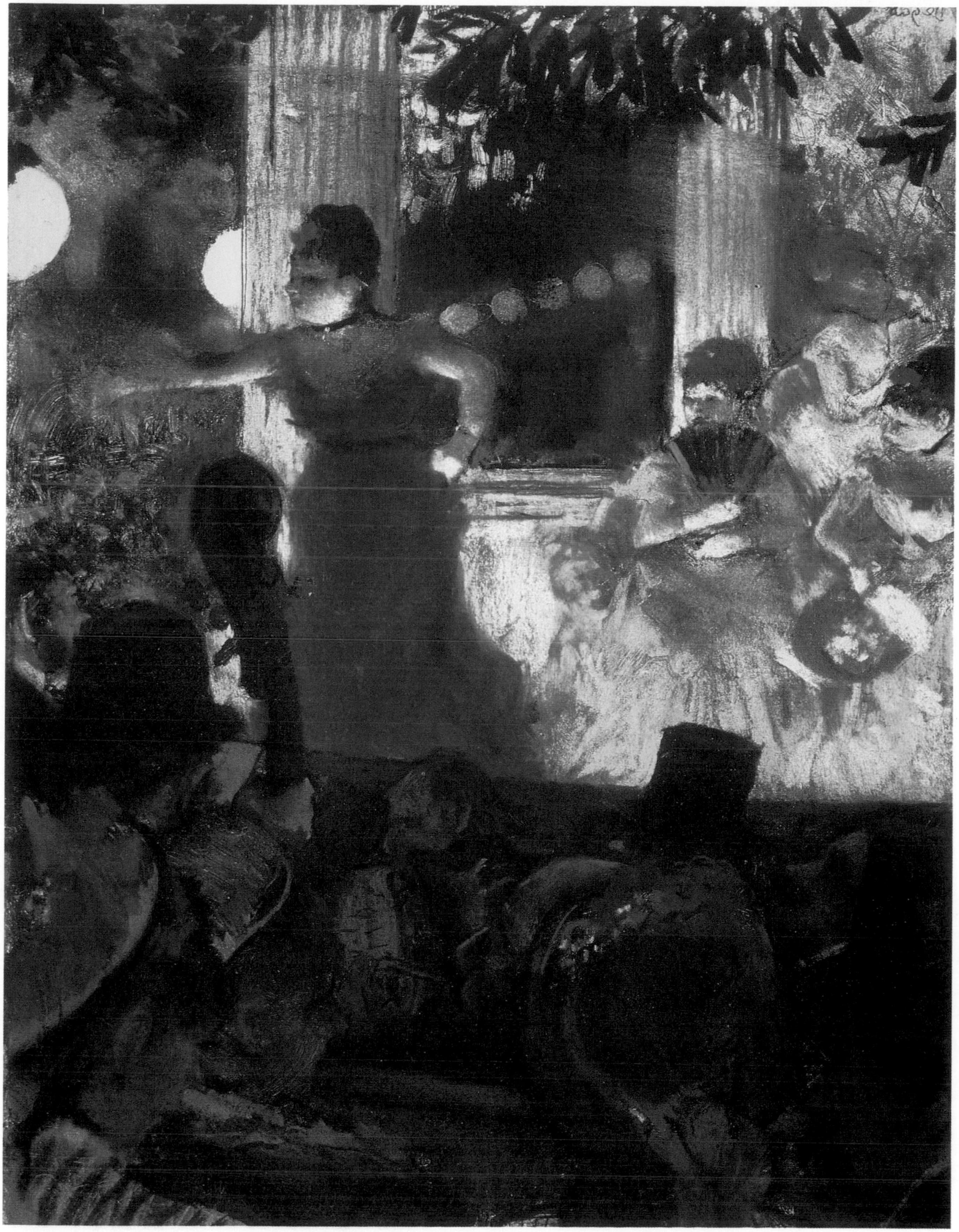

A Bar at the Folies-Bergère

1881–82, oil on canvas, 96 x 130 cm (38 ½ x 52 in), Courtauld Institute Galleries, London, England

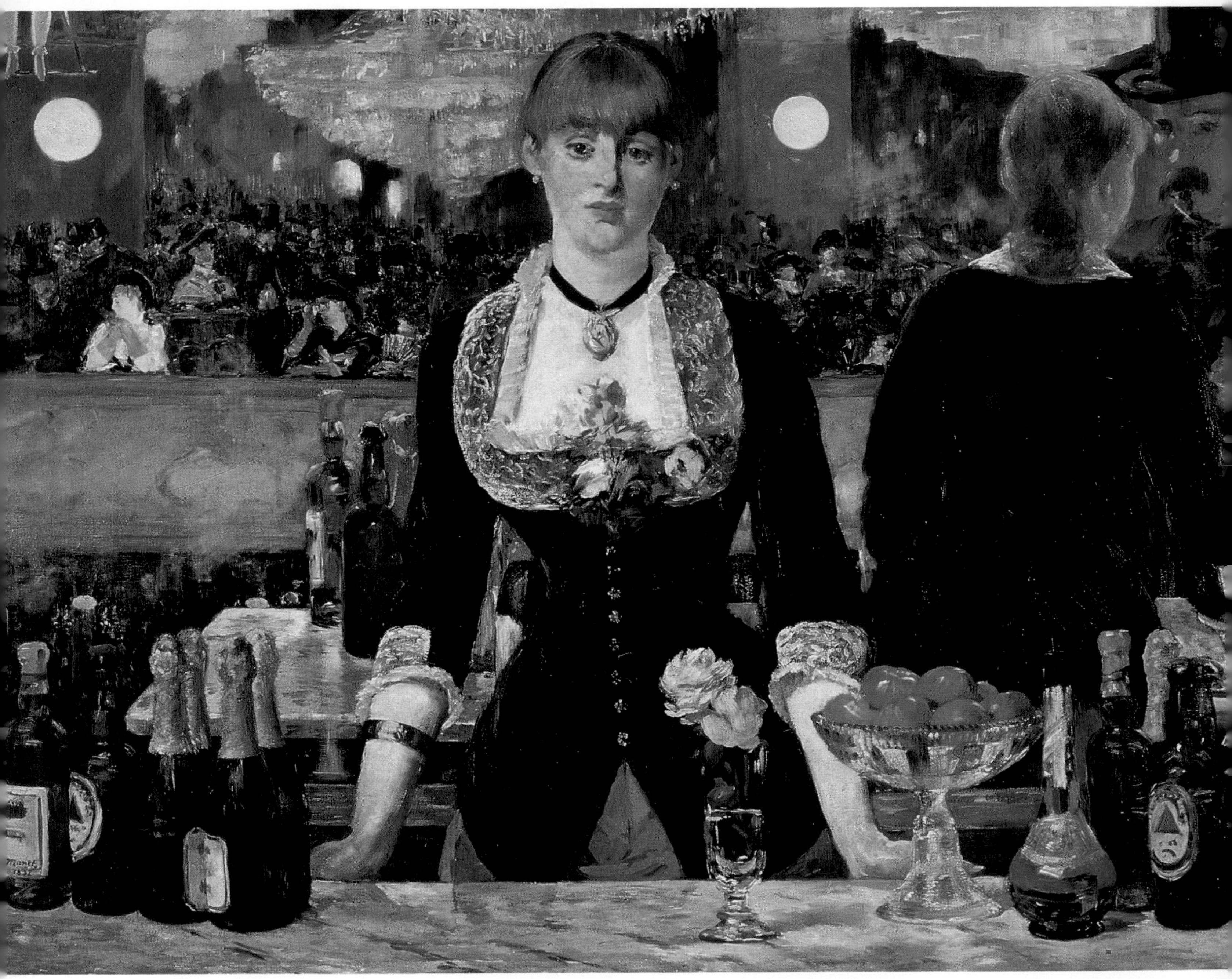

Café life features heavily in any "history of Impressionism." Cafés had always been regarded by the establishment with suspicion; they were places where people could gather informally, to relax, gossip, read newspapers and journals and also to discuss and debate the issues of the day. In the eyes of any government, such places, being unpoliced, could be seen as real or potential hotbeds of political unrest. The depiction of such places in the work of

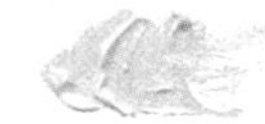

the avant-garde, whether writers or artists, could only further suspicion that they were places that reflected the instability of a society that was trying hard to represent itself as stable and ordered. It has been pointed out by Paul van den Abeel and Juliet Wilson-Bareau that Manet's drawing *Au Café* was published in lithographic form in a subversive journal as part of an article that clearly marked out such institutions as centers for political discussions. The names of many of the establishments frequented by the painters are almost as well-known as the artists themselves, because they feature in many of their most famous paintings. Courbet's favourite drinking spots have already been mentioned. Manet used to frequent the fashionable Tortoni's and the Café de Bade on the Boulevard des Italiens, where the literary clique had included Baudelaire and Duranty in the early to mid-1860s.

Manet later switched his allegiance to the Café Guerbois near the Place de Clichy, where he socialized with Zola, Duranty and the future Impressionists. He considered the café the "only resource" during the siege of Paris. This was the setting for many of the encounters and discussions that were such an integral part of Impressionism. It was here that Cézanne greeted Manet in such a deliberately provocative manner that, some think, it helped confirm the older artist's antipathy toward exhibitions with the group. Such events may also have decided the fastidious Manet to move on with Degas to the more salubrious Café de Nouvelle-Athènes in the Place Pigalle, which became their favored meeting place during the 1870s. There were many other establishments they visited, including the Ambassadeurs, the Moulin de la Galette, the Folies-Bergère and the Brasserie de Reichshoffen. Each attracted a different clientele and each had their moments of popularity.

Cafés were male preserves and, with certain exceptions, were out-of-bounds to middle-class women, except for those of a certain class and profession. Prostitutes were not meant to enter cafés in the 1860s and 1870s, though, in reality, they were frequently found in such establishments. Above all, cafés were a place to observe the world passing by past their windows and terraces. The living signs and emblems of a city were described by Augustus Sala in 1878–79, in his travelogue, *Paris Herself Again*,

> ***The daily and nightly crowds on the boulevards are as great as ever… the open-air concerts at the Champs-Elysées and the Orangerie of the Tuileries, the Hippodrome, the dancing saloons and Alcazars, the al-fresco cafés and brasseries, are continuously thronged … Paris to me is what it has been any time these forty years, a perpetual and kaleidoscopic fair.***

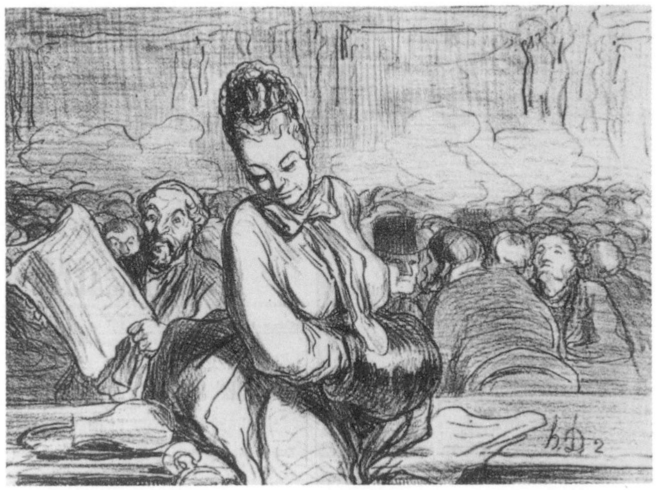

Honoré Daumier,* The Muse of the Tavern, *lithograph, 1864. Manet's debt to this homage of a barmaid is manifested in his work.

Such public spectacle had been depicted by artists such as Daumier and Gavarni in the popular press of the day and these images, together with similar subjects found in Japanese *Ukiyo-e* prints, based on scenes from the transitory world of courtesans, the theater and the arts, suggested novel and informal models of representation that the Impressionists could develop in their own work. As we have seen, traditional models taken from high art could also be adapted with positive and occasionally perturbing results. Whether sketched on the spot or in the studio, the subject of the café or bar interior allowed artists to represent their chosen urban types lost in reverie or animated in social interaction, exploring novel codes of conduct and displaying informal gestures and actions.

These works are obviously locked into the social mores of their times. A comparatively innocent-looking picture such as Manet's famous *A Bar at the Folies-Bergère*, painted in 1882, is a case in point. Since the early 1850s, imported German beer had become popular in Paris, and fashionable brasseries were opened to capitalize on this. Instead of the traditional male waiters, the drinks were served by barmaids, many of whom supplemented their income with prostitution. This gives the male customer, visible in the mirror, an ambiguous role. Like Degas, Manet has a vision so precise that it is easy to empathize with his model's world-weariness. She was a real waitress, Suzon, who agreed to pose for the painting behind a purpose-built bar in Manet's studio. The composition is vivid and complex, inspired by Daumier's powerful lithographs and possibly by Renaissance depictions of the Virgin Mary. In such images, the mother of Jesus is often set behind a marble entablature, protected from the impurities of the world; Manet ironically uses the same compositional device to very different effect.

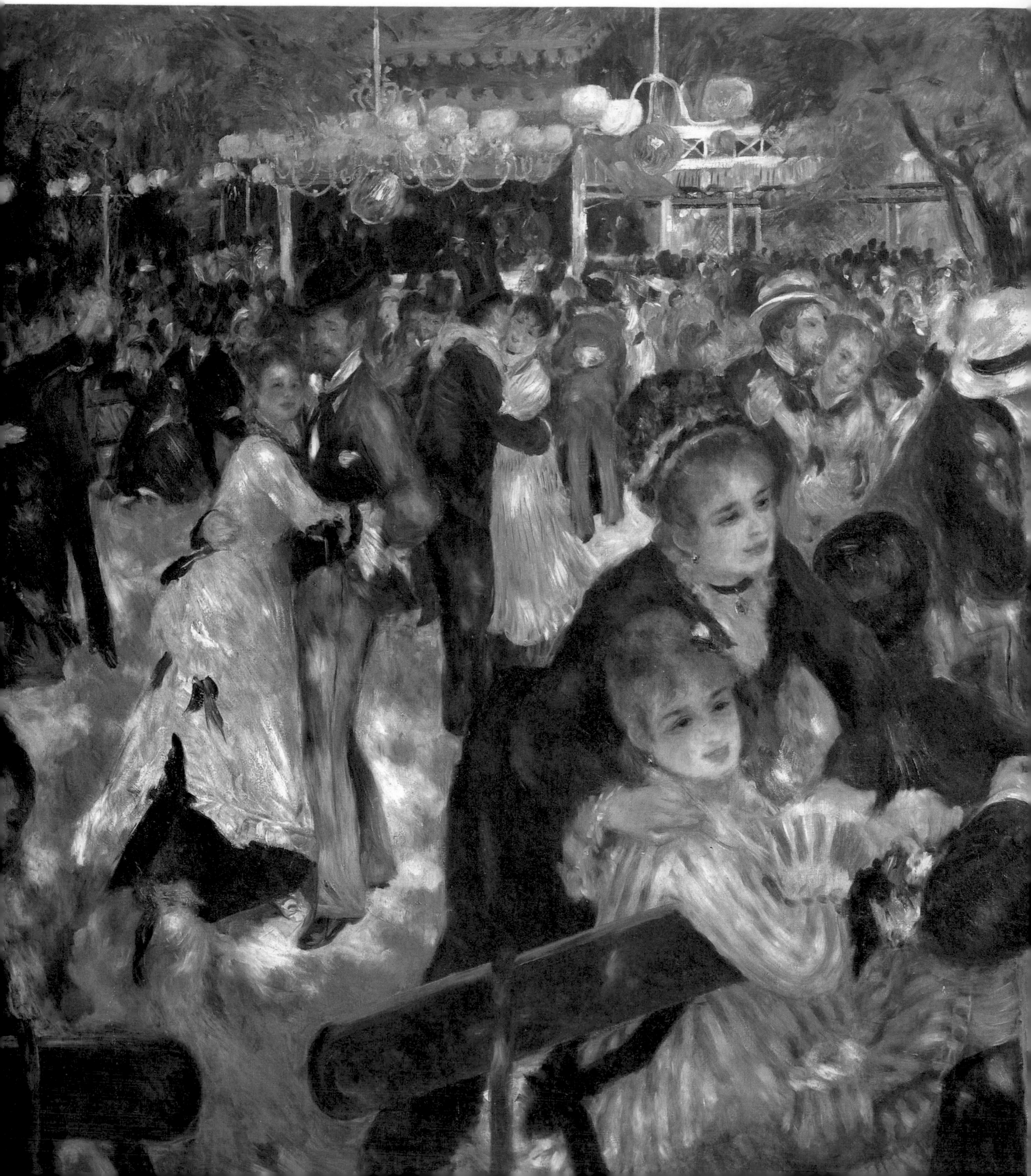

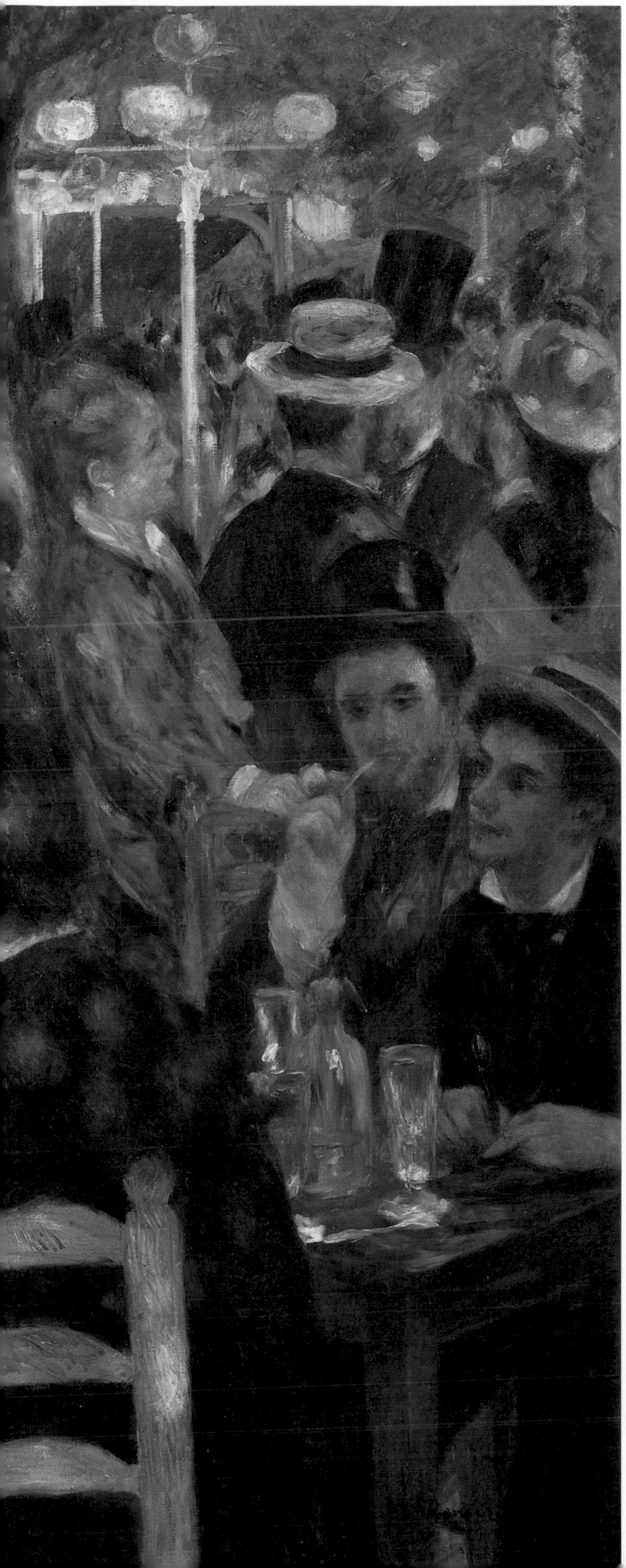

The Moulin de la Galette

1876, oil on canvas, 131 x 175 cm (51½ x 69in), Musée d'Orsay, Paris, France

In 1876 Renoir moved to 12 Rue Cortot in Montmartre in order to be close to the famous dance hall, the Moulin de la Galette. He had chosen this site as the setting for an ambitious painting, a reprise of his experiments with figure painting in the open air. It was the more acceptable, Sunday afternoon face of the dance hall that Renoir chose to depict in *The Moulin de la Galette.* The painting includes many of Renoir's friends, including the painters Pierre Lamy, Norbert Goeneutte, Frédéric Cordey, and Henri Gervex, Lestringuez, an occultist, and Georges Rivière. It was Rivière who recorded Renoir telling him that "... after that painting, he profoundly changed his handling, his palette became richer, and, he said, he knew better than ever before how to compose his pictures." The mood is one of gaiety and informality; the figures are lit by the fall of afternoon sunlight through the acacia trees casting pools of dappled light and shade across their bodies. These alternating rhythms create a pattern that is counterpointed by the spiraling composition that leads the viewer past the people gathered around the table, one of whom is the young poet Rimbaud, through the group under the tree and then shifting direction, across to the left into the swirling movement of the dancers themselves. The surface of the canvas is enlivened by a medley of warm and cool colors set off by small touches of rich color that appear and reappear at intervals across the composition, creating visual rhythms that suggest the music and movement of the dance hall.

The alternating lights and shadows of the picture and the contrast between the figures of the foreground and those seated in the distance create a wonderful sense of depth. Each couple suggests a different moment of the dance, which again suggests the movement of the dancers within the enclosed space of the dance floor. The brilliance, the ease and fluency of composition, apparently casual yet carefully considered, almost convince one of the truth of Renoir's claim that the painting was painted entirely in the open air. It was exhibited at the 1877 Impressionist exhibition; it is a demonstration of Renoir's skill and his ability to preserve the spontaneity of sketches made out of doors in what is essentially "*un grand machine*" of Impressionism.

Miss Lala at the Cirque Fernando

1879, oil on canvas, 117 x 76 cm (46¾ x 30½ in), National Gallery, London, England

After painting portraits seen from above, I am now going to paint some seen from below.
– Edgar Degas

La Cirque Fernando was Paris's first established circus. It was founded in 1877, and under its later name of La Cirque Medrano became known to Seurat, Toulouse-Lautrec, Bonnard and Picasso. The circus, although such a popular subject for Post-Impressionist painters, did not exert the same power over the Impressionists. Only Renoir and Degas made it the subject of a number of their compositions; in fact, only three Degas images of circus performers survive, although they include *Miss Lala*, one of his most effective and innovative compositions. It is a sign of Degas' voracious hunger for novelty that he chose this as the subject of one of his most carefully considered oil paintings. Degas shared his fascination with such performers with Edmond de Goncourt, whose novel based on circus life, *The Zemganno Brothers*, explored the relationship between performers and their art in a society that viewed circus performers as outsiders.

Acrobats and circus entertainers were figures of a profound and disturbing ambiguity, for they represented all that was not of the bourgeois order: often foreign or exotic, they were free to display their bodies and to dress and act in a manner foreign to that of their audience. As in Edmond de Goncourt's *The Zemganno Brothers*, they could also be presented as the living embodiment of a classical ideal, a model of physical perfection that many social commentators felt at the time to be under threat, the physical decline of French manhood being a *bête noir* of the mid-to-late nineteenth century.

The figure of Miss Lala typifies these often unstated concerns. She appeared at the circus in 1879 and Degas made numerous studies of her in pencil, pastel and oil; he also made punctilious analyses of the cast-iron architectural details of the circus itself. The coloration of this painting is arbitrary: one of his studies for the painting shows Degas experimenting with completely different colors to describe the interior. Degas has presented the scene to the viewer as if seen through binoculars; the audience and all reference to the lower area of the circus are abandoned in order to heighten the impact of this magnificent figure hovering in space above us. Miss Lala was a mulatto acrobat who specialized in feats of strength, endurance and daring. She was known also as *La Femme Canon*, but Degas has chosen not to show her being shot from a canon; rather, she is in the very act of being hauled to the ceiling of the circus by a leather thong firmly gripped between her teeth. Her suspended body, clad in a glamorous pink costume edged with golden tassels, combines the grace and poise of a ballerina with the unmistakable strength and power of the acrobat.

As Degas had said, he wanted to paint portraits "seen from below," and in saying this he was drawing attention to the consideration he showed in finding new and unusual viewpoints for his subjects. The vertical composition is quite startling, with the figure of Miss Lala situated high in the top left-hand quarter of the composition; her soft form is set against the cast-iron supports that so cunningly echo the line of her body and outstretched arms. The supporting rope extends from top to bottom of the canvas, subtly set off-center to enhance further the vertiginous effect of the composition as a whole. The critic and novelist Huysmans saw this painting at the 1879 Impressionist Exhibition, and later remarked that "in order to give the exact sensation of the eye following Miss Lola (as she was mistakenly referred to in the exhibition catalogue) climbing to the very top of the Cirque Fernando, Degas dared to make the circus roof lean wholly to one side."

The painting continues Degas' concern with depicting people in their professional environment, fully occupied with their work. In doing so, he has once again found a modern-day equivalent for the subjects that would have been the business of the artists of the past. To modern eyes, at least, the arcs of the circus roof may suggest the wings that help this latter-day angel make her ascent, not toward the glory of God, but for the benefit of an earth-bound crowd.

Interestingly, Degas enjoyed a *jeux d'esprit* in the painting; matching the bravura of Miss Lala's performance, he incorporated his signature following the architectural perspective of the interior.

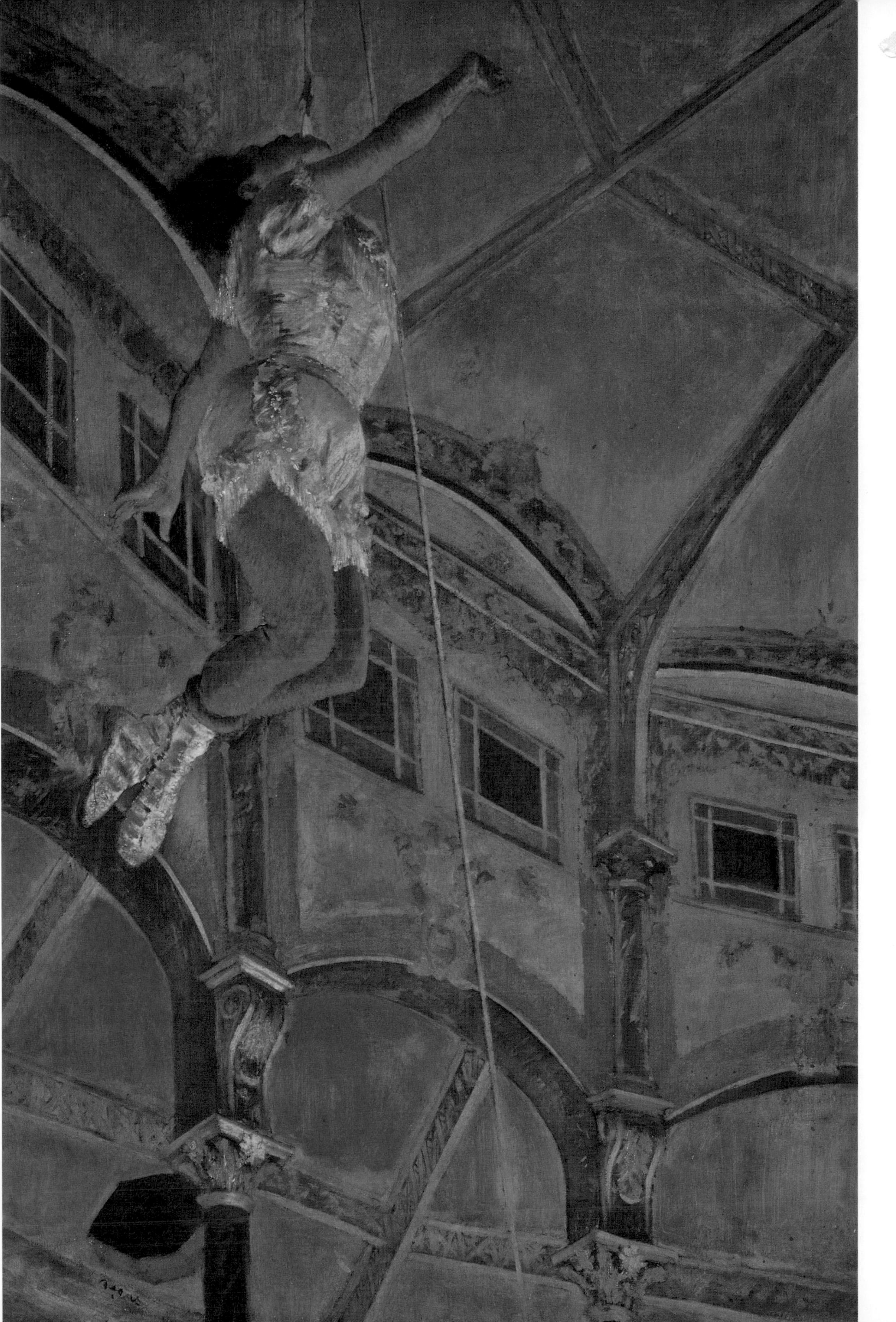

Theater and Ballet

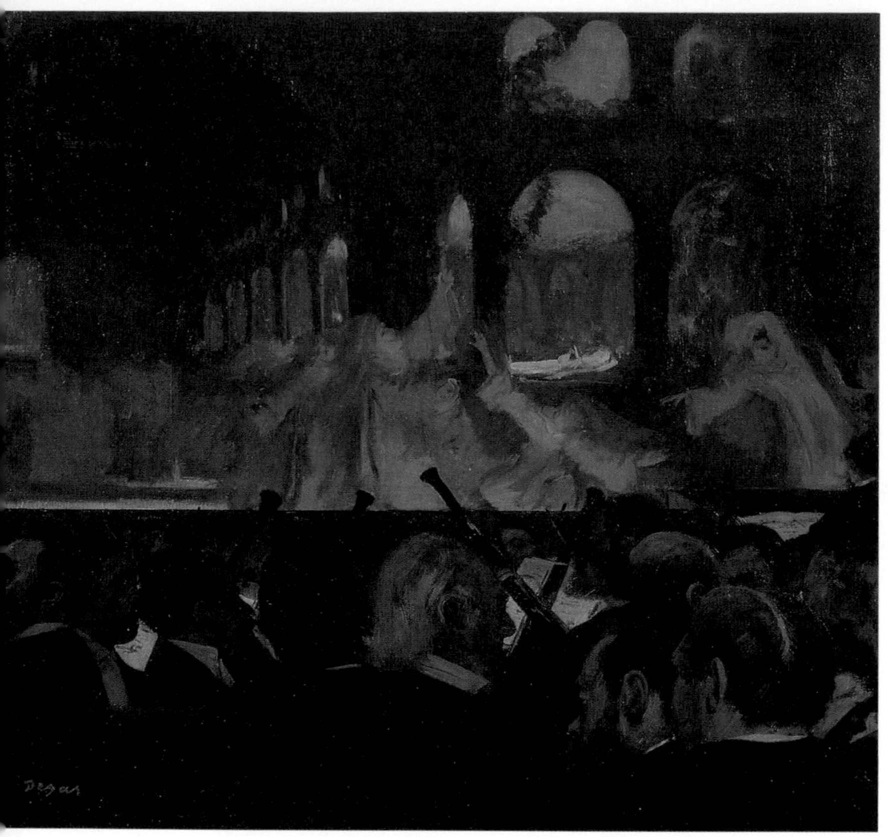

Degas, **The "Ballet Scene" from Meyerbeer's Opera, Robert le Diable,** *1876. Degas' interest in the artifice of the theater and in recording portraits of professionals at work coalesce in this scene.*

Degas' fascination with the quite different worlds of ballet dancers and laundresses is vividly recorded by Edmond de Goncourt in a journal entry for February 12, 1874:

> ***Yesterday I spent the whole afternoon in the studio of a strange painter named Degas. After a great many attempts and experiments and trial shots in all directions, he has fallen in love with the modern life and, out of all the subjects in modern life, he has cast his eyes upon washer-women and ballet dancers … It is a world of pink and white, of female flesh in lawn and gauze, the most delightful pretext for using pale, soft tints. He showed me, in their various poses and their graceful foreshortening, washerwomen and still more washerwomen … speaking their language and explaining their technicalities of the different movements in pressing and ironing. Then it was the turn of the dancers. There was their green-lit room with, outlined against the light of a window, the curious silhouette of dancer's legs coming down a little staircase, with the bright red of tartan in the midst of all those puffed-out white clouds, and a ridiculous ballet-master serving as a vulgar foil. And there before one, drawn from nature, was the graceful twisting and turning of the gestures of those little monkey-girls.***

The painting of ballet dancers Goncourt referred to in his journal is the painting seen opposite and which now forms part of the Burrell Collection in Glasgow, Scotland. The painting features not only the famous ballet teacher and former dancer, Jules Perrot, but also the artist's housekeeper, Sabine Neyt, draped in tartan and attentively adjusting a ballet "rat's" costume. From such unpromising subjects, Goncourt wrote, Degas had become "… the man I have seen up to now who has best captured, in reproducing modern life, the soul of this life."

Rediscovering the Greeks

Paradoxically, and Degas was nothing if not paradoxical, when asked by the American patroness of the arts and collector of Impressionist paintings, Louisine de Havemeyer, why he painted so many paintings of dancers, Degas made the famous answer, "Because, Madame, it is only there I can rediscover the movements of the Greeks."

Degas was clearly obsessed with the little "rats" of the Opéra, finding in their repeated movements the equivalent for the paintings of the old Masters he adored. He used all kinds of contrivances to gain a sense of immediacy, borrowing from Renaissance artists like Mantegna and others low or high viewpoints, cropping and unusual color effects. His knowledge of photography and Japanese prints confirmed the validity of such techniques and no doubt gave him the impetus to push the possibilities they offered ever further, but always with the validity of constant reference to the model.

For all their apparent realism, these works were actually the products of a studio-based art practice. In the early 1880s, Degas wrote to a friend to ask him for a pass to the Opéra, giving as his reason that "… I have done so many of these dance examinations without having seen them that I'm a bit ashamed of it."

Elsewhere, Degas said, "They call me the painter of dancers without understanding that for me the dancer has been the pretext for painting beautiful fabrics and rendering movement."

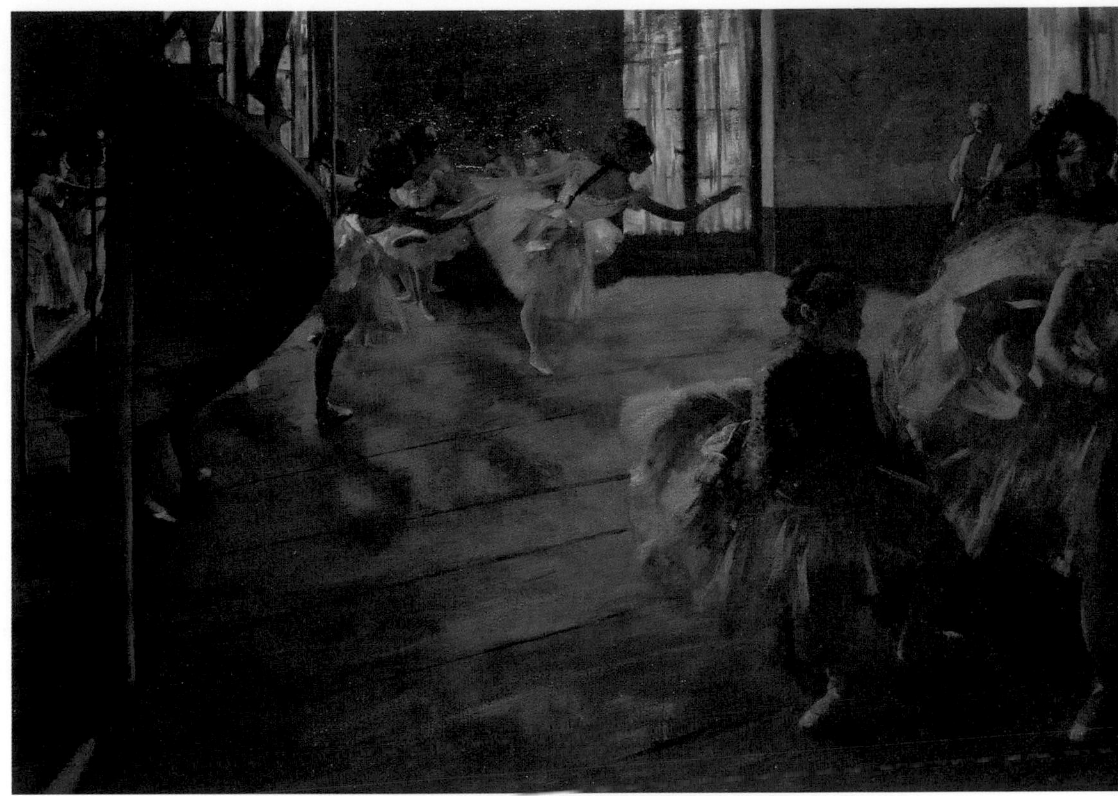

Degas, **The Rehearsal,** ***1873–74. The spiral staircase acts as a metaphor for the movements of the "rats" and the empty space of the floor creates a diagonal leading to the watchful dance master.***

He spent a lifetime studying the peculiarities of the body's movement, its articulation, weight and tension, and savoring the moments when the dancers are caught at moments of greatest physical tension, or when their bodies, fully relaxed, fall into the relaxed postures of habitude. Such moments allow him to study the human body, not at moments when it is displayed for public consumption, but when it is unaware of its audience. Degas showed surprisingly little interest in painting the stars of the stage or even of depicting actual performances. As in his paintings of horses and jockeys, he was fascinated not by the main event, but by the moments of preparation or recovery immediately before or after.

The subjects that Degas studied, while they were of interest to him in their own right, were always ones that allowed for the study of unusual light effects, interesting fabrics and textures and unusual perspectives and viewpoints. Not least significant were the opportunities they offered to experiment with different and unexpected color or tonal effects.

A world of intrigue

There is also no doubt that Degas was fascinated by the world of sexual intrigue the subject offered, including the little girls under the lustful eyes of their "lions," or would-be protectors. Such figures are a recurrent element in the ballet paintings, and remind the contemporary viewer of the sordid realities of the dancer's life, which was dedicated to the art of display, dominated by the male viewer, either the *abonné* (subscriber) or the wealthy benefactors, who were allowed special privileges, to wander backstage and to watch performances and rehearsals from the wings. Such figures remind us of our own role as the viewer of the image before us and ask us to question our own relationship with that image.

The example of Daumier and Manet further confirmed Degas in his exploration of various experimental compositions and in the validity of his choice of subject matter. His bold and imaginative compositions feature the most ordinary to the most bizarre of effects, including cutting off figures by the fall of curtains or the edge of theater flats. As Degas grew older, so his paintings became less descriptive and more evocative, moving from images that suggested the preservation of a single moment to ones that suggested the flux of experience and, like the statues of the Greeks, extended movement into time. As he moved away from the precisionist recording of a supposed external reality toward something more elusive and imaginary, so Degas came ever closer to fulfilling Baudelaire's definition of modernity: "By 'modernity,' I mean the ephemeral, the contingent, the half of art whose other half is eternal and immutable."

The Race Course

The image of the horse and rider is a familiar one in the history of art. One of Degas' earliest copies was of a fragment of the Parthenon that included horses. During the Romantic period in French art, particularly in the paintings of David, Gros and Géricault, the image became the paradigm of the heroic victor, astride a rearing horse, triumphing over his enemies and personifying man's power and control over the forces of nature.

Horse racing had been popular in England for a long time but it had only become a really fashionable activity in France during the Second Empire. The Longchamps race course in the Bois de Boulogne had been remodeled in 1857 and had become one of the main places to see and be seen: people watching was as important as the horse racing. The race course was a place where people from different social backgrounds could mingle; as such it was the ideal spot to paint a comprehensive catalog of modern types. In England, W.P. Frith had done just this in immense detail in his versions of Derby Day, though such attention to the minutiae of actuality evident in Frith's paintings was far from Degas' and Manet's ideas of picture-making.

Emile Zola visited the Longchamps racetrack on June 8, 1878, to witness the Grand Prix and made it the setting for a key scene in *Nana*, one of the most important of his epic novels of Second Empire life. He recognized the event as an illustration of the profound ambiguities that troubled Second Empire society. In the section dealing with the race, Zola made reference to the confusion of identities and the sexual intrigue inherent in the event, making great play with the difficulty of distinguishing the women of the *demimonde* and those allied to the aristocracy or those attached to immensely rich captains of industry. He also made clear his association of women and the horses as instruments designed for male pleasure, one of the horses coincidently even bearing the same name as the heroine of the novel, the courtesan Nana.

Degas was not a horseman, but he had been associated with horses since his youth and he drew and sketched them from childhood. As one might expect, most of his sketching was done after English sporting prints, or from prototypes from Greek and Renaissance art and the work of contemporaries and near-contemporaries such as Géricault, Alfred de Dreux, John Lewis Brown and Meissonier, all of whom produced work that capitalized upon the vogue for horse racing.

In spite of the apparent verisimilitude and spontaneity of their racetrack paintings, both Manet's and Degas' art was unashamedly studio-based. As Manet wrote to Berthe Morisot, "Not being in the habit of painting horses, I copied mine

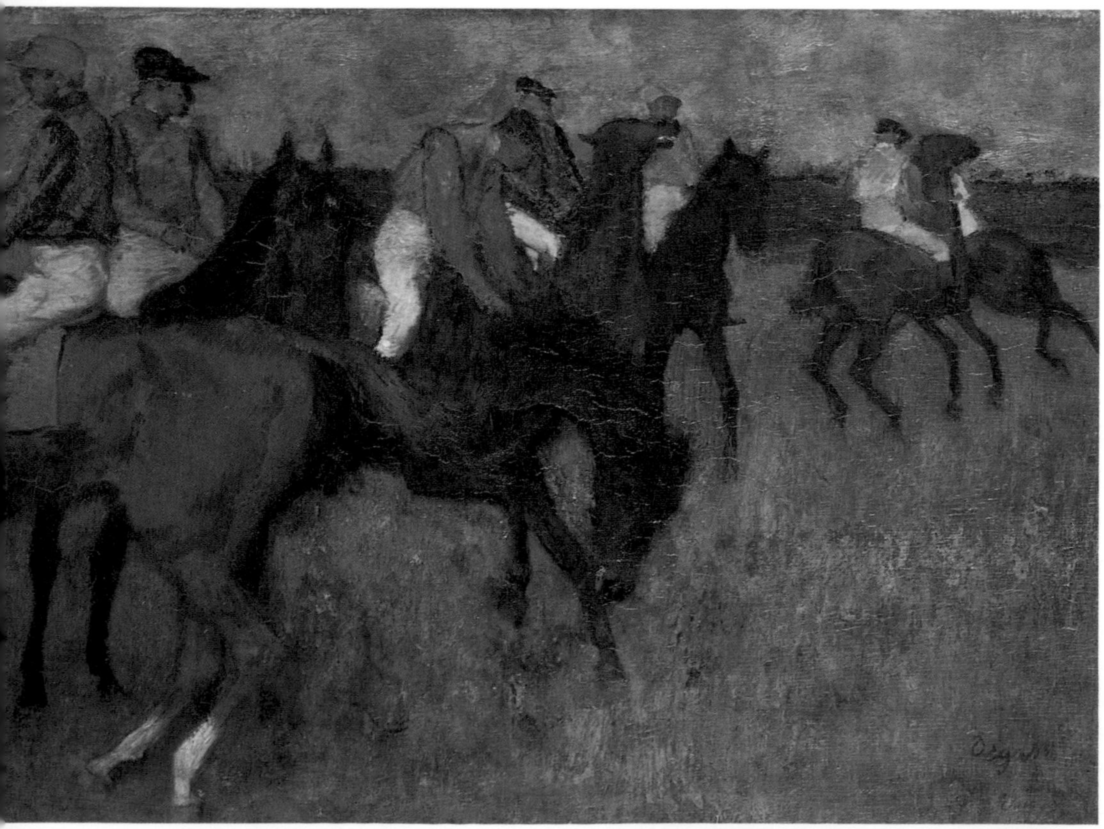

Edgar Degas,* Jockeys, *1886. In this frieze-like procession of forms, one can almost feel the nervous energy of horses and riders as they prepare for the race.

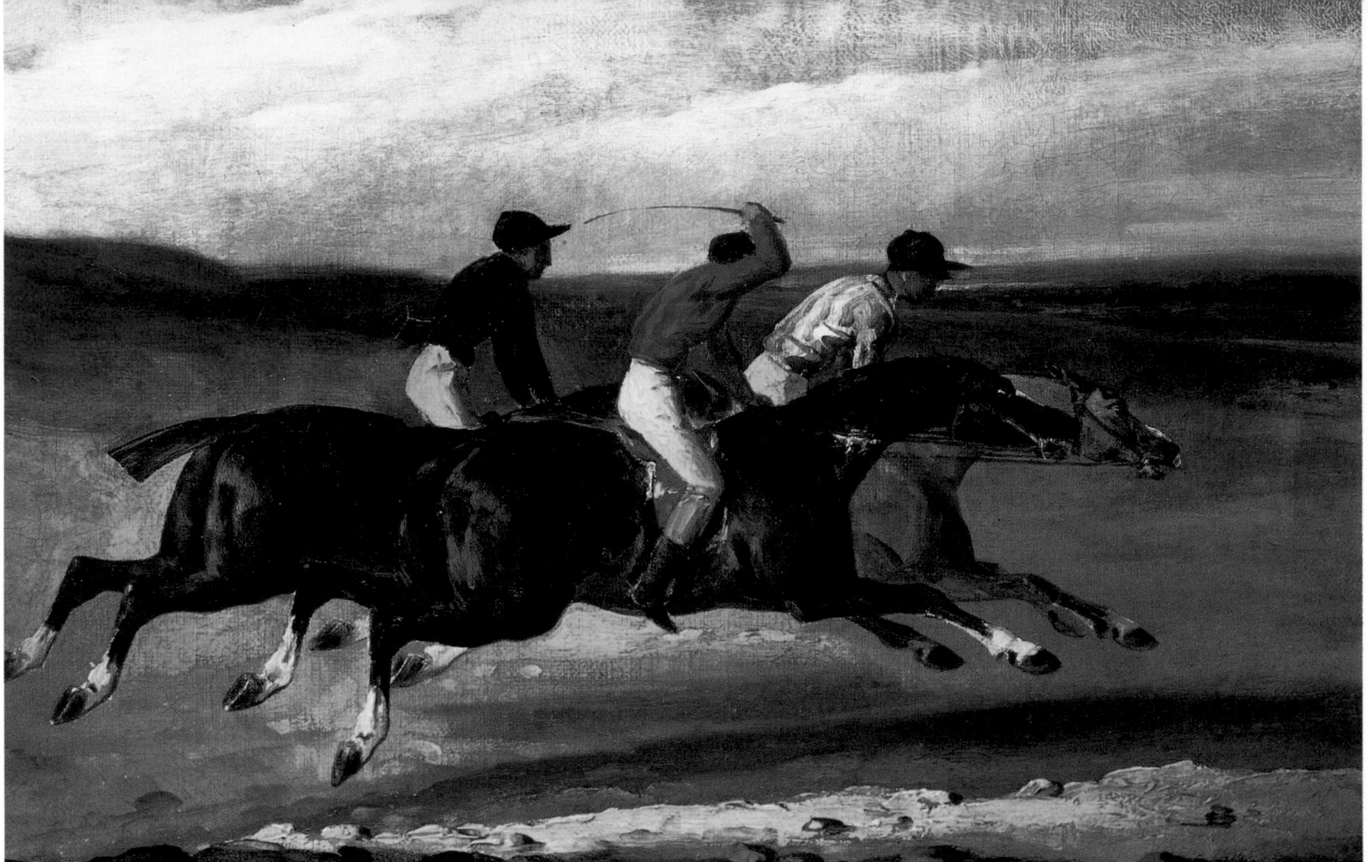

Géricault, **Horse Race,** *c.1820. Géricault much admired English sporting paintings and prints and, in turn, Degas held his representations of horses and their riders in high regard. Here the movement of the horses is conveyed even though all four legs are off the ground.*

from those who best know how to do them." In one of Degas' early genre scenes from the 1860s, called *Sulking*, an English sporting print appears prominently placed between the two main protagonists.

The horse is central to most of Degas' early history paintings, his first modern subject being *Scene from a Steeplechase* (1866), a 2-meter (6-foot) canvas featuring a fallen jockey. In such works, Degas reveals his deep love of horses; like Zola, he merges their identities with his images of women, so often seen naked, their faces obscured, all interest centered not on their personalities, but the magnificence of their anatomies.

The influence of Muybridge

One of the most significant elements in Degas' work was his discovery of the photographs of the English-born photographer, Eadweard Muybridge, (1830–1904). Muybridge moved to America in the 1850s and, financed by a governor of California who was also a wealthy horse-breeder, began to photograph horses in such a manner as to record in a series of single photographs the sequential movement of the bodies in movement. In 1878, the first articles showing photographs of animals in motion were published. When seen in France, they caused a sensation, particularly among artists, who at once realized how far from the truth was the conventionalized way of showing horses in movement, with all four legs off the ground. Degas was fascinated and made studies from the photographs to learn how the horse moved, developed into three dimensions in his sculptural studies, but perhaps more importantly, they must have affirmed his belief in the significance of sequential poses as suggesting the passage of time in a single static artwork. The separate photographs revealed the unpredictability and awkwardness of real-life movements.

Degas used a variety of formal devices to suggest the things he discovered in these photographs. His techniques of overlapping forms on top of each other, using a sequence of related movements in different individuals or horses, can be seen as attempts to capture a sense of movement through time, something that Muybridge's photographs suggest so evocatively. Such information was used together with his own experience of horses and the borrowings he made from other sources to paint modern-day equivalents of the battle scenes and processions of former times.

Degas disregards the main event, the race, and centers his interest on the moments just before it starts. It has been pointed out that he rarely depicts any particular course and that his jockeys are usually "gentlemen jockeys": horse owners who were allowed to race, once a season, in their own colors. They are the latterday equivalents of the rich Florentine banking dynasty in Gozzoli's fresco or the young Athenians parading on their horses in the Pan-Athenian procession. They are cropped like photographs or as the slabs of marble from the Parthenon are, allowing the spectator to continue the scene in their imagination.

Woman with Binoculars

1869–72, oil on card, 48 x 32 cm (19 x 12½ in), Gemäldegalerie Neumeister, Dresden, Germany

This extraordinary study has as its subject Lydia Cassatt, the sister of Mary Cassatt. It is one of a number of studies, one of which includes as her companion Degas' rival in the painting of *modernité*, Edouard Manet, for a painting that was never completed, *At the Racetrack*, now in the Weill Bros-Cotton, Inc. collection, Montgomery, Alabama. It illustrates once again the intense preparation and the artifice that were necessary to create an apparently spontaneous image.

Degas' eloquent study has caught the imagination of many contemporary writers upon nineteenth-century art, not least because it epitomizes the questions that so many Impressionist images raise. The subtlety of its psychological content, its grace, the concern with costume, its exactitude of pose and anatomical correctness, and its ambiguity recall Degas' appreciation of Watteau's work. The image demands that we take responsibility for our presence before it; as we are gazing upon this fashionably dressed young lady so she, in her turn, scrutinizes us. Who is watching whom?

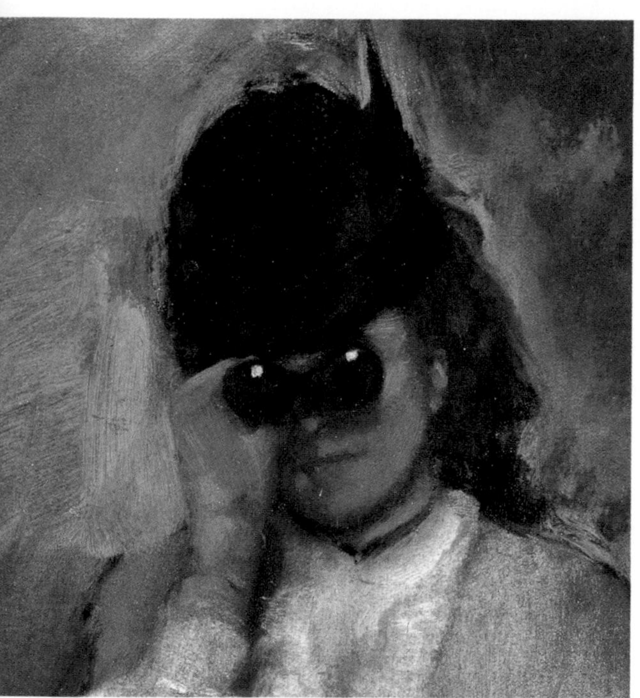

Arsène Houssaye tells of an encounter with Ingres in 1850. They are seated in a theater box at the Théâtre Français, Ingres having just pressured Houssaye as its general manager into allowing him as a member of the Académie an extra free *loge* ticket for his wife when, "turning towards the orchestra seats, he shouted to some young people who were ogling the boxes, 'You wretches, be respectful.'" Unlike many of the women in Degas' paintings, this woman questions by her actions our right to survey her and in turn demands her right to survey us. In this confrontational image – one, incidentally, that was never publicly displayed in Degas' lifetime – we have an example of the way in which the Impressionists were intent on upsetting conventional means of depiction and, in the chosen manner of their representation, on upsetting conventional notions of behavior too. This, as much as the manner in which such images were made, is what makes Impressionist paintings so open to exploration.

As many commentators have pointed out, despite the fact that she appears to be such an arrestingly contemporary image, the pose of the *Woman with Binoculars* is, once again, taken from antique statuary. In its transformation to modern *Parisienne*, the pose has given the woman a powerful sense of independence; she stands assured of her own space and of her right to be there, in a perfectly stable geometric stance. Not the least disconcerting element of the study is the way in which she appears to be inclining her head downward and at a slight angle, the better to scrutinize the object of her study: the viewer.

In Griselda Pollock's chapter, "Women with Binoculars – A Question of Difference" in *Dealing with Degas*, the author quotes from Eunice Lipton's book *Looking into Degas*,

> ***Standing frontally, ironically and staring out through binoculars, this woman is an imposing personage whose monumental form and act of bold looking expresses tremendous power, power which at that time was by definition male.***

Such behavior, the author implies, in a society where women were normally expected to behave in an altogether more demure and submissive manner, could identify her as a woman whose act of visual engagement with the viewer is provocative. The sense of shock at being the subject of this penetrating gaze rebounds upon the male viewer more accustomed to the active and safer role of being the originator and not the recipient of the gaze. The painting, ingeniously, is a visual metaphor for the usually active citizen now become the passive observer, increasingly self-centered, but increasingly powerless, seeing others like himself, but unable to communicate with them.

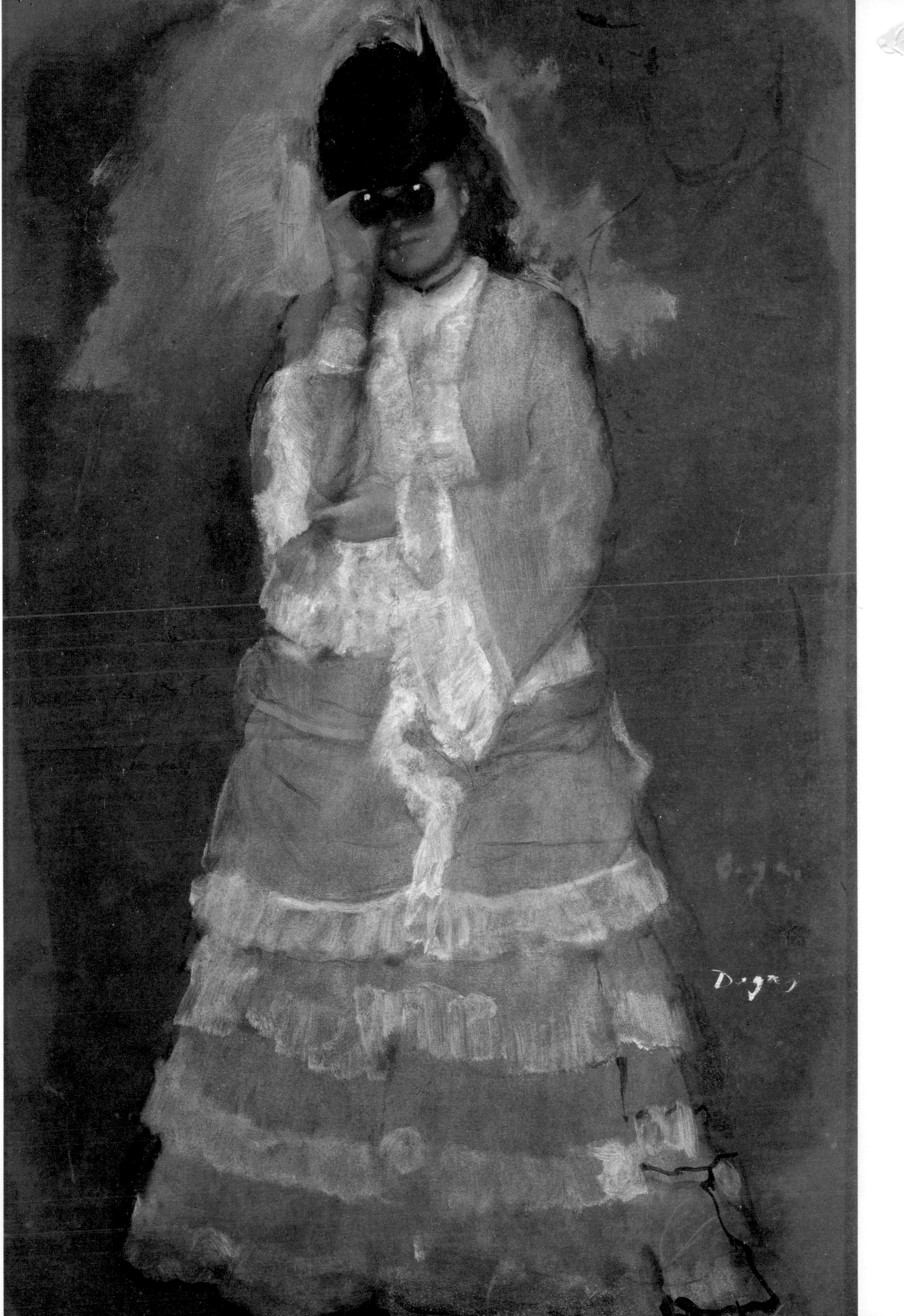

The Demimonde

A contemporary guide, written for the benefit of English travelers, made clear the extent of prostitution in Paris: "You cannot go into any public place without meeting one or more women that you will recognize at a glance as belonging to the class known in French society as the *demimonde*. You will find them in the theaters, in the concert halls, in the cafés."

Paris was renowned for its brothels, or *maisons clos*. It was the custom of young Frenchmen to lose their virginity in such places; Guy de Maupassant, in one of his short novels, relates how on public holidays regular clients in brothels would be ousted by schoolboy customers. In the final scenes of Flaubert's influential novel of contemporary life, *Sentimental Education*, the hero, Frédéric Morel, reveals that it was only in a brothel that he had ever been really happy.

The prostitute was the personification of high capitalism, her body and person becoming just another commodity to be exchanged or bartered on the open market. Selling her body for money, she became a travesty of bourgeois notions of love and marriage: her glittering image of available sexuality provided an officially sanctioned outlet for lust divorced from love or social obligation.

The publicly propagated ideal of womanhood was wreathed in an aura of romantic love. A well-bred young woman was expected to marry well and to provide her husband with children. Her husband, however, was expected to make use of the prostitute, not only for sexual pleasure, but also for the preservation of his health. It was a normal and accepted practice for healthy men to visit brothels. As a result, syphilis was the great fear of the age: as Flaubert wrote in his *Dictionary of Received Ideas*, like the common cold "... more or less everyone is affected by it." Baudelaire, Manet, Maupassant and Gauguin all suffered from the malady.

Although officially the number of brothels declined in the 1860s and 1870s, such estimates did not take into account the clandestine brothels or the work of the casual or part-time prostitute.

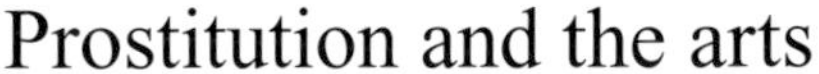

Prostitution and the arts

Given the widespread, though unspoken, acceptance of prostitution in Paris, it is not surprising to find it appearing in the work of artists and writers from the time of the Second Empire. In the mid-to-late 1870s, a number of writers began to treat the subject openly, the theme having already been broached by Baudelaire who made the prostitute one of the prime icons of Haussmann's Paris. Edmond de Goncourt's novel *The Whore Elisa* was published in March 1877, Joris-Karl Huysman's *Marthe, the Story of a Prostitute*, appeared in September 1876,

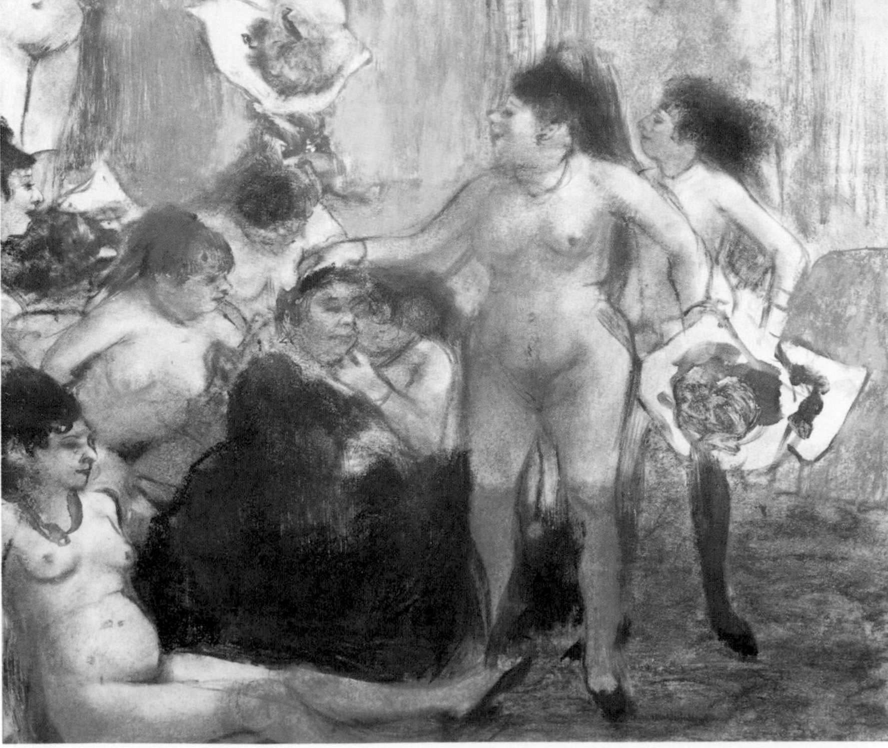

Degas,* Nameday of the Madame, *monotype and pastel 1876–77. Wit and humor vie with brilliantly incisive draftmanship in this monotype, one of two that belonged to Picasso.

and Guy de Maupassant wrote numerous short stories and a number of novels featuring aspects of the *demimonde*.

Early in 1878 Emile Zola began his assiduous research for a moral narrative concerning the rise and fall of the prostitute Nana. In the novel, Nana's spectacular reign as one of the leading *Grandes Horizontale*s of her time is cut short by her death from smallpox, graphically described by Zola in the book's last pages, at the very moment that the French troops march out of the capital toward their fatal encounter with the Prussians.

A passage from *Nana* matches Degas' frankness and his interest in seeing humanity as another species of the animal kingdom:

> ***Look around, you find him among us. How many sinister comedies you can see, how many men who will throw to one side their dress-coat like a theatrical costume and roll on the carpet, playing the dog and begging to be kicked!***

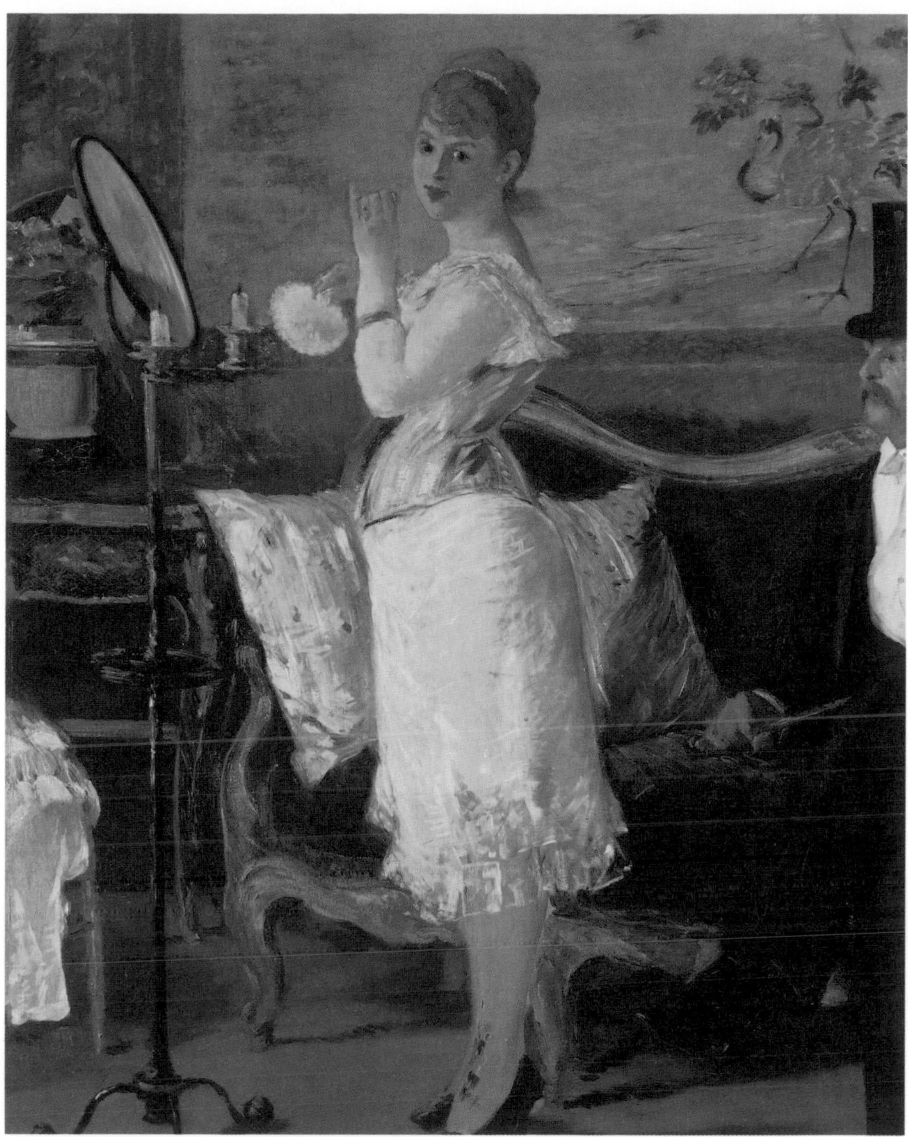

Manet,* Nana, *1877. The woman portrayed was Henriette Hauser, mistress of the Prince of Orange, who was accordingly called* Le Citron *(The Lemon).

Elsewhere in the novel, Nana is described as "giving herself to friends or passers-by, like a good natured animal."

Unlike Zola's writing, Degas' art does not indulge in heavy moralizing, but there is an uneasy parallel between his depictions of women, specifically bathing women, and his fascination with the horse. Women's anatomies are depicted stripped of the trappings that mark them as social beings and are analyzed, naked and as unself-conscious as animals.

A small group of monotypes made by Degas around 1879–80 give a frank portrayal of brothel life. His near-caricature depictions are not devoid of sympathy for the lot of the prostitute, and some of them reveal a great understanding of the monotony, loneliness and deep sadness of their lives. Equally, he is able to show happier moments, especially when the women are depicted without the overbearing presence of the male clients. The customers are just as frequently subjected to his pitiless analysis, portrayed as privileged, self-absorbed and often as being rather witless.

In their subject matter and in the brevity and wit of their representation, Degas' monotypes reveal the artist as having thoroughly assimilated the example of Japanese prints, which frequently represented the daily round of the courtesan. Another celebrated depicter of prostitution, Pablo Picasso, whose brothel picture, *Les Demoiselles d'Avignon*, is often claimed to have changed the course of twentieth-century art, acquired two magnificent examples of Degas' brothel scenes late in life.

Since such works were always intended for a limited and exclusively male audience, it is not known how many brothel-life monotypes Degas actually made, particularly as his brother destroyed some examples on the artist's death, presumably to preserve his reputation.

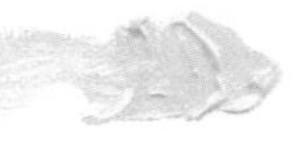

The Nude:
Gauguin and Degas

For three centuries or more in Western art the nude had been regarded as the embodiment of beauty in its most absolute form. Artists were encouraged to use the idealized naked figure as the basis of their art, sustaining a tradition that was seen to continue the ideals of antiquity and the Renaissance. In the late eighteenth and early nineteenth centuries, David had succeeded in making heroic images of the nude or semi-nude male in paintings such as *Homage to Marat* and *Leonidas and The Spartans at Thermopolae*.

Later, Géricault had drawn from the work of Michelangelo and Rubens as well as the Davidian tradition to create his tragic and contemporary image of shipwreck and starvation, *Raft of the "Medusa"* (1819). Ingres, in his turn, continued the Davidian tradition, creating images of heroic males and languorous females, drawn with a brilliancy and contained eroticism that allowed critics to make comparisons with antique art. Delacroix, who had posed for Géricault's *Raft of the "Medusa,"* continued the bravura qualities found in Rubens in his own romantically charged paintings.

By the 1850s, this tradition was growing increasingly unworkable, challenged most visibly by the fleshy, un-idealized nudes of Courbet. Baudelaire's Salon review of

Degas,* Nude in a Tub*, pastel, 1886. The extraordinary viewpoint makes the dresser a startling vertical; on its surface, the jugs make a commentary on the crouching woman.

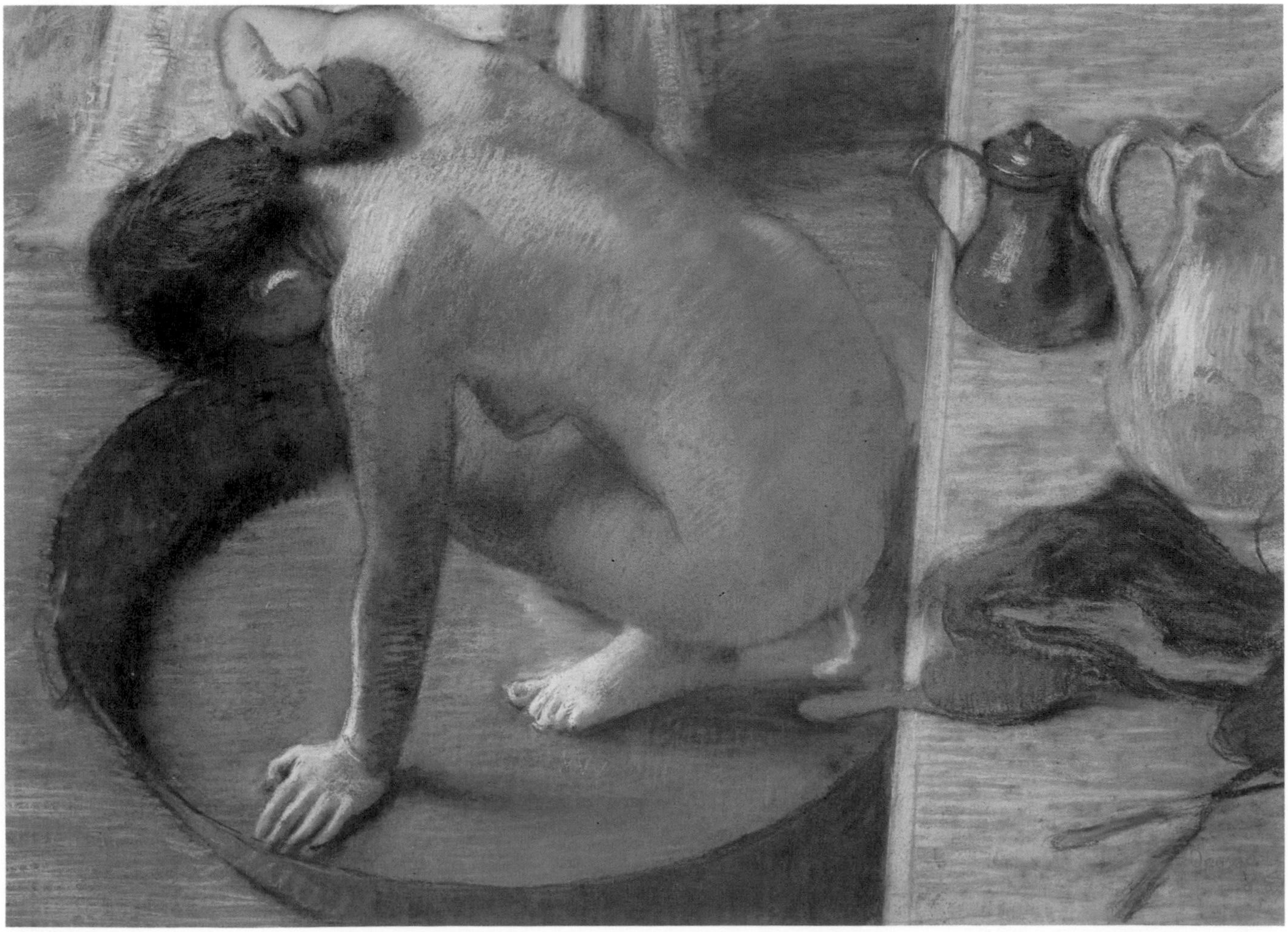

1846 included a call to reestablish the nude as an important element of modern art practice, the critic writing that:

> ***The nude – that darling of the artists, that necessary element of success – is just as frequent and necessary today as it was in the life of the ancients; in bed, for example, or in the bath, or in the anatomy theater. The themes and resources of painting are equally abundant and varied; but there is a new element – modern beauty.***

The two most radical paintings of the 1860s, Manet's *Luncheon on the Grass* and *Olympia*, were reworkings or subversions of this tradition. Monet and Sisley showed no interest in painting the nude; as women, neither Mary Cassatt nor Berthe Morisot had ready access to the nude model; but for Renoir, Cézanne and Degas the nude figure kept its position at the core of their creative energies. Even Pissarro produced paintings of nude peasant girls bathing in woodland streams.

Shown at the sixth Impressionist exhibition of 1881, *Study of a Nude: Suzanne Sewing* was a new departure for Gauguin, who until then had been an amateur artist. The critic Joris-Karl Huysmans enthused over its mundane qualities, registering it as a painting, "of our own times … a girl who does not pose for spectators, who is neither lewd nor affected, who very nicely busies herself with repairs to her old clothes."

Gauguin's Danish wife, Mette, may have instrumental in his use of the family maid, Suzanne, as a model for this study, possibly because she did not trust her husband with a hired model. This unidealized figure of a mature woman could hardly be further away from the academically idealized beauties of contemporary "official" artists such as Cabanel or Gérôme. Nevertheless, the painting is thoroughly artificial: the image of a woman doing needlework in the nude is hardly a scene from everyday life. Its designation as an *étude* denotes the work as a study rather than one of the normal allegories used to sanction the depiction of naked nubile young women.

The naked female was Degas' main preoccupation. During the mid-1880s he worked on a number of pastels of women at their toilette, washing and drying themselves. At the Impressionist exhibition of 1886, he exhibited a series of these works under the heading "Sequence of Nudes, of Women Bathing, Washing, Drying, Wiping Themselves, Combing Their Hair or Having it Combed." This almost scientific cataloging of these intimate female activities is paralleled by the artist's intense scrutiny of the figure performing the routine tasks that normally would be undertaken in private. Degas told the Irish writer George Moore that he wished to show woman as:

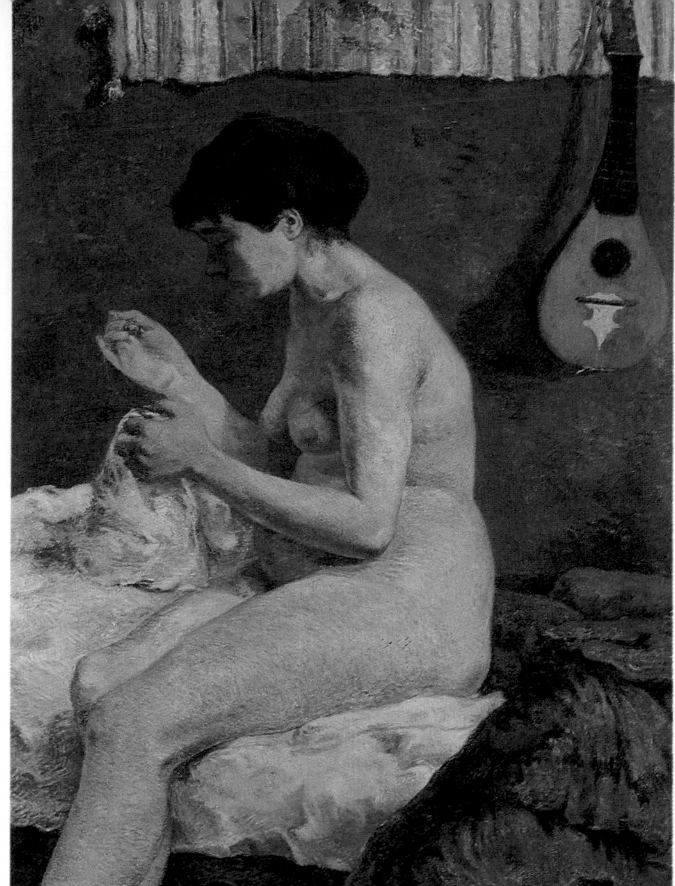

Gaugin,* Study of a Nude, Suzanne Sewing, *1880. A studied composition, painstakingly organized gives this prosaic action a rather bizarre quality.

> ***A human creature preoccupied with herself – a cat who licks herself; hitherto, the nude has always been represented in poses which presuppose an audience, but these women of mine are honest and simple folk, unconcerned by any other interests than those involved in their physical condition … it is as if you looked through a keyhole.***

This apparently innocent statement has become a notorious definition of the artist and, by extension, the viewer as voyeur. Some commentators consider "these women" to have been prostitutes, their act of bathing therefore being a necessary professional practice.

Many at the time regarded these pastels as being brutally misogynist images of women, deformed by the harsh realities of their lives, their ageing bodies bearing the marks of childbirth and hard labor.

Formally, Degas' images, like Gauguin's, belong to the tradition of Rembrandt's clear-eyed and minutely worked etchings of naked women in which all the blemishes and marks that define us as individuals are presented with a sympathy and a humanity that is rare in European art. Whatever may have been Degas' personal reasons for making these images, the pastels themselves stand as remarkable documents of our shared physical condition.

Man at His Bath

1884, oil on canvas, 166 x 125 cm (65 x 49 in),
Private Collection, on loan to the National Gallery, London, England

This painting is one of two large paintings featuring the male nude by Caillebotte. They are most unusual in nineteenth- and even twentieth-century art in their frank and raw depiction of the male physique. Degas' notion of looking through a keyhole is given a subversive dimension in this painting, in which the viewer is confronted by the back of a mature man, drying himself and oblivious to the fact that he is being observed.

The actions of the man are vigorous, the wet footprints denote the passage of time and suggest that this is not a model posing in a studio but an intimate and highly unusual genre scene of everyday life. This is no male Adonis but an unidentifiable male, seen from the rear, whose discarded clothing and neatly arranged boots suggest that his actions are brusquely undertaken as a necessary and mundane part of his daily routine.

A sequence of curves are repeated across the surface of the surface. The man's buttocks, his head and shoulders, his discarded clothes, the curve and reflective surface of the bath and the simple wooden chair all play a part in making a lively dialogue between rigorous order, suggested by the horizontals and verticals of the setting, and the malleability of the human frame.

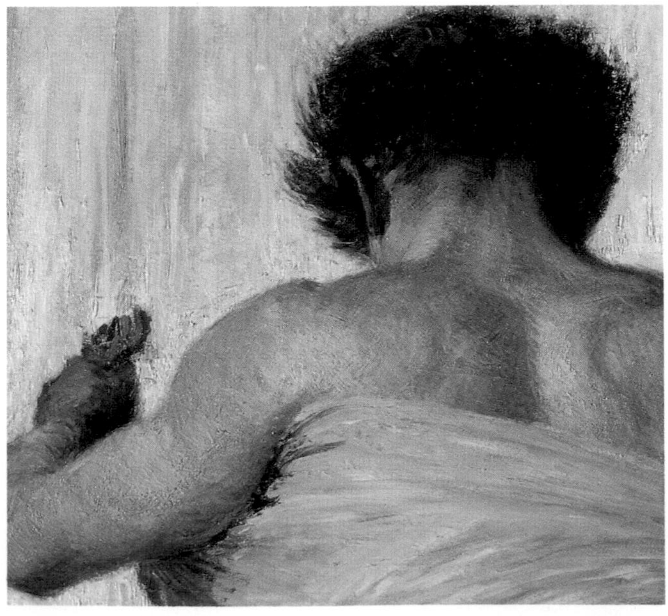

The color is muted, although the reds in the painting are vivid, particularly where a single line of paint describes the form of the buttocks, between which, in a startling note of realism, may be glimpsed a hint of scrotum.

The painting was exhibited in Brussels at the exhibition called *Les XX* in 1888, and the art historian Gloria Groom has noted how it was probably displayed in a closet room apart from the main exhibition hall, hence the fact that this startling image escaped critical mention. Caillebotte owned a particularly fine example of one of Degas' pastel monotypes, and it may well be that this painting was a knowing riposte to the work of his fellow artist, as much as to the clichéd depictions of female bathers that were so popular throughout this period.

The perfect male nude was considered by the Greeks and the artists and thinkers of the Renaissance to be the most suitable means of representing human aspirations. Leonardo da Vinci's famous depiction of Vitruvian man, represented naked at the center of a circle, which was then superimposed on a square, makes visible the traditional notion of the male body as holding some kind of mystical correspondence with the hidden order of the universe; a model of rationality, balance and harmony or as a signifier of the "manly properties" of strength and vitality. Against this model, as can be seen many times in this book and famously subverted by Manet, women were depicted as being passive and "natural" – objects of male desire.

In the 1870s, the Empress Eugènie ordered that the naked male statues situated in the Tuilieries were to be suitably adorned with fig leaves to hide from view the offending parts of the male anatomy. She had decreed that the classical culture that had fired the artists of Ancient Greece, Rome and the Renaissance was to be suitably tidied up and made safe for the Parisian middle class.

In such a context, Caillebotte's frank study of a naked man seen from behind in the apparent privacy of his own bathroom comes as a shock. With Baudelaire's writings in mind, perhaps, Caillebotte has rejected any temptation to turn his subject into a carrier of clichéd ideas so familiar in the work of his more academically minded contemporaries.

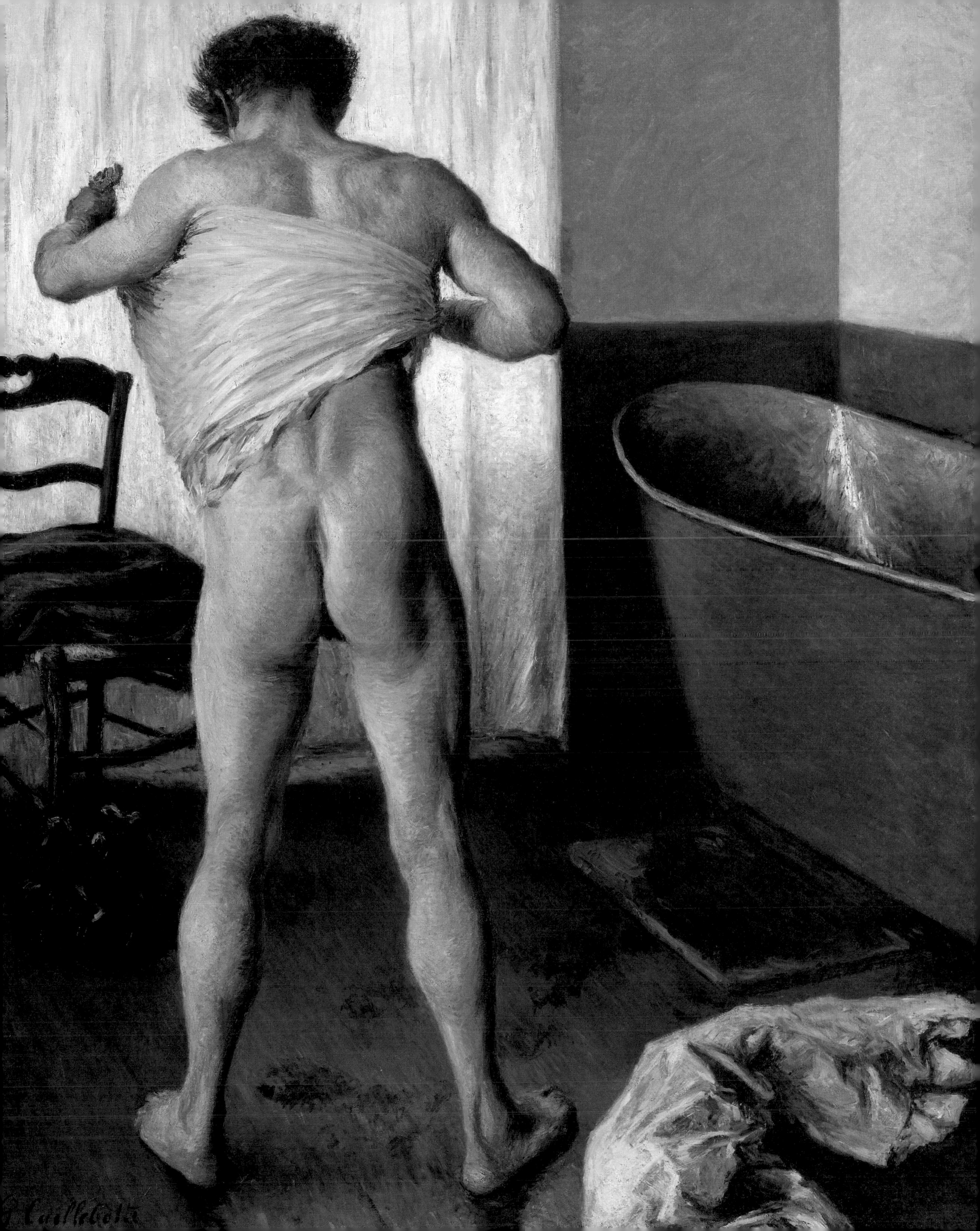

Berthe Morisot: "the one real Impressionist"

***Berthe Morisot's life was a singular one, she lived her painting and painted her life as if it were a natural and necessary function.* – Paul Valéry**

Berthe Morisot was one of the few professional female artists of her time, by accepting in 1873, Degas' invitation to join what was to become the Impressionist group, she was in fact, breaking into an all-male preserve, an exclusive and distinctive exhibiting body that would begin the slow attrition of the male dominance of Fine Art practice.

Morisot (1841–1895) was born in Bourges into an upper middle-class family; her father was a highly placed government administrator who took a lively interest in the artistic leanings of his two daughters, Edma and Berthe. In an age when women were not expected to excel in the arts, both girls showed more talent for art than was considered to be either proper or necessary for a middle-class girl. The professional world of art was an almost entirely male preserve: female students only gained the right to enter the Ecole des Beaux-Arts in 1897. The Morisot sisters were lucky in that the family supported their ambitions and in 1855, after the family's move to the chic Parisian district of Passy, close to the fashionable Bois de Boulogne, they began lessons with the painter Guichard.

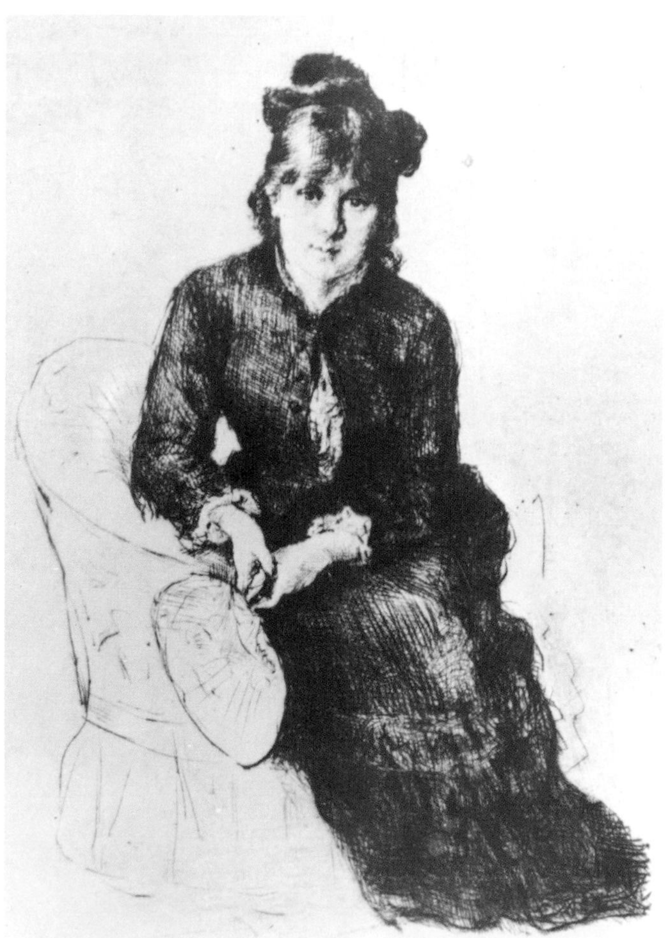

Marcel Desboutin, etching of Berthe Morisot, 1876. An engaging informal portrait of the artist, shown holding a Japanese fan.

In a revealing letter to Berthe's mother, Guichard exposed the strength of prejudice felt against female painters:

> ***Considering the character of your daughters, my teaching will not endow them with minor drawing-room accomplishments; they will become painters. Do you realize what this means? In the world of the grande bourgeoisie in which you move, this will be revolutionary, I would even say catastrophic. Are you sure that you will not come to curse the day when art, having gained admission to your home, now so respectable and peaceful, will become the sole arbiter of the fate of your two children?***

This did not deter the girls' parents, who had constructed a studio for them in their large garden. They were soon receiving lessons from Corot and Fantin-Latour, who converted them into keen adherents of *plein-air* painting, so that they used their summer holidays to sketch and paint in the countryside of Normandy.

The two sisters successfully submitted to the Salon of 1864 and, at the Salon of 1866, Berthe's painting was admired by Manet. He belonged to the same social class as the sisters and began to give them his advice and friendship. Her elegant features may be recognized in many of Manet's paintings from 1868–74, perhaps most notably in *The Balcony* of 1868–69. Although her painting style is hers alone, she benefited enormously from the privilege of watching Manet at work. But Morisot was an extremely independent person and was mortified at Manet's retouching of her successful Salon submission of 1870, a portrait of her sister Edma and their mother. This was the last occasion she exhibited at the Salon.

Through Corot, Fantin-Latour and especially Manet, she became acquainted with the avant-garde group of painters, later to become known as the Impressionists. She was a founder member of the *Société Anonyme des artistes, peintres, sculpteurs, graveurs, etc.*, as the Impressionists called themselves for their first independent exhibition, and, unlike Manet and Fantin-Latour, she threw herself wholeheartedly into the Impressionist enterprise, taking an active role in the organization of their exhibitions. She remained dedicated to the Impressionist cause, employing her considerable social and personal skills in holding the group together, despite her colleagues' propensity for bickering and back-biting.

She was friendly with Degas, Renoir and Monet and was considered by them to be an equal. Her financial security protected her from the money problems that beset so many of her painter friends. She kept her distance from the social and business side of their shared ventures, but she exhibited in seven out of the eight Impressionist exhibitions and took an active role in the disastrous Hôtel Drouot auction of 1875.

At the first Impressionist show in 1874, she exhibited nine works of various subjects. Her paintings were generally praised, both within and without the Impressionist circle, for their lightness of touch and her skilled rendering of outdoor effects. Beneath the atmosphere of ease and relaxation apparent in her work, there is an underlying quality of melancholy and introspection that characterizes her work. Her paintings are light-filled and brilliantly informal, both in subject and technique, characterized by a sense of sketchlike improvization informed by close observation.

The critic Paul Mantz described her in 1874 as the "one real Impressionist." She came to be regarded as one of the prime exemplars of the movement, faithfully adhering, along with Monet and Sisley, to the original tenets of Impressionism. In 1881, she and Mary Cassatt, with whom she had become friendly during the 1870s, were thought by one critic to be the only interesting artists exhibiting in the group show of that year. Gustave Geffroy went even further, writing that "no one represents Impressionism with more refined talent or with more authority than Morisot."

Edma Morisot, thought by some to be as talented as Berthe, had given up painting on her marriage in 1869. Berthe's marriage to Manet's brother Eugène in 1874 only strengthened her commitment to art. Her daughter, Julie, was born in 1878 and from then on Morisot's art centered even more firmly upon the immediate circle of her own family.

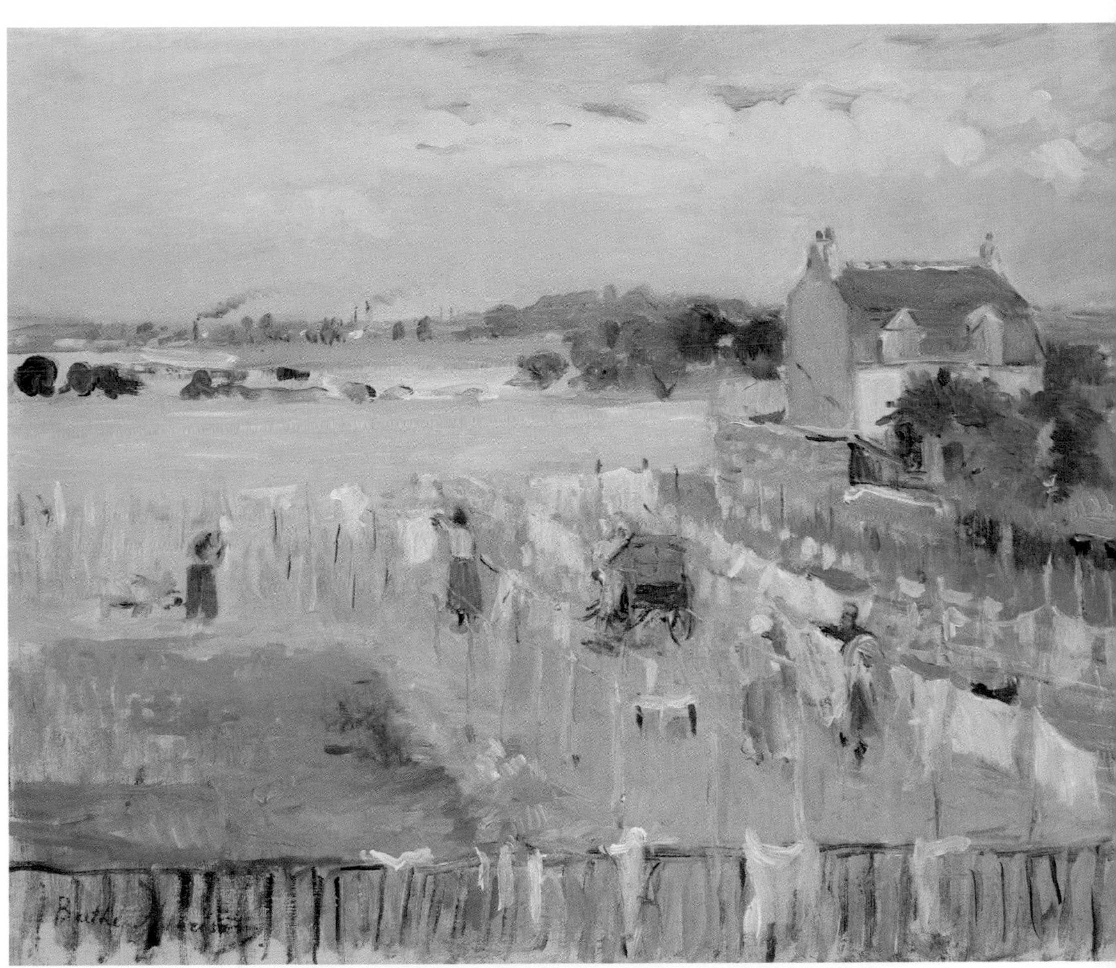

Morisot, **Laundresses Hanging Out the Wash,** ***1875. Shown at the second exhibition, this is an exquisite harmony of pinks, lilacs and blues.***

In the last decade of her relatively short life – she died at the age of 51 – her Thursday night suppers at her home in the Rue Wéber became the setting for the reunion of the Impressionist community. Degas, Monet, Renoir and Whistler gathered there in friendly conviviality, mingling with assorted politicians, poets and musicians.

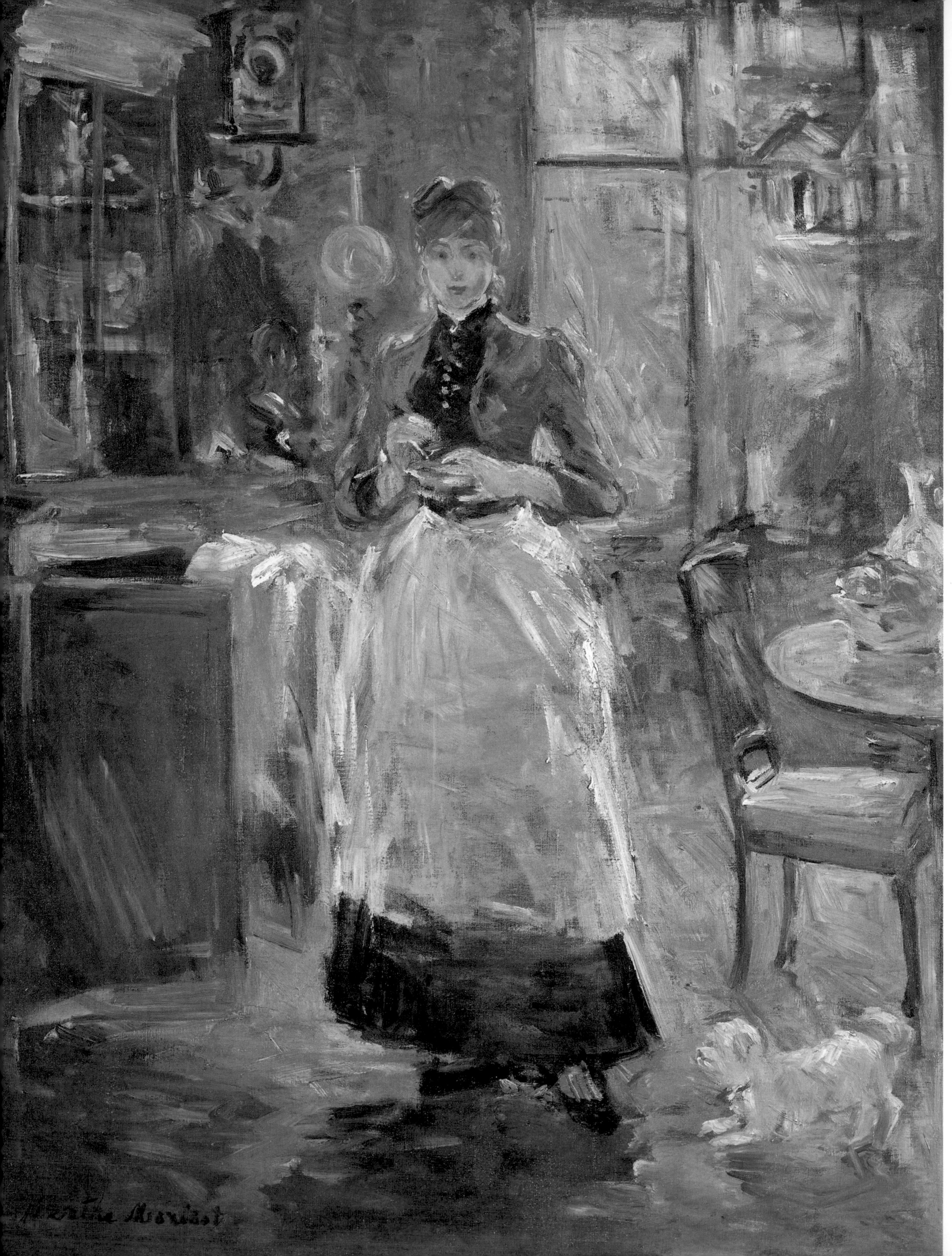

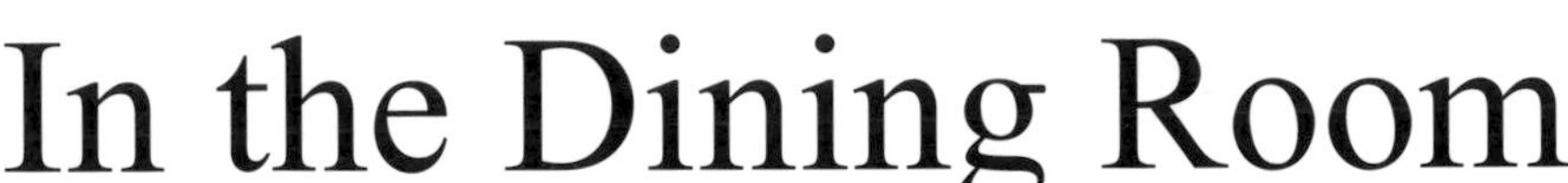

In the Dining Room

1886, oil on canvas, 61.6 x 50.2 cm (24¼ x 19¾ in), National Gallery of Art, Chester Dale Collection, Washington DC, USA

This charming painting of Berthe Morisot's maid-servant, Pasie, reminds us that the ease and sense of leisure present in so many Impressionist paintings was only made possible by the labors of domestic servants. The young woman looks out as if disturbed mid-task, from a corner of the dining room of Berthe and Eugène Manet's new house in the Rue de Villejuste.

Morisot shared with Cassatt an ability to create a sense of intimacy by reducing the distance between the viewer and the depicted scene. The painting is extremely informal in handling and subject matter: this is not a commissioned portrait, but a record of one of the members of the artist's household. The maid's open and smiling face presents a very different image of service from the world-weary expression found on the face of Suzon, Manet's model for *A Bar at the Folies-Bergère* of 1882.

The painting was shown at the Impressionist exhibition of 1886. With its characteristic sketchiness, bravura brushwork and spontaneity of handling, it contrasted markedly with the innovative Pointillist paintings of Seurat and Signac at the exhibition. Morisot was seen as a representative of the old style of Impressionism and it was noted that, in comparison with the more structured paintings of Mary Cassatt, her work appeared the more feminine. A contemporary noted that "in Paris, she was accustomed to paint in her drawing-room, laying aside her canvas, brushes and palette in a cupboard as soon as an unexpected visitor was announced."

In the Dining Room shows Morisot's distinctive style at its most effective and elegant. The scene is animated by a dialogue between areas that are relatively finished and others that remain barely suggested, and her tremulous, flickering touch and open brushwork perfectly conjure up the atmosphere of a light-filled room.

Standing between an open cupboard door and the dining table, the maid is seen framed by the glass front of the cupboard and the window, through which can be seen a glimpse of the garden beyond. Areas of animated brushwork are not restricted to the forms they describe but are used to animate the whole canvas and to suggest the enveloping atmosphere. The silvery tones and the predominance of blues, greens, greys and white give a strong sense of the light shimmering into the room. The open window, the cupboard door left ajar and the lively presence of the dog give the scene an air of openness, informality and ease.

This small painting is charged with great energy, the paint laid in wet on wet, areas of impasto contrasting with thin veils of color which allow the canvas to show through. The looseness of the brushwork is held in check by strongly defined slashes of paint, which serve to unite the figure of the maid with her place of work. Morisot's lack of interest in contemporary notions of finish may well have been a result of

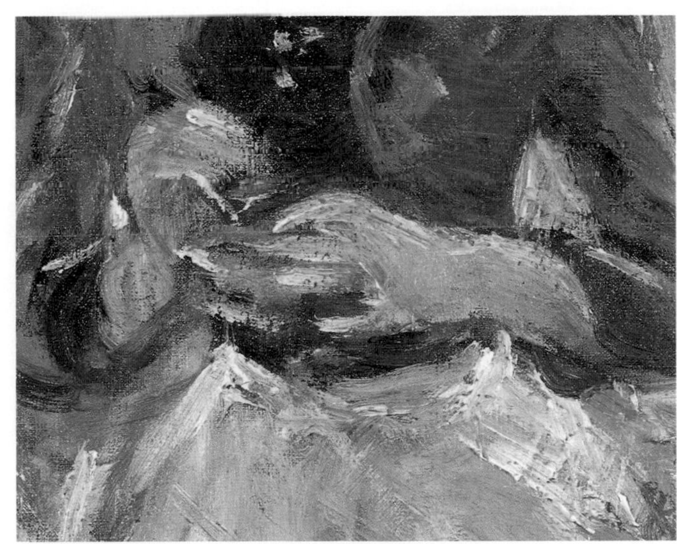

her affluent circumstances; like Manet, she did not have to pander to dealers or a public, but could paint for her own reasons.

As a woman of a certain social standing, Morisot, like her artistic contemporary, Mary Cassatt, was circumscribed in her dealings with the outside world and her portrait work was restricted to painting her family and friends.

In the Dining Room shows Morisot's art at its most sympathetic and engaging. Later in her career, during the 1880s, Morisot, like so many of her fellow Impressionists, became dissatisfied with so many of the qualities apparent in this painting and moved closer to Renoir, whose monumentalizing ambitions she assimilated into her own domesticated vision.

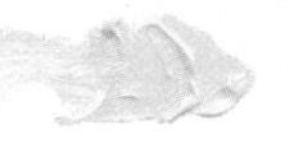

The Family

In his pamphlet, *The New Painting*, published in 1876, Degas' friend and supporter, Edmond Duranty, called for the modern artist to depict both the public world of the streets and the private world of the middle-class interior. "The person to be portrayed should be depicted at home, on the street, in a real setting, anywhere except against a polite backdrop of empty colors...," he wrote. In other words, painting should become a part of the "mapping" of the new world of Paris – a world that demanded a new means of representation.

Degas, Cassatt, Morisot and Caillebotte were all members of the haute-bourgeoisie and in their paintings of friends and family they have left a tangible record of the inner workings of family life at this period. The notion of home and family was a critical element of modern life; it was at one and the same time a retreat from the harsh realities of public life and the dynamic source that generated and sustained the engine of modern society. It was seen as a model that reflected the harmonious workings of an ordered and regularized society. Art historian Linda Nochlin, writing about the status of family life in nineteenth-century France has revealed how the family represented:

the chief pillar of the state, a bulwark against the chaotic and uncontrolled energies and desires of the masses, and on the necessity for the middle-class family to instill the virtues of industry, honesty, loyalty and self-sacrifice in its members – through the instrumentality of its female members above all.

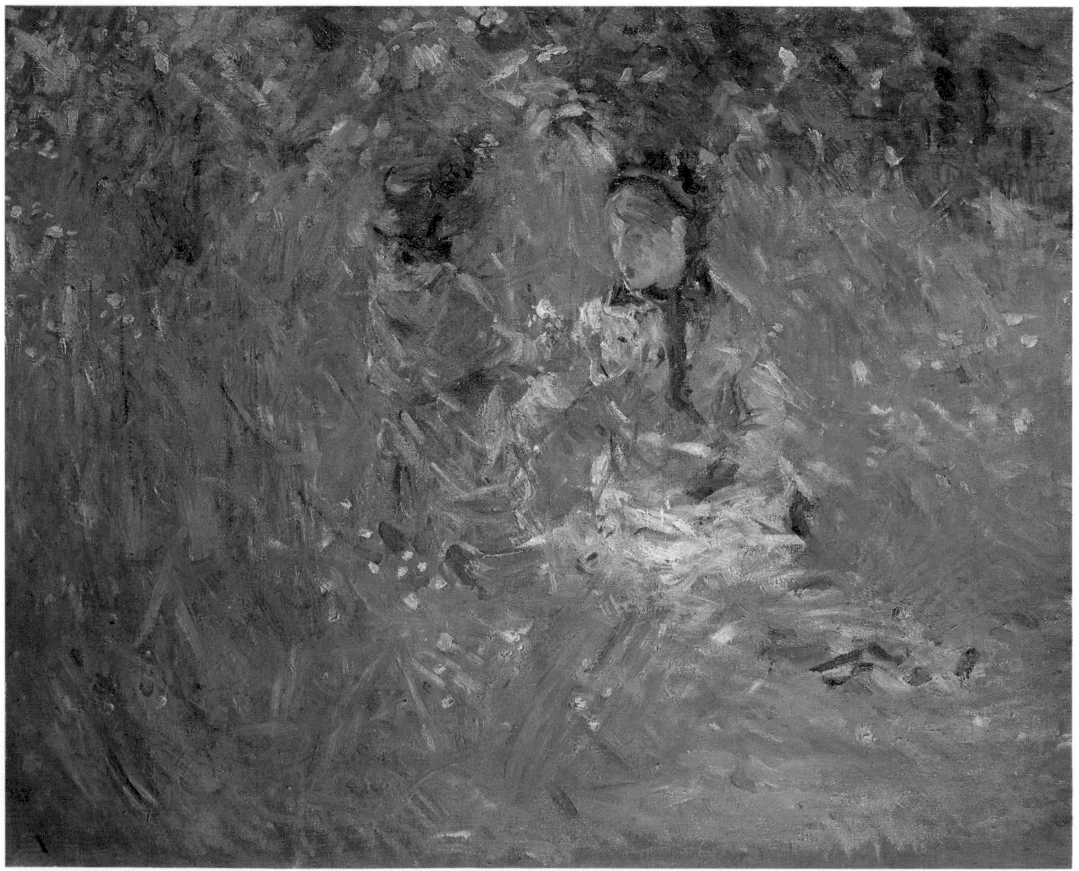

Berthe Morisot,* In the Garden, *1883–84. The dynamic brushwork suggest the security and shared affection that the Impressionists strove for in their desire for harmony, both in public and private life.

Artistic images of the family, corresponding to this need to create and sustain this public image, do not necessarily relate to the actuality of any one domestic situation. The *année terrible* of 1870–71 was thought to have been evidence of the spiritual and moral weakness of France. Now, in the new Republic that had replaced the decadent Second Empire, the family unit was promoted as a means of regenerating the country, both physically and metaphorically. Family portraits that set the individual within the harmonious

structure of the family unit and emphasized the role of the mother became a common subject at this time. The promotion of this ideal, still prevalent today, is an important factor in the continued popularity of Impressionism.

Occasionally in the compositions of Monet, and frequently in the portraits of Degas, the tensions that are an inevitable part of family life are given visual form. Degas' first masterpiece, his formal portrait of the Bellelli family (*c.*1860), is an unparalleled study of a dysfunctional family. The paintings of Morisot, Cassatt and Renoir, in contrast, invariably project the image of a happy contented family unit where children do not scream and parents keep their cool.

The woman's role as the guardian of the family is clearly celebrated in Renoir's famous painting of Madame Charpentier and her family. A fascinating comparison could be made with Degas' Bellelli family portrait that equally shows the mother in a protective and controlling attitude, but in this image there is an ease and informality that suggests a happy family unit, the children are dressed charmingly and expensively and wear their gorgeous hair long. The family dog, remains firmly part of the scene, unlike Porto, the dog in Degas' painting, even if he does look less than happy about his role as a surrogate chair.

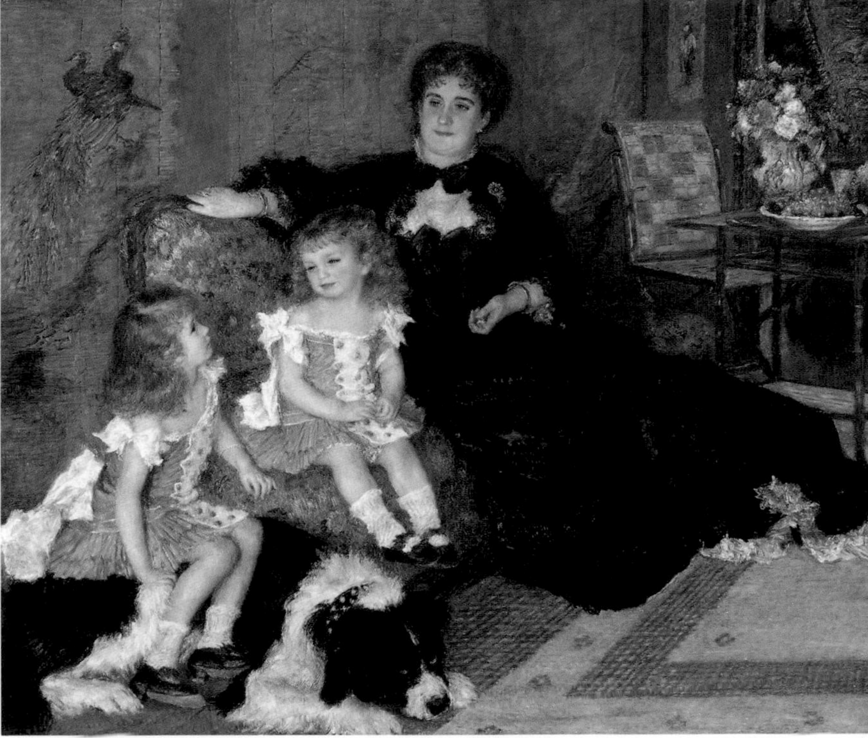

Pierre-Auguste Renoir,* Portrait of Madame Charpentier, *1878. Seated amid her* objet-de-luxe *and in her designer gown, Madame Charpentier shows she is still a loving and protective mother.

Intimate records

Perhaps what sets Impressionist portraits apart from previous commissioned portraits of the family group, and is another reason for their continued popularity, is that they were often painted as an intimate record of the artist's own family. During the period the Impressionists were painting, photography was becoming increasingly available to ordinary people, beginning the practice of the casual recording of private lives that we today take so much for granted. Where, in art, the family is normally seen from the viewpoint of the father, frequently in Impressionism, the father figure is the artist who, busily occupied painting the scene, is inevitably absent from the resulting image.

One of the major innovations that still makes Impressionist paintings of the family so eloquent was the introduction of the woman's viewpoint, to be found in the work of Berthe Morisot and Mary Cassatt. As women they were denied a complete professionally oriented fine art training. Excluded from life classes, they were lacking that essential element of the serious artist's repertoire, the nude figure, which was a necessary adjunct of history painting. Their social positions, and it would seem their own preferences, restricted them to the domestic world, with occasional forays into those areas of existence beyond the family home that were deemed socially acceptable. The beneficial result of this constraint was that the family, instead of being seen through the normal channel of the male gaze, now came under the scrutiny of a female sensibility.

The complexities and difficulties involved in painting and at the same time, sustaining a "correct" role within society was tellingly identified in this extract from a letter from Morisot to her sister Edma, who had given up painting on her marriage.

> ***Men incline to believe that they fill all one's life, but as for me, I think no matter how much affection woman has for her husband, it is not easy for her to break with a life of work … Affection is a very fine thing, on condition that there is something besides with which to fill one's days. This something, I see for you, is motherhood. Do not grieve about painting, I do not think it is worth a single regret.***

Such a letter reveals the evident complexity of Morisot's thinking about her own professional practice and her concerns about the role of the woman within the family, the fact that she was able to combine both roles in her own life is a sure sign of the determination that was such a key element in her personality.

Children

Portraits of children are characterized by an inevitable poignancy, due partly to the fleeting nature of childhood, and partly to an adult propensity to regard that period in our lives as a time of innocence, a moment when we were open to the magic of the world. Memories of childhood are often tinged with nostalgia for a time that can never be regained except through memory or vicariously through images such as these. The process of childhood and adolescence has been shared by us all, and unlike portraits of adults, whose histories are there to be read on their faces, images of children suggest the inevitability and essential unknowable face of the future: these are people whose histories are waiting to be written.

For today's audience, Impressionist paintings of children have an added poignancy, similar to that experienced in looking at old photographs. The children in these paintings have moved on from childhood to adulthood and old age, leaving us to ponder upon the inevitable passage of time. However much we may project our own feelings upon these images and however informal and psychologically acute the representations may be, the children portrayed in such paintings as these retain their essential privacy.

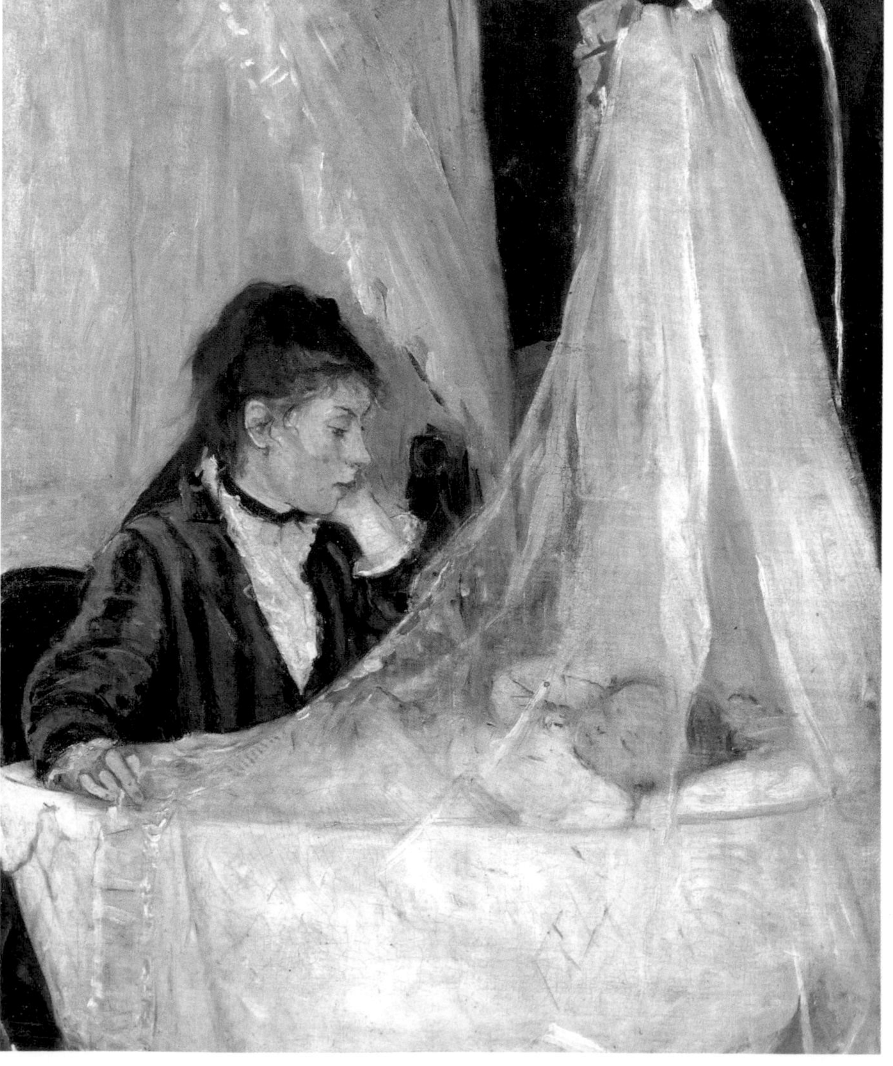

Impressionist portraits of children are, with few exceptions, extremely informal unlike many of their earlier counterparts. Historically, paintings of children were usually commissioned from artists in order to celebrate and substantiate the line of succession and the legitimacy of an important child's birth. Compared with such portraits, Impressionist paintings of children are characterized by their intimacy, vitality, and affection. For the most part, these paintings were uncommissioned and undertaken by the artists as records of their own, or of friend's parenthood. However close these adults may have been to their subjects, they were still adults and could only paint from an adult's point of view; the child's emotions and thoughts remain unexpressed, except in as much as they coincide with accepted norms of behavior. The children are subject to someone outside their own world, and the resultant image can never be a record of how the child sees himself or herself, but of how the world wishes to see the child.

Berthe Morisot,* The Cradle, *1872. The artist shows her sister, Edma, like a latter-day Madonna, looking down protectively upon her sleeping baby.

A natural informality

One of the great achievements of Impressionism was the introduction into painting of a sense of the natural and informal. Impressionist representations of children show them as secure within the family unit, this security usually signified by the presence of the mother or the implied presence of the father, represented by the viewer–artist figure. These children inhabit comfortable interiors, or occupy themselves within the secure boundaries of gardens, parks and nurseries, always happy and well fed. Gender roles are carefully and tactfully reinforced; boys are usually represented as actively operating in the world, or with an air of inherent authority, whereas girls are shown at the piano, reading or doing little of anything in particular. These idealized images of a protected existence stand as a powerful icon of an ideal world: the garden of Eden regained through the adult's re-creation of childhood experience.

One of the most appealing of the many subjects treated by the Impressionists is that of the mother and child. The prototype for this scene of domestic bliss is the image of the Virgin and Child, the mother invariably being portrayed as meek, loving and tender, untroubled by her charge. In this context, the paintings of Mary Cassatt and Berthe Morisot may be considered as variations on the traditional theme of the Virgin and Child adapted to a secular world, which invest the depicted intimate relationship of mother and child with an almost religious aura. It is not therefore surprising that there is a sense of that serenity, reverence and tenderness in the paintings of Berthe Morisot and Mary Cassatt.

The popularity of such subjects was widespread, as it is today, and the countless Madonna and Child images very obviously lend to the theme of motherhood an odor of sanctity and purity that was very much an element of bourgeois ideology and something of their success creating such memorable paintings of such subjects relies upon their innovative development of such standard compositions.

However, their sense of this bond between mother and child is informed by very different circumstances from those that were part of their illustrious model. It is perhaps a measure of their middle-class status that their paintings celebrate only positive aspects of parenthood; one suspects that a nurserymaid was never far away to deal with less appealing moments.

In reality, in many of the households painted by the Impressionists, such activities as feeding and changing the child would have been undertaken by others. Renoir is unusual in his depictions of his own wife, who was from Burgundian peasant stock, breast-feeding their child.

Impressionist portraits of children are with few exceptions extremely informal unlike so many of their counterparts.

Cézanne has used his son Paul, as a model perhaps because he was available and could be trusted, as the painter's son, not to move. For all that he loved the boy, the image as painted remains impersonal, no attributes or symbols are introduced into the painting, it is essentially a study of color and form, which preserves the privacy of the boy's own thoughts.

Consciously or otherwise, the fact that such images were painted by women adds a subtle twist to the usual position of the artist as surrogate father-figure. In particular, it allowed Morisot the opportunity to paint her husband Eugène Manet playing in the garden with their daughter Julie, looking out of the canvas at his wife, his gaze including her in this intimate moment with their daughter. It may be that the most significant aspect of Impressionist portraits of children is that unlike their English counterparts, they had a comparative lack of interest in moralizing a subject we now realize is fundamentally an adult invention – the innocence of childhood.

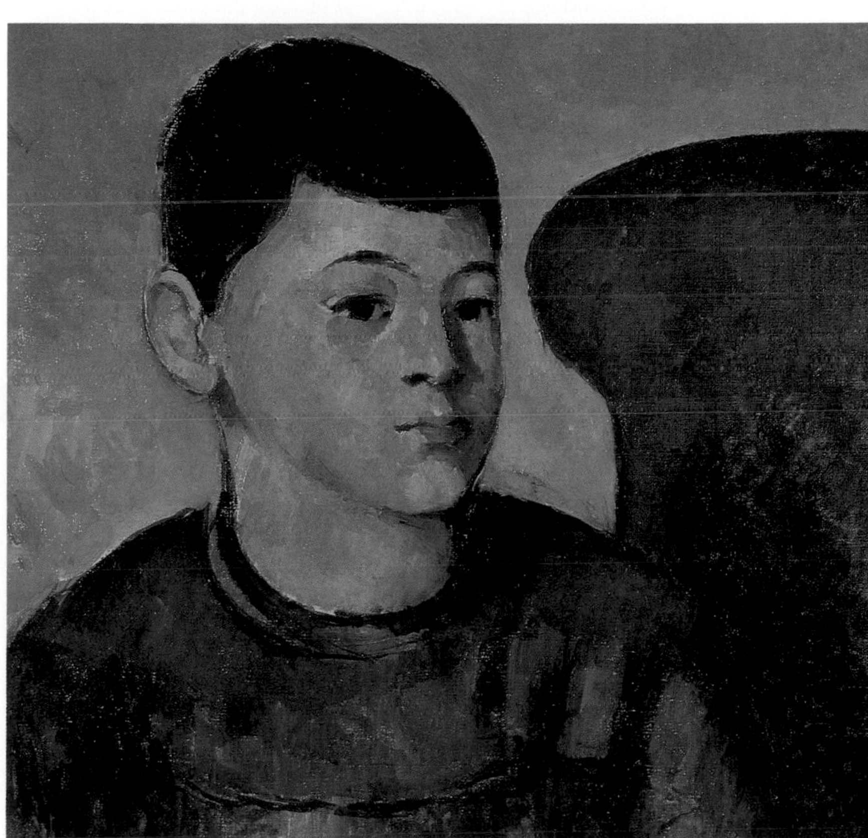

Paul Cézanne,* Portrait of the Artist's Son, Paul*, c.1884. A cool and beautifully phrased portrait of Cézanne's much-loved, much-spoiled only son.

Parks and Gardens

The urban park or domestic garden represents nature brought under man's control and made safe for civilized behavior. As such, it is a mark of affluence and leisure, a public or a private space separate from the world of work. Included in the development of Paris in the 1850s was a whole system of open parkland intended to bring health to the inhabitants of the capital and to create a place for relaxation and display. Many parks were based upon the *jardin anglais*, with promenades and lakes, trees and bushes, the planned and nurtured landscape organized to become an informal setting and a carefully managed piece of the natural world.

Parks and gardens feature in the work of every Impressionist painter with the exception of Degas. Domestic gardens were private extensions of the domestic interior and were regarded as a sign of affluence, ease and security, away from the cares of the outside world where the family could relax among themselves and their friends.

The labor necessary to sustain these spaces is rarely depicted; instead, like the garden of Eden, everything appears to flower of its own accord, the inhabitants not naked, but dressed in the height of fashion. Monet's first major works, the large, never-finished *Luncheon on the Grass* and his *Women in the Garden*, take the image of sophisticated urban dwellers occupying themselves with the pleasures of life. The women are represented as doing quite literally nothing: like the garden they inhabit they are there for our delectation, artificial, cosseted and beautiful. For artists, the colors and arrangement of the flowers and foliage in a garden gave them

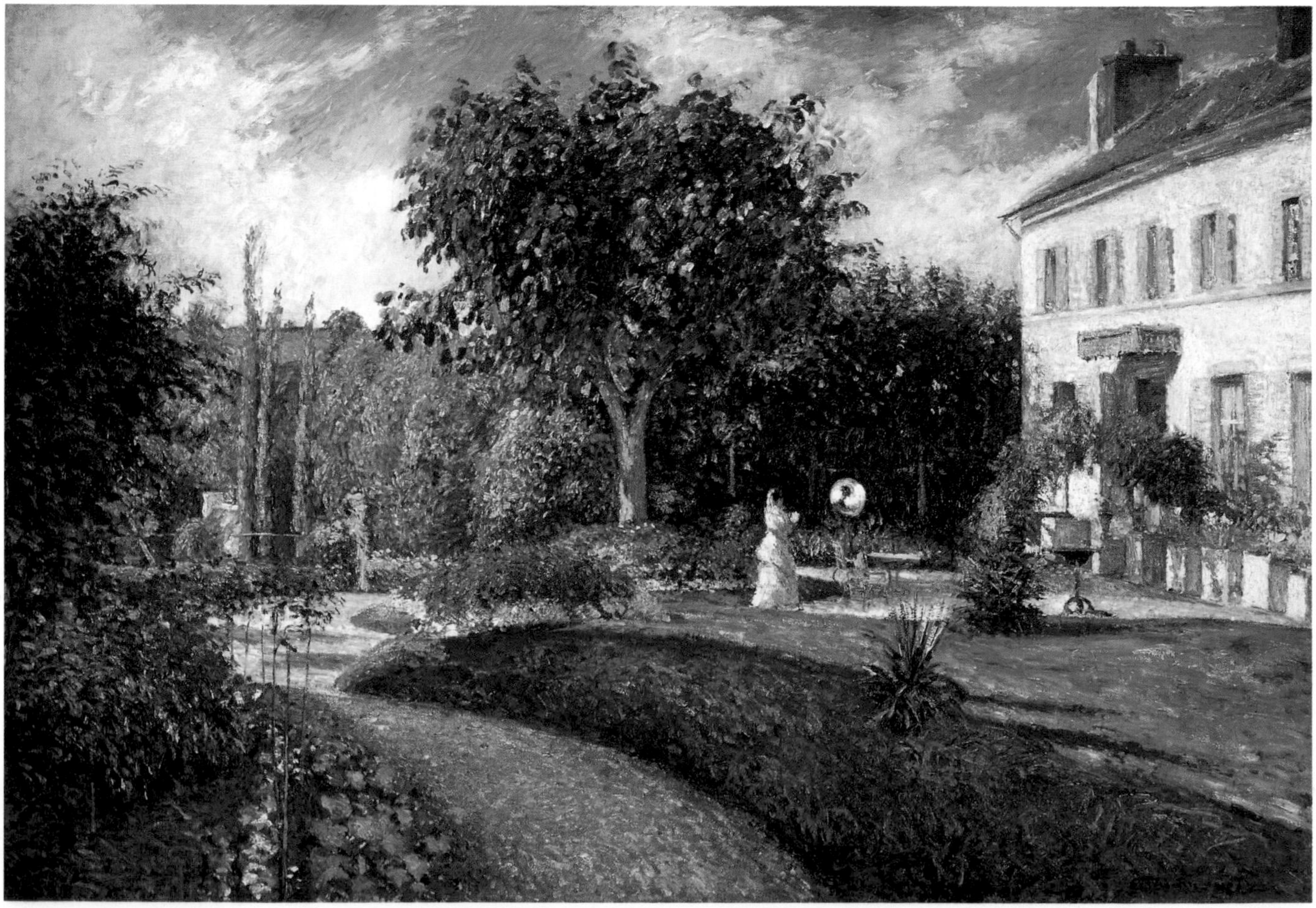

Camille Pissarro,* Garden at Les Mathurins at Pontoise, *1876. Here Pissarro celebrates the safety and security of the suburban garden.

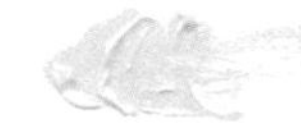

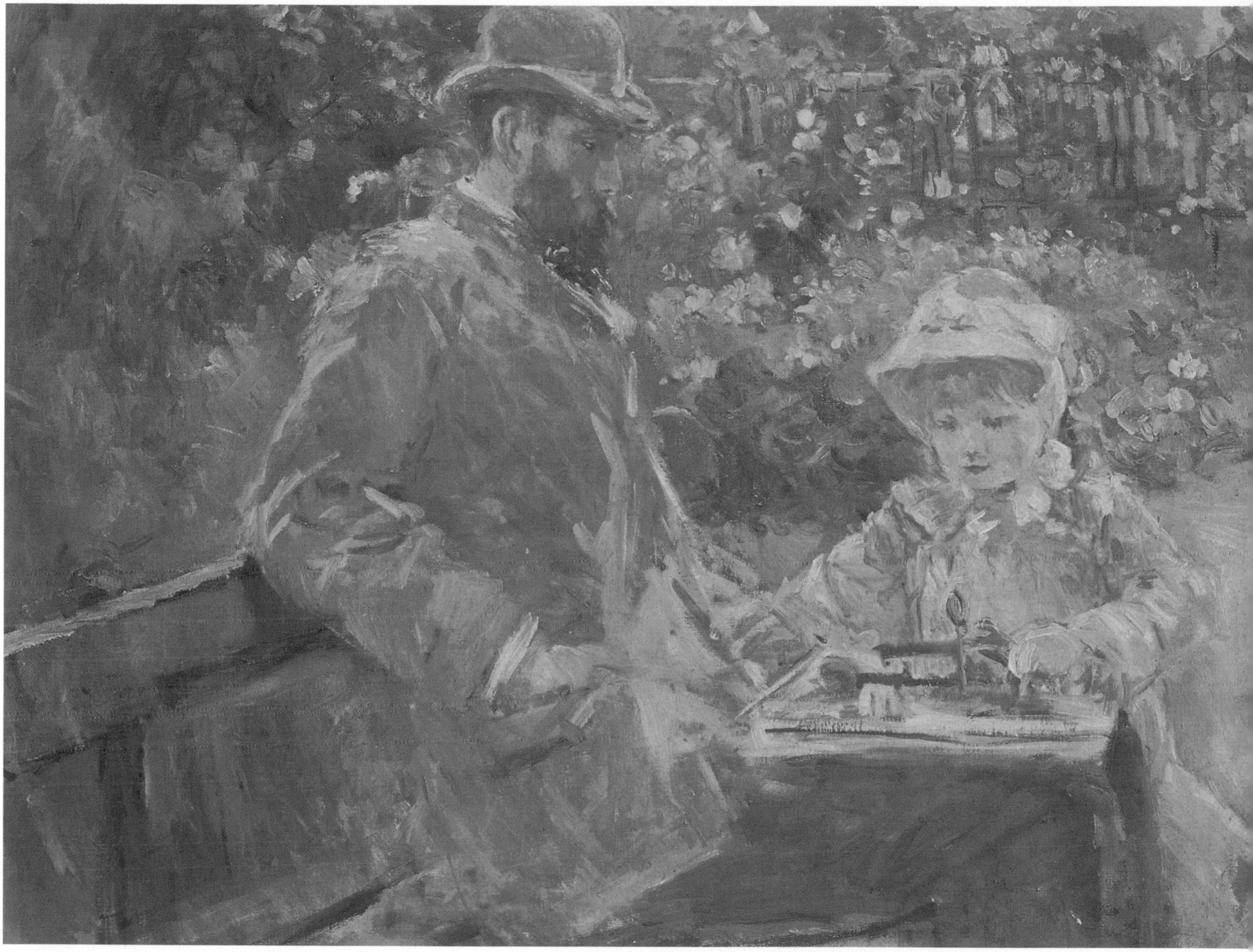

Morisot, **Eugène Manet and his daughter Julie in the Garden at Bougival,** ***1881. An unusual representation of a father, Morisot's husband Eugène Manet and their daughter Julie.***

a corresponding freedom in their own painting allied with an ease of access that gave someone like Berthe Morisot a private and secure miniature landscape in which to work. For Manet, whose illness prevented him from moving far from home, his garden at Versailles gave him the opportunity to paint some coolly observed, virtuoso paintings of his suburban garden. While most of his friends painted the managed gardens of the town, Pissarro identified himself more often with the market gardens of Pontoise and Eragny.

Monet's love of gardens and flowers is evident in many of his paintings from all periods of his life. From the mid-1870s he was able to afford a gardener and by the late 1880s, when he became financially successful, he wasted no time developing the property around his house at Giverny, employing at one stage of his life over a dozen gardeners. These employees tended an extended garden that in the last twenty-five years of his life became the focal point of his artistic investigations. Caillebotte, too, shared Monet's passion for horticulture and Renoir enjoyed the opportunity to create relaxed compositions of flirtation and dalliance that recalled the *fêtes galantes* of Watteau and other artists of his beloved eighteenth century.

The Impressionist Portrait

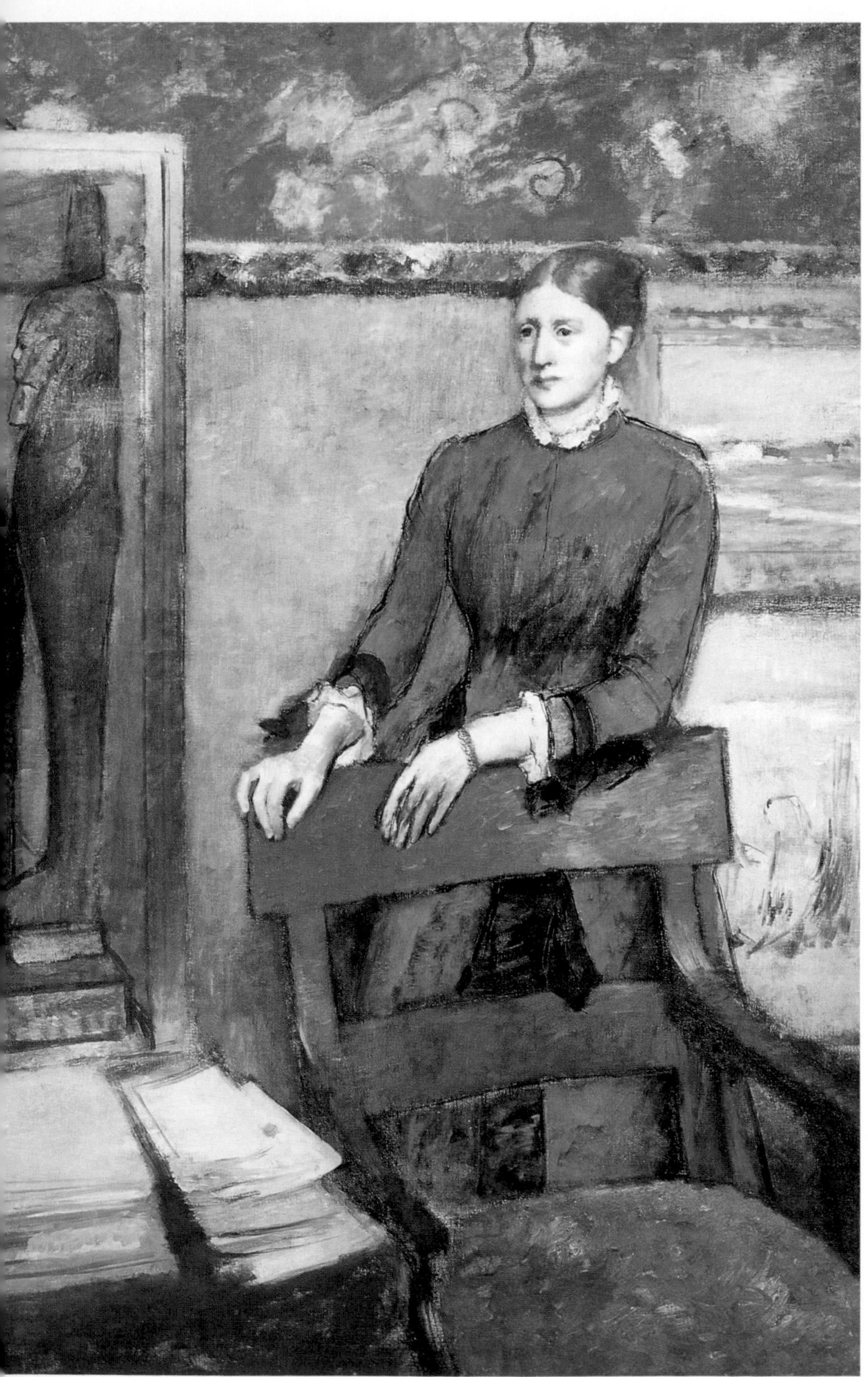

Degas, **Portrait of Hélène Rouart in her Father's Study,** *1886.* ***The daughter of Degas' friend and collector, Hélène is situated in her father's study surrounded by objects from his collection.***

The characters depicted by the Impressionists have become almost as much a part of our lives as the familiar faces of old Hollywood movies. They populate our memories like old friends and accompany us as constant companions through our lives. Like Shakespeare, Rembrandt, Dickens and van Gogh, the Impressionist painters have created a vivid, populous world alive and parallel with our own.

As in every other genre, the Impressionists broke the portrait-painting mold. They created a new kind of portraiture that would be a vehicle for the depiction of modern feelings. Following the example of novelists such as Balzac and Zola, they made use of contemporary interest in the pseudo-science of physiognomy to record and interpret an age that seemed so different from previous epochs. Earlier modes of expressing feelings and emotions through the conventionalized language of gestures and facial expressions no longer seemed adequate. Meaning need not be confined to the body and its gestures but could also be formed by clothes and accessories.

Degas' notebook jottings made in May 1879 are particularly striking examples of this quest:

> ***Do all kinds of objects in use, placed, associated in such a way that they take on the life of the man or woman, corsets which have just been taken off, for example, and which still retain as it were, the shape of the body, etc. etc. … A series on instruments and instrumentalists, their shapes, the twisting of the violinist's hands and arms and neck, for example. The swelling and hollowing cheeks of a bassoonist, and oboist, etc.***

Elsewhere, Degas noted his ambition to find an equivalent to the conventionalized academic studies of particular facial expressions to denote particular emotions: "Make a *tête d'expression* – it is Lavater, but Lavater more relative as it were, with accessory symbols at times." Lavater was an eighteenth-century Swiss specialist who codified physiognomic expressions into a coherent program. Famously, Edmond Duranty wrote in his 1876 pamphlet, *The New Painting*, composed specifically with his friend Degas in mind, that:

By means of a back, we want a temperament, an age, a social condition to be revealed; through a pair of hands, we should be able to express a magistrate or a tradesman; by a gesture, a whole series of feelings. A physiognomy will tell us that this fellow is certainly an orderly, dry, meticulous man, whereas that one is carelessness and disorderliness itself. An attitude will tell us that this person is going to a business meeting, whereas that one is returning from a love tryst. A man opens a door, he enters; that is enough; we can see that he has lost his daughter … Hands that are kept in pockets can be eloquent …

Financial importance

More prosaically, portraiture was a means of making money, appealing to the vanity of those able to afford such paintings, and was thus a necessary part of a painter's life. Renoir's *Madame Charpentier and Her Children*, painted in 1878 and exhibited to great acclaim in the 1879 Salon, is a good example of the artist creating a carefully orchestrated public image for a private patron in the hope of securing more equally lucrative commissions. Earlier in his career, Monet had also on occasion painted portraits in the hope of gaining some necessary money. His extraordinary 1876 portrait of Camille in a red kimono, *The Japanese Woman*, was painted as a public relations exercise to advertise his ability to transform any woman into a glamorous icon.

Many Impressionist portraits are intimate informal affairs, paintings of family and friends. Among the most moving of them is surely Monet's portrait of his wife, Camille, on her deathbed. She appeared in many guises in his paintings of the 1860s and 1870s, sometimes the focus of attention, as in *The Japanese Woman*, sometimes just an incidental presence within a larger scene. This portrait of Camille on her deathbed, like the contemporary paintings of Eugène Carrière, goes beyond mere description to suggest a metaphysical reality beyond the physical. Seated by his dying young wife's bed in 1879, Monet found himself,

… automatically searching for the succession, the arrangement of color gradations that death was imposing upon her motionless face … that was the point I had reached … even before I had the idea of recording those features to which I was so profoundly attached, my organism was already reacting to the color sensations, and in spite of myself, I was being involved by my reflexes in an unconscious process in which I was resuming the course of my daily life.

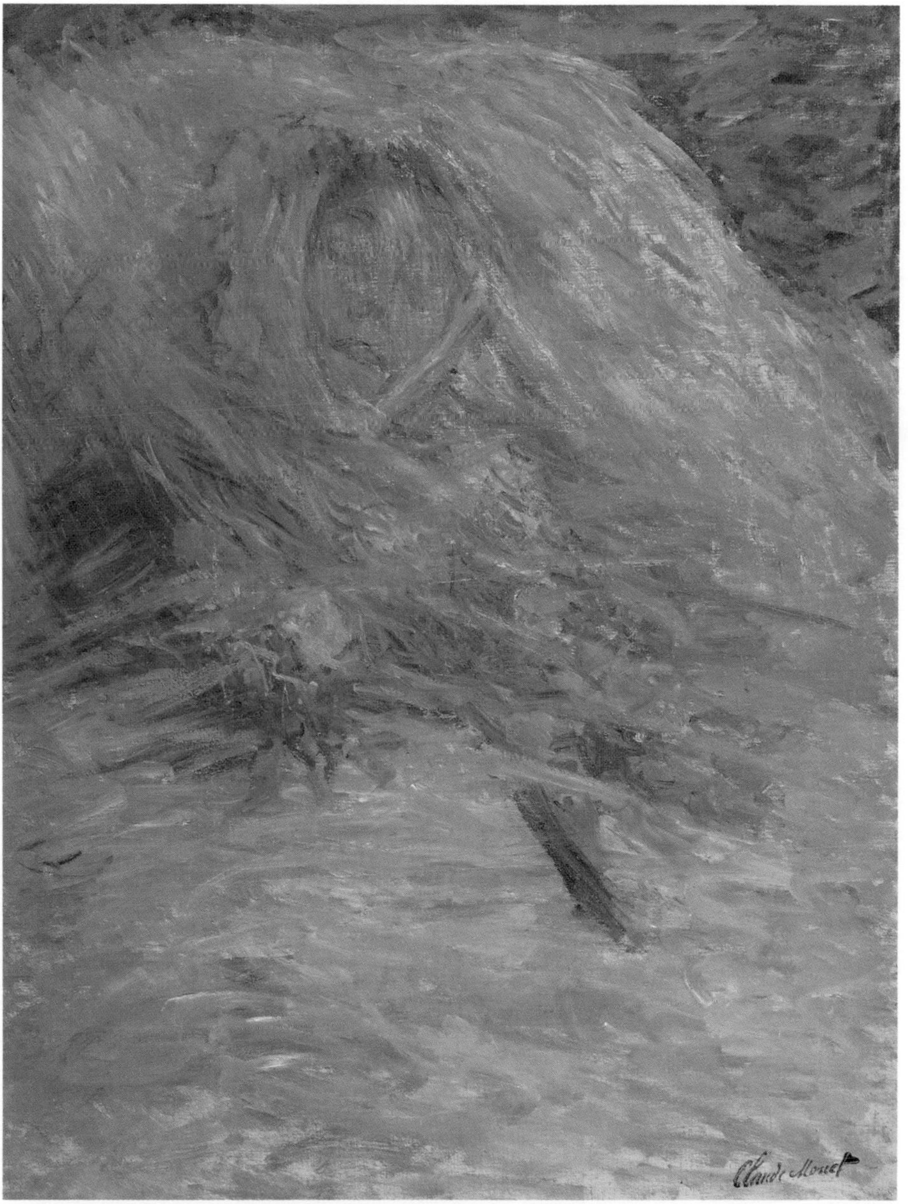

Monet,* Portrait of Camille on Her Deathbed, *1879. One of the most moving portraits ever painted, Camille's form seems caught midway between life and death.

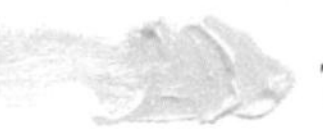

Mary Cassatt:
the American Impressionist

Mary Cassatt (1844–1926) was the fifth child of Robert Simpson Cassatt, a wealthy American broker and was born in Allegheny City, Allegheny County, Pennsylvania. Her sister, Lydia, who features in so many of her paintings was older than she, having been born in 1837. In 1851, two years after the family had moved to Philadelphia, they embarked on an extended European tour, returning to America in 1855.

Cassatt,* Girl Arranging Her Hair, *1886. With its strong and daring composition of colors, this painting makes it easy to understand Degas' high opinion of Cassatt.

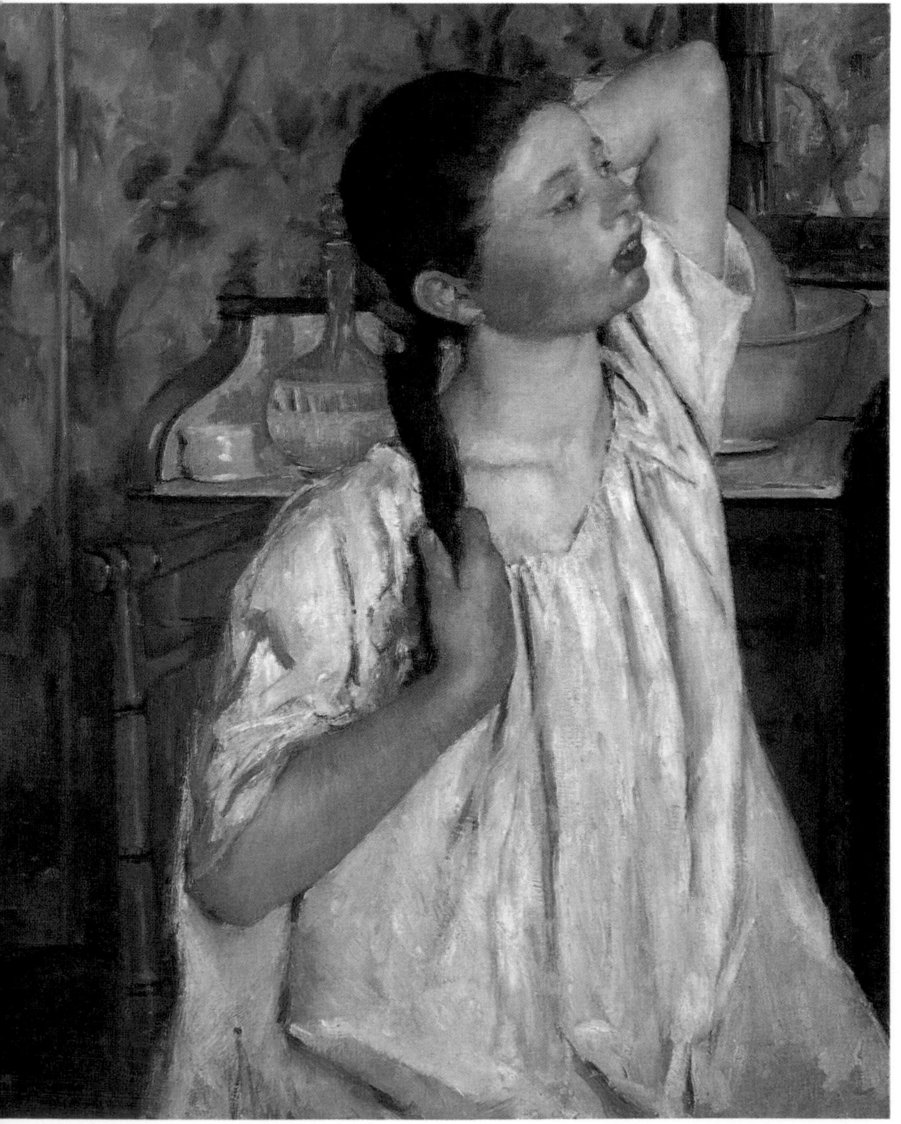

In her mid-teens, already determined on her future career, Cassatt enrolled at one of the very few art schools in the United States, the respected Pennsylvania Academy of Fine Arts, undergoing a thorough academic training until 1865. By now, she was telling her parents that the teaching was dull and stifling and that she strongly desired to return to Europe to study amongst the museums and galleries there. In 1866 her family agreed to her wishes and in that year she entered the Paris studio of a successful Academic painter, Charles Chaplin.

In 1871–72 she visited Rome and, most significantly, spent eight months in Parma studying the works of Correggio. Her early years were thus a prolonged and arduous studentship. She was settled in Paris by 1874, where she had already fallen under the spell of Manet's painting. Her first appearance at the Salon was in 1874 with a picture of three people on a balcony, entitled *During the Carnival,* which now hangs in the Philadelphia Museum of Art. She showed again in 1875, represented by two assured exercises in *Espagnolisme.* She knew Paris well, having visited it frequently since that first childhood visit in 1851, she spoke French fluently though always, like her fellow American Whistler, with a pronounced American accent.

In 1873, at the age of 28, she had her first encounter with a painting by Degas, *The Ballet Rehearsal.* Her friend Miss Louisine Waldron Elder, then in her teens, later to become Mrs. Henry O. Havemeyer, bought the picture, which was to be the first of many such purchases inspired by Cassatt. Although Cassatt kept herself somewhat aloof from the American expatriate crowd, she was well connected among the avant-garde artistic circles of Paris; she knew Whistler and Courbet, and in 1874 her painting *Madame Cortier,* listed for the first time under her own name, was seen by Degas. "C'est vrai. Voila quelqu'un qui sent comme moi" ("At last. Someone who feels as I do"), he said.

She was thirty at the time of this decisive encounter and had reached her maturity as a painter. Degas invited her to exhibit with the independent group in 1877, by which time she knew many of the Impressionists, including Berthe

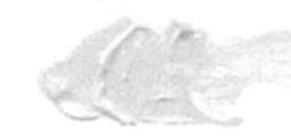

Morisot. Cassatt made her first appearance with them in their 1879 exhibition, exhibiting with them again in 1880, 1881 and 1886. She was recognized by her associates and critics as a professional and as their equal.

Cassatt soon became intimate with Degas and her familiar elegantly turned and well-tailored silhouette and sharp, self-assured features reoccur in many of his works. He greatly admired her taste in hats and she features particularly in many of his pastels of the early 1880s of the interiors of millinery shops.

Initially, there was a perceptible tension between Berthe Morisot and Cassatt, but it disappeared and developed into a warm friendship. Although very different artists, critics persisted in seeing their work together. Usually, Morisot was seen as being more feminine, whereas Cassatt's work was characterized by its firm drawing and clear articulation of forms. J.K. Huysmans felt Cassatt was the superior artist, noting on one occasion that "Miss Cassatt has … a curiosity, a special attraction, for a flutter of feminine nerves passes through her painting that is more poised, more peaceful, more capable than Mme. Morizot [sic], a pupil of Manet."

Despite Huysman's mention of Manet, the two most significant encounters in Cassatt's life were undoubtedly the art and personality of Degas and her deep love for Japanese prints, which began to affect her work after the 1880s. She was able to assimilate both to create a powerful and highly personal art. Her work reveals a strong decorative sensibility, combined with a particular fondness for unusual perspectives, asymmetrical compositions, clean coloration, sharp incisive drawing, and a shrewd and sympathetic characterization of her subjects.

Cassatt's favored subject matter was the relationship between her family and friends, and especially the relationships between women and between mothers and their children. Her work is confident and assured and, although there is a great sense of intimacy in her compositions, her work is never overtly sentimental or coy. Two paintings by Cassatt were on view at Durand-Ruel's Impressionist exhibition in London in 1883, and others in his major New York exhibition in 1886. In 1893 she painted a large decorative mural for the Women's pavilion at the World's Columbian Exposition in Chicago.

By now, Cassatt's style of painting had moved to a drier, more brightly colored and discriminating decorative quality tied to her innovative experiments in color printing. Cassatt's unique achievement in her creation of color drypoints and aquatints of women at home, engaged in domestic affairs or occasionally in the wider milieu of the city, as in the well-known etching *The Omnibus* (1891), has long been recognized.

Like Berthe Morisot, with whom she became intimate, she remained fiercely loyal to the notions of independence common to the Impressionist painters. She refused to serve on juries, despite being asked many times, and thereby she threw herself into opposition with the American art establishment.

She never married and only made rare visits to the country of her origin, although she had a profound and lasting impact upon the growing American taste for French Impressionist painting. She was able to exert a powerful influence upon developing art collections in America partly because of the social position and wealth of her brother, Alexander Cassatt, who was President of the Pennsylvania Railroad. Her friends, Mrs. H. O. Havemeyer and James Stillman, bought not only Impressionist paintings at her suggestion but also works by El Greco and Goya. Toward the end of her long life she lost her sight and from 1912 was unable to produce work, pastels having occupied much of her time until then. She died, fiercely independent to the last, at her home, the Château de Beau Fresne, near Paris.

Degas,* Portrait of Mary Cassatt, *c.1880. Although she admired it as a work of art, she disliked this portrayal of herself immensely.

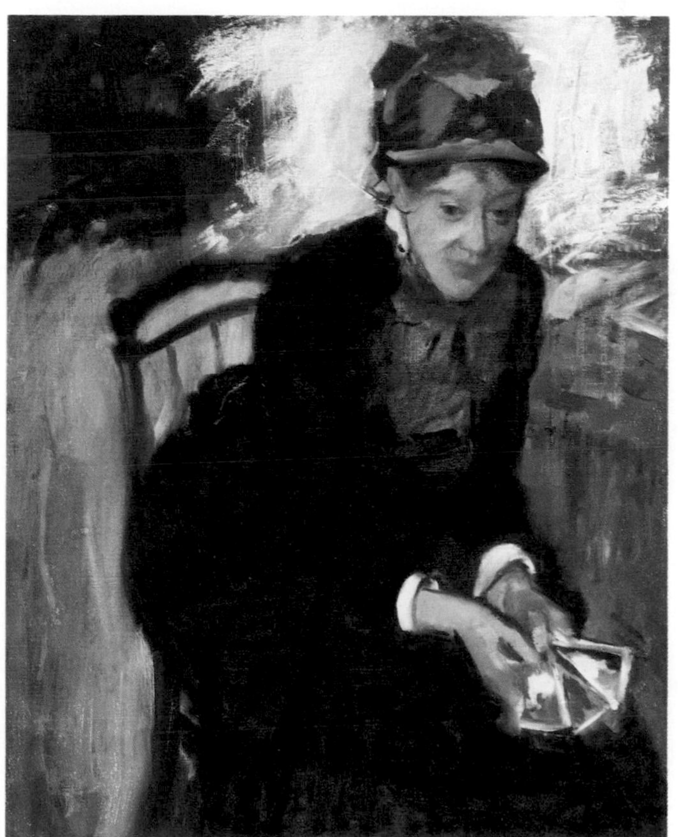

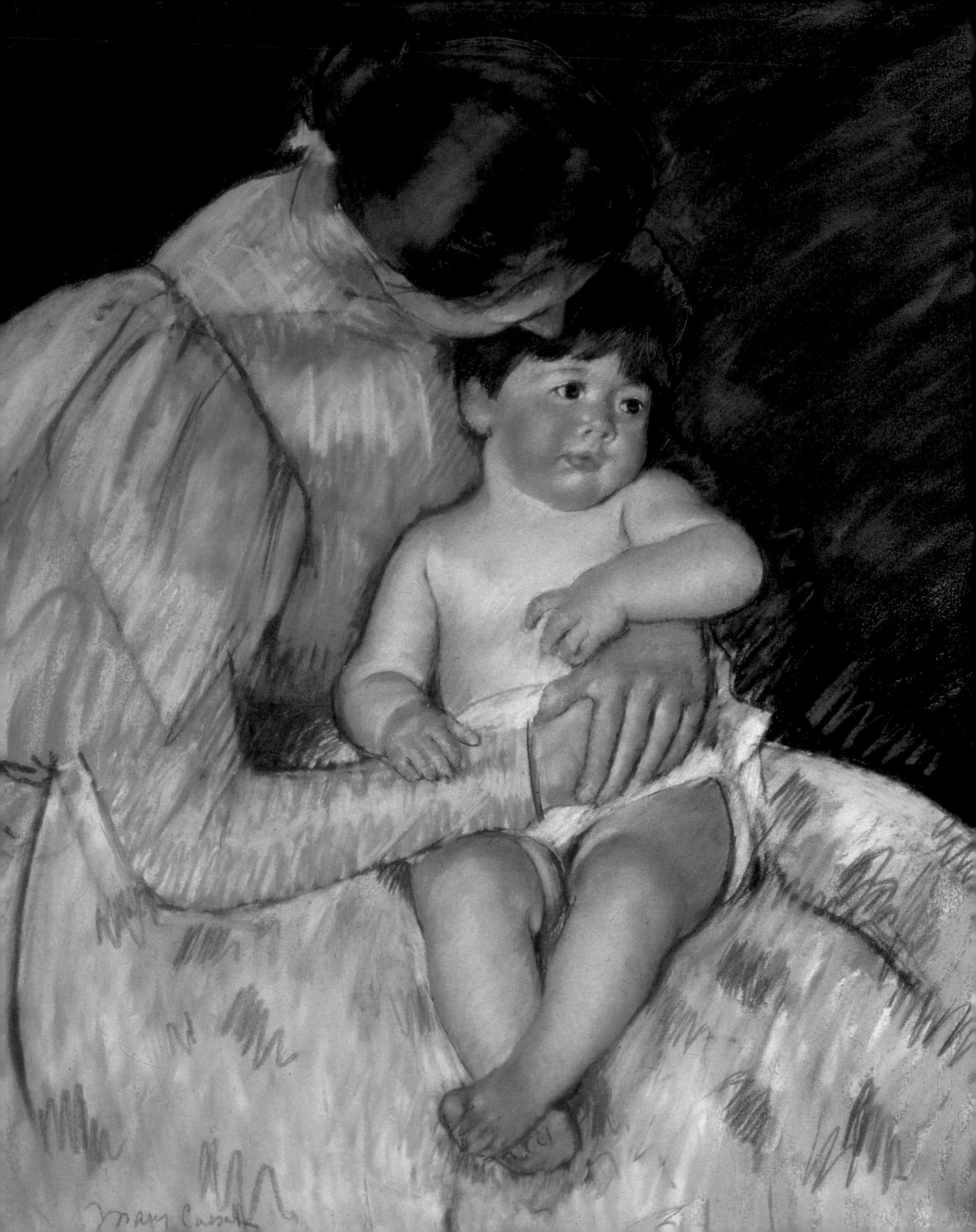
Mary Cassatt

Mother and Child

c.1890, pastel on paper, 81 x 65 cm (32 x 25½ in), Pushkin Museum, Moscow, Russia

Degas wrote that Cassatt's preoccupation was with the study of "reflections and shadows on skin and costumes for which she has the greatest feeling and understanding."

This is certainly true of this intimate pastel. Vigorously modeled, with incisive contours and powerfully drawn sweeps of vibrant pastel colors, it suggests the close relationship between the mother and child, although the child looks away from the security of his mother's enclosing embrace. The dark background is enlivened with traces of blue and pink and rapidly drawn pastel zig-zags that are repeated in the greater mass of the mother's dress. The painting's debt to Degas is obvious but equally evident is Cassatt's own distinctive style and her ability to create an image that is at once tender and strong.

Cassatt's expression of the strength and fleshy bulk of the infant is completely convincing, as is her drawing of the mother's relaxed hands interlocked around the infant's waist. The foreshortening, especially in the area describing the mother's downward turned face is consumate, her invisible gaze locked upon the fully modeled child's face, its pink cheeks picking up the major color note of the pastel.

The more finished working of the child's face is counterpointed by the freely drawn body of the woman, whose pink blouse is an open weave of overlaid movements of the pastel, usually darker pinks over a pale pink white ground. Areas of green–blue pastel are worked into the child's body to create an impression of its rounded form, not through gradations of light to dark, but purely in terms of color contrast; freely drawn squiggles of charcoal break away from the child to position its body more coherently within the picture area. The dark area of the mother's dress where it meets her blouse is particularly interesting, revealing Cassatt's initial drawing line to establish the basic form, then her overworking in charcoal and green pastel to create a convincing effect of shadow.

Loose hatchings and conscious use of composition create the physical and emotional link between mother and child. There are many examples on the subject of mothers embracing their children, but Cassatt made the subject her own. *Mother and Child* is almost sculptural. We see a subtle and dynamic balance between embracing figure and child and rhythms of arms, hands, legs and feet. The relationship of the two figures through the artist's choice of viewpoint, and establishment of the subject's gaze, give the child a sense of its own independence within the confines of its mother's protective embrace that was rare in art of the time.

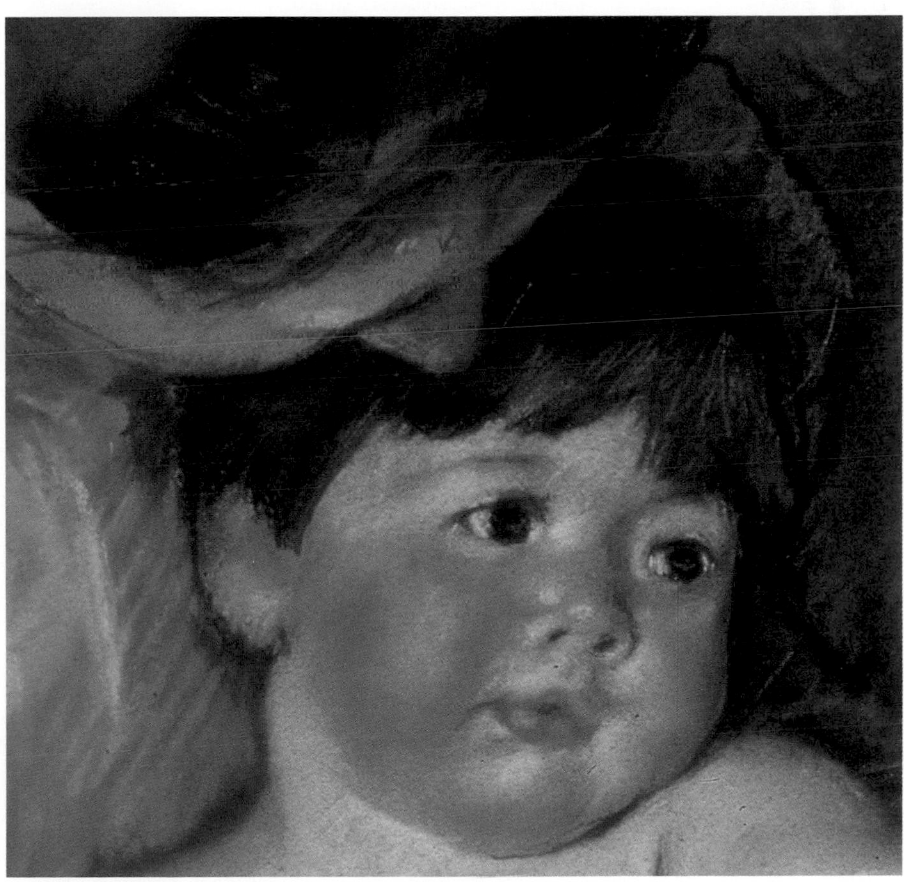

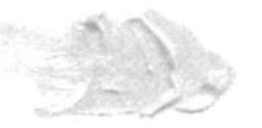

CHAPTER FOUR

Out of Paris

Paris had six railway stations, of which the Gare Saint-Lazare was the largest. It was also the one with which the Impressionists were most familiar because it served the suburbs of Bougival, Marly and Argenteuil and the towns of Pontoise and Auvers, as well as destinations further afield, such as the towns and ports of Normandy and Brittany.

In this chapter, we begin our journey from that station and visit the places outside Paris where the artists lived and painted. The Impressionists did not merely record these places, they also celebrated the means by which they were made so accessible: the modern railway, given center stage by Zola in *La Bête Humaine*, published in 1890, and painted by Caillebotte, Manet and, most famously, by Monet.

The area of Paris to the north of the station was known as the Batignolles quarter and had long been popular with writers and artists. In 1879, Manet moved into a new studio in the Rue d'Amsterdam, where Baudelaire and Alphonse Daudet had both once had apartments; before this, Manet had lived in the Boulevard des Batignolles and the Rue de St-Petersburg (now Rue de Moscou), which faced on to the Place de l'Europe and the railway line where it enters the Batignolles Tunnel.

It would have suited the artist well; he had ridden with the engine drivers on the Versailles–Paris run and had admired "their *sang-froid*, their endurance." His plan to celebrate their achievements on an epic scale within the newly rebuilt Hôtel-de-Ville never came to fruition. Instead, in his oblique homage, *The Railway*, painted in 1872–73, the subject of the painting, the railway, is seen only incidentally, the train identified by a wisp of steam. In the foreground, looking up as if disturbed by our presence, a young woman sits against some iron railings with a lap dog and a book while her young companion, adorned with a blue ribbon, looks down on the very scene that Monet was soon to celebrate so enthusiastically.

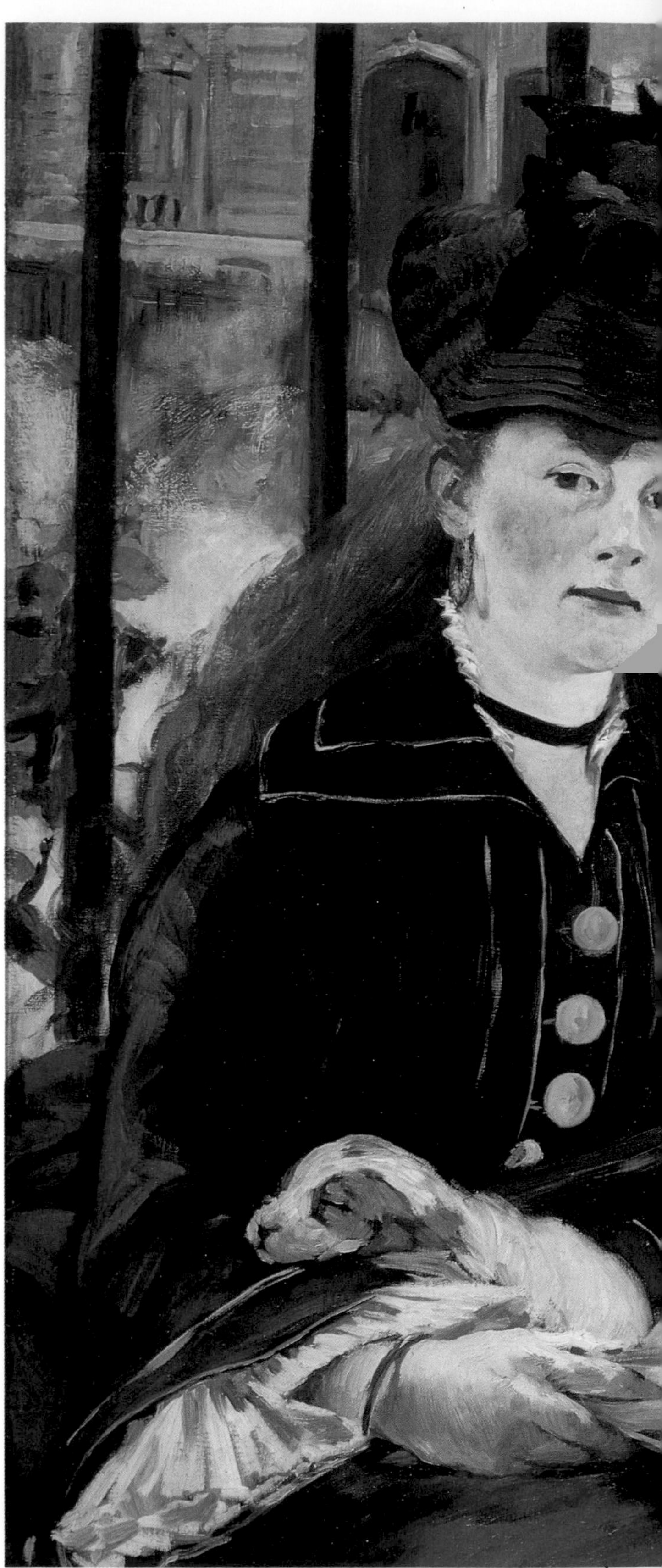

The Railway, ***1872–73. Startling in color and composition, this work had a powerful influence on Manet's friends Caillebotte and Monet.***

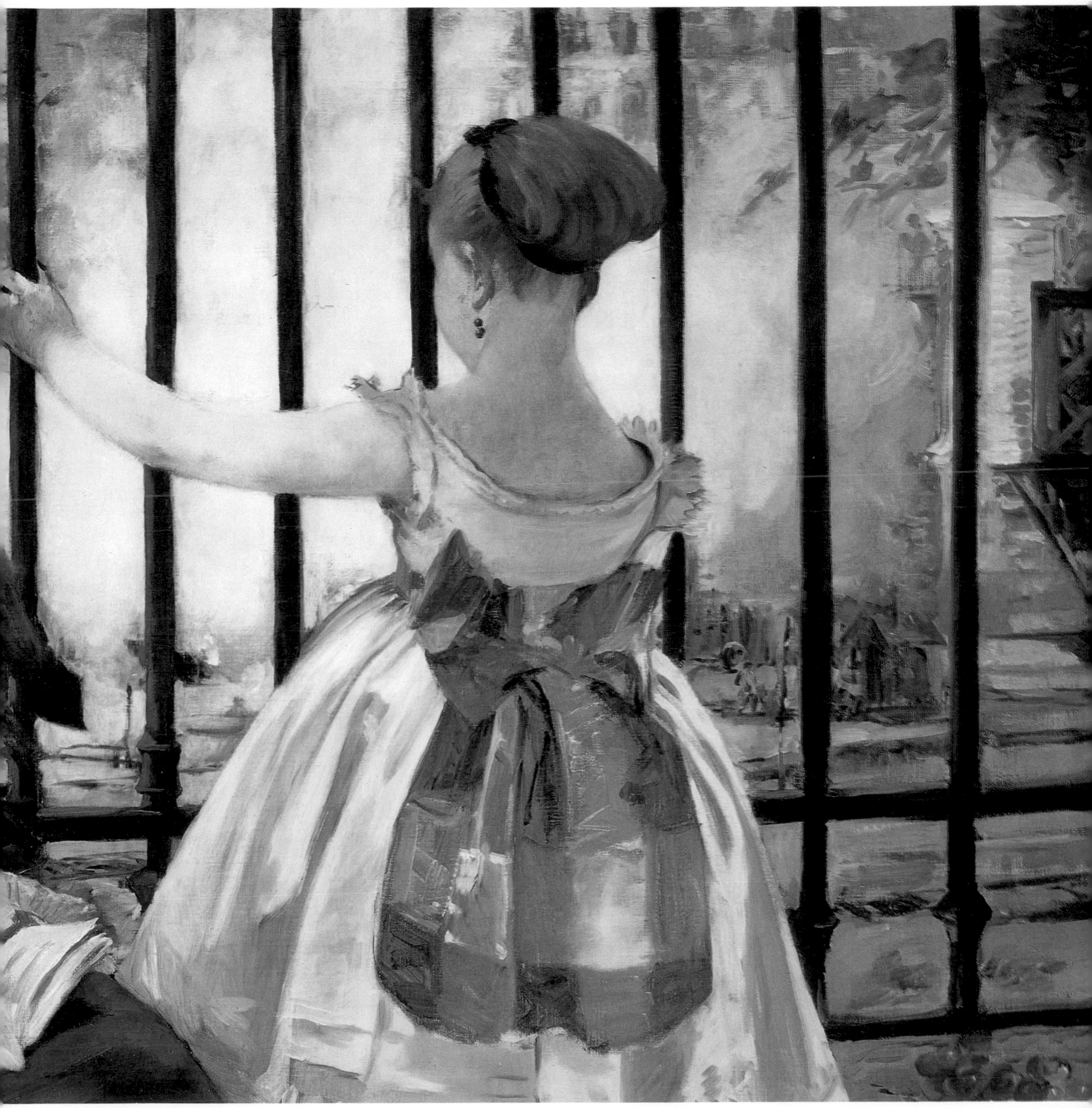

Gare Saint-Lazare

1877, oil on canvas, 75.5 x 104 cm (29¾ x 41 in), Musée d'Orsay, Paris, France

The railway terminus presented an unprecedented challenge to the architects and engineers of the nineteenth century. It was a genuinely modern phenomenon, with no equivalent in previous ages. Even so, most railway termini of the period had large, imposing and even pretentious entrances, betraying all too easily their roots in medieval or classical architecture; out of view, behind the impressive façade, stretched out skeletal spans of cast iron and glass arching over the railway platforms.

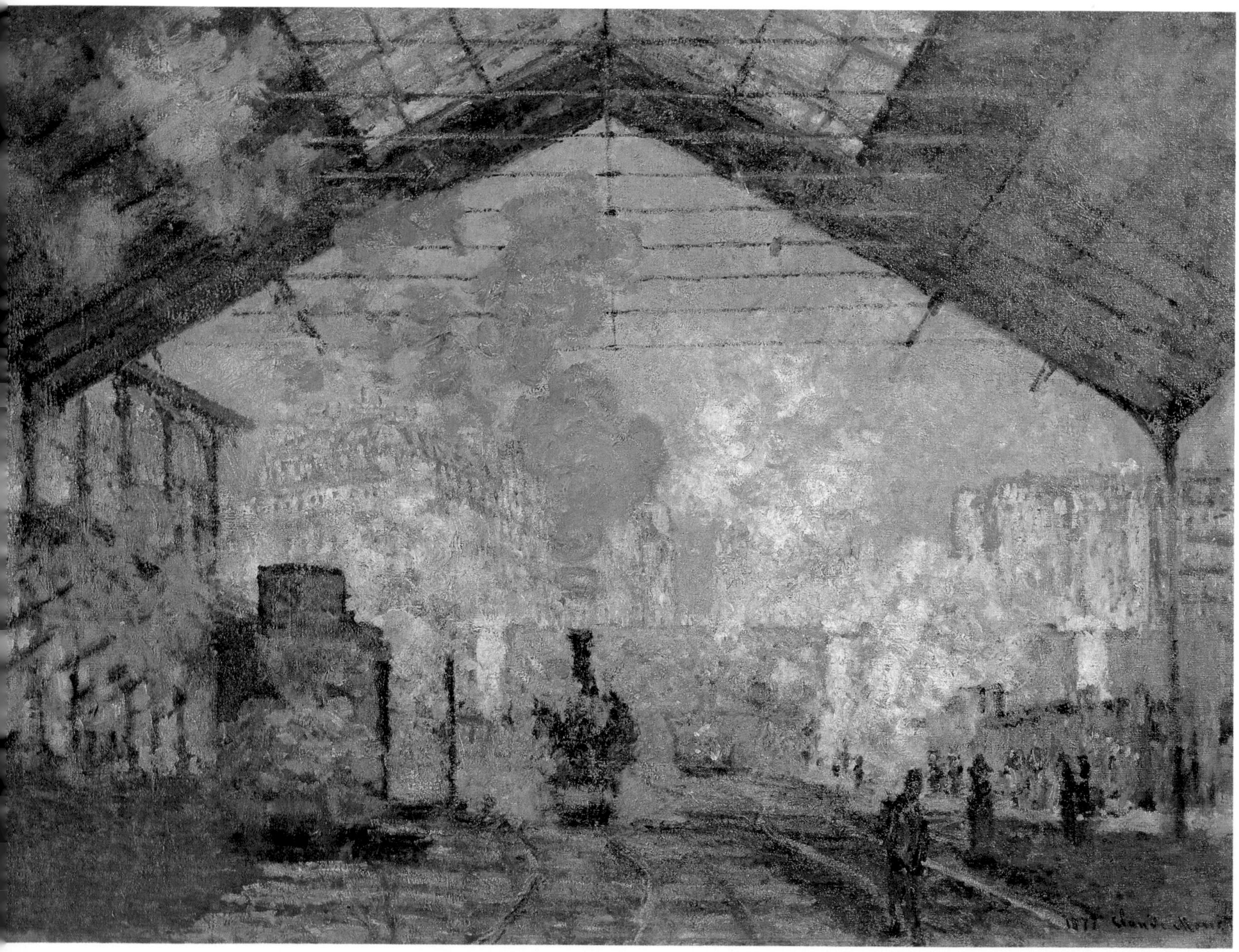

Unlike Daumier, for instance, Monet showed little or no interest in the dramatic and narrative potential of such a subject, in Monet's case the great Gare Saint-Lazare; he paid hardly any attention at all to the human aspect of the station. His deliberate avoidance of any form of sensationalism is

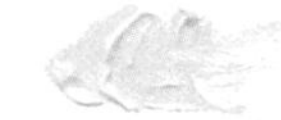

evident when his paintings of the Gare Saint-Lazare are compared with Zola's great novel *La Bête Humaine* (*The Beast in Man*), in which the same station is the backdrop to a torrid and melodramatic narrative of love, betrayal and murder.

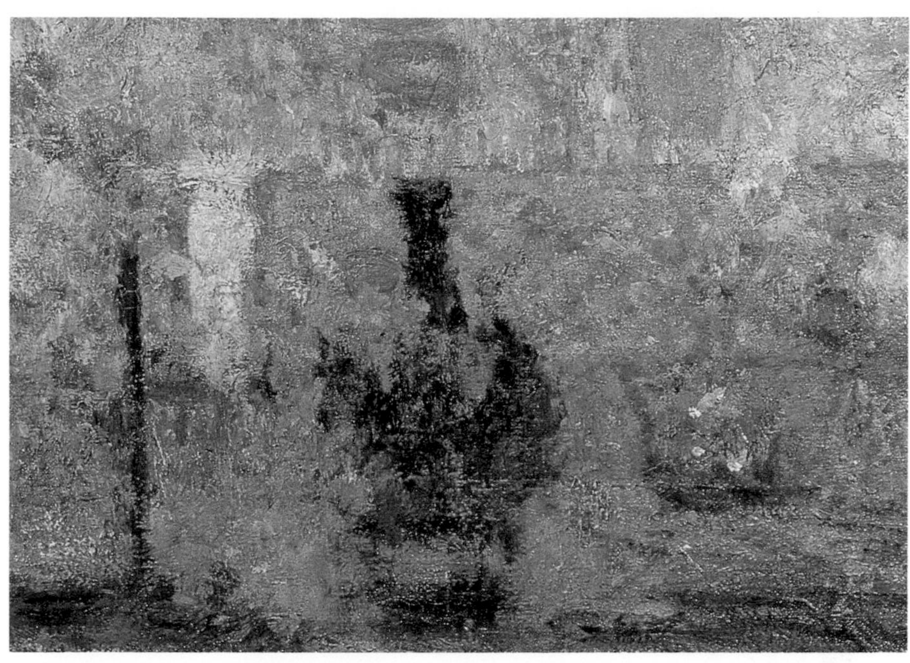

Although something of the power of the huge train engines, which had clearly fascinated Zola, is evident in Monet's paintings, his real interest lay in translating into paint the effects of light filtering through the glassed canopy. He could hardly have chosen a more challenging and complex scenario, for the atmospheric effects caused by steam rising from the engines were set against the brilliant daylight playing on the buildings of Paris, framed in the arched end of the station's glass canopy, facing north toward the Pont de l'Europe.

Monet obtained permission to paint inside the station in January 1877, and Caillebotte helped him locate a studio close by in Rue d'Edimbourg. In three months Monet had completed at least eight works, seven of which were exhibited in the third Impressionist exhibition in April 1877. Jean Renoir, Pierre-Auguste's son, has told how Monet intimidated the director of the station into submitting to all his requests: "The trains were all halted; the platforms were cleared; the engines crammed with coal so as to give out all the smoke Monet desired," he recalled.

The paintings, which included one titled *The Pont de l'Europe*, quite different in treatment from Caillebotte's of the year before, are very different from each other in composition, viewpoint and finish. At least one has been left in an extremely sketch-like state, with thin washes of paint enlivened by rapid calligraphic notations that describe the atmosphere and furniture of the train shed; others have a surface like heavy damask, with thickly encrusted swirls of paint worked across the surface of the canvas. The repeated application over already dry or near-dry paint has created ridges that catch the brush as it moves across the canvas to create a diffusion of color and form. In this way, Monet has brilliantly succeeded in evoking the rainbow-like effect as the sunlight hits the droplets of water hanging in the atmosphere.

The effect of these paintings seen together in the same room as Caillebotte's masterpieces of urban life must have been astounding. Their friend and supporter, the critic Georges Rivière, wrote of Monet's paintings in *L'Impressioniste* on April 6, 1877:

> ***These paintings are amazingly varied, despite the monotony and aridity of the subject. In them more than anywhere else can be seen that skill in arrangement, that organization of the canvas that is one of the main qualities of Monet's work … Looking at this magnificent painting, we are gripped by the same emotion as before nature, and it is perhaps even more intense, because the painting gives us the emotion of the artist as well.***

Rivière here articulates an important concern that still occupies artists and writers today. Does the significance of a painting depend upon the beauty and dramatic possibilities of its subject matter or does it reside in the manipulation of the medium to express the artist's inner feelings? Another critic, seeing Monet's paintings, felt that neither possibility had been convincingly explored by the artist, the paintings being mere vehicles for empty virtuosity. They contained "no inner feeling, no subtlety of impression, no personal vision, no choice of subject to show you something of the artist," he wrote. "Behind his eye and hand, one looks in vain for a mind and a soul."

Gare Saint-Lazare was the first group of paintings consciously undertaken by Monet as a series of related works. Later in his life, he was to return to painting series, with spectacular results; perhaps, in painting the Rouen Cathedral in the 1890s, Monet was consciously painting it as an antecedent of the cathedrals of the modern age, the great railway termini.

Argenteuil

In the early years of their careers, the Impressionists painted the coast of Normandy and the forest of Fontainebleau, sites already made popular by artists such as Boudin and Jongkind and the Barbizon painters. They also centered their activities around the Ile de France: the countryside, towns and villages that lay within easy reach of Paris, including Bougival, Chatou, Louveciennes and Marly-le-Roi. After the Franco-Prussian War of 1870 and the Commune, many of them moved further afield, only Sisley remaining completely faithful to the sites that saw the birth of Impressionism. Monet moved west to Argenteuil and Pissarro north of Paris to the busy market town of Pontoise and to Auvers-sur-Oise, where Cézanne also lived for a time. Renoir remained based in Paris but moved freely around the various places, visiting and painting with his friends.

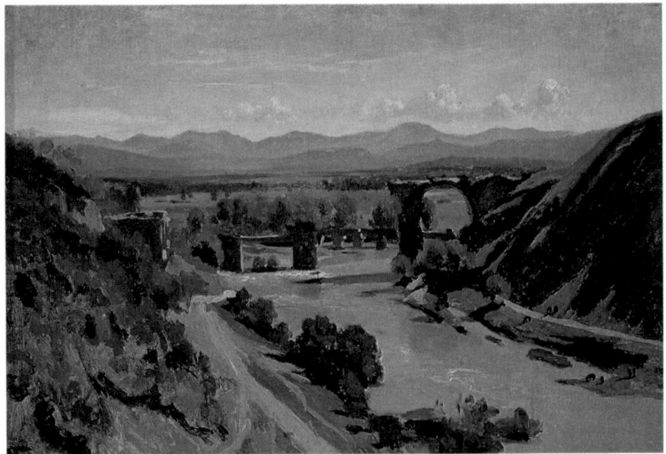

Corot,* The Bridge at Narni, *1826, A work far removed from the paintings of Monet, Renoir and their colleagues.

These frequent contacts were mutually stimulating, although Monet, ever an individualist, felt uneasy about too close a contact with his fellow artists. Although Paris remained their professional base, improvements in transport, especially the railways, allowed the artists to move further afield. The opening of new and constantly improved railway lines enabled Cézanne to make his frequent sorties from the capital to his family home in Aix-en-Provence with relative ease.

The middle classes were able to leave the city and enjoy the charms of a managed countryside while living within commuting distance of their places of employment – which is essentially just what the Impressionists did. In many ways they were the painters of suburbia. For them, as much as for the commuters, stations and roads were an important part of their lives, taking them to work and home again and, during holidays and weekends, to the country and the coast.

The landscape held a different significance for each artist, and each interpreted it according to his or her own concerns. Pissarro and Cézanne were drawn toward a nature transformed by the presence of man. Monet and Renoir, on the other hand, together with Caillebotte and on occasion Manet, made expeditions around Argenteuil in the 1870s to paint a landscape familiar to most Parisians as a place for relaxation and pleasure.

Only nine kilometers (6 miles) from the capital, and just half an hour away by train from the Gare Saint-Lazare, Argenteuil was a desirable place to live and, in consequence, was rapidly becoming an outreach of the capital. It was a thriving industrial town and a rapidly developing center for yachting, rowing and swimming. In painting such subjects, the Impressionists were identifying themselves resolutely with a landscape in the process of change, a place where leisure and industry coexisted and the presence of man was leaving an indelible mark on the landscape.

Edited views

Recent writers such as Paul Tucker and T. J. Clark have pointed out that the painters were extremely selective in their choice of the aspects of the town they chose to represent. They carefully edited their field of vision and their paintings played down, for obvious reasons, the visual evidence of industrial activity and the sewage works that polluted the river – such omissions were noted by some of the caricaturists of Impressionist paintings. Although the factory chimneys that flanked the rivers around the capital featured in their paintings, they were never treated as subjects in their own right, except in earlier paintings by Pissarro.

Even in these works, there is little sense of the factories being in any way connected to the lives of the people whose leisure activities are being celebrated in so many Impressionist

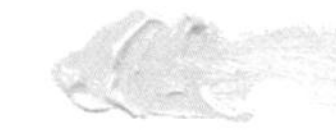

canvases. More frequently, the factories and their chimneys are simply ignored or painted out of the landscape in which they were situated. Such actions reaffirm Impressionism's role in constructing an idealized image of the countryside acceptable to the newly empowered middle class, and reveal the foolhardiness of equating an avant-garde artistic style with correspondingly avant-garde political sensibilities.

The Bridge at Argenteuil

Monet's fascination with trains and the river resulted in a series of paintings that have been seen as celebrating, consciously or otherwise, the reconstruction of France after the disaster of the Franco-Prussian War. The very bridge that features so prominently in this painting, *The Bridge at Argenteuil*, had only just been rebuilt after its destruction during the Franco-Prussian War.

It is only necessary to compare, as Robert Herbert has done, the beautifully weathered stone bridges that appear like natural extensions of the landscape in Corot's paintings with Monet's structures to see how far his works depart from the promotion of the landscape as a timeless idyll. In Corot's paintings the countryside and man's presence within it are seen as something fixed, as part of a nurturing natural order, whereas in Monet's paintings and those of his friends, the modern bridges are represented in such a way as to highlight their uncompromising modernity.

The gap between the harassed town-dweller's dream of a clean and innocent natural world as the source of spiritual renewal and the actualities of that landscape is perfectly caught in the following quotation, cited by T. J. Clark in his book, *The Painting of Modern Life: Paris in the Art of Manet and his Followers*:

> ***Monsieur Bartaval, a caricatural member of the bourgeoisie, on setting foot in the countryside reveals his disillusionment with the following words: "When I set off I said to myself: 'And there, I shall have some air, some sun and greenery … Oh, yes, greenery! Instead of cornflowers and poppies, great prairies covered with old clothes and detachable collars … laundresses everywhere and not a single shepherdess … factories instead of cottages … too much sun… no shade … and to cap it all, great red brick chimneys giving out black smoke which poisons the lungs and makes you cough!'"***

Monet,* The Bridge at Argenteuil*, 1874. A small miracle of painting, the solid presence of the bridge perfectly balances the rocking boats.

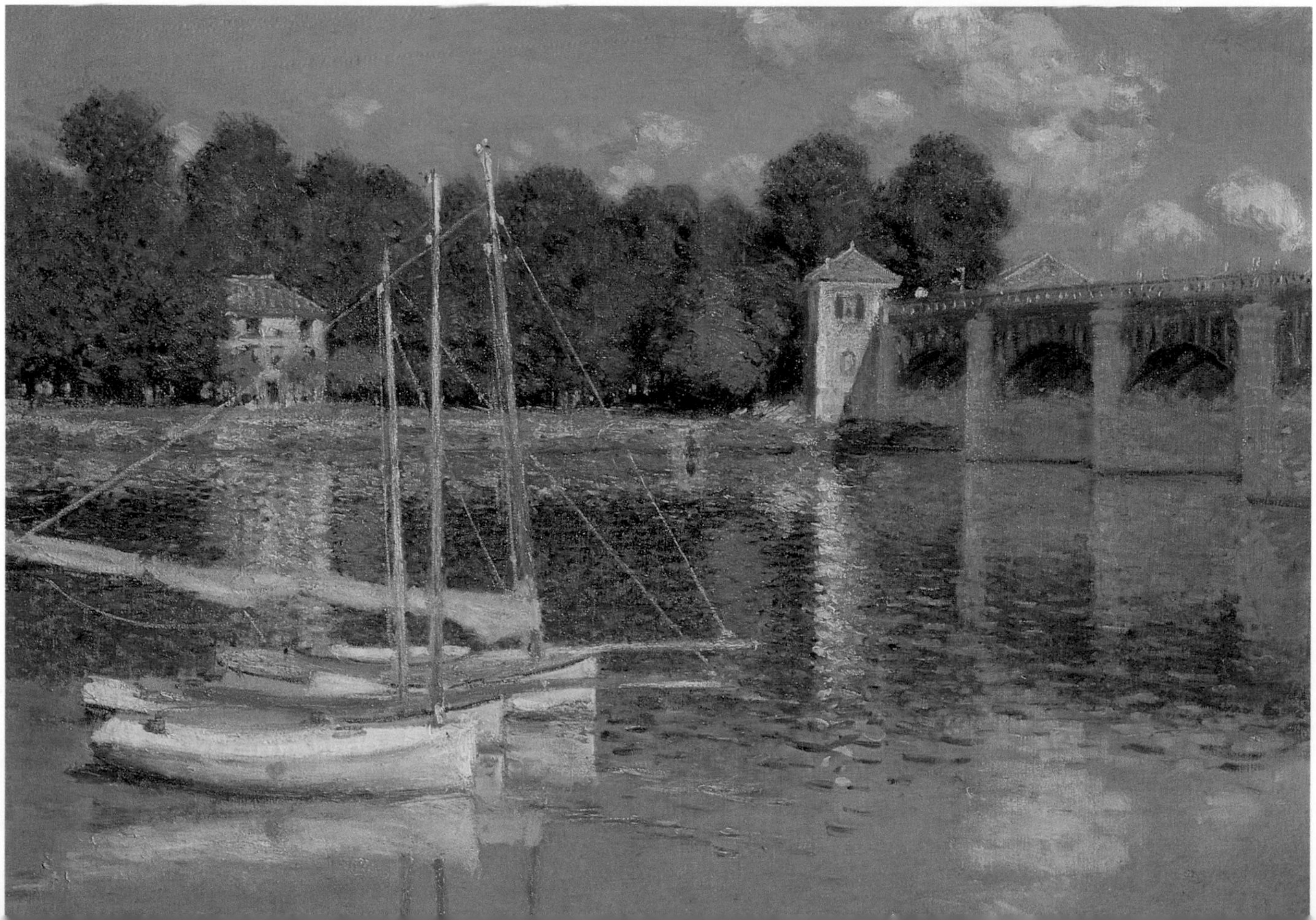

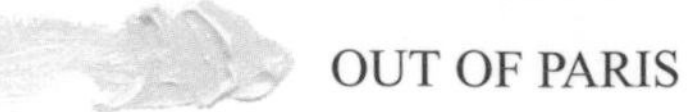

Boating and Yachting

Charles Daubigny (1817–78) was a major liberating force in the development of modern landscape painting, not only in his own work but also in his support for younger artists specializing in the genre. He was a sociable man, whose home at Auvers-sur-Oise was an open house for young painters. During the 1860s he attempted, with some success, to convince fellow jurors at the Salon to accept the paintings of his friends Monet, Pissarro, Renoir and Sisley. The qualities that attracted younger artists to his work are revealed in this far from favorable review written in 1861 by the popular critic and poet, Théophile Gautier: "It is a real pity that this landscapist whose sentiment is so true, correct and natural is content with an impression ... M. Daubigny's landscapes are merely dashes [taches] of juxtaposed color." Daubigny painted many of his canvases from a boat which he had converted into a floating studio; launched in 1857, and

Cassatt,* The Boating Party, *1893–94. An unusual variation on the mother and child theme.

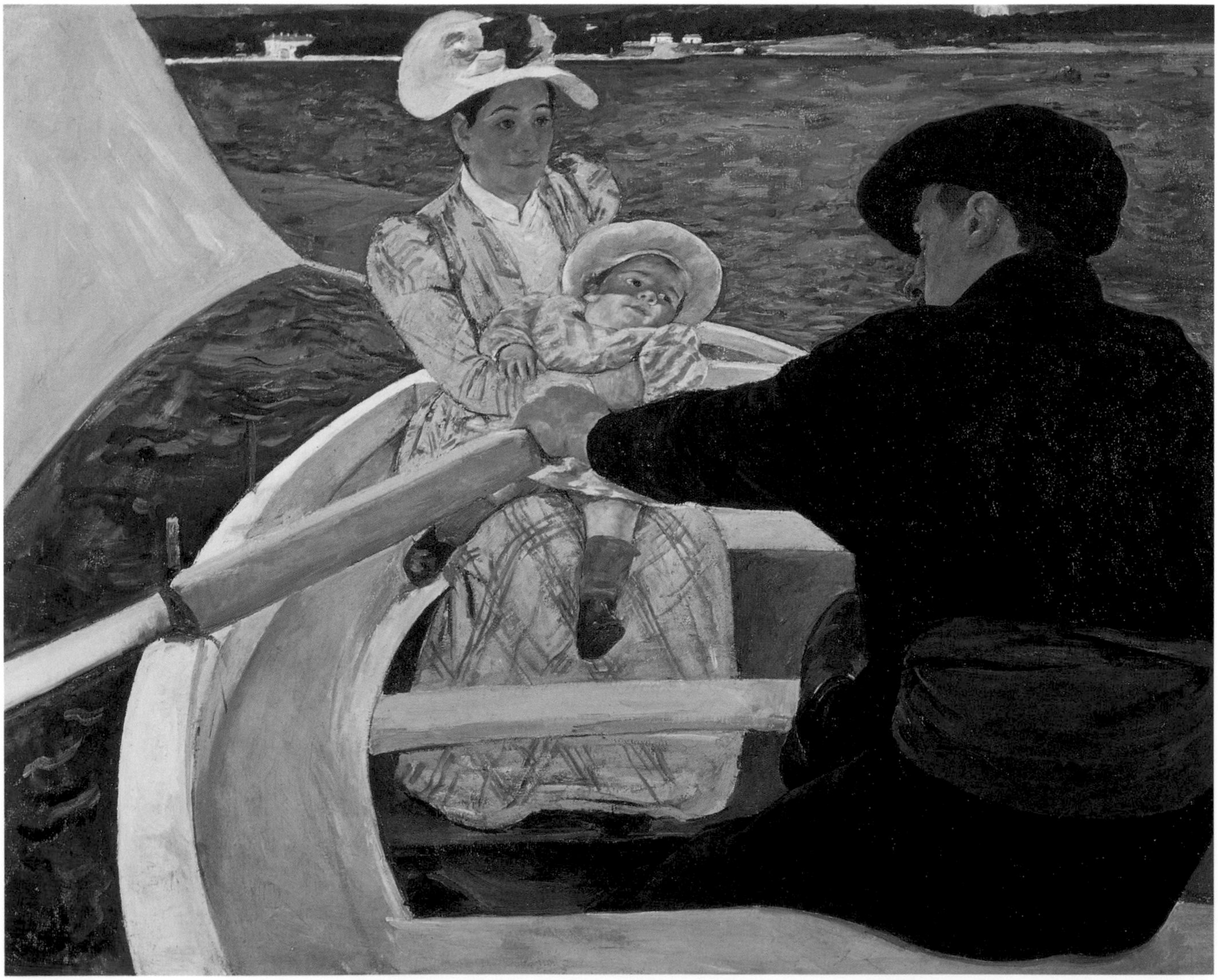

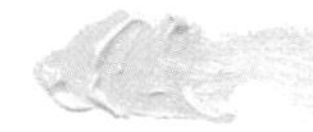

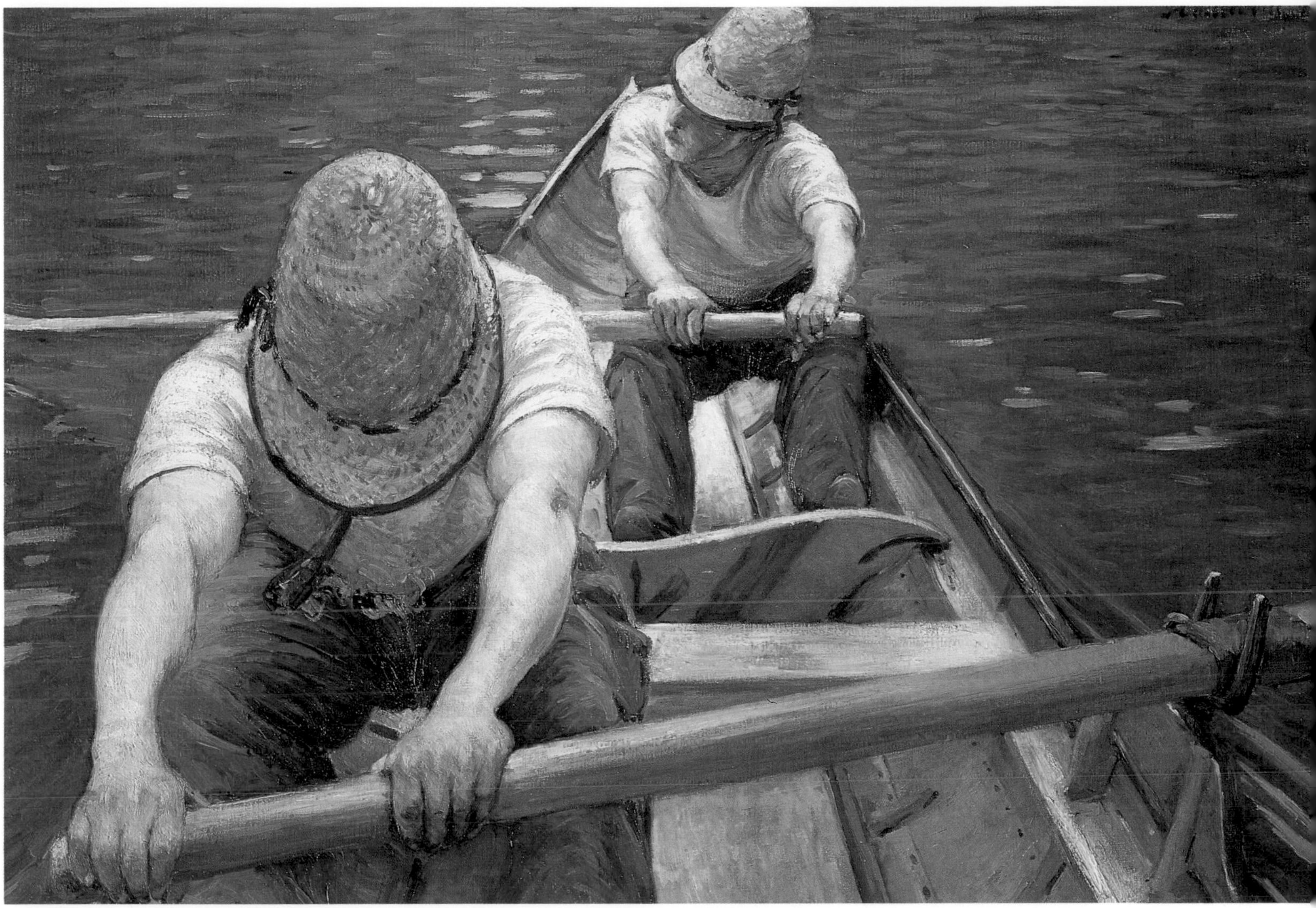

Caillebotte, **The Oarsmen,** *1877. This daring composition conveys a powerful sense of movement.*

called "le botin," it served not only to increase his mobility but also offered innovative compositional opportunities. The boat allowed him to enjoy to the full an aquatic *vie bohème* along the rivers Oise and Seine. Monet and his colleagues were, therefore, not without models in developing their views of the landscape.

Almost as important as the work of Corot, Daubigny, Courbet and others, were the many guidebooks and travelogues that catered for the developing tourist industry. Such publications had been produced in France since the 1820s and had originally concentrated upon the picturesque historical monuments of the French provinces. As the century progressed, interest shifted to the countryside itself, its inhabitants and their customs. These works were sometimes illustrated by artists like Daubigny, whose *Le Voyage en Bateau* of 1862 had a particular significance for Impressionist art; they were extensions of the romantic topographical tradition, and juxtaposed vignettes of trains and steamboats, modern bridges and roads with the natural landscape. These unpretentious representations, appearing within factual texts, had an aura of truth and as such would have been embraced by the Impressionists as sanctioning their own compositional arrangements and subject matter.

The more wealthy of the Impressionists could afford to buy property along the Seine. The Manet family owned property at Gennevilliers, Caillebotte was close by, the Cassatt family had property at Marly, and Morisot's family had a summer home at Maurecourt. Never at ease in the capital, Monet lived close to the water all his life. He had a home at Argenteuil between 1872–78, then moved north of Paris to Vétheuil, only to move downriver towards Rouen, making his final home at Giverny. Monet's period of residence at Argenteuil coincides with the period of "high" Impressionism. The river and bridges of the town are the subjects of some of the best-known paintings of Impressionism.

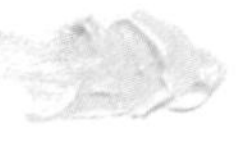

Monet Painting in His Floating Studio

1874; oil on canvas; 80 x 98 cm (31½ x 38½ in), Bayerische Staatsgemäldesammlung, Munich, Germany

In about 1874 Monet followed Daubigny's example and had a studio boat built to allow him to paint the river scene around Argenteuil. Manet was staying nearby at Gennevilliers, and his double portrait of Monet and his wife, Camille in the studio boat is a lasting testimony to the artists' friendship. The banks of the river clearly show the signs both of the tourist impact upon the scene and the substantial industrial development of the neighborhood. Monet's boat, less ungainly than it appears in Manet's painting, was maneuvered by oars and possessed a fine striped awning to protect the artist from the effects of either rain or sun. "It was like a large sort of boat in which one could sleep. I lived there with my painting materials, keeping a sharp eye out for the changing effects of light from dawn to dusk," Monet recalled later.

The effects of this unusual practice are evident in many of his paintings of the 1870s. The mobility of his craft and the low viewpoint it afforded allowed the artist to paint scenes of the river without the intrusion of a foreground that would immediately set the viewer at a distance from the scene. The proximity to the water also enhanced the brilliance of the light, which, rather than being absorbed by the surrounding landscape, was reflected directly off the surface of the water. Another important factor was the seclusion and security that being in a boat afforded the artist. Monet was not alone in this practice, as Berthe Morisot, too, on occasion made paintings from a boat.

For his painting, Manet was moved to adopt in a modified form the lightened palette and variegated brushwork of his friend. He remained faithful to his love of black, but used it only as one element among many. The informality of the composition and the apparent ease with which it has been painted belies the considerable trouble the composition caused Manet. He painted a number of versions, each characterized by his verve and wit. Monet, dressed in the costume of a holiday-maker, is represented painting the banks of the river but the framing of his wife in the doorway of the cabin almost suggests that she is the subject of his attentions.

The directional brushwork and the application of the paint show the work to have been very rapidly painted. Despite its size, it retains a pleasing sketchy quality that admirably suits its subject matter. In places Manet has copied Monet's characteristic slablike brushwork, but his handling is far more fluid and arbitrary, informed by a very different sensibility. The shifts of contrast in the water around the hull of the boat and the treatment of the reflections in the water are the result not so much of observation, but of painterly decisions. Nothing seems fixed, factory chimneys alternate with the masts and rigging of the pleasure craft, and even Madame Monet's features are only suggested by a few well-chosen strokes of the brush.

Monet later recollected, "… those …wonderful hours I spent with Manet on that little boat! He did my portrait there…Those wonderful moments with their illusions, their enthusiasm, their fervor, ought never to end."

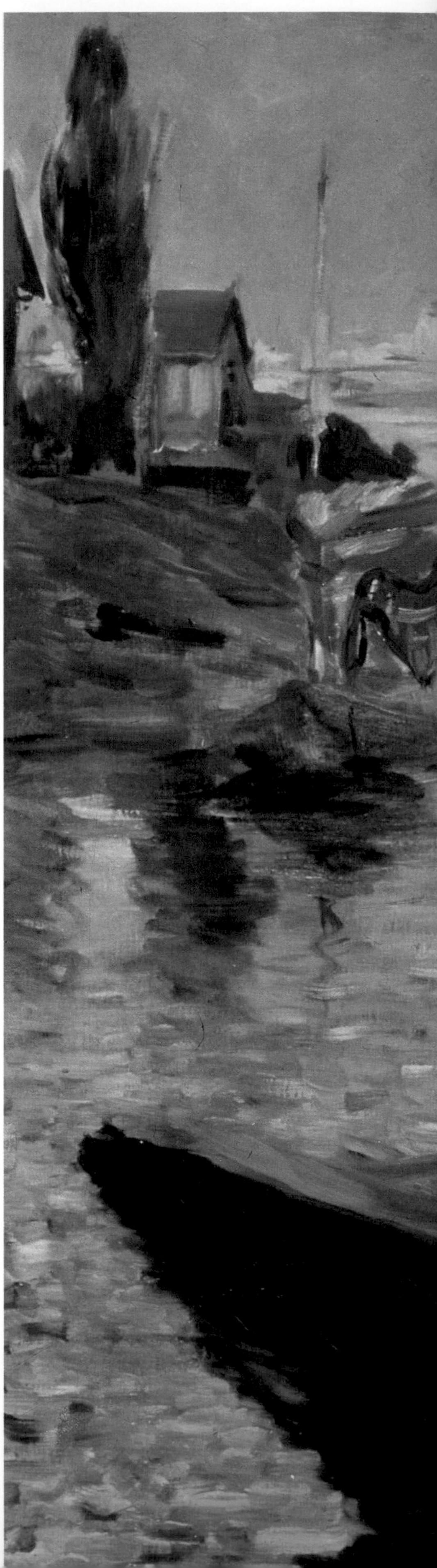

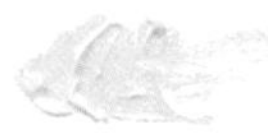

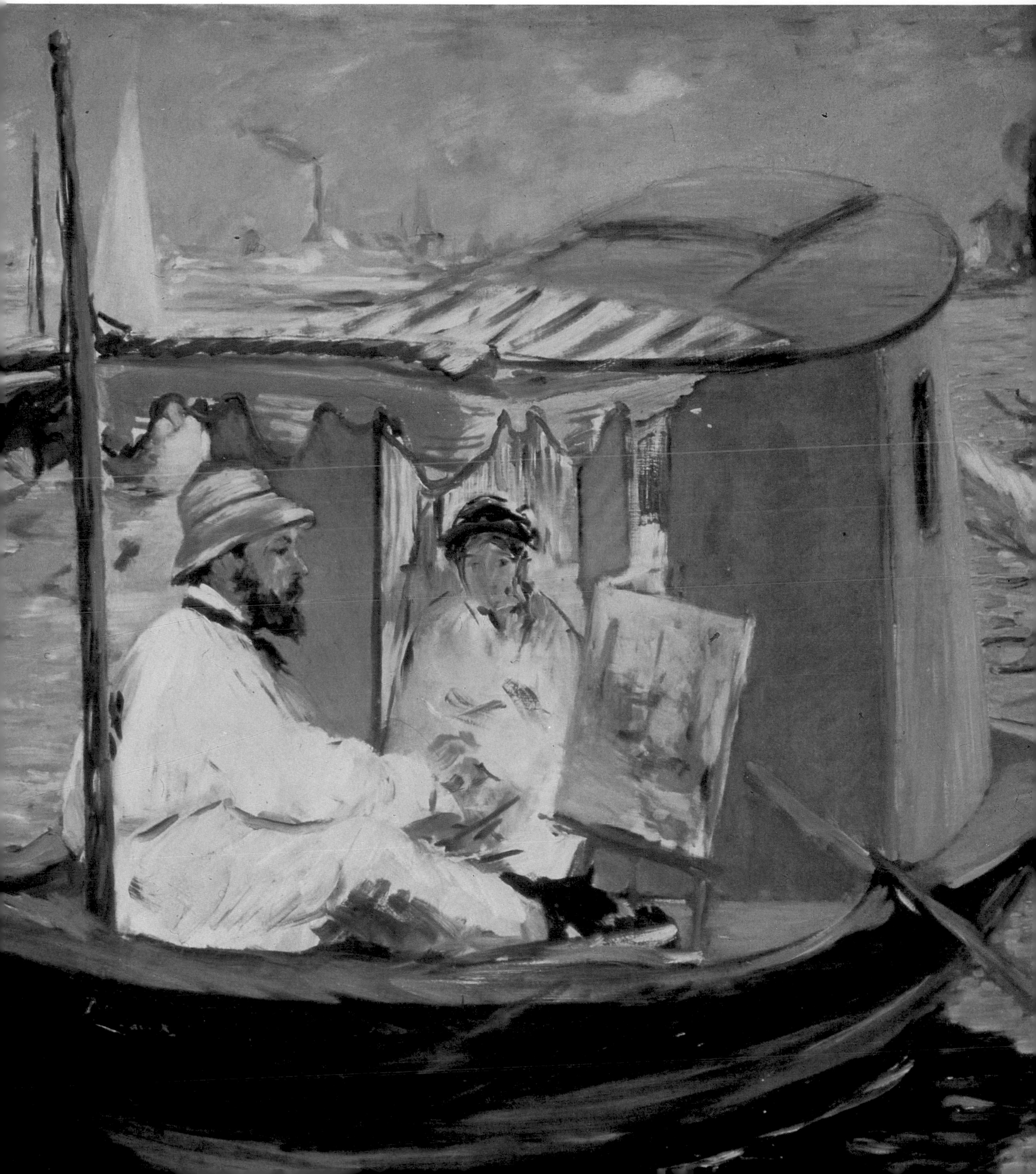

Monet by the Sea

The picturesque charm of the landscapes of Normandy and Brittany and their inhabitants had attracted the attentions of artists as diverse as Bonington, Delacroix and Whistler. During the nineteenth century, the landscape of France became an increasingly important means of developing and sustaining a national identity. Many city dwellers had their family origins in the provinces, and scenes of rural life were a staple ingredient of each year's Salon. By the 1850s and 1860s, the rapid development of the French railway system meant that "*trains de plaisir*" could take increasing numbers of Parisians to enjoy the peace and tranquility of the Normandy coast. The rail link from the capital to the coast was opened in 1847, cutting a journey that had previously taken days to a mere five hours. As the century progressed,

Monet,* The "Pyramids" at Port-Coton, Belle-Ile-en-Mer, *1886. Rugged and romantic, these rocks are a well-known tourist site.

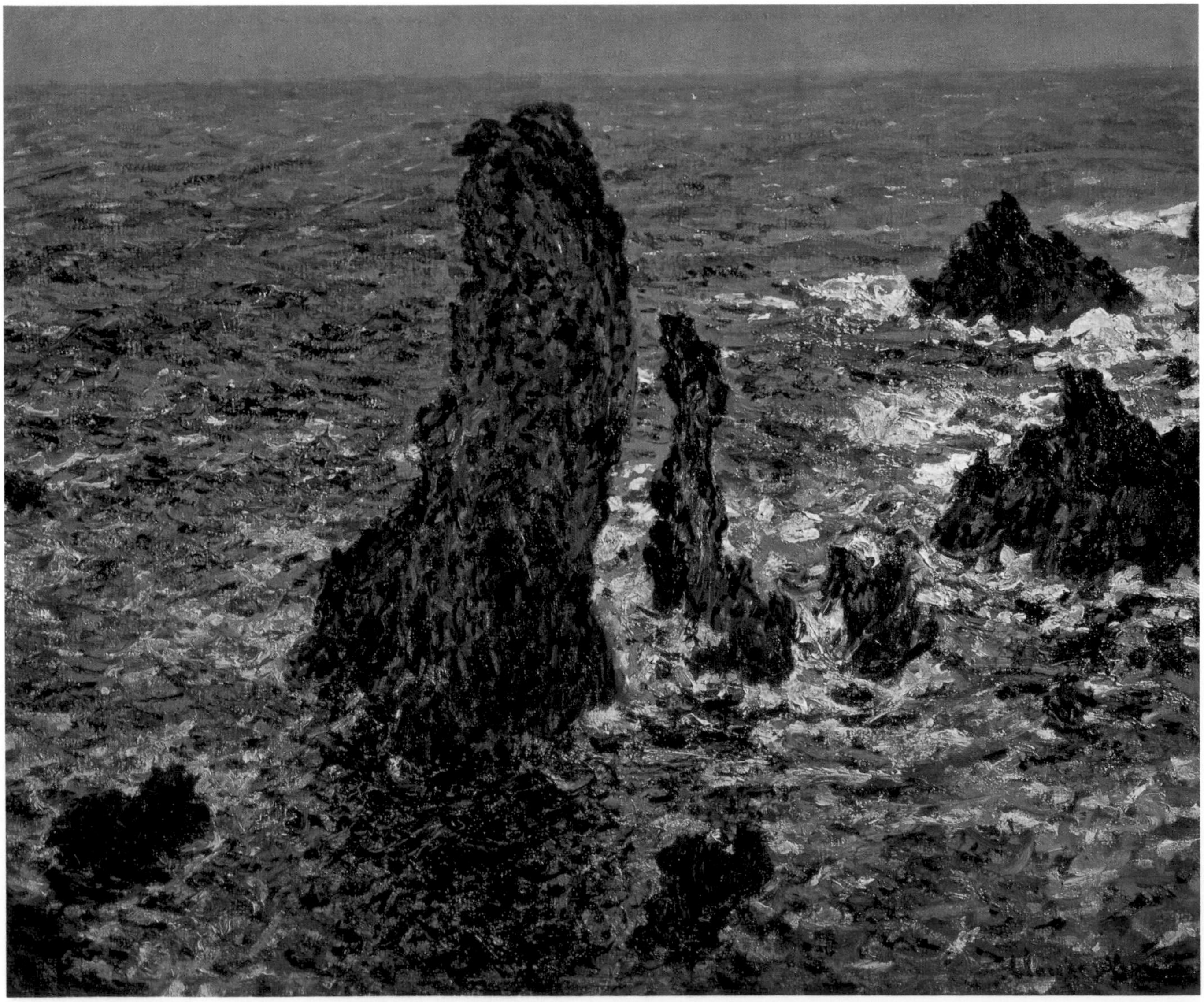

the public interest in historical sites was largely overtaken by a desire to visit sites of natural interest and, correspondingly, the need to record those landscapes for an urban audience developed apace.

The effect of this development was the transformation of the Normandy coastline to cater to this new phenomenon. The small fishing ports became tourist centers and local populations gave up traditional ways of earning a living to meet the demands of a new and transient population. Impressionist paintings were an integral part of this development as they celebrated and recorded the landscape the tourists came to see and, in so doing, propagated the notion of the landscape as a site for leisure.

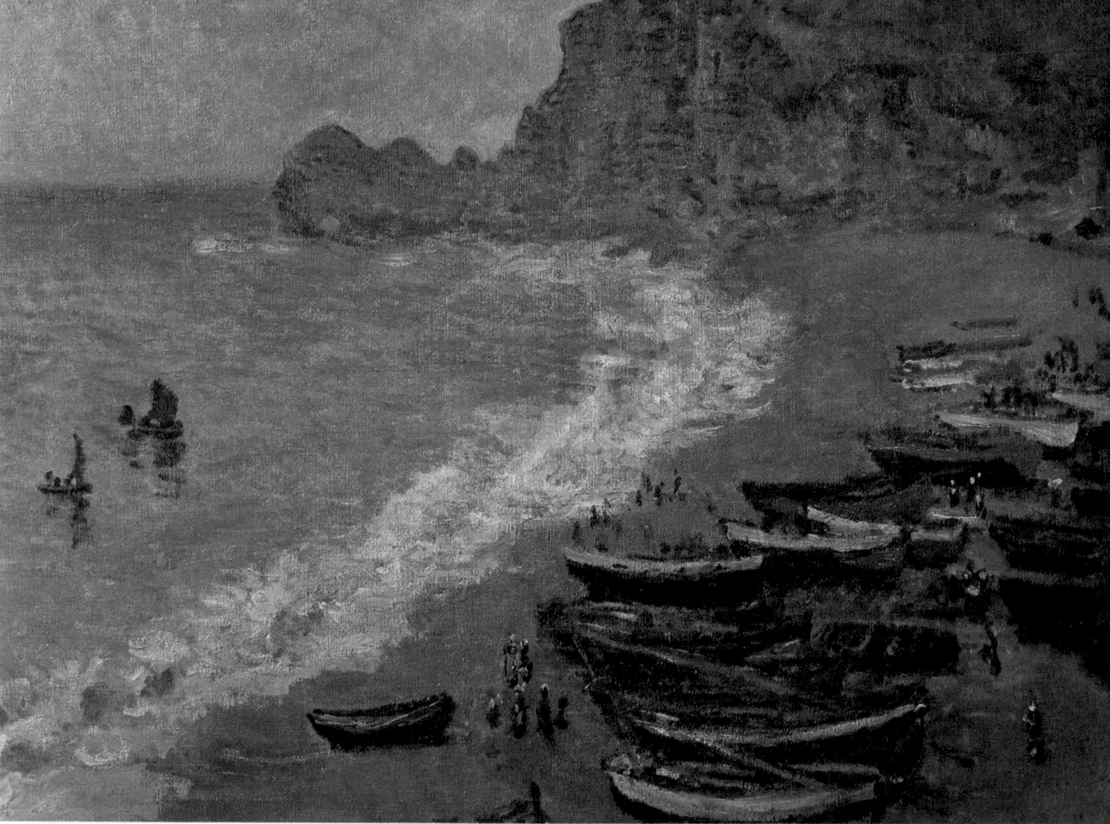

Monet,* Etretat, *1883. A picture postcard of a painting, all reference to the village as a resort is excluded in this cosy image.

Because of its proximity to the capital, the Channel coast of northern France became very popular with those rich enough to stay in the hotels and villas that sprang up in the villages and fishing ports along the coast. Those who could bought properties. Monet had family connections in Sainte-Adresse and stayed in the best hotels in Etretat, Les Petits-Dalles and elsewhere; the Morisot family regularly took their vacations on the Normandy coast. "She would vanish for entire days among the cliffs, pursuing one motif after another, according to the hours and slant of the sun," it was noted of Berthe Morisot.

Nature was now an extension of the urban, and the visitor was encouraged to experience it in a particular way; guidebooks, travel books with their maps and wood engravings, presented the would-be holiday-maker or day-tripper with a ready-made program of what to see and how to see it. Monet had incorporated images of contemporary life into his paintings of Normandy in the 1870s, but during the 1880s, he began to underplay any reference to the sites as tourist centers. Monet resolutely set his back against the railway stations and hotels and ignored the fashionably dressed visitors to paint a view of nature that stressed its unspoilt aspects.

Although born in Paris, Monet had been raised in Normandy and spent most of his life there. The cliffs and beaches had attracted painters like Delacroix, Courbet and scores of romantic landscapists: even Degas had fallen under the spell of the region. Monet was drawn to the epic grandeur of the cliff faces set against the ever-changing sea and sky. This had always been a highly marketable subject and was common enough in the Salon, but Monet made it his own, seeing himself as a romantic and heroic painter of elemental nature. Much of the writing on Monet has sustained this chosen identity, describing his paintings as if they were the result of an act of nature rather than a highly sophisticated system of representation.

Guy de Maupassant, the famous short story writer and friend of the artist, wrote the following account for the journal *Gil-Blas* in September 1886:

> ***Last year, right here, I often followed Claude Monet, who was in search of impressions. Actually, he was no longer a painter, but a hunter. He went along followed by children who carried his canvases, five or six all depicting the same subject at different hours of the day and with different effects … Another time he caught with both hands a torrent of rain on the sea and flung it on his canvas.***

Monet's romantic engagement with the sea on one occasion almost caused his death. So absorbed was he in his painting among the rocks at Etretat that he was swept away by a wave and was saved from being drowned by the prompt action of some local fishermen, who pulled him out, paint from his canvas smeared over his beard. Monet loved water; even as an old man he would make special visits to the seashore to reinvigorate himself, and once suggested that when dead he wished his body to be placed in a buoy so he could spend eternity cradled in the element he loved so much.

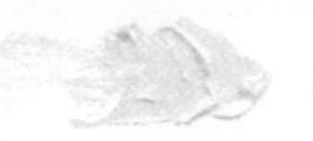

Portrait of Alphonsine Fournaise

1879, oil on canvas, 73.5 x 93 cm (29 x 36⅔ in), Musée d'Orsay, Paris, France

This painting dates from one of the most idyllic periods of Renoir's life, centered upon the restaurant owned by the Fournaise family. Apparently he was rarely presented with a bill at their restaurant, instead he would give them paintings. His son, Jean recalled Renoir's account of those halcyon days:

> ***"You've let us have this landscape of yours," they would say. My father would insist that his painting had no value: "I'm giving you fair warning; nobody wants it."***
>
> ***"What difference does it make? It's pretty isn't it? We have to put something on the wall to cover up those damp patches."***

Renoir's painting of Alphonsine Fournaise, known as "the lovely Alphonsine," posed casually on the balcony of La Grenouillère, her parent's restaurant at Chatou, is one of a number of paintings that he produced in the late 1870s celebrating the cafés and *guingettes* that lined the Seine from Argenteuil to Bougival. The masterpiece of this period is his spectacular *Luncheon of the Boating Party* of 1881, in which Renoir included Alphonsine. This was a carefully considered painting, the result of two years' planning and was as ambitious a project as *The Moulin de la Galette*. These two paintings represent Renoir's continued ambition to use the techniques and subject matter of Impressionism in order to create major paintings that would equal the seriousness of Salon painting.

This portrait, although painted before *Luncheon of the Boating Party*, could be read as a continuation of the narrative suggested in the larger work: the guests have departed and the viewer is left to enjoy a *tête à tête* with this engaging girl. Alphonsine, who was one of Renoir's favorite models, also modeled for Degas and eventually married an aristocratic painter. According to Renoir's son, she invested her fortune in Russian bonds and died penniless at the age of 92, in 1935.

No disturbing elements upset this image of suburban delight; the girl is pretty, the scene is tranquil and picturesque, a pleasure craft and the bridge glimpsed in the distance establish the scene as a holiday idyll, but make no reference to the pollution, which even then was evident to visitors.

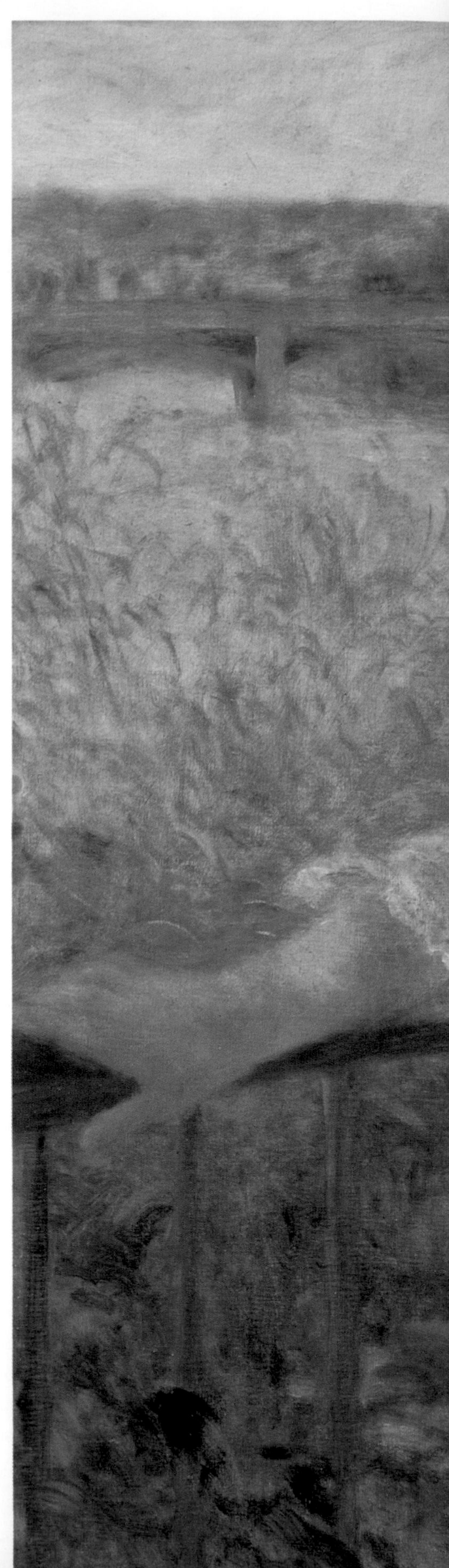

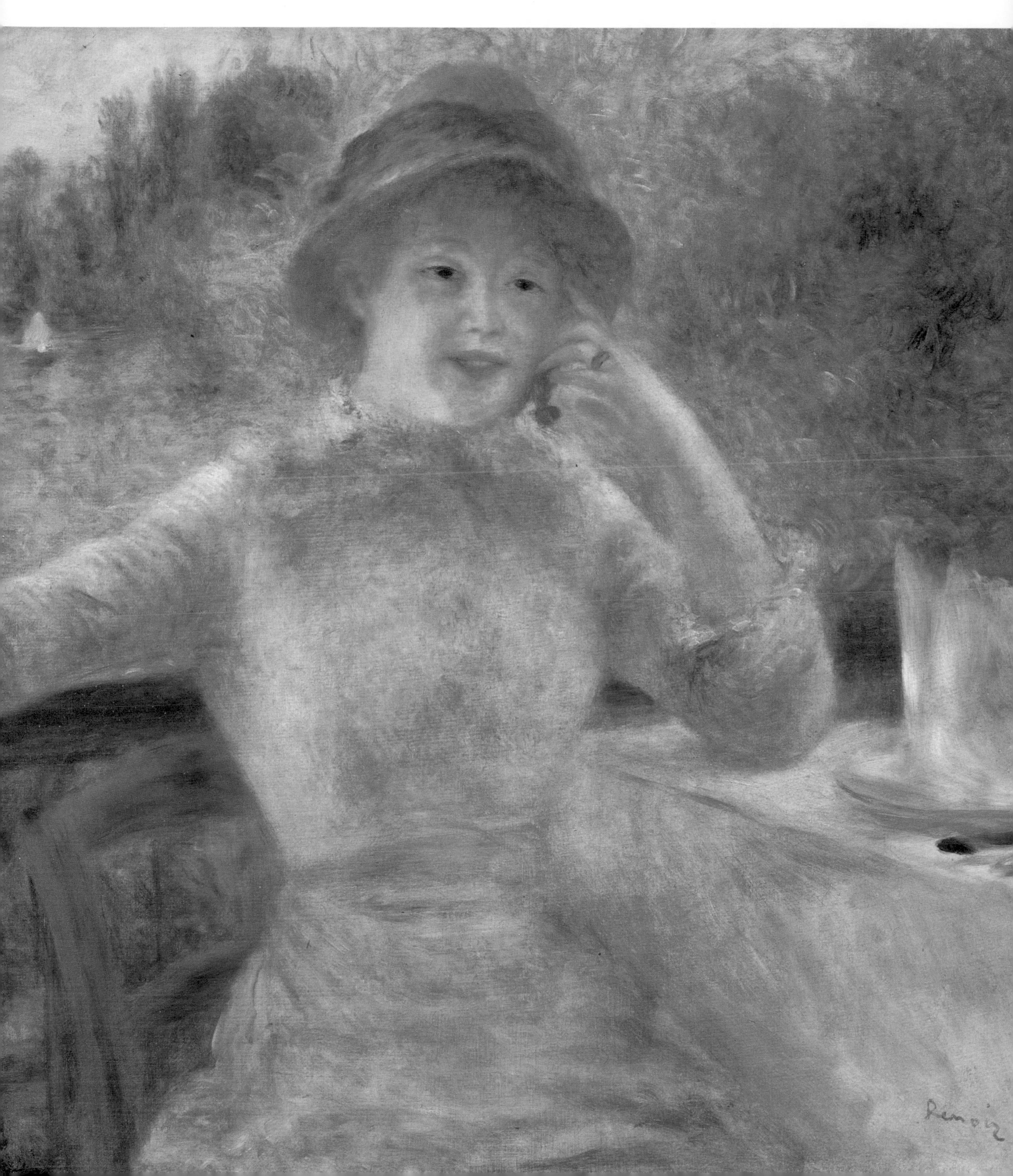
Renoir

Nude in Sunlight

1876; oil on canvas; 81 x 65 cm (32 x 25½ in) Musee d'Orsay, Paris, France

The notion of the countryside as a kind of garden of Eden, an escape from the pleasures of city dwelling, finds expression in this study, which presents the viewer with a modern Eve, set within some shady bower or secluded corner of a suburban garden or, as seems more likely, in the landscape of the artist's imagination. Whether naked or clothed, placed in a real or imaginary setting, there is no denying that Renoir's images of women are presented to the viewer as lush embodiments of sensual delight. Even in his earliest paintings, Renoir, like his favorite painters of the rococo period, represented the world as an earthly paradise. In the late 1860s, and for the decade of the seventies, he was attracted by the example of Monet and painted with him scenes of contemporary life. His abiding love for the female figure was never dormant, and he returned often to the motif of the naked female and made it the focus of his artistic activity.

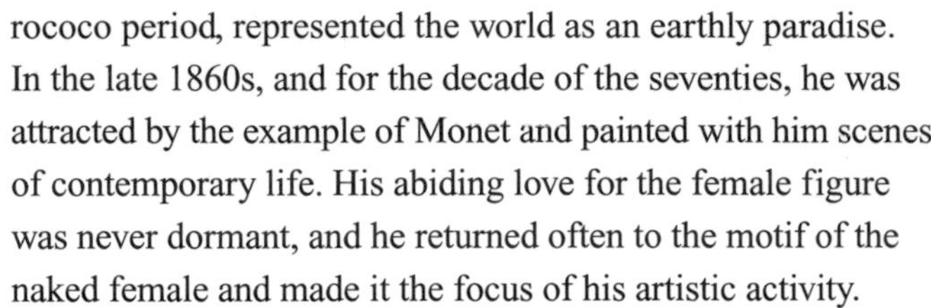

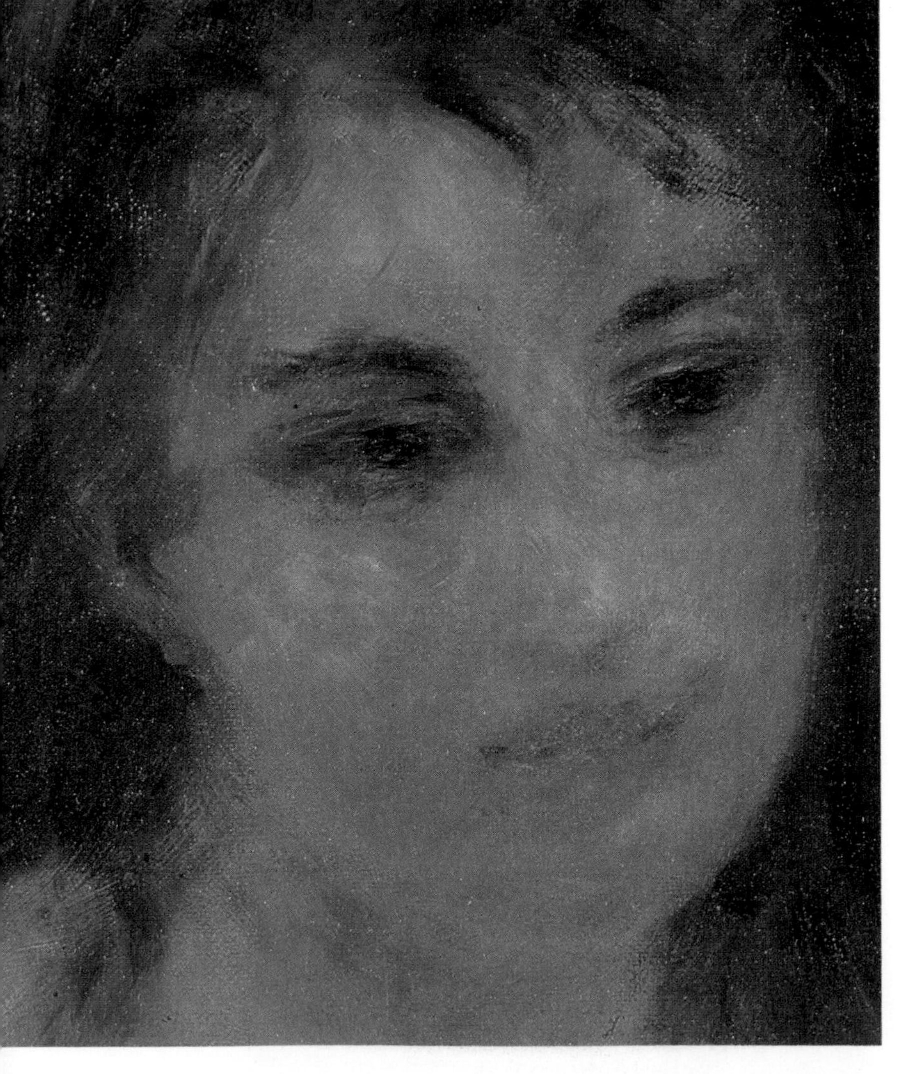

Renoir has set this intimate study of a pretty but unidealized naked young woman within a light-dappled bower of summarily indicated foliage. His modern Eve stands midway between his statuesque early depictions of Diana the Huntress and the full-blown monumental nudes of his final years.

The painting was shown at the second Impressionist exhibition in 1876 as a study, possibly to shield it from criticism for being unfinished, where it attracted the attention of the conservative critic, Albert Wolff, whose reaction to the painting has become one of the most famous of the many attacks on Impressionist practice. The writer deliberately misread the painterly equivalents for the fall of light through the leaves as being a "mass of flesh in the process of decomposition with green and violet spots."

Such an extreme reaction reminds us that art criticism is a branch of journalism and will often sensationalize to amuse, attract and occasionally educate its readers. The passage does, however, highlight the radical nature of Renoir's technique. The painting relates strongly to the work of those painters such as Rubens, Fragonard and Ingres, who were equally in thrall to the beauties of the female body and who, like Renoir, imposed their vision upon the passive female form. Renoir's unique achievement is to endow what is after all only canvas and paint with the palpitating vitality of living flesh. The foliage is painted in an abbreviated manner, while the translucent quality of the flesh is built up by a variety of means. In some areas the paint has the consistency of watercolor built up in a series of glazes, and in others the forms are accentuated by touches of thick impasto. Uniting the whole is a lightness of touch and a sense of improvization that give to the whole canvas a freshness and sparkle that endows the painted figure with the pulse of life.

The painting was bought by Gustave Caillebotte and was part of his bequest that was accepted by the French state. It has since become one of the best-known and best-loved of all Impressionist images.

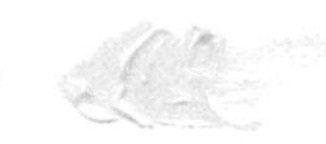

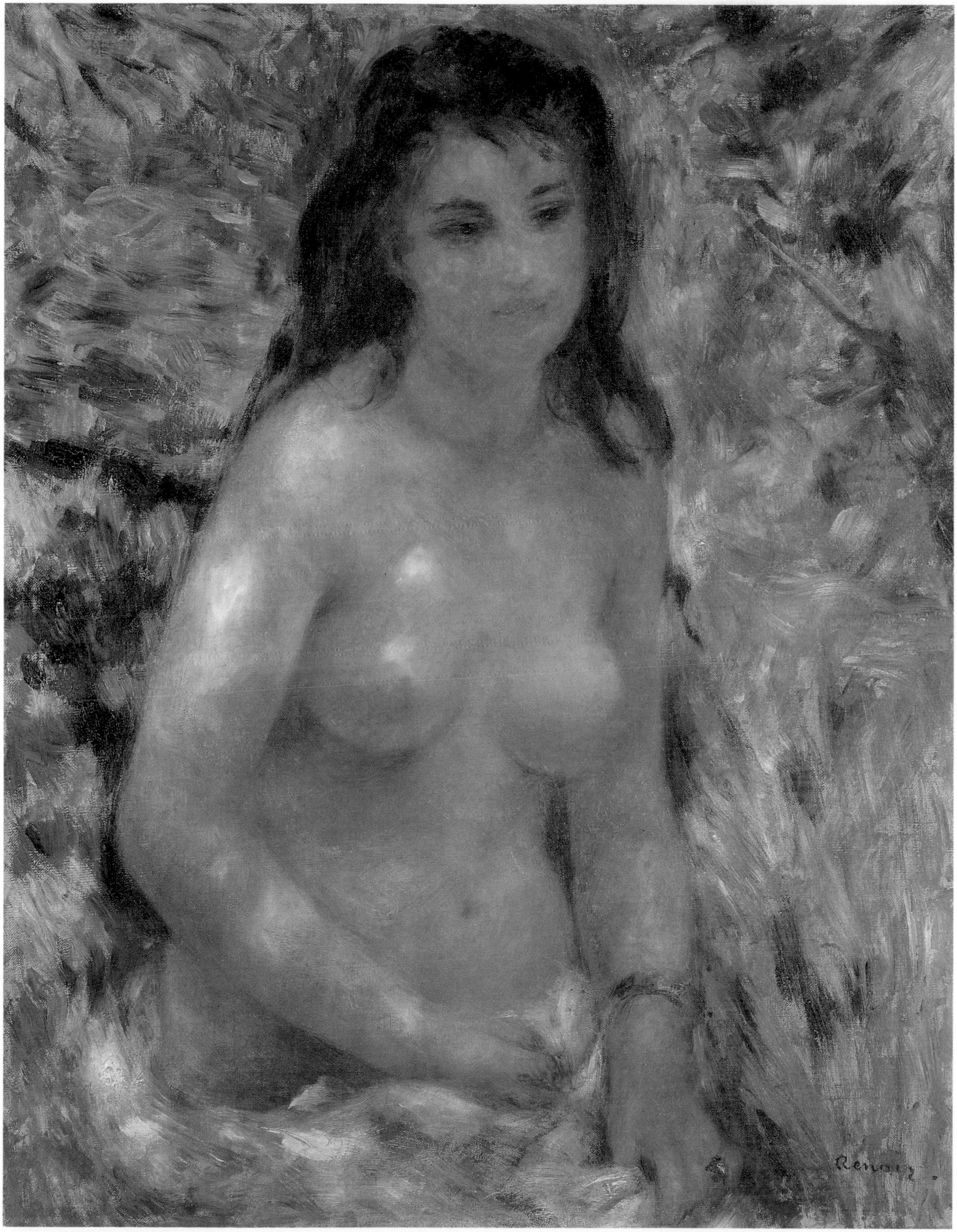

Cézanne in the South of France

Cézanne told a journalist in 1870, "I paint as I see, as I feel – and I have very strong sensations." His paintings chart a journey from unrestrained romanticism based upon his love of the masters and his own erotic fantasies to an art that records his struggle to achieve a balance between his perceptions of the world and his chosen means of representation.

Cézanne was fiercely loyal to the land of his birth."When you were born there," he said, "nothing else has any meaning." It was to his family home in Aix that he returned in despair after his failure to achieve any favorable response to his pictures shown at the 1874 and 1876 Impressionist exhibitions. Aix-en-Provence was then an isolated part of France, and only recently had the rail link to Marseilles made his trips back and forth to the capital relatively easy.

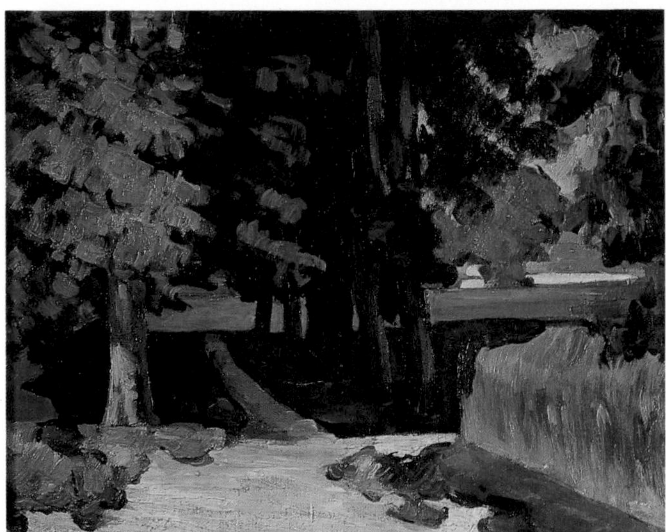

Cézanne, **The Chestnut Trees and the Pool at Jas de Bouffan,** ***c.1871. His aim was to create a strong equivalent to visual experience.***

Cézanne felt a deep love for the tortured Provençal landscape, where he spent what he regarded as the happiest years of his life, among the twisted pines, brooks, rocks and quarries that surrounded the city. He spent more and more time at the Jas de Bouffan, the estate on the western outskirts of Aix that his father had purchased in 1859. In the familiar surroundings of his childhood home, he lived in relative seclusion. The Jas de Bouffan was an impressive eighteenth-century property, bounded by an extensive walled garden. Once the residence of the governor of Provence, the house and its estate included a garden with an ornamental pond watched over by tall trees, stone lions and dolphins.

Any tranquility Cézanne may have found there was constantly threatened by the overbearing presence of his father, who opened his mail and kept a close watch on his finances. This must have been intolerable for Cézanne who, close to forty years old, could only consider himself a failure as an artist. He could not even bring himself to disclose to his father his relationship with Hortense Fiquet, nor the existence of his son, Paul. He settled his family in various lodgings in the outlying villages of Aix and would visit them while painting.

Cézanne was a great walker and found an immense variety of motifs within walking distance of his home. His paintings of the 1880s are characterized by his interpretations of the countryside, including Mont Sainte-Victoire, the garden of the Jas de Bouffan, and paintings of the coast around the Gulf of Marseilles. At home, he concentrated upon a succession of still lifes and portraits and continued to develop his ambition to produce a series of major paintings of male and female bathing figures. In time, the eroticism and violence of his earlier works was brought under control and his approach to his subjects became ever more rigorous, his paintings increasingly becoming sites of his struggle to bring order to the fugitive effects of nature as experienced through his senses.

Cézanne continued his work toward analytical, structured and considered interpretations of the visual world. The examples of Monet and Pissarro had taught him to base his art upon the dialogue between seeing and feeling. Cézanne strove to capture the rhythms and structures of the Provençal landscape, trying to reconcile the lessons he learnt in the Louvre with his own experiences before nature. Few of his works were ever signed as there was no reason why the process in which he was involved should ever be seen as having an end.

Cézanne spent most of 1878 and numerous periods in the early 1880s living on the Mediterranean coast at L'Estaque, with the example of Pissarro's paintings firmly in his mind. In 1876, he wrote to Pissarro,

I have started two little motifs with the sea for Monsieur Chocquet … It's like a playing card. Red roofs over blue sea… The Sun here is so tremendous that it seems to me as though objects were silhouetted not only in black and white but in blue, red brown, and violet. I may be mistaken but this seems to me the opposite of modeling…

Cézanne's revelation meant that he regarded form in a completely new light. Instead of being bounded by contour or seen in terms of light and shade, the motif was considered in the terms of dynamic modulations of color. He would begin his canvases with a thin blue outline to fix the basic forms of the composition, and on to this scaffolding he would place small repetitive strokes of color, dashes and dabs, building a record of his sensations before the motif in a structure of bricklike applications of pigment.

In 1886 Zola sent him a copy of his latest novel, *L'Oeuvre*, in which the hero Claude Lantier, regarding himself as a failure both as a man and an artist, commits suicide before his canvas. Stung by resemblances between the fictional painter and himself, Cézanne acknowledged the receipt of the book but never spoke to Zola, his oldest friend, again. A few weeks later, on April 28, he married Hortense in Aix. Six months later his father died: "My father's a genius," Cézanne declared, "he's left me with an income of 25,000 francs." Free from parental control, loved by his mother and his sister Marie, he settled down "to work without troubling myself about anybody in order to become strong."

Cézanne,* The Gulf of Marseilles, Seen from L'Estaque, *1878–89.

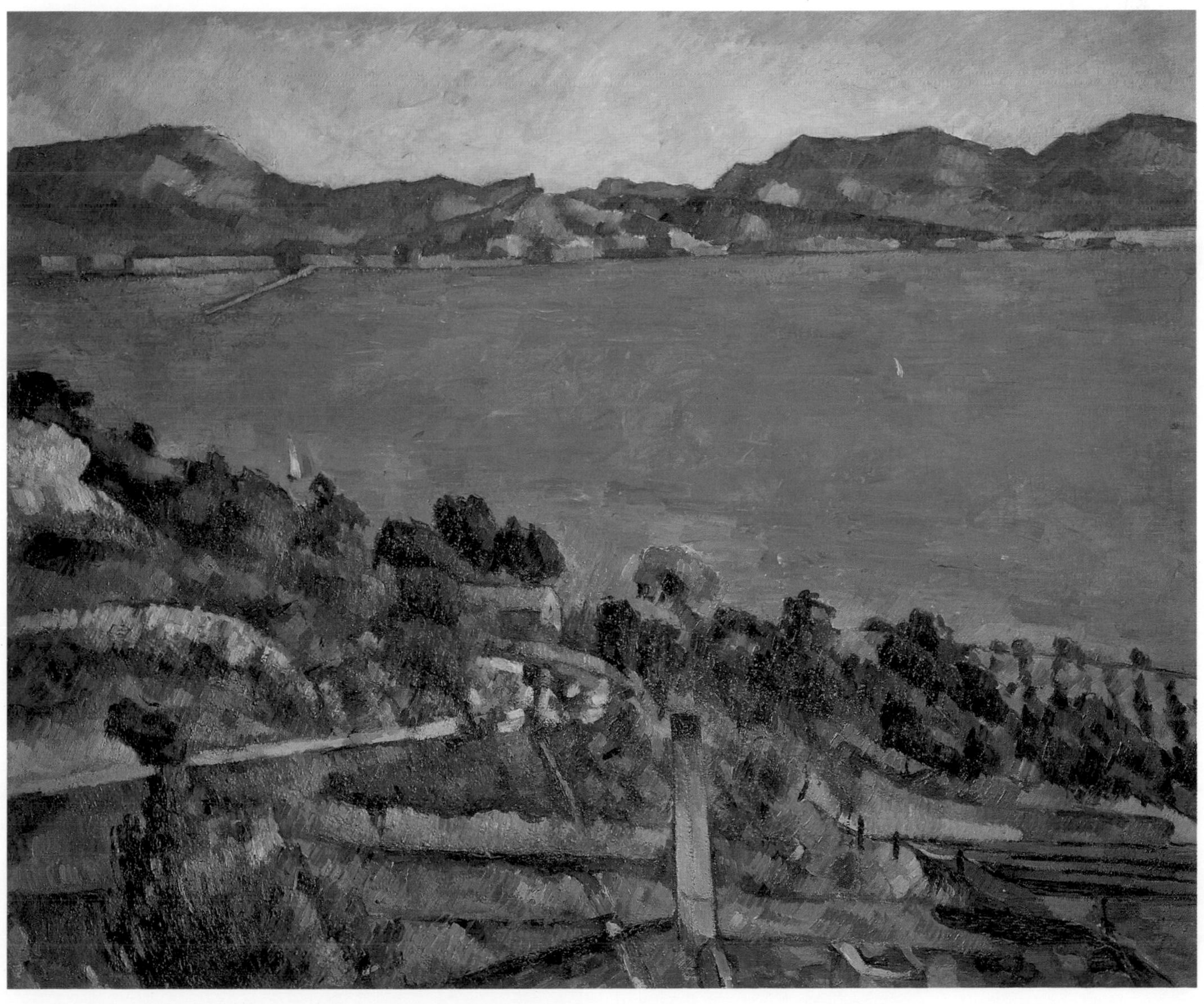

CHAPTER FIVE

Still Life

Paintings such as these reproduced over the following pages, represent an ordered, enclosed world of physical objects, translated by the skill and sensitivity of the artist into permanent form. Still life functions best in mercantile societies, which have a special interest in depicting the world as a place where consumerism can flourish and natural objects can be manipulated for the use of man. Normally speaking, with the exception of the golden age of still-life painting in seventeenth century Holland, the genre was considered to be of lower significance that other more highly regarded types of painting.

Often occurring in larger compositions as a coda or symbolic commentary to the main action, still life and flower painting enjoyed an ever-increasing popularity as subjects in their own right in the middle years of the nineteenth century. The genre was regarded by most of the Impressionist circle as a means of making ready money when their more ambitious canvases proved hard to sell. Decorative, unassuming and pleasant to look at, such works appealed to connoisseurs with modest pretensions and a limited budget.

The Impressionist painters, Cézanne in particular, raised this genre beyond its previously narrow confines to establish it as the equal in significance of any other form of serious artistic expression. The humble nature of the subject matter could act as a carrier for the artist's sensibilities as much as it could be seen as a celebration in color, line and form of both the natural and the man-made worlds. The blurring of the distinctions between the relative significances of subject matter meant that even the most ordinary object could be invested with allegorical implications normally reserved for grander subjects.

***Renoir,* Still Life with Roses, 1875.**

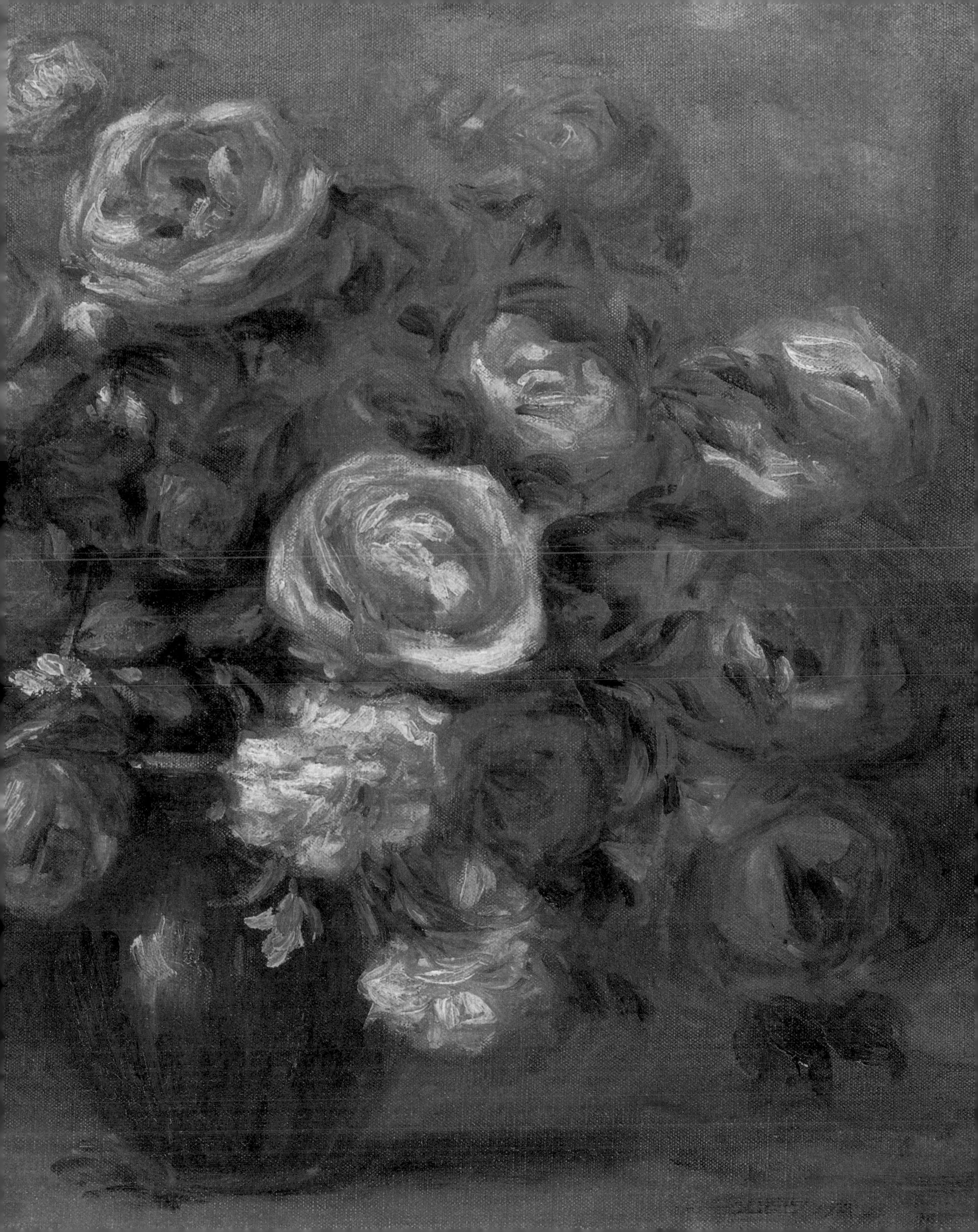

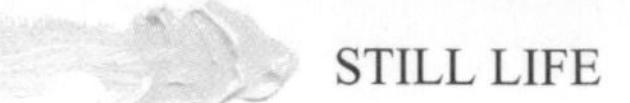

Cézanne's Still Life

In the nineteenth century still-life painting was habitually regarded by critics, collectors and artists as a minor genre, much inferior to history painting. As such, it received very little notice in most Salon reviews. Even the much revered eighteenth-century still life painter Chardin, was esteemed almost in spite of his choice of subject matter rather than because of it.

More recent artists had included stunning still lifes within their compositions: for example in Delacroix's mural painting, *Jacob Wrestling with the Angel*, the detail of the discarded clothes and weapons was the subject of much admiration. Like other artists Delacroix, on occasion, painted remarkable still lifes and flower pieces in their own right, but such works were always regarded as being of lesser importance than figurative works. Courbet's late still-life compositions are something of an exception, containing as they do intimations of allegorical significance.

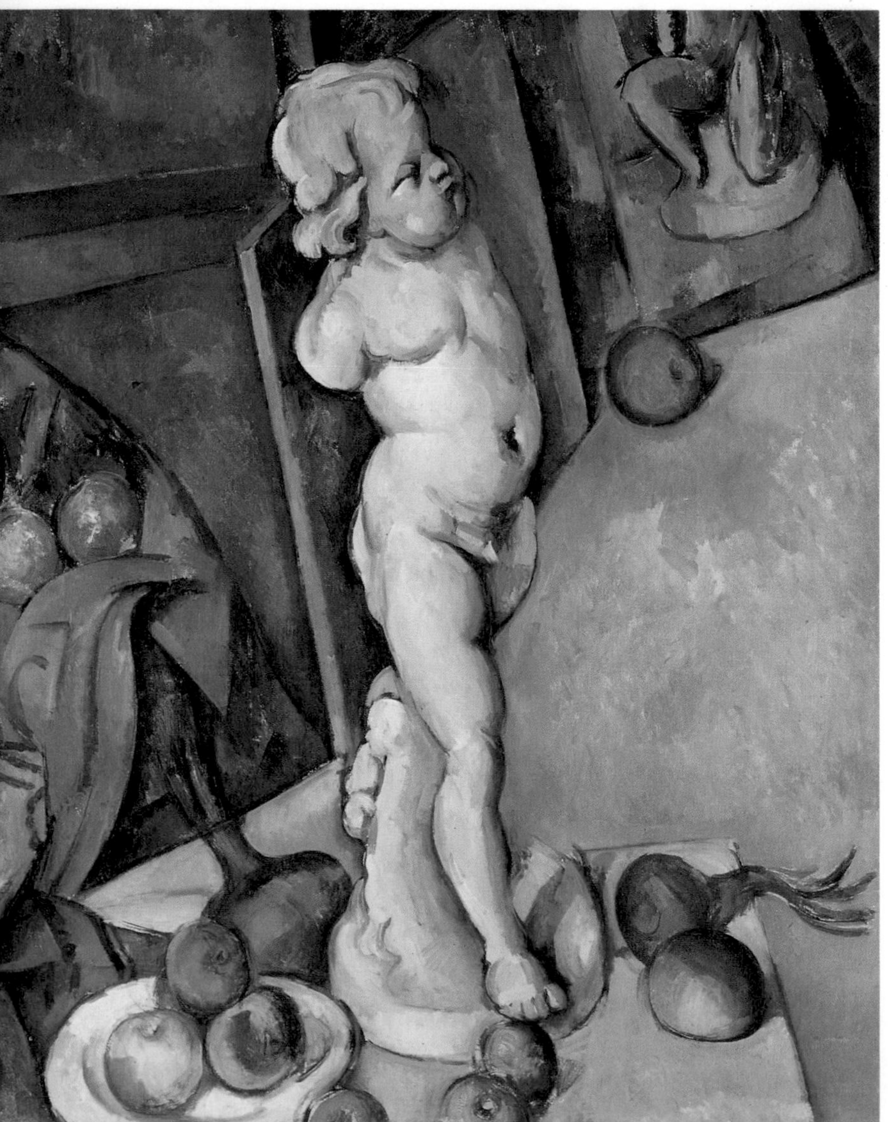

The Impressionists' interest in still-life painting is clear evidence of the gradual breakdown of the system of established hierarchies for certain kinds of subject matter. Part of this process, beginning in the 1830s, was fed by the desire for an art that would celebrate the common things of the world rather than the deeds and objects associated with the old order of the aristocracy. By the 1840s, artists such as Bonvin and Vollard were making a good living painting Chardinesque paintings of glistening pots and pans and kitchen scenes reminiscent of Dutch and Spanish seventeenth-century painters, overflowing with a sense of the inherent goodness of humble objects. Like the still lifes of Chardin, such works proclaimed the worth and value of ordinary things. Indeed, the "lowliness" of the genre and the relative insignificance of the objects under scrutiny were, like landscapes, seen as a means for artists to express their own will and feeling as transparently as possible.

A safe arena in which to experiment

While such scenes and subjects were painted by artists hoping to find a ready sale among the newly affluent middle class, they served another purpose in offering the artist a relatively safe arena in which to experiment with composition, color and expression.

Unlike a portrait or a landscape, a still life offered the artist as near as possible complete control over stable and – relatively speaking at least – unchanging subject matter: an apple or a pot cannot throw a tantrum or complain of the artist's inability to capture their likeness.

Cézanne,* Still Life with a Plaster Cast*, 1895. A powerfully constructed painting, exquisitely colored, the small figurine is studied and painted in accordance with the surrounding space.

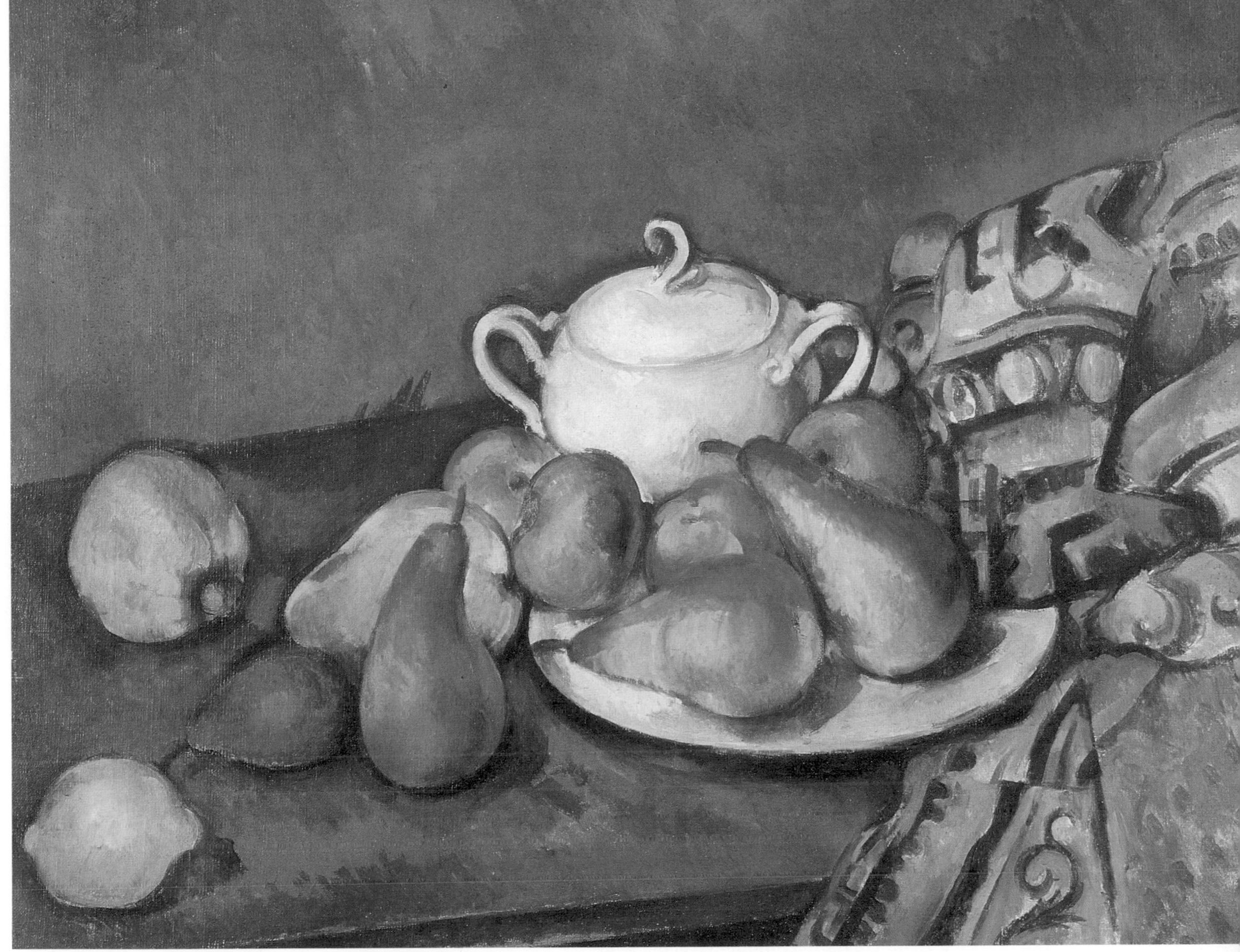

Cézanne*, Curtain, Jug and Fruit Bowl*, 1893–94. The artist's organizational skills are clearly discernible in this beautiful study.

With a still life, the artist is free to arrange and rearrange a composition according to his own desires, allowing him to experiment within a controlled environment, almost like a musician doing exercises. No other genre allows artists such freedom to pursue formal enquiries into their own craft. However, at the heart of this seemingly simple genre there lies an irresolvable contradiction: is the purpose of painting to reproduce the natural world as realistically as possible or is it a forum to display the technical achievements of the artist?

Perhaps no one has investigated this genre with such subtlety and dedication as Cézanne. He made it his own and was more responsible than any other artist for the elevation of the once-humble genre to the heights normally reserved for paintings of more seemingly significant subject matter. He took an obsessive care in choosing the objects he would paint, composing them with a finesse and judgment to reveal their forms, colors and textures to best advantage. Sometimes his canvases are small and intimate, the study of just a few pieces of fruit; other paintings are large, complicated arrangements that recall the massive still lifes of the baroque era. Like old friends, objects appear and reappear in Cézanne's compositions over the years; some of them still survive and may be seen today in his studio in avenue des Lauves, in Aix.

Cézanne's paintings not only offer the viewer a superb visual feast, but they are also profound meditations upon the act of painting and the relationship of the individual to the world of sensual experience. In the "Introduction to his [own] Paintings," the English novelist and occasional painter D.H. Lawrence wrote in 1929, " Cézanne's great effort was, as it were, to shove the apple away from him and let it live of itself … [he] makes us realize that it exists absolutely since it is compact energy in itself." Lawrence grasped this fundamental point and, for all his partisanship, he perhaps came closer than anyone to presenting in words the unique achievement of Cézanne's still life.

Fruit Displayed on a Stand

1880–82, oil on canvas; 76.5 x 100.5 cm (31⅛ x 39⅝ in); Fanny P. Mason Fund in Memory of Alice Thevin, Museum of Fine Arts, Boston, USA

One of the most famous anecdotes in the history of art is that of Zeuxis' competition, Zeuxis being an Ancient Greek painter. A competition took place between two painters as to who could paint the most realistic painting. One painter painted a wonderful still life that everyone praised and which was thought to be the sure winner – until the birds descended to eat the grapes painted by his rival. The story demonstrates the fundamental duality of painting that still life embodies so well. Should we appreciate the illusionistic ability of the artist to represent the world with such skill as to make the means of representation invisible or should we admire the means by which the artist is able to re-create the world in paint?

In Degas' notebooks for 1877–83 is this *aide-memoire* for a future program of work inspired by a visit to a baker's shop:

> ***At the baker's, bread. Series on* mitrons *seen in the cellar. Also a view across the ventilators leading to the street. Color of flour, lovely curves of dough. Still lifes on the different breads. Large, oval, fluted, round, etc. Experiments in color, on the yellows, pinks, greys, whites of breads. Perspective views of rows of bread, ravishing layout of bakeries. Cakes, the wheat, the mills, the flour, the sacks, the market porters.***

Such enthusiasm! Degas' excitement is infectious and one can only regret that such notes did not lead to the paintings they suggest. The variety of bread, the interest in its production and consumption marks such comments and paintings that are their parallel with a precise image of the visible conspicuous consumption that characterizes modern capitalist society.

Caillebotte's painting, *Fruit Displayed on a Stand* is almost an inventory of plenitude, presented in a most forthright manner possible, literally as a shopkeeper's display. The artist painted a number of still lifes celebrating the availability of produce in late nineteenth-century Paris.

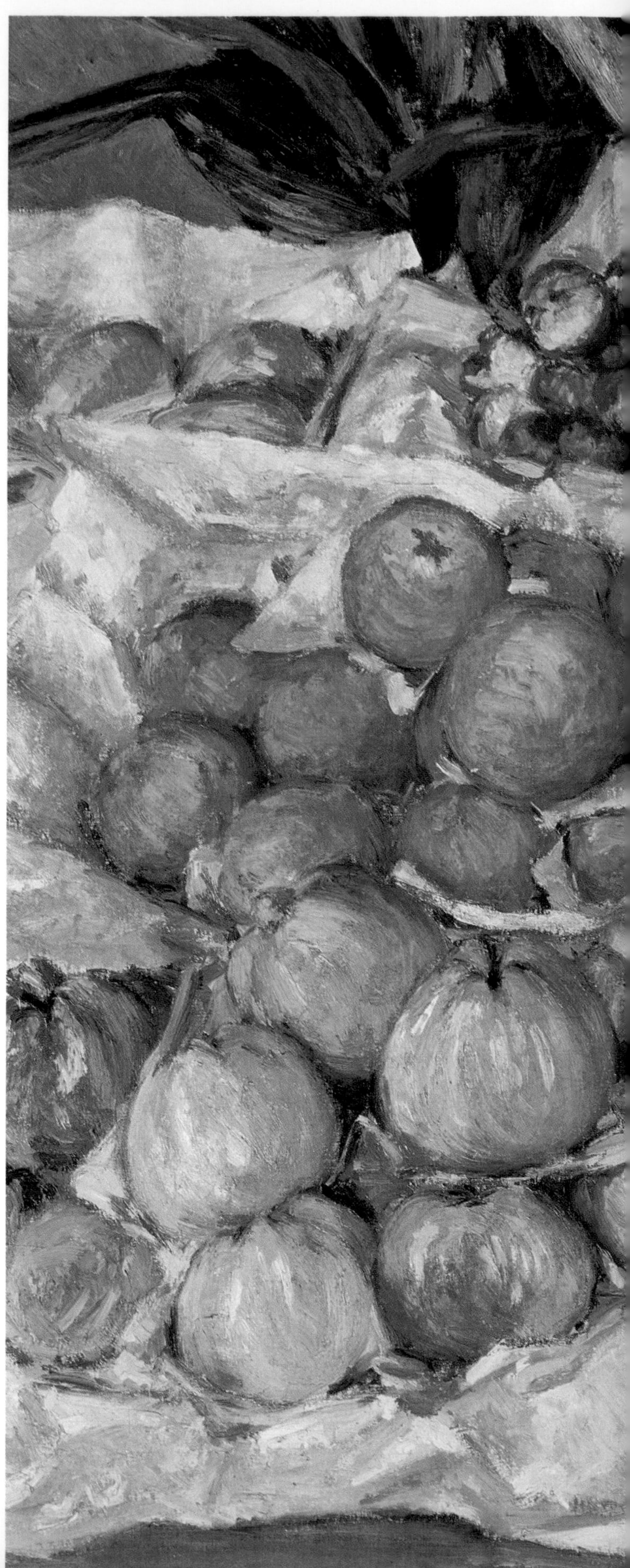

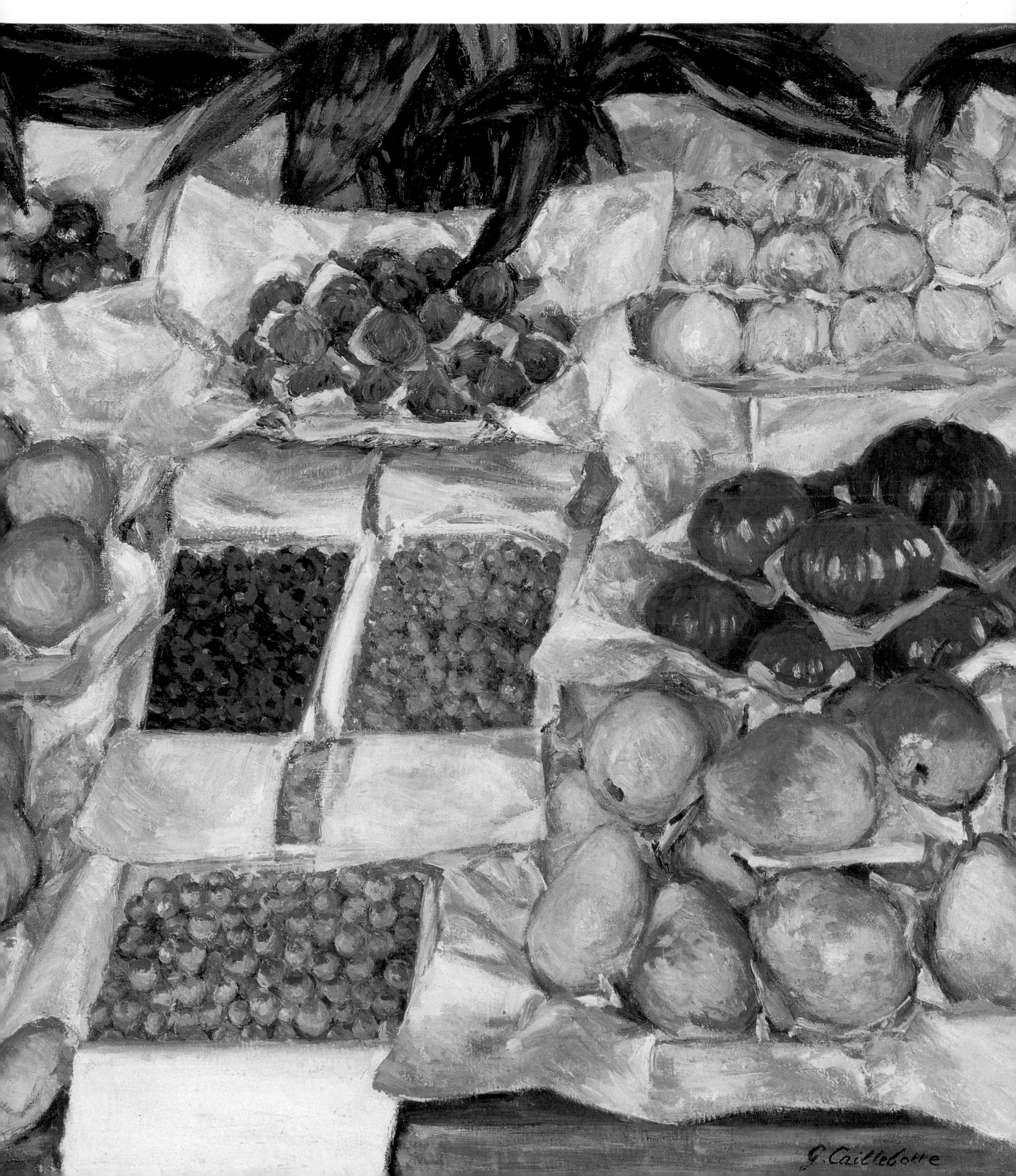
G. Caillebotte

Flowers

Cézanne, **Vase with Flowers,** *1900–03. One of the artist's many quirky flower studies.*

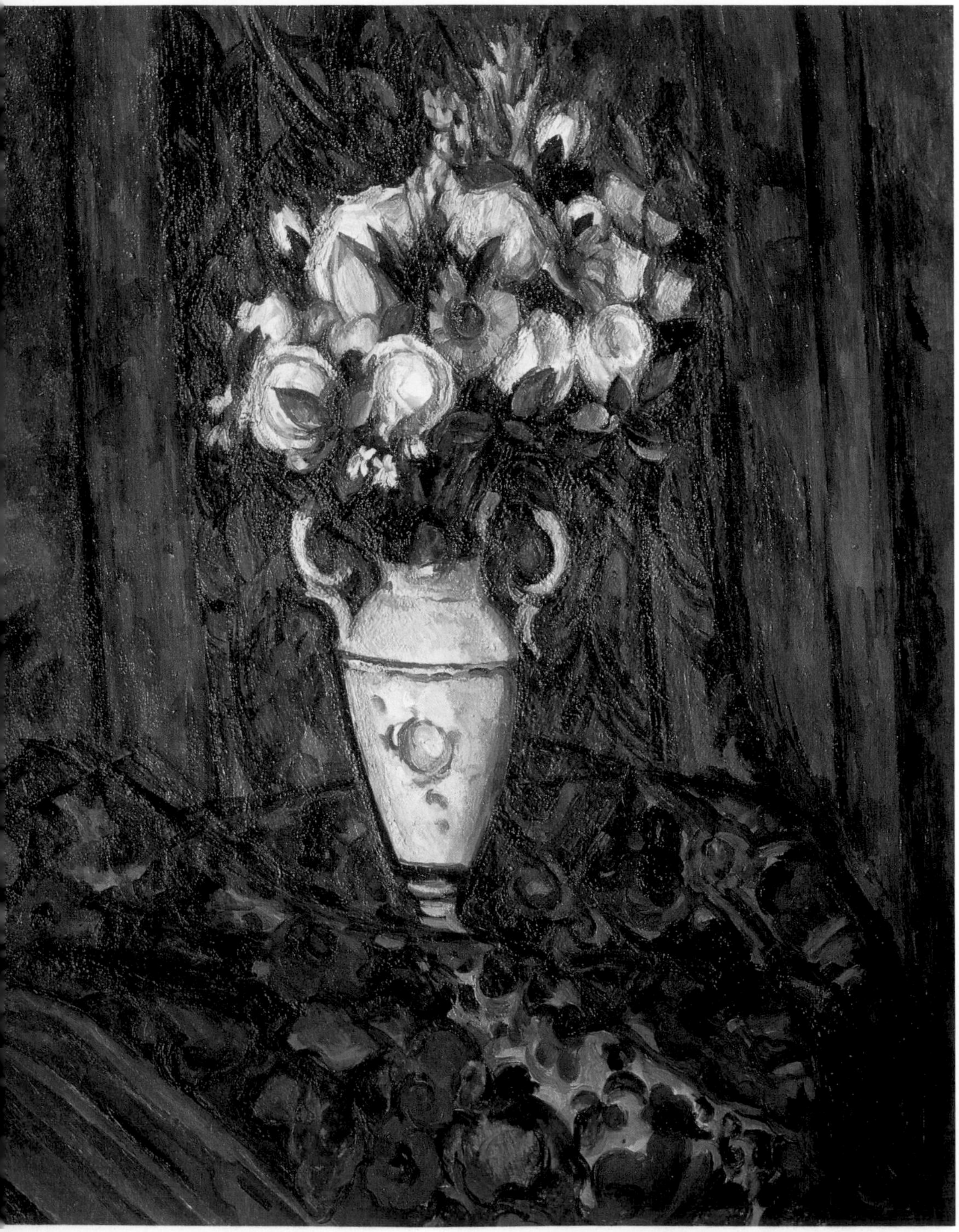

Their fragrance, colors, shapes and textures make flowers a never-ending source of delight. For centuries, artists have attempted to rival nature in their depictions of blooms and blossoms. There is a powerful analogy between the arrangement of a group of flowers in a vase and the artist's distribution of colors on a canvas: this is painting as pure delight. Inevitably, flower paintings have their own poignancy. The pleasures they offer are bittersweet, for, like ourselves, their existence is limited by time, and any painting of flowers inevitably bears this message: *vanitas*.

Without being burdened with symbols or recondite allegorical programs, flower paintings, despite their simplicity, can carry the most fundamental of meanings. Like landscape painting, flower paintings were long popular with a middle-class clientele in Europe and many such paintings were painted with an eye for the market, an ideal subject for those times when illness or the weather prohibited jaunts out into the country.

Although depictions of flowers are abundant in many cultures, those painted by the Impressionists belong to a tradition going back to seventeenth-century Holland, when the wealthy merchants of Amsterdam and elsewhere invested their money in flowers and saw paintings of their investments as visual analogies of their wealth and, perhaps, their control over a cultivated nature. Flower paintings were images of visible consumption, luxury items of a high order resplendent in their meticulous

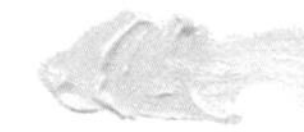

rendering of the minutiae of each bloom, and testaments to the owner's ability to afford an expensive artifact. For the artist, flower paintings were opportunities to display his talent, with the flowers arranged at will to create any wished-for color and textural balance.

Degas could not abide flowers, which he saw as Nature's rivals, and had been known to take flowers out of a room he was invited into. Despite this, he painted one of the most stunning floral compositions of the time in *Woman with Chrysanthemums*. Manet loved flowers and during the winter of 1880, when he was desperately ill and able to work only for the shortest of periods, his friends sent him flowers. "I would love to paint them all," he said and produced at least sixteen small elegant and brilliantly rendered studies of flowers, each a variation upon a single theme. They tremble with the brevity of their existence and, with our knowledge of the artist's death so soon after their completion, are almost unbearably poignant signs of the shortness of his own life and the fragility of our own existence.

Each artist brings a different sensibility to the genre. Renoir's flower paintings are brimful of the artist's open enthusiasm for life, whereas Cézanne's are more consciously formed out of the imperative to create an analogy in paint for the unattainable richness of the natural world. For both artists, the issue was not to achieve botanical accuracy, but to construct a well-knit, sonorous composition.

For a long period, flowers were an adjunct to religious art, their inclusion within religious paintings adding another layer of meaning to the scene depicted. Surely the blooms and corsage so prominently displayed in Manet's *A Bar At the Folies-Bergère* act similarly, those on the marble-topped bar giving Suzon the air of a Madonna whilst those suggested with the minimum of means at her breast celebrate her sexuality. Both groupings connote the signifying mysteries of paint itself: the flowers on the bar are richly worked, those at her breast are sketched in against the revealed ground of the canvas. As Vincent van Gogh was to write to his brother, Theo: "Manet's flowers are as much flowers as anything could be."

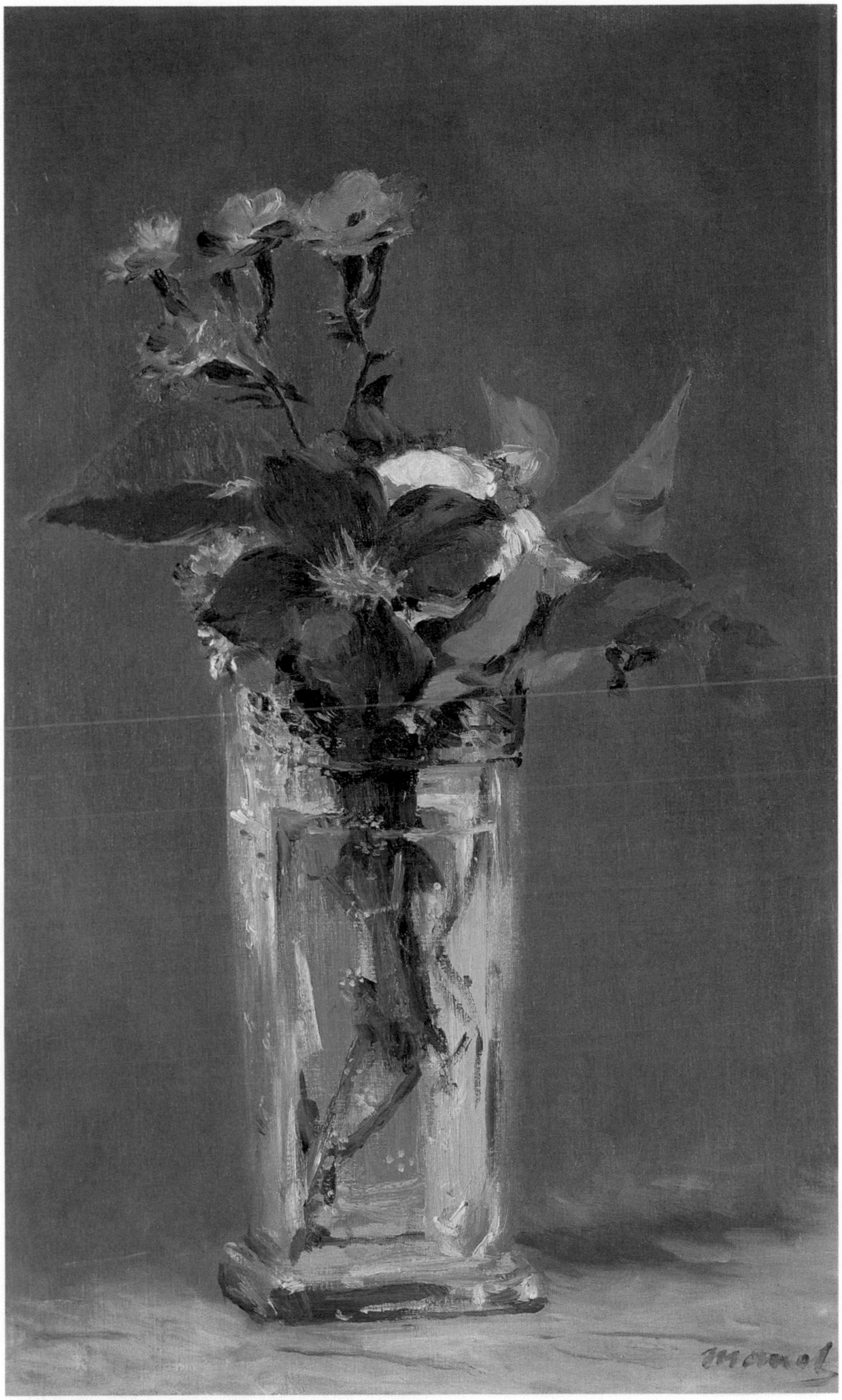

Manet,* Pinks and Clematis, *c.1882. A small miracle in paint.

Bouquet of Sunflowers

1881, oil on canvas, 161 x 81.3 cm (38¾ x 32 in), bequest of Mrs. H.O. Havermeyer, 1929, Metropolitan Museum of Art, New York City, USA

Monet was happier painting flowers within their natural habitat rather than in vases, and flower-pieces such as this are relatively rare in his output. However, between 1878 and 1882 he produced a number of vigorous still lifes and among them were a number of flower paintings including this one, *Sunflowers*.

After this period, Monet's growing reputation as a landscapist, allied to Durand-Ruel's ability to sell his work easily, meant that he could concentrate his energies upon that aspect of his art and leave still life, which he found troublesome, well alone.

The composition of most of Monet's still-life paintings is disarmingly simple, although their effect of a healthy vitality and their overpowering, almost vulgar, vitality has been achieved with great artistry. With *Sunflowers*, the paint is laid on with great gusto in a lyrical curvaceous movement that describes the forms of each individual leaf and flower head. The surface is richly worked into a thick impasto, the ridges of paint catching the light and further defining the crisp forms of the blooms.

These sturdy specimens are redolent of the heat and movement of the sun. They are precariously balanced in a small, simple vase, the green leaves creating a living frame that encloses the central blooms, and others spiral out to the very edges of the canvas.

Compared with several of van Gogh's paintings of sunflowers, all Monet's blooms are healthy and brimming with life, their stalks scarcely able to bear their weight. Van Gogh's flowers are emblematic of time, some of them having lost their petals, and each is shown at a particular stage of its development: the crisp geometrical outlines contrast with the organic shapes of the flowers, a contrast followed through in the organization of the paint on the canvas, with taut, mainly horizontals and vertical movements of the brush, defining the background.

In Monet's painting, everything is lyrically imbued with the dynamism of growth. Monet has conquered time, denying its inevitable victory over something as ephemeral as a flower; because his sunflowers are painted indoors, there is no precise effect of light to give a sense of the hour. Van Gogh's sunflowers are hymns to yellow: the color of the sun and these flowers. Monet uses a crude but carefully sustained mixture of blues, greens, reds and golds to blitz our visual senses.

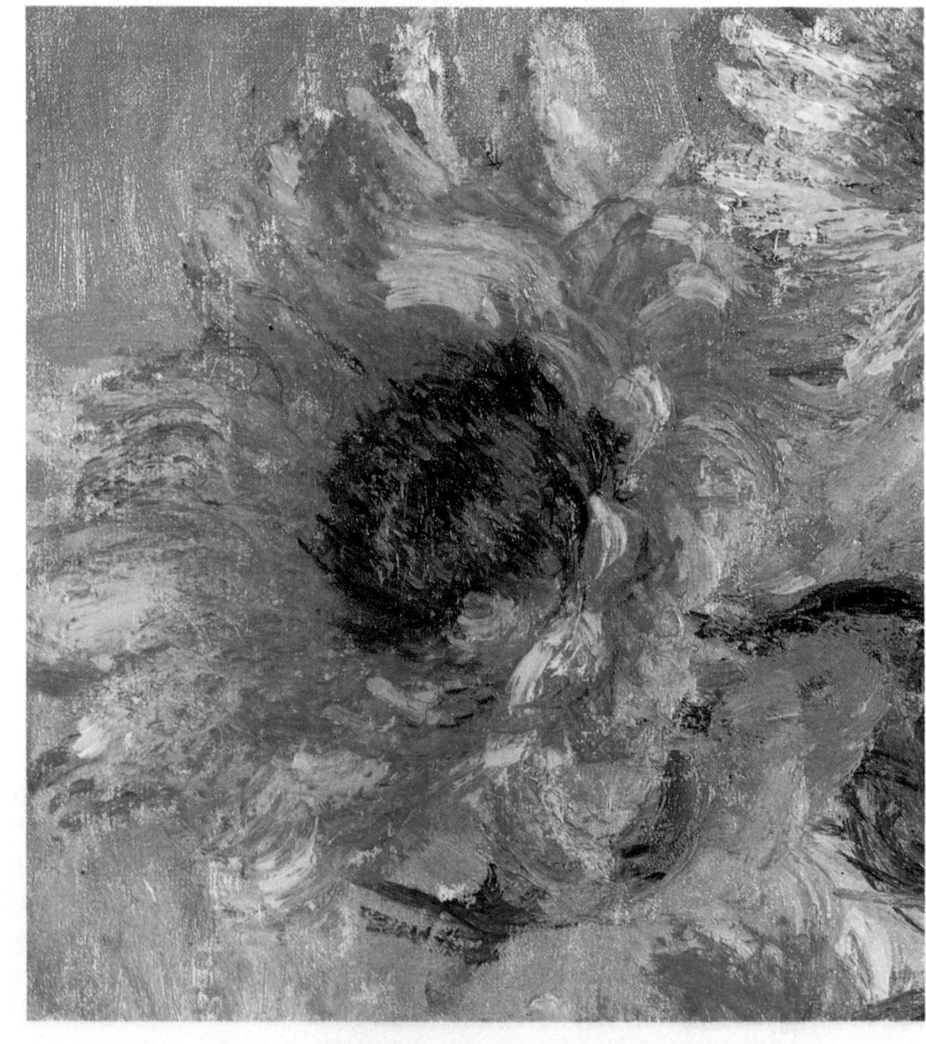

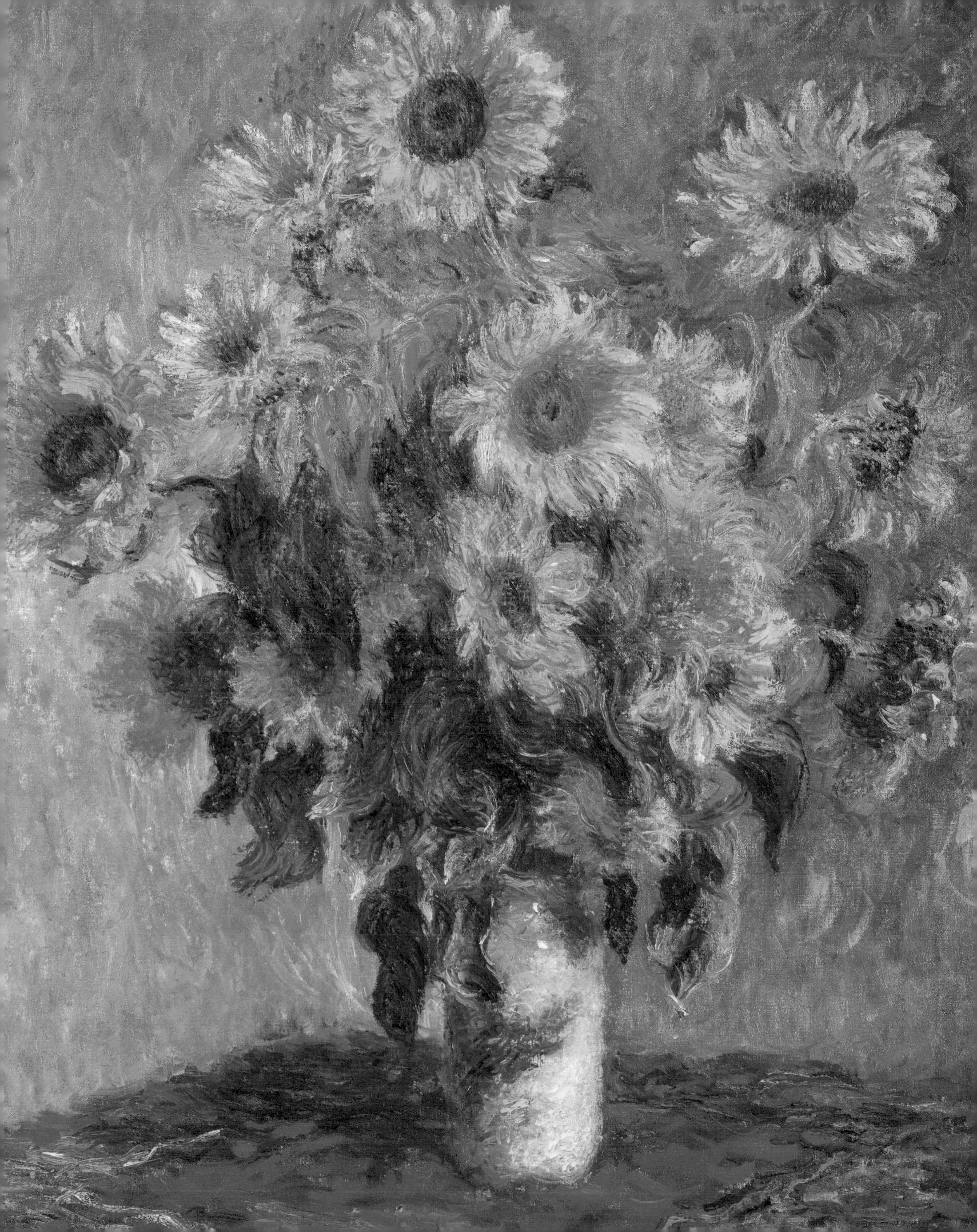

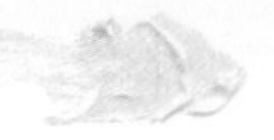

CHAPTER SIX

Techniques and Materials

A new technique for a new age: it is as simple as that.

One of most engaging aspects of Impressionism is its continual engagement with experimentation in subject matter and technique. Because their art was based upon their individual perception of reality, the means by which the Impressionist artists gave form to their vision could not be allowed to become tired or formulaic. Their work is marked by a continuing questioning and regeneration as they adapted their working methods to their own experience. The Impressionists consistently refused to be hidebound by theory and their technical practices were always filtered through their intuitive response to the motif.

Monet's painting reproduced opposite reveals the essentially improvisatory approach that the Impressionists took. The color is deceptively simple: small multicolored flecks of paint dance across the irregular wave of the canvas to create the impression of sparkling sunlight. The trees on the left-hand side have richly worked-in layers of paint to create a raised surface of pigment, which the artist has then drawn to with the "wrong" end of his paint brush to produce the exact effect of the open weave of branches and leaves catching the brilliancy of the sunlight.

The world of reality and its reflections on the water merge into a single mass of color and a band of clear color indicates the fall of light, which underscores the distant town.

As Renoir said, "Before nature theories melt away."

Monet,* Autumn Effect at Argenteuil, *1873.
This was probably painted by Monet from his studio boat.

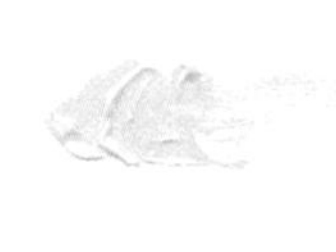

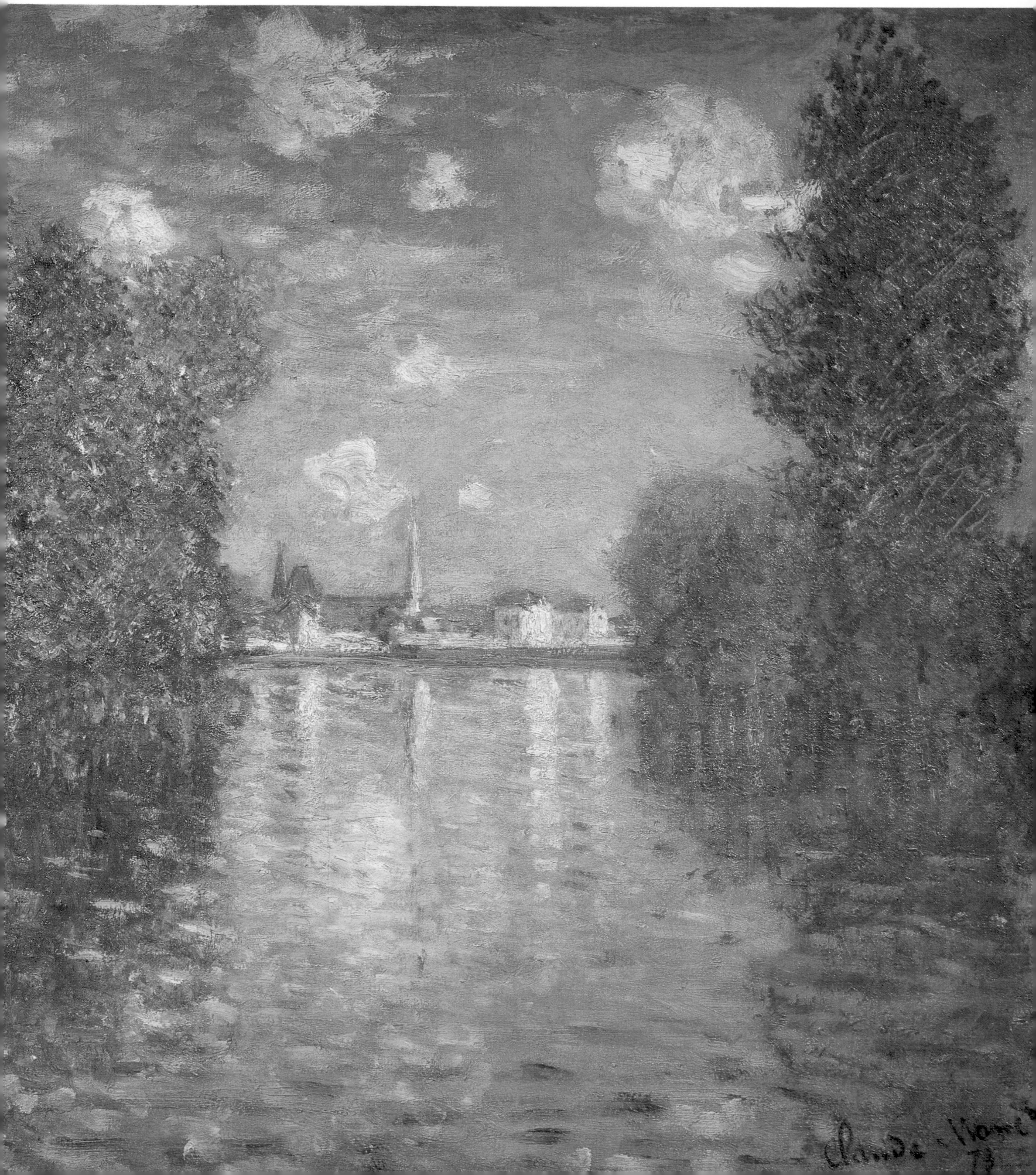

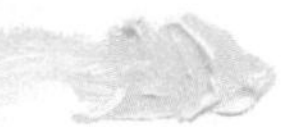

Paints and Palettes

The Impressionists lived in an age of radical technical innovation as well as great social change, both of which affected their professional as well as their private lives. The most evident of such changes was the intervention of middlemen into a profession which, at least as far as Delacroix claimed in 1857, had once been the business of artists alone. The result of this was a sense of loss, in an age already marked by deep uncertainty. Artists felt that they no longer possessed the autonomy or total knowledge of their craft they believed the masters of the past had enjoyed: now they were deeply anxious about the fundamental aspects of their art. On January 13, 1857, Eugène Delacroix wrote in his journal: "Decadence: the arts since the sixteenth century, the peak of their perfection have shown steady decline."

Cézanne's utensils – an image that clearly demonstrates the constituent parts that construct the paintings that fetch millions of dollars worldwide.

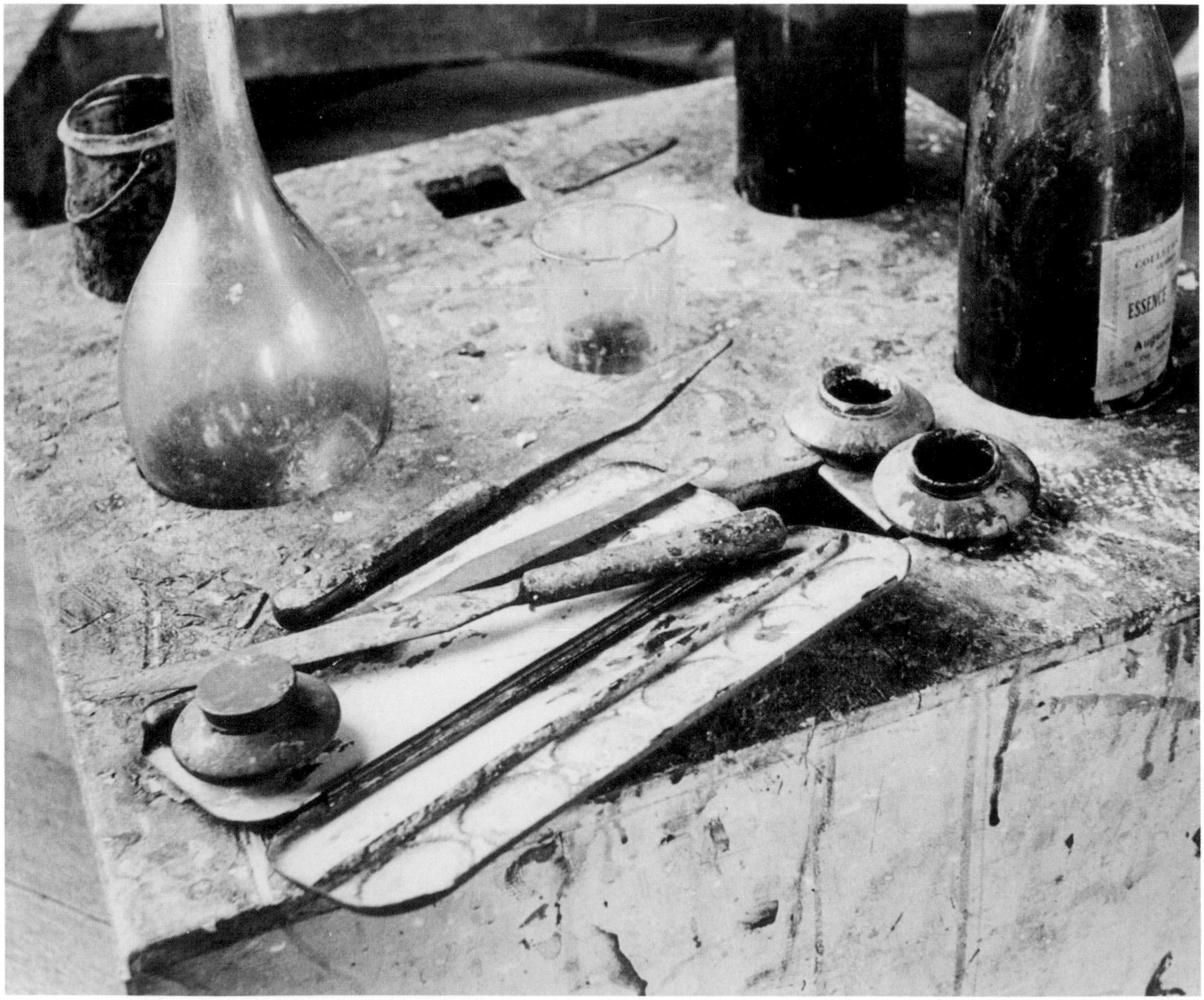

The artist's theories and painting practice were of great importance to the Impressionists, a point reiterated by Cézanne's comment, "We are all Delacroix."

In 1865, just two years after the Romantic master's death and at the very moment that Monet and his friends were painting in Fontainebleu forest, the following notes by Delacroix were published:

At last I have convinced myself that nothing exists without the three primary colors … Every reflection [in a shadow] partakes of green, every edge of a shadow, of violet … Banish all earth colors … Flesh reveals its true color only in the open air and above all in sunlight … hence the folly of making studies in the studio.

Young would-be artists were no longer subject to the prolonged apprenticeships with established artists in whose studios they learned all the necessary elements of their craft, including such basics as the mixing of colors, the preparation of canvases, and, not least, their master's studio secrets. In the journal *L'Artiste*, of May 1, 1877, Frédéric Chevalier wrote,

The disturbing ensemble of contradictory qualities which distinguish the Impressionists, the crude application of paint, the mundane subjects, the appearance of spontaneity, the conscious incoherence, the bold colors, the contempt for form, the childish naïveté that they mix heedlessly with exquisite refinement, all this is not without analogy to the chaos of contradictory forces that trouble our era.

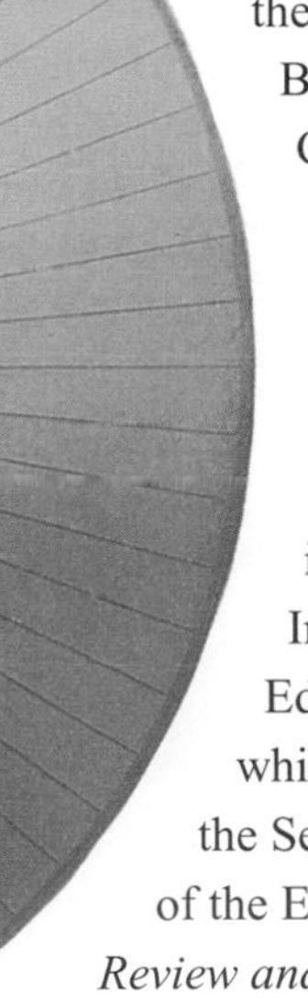

Eugène Chevruel's color wheel (published 1839), illustrates his "Law of Simultaneous Contrast of Colors," which justified his claim that complementary colors, juxtaposed, mutually enhance each other's properties.

A shared body of knowledge

To us, looking back, there does seem to be a certain degree of truth in this interpretation of the breakdown of a shared body of knowledge, handed down from master to pupil. For instance, by the middle of the nineteenth century, most artists bought their paint ready-made in tubes and their canvases ready-stretched and primed. Even artists who had received a thorough training, like Renoir and Degas, felt a deep unease with their level of technical expertise. Indeed, none of the artists in this book, with the possible exception of Sisley, felt secure in their art practice. It is possible that it is their very struggle with their means of expression that gives their work its edge.

Both Manet and Cézanne talked about the process of painting as "diving off a plank into the water." Stéphane Mallarmé, in an article, "The Impressionists and Edouard Manet," which first appeared in the September 1876 issue of the English *Art Monthly Review and Photographic Portfolio* wrote of Manet:

Each time he begins a picture, says he, he plunges headlong into it, and feels like a man who knows that his surest plan to learn to swim safely, is, dangerous as it may seem, to throw himself in the water. One of his habitual aphorisms then is that no one should paint a landscape and a figure by the same process, with the same knowledge, or in the same fashion; nor, what is more, even two landscapes or two figures. Each work should be a new creation of the mind. The hand, it is true, will conserve some of its secrets of manipulation, but the eye should forget all else it has seen, and learn anew from the lesson before it.

Impressionist Color

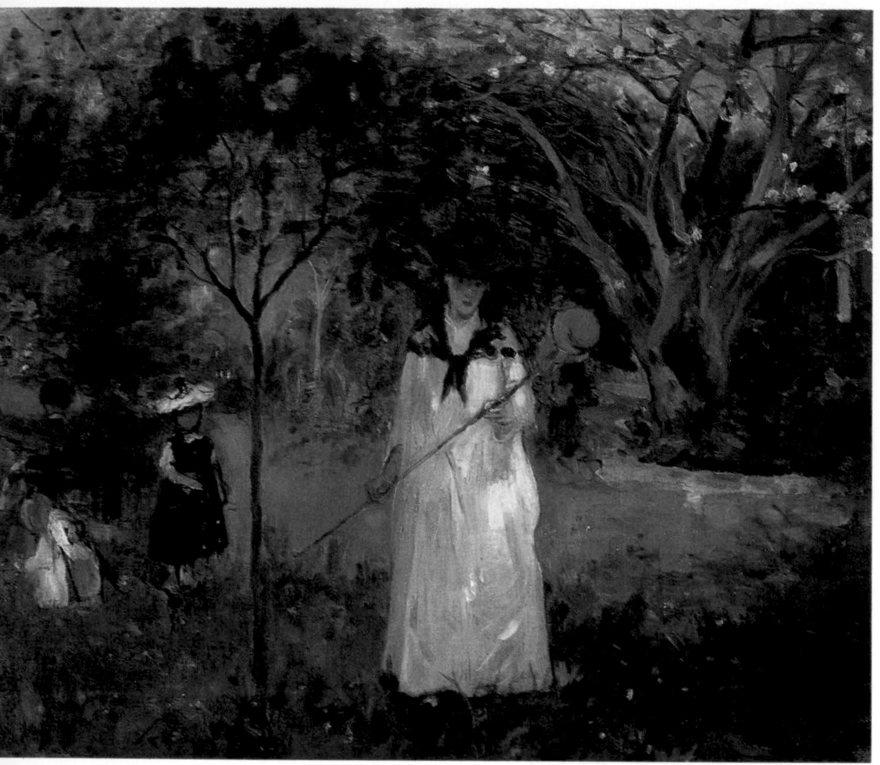

Morisot, **Catching Butterflies,** *1874. Like Renoir, Berthe Morisot had a special regard for the color black.*

***If Veronese disembarked on the banks of the Seine ... it would not be to Bouguereau, but to me that he would give his hand as he stepped down from his Gondola.* – Degas**

Veronese's massive *Marriage at Cana* was one of the major attractions of the Louvre and was much admired and studied by young artists. Degas' splendid fantasy of the great sixteenth-century Venetian colorist sailing down the Seine emphasizes not only the respect Degas had for the art of the past, but also the important role color played in the works of the Impressionists.

Their innovatory use of color was probably the single most unifying factor of Impressionism. Although each of the painters used color in an idiosyncratic way, their common ambition to bring drawing and painting together links their work and was one of the major achievements of their art.

Drawing and color had often been regarded as separate elements of the artist's craft. Ever since the time of Vasari, who worked and wrote in the sixteenth century, drawing had been associated with the Florentine tradition, whereas color had been seen as the defining feature of the Venetian school, the implication being that drawing was the rigorous intellectualizing element of art and, as such, the basis of art. Color was expected to play a subordinate role within a picture; it was considered too emotionally charged, a sensuous addition that disrupted the intellectual aspect of the image. By the nineteenth century, these attitudes had hardened into something easily caricatured, as with Ingres and Delacroix, representing the two extremes, who were famously caricatured doing battle royal outside the Academy, each defending his own preserve.

The nineteenth century saw painters rejecting this prohibitive code and artists of the Impressionist generation dedicated themselves to the abolition of such prejudices. The tonal basis of much of traditional art practice was subverted by their preference for white or creamy colored grounds and by their attempts to represent depth and recession not by the time-honored systems of tonal recession but by the juxtaposition of warm and cool colors. The abandonment of the tonal basis of representation was not completely rejected by all of them; Richard Kendall has shown how Degas, for example, did not reject traditional procedures but radically re-worked them to suit his own purposes.

Other artists took different views. Monet and Sisley were careful students of Delacroix, whose mural paintings at the church of Saint-Sulpice in Paris had a liberating effect on the young artists as they would later have on Seurat and van Gogh. Delacroix, who had studied the color harmonies of Veronese and Rubens, had also paid heed to the researches of the chemist Eugène Chevreul, the director of the Gobelins tapestry works who had been given the task of regenerating the tapestry works to their former glory. As a result of his researches into the effects of color, Chevreul developed a color wheel, which revealed how complementary colors affect each other. By the time of the Impressionists, such ideas were well-known among artists and the effects of such knowledge may be seen in the tapestrylike weave of color strands that are evident in Delacroix's mural.

Following Delacroix's example, certain artists began to banish dark tones from their palettes and to apply paint in single dashes (taches) of the brush.

While Delacroix's palette was extremely sophisticated, that adopted by the Independent painters was, in comparison, relatively uncomplicated. It was based upon the practice of painting on cream or off-white grounds and using white to lighten the overall tone of the painting. This was partly developed from Corot's practice of *peinture claire* – the admixture of white to the colors – modified by the adoption of *peinture au premier coup*, in which the paint is applied directly to the canvas at a single sitting. The most famous example of this in Impressionist painting is Monet's *On the Beach* (1870), in which the sand can be clearly seen mixed with the paint.

Of course such techniques varied from artist to artist, most spectacularly in the working methods of Degas, who showed no interest in the methods adopted by Monet, Renoir, Pissarro and Sisley. Morisot's practice was based upon Manet's procedures but informed by her experience of *plein-air* painting. Although the Impressionists avoided the use of earth colors and adopted a palette dominated by pure brilliant colors, black was never abandoned and appears frequently in the work of Renoir and Morisot, although it is rarely used to darken tones.

Monet's techniques went through spectacular changes throughout his career. Basing his technique not on the physical characteristics of what was before him but on how such forms were affected by the fall of light, he built up his paintings through the repeated application of paint, often painting wet on dry to produce the encrusted paint surface so typical of his work, and often painting wet on wet, which allowed former strokes of color to be modified by subsequent applications of pigment. Black never appears in his later works. Monet's color preferences had a marked impact upon Manet's later style. "I have discovered the color of the atmosphere," the latter once said, "it is violet!" In 1865, Pissarro prohibited himself the use of earth pigments; instead, he used colors of a high chromatic range juxtaposed to create the harmonious, even muted quality evident in so many of his canvases.

Monet,* The Poppyfield, *1885. Using the natural color of the poppies, Monet has made this painting an excuse for a pattern established by the use of the complementaries green and red.

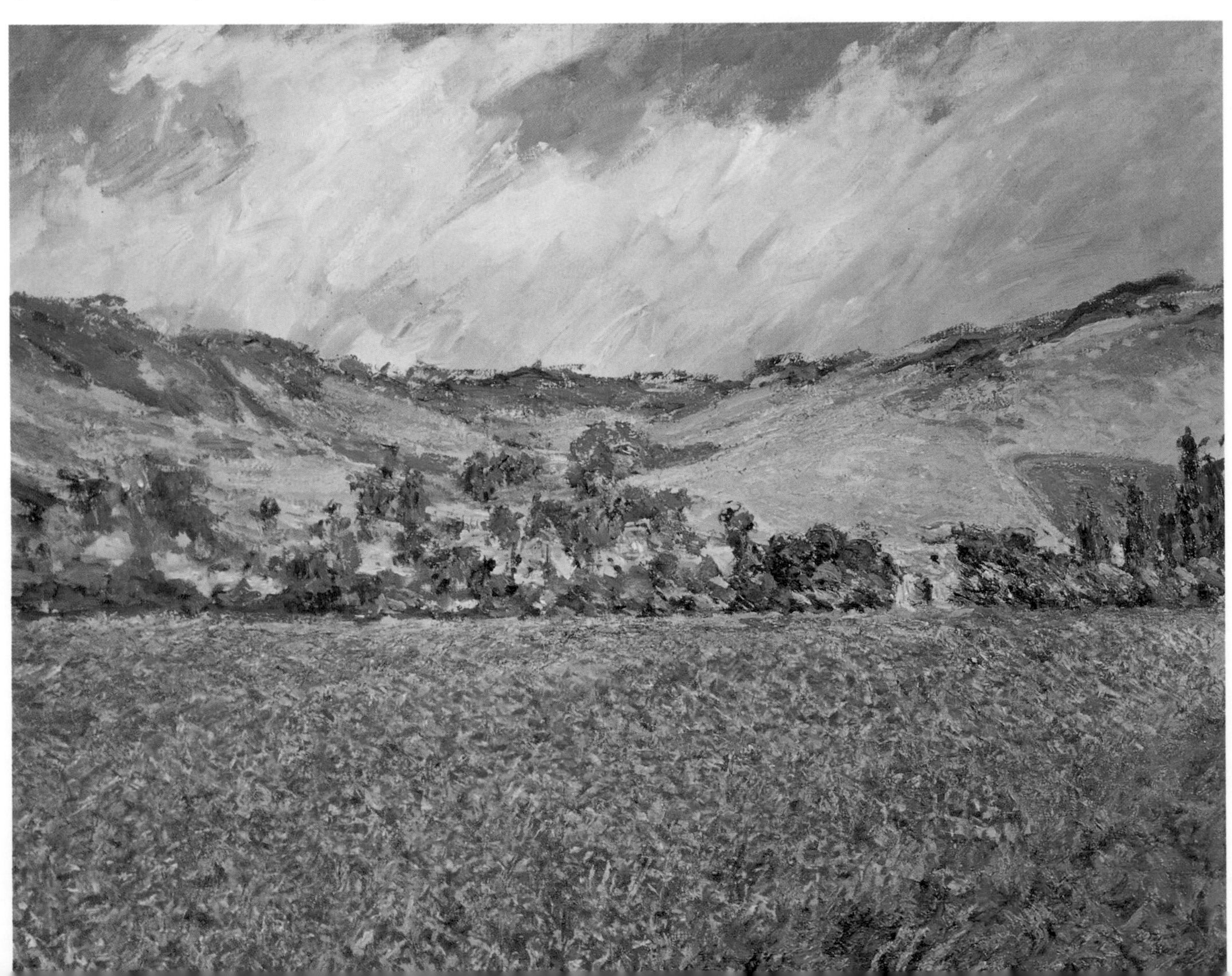

A Painting Lesson from Pissarro

Berthe Morisot said that Pissarro was such a good teacher, he could teach even the stones how to paint. In a letter to a young artist, Louis le Bail, written in the mid-1890s, Pissarro wrote these words of advice:

Pissarro,* Farm at Montfoucault, Snow Effect, *1874. Painted twenty years before Pissarro's letter, this charming work reveals the artist's approach to painting.

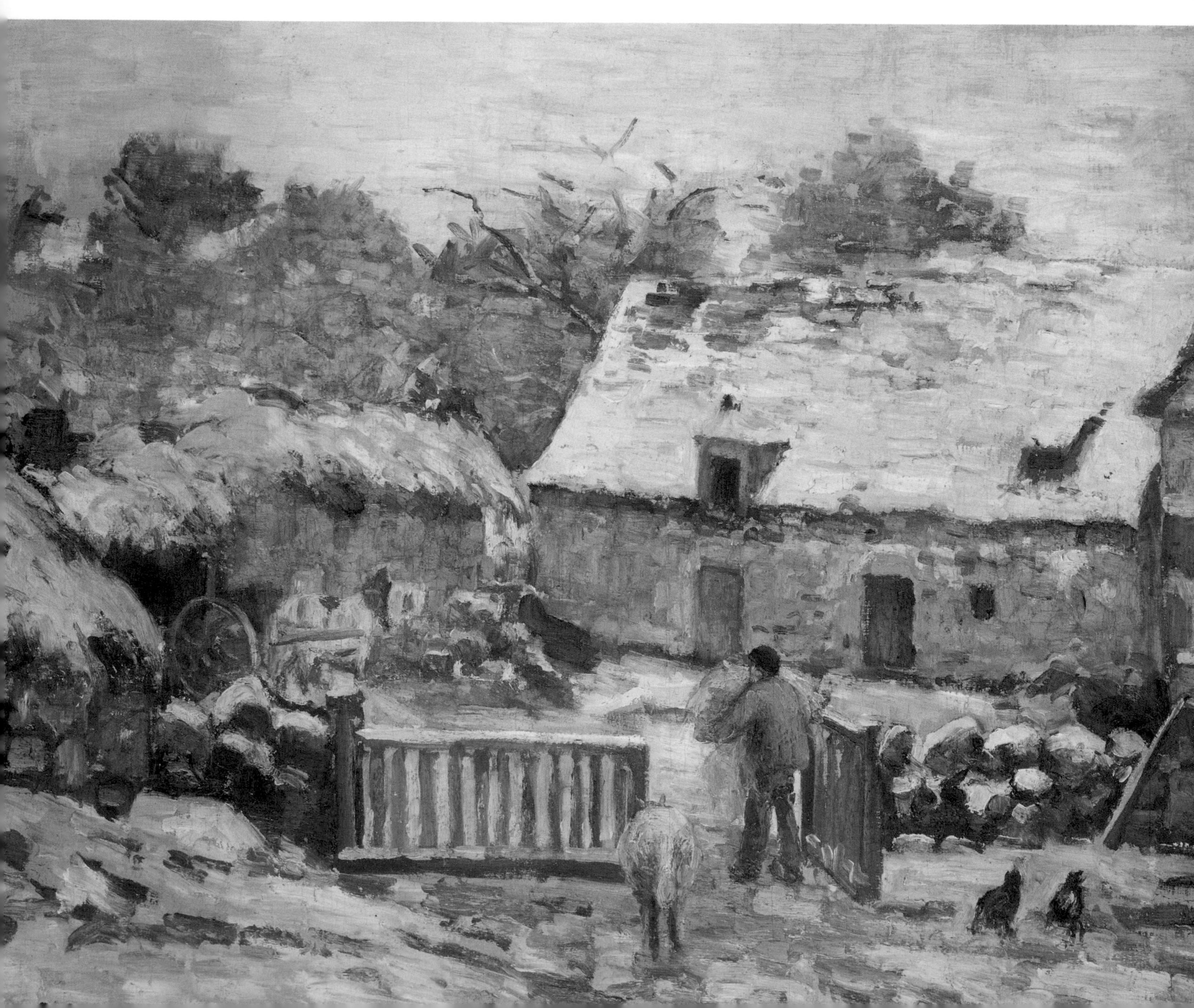

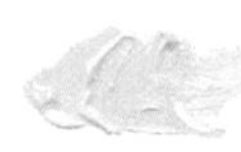

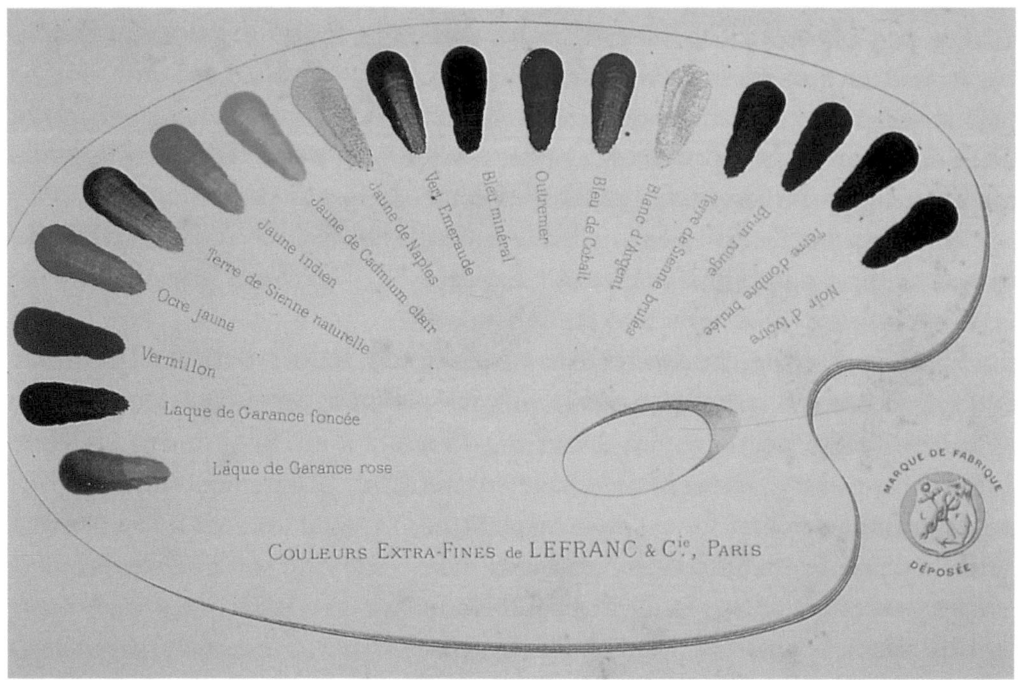

Look for the kind of nature that suits your temperament. The motif should be observed more for the shape and color than for the precise drawing … Precise drawing is dry and hampers the impression of the whole, it destroys all sensations….

Do not define too closely the outlines; it is the brushwork of the right value and color which produces the drawing … Paint the essential character of things; try to convey it by any means whatever, without bothering about technique. When painting, make a choice of subject, see what is lying at the right and left, then work on everything simultaneously. Don't work bit by bit, but paint everything at once by placing tones everywhere, with brushstrokes of the right color and value, while noticing what is alongside. Use small strokes and try to put down your perceptions immediately. The eye should not be fixed on one point, but should take in everything, while observing the reflections the colors produce on their surroundings. Work at the same time on the sky, water, branches, ground, keeping everything going on an equal basis and unceasingly work until you have got it. Cover the canvas at first go, then work at it until you have nothing more to add.

Observe the aerial perspective, from the foreground to the horizon, the reflections of the sky, of foliage. Don't be afraid of putting on color, refine the work little by little. Don't proceed according to rules and principles, but paint what you observe and feel. Paint generously and unhesitatingly, for it is best not to lose the first impression. Don't be timid in front of nature; one must be bold, at the risk of being and making mistakes. One must always have only one master – nature; she is the one always to be consulted.

Impressionist Drawing

Drawing is not the same as form, it is a way of seeing form.

Degas' aphorism is one of the most simple and effective ways of understanding the role of drawing in modern art. In 1859, Degas' father wrote a stern letter to his young son, saying,

> ***You know how far I am from sharing your opinion concerning Delacroix, this painter who has abandoned himself to the fury of his ideas and has sadly for him neglected the art of drawing, the sacred arch on which everything depends, he is completely lost. As for Ingres, he is elevated through drawing …***

Degas, **Three Dancers in Yellow,** *c. 1899–1904. The working and reworking of the lines define the image.*

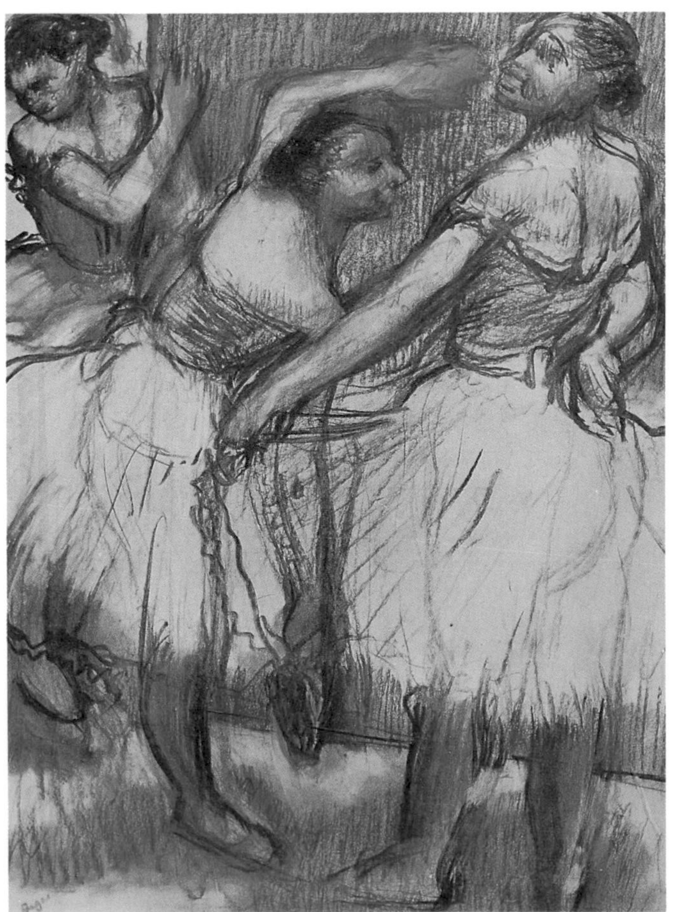

The artist's father was repeating the commonly held assertion that drawing was the elevating element of art and as such central to art practice. Over the years it had acquired an intellectual role, even a moral one, sustaining academic practice as a rigorous discipline of the liberal arts. By the 1860s, however, this view had become increasingly outmoded, as the influence of the Ecole des Beaux-Arts waned and what were once considered radical art practices became accepted by the state.

The liberation of drawing from its circumscribed role that had begun with Delacroix and the romantics was completed by the Impressionists. Cézanne told a young Emile Bernard, "Drawing and painting are no longer different factors, as one paints, one draws; the more harmony there is in the colors the more precise the drawing becomes. When color is at its richest, the form is at its fullest. Contrasts and harmonies of tones, there lies the secret of drawing and modeling."

The graphic arts – watercolor, drawings, pastels and etchings – played an important part in the Impressionist exhibitions. In the 1886 show, for example, over a third of the exhibits were works on paper. This was partly a result of commercial considerations, works on paper being less expensive to purchase than oils on canvas, but it was also to do with drawings being considered as works of art in their own right.

The role of drawing in art

To most artists, drawing is an integral part of the process of making art; drawings can operate as initial compositional sketches, notations capturing a particular object, effect or gesture that could be incorporated into a painting. Drawing can also encompass rapid responses to nature, which then may function as a crucial part of the process of transformation from the initial act of seeing into the resolved painting.

Each of the Impressionists followed their own agenda and worked in media suited to their own particular activities. Monet's drawings were almost always tied to the making of his oil paintings, his looping serpentine pencil line playing the same unifying role as the great cursive sweeps of his brush. Few works on paper survive by Sisley, but Pissarro

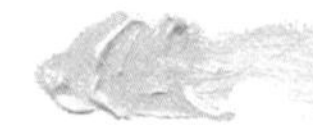

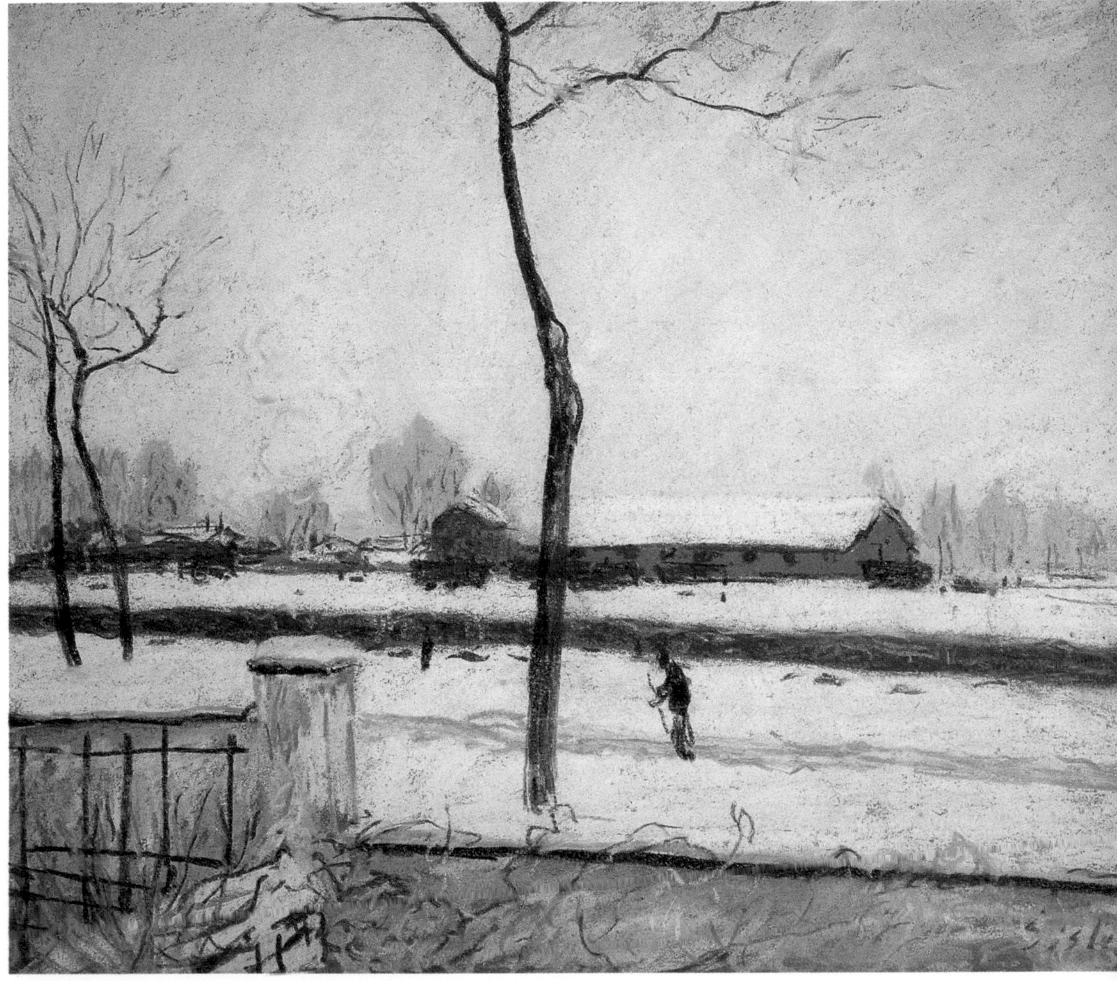

Sisley,* Railway Yards at Moret. *A simple effective composition that uses color and pastel to evoke a chilly winter's day.

and Degas were compulsive draughtsmen, drawing for them being an integral and everyday activity.

The most spectacular achievement of Impressionist graphic art, outside Degas' superlative draftsmanship, is to be found in their practice of uniting, each in their separate ways, drawing and color.

As Degas once said, in typically provocative fashion, "*Colorer, c'est poursuivre le dessin plus en profondeur*" ("Coloration is only drawing pursued in more depth"). This comes close to explaining the ability of art to suggest color through the knowing manipulation of black and white and also alludes to Degas' practice of introducing pastel color on to his black and white monotypes: nothing could be further from the usual notion of Impressionist art as being only concerned with *alla prima* painting.

Degas was fascinated by the Venetian practice of painting in glazes upon a tonally structured underpainting, and attempted to find a modern equivalent for this way of working. His late pastels and oils may be interpreted as modern attempts to find equivalents to these traditional techniques. If Degas could draw with the volumetric power and emotional intensity of Michelangelo, he could also draw with the precision and elegance of Watteau. From the 1880s, Degas' interest in sequential drawings developed apace, the artist exploring the same pose or gesture countless times, tracing the drawing through on to another sheet of paper the better to investigate the mysteries of movement that fascinated him so much.

Ingres' advice to him so many years earlier is borne out in his countless variations on a single theme: "Draw lines, my boy, many lines, using a weave of line or color to capture, like a fisherman's net, a sequence of movements." In his later works, as in that of his colleagues, a movement away from the more precise drawings of the 1870s may be discerned. Degas' art and especially his drawings in different media, hint at some thing more allusive, more mysterious, the breath of life itself as expressed through movement.

Cézanne and the importance of drawing

For Cézanne, drawing was an essential practice, part of his very being, not simply a space in which to solve painterly problems, but an activity that, like his painting, was based upon his most profound beliefs.

Through the intense study of the landscape or whatever else he was confronting, a Cézanne drawing is a record or a trace of his attempts to bring his perceptions to an ordered conclusion, to organize them into a harmonious and unified structure, without recourse to the conventionalized solutions he abhorred so much.

The attraction of the artificial or abstract nature of drawing may be defined by two illuminating statements by Cézanne. One of these was quoted by Léo Largier: "Cézanne regarded drawing as a function of color. 'Pure drawing is an abstraction, drawing and color are not distinct points, everything in nature is colored,' he said."

The other Cézanne statement is equally terse: "Art is personal perception. This perception I place in feeling and I ask of feeling that it should organize itself into a work."

Japonisme

Before Japanese art arrived the painter always lied. Nature, with its bold colors was there for all to see, but on the canvas all you ever saw were anemic colors, drowned in an overall half-tone … As soon as people looked at Japanese pictures in which the most vivid, piercing colors were set side by side, they finally understood that there were new ways of reproducing certain effects of nature which had been until then considered impossible to reproduce … Japanese art conveys the real appearance of nature by bold new means of coloring, and so strongly influenced the Impressionists.
– Théodore Duret, *Les Peintres Impressionistes*, 1878.

Duret's claims for the impact of Japanese art upon Impressionism may be somewhat exaggerated, but they bear witness to the incalculable effect of the importation of Japanese goods and artifacts into Europe, particularly France, that began on a large scale in 1855 with the opening up of the Japanese port of Yokohama to trade with the West. The term "Japonisme" was coined by Philippe Burty to describe the phenomenon. Burty was a well-known art critic and wealthy collector who in 1872 promoted Japanese art as a suitable model for the restoration of French art and design to the position it had enjoyed in the eighteenth century. Thus, Japonisme became a tool for the restoration of French national identity. French artists and designers were encouraged by numerous books, journal articles and exhibitions to integrate Japanese elements of art and design into their own practice. Each artist reacted differently to this pervasive influence.

The man credited with popularizing Japanese *Ukiyo-e* prints in Paris was the printmaker Félix Braquemond (1833–1917). He had apparently discovered one of Hokusai's *Manga* (sketchbooks) in his printer's studio. The book was filled with sketches depicting every aspect of Japanese life, captured by the master draftsman. A little later, he acquired the volume and carried it around with him everywhere, "as if it were his prayer-book," someone quipped, showing it to his friends and acquaintances in the hope of finding new converts to the cause.

Orientalism in France

In their country of origin, Japanese prints were not thought of as possessing any particularly high cultural or monetary status. They were sold in markets for a few pence, and could be regarded as a truly democratic and popular art form. They were not exported for their worth as art, but were used as packing material to protect the luxury goods that were brought over to Europe in such vast quantities. A number of shops specializing in Japanese goods opened in the 1850s and were frequented by Burty, Degas and Baudelaire among others. Thanks to their enthusiasm for these discarded

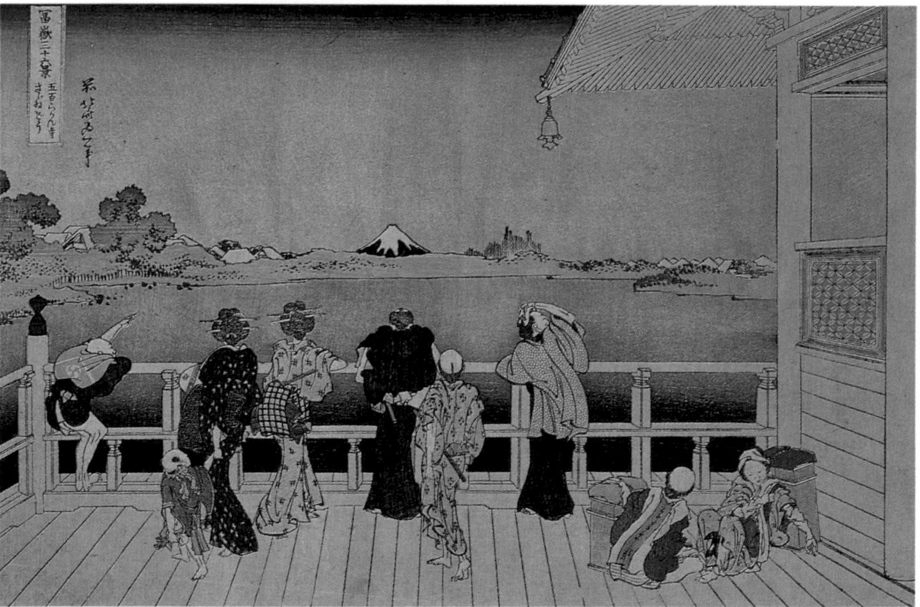

Katsushika Hokusai,* The Sazai Pavilion of the Temple of Five Hundred Rakan *from* Thirty Five Views of Mount Fuji, *woodblock print 1829–33. The print greatly influenced Monet.

wrappings, the prints rapidly became collectible, particularly among their friends of the Café Guerbois set. A number of bric-à-brac shops specialized in Japanese art and culture, Madame Desoiye's *La Porte Chinoise* under the arcades at the Rue de Rivoli being the most famous, and in 1867 and 1878 the Exposition Universelle further popularized the vogue for all things oriental. The prints were known to the Japanese as "*Ukiyo-e*," images of the floating world, and took for their inspiration scenes of everyday life, including the brothels of Edo, the capital of Japan (now called Tokyo), popular legends, scenes from the theater and the landscape; portraits of prostitutes, actors and famous warriors were also popular.

The French avant-garde was quick to see in such images confirmation of their own interest in such subjects and affirmation of their stylistic experiments. Many of these were familiar already in European art, but had never been treated with the forthrightness and sophistication they found in the work of their Japanese counterparts. The prints were heavily stylized, elegantly drawn with clear and simple contours, distance suggested not by single viewpoint perspective and tonal recession, but by overlapping forms and cropping. Compositions were asymmetrically oriented with shapes organized into bright areas of flat color. Such works confirmed and sustained the artists in their own practice.

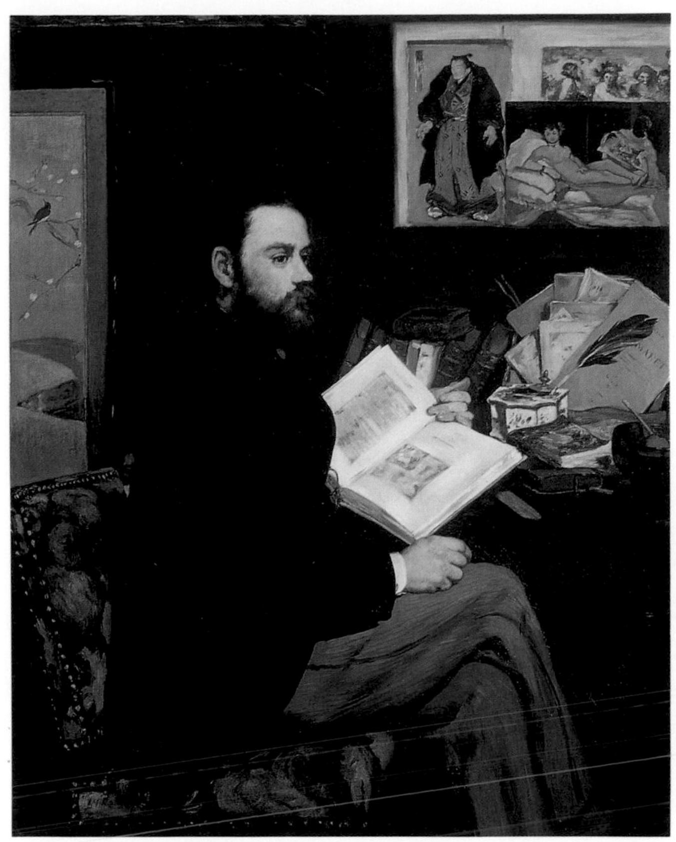

Manet,* Portrait of Emile Zola, *1868. Painted to thank the critic for his support, Manet's painting presented the viewer with an inventory of his artistic interests.

Japonisme in European art

The influence of such works was not limited to avant-garde artists, and fashionable painters like Stevens and Tissot, and Whistler in England, incorporated Japanese prints, kimonos and ceramic pots into their work in the hope of improving their marketability.

The clearest image of the impact of Japanese art upon French painting can be seen in Manet's *Portrait of Zola*, completed in 1868 and shown at the Salon of that year. Painted to thank his friend for his critical support, the work is an inventory of Manet's interests at the time. The overall composition is based upon the example of seventeenth-century Dutch artists, while the print after Velazquez's *The Topers* and his own painting, *Olympia*, are placed immediately next to a Japanese print of a Sumo wrestler. The peacock feather and Oriental screen further indicate the eclectic nature of Manet's artistic interests.

To borrow from the Japanese was a sign of *modernité*, of showing oneself open to novel means of expression with which to represent the modern age. In Manet's *The Balcony* (1868–69), while the composition is essentially taken from Goya, the sensibility is Japanese, the bizarreness and ambiguity of the images found in *Ukiyo-e* prints being adapted to this very Parisian subject to give it an *outré* quality that marked it as distinctively of the moment.

Two painters of the next generation, Monet, who as early as 1868 was known as a "*fidèle émule d'Hokusai*" ("Hokusai's faithful disciple"), and Degas, were the artists most influenced by the Japanese print. Both thoroughly assimilated those aspects they found most in line with their own researches and both built up impressive collections of prints. Monet's enthusiasm led him to design his house and gardens at Giverny along Japanese lines.

Paradoxically, Japanese art was seen as being at once sophisticated and, as Burty's quote implies, naive and even "primitive." The Japanese artist was thought to be fully integrated both into the world of natural beauty and into the society of which he was a part. It was these aspects of the craze for things Japanese that most influenced the next generation of artists, among them van Gogh and Toulouse-Lautrec, for both of whom the art and the land of Japan stood for an ideal. Both wished to visit the country and to live and work there, and, tragically, neither of them achieved their dream.

Photography

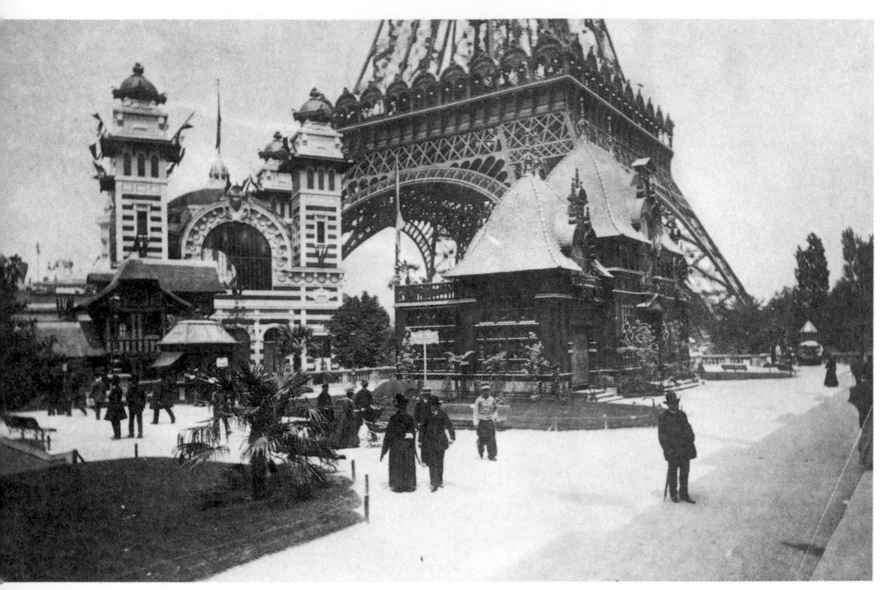

Gustave Eiffel's 300m (984ft) tower, constructed for the Universal Exhibition of 1889, the subject of many contemporary photographs.

Impressionism coincides precisely with the development of photography, which began as an exclusive pastime for the wealthy and became, as the century progressed, the most accessible means of recording the visual world. Photography had been around for a long time. In the seventeenth century Vermeer had used a camera obscura, but it was not until the nineteenth century that ways were found to capture the image permanently, first on glass and then on paper. As a result, the nineteenth century is littered with claims of "the death of painting."

Rather than killing off painting, however, the growing popularity of photography freed the artist from the enslavement of being mere reproducers of the visual, for now the photographer's studio could take care of that. The artist may have had one role taken away from him, but he was free to explore others. The camera as a mechanical means of representation revealed through its development many different images of reality. In the process it exposed the arbitrary nature of systems of representation and discredited the notion of any one kind of image being uniquely "true." Many of the "accidents" evident in early photographic prints may be found in Impressionist art, because they relished the distortions and peculiar effects that the mechanical process imposed upon visual reality.

Like the Japanese print and the popular images of Daumier and others, photography in all its various guises supported the Impressionists in their search for alternative means of representing reality. Nineteenth-century photography shared with Japanese prints a number of features that were adopted by painters to give a twist of the unexpected to their works, enabling them to create compositions that were very different from the models traditionally used to construct images of reality.

One of the major novelties of photography was its ability to bring every element situated in the visual field covered by the viewfinder into perfect focus, with no particular aspect given a greater or lesser significance than any other. This,

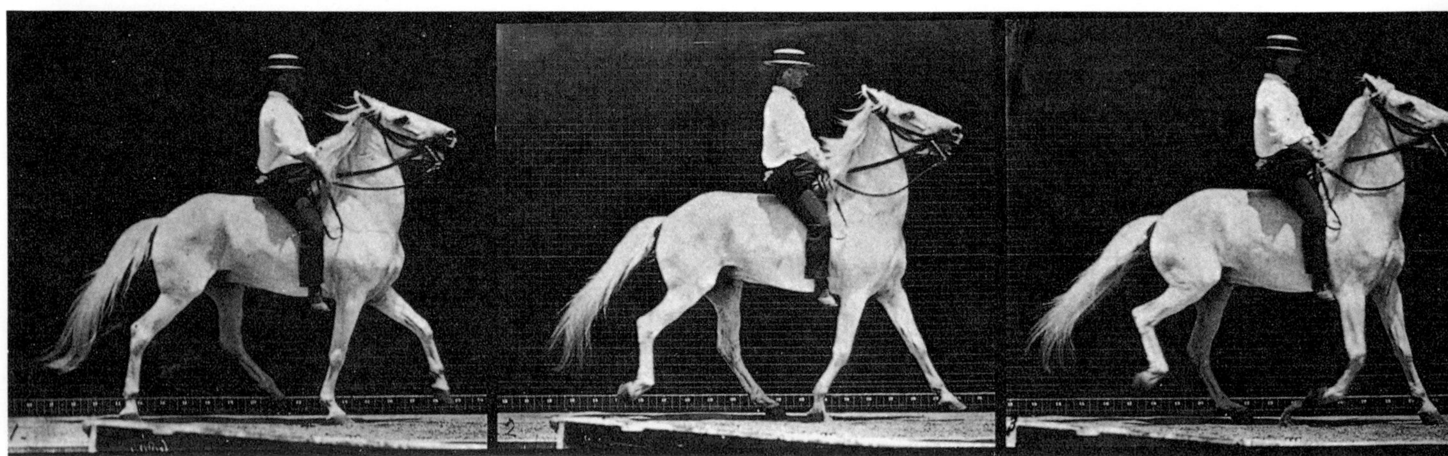

when translated into painting, gave the works of the Impressionists a curiously unposed look that acted as a metaphor for the arbitrariness of real experience.

The photographic process also froze the moment, catching figures off guard in the awkward poses of everyday activities, or reduced them, through slow exposure, to a blur – as can readily be seen in Monet's *Boulevard des Capucines* of 1873. Painters actively exploited the blurring effects in their paintings, often introducing unusual or unexpected cropping of figures and buildings to create informal asymmetrical compositions.

Photographs could also capture a sense of movement, they could preserve fortuitous juxtapositions and give a sense of immediacy, represented not by the posed conventions of traditional art practice, but by the realities of everyday life. One of the pioneers of the photography of movement was the English photographer, Eadweard Muybridge, whose work was especially important to French artists. In 1887 he published a book called *Animal Locomotion,* which featured photographs of humans and animals caught in sequential movement. When these photographs appeared in France they had an immediate impact upon artists of all persuasions, most spectacularly upon Degas, whose whole life was marked by his obsessive investigations into the depiction of movement which was the *raison d'être* for his countless images of ballet dancers and horses. Paul Valery, who was intimate with Degas, recalled the artist explaining how

> ***... a horse walks on its toes ... No animal is closer to a première danseuse ... than a perfectly balanced thoroughbred ... He was among the first to study the real positions of that noble animal in movement, as seen in the "instantaneous" photographs of M. Muybridge.***

Traditionally, one of the most common ways of suggesting movement had been to show different people acting out different stages of the same movement; this can be found in Degas' *Young Spartans* and Renoir's *Moulin de la Galette*. The example of photography offered much that could be picked up and used by artists. Degas worked hard to replicate the camera's sense of immediacy. Monet, too, was fascinated by photography and he owned four cameras in the 1880s, while Degas bought one in 1896 and took many fascinating photographs of his own.

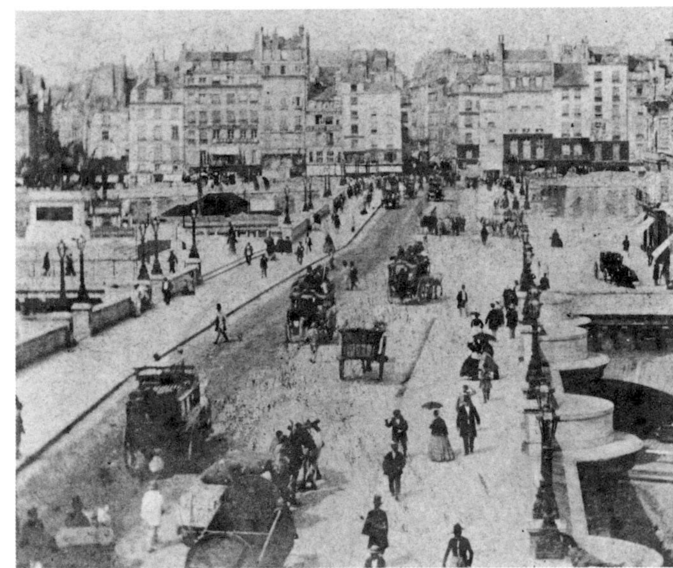

Contemporary photograph of the Pont Neuf; this print makes a fascinating parallel with Renoir's painting of the same subject.

Baudelaire had expressed his doubts as regards the new medium; like Delacroix, he could see that it might have its uses as an effective recording agent for artists, but he stressed how important it was for the artist to transform such prosaic material into art through the intervention of his "genius." The paintings of Manet and Degas reveal just how far the artist could use photography to enrich their own relationship to their art.

Muybridge's photographic study of bareback riding, 1884–85. Such photographs shocked and thrilled the sophisticated Parisians.

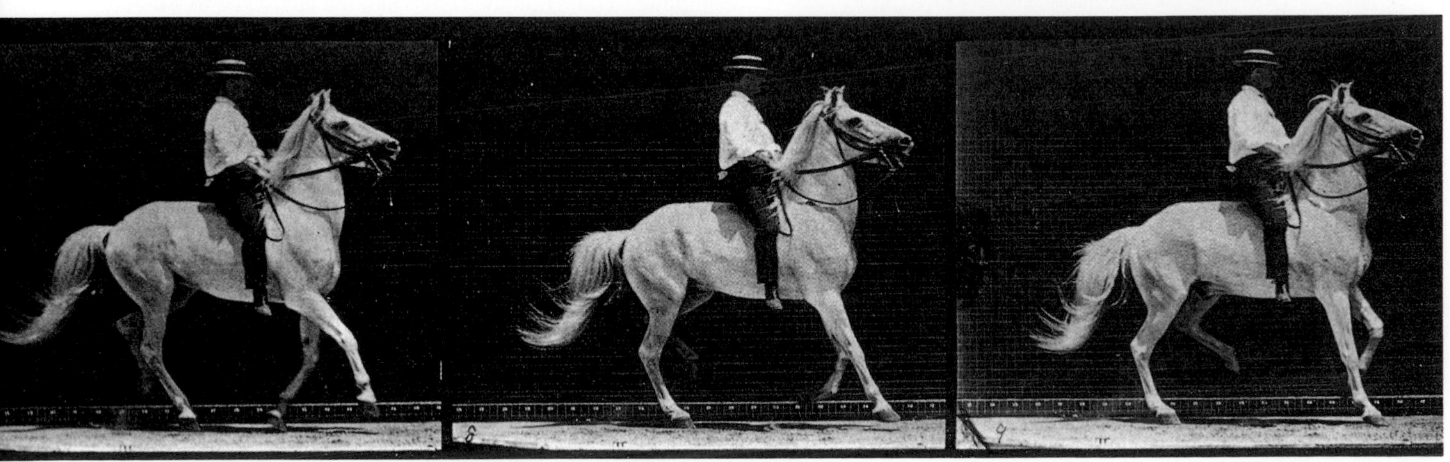

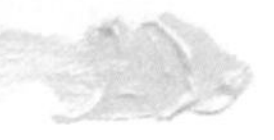

Paul Gauguin: rejecting Impressionism

***I love Brittany. I find something savage, primitive here. When my clogs echo on this granite earth, I hear the dull, muffled note that I am seeking in my painting.* – Gauguin**

If an absolute innocence of vision can never be achieved, then an apparent innocence or *naïveté* before nature can be signaled by a deliberate avoidance of conventional structures of representation or the deliberate adoption of alternative models. One of the most attractive of these models was the appropriation of so-called "primitive" art forms. Nothing can be more sophisticated than a cultivation of primitivism. The problem inherent in such a decision is that eventually these strategies in turn become conventions.

In different ways, Courbet and Cézanne had played the savage, but it was an ex-stockbroker amateur painter who made the genre his own. Paul Gauguin (1848–1903) was born in Paris in the year of revolutions throughout Europe. His mother and father were well-known political activists who, having to leave Europe, took their little boy to Peru, where he grew up in exotic splendor. In 1854 he returned to France, staying in Orleans with his wealthy uncle Gustave Arosa, who had a large collection of paintings by romantic artists and the painters of the Barbizon school.

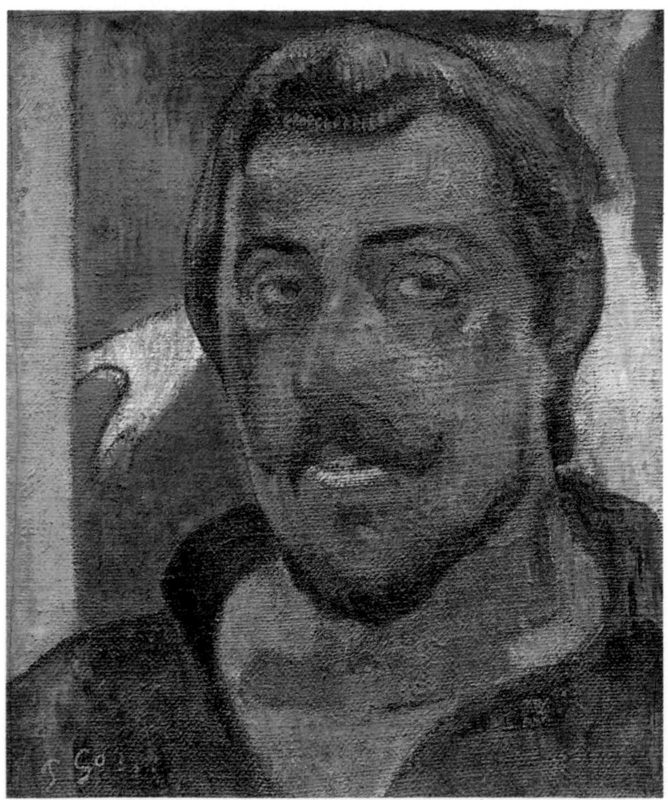

A self-portrait by Gauguin. The haunted look is very different from the usual self-confident self-images produced by the Impressionists.

Gauguin attended pre-naval college in 1862 and during 1865–67 traveled the world as a merchant sailor, joining the navy in 1868 and seeing action during the Franco-Prussian War. On his return to Paris in 1871, his uncle found him a job as a stockbroker connected with the Banque Bertin, which he kept until the financial collapse of 1882. During the boom years immediately after the war, Gauguin became a wealthy collector of Impressionist paintings and an amateur artist. Wooed by the Impressionists as a patron, he exhibited with them and as the economic situation worsened, he took the decision to become a full-time modern painter, encouraged by a favorable review of his nude study of his maid Suzanne sewing, shown in the sixth Impressionist exhibition in 1881.

Paintings from earlier and later in Gauguin's Pont-Aven period reveal the shift that was apparent in the work of most artists associated with Impressionism. While still an amateur painter, Gauguin had received lessons from Pissarro, who had encouraged him to show at the fourth Impressionist exhibition of 1879. By 1883 he had made the momentous decision to become a professional artist and, like his mentor, was attempting to integrate the figure into the landscape to suggest the harmony between man and nature that was so difficult to attain in the urban centers.

Like many artists seeking cheap accommodation and picturesque subject matter, he traveled to Brittany, which was even then being developed as a romantic holiday destination. Images of rural life were popular and saleable in the city, and artists, whatever their stylistic persuasions, offered their audience images of the countryside as a place where traditions and community values were still significant factors in life and where simple people were locked into a round of existence that owed much to the essential rhythms of life. Many modern commentators have exploded this myth and shown that many of the customs that gave Brittany its distinctness had been artificially sustained to create an identity that would perpetuate its reputation as a mysterious, primitive region.

Gauguin's association with the area around Pont-Aven and Le Pouldu, where he stayed between 1886 and 1890 (apart from two trips abroad and a disastrous stay with van Gogh in Arles), resulted in two very different kinds of paintings. *The Breton Shepherdess* shows a young peasant girl watching over her sheep and in style and subject reveals a clear debt to Pissarro. Gauguin, like his mentor, has not attempted to depict a particular moment in time but has concentrated on suggesting the young girl's mood of abstracted reverie, secure within the rural community that surrounds her. The brushmarks and the overlapping forms owe much to Cézanne, several of whose works Gauguin had bought in his more prosperous days.

Two years later, in 1888, Gauguin completed *The Vision After the Sermon*, sometimes called *Jacob Wrestling with the Angel*, an extraordinary painting that is a complete volte face against the principles of Impressionist *plein-air* practice. Gauguin had returned to Brittany from a disastrous sojourn on the tropical island of Martinique. He always felt that he was a half savage, half civilized man: "This year I have sacrificed everything – execution, color – for style, because I wished to force myself into doing something other than what I know how to do."

This meant a thorough and complete rejection of Impressionist principles. He looked to many of the same sources of inspiration as they did, but with different ends in view. He studied Japanese prints, children's drawings, popular prints, stained glass and religious art and fused all these disparate strands into a personal symbolic art. He was not alone in his ambitions to create an art that was more mystically inclined and more abstract than that of most of his contemporaries. Van Gogh, Aquentin and Emile Bernard were all seeking for a means to renew art, to create a religious painting for a secular society. Emile Bernard stayed at Pont-Aven in the summer of 1888 for a few weeks, and Gauguin was much influenced by his painting techniques.

The painting is a reworking of Delacroix's monumental mural of *Jacob Wrestling with the Angel* in the church of Saint-Sulpice in Paris. Gauguin has interpreted this painting through an adoption of Bernard's decorative *cloisonné* style, which he had derived from his admiration of stained glass and medieval art. The peasant women, dressed in their traditional garb, have been inspired by the priest's sermon and are experiencing the vision. In order to heighten the mystical content of the work, Gauguin has made the simple decision to paint the field outside the church vermilion, rather than its normal green. The wrestling figures are taken from Hokusai's *mangwa* and the detail of the kneeling cow and tree trunk can also be traced to models in similar sources. The female figures are separated from the spiritual action taking place by the diagonal of the tree. The artist–priest figure is significantly on the side of the spiritual, as it is through him the women have received their vision. It is no accident that the priest appears to bear the features of Gauguin himself. He offered the painting to the priest at Nizon where it could be seen "surrounded by bare stone and stained glass … it would look out of place in a drawing-room," as he wrote. It was refused.

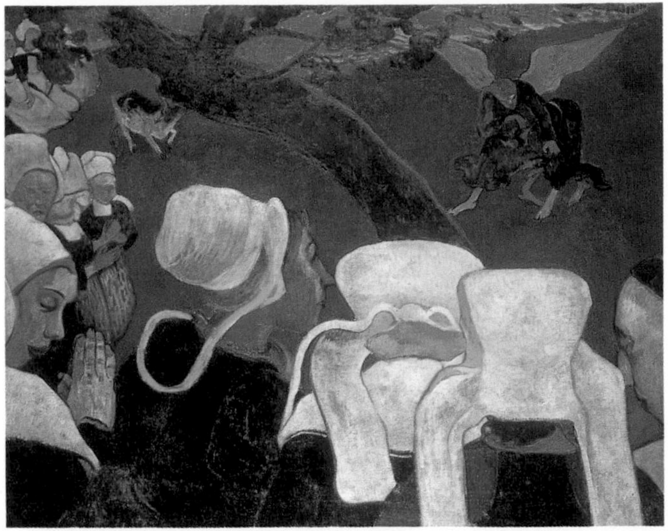

Gauguin,* The Vision After the Sermon, *1888. A painting that, quite rightly, was seen by critics as being the antithesis of Impressionist practice.

Pissarro was not amused at his friend's development. "I do not blame Gauguin for having painted a vermilion background, two warriors fighting, and the Breton peasants in the foreground," he said. "I reproach him for having stolen this from the Japanese, from Byzantine painters and others. I reproach him for not applying his synthesis to our modern philosophy, which is absolutely social, anti-authoritarian, and anti-mystical."

In this work, Gauguin created one of the key images of expressive and symbolic art in which the primitive and mystical are celebrated at the expense of the sophisticated achievements of a materialistic society. He hoped his work would help to reintroduce people who were becoming increasingly distanced from nature and their emotions to the reality and mystery of their inner lives. When he died in poverty and illness in the Marquesas in 1903, aged only 54, Paul Gauguin left a testimony that was to be taken up by many of the young avant-garde painters of the early twentieth century. He wrote "You have known for a long time what I have tried to achieve: the right to dare anything."

Printmaking

The era of Impressionism was a golden age of prints and the making of prints was an integral part of Impressionist practice. Degas, Pissarro and Morisot often exhibited prints and other works on paper with their paintings in the group shows from 1874–86. In 1862, the *Société des Aquafortistes* was formed by Alfred Cadart, a

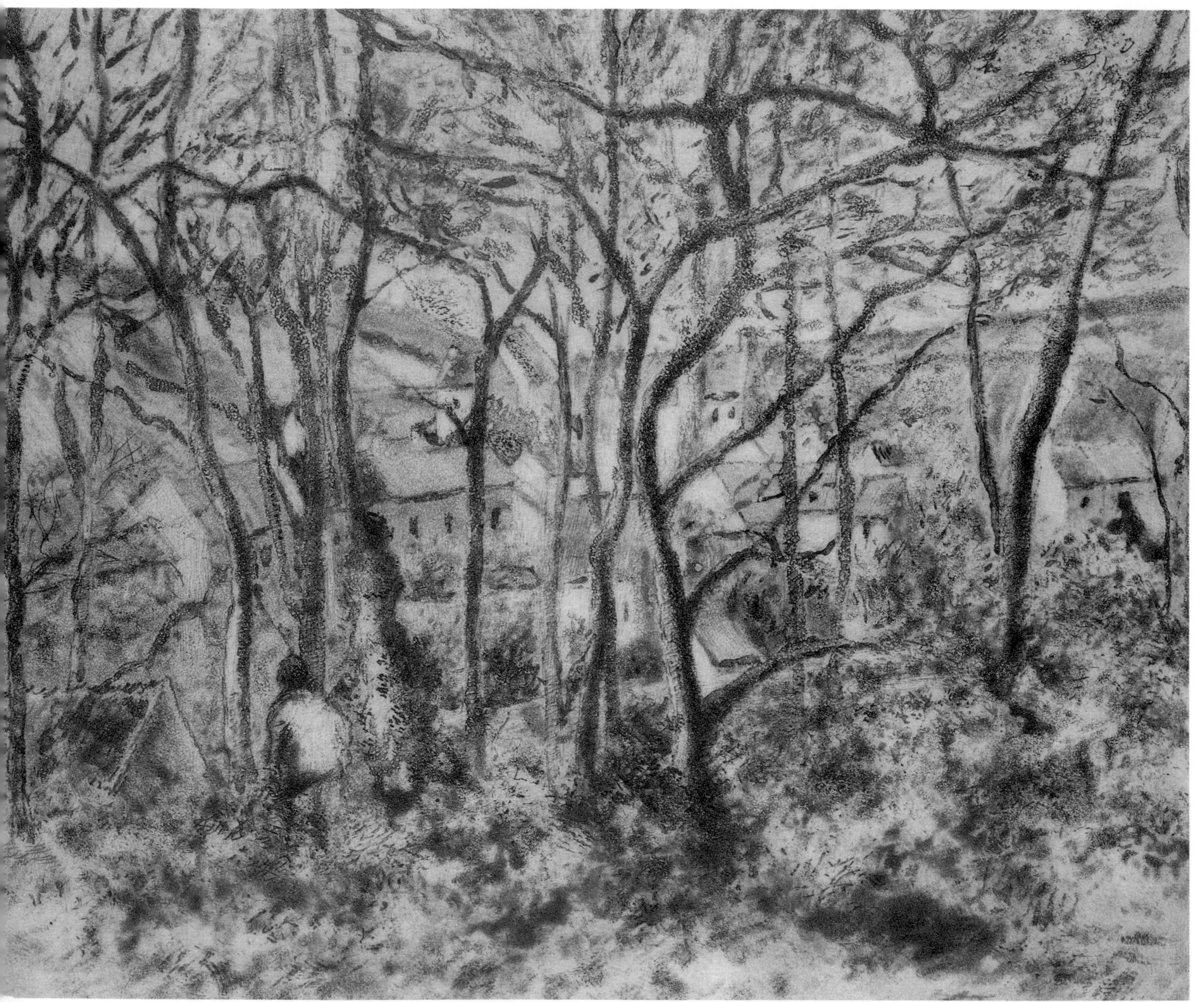

Pissarro, **Sous-bois landscape at L'Hermitage,** *Pointoise, 1879. Soft-ground etching aquatint and drypoint.*

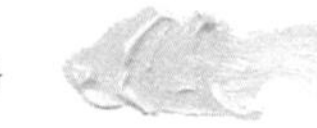

publisher and print enthusiast, the master printer Auguste Delâtre and Félix Bracquemond. Manet was a founding member, and Pissarro was briefly a member but never produced any work for their portfolios.

Inspired by the etchings of Rembrandt, the Society's members experimented with varying the inking of the copper plate to enrich and vary the tone of the print. Following the example of the great Dutch master, they made great use of dry point, cutting directly into the copper with the burin to raise a burr or edge on the discarded material which, catching the ink, would create a rich and sonorous velvety black line when printed. These experiments encouraged Vicomte Lepic, a friend of Degas, to discard the etched line altogether, creating the image merely by the subtle manipulation of the ink on a clean plate. This process only allowed one or, at most, two proofs to be achieved from each plate. This painterly method of print making appealed to Degas, who made the medium his own.

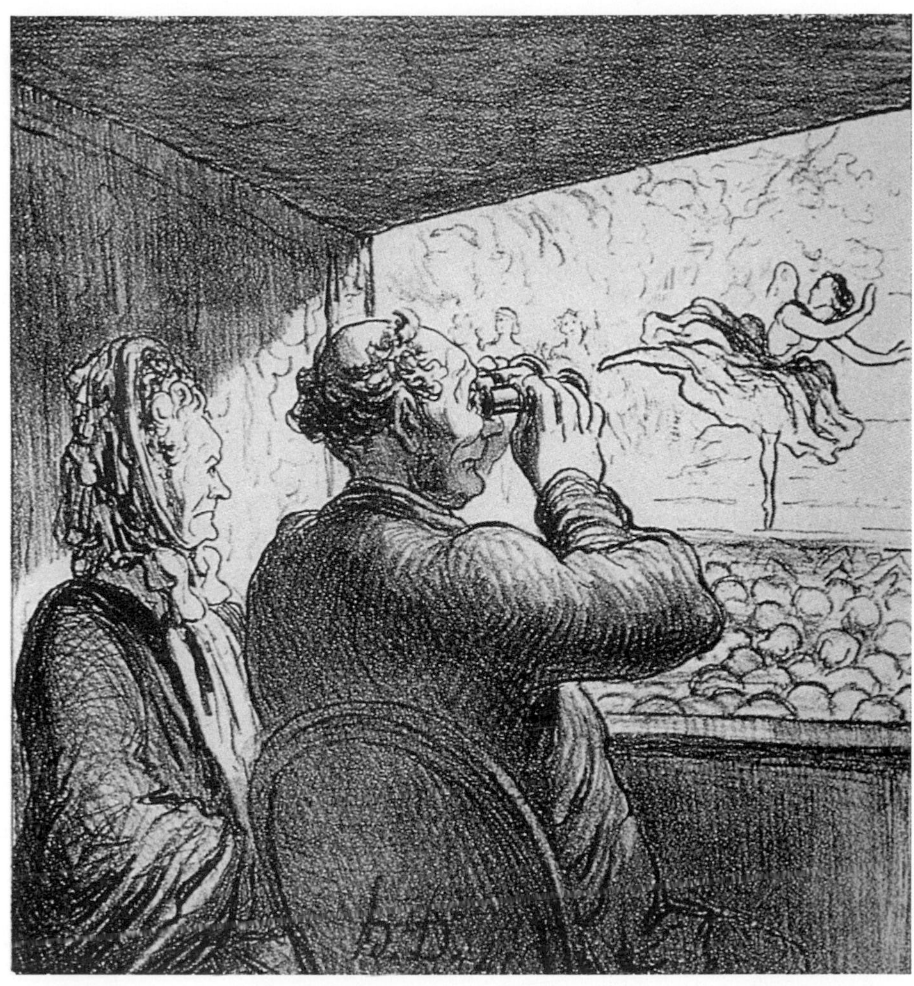

Honoré Daumier,* Theater Sketch, *lithograph, 1864. The great lithographer's impact on Impressionism should not blind us to his own mastery, wit and humanity.

None of the artists was particularly interested in the most obvious property of printmaking: its ability to reproduce the same image many times, the resulting prints being saleable relatively cheaply. The commercial aspects of printmaking were outweighed by its appeal as an innovative medium. Monet showed no interest in prints; Sisley made a few prints after his paintings, and Renoir made a few essays in etching and lithography, but it was really Pissarro and, in particular, Degas and Mary Cassatt who were seduced by the unconventional techniques that print making offered artists. Each had his or her own particular attitude to the medium and made distinctive experiments in it.

Cassatt and Degas as printmakers

In April 1890 Mary Cassatt wrote to Berthe Morisot, friend and neighbour, telling her of a major exhibition of Japanese prints. "You must not miss it. You …couldn't dream of anything more beautiful. I dream of it and don't think of anything but color on copper," she wrote.

In 1879, Cassatt was involved with Degas and Pissarro in plans for a fine art journal; Caillebotte and the banker Ernest May were to underwrite it. Pissarro was excited and began work on the project, but the journal, tentatively entitled *Le Jour et la Nuit*, never appeared: Mary Cassatt's mother, complaining to a friend a week after the closing of the 1879 exhibition, thought it was all Degas' fault:

> ***Degas who is the leader undertook to get up a journal of etchings and got them all to work for it so that Mary had no time for painting and as usual with Degas when the time arrived to appear, he wasn't ready – so that* Le Jour et la nuit *(the name of the publication) which might have been a great success has not yet appeared – Degas is never ready for anything – This time he has thrown away an excellent chance for all of them.***

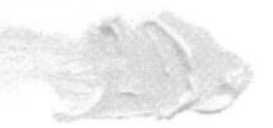

At the Louvre, Mary Cassatt in the Etruscan Gallery

1879–80, soft-ground etching, aquatint and drypoint, 27 x 23cm (10½x 9 cm) Fitzwilliam Museum, Cambridge, England

Created at the height of his enthusiasm for printmaking, this image is the result of a prolonged and complicated series of procedures. The composition is taken from a pastel that was then transferred onto the copper-etching plate, although the printing process necessarily reverses the original image. Curators Sue Welsh Reed and Barbara Stern Shapiro have calculated there were as many as nine separate states of this print, each marking a stage in artist's search for the absolute expression of his idea.

The first recorded state depicts the two women, with no hint of the eventual gallery setting. Step-by-step, using a wide variety of techniques, including the burnishing of some areas, and engraving directly onto the plate with a needle or carbon rod, Degas gradually brought the print to completion. The soft atmospheric quality owes much to his use of soft-ground etching, which creates a fuzzier broken line than hard-ground etching. The light and dark areas are the result of cross-hatching, parallel hatching and the use of aquatint, which creates a pitted surface on the plate etching the ink in a distinctive way that results in an overall tonal effect. All these effects are utilized to create an image of great charm and power.

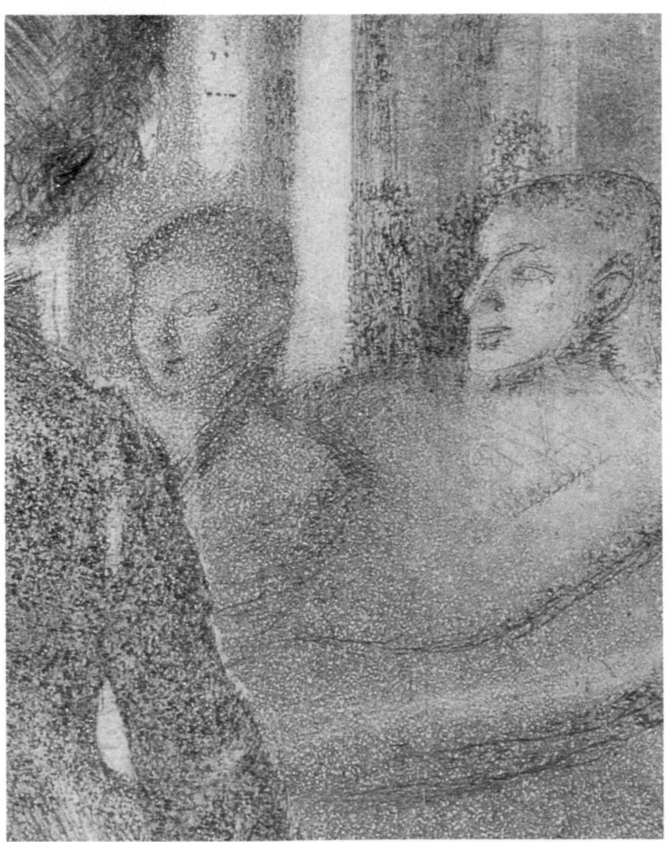

It is likely that the print, although not necessarily this proof, was exhibited at the 1880 Impressionist Exhibition, along with prints by Pissarro and Cassatt

The identity of the two gallery visitors was not noted by Degas, but friends recognized the distinctive and elegant silhouette of Mary Cassatt in the standing figure, which is drawn with a Japanese elegance and economy of means. Cassatt was known for her fashionable dress and particularly for her taste in flamboyant hats.

The figures reappear in a related etching *Mary Cassatt at the Louvre: The Paintings Gallery*, which owes more to his interest in Japanese popular prints

It is difficult not to appreciate the humor of this engaging image, a humor that may be made at the expense of his friends. The woman who lifts her face from the guidebook appears to suggest that this woman, like so many can only enjoy the museum objects before her through the means of her guidebook. Even Mary Cassatt's elegance may suggest that her presence in the gallery is more a statement of her class and education rather than a natural engaged interest. The object being scrutinized is an Etruscan sarcophagus in the Galerie des Antiquities. One can see how Degas' incisive interest of lights, half-lights, shadows and reflections, lends itself to the complex nature of the medium through the nine states using different *intaglio* techniques to capture the complexity of the scene. There is a contrast between the two single women (Mary Cassatt never married) looking at the sarcophagus that famously celebrates the dead Etruscan couple: Everything is given equal emphasis: reflections and objects are brought together in a harmony of carefully calculated tonal relationships.

Degas authorized the master-printer Salmon to print an edition of fifty proofs for the proposed journal *Le Jour et la Nuit* that was going to include prints by his friends Cassatt, Braquemond, Pissarro and others.

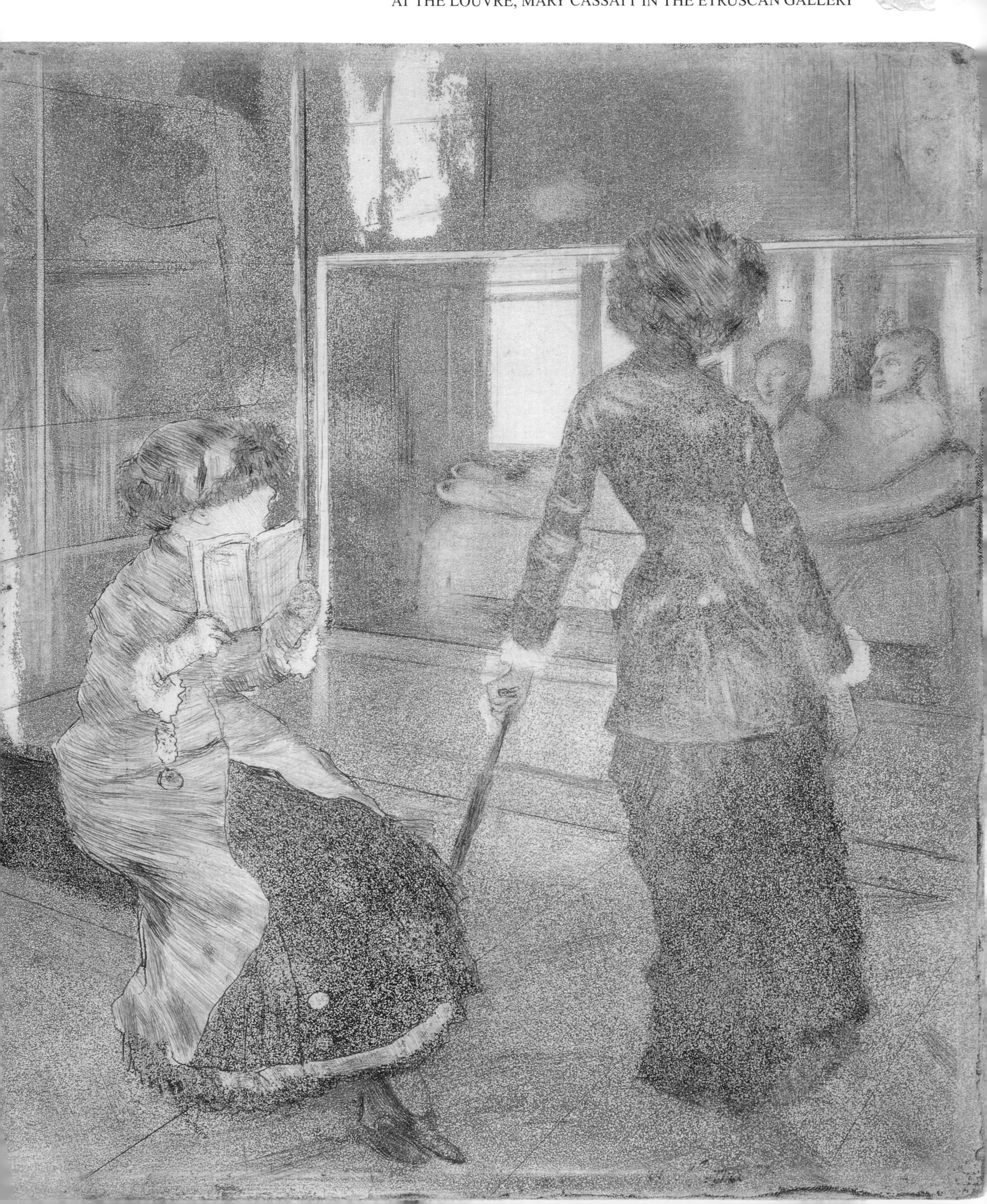

Degas' Sculpture

A sculptor capable of rivaling the ancients.
– Renoir on Degas

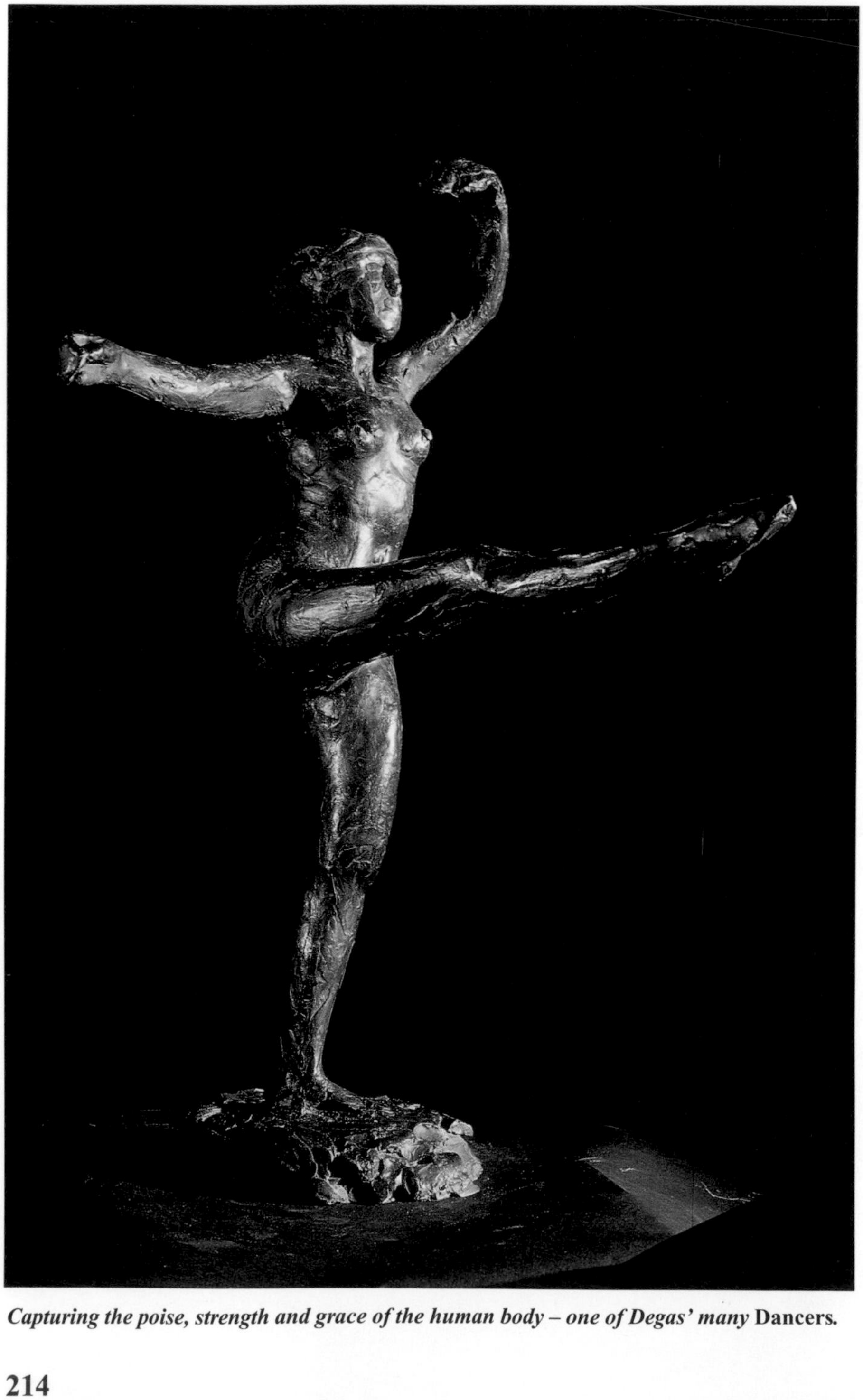

Capturing the poise, strength and grace of the human body – one of Degas' many **Dancers.**

Degas' sculpture was almost completely unknown during his lifetime, and the extent of his sculptural practice was not revealed publicly until 1921, four years after his death. Over one hundred and fifty wax models of dancers, bathers and horses were found in various states of repair in his studio. Completely captivated by the process of modeling, Degas kept his works in their wax form and never had any of them cast into bronze. He seemed not to have considered keeping these works available for posterity, his working practice not being conducive to the work's extended survival in time.

Degas' sculptures are constructed mostly from wax built around improvised armatures, which occasionally included paint brushes, with corks from discarded wine bottles and bits of wood being used to bulk out the wax. Other materials were mixed with the wax itself, making the pieces extremely fragile. The advantage of working with wax was that it allowed Degas continually to rework the pieces; if they over-balanced or slipped, then he simply extended the armatures to support the models in the desired positions.

After Degas' death, over half his sculptures collapsed before they could be cast. Most of the surviving waxes can be found in the Mellon Collection, at Upperville, Virginia. The bronze versions have a spurious academic air that is completely dispelled in the presence of the originals which, being wax, have the translucency of living flesh.

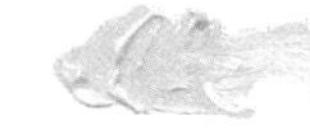

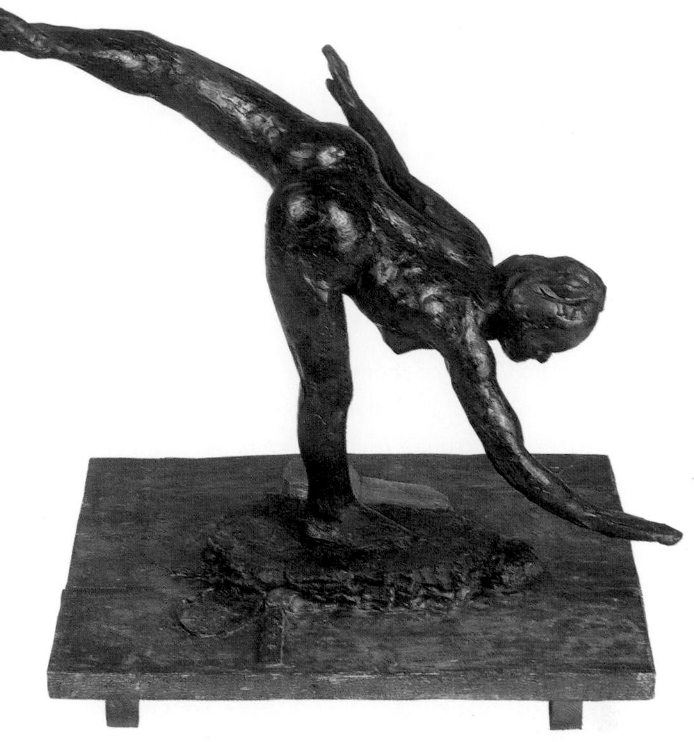

Degas' sculptural prowess was recognized in his lifetime by his intimates. Renoir is recorded by his dealer Vollard as saying, "If Degas had died at fifty, he would have been remembered as an excellent painter, no more; it is only after his fiftieth year that his work broadens out and he becomes really Degas."

Certainly, there is a distinct difference between the artist's early and later sculptural work. Any overt narrative or documentary detail slips away to be replaced by a grander more monumental vision, apparent in the smallest and most modest of his works; everything seems focused upon the essentials of describing movement through mass and light. The figures twist and turn, bend and stretch, the tensions of their bodies described in a firm and robust modeling that, without recourse to detail, creates a simulacrum of our everyday experiences of having a physical frame. They are the counterparts of their partners that appear in the artist's graphic work and painting. Just as in Matisse's work, Degas' sculptures are complete in themselves and yet inform the work in other media, dominated by the central controlling intelligence of the artist. Like his pastels, drawings and paintings of his later years, they are worked on over and over again, to such a degree that Degas said to Vollard, that the only purpose of doing the sculpture was destroying it in order to begin again.

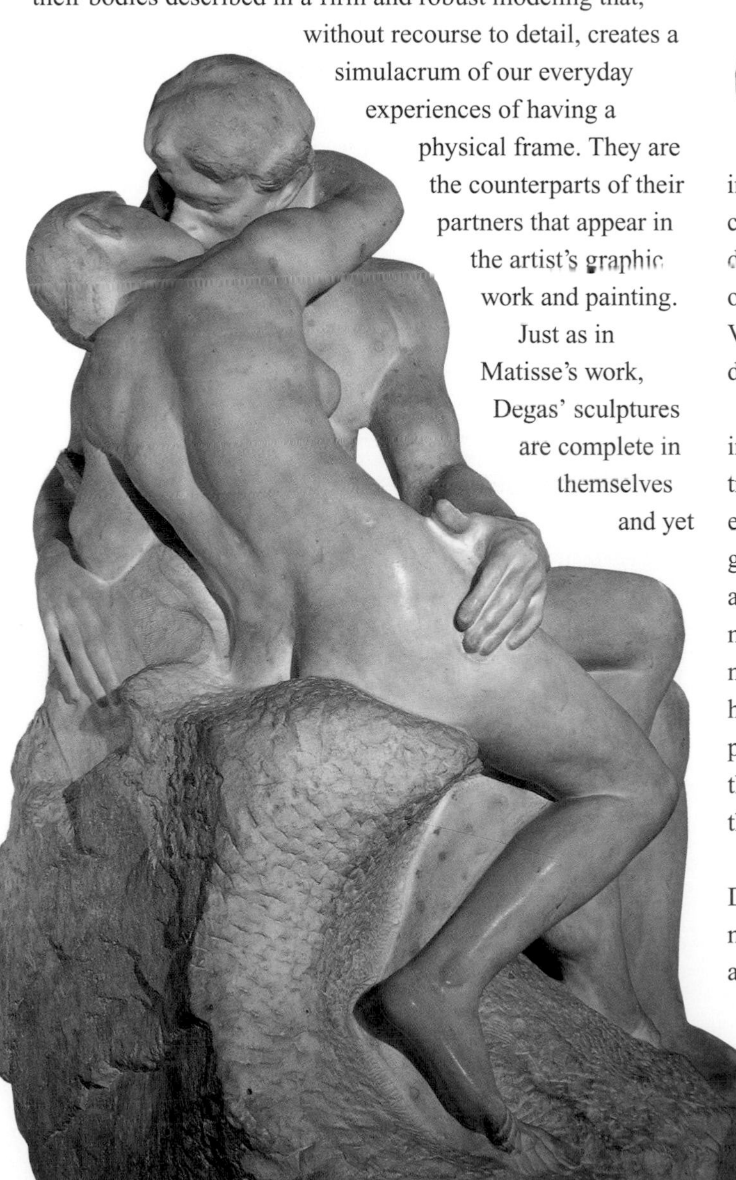

Degas' sculpture is unusual in that many of his pieces, instead of being centered upon a gravitation base, as in traditional sculpture, appear to be fired by the artist's desire, evident in so much of his two-dimensional work, to conquer gravity. Again and again, he appears drawn to the continued and obsessive reworking a small group of motifs, his source material being his own drawings, memories and a small number of hard-working models, whose trained bodies could hold what were often excruciating poses for protracted periods of time. Their personalities are not what concerned the artist, just the mass of the bodies and the eloquence of their gestures.

In 1903, Gauguin wrote in *Avant et Après* that "... the Dancers of Degas are not women. They are machines in movement with graceful and prodigious lines of balance, arranged like a hat from the Rue de la Paix and with the same lovely artificiality."

ABOVE:* *Another of Degas'* Dancers. *Over one hundred and fifty wax studies were found after Degas' death; many crumbled to dust before they could be cast into bronze.

LEFT:* The Kiss, *by Degas' contemporary, Auguste Rodin, marble version, 1886. Rodin's large sensuous public sculpture occupies the opposite end of the spectrum to Degas' small, intimate and private studies.

The Little Dancer Aged 14 Years

1881, wax and other materials, Tate Gallery, London, England

In an undated letter of about 1880, Gauguin made reference to the feverish enthusiasm for sculpture that had gripped his painter friends; Degas was making maquettes of horses, Pissarro was modeling cows and even Renoir was involved in three-dimensional activity, which he would take up again to great effect, with the help of Italian assistants, in the last years of his life.

It was common practice for academic artists to turn to modeling, either to help with visualizing their compositions or as a means of solving painterly problems. For Gustave Moreau, such a practice was an essential part of his working procedure, and his small studies may well have had an influence upon Degas. However, for Degas, modeling quickly became not simply a useful aid to his two-dimensional work but an obsession.

Degas' first major work, and the only piece of sculpture he ever exhibited in public, was *The Little Dancer Aged 14 Years*. It was produced in 1881 and shown in the sixth Impressionist exhibition that year. Earlier, Degas had written to his artist friend James Tissot, "The realist movement no longer needs to fight with others. It is, it exists, it has to show itself *separately*; there must be a *Realist Salon*." Degas always considered himself an independent realist and made many moves to commandeer the Impressionist exhibitions and turn them into realist ones by the introduction of his protegés.

The Little Dancer explores the boundaries separating reality and artifice. Although not modeled lifesize, she is startlingly realistic, even in the bronze versions that are displayed in museums throughout the world. At the sixth Impressionist exhibition, she was exhibited in her original state, modeled in tinted wax to give her a convincingly life-like appearance. Her black hair, tied with a green–blue ribbon, was real, as were her silk faille bodice, gauze and tulle skirt and fabric dancing shoes. The whole figure was coated in a thin layer of translucent wax, which enhanced the illusion of reality.

Some critics found the *The Little Dancer Aged 14 Years* ugly, even bestial, and found the upturned features of the dancer, in particular, deliberately unpicturesque. Huysmans, in contrast, relished the startling and unnerving realism of the sculpture and wrote about it at length in his review in *L'Art moderne* in 1883,

> ***Degas has exhibited a statue of wax entitled* The Little Fourteen Year Old Dancer *before which an astonished public [runs away], as if embarrassed. The terrible realism of this statuette makes the public distinctly uneasy, all its ideas about sculpture, about cold, lifeless whiteness, about those memorable formulas copied again and again for centuries are demolished. The fact is that, at the first blow, M. Degas has overthrown the traditions of sculpture, just as he has for a long time been shaking up the conventions of painting … At once refined and barbaric with her costume and her colored flesh, palpitating, lined with the work of its muscles, this statuette is the only truly modern attempt I know in sculpture.***

The model for the sculpture was a Belgian girl, Marie Van Goethen, one of the "rats" at the ballet school at the Opéra. Her perfectly poised athletic body and distinctive face with its high cheekbones and heavy-lidded eyes are immediately recognizable in the many drawings and maquettes that were part of Degas' painstaking preparation for the final version. Contemporaries would have compared the work with Gérôme's exquisite polychrome sculptures; in the 1881 exhibition itself, the precise modeling of the girl's features could have been compared with Degas' physiognomic pastel studies of two murderers.

Although Degas' consuming interest in sculpture was essentially a private one, since his death in 1917, he has been increasingly regarded not only as one of the greatest sculptors of his age, but also one of the most significant influences on modern sculptural practice.

The Little Dancer Aged 14 Years is today regarded as a masterpiece of nineteenth-century sculpture. Over the years it has lost none of its authority; situated as it is midway between art and reality, it exerts a pull on the imagination that has lost none of its mysterious effect.

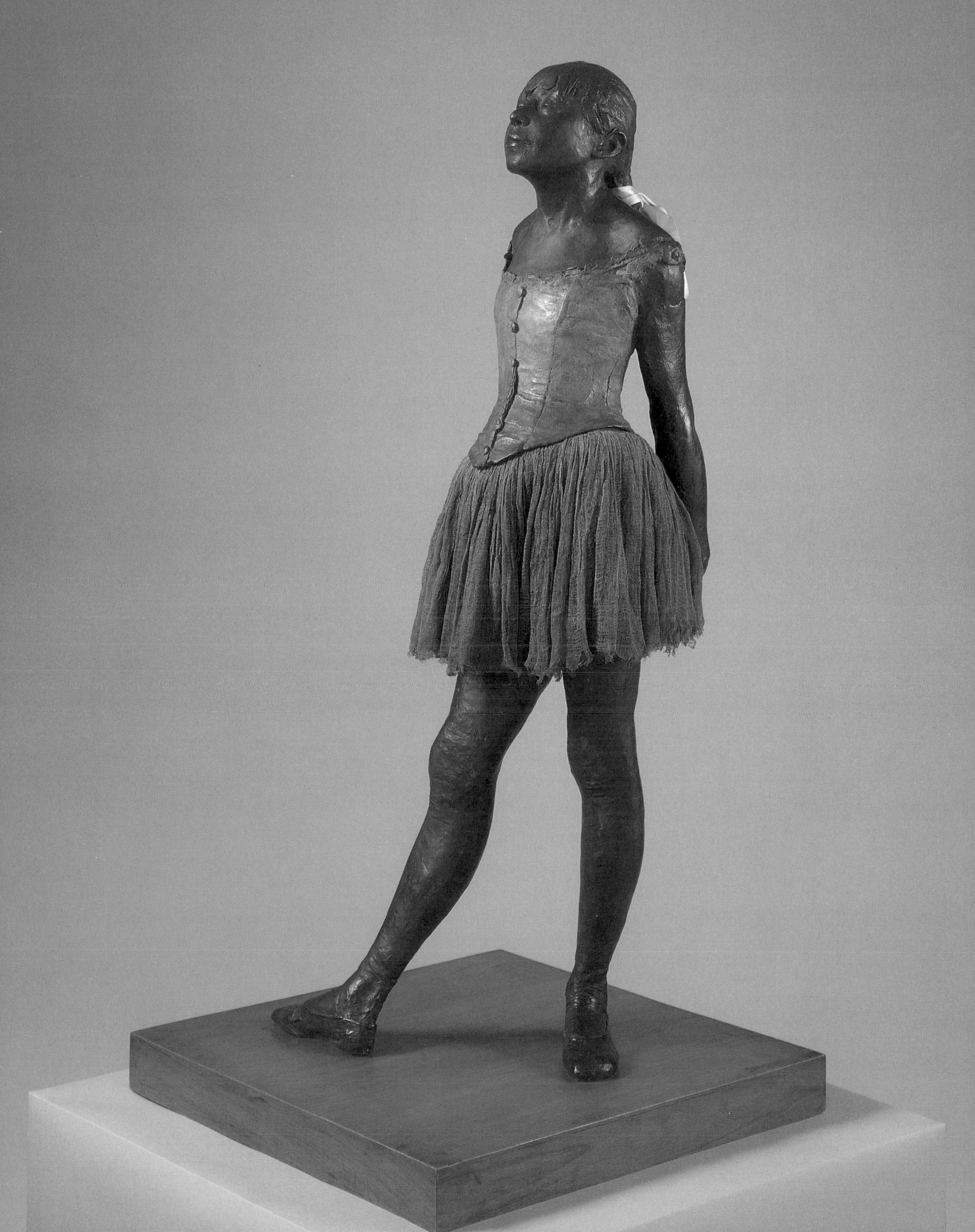

Fans

In 1879, Degas, who was in the midst of organizing the fourth Impressionist exhibition, wrote enthusiastically to Félix Bracquemond: "There is one room with fans, do you understand Mme. Bracquemond? Up to now, Pissarro, Mlle. Morisot and I are depositing things there. You and your wife should contribute too."

At this time, fans were fashionable, both as decorative objects and as fashion accessories; framed fans were often hung on apartment walls as decoration alongside paintings and prints. Large numbers of fans were imported and one major French company, Desrochers, Alexandre and Duvelleroy, both mass-produced fans and commissioned artists to make special designs for fans.

Durand-Ruel encouraged Pissarro to paint fans, along with more finished paintings and decorative pieces, and bright landscapes. The dealer wrote to the artist on October 18, 1882,

> ***I'm sure that in our next exhibition it will be these small compositions that will sell the best and fastest. Spend your rainy days on these studies. Think, too, about fans, as we discussed. You must think about varying your exhibition as much as possible, and it is through this diversity that you will attract the public.***

It would seem that, aside from the compositional challenges set by the unusual format of fans, the main reason for their production by artists was financial. When sold, they attained modest prices compared with oils. In the early 1880s, Degas' top price for a fan was 120 francs, and Pissarro's best price for a fan was 200 francs. Even so, in 1885 Pissarro wrote that he "had got to churn out fans, because times are hard and for the moment one can only find a market for them, one mustn't count on paintings."

Fans were part of the growing interest in the fine and applied arts during the latter part of the nineteenth century in Europe, sustained by the Great Universal Exhibitions that had taken place in England in 1851 and in France in 1855, 1867, 1878 and 1887. Such exhibitions, both in France and elsewhere, proclaimed the national concern that France should regain her place as the world leader in decorative and fine arts. There was a particular interest in the rococo style, the Goncourt brothers having published their study on eighteenth-century art between 1856 and 1875. The popularity of French eighteenth-century art had never faded away, but the Goncourts' work promoted an interpretation of the rococo, in which special attention was given to the painters Watteau, Boucher and Fragonard. Those concerned with publicizing this interest in eighteenth-century culture, like those (including the Goncourts) propagating Japanese art and design, were a small but influential minority; both fads were elitist in intent.

Many of the Impressionists were caught up in the debates concerning the bringing together of the fine and applied arts. Mary Cassatt became involved with Chapu, the great ceramist, as did Gauguin.

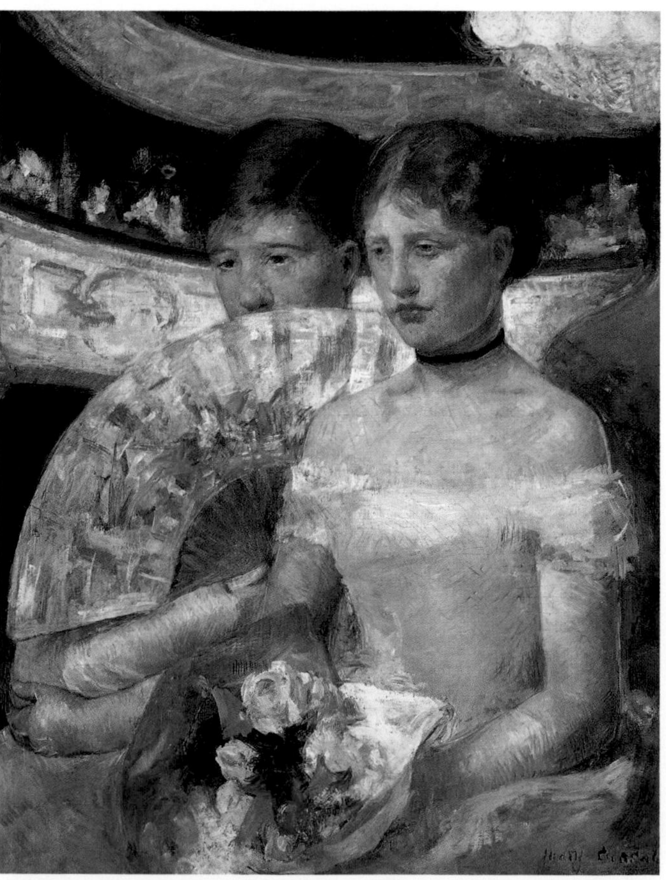

Cassatt,* Two Women in a Loge, *1882. The two girls are objects of display, just as the flowers are that feature so prominently.

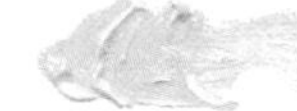

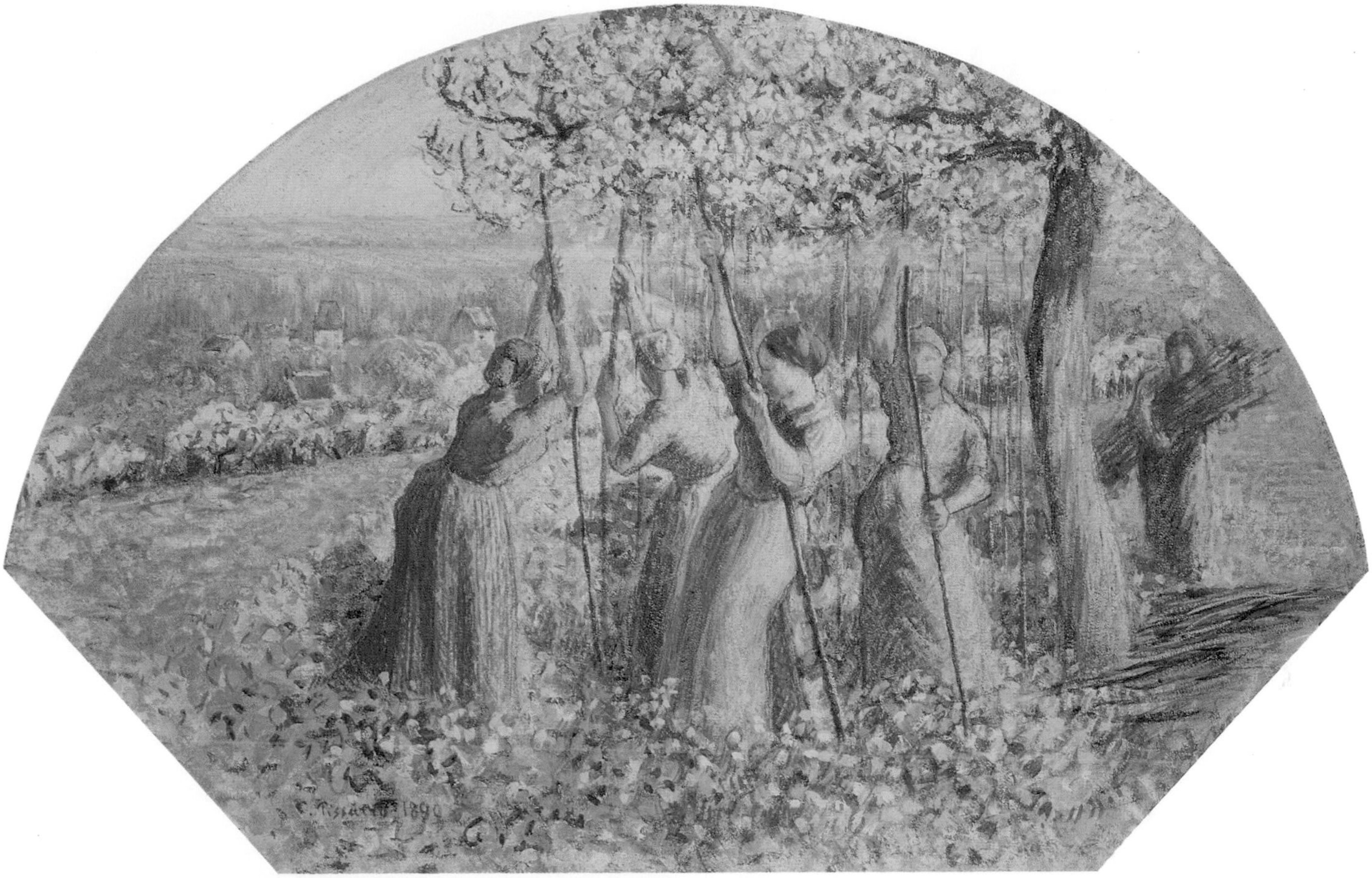

Pissarro, **Peasant Women Planting Pea-Sticks,** *1890, gouache and black chalk on gray-brown silk in the shape of a fan.*

Mary Cassatt's painting *Two Women in a Loge*, is just one of many Impressionist depictions of women with fans in Impressionist art. The two women in question are a visiting American called Mary Ellison and Mallarmé's daughter, Geneviève. They are linked together by the sloping shoulders and the arc of the extended fan. Behind them is a mirror, which rather unconvincingly sets them in a theater. Unlike women in similar situations by Renoir, these are obviously highly eligible young women who are being displayed as part of the middle-class ritual that would lead to courtship and marriage. The fan covers what is so openly exposed on the right-hand woman and signals the fan's purpose to attract the eye to the very area it covers.

Twenty-five fans by Degas are known, three dating from 1868–69 and the rest from the period 1878–85. For the 1879 Impressionist exhibition, Degas had pushed for a separate room decorated with fans painted by himself and his colleagues; for whatever reason, when the exhibition opened, only Pissarro and Forain were represented in the room set aside for the display of painted fans. Degas had produced five for the exhibition, Forain four and Pissarro twelve. The arcing contour of the fan encouraged Degas to create exciting visual *tours de force* in which the illustrational properties of the scene depicted vied with the strictly decorative aspects of color, line and form.

The relationship of Degas' fans to Japanese fans is evident, not just in the choice of the fan as the support for the design, but also in the wit and imagination Degas reveals in playing with the dialogue between the surface patterns of the composition and the imaged depth of field. In a number of his fans he used gold dust to enhance the exotic effects of his color. It has been suggested that the colors Degas chose to use – pinks, ochres, browns and whitish tones – and the play he made between decorative and illusionistic effects show that he was aware of the work of Tawaraya Sotatsu (c.1570–1640), the Japanese court fan painter who lived in the Daigo-Ju Temple in Kyoto.

Pissarro's design reveals his penchant for idealizing rural labor, and his interest in adapting a composition to the particular shape of the fan. The women's rounded and curvaceous forms are set against the straight lines of their sticks and both the women and their implements are set under the tree to create a pleasing interplay of line, color and form within the usual format of the fan.

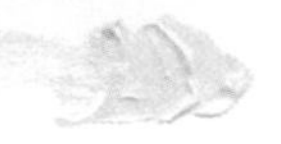

CHAPTER SEVEN

Toward a Grander Vision

Impressionism was never a fixed or easily definable movement; each artist investigated his own relationship to his craft and the associated problems of visualizing his sensations of the world on canvas. Such concerns were a continual source of anxiety to the artists. As they grew older and more successful, they continued to question the very basis of their art practice: its relationship to the reality of visual experience. Monet himself expressed his dissatisfaction with any over-simple definition of his art. Referring to his recent (that is, early 1890s) work painting the cathedral at Rouen, he told his friend, the American painter Theodore Robinson, that he was now occupying himself with what he referred to as "more serious qualities." In a similar fashion, Degas told his friend Georges Jeanniot,

> ***At the moment, it is fashionable to paint pictures where you can see what time it is, like on a sundial. I don't like that at all. A painting requires a little mystery, some vagueness, some fantasy. When you always make your meaning perfectly plain, you end up by boring people.***

Degas' comment clearly indicates a dissatisfaction with the limitations of too precise a definition of Impressionists' aims. "The ceiling of Impressionism is too low," Gauguin had claimed, and he stressed the need to "get away as far as possible from that which gives the illusion of the thing." It is possible to see the later work of Degas and his erstwhile colleagues in the light of these two statements. Their long-term investigation into giving expression to the sensations felt in their confrontation with an ever-changing reality became increasingly personalized researches into their art.

Monet, **Waterlilies** *c.1922–24. This painting represents Monet's ability, lon fought for, to synthesize apparent opposing ends: the actuality of the painti as a surface covered in pigment and its quality as a decorative object recording his own experience of visual reality.*

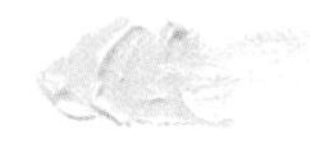

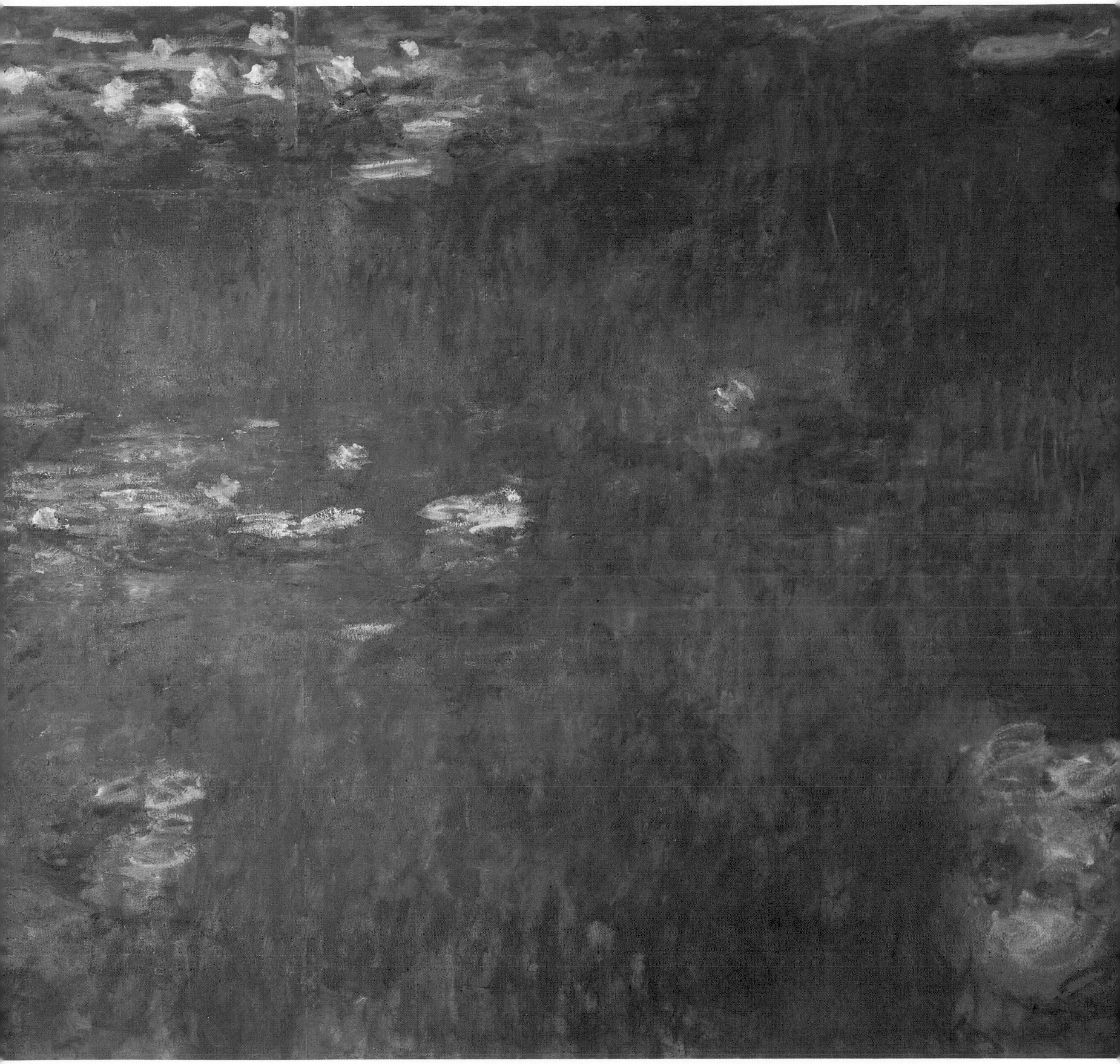

Monet: The Series

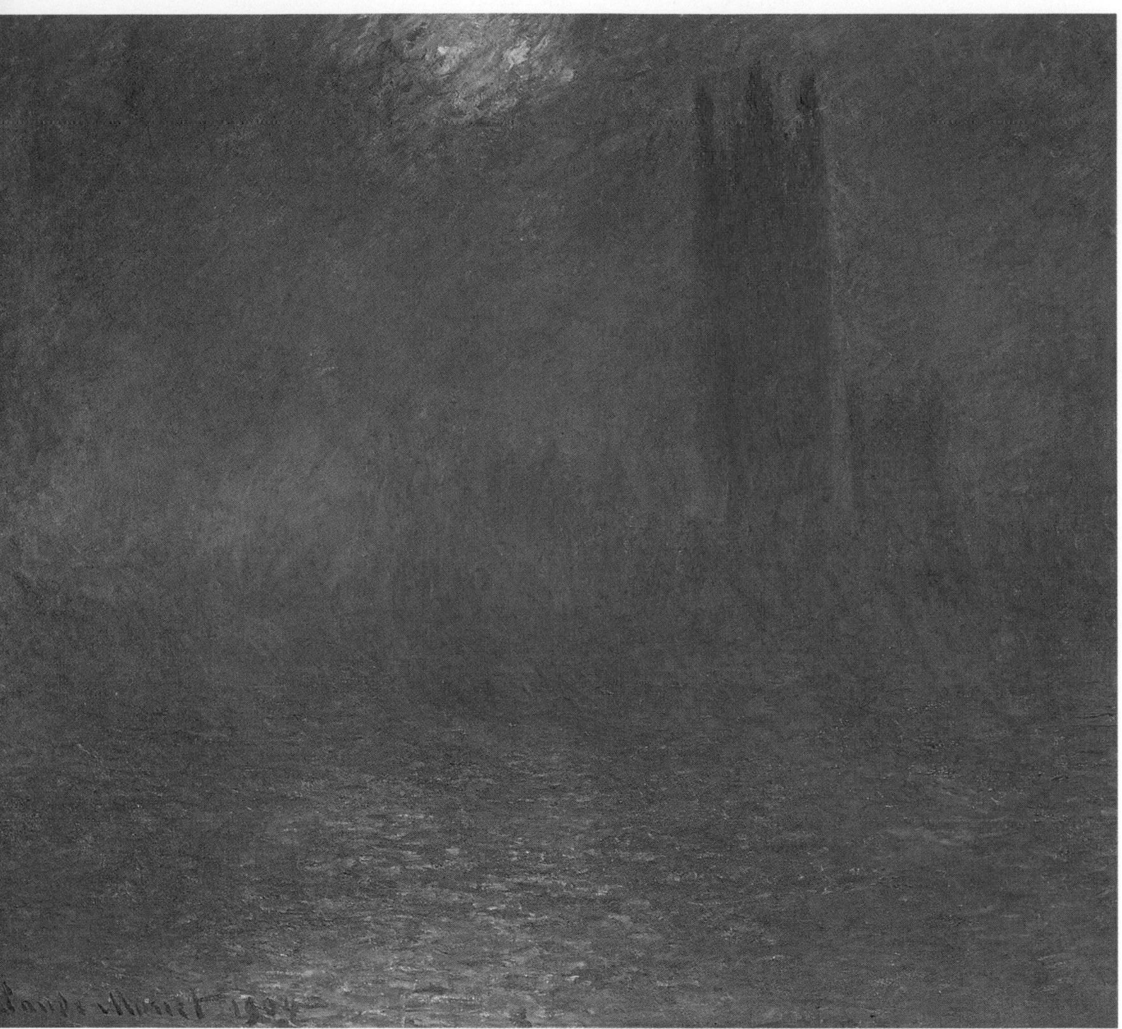

Monet, **Houses of Parliament, Sun Shining Through a Gap in the Fog,** ***1904. One of a series of paintings painted in response to the changing atmospheric conditions that have transformed the British government into a mysterious, almost insubstantial entity.***

Off he went, followed by children carrying his canvases, five or six canvases representing the same subject at different times of the day and with different light effects. He picked them up and put them down in turn, according to the changing weather.
– Guy de Maupassant, 1886.

Early in his career Monet told his friend Bazille that his ambition was "to paint directly from nature, striving to render my impressions in the face of the most fugitive effects." This program remained the guiding principle of his art until the end of his life. The series paintings of the 1890s are not an isolated phenomenon in Monet's *oeuvre*, but are the considered outcome of his many attempts to fulfill that stated aim. Even in his early work of the 1860s, such as his paintings at La Grenouillère and Sainte-Adresse, and in his paintings of the Gare Saint-Lazare in the next decade, Monet, like many artists before him, was interested in seeing the same motif at different times of the day and from various viewpoints.

During the 1890s, Monet began consciously to paint sequences of pictures of the same subject, painted together as a group at the same time, and with each one relating to a precise time of the day, or atmospheric effect. With the benefit of hindsight, Monet's practice appears to be a logical conclusion of his researches. Monet was an empiricist: as time never stands still, so it is illogical to paint one unique image of a particular moment when the scene before the artist is in a continual state of flux.

A brief moment for each canvas

Monet developed the practice of working on a number of canvases, each one for the briefest of moments, to capture the particular effect of ever-changing qualities of light on his chosen motif. These on-the-spot reactions to the motif were then taken back to the studio to be worked on with the others, in order to create a harmonious unity to the group while preserving and enhancing the evocation of a particular atmospheric effect.

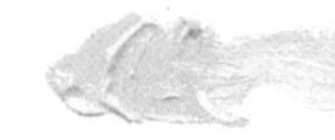

Degas told the story of Monet arriving in a carriage at Varengeville, stepping out and, after one look at the sky, saying "I'm half an hour late; I'll have to come back tomorrow."

Monet encouraged the circulation of stories which propagated the theme of his complete dedication to painting directly from nature; however, we know that, despite working on a hundred canvases (his estimation) recording the effects of the London atmosphere on the Houses of Parliament during visits in 1899, 1900 and 1901, he nevertheless spent two years reworking them in the studio before finally allowing Durand-Ruel to exhibit them in 1904.

Artists had painted series before, to suggest the cycles of the year, or as a means of studying the changing effects of light, or as replicas or near-replicas of successful and saleable works. What is impressive about Monet's cycles of paintings is the oddness of his choice of subject matter. The series paintings began with his paintings of haystacks, which occupied the field adjacent to his house at Giverny one summer. It would seem that he began painting them in a spirit of research, but became more and more intrigued by their endless color shifts as the day progressed and the atmospheric conditions varied. It was impossible for Monet to reproduce all these shifts within one or even two pictures; as the fugitive light changed, so another canvas had to be begun.

Capturing the moment

Within this practice is the built-in admission of the failure of art to capture a single moment and the realization that a single painting records a prolonged period of time. The endless painting and repainting of the same subject under different atmospheric effects is a tacit admission of the impossibility of painting reality and a celebration and investigation into achieving that impossible end.

In many ways, it was an agenda Monet shared with Cézanne and Degas and even Renoir, working contemporaneously on a restricted number of subjects, their art enriched by their experience of painting modern life. Should art be a record of the phenomenal world or could it only ever be an expression of the artist's own subject experience of reality made public through his painting?

Unlike his colleagues, Monet never felt the need to measure up to the art of the museums: he kept his eyes firmly fixed upon the world around him. His choice of subject was determined by his working practices and his newly won financial security allowed him the freedom to follow his own agenda. He saw no reason to participate in group exhibitions and increasingly asserted his own independence as a man and an artist. He took real risks: the collector de Bellio wrote to Pissarro that Monet was going to exhibit "nothing but grain stacks" at his one-man show at Durand-Ruel's gallery in 1891.

The Haystacks show, Monet's first true series show, was successful and he was encouraged to carry on his interest in painting groups of related subjects. He began a sequence based upon the poplar trees that edged the River Epte near his home. They began as relatively naturalistic studies, but as the year progressed, they became increasingly decorative. His attitude was pragmatic; as the leaves began to sprout from the trees, he paid the purchaser of the wood to refrain from pruning the trees until his paintings were finished. From poplar trees he moved on to paintings of Rouen Cathedral and the Houses of Parliament in England.

From 1906, Monet's creative energies were taken up by paintings of his waterlily garden. Like Cézanne, he rarely signed his canvases, each being seen as a work in process, becoming increasingly difficult to bring to a conclusion. As he told his politician friend Georges Clemenceau, "What difficulties I have in rendering what I feel. I tell myself that whoever thinks that he has finished a canvas is terribly arrogant."

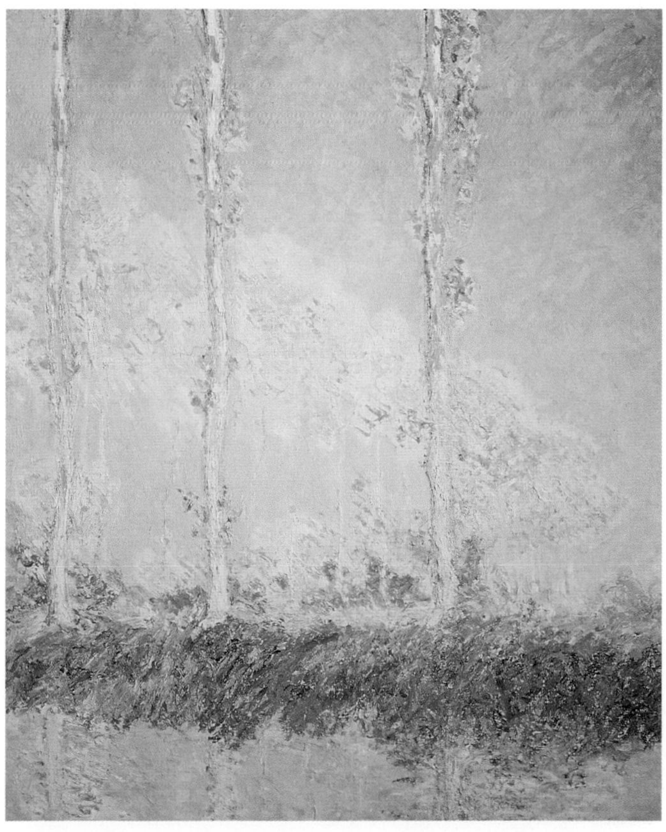

Monet,* Poplars, *1891. His reordering of nature for his own decorative ends is evident in this geometrically rigorous work.

Monet and Rouen Cathedral

No artist exists within a vacuum and Monet's paintings, however private their genesis and execution, were cultural artifacts, publicly exhibited and seen within the context of their own time. Paul Tucker has shown that, like his *Haystacks* and *Poplars* series, Monet's *Rouen Cathedral* paintings were not devoid of meaning, but were readable as images of national identity. The last decade of the nineteenth century was notable for the intensity of debate concerning questions to do with national identity. Above and beyond any other consideration, Monet's paintings were art and therefore had an inescapable relationship to the morals and beliefs of the time.

His paintings of the French landscape can be easily read as poetic celebrations of the Gallic countryside, and his paintings of Rouen Cathedral, however he may have thought of them, are portraits of a Christian place of worship intimately associated with Joan of Arc, the fourteenth-century French martyr, burnt as a witch by the English. Precisely at the time Monet was painting the Cathedral, Joan was being held up to the French nation by the right-wing Catholic monarchist groups as an image of "La France." Even if this was not openly admitted by those looking at Monet's paintings of Rouen Cathedral, the very fact that it was an old medieval Gothic structure gave his paintings a respectability and an aura of spirituality that helped their successful reception by public and critics alike. There was even an attempt to purchase for the nation the entire sequence of works, but it came to naught.

Monet painted the views of the cathedral's facade from the Hotel d'Angleterre and, later, from the front rooms of a draper's shop across from the square, which gave him the view that appears in most of the paintings. As always, the pictures gave the artist intense difficulties, which threw him into despair. He had vivid nightmares of the cathedral in various colors – pink, blue and yellow – falling upon him. He wrote to Alice Hoschedé, who became his second wife in 1892, the year he started the cathedral series, "Things don't advance very steadily, primarily because each day I discover something I hadn't seen the day before … In the end, I am trying to do the impossible." The impossibility he meant was the halting of time in a single image and the realization in paint of his own experiences of the medieval building. Monet spent almost six months before the cathedral, responding to the infinite shifts of color and light as the sun rose in the morning and set in the evening, each image charting a brief instance of this progress. The eroded stonework of the cathedral, transformed into the ridges and hollows of his encrusted paint surface, is described not in all its antiquarian detail but as it is affected by the light. Monet appears to have

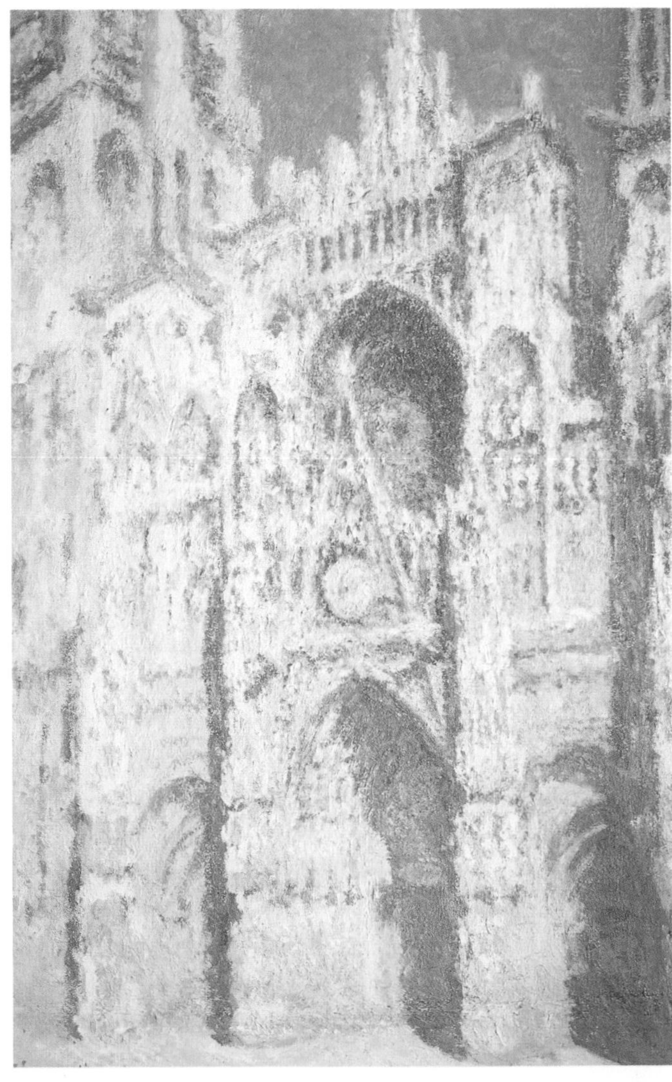

Rouen Cathedral, Sunlight, ***1874. One of the group of forty canvases that Monet painted of the Cathedral.***

begun with a thin and fluid brushwork, which is slowly worked on until the oil paint stands proud of the surface, color applied in a wide range of hues, the dry paint catching the brush as it moves delicately over the painting's surface, creating a shimmering effect.

Monet never indulges in the play of color or brushwork for its own sake, the sense of the building's architectural structure is never lost and the results apparent on the surface are the result of his close scrutiny of the building. The finished paintings are a balance between two opposing systems of representation, one based upon his observation, the other upon the need to bring that experience into a harmonious unit, which in turn must relate decoratively to the entire sequence of related works. This poetic aspect is evident in the titles of the paintings, which are highly specific and are obviously intended to evoke a specific mood: "*Harmonie bleue*," "*Harmonie blanche*," "*Effet de matin*," "*Harmonie bleue, soleil matinal*."

By May 1895 Monet had finally brought his paintings to the required state of finish and they were exhibited in Paris. A shrewd businessman, no longer needing to sell through exhibitions, he could afford to sell privately at high prices; the sale of one for 15,000 francs to a private patron allowed him to bully Durand-Ruel to up the exhibition prices.

The exhibition was well received by the public, critics and fellow artists. Pissarro wrote that he was "thrilled by that extraordinary mastery" and, like Sisley, was inspired to paint his own very different versions of the same building. "I am carried away by their extraordinary deftness, Cézanne is in complete agreement … this is the work of a well balanced but impulsive artist who pursues the intangible nuances of effects that are realized by no other painter."

Rouen Cathedral, Portal, Morning Mood, ***1873. The series provided Monet's interpretations of the cathedral as its appearance changed during the progress of the day.***

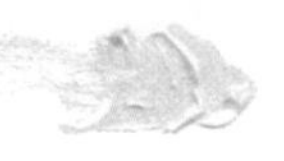

The Roofs of Old Rouen, Grey Weather

1896, oil on canvas, 72.3 x 91.4 cm (28½ x 36 in), The Toledo Museum of Art, Toledo, Ohio, USA

Pissarro's enthusiasm for Neo-Impressionism was not sustained for long. As he explained to the Belgian adherent, Van der Velde in 1890, he had found it "impossible to follow my sensations, and consequently to give a sense of life and movement, impossible to give a sense of life and nature, so fugitive and so admirable, impossible to give my drawing an individual character."

Pissarro began to paint at Rouen in 1883; he found the city's industrial quayside as inspirational as the medieval streets with their gabled houses, narrow thoroughfares and, not least, its cathedral. In 1896, he wrote to his son Lucien from the Hôtel Jeanne d'Arc, "It's as beautiful as Venice … It has an extraordinary character and really it's beautiful."

He enjoyed Rouen, including the contrasts between the old and new. "How hideous the new quarter is, what a slap on the bourgeois' cheek … but so what, they've no conscience and don't care about it." In Pissarro's paintings, the cathedral keeps its architectural and social identity, firmly set within the context of the old town. Its imposing bulk rises up above the roofs, and no modern buildings intrude to set the scene in the nineteenth century; instead, in its subject matter and technique, the repeating of blocks of color and the variegated but unified brushwork that is evident across the canvas, there is a sense of integration, harmony and poetry of a scene that, perhaps, is meant to echo the balance and harmony of an ideal society.

Pissarro admired Monet's paintings of Rouen Cathedral for their ambiguous mysterious qualities; they were "all executed with a very veiled effect which gave the monument a certain mysterious charm," he wrote to Lucien in 1896. His paintings of the cathedral seem to have no religious intent but rather romantically suggest the medieval period as one of harmony and belief. Superficially less poetic than Monet's personalized interpretation, Pissarro's cathedral represents the achievement of a community working together to construct a coherent metaphor of their beliefs, which he in turn has restated in this composition.

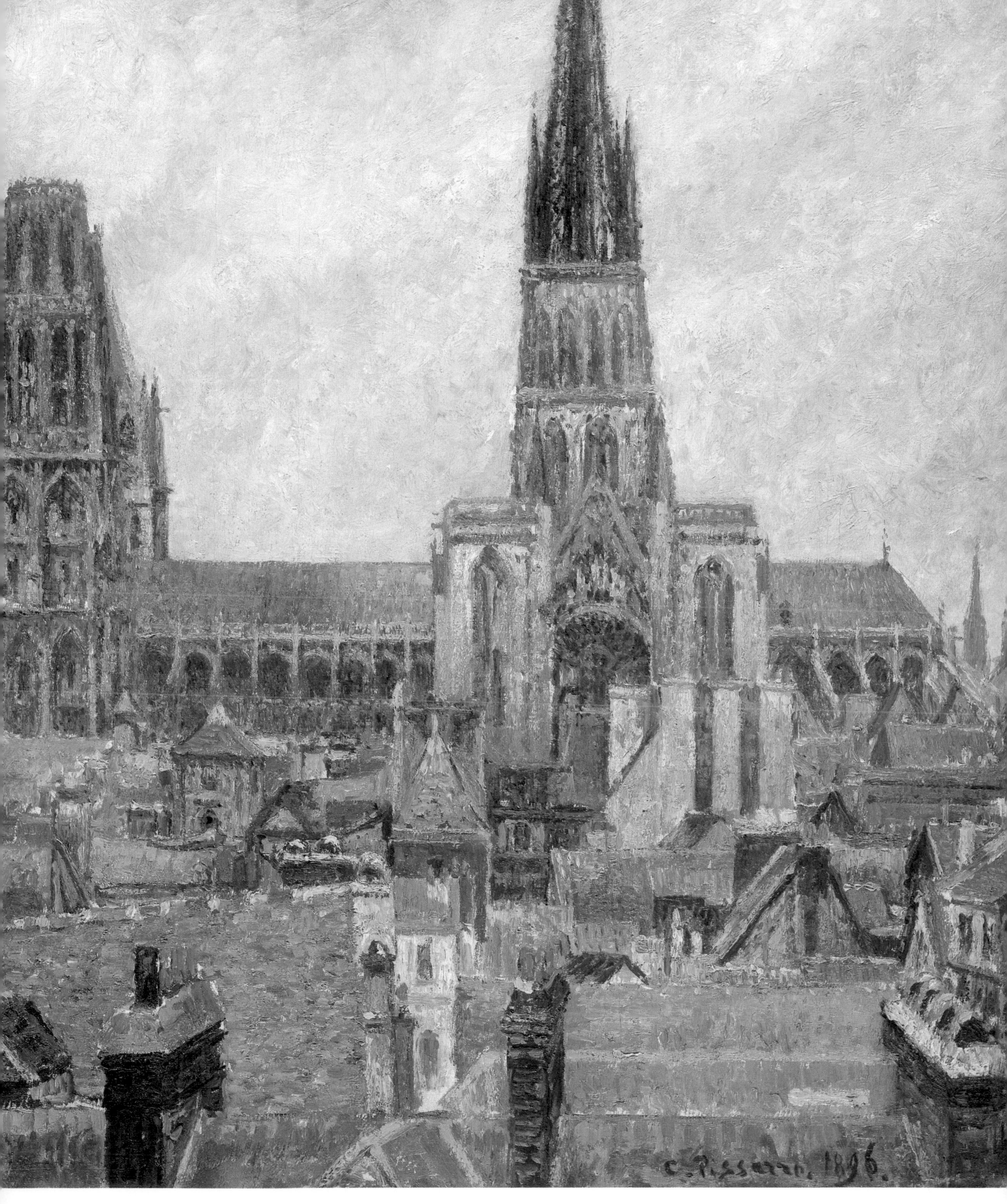
C. Pissarro. 1896.

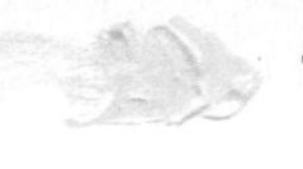

The Church at Moret, Frosty Weather

1893, oil on canvas, Private Collection

In October 1883, the Sisley family moved to Moret, not far from the historic town of Fontainebleau; in November 1889 they moved again, this time into the center of Moret, to a small house near the church at the corner of Rue du Château and Rue de Montmartre. While living there, Sisley completed twelve canvases of the local church under the most difficult of conditions. He had enjoyed none of his friends' financial success, and his last exhibition, organized in 1897 by Georges Petit, Sisley having fallen out with Durand-Ruel, would be another failure. By now, Sisley was extremely ill and in great pain from rheumatism and facial paralysis.

His paintings of the church at Moret certainly owe a debt to Monet's work at Rouen. Like Monet, he was happy to paint the same motif in different weather conditions or from different viewpoints, but his sensibility was markedly different from his friend's. It is unlikely, though not impossible, that he would have seen any of Monet's *Rouen Cathedral* paintings; Monet was very secretive and none of the works was shown until 1895. However, Sisley would certainly have heard of what Monet was doing. In the end, perhaps, it is relatively unimportant. Monet's cathedral paintings are a sequence of captured moments and Sisley's have a bulk, a physical weight that suggests permanence and solidity. His paintings of the church are closer in spirit and style to those of Pissarro who, like Sisley, placed his buildings within a recognizable topographical site. Sisley shared with the older artist a feeling for the architecture of the buildings and their relationship to their environment. And as with Pissarro's work – although on close investigation one is struck by the invention of the color work – the overall sensation coming from Sisley's paintings is one of harmonious tonal values that exquisitely evoke a sense of atmosphere and also the specifics of a precise geographical site. His subdued brushwork never interferes with his highly refined delight in proportion and balanced compositions.

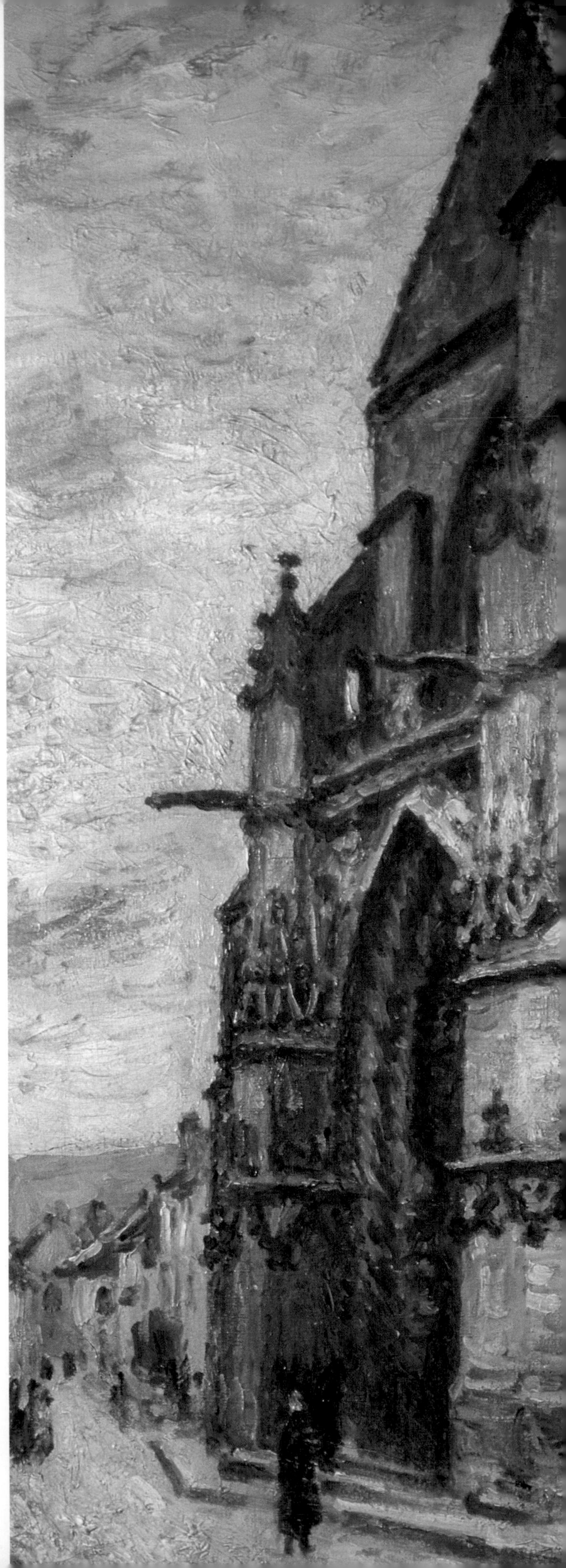

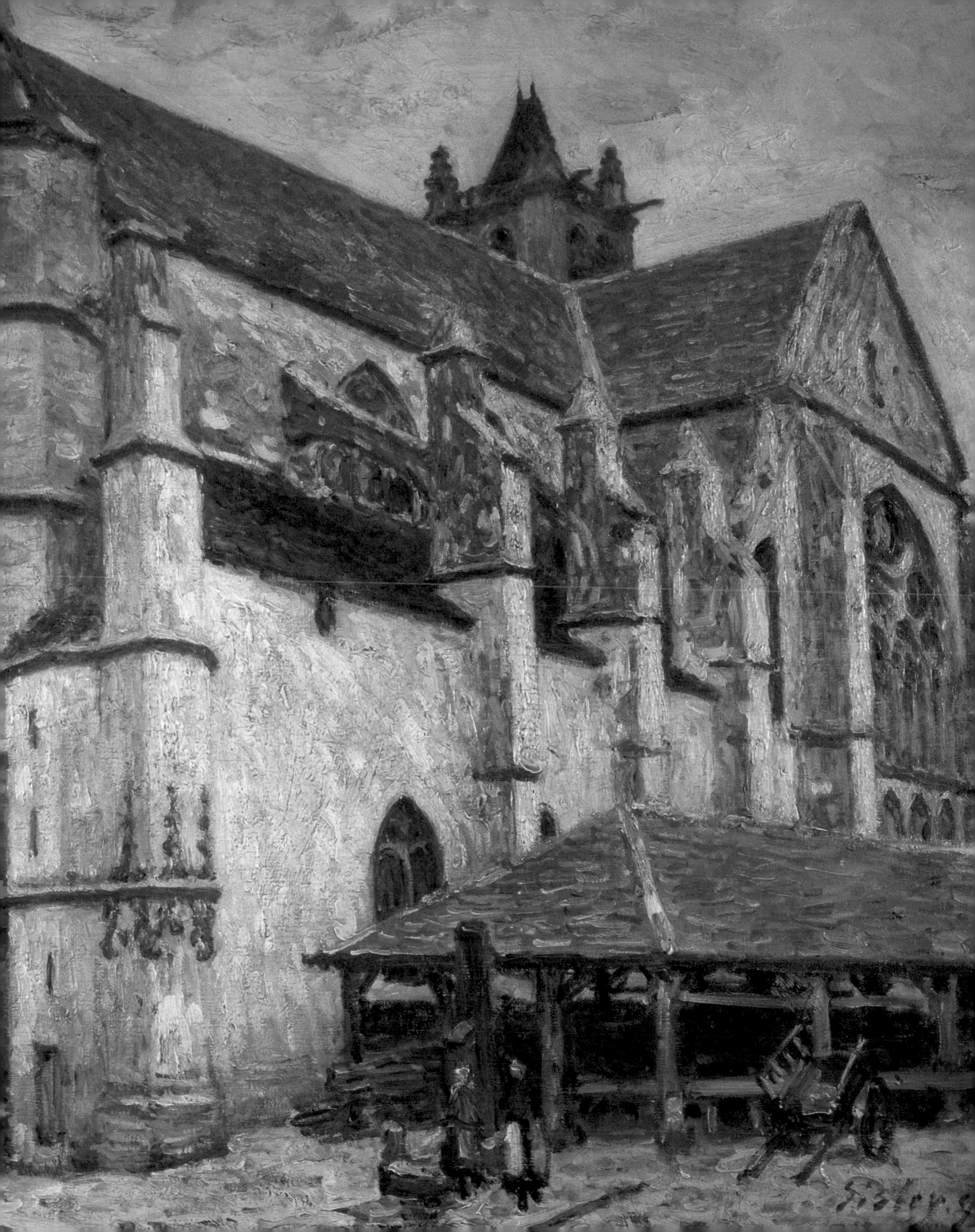

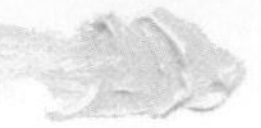

Monet's Waterlilies

Monet lived until 1926 and, despite severe eyesight problems, continued to paint well into that decade. The latter part of his life was dedicated to painting the immediate surroundings of his house at Giverny. The outside world had ceased to exist as subject matter for him, despite the fact that during the First World War, trains carrying troops and munitions to the front line regularly passed by his garden walls and Giverny was so close to the war zone that the cannons could be heard. Even in the midst of such turmoil, the artist continued to be directed by the ambition first stated to his friend Bazille as early as 1868: to make his art "simply the expression of my own personal experience." Although the physical boundaries of his world may have closed in, he remained faithful to the phenomena that had nurtured his art for over fifty years, the qualities of light and atmosphere, and the effects of transparency and reflection.

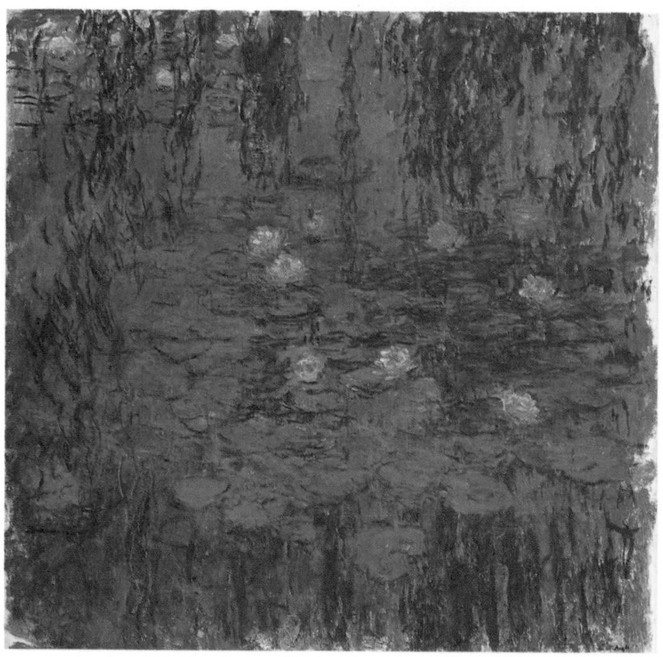

Monet,* Waterlilies and Japanese Bridge, *c.1900.

His paintings of waterlilies may seem a sign of his withdrawal from the world of contemporary events, but like Degas and Cézanne, Monet had only limited his subject matter the better to create an art that would be fully resonant in every sense of the word. In his final paintings the world is not perceived as a sequence of frozen moments, bound by the arbitrary events of day-to-day affairs, but as documents recording a passionate and sustained search for a unity of self and the world. Monet was not a particularly religious man and only ever talked about his art in the most prosaic of terms; however, through his working practice he gave expression to an almost pantheistic regard for nature.

Monet had a lifelong interest in gardens and at Giverny he was able to indulge his passion to the full, helped by a large team of gardeners. Today his garden – in reality, two gardens, a flower garden and a water garden linked by an underground passage – fully restored to its original splendor, is one of the most visited tourist sites in Europe. Monet was much inspired by Japanese culture and the garden is a happy mixture of Oriental and Occidental influences. In 1891 he had a visit from a Japanese gardener who gave him advice on its layout and gradually, almost without realizing it, his private domain became the most prominent subject of his art. In 1901 he enlarged the garden so that its oval pond, spanned by a Japanese bridge, stretched 55 meters (180 ft) from end to end and 18 meters (59 ft) across its widest point. The surrounding banks are a mass of carefully situated clumps of bamboo, peonies, irises, weeping willows; floating on the surface of the pond are the waterlilies that feature so frequently in the paintings of these years.

His initial paintings of the waterlilies, *Paysages d'Eau Nympheas*, twelve of which were exhibited at Durand-Ruel's gallery in 1900, were relatively straightforward representations of the lake and surrounding gardens. His second exhibition of forty-eight canvases in 1909 revealed a spectacular development in his vision that would culminate in the great decorations now in the Orangerie in the Tuileries Gardens, Paris. In these paintings, the lily-strewn surface covers the entire canvas, with the only reference to the sky or the surrounding environment to be found in the reflections on the surface of the water or occasionally where the trunk or branches of the willow tree may be seen standing against the water's surface.

Monet, encouraged by Georges Clemenceau, donated a cycle of these paintings to the French nation as a memorial to the dead of the First World War. Without recourse to heavy allegorical programs or clichéd images of idealized soldiers dying for their country, Monet created an environment for meditation and remembrance. In an article in the *Revue de l'Art* of July 1927, Thiébault-Sisson quoted the artist as saying,

> ***I have painted these waterlilies many times, modifying my viewpoint each time in accordance with the season and the different light effects each season brings. Besides the effects vary constantly, not only from one season to the next, since the water-flowers are far from being the whole scene; really they are just the accompaniment. The essence of the motif is the mirror of water whose appearance alters at every moment, thanks to the patches of sky which are reflected in it, and which give it its light and movement. The passing cloud, the freshening breeze, the storm which threatens and breaks, the wind that blows hard and suddenly abates, the light growing dim and bright again – so many factors, undetectable to the uninitiated eye, which transform the coloring and disturb the planes of water.***

Monet's radical use of a displaced perspective and the rich swathes of pigment that weave across the canvas surface link these paintings with the works of Monet's young contemporaries, the Cubist works of Picasso and Braque and the Orphist works of Delaunay. Monet pointed the way for artists who have used art as a means of creating a synthesis of self and experience; such qualities, together with the sheer size, color and texture of his canvases, were to play a determining role in the work of American artists such as Jackson Pollock and Mark Rothko.

Like so many of his waterlily paintings, Monet has omitted any reference to the bank of the pool on which he stood.

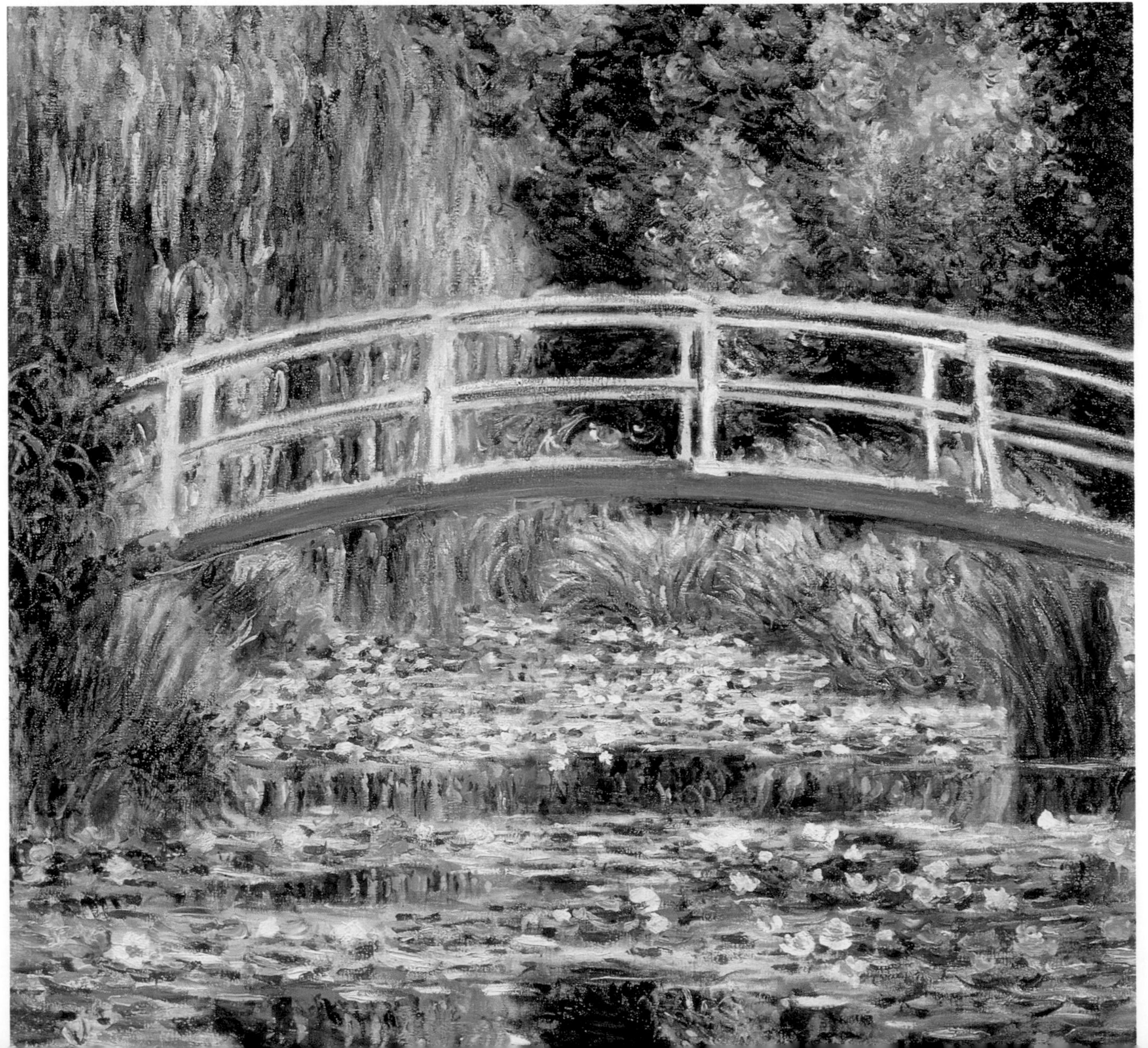

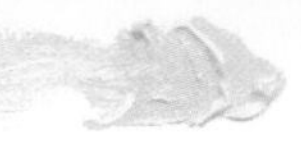

Degas' Late Work

Degas' reputation as an Impressionist, as a painter of the ballet and of modern Paris, has obscured the full nature of his artistic achievement. Like Monet, Degas was producing work well into the twentieth century and his late work should be seen within the context of late nineteenth century and early twentieth century art. Degas lived in Montmartre, the center of avant-garde art, close to the galleries of Bernheim-Jeune, Vollard and Durand-Ruel. Living in such a district and with such a reputation as his, he could not have failed to be aware of the paintings of artists such as Matisse, Picasso and Braque. Richard Kendall, in his illuminating and scholarly investigation into the late years of Degas' life, *Degas: Beyond Impressionism*, notes the supposed reaction of the aged artist to the paintings of the young tyros.

Degas,* Return of the Herd, *1896–98. A haunting, melancholic, evocation of a small street in the port of Saint-Valéry.

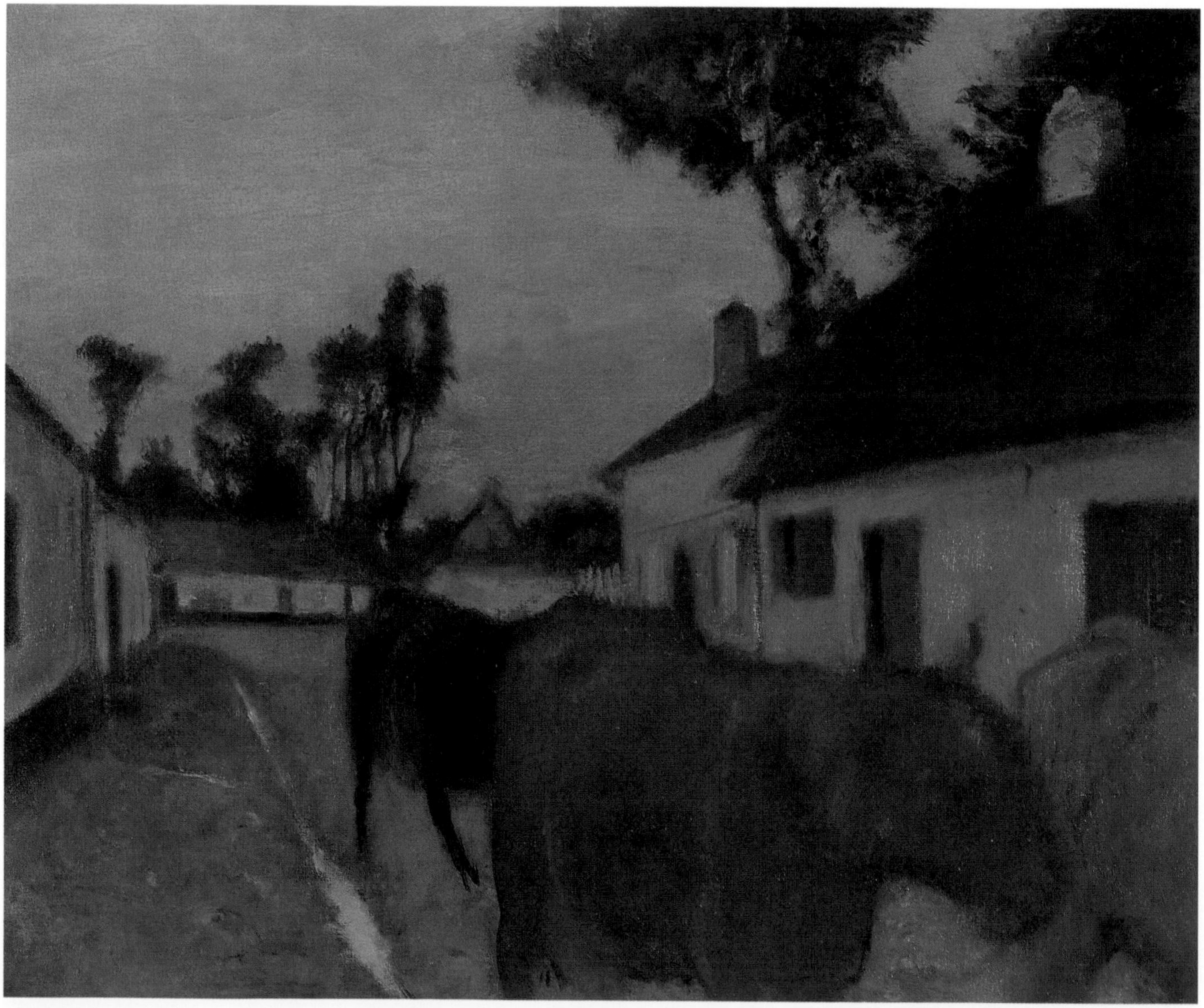

Deeply paradoxical as a man and an artist, Degas said that he wished to be at once famous and unknown. His virtuosity as a draftsman and colorist were of the highest order, yet he never fell into empty displays of skill. He had the utmost disdain for art produced specifically for a market and his art became increasingly the product of his own personal researches.

For Degas, the 1880s were a period of crisis. Like so many, he was deeply depressed by the political and social climate of his times, and was also troubled by various personal concerns. There is evidence to suggest that he may have regretted his decision to remain celibate. His artistic life, too, was not without its problems. He had been experiencing a progressive sense of unease with the Impressionist program and his deteriorating eyesight, together with uncertainty of his own artistic worth, made these difficult years for the artist.

In 1890, aged 55, Degas moved to an apartment at 37 Rue Victor Massé, which served not only as a living quarters but also as a personal museum. On the fourth floor was a large and somber studio. He remained here, locked in his own private world surrounded by a concerned body of friends, admirers and acquaintances, until he was forced to move to an apartment on Boulevard de Clichy in 1912. The enforced move was catastrophic for the elderly artist and he did little work thereafter. After his death in 1917, his studio contents and his collection, which he once had thought of preserving as a museum, were dispersed.

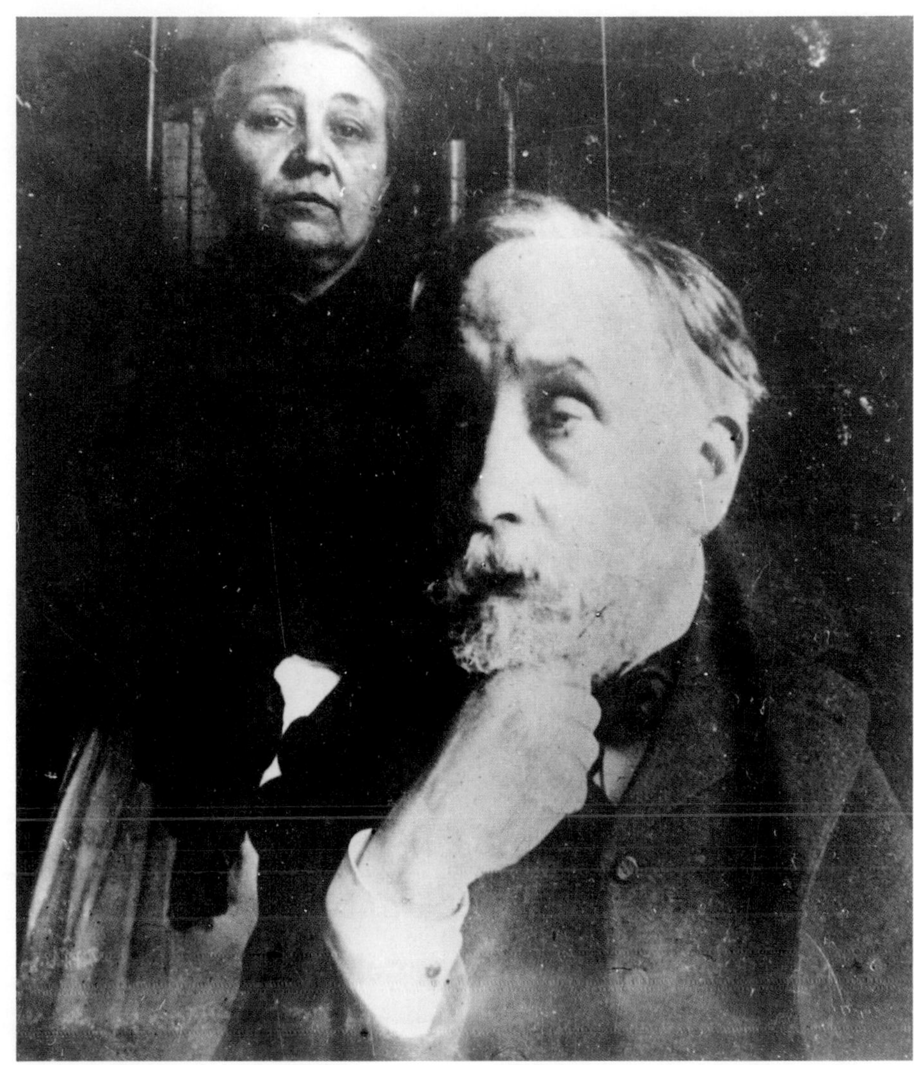

Passionately interested in photography, this is an arresting self-portrait of the artist and his proprietorial but faithful housekeeper, Zoë.

Bathers and dancers

His late work is marked by continual experimentation and the artist's obsessive working methods. His relationship with Impressionism had always been fraught. As Degas grew older, so his art became increasingly less interested in the specifics of actuality and more concerned with expressing the generalities of experience. This does not mean his art became duller or blunter, but rather that while his range of subject matter grew ever narrower, so it increased in profundity and daring. Like Renoir and Monet, he abandoned the varied subject matter of his early career to focus increasingly upon a limited area of study, eventually concentrating upon one central theme – the depiction of women as bather or dancer.

Progressively precise detail is discarded, narrative elements, such as the male figure, are avoided as the single figure is left to hold center stage, the action being merely a pretext for the celebration of the nude in itself. His bathers are not the polite, sun-filled fantasies of his colleague Renoir, nor are they the obviously sexually alluring images of the same subjects produced in such number and variation by his contemporaries. Rather, they are a private scrutiny which breaks all kinds of taboos and boundaries and, in doing so, reveals an intensity of investigation and identification with the human frame that may have been equalled by others, but never surpassed.

Combing the Hair

1892–95, oil on canvas, 114.3 x 146.1 cm (45 x 57½ in), National Gallery, London, England

Degas had always been fascinated by the intimate details of women's lives and instilled his depictions of even the most mundane of these actions with a ceremony found in the Japanese prints of the pleasure houses of Edo. This painting is the culmination of a number of similar works. All the detail and precision of earlier works have been exchanged for something much more ambiguous. For all these qualities, the painting possesses a precise, if indefinable mood; each woman is thoroughly preoccupied within their own world, linked only by the repeated movements of this timeless ritual. The young, possibly pregnant, woman leans back as her maid-servant combs the heavy mass of her Titian red hair.

Matisse's ownership of this painting (he acquired it shortly after World War I) and the high regard in which it is held by many modern artists, draws attention not only to Degas' genius in suggesting atmosphere but also his bravura use of color and his virtuoso draftsmanship. Using a relatively limited range of reds, Degas created a rich harmony of saturated color, enlivened by the admixture of white, black and two highly significant touches of yellow. The setting is ambiguous; the heavy swathe of curtain and hint of gilded frame operate more as devices rather than signifiers of a particular environment, although the suggested opulence could situate us within the confines of a courtesan's chamber. The two bodies form a complex interchange of echoing forms, that switch back and forth in a twisting diagonal from top right to lower left. Like so much of Degas' work, the final painting bears the imprint of his premeditation and spontaneity; nuances and traces of previous decisions are clearly distinguishable throughout the composition. The woman's upraised arm is repeated in the heavy curtain on the left of the canvas and repeated in reverse in the maid's lower arm creating a quite extraordinary figure eight movement in the center of the picture. Flat patches of color and tone are tracked by a blurred and muted line that describes the form with minimal detail. Degas' control of tone is absolute and innovatory; the indeterminate light source creates a theatrical space in which there is no clearly distinguishable difference between foreground and background space.

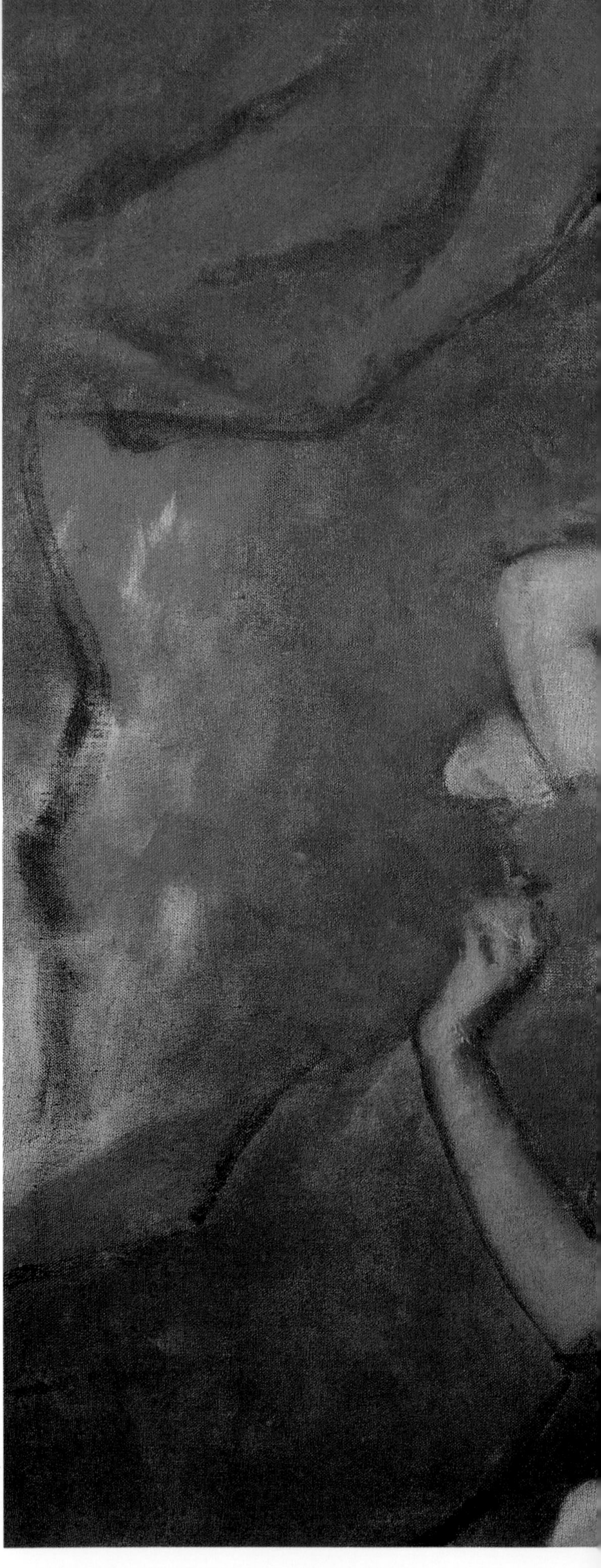

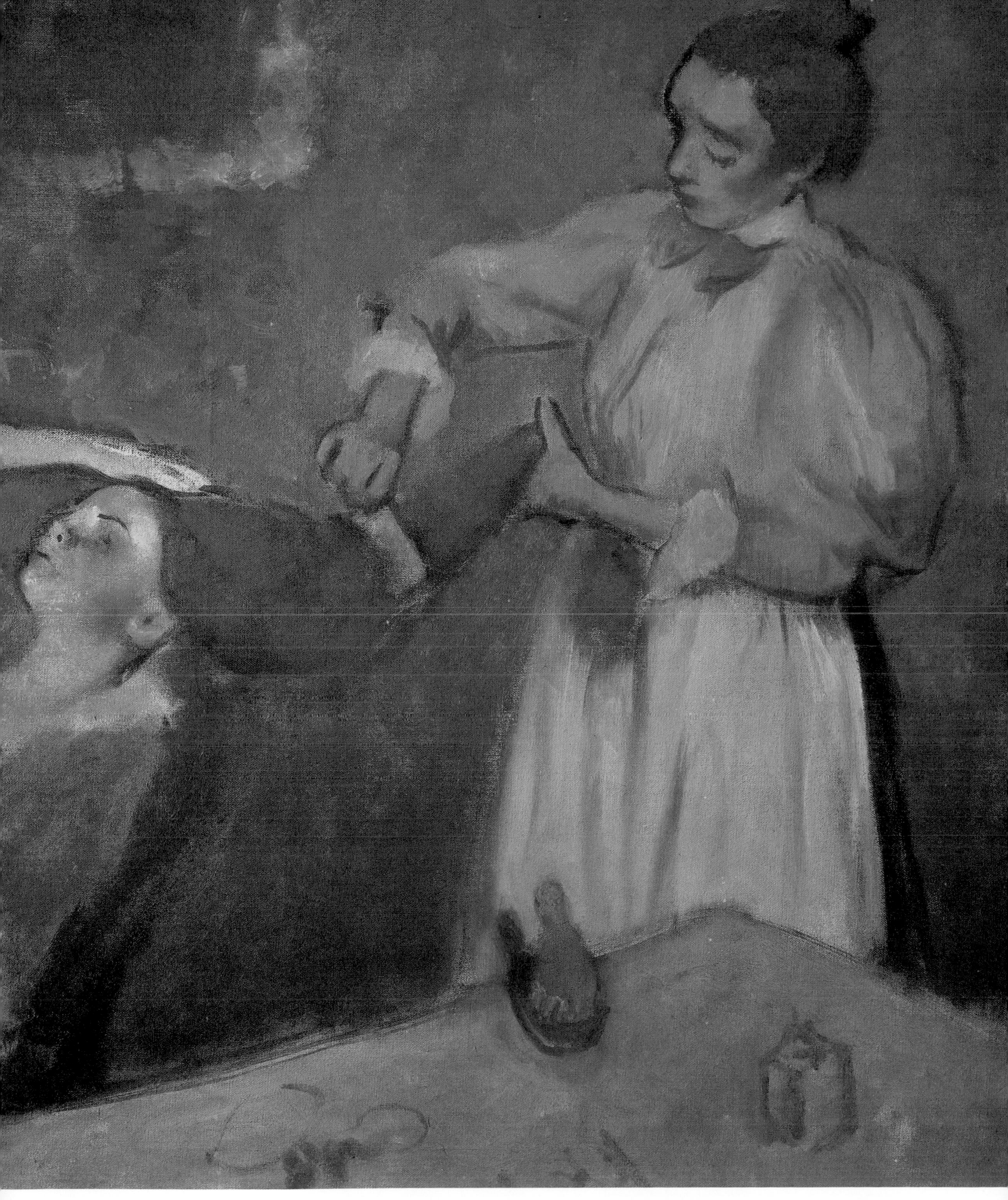

Cézanne's Late Work

Like the paintings of Constable or van Gogh, Cézanne's paintings, though rooted in reality, are visionary in intent. He once wrote:

Finally I must tell you he wrote only six months before his death, that as a painter, I am becoming more clear-sighted before nature, but that with me the realization of my sensations is always painful. I cannot attain the immensity that is unfolded before my senses. I have not the magnificence of coloring that animates nature.

Nature can never be captured in words or images, but may only be alluded to, it will always escape our efforts to enclose and contain it. Cézanne's paintings, especially those of the country round his home in Provence, come close to giving back nature something of its own self. The distinctive

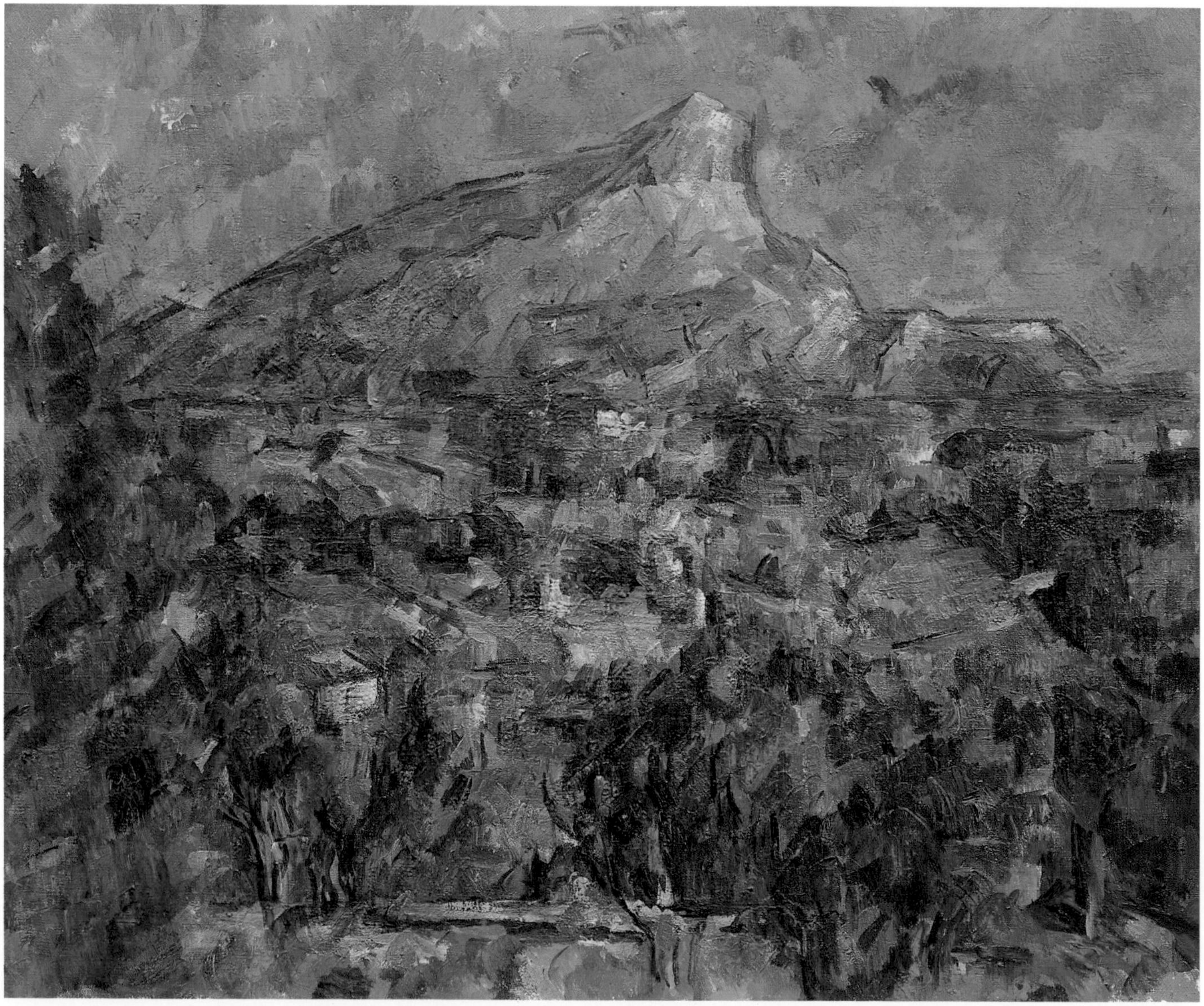

Cézanne,* Mont Sainte Victoire, *1902–06. A densely worked mosaic of color patches.

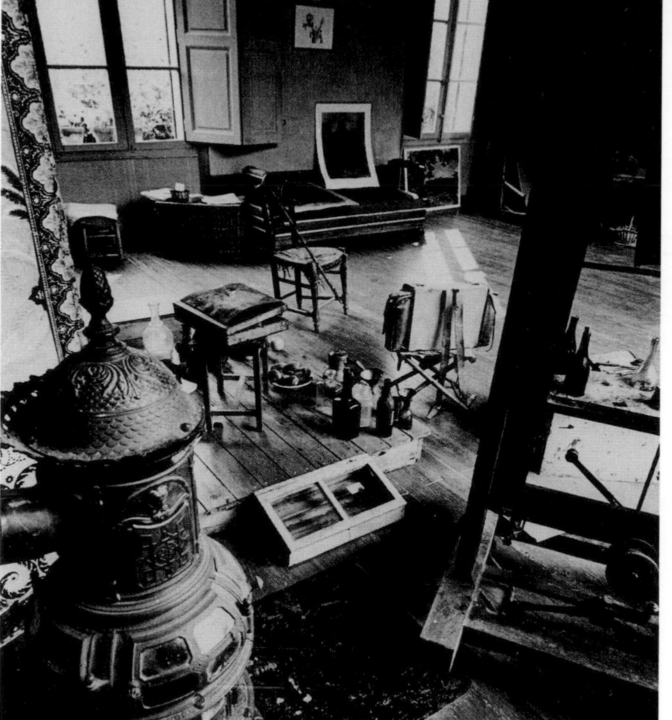

Cézanne's famous studio at Les Lauves, built on what was then the outskirts of Aix-en-Provence.

silhouette of Mont Sainte-Victoire, which had featured earlier in Cézanne's painting, in the last years of the artist's life became an abiding presence, dominating his art as it dominated the landscape around Aix-en-Provence.

During the last years of his life, Cézanne increasingly became the object of intense admiration among younger artists and writers, numbers of whom wrote down or "remembered" conversations with the so-called "Hermit of Aix." While these recollections have to be treated with caution and read within their original context, they give significant insights into the artist's continuing struggle to realize his sensations before nature – as does this "recollection" of remarks by Cézanne:

> ***Now being old, nearly seventy years, the sensations of color, which give light, are for me the reason for the abstractions that do not allow me to cover my canvas entirely or to pursue the delimitation of objects where points of contact are fine and delicate; from which it results that my image or picture is incomplete.***

In fact, Cézanne signed very few of his works, the imposition of a signature artificially calling an end to what he saw as a continual process of investigation. His paintings are not descriptions of the world but analogies for his experience of it in paint. Cézanne's work process could not be based upon standardized responses or clichéd conventions: nature has no contours, as Delacroix famously observed, and perspective and traditional notions of aerial perspective only serve to distance the viewer from the immediacy of the artist's experience. Cézanne's paintings evolve from a sketched-in scaffolding of loosely defining contour lines over which are superimposed a patchwork of cool and warm colors. Reds and ochers are set against blues and greens to create a coloristic drama equivalent to that found in nature.

Cézanne ceaselessly overworked his paintings, re-adjusting them in the light of each contact with the motif and registering each response with a single touch of color, regulating the color balance constantly to preserve the harmony he wished to achieve in his picture. Cézanne used the metaphor of interlocked hands to suggest the tension, strength and unity that he wished to create within his work. For him, as for Monet, each work represented a genuine struggle for completion, success could never be guaranteed and no motif set him as great a challenge as the awesome silhouette of the looming Mont Sainte-Victoire.

He painted the mountain all year round. By five or six o'clock in the morning he could be found making his way along the Le Tholonet road to the east of Aix, to walk the five kilometers or so to his chosen point of view; later he could walk up the road just outside his purpose-built studio on Avenue des Lauves where he would also find a panorama suitable for his purposes. Cézanne's paintings are intuitive and immediate and he never relinquished his faith in his initial response to the motif, even though, as with Monet, this process could result in overwhelming fits of despair; often, according to his friend, the dealer Ambroise Vollard, he would abandon his canvases in hedgerows and ditches.

The subject of his work became the depiction of a diverse universe in a constant state of flux, brought into a harmonious unit within the picture surface. This operated hand-in-hand with his desire to "redo Poussin over again according to nature." His landscapes are animated by the pulse of life, the expression of the continuity of nature in the face of our transient experience of life; Cézanne had little interest in the actions of humans in the landscape, despite the fact that the landscape is obviously the result of human interaction with the land. Any narrative content within the work is minimal; in its place is the rhythmical repetition of interrelated forms that bring order to the confusing variety of the world he was contemplating.

"Art is a harmony that runs parallel with nature," he wrote in 1897. Sometimes this harmony is a classically balanced order; at other times it is an order barely held in place. Things are not seen as fixed, relations with the world are part of a endlessly changing cycle of transmutation; what may seem permanent to us, a huge outcrop of rock or the lie of the land, are in fact as transitory as the clouds that pass overhead.

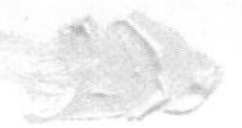

The Large Bathers

c. 1900–05, oil on canvas, 208 x 249 cm (82 x 98 in) Philadelphia Museum of Art, Pennsylvania, USA

During the last ten years of his life, Cézanne attempted to produce a series of coherent paintings of groups of nude figures fully integrated into a landscape setting. This subject had interested him from the beginning of his career and he had returned to it at intervals throughout his life.

Cézanne enjoyed none of Renoir's facility and his major paintings of this subject, for all their power, remain unresolved. He had set himself an almost unrealizable task, the inherent contradictions of which went right to the heart of the anxieties that plagued the artist: how to make coherent a painting practice authorized by instinctual responses before the motif but also influenced by his deep awareness of the work of the great masters. How could he apply the effects he witnessed *en plein-air* with the images of the nude that he could only produce from memory and sketches?

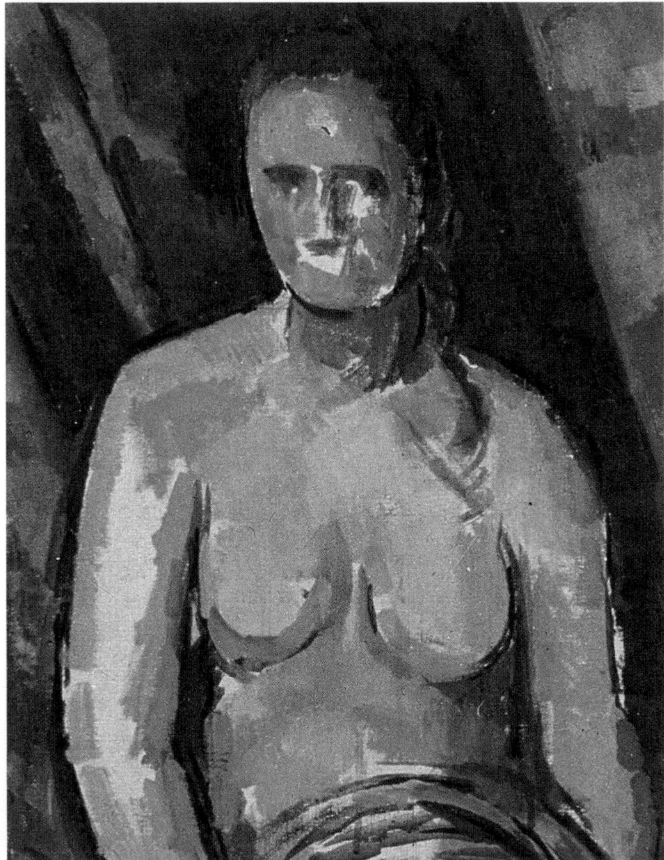

***Detail from* The Large Bathers.**

In the light of these ambitious studio creations, a letter he had written much earlier in his career to Zola is especially poignant. In it, he wrote

> ***But you know that all pictures painted inside in the studio, will never be as good as those done outside. When outdoor-scenes are represented, the contrasts between the figures and the ground are astonishing and the landscape is magnificent. I see superb things and I shall make up my mind only to do things out-of-doors.***

Cézanne's own curious personality made it difficult for him to work from a living model; also, the provincial nature of life in Aix-en-Provence made it impossible to work from the naked figure. As it was, he was a figure of fun around the town. He had to make do with his accumulated drawings made from earlier encounters with the life model, drawings from the Louvre and from illustrated magazines and from a fortuitous encounter with a group of soldiers bathing in the river.

Innumerable nuances of color tremble on the surface of these canvases, laid over and redefined by a network of contours that are revealed and concealed by further applications of paint, shifting and breaking, their very discontinuity creating a feeling of movement and space. Every element of the composition is governed by what Cézanne called *réflexion*, or prolonged meditation. These paintings suggest the subject matter of the *artistes pompiers* of the Salon as much as the heroic subversions of Courbet and Manet. His compositions suggest such well-known images as the goddess Artemis (Diana) being espied by the hunter Actaeon, the finding of Moses in the bulrushes, or Michelangelo's bathers at Cascina. Cézanne's figures of uncertain anatomy and indeterminate sexuality are like actors on a stage unsure of their roles. These are extraordinary paintings, willed efforts to create academic art without recourse to academic practices.

Although his choice of subject matter was one that belonged to the world of establishment and avant-garde

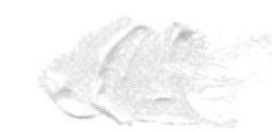

culture, it was also one that was deeply ingrained in his psyche. These works are informed by memories of his youthful happiness rambling and bathing with his friends in the countryside around Aix. His *Bathers* are as much reconstitutions of a never-to-be-recaptured past as they are homages to Veronese, Rubens or Poussin. "Art is a religion," he told Largier. "Its goal is the elevation of thought." With these paintings, we have come full circle, the academic ideal of art as a moral and intellectual activity, apprehended through the senses has been reinvented to suit a new age. The compositions of Cézanne have continued to reverberate throughout our century, and have retained their power as disturbing and challenging documents to aid us in our quest for an understanding of the universe and of our place within it.

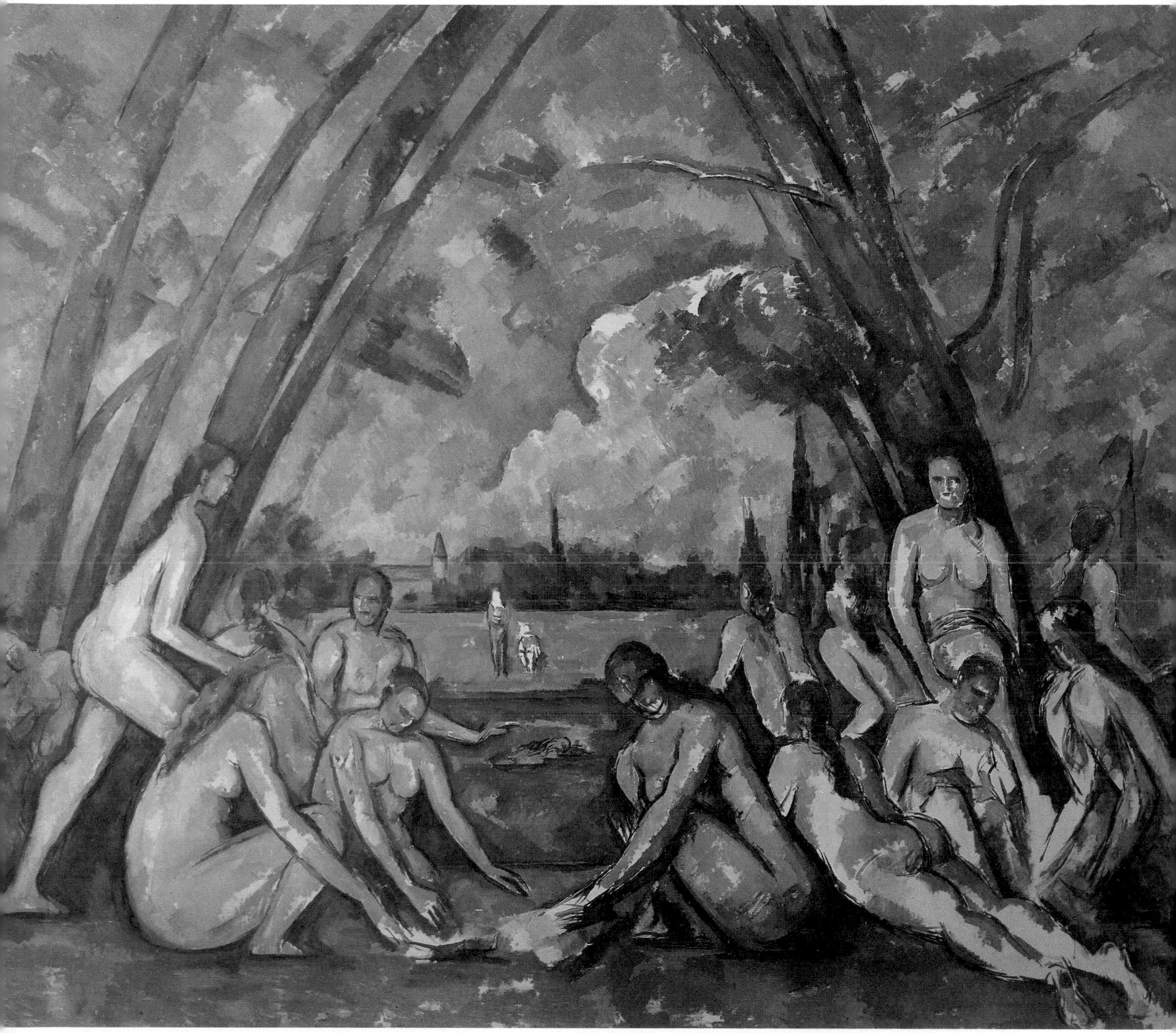

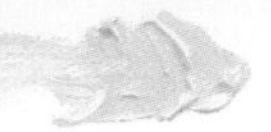

Late Renoir

"The simplest subjects are eternal," Renoir told his friend and most famous pupil, André late in life. "A nude woman getting out of the briny deep or out of her bed, whether she is called Venus or Nini, one can invent nothing better." Renoir's late nudes are direct descendants of the full-bodied voluptuous beauties of Rubens, Fragonard, Boucher and Ingres and, like the paintings of those artists, are made primarily for the male gaze, though they remain accessible to all. The skins of Renoir's nudes exude a healthy vitality, as if they have soaked up the warm golden sunlight of the Mediterranean. Unlike Cézanne's bathers or those of Degas, Renoir's nudes are untroubled, at complete ease with themselves and their surroundings.

During the 1880s, Renoir, who had been a healthy, sociable young man, became increasingly troubled by ill-health and by 1905 his various ailments kept him confined to a wheelchair. Although he was in almost constant pain, his art reflects none of this personal tragedy. Indeed, his work seems to have been a palliative, a visualization of the health and vigor he had once enjoyed. His crippled hands caressed into life countless women in robust and carefree health. Renoir had painted bathing figures all his life, whether posed as goddesses of the classical era or as contemporary Parisians, modishly garbed in their bathing costumes at La Grenouillère. He returned to the image of the bather with renewed vigor in the 1880s, and continued to work on the theme until his death in 1919.

In December 1883, Renoir and Monet worked together in the south of France. The experience acted as a catalyst for Renoir, because, together with his recent trip to Italy, it revealed not only his dissatisfaction with Impressionist practice but also his continued desire to succeed as a painter of the figure. He dedicated himself to the production of a single masterpiece, and after three year's hard work, during which time he produced preparatory studies in all media, he exhibited the finished work in the spring of 1887. The title he gave it was significant, serving to remove it from the expressions of *la vie moderne* that had preoccupied him during the previous decade: *Bathers: Trial for a Decorative Painting*. It was exhibited, not at Durand-Ruel's gallery because the dealer found his new style unappealing and potentially unattractive to buyers, but in Georges Petit's fashionable gallery. The painting was worked on in Paris, and is illuminated not by the light of nature, but the light of the museum: the fickle transient effects of the outdoors has been exchanged for a timeless light, regulated to integrate the female figures into their setting. Each figure is encased in a firm but supple outline, inside which the forms of the body are described in high-toned color. Renoir has avoided the light, feathery touch of his earlier canvases in favor of a dry matte finish intended to lend the composition the sense of gravitas found in the frescoes of Pompeii he had so admired in 1881. The composition owes much to the famous painting, Boucher's *Diana at her Bath* and (almost directly) from the famous low-relief by the seventeenth-century sculptor, François Girardon at Versailles, representing Diana bathing with her Nymphs – a term Renoir habitually used when referring to young girls and his models.

Stephane Mallarmé, the **eminence gris** *of Impressionism, a great enthusiast of Renoir and his fellow Impressionists.*

For Renoir, women were, above all, sensuous animals, and although he depicted peasant women, washerwomen and even mussel gatherers, their professions were merely the excuse to portray well-fed, well-rounded women in idealized settings.

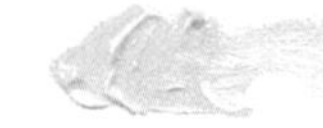

Unlike in the images of modern life that dominated his work of the 1870s, in his later work he made no attempt to paint the stuff of actuality: instead his art is a contrived display in which his models have been manipulated to the artist's will.

The image of the idealized woman has been a prevalent theme in the Western tradition with which Renoir so passionately identified; the theme of *L'Age d'Or* (the Golden Age) was popular with many artists, reactionary and avant-garde, a response to the deep need in us all to imagine a place were humans might live at ease within a kindly, nurturing nature. Renoir never populates his imaginary landscapes with men (except for the occasional image of Paris, judging the three Goddesses). Renoir's friend, Stéphane Mallarmé, matched the artist's vision of femininity in his poem, *L'Après-Midi d'un Faune*, published in 1876:

Ces nymphes, je les veux perpétuer.
… Si clair, Leur incarnat léger, qu'il voltige dans l'air
Assoupi de sommeils touffus.
Aimai-je un rève?

("I wish to perpetuate these nymphs.
So bright, their light rosy flesh that it floats in the air
Sleepy with tufted slumbers.
Did I love a dream?")

Like Mallarmé's faun hidden in the reeds, Renoir's *Bathers* presents the viewer with an intangible glimpse of perfect beauty, impossible to possess except through the operation of art. Renoir's women are of a similar type to those used by Impressionism's arch enemy, Alexandre Cabanel, as in the latter's popular but now much-derided *Birth of Venus*. They are presented in terms of luxuriant hair, unfurrowed brows, full breasts and well-described buttocks. *Bathers* is enclosed within the fantasy world created by the artist. No reference to modern times intrudes and no hint of irony allows the viewer to see this as anything other than a celebration of that age-old scenario, the "Nymph surprised." Renoir's masterful draftsmanship and composition hold the picture together, sustaining its status as a successful addition to a singular genre that would be so intelligently continued by Matisse and so brutally disrupted by Picasso.

Renoir,* **The Bathers**, *1887. Renoir's later work is as artful and contrived as that of his erstwhile colleagues.

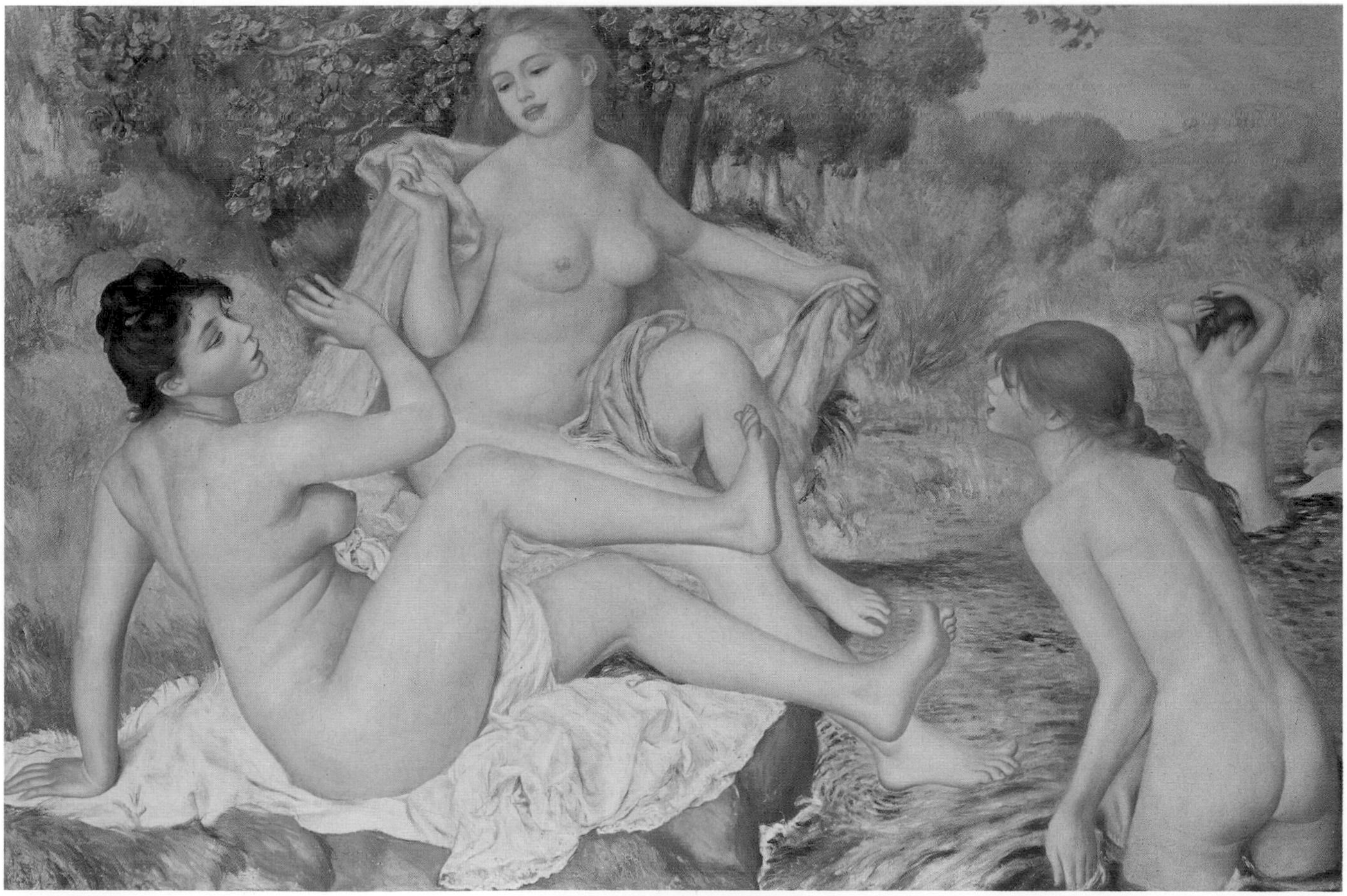

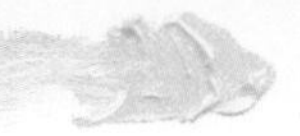

English and American Impressionism

Into the hothouse of sentimentality in the late 'eighties it blew again the fresh breath of the open air, of the vitality of the thing seen, of reality faced and its beauty sought out.
– Alfred Thorton, *Fifty Years of the New English Art Club,* 1935

Philip Wilson Steer, **The Beach at Walberswick,** *1891. A mixture of pre-Raphaelitism and French avant-garde painting was possibly shown at the 1889 London Impressionist Exhibition.*

Toward the end of the nineteenth century Impressionism, as exemplified particularly by Monet's painting, had become an international style; modified forms of Impressionism were adopted not just by French painters, but by artists of many nationalities. American, German and English painters made France a place of pilgrimage, flocking to paint the subjects and sites made famous by Monet and his fellow Impressionists.

The artists who thoroughly investigated Impressionism soon found themselves creating very different works from their forebears, although most were content to play down the more daring aspects of Impressionist practice to suit a conservative clientele.

Impressionist paintings had been available to English artists since 1870, although most people were unaware of the existence of the movement. The most radical painter in England was a friend and early associate of the Impressionists, the American artist James McNeill Whistler had moved from Paris to London and had made the city the centre of his activities. His wit, charm and charismatic personality as much as his art and his connections with France made him a figure of considerable influence on many of the most talented younger painters of the time. His writings and his art reveal a striking and unexpected correspondence with Monet's mature work. In his famous "Ten O'Clock Lecture" staged in 1885, Whistler declaimed:

And when the evening mist clothes the riverside with poetry, as with a veil, and the poor buildings lose themselves in the dim sky, and the tall chimneys become campanili, and the warehouses are palaces in the night, and the whole city hangs in the heavens, and fairyland is before us – then the wayfarer hastens home; the working man and the cultured one, the wise man and the one of pleasure, cease to understand, as they have ceased to see, and Nature who, for once, has sung in tune, sings her exquisite song to the artist alone, her son and her master – her son in that he loves her, her master in that he knows her.

Whistler's doctrine of creating an absolute beauty out of the dross realities of the urban scene had a invigorating effect upon the younger artists of the time. There was a strong interest in reviving naturalistic painting among British artists

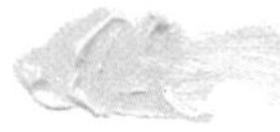

and the New English Art Club became the focal point for artists who shared this ambition. At their first meeting, a year after Whistler's speech, it was proposed unsuccessfully that the group be called "The Society of Anglo-French Painters." Many had been trained in France and most of them produced work that was acceptable to the Royal Academy, based upon a synthesis of the work of Millet and Bastien-Lepage. Despite their avowal to paint "vivid and simple studies" from nature the paintings of artists such as Clausen, Lathangue, Stanhope Forbes, Fred Brown and others were still touched by the sentimental and anecdotal values common in the more conventional art of the time.

Into this set came Walter Sickert, born in Munich of Danish and Irish descent, he had lived in England since childhood. He became Whistler's studio assistant and was asked by him to visit Degas in Paris. This encounter drew him away from his American mentor and toward the art of both Degas and Manet, although his work never lost its particular quality of "Englishness."

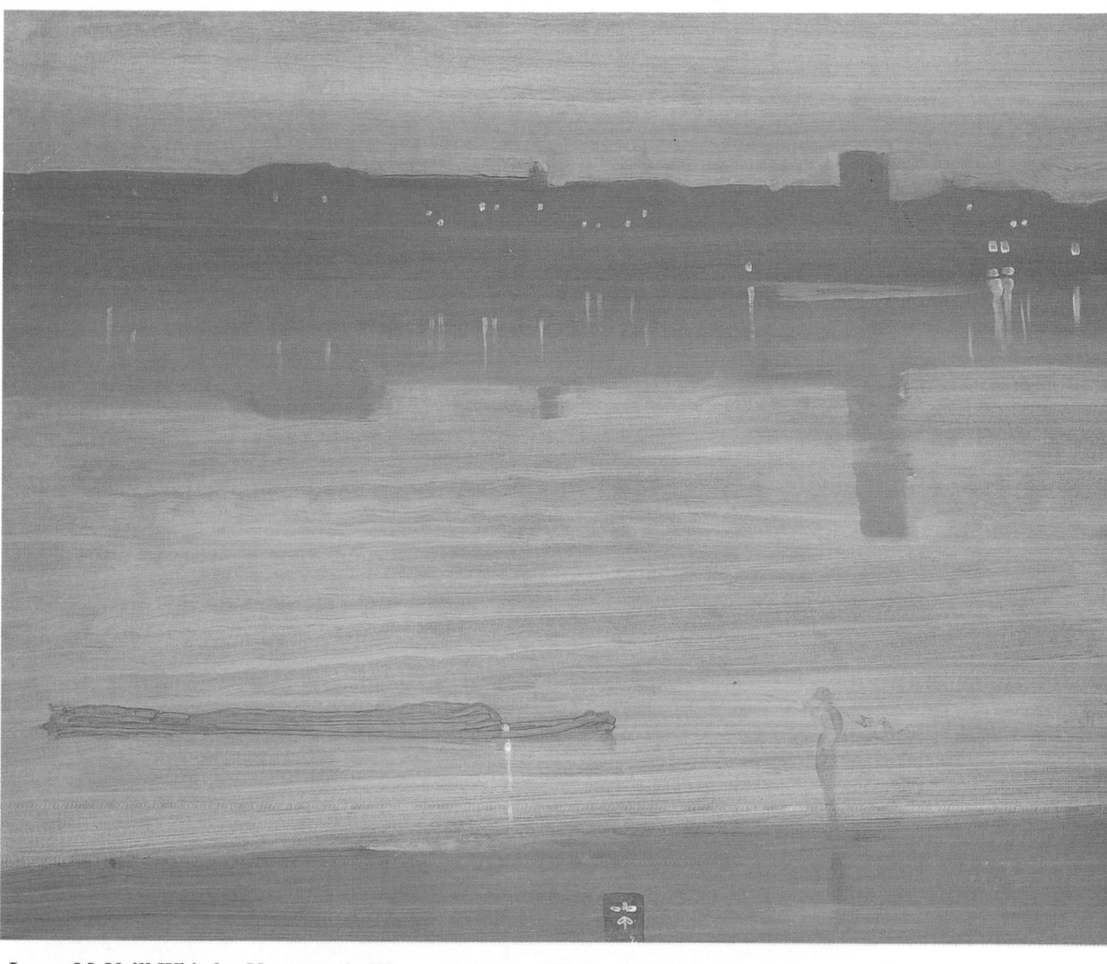

James McNeill Whistler,* Nocturne in Blue and Green: Chelsea, *1871. This painting reveals unexpected affinities between Whistler's painting and that of Monet and the Impressionists.

Sickert joined the New English Art Club in 1888 and attracted a small group around him who made up the core of painters represented in the London Impressionist exhibition, which opened on the December 2, 1889, and included 70 works. *The Times* newspaper noted that the most characteristic of the paintings bore the evident influence of Monet. Indeed Monet had shown at the same gallery only a few months before, although in real terms the work of the British artists was in fact, very different from that of the French master, showing as it did the influence of Whistler's aesthetics. When asked to define Impressionism, Sickert replied, "I don't know. It is a name they will give us in the press."

The word Impressionism had become a cliché – a flag of convenience to declare an artist's distance from conventional art practice. "Our theories were perfectly simple," wrote Alfred Thorton in his memoires, "we were in utter revolt against the prettiness and anecdotal nature of the work at home [in England], and enthusiastic for the Impressionism of Monet, as well as Manet, whose 'Olympia' was still the cause of fierce controversy … Our slogan was 'effects not facts.'"

Philip Wilson Steer visited Paris in the early 1880s where he saw Manet's retrospective exhibition in 1884. This confrontation encouraged him to develop a more experimental approach to his art. The impact of Whistler and Monet led him to the use of a much more painterly style which varied from thin washes of pure color to works that reveal a relationship with the pointillism of Seurat. His painting of these years is characterized by a pervasive charm and an atmosphere of reverie associated with certain paintings by the English pre-Raphaelite painters of the mid century. He only managed to sustain this mixture of French and English qualities for a few years before reverting to a style of painting based upon the work of Constable and Gainsborough.

Walter Sickert in *The New Life of Whistler*, December 1908 said, "Whistler… has sent the more intelligent of the generation that succeeds him to the springs whence he drew his own art – to French soil."

The Aftermath of Impressionism

Impressionism will always escape any simple definition. Monet, Renoir and Degas lived well into the twentieth century, and artists from France and elsewhere who had nothing to do with the famous group exhibitions of the 1870s and 1880s have since become defined as Impressionists. Indeed, for many, Impressionism was not simply confined to paintings produced in the nineteenth century but was considered to have been a permanent feature of Western art of which Velasquez, the great seventeenth-century Spanish master, was the greatest exponent.

However, if Impressionism is taken to be the work of the artists represented in this book, then the impact of the paintings, pastels, prints and drawings produced by this small loosely associated group of friends upon young avant-garde artists of the late nineteenth and twentieth centuries becomes all the more immense.

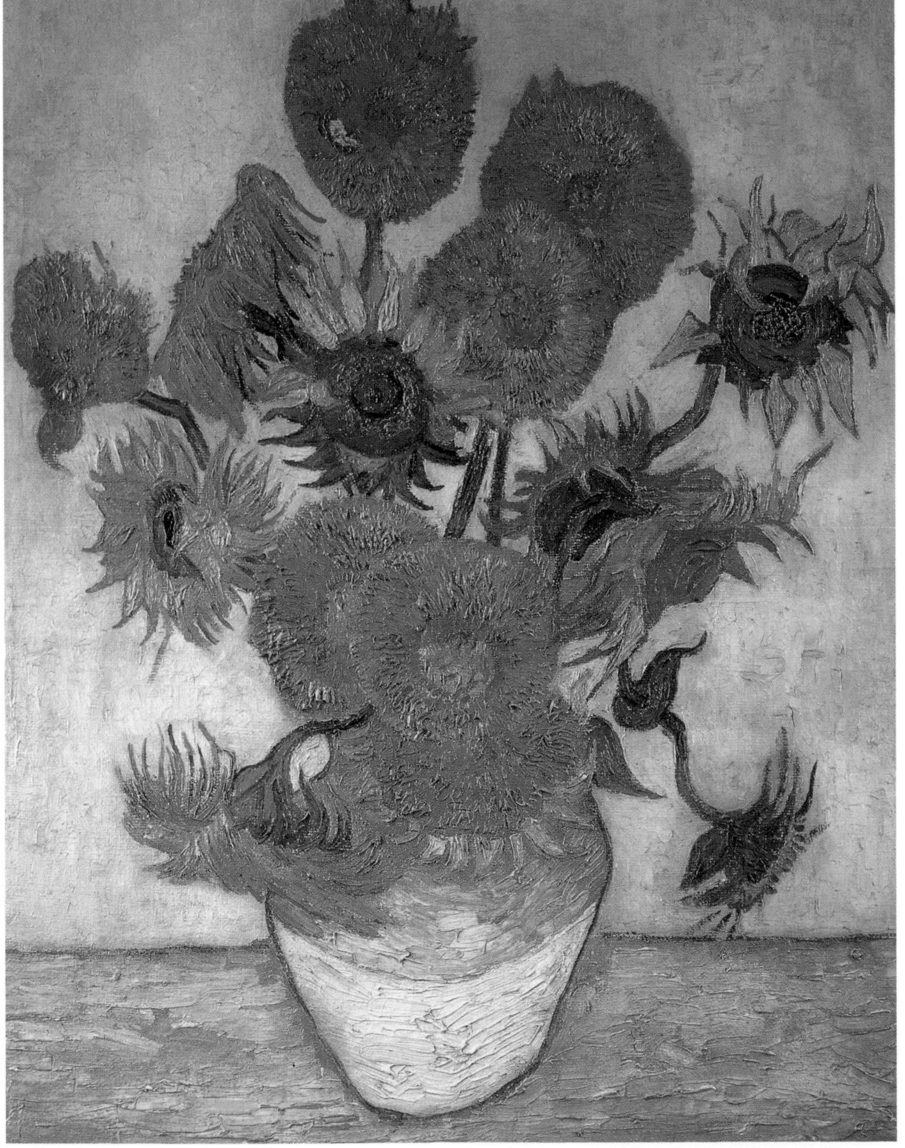

Van Gogh,* Sunflowers*, 1888. To his brother Theo: "Who will be in figure painting what Claude Monet is in landscape?… the painter of the future will be a colorist such has never been …"

The artists commonly termed Impressionists left no coherent manifesto or publication to summarize their aims or ambitions, only their work and reputations. Young artists at the end of the nineteenth century were looking not at the work that had been produced in the 1860s, 1870s and early 1880s but at the later work of Manet, Monet, Renoir, Cézanne, Seurat, van Gogh and Gauguin. When the English writer and critic, Roger Fry, put together an exhibition to catalog the significant artists and tendencies of late nineteenth-century French painting, he invented the title *Manet and the Post-Impressionists*, dismissing out of hand the painters of Impressionism as being irrelevant to the development of modern art.

Perception versus the cerebral

Monet's reputation as an influence on Twentieth-Century art has suffered in comparison with that of Cézanne mainly because he was categorized as an artist whose work was based on perception, a categorization influenced by Cézanne's

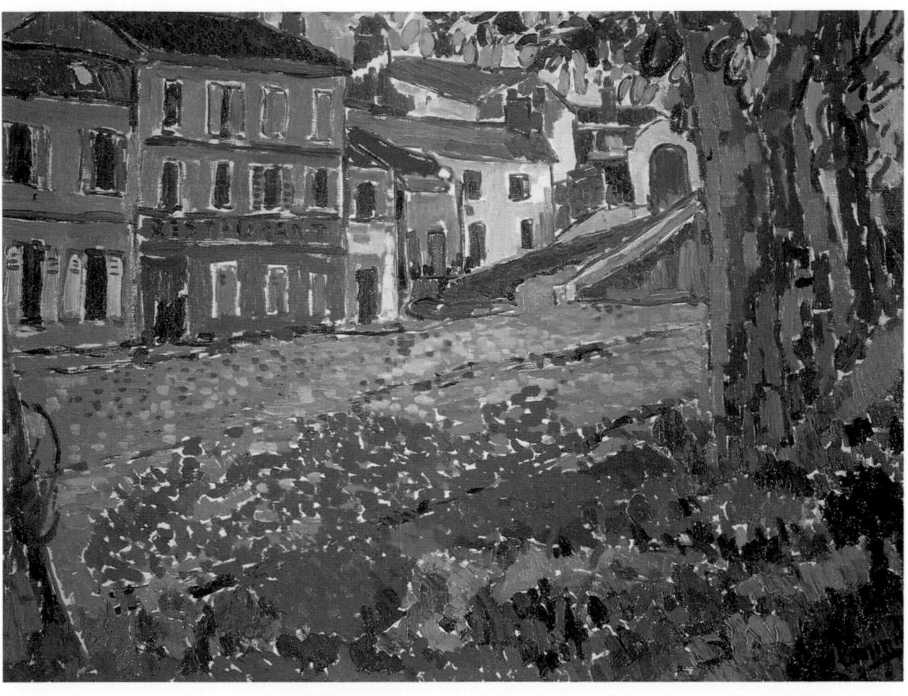

Maurice de Vlaminck,* Restaurant de la Machine à Bougival, *1905. Like Matisse and Derain, Vlaminck used the Impressionist interest in a direct response to the motif as a basis for his art in the early years of the twentieth century.

infamous comment, "Monet is only an eye, but my God, what an eye!", whereas Cézanne's supposedly more cerebral approach to his art was used to validate a certain construction of Twentieth-Century art history which saw him as the progenitor of modern art.

In 1899 Henri Matisse made a considerable financial sacrifice and bought Cézanne's *Three Bathers,* which later, in 1936, he donated to the City of Paris. "It has sustained me morally in the critical moments of my venture as an artist," he wrote.

Books such as *Cubism and Modern Art* by Robert Rosenblum have reiterated the debt Picasso and Braque owed to the Master of Aix. Young artists working in Paris in the early years of the Twentieth Century were shameless in their plundering of any element from previous artists' work that might help with the formulation of their own working practices. However, as this book suggests, seeing artists such as Monet, Cézanne and Degas principally as forerunners of Ttwentieth-Century art movements may obscure or even suppress their real achievement and hinder our appreciation of their work within its own terms.

The links between Cézanne and Pissarro in the 1870s, or that between Gauguin and Degas in the late 1880s and early 1890s, are just two examples of the relationship between the Impressionists and the so-called Post-Impressionist painters. Such terminology is rarely helpful and it is probably more useful to consider Impressionism as part of a much wider development in the visual arts that began with Romanticism. Although an equally vague term, Romanticism has at its center the visualization of the artist's personal feelings on canvas using an individualistic and flexible style of painting.

Romanticism also propagated a respect for the natural world, the liberation of color as an emotive tool and the right of the artist to choose his or her own subject matter. Such actions contributed to the breaking down of conventional art practices into something that was much more personal and resonant – the right to be "of one's age" and to find one's own audience.

Fauvism

The continuation of Impressionist ideas into the twentieth century can be seen most clearly in the work of those artists associated with Fauvism, often considered to be the first avant-garde movement of the new century.

The name "*Les Fauves*" – "wild beasts" – was, like Impressionism, a label thrust upon a group of painters by a journalist. The group included Matisse, Maurice de Vlaminck, André Derain and Raoul Dufy, who developed some of the central themes of Impressionism in a new and distinct manner.

They too painted *la vie moderne*, city scenes and landscapes, nudes by the seaside and countless river scenes. Their centers of activity were Chatou, which forty years earlier had been "the cradle of Impressionism," they were also inspired by the coasts of Normandy and the Mediterranean. They placed great faith in the primacy of instinctive and expressionistic painting, produced *en plein-air*. Even their compositions and techniques are adaptations of those used by Monet, Sisley and Renoir.

Like their forebears, *Les Fauves* painted in an extremely individual style, priding themselves on their fierce anti-intellectualism and setting themselves to see and paint afresh according to their own feelings and perceptions, without conscious recourse to the conventions established in previous generations. All these factors reveal Impressionist notions as being a fundamental feature of the development of Twentieth-Century art.

Prices and Reputations

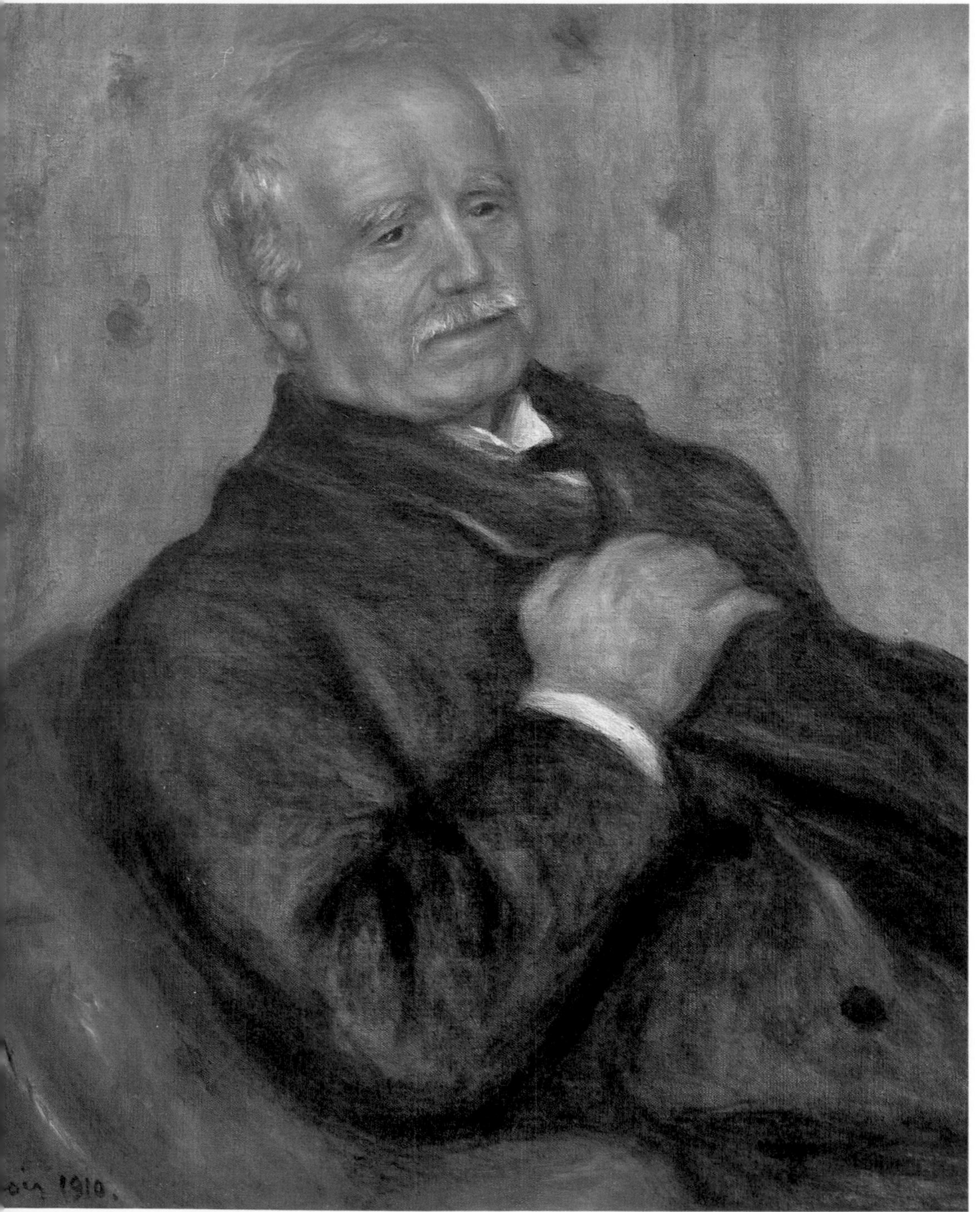

Renoir, **Portrait of Paul Durand-Ruel,** *1890. A late canvas of the dealer whose support of the Impressionists and entrepreneurial skills were so important to their survival.*

The eventual success of Impressionism exceeded anyone's wildest dreams. In 1885, Durand-Ruel, on the verge of bankruptcy and desperate to find new buyers for his Impressionist stock, exhibited first in London and then, at the invitation of James F. Sutton, in New York. At the American Art Association, Durand-Ruel displayed three hundred works, including 23 by Degas, 17 by Manet, 48 by Monet, 42 by Pissarro, 38 by Renoir, 15 by Sisley and several by Boudin and Morisot. The introduction of Impressionism to America was a slow but eventually completely effective operation.

American and German interest

Mary Cassatt, who had given financial assistance to Durand-Ruel and her fellow Impressionists, also encouraged her wealthy American friends to buy their work. This helped to establish Impressionism as a major force in America, represented in many museums and private collections. Cassatt's friend Louise Havemeyer, who was introduced by Cassatt to the work of Degas in Paris, built up, with her husband Henry Havemeyer, a sugar millionaire, a large collection of Impressionist works. On their deaths, most of these works were donated to New York City's Metropolitan Museum of Art.

German museums and collectors were also quick to begin collecting Impressionist canvases and helped define its role in the development of modern art. As the fame of the artists grew, so did the prices paid for their works: just

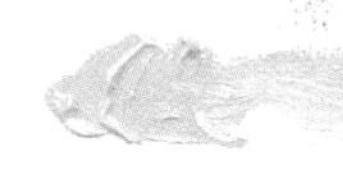

before the outbreak of the First World War Degas commented caustically on the perceptible rise in his stock, comparing his situation with "a horse which has won the Grand Prix and has been given another bag of oats."

Putting a price on art

The price of a painting is never a permanent fixture. A painting in itself has no intrinsic worth and its financial value can only correspond to the amount of money that has been exchanged at any one time in order to secure ownership. At a subsequent date, the painting may be sold again, for a greater or lesser price, depending upon market forces. These may include the status given to the work in question, its desirability and its rarity value. The physical properties of the painting will not have changed; rather the set of circumstances surrounding its sale will have altered. The principal considerations in fixing a painting's value are not its aesthetic worth alone, but also the significance it holds at the moment of sale, what the work signifies for its purchaser and the aura of privilege, taste and glamor such a work can bring a collector. Normally, the status of a high-art object is dependent upon its being seen as a unique luxury item, its proven association with a particular individual, its historical significance, its rarity, condition and, not least, its identity as a beautiful object and its value as an investment.

Traditionally, the biggest-spending collectors of the Impressionists have been the Americans who took them to their hearts and embraced the values they appeared to represent. This was particularly the case just after the Second World War, when the German-born art historian John Rewald produced in 1946 the fruit of many years' research, his magisterial *History of Impressionism*, published by the New York City's Museum of Modern Art. This was to become a cornerstone of Impressionist studies and to spawn a rolling program of exhibitions dedicated to the Impressionists that continues to this day.

Just as earlier entrepreneurs had collected Old Masters and English eighteenth-century paintings, so new generations collected the Impressionists. Encouraged by tax concessions, collectors often donated such works to local museums, thus giving America the finest public collections of French Impressionist painting in the world and the donors a modest form of immortality.

The worldwide popularity of Impressionism shows little sign of abating. In May 1986, sixteen Impressionist canvases were sold at Sothebys, New York, by the estate of Mary Cassatt's daughter-in-law. The prices for some of these canvases reached incredible proportions and Impressionist art still continues to attract high prices at auction. In the recent sale of Impressionist works of art from the Shelbourne Museum held at Sothebys in New York City, individual pieces surpassed the records for Impressionist works set in 1988–90. Degas' sculpture of the *Little Dancer Aged Fourteen Years* attracted, in November 1996, a record price of $11,882,500 (approx. £8,000,000), while his pastel of the *Young Dancer* was sold for $8,692,500 (approx. £5,500,000) – a world record for a Degas work on paper.

As the decade progressed, so such prices were sustained and even surpassed. It would seem that the world presented to us by the canvases, pastels and drawings in this book, together with the mystique associated with their creators, strikes a chord that is in particular harmony with our own times.

Despite the many dramatic changes in our way of life over the past century, the surface of Impressionist painting carries in its fabric a world with which many still identify, allowing the viewer to weave any number of narratives and dreams from the familiar and well-loved scenes that these works present.

Impressionist paintings are often sold through the large auction houses of Sothebys (seen here) and Christies.

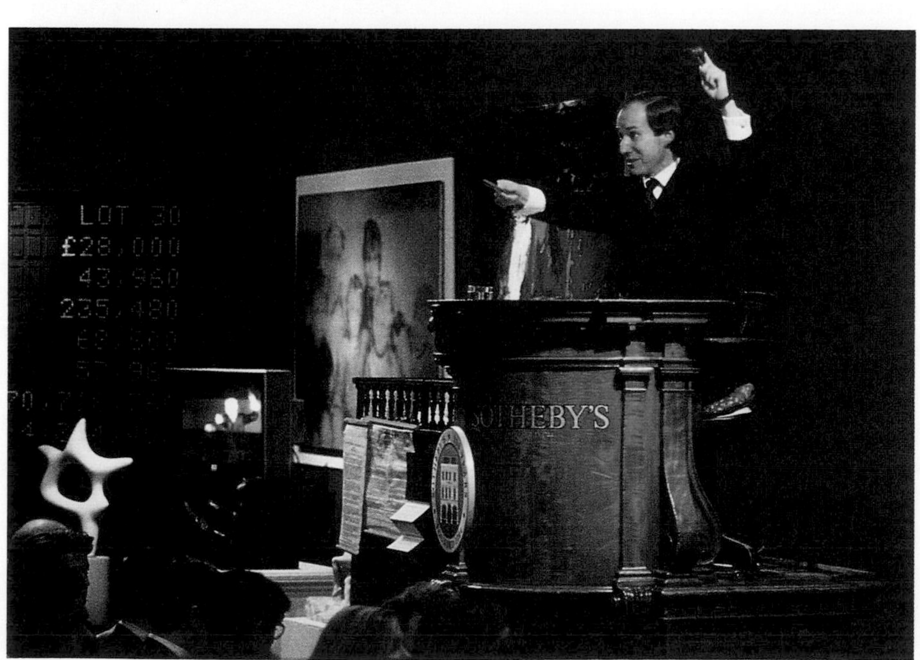

Impressionist France

This map represents the major sites visited and painted by the Impressionists. It tells us much about Impressionist practice: the centering of so much of their activity on the environs of the capital and their use of the newly established network of communication systems, principally railways, to travel to places of natural beauty. France is a country of great contrasts, and the Impressionists, especially Monet, traveled widely in search of suitable motifs for their work. It is still possible to visit these sites and to witness the landscape that so inspired them and to compare our experience of nature with that painted by Monet, Cézanne and their colleagues. When read in conjunction with the main text, the map will reveal patterns of activity and movement unique to each artist, hence the provincial roots of Cézanne and his return to the land of his birth is made evident, as is Monet's abiding love of the Normandy landscape and the surrounding countryside of the River Seine. The relatively conservative nature of Sisley's movements are also clear, as is Degas' still little-known concern for the landscape.

A trip to the sites painted by the Impressionists provides much food for thought, most of the urban and rural locations have changed beyond recognition, for example, Pointoise and Louveciennes. Others, like Giverny and Pont-Aven, have become major tourist attractions centered upon their association with those painters who spent time there. But almost always, especially when visiting natural sites such as Belle-Ile and certain of the Parisian motifs, such as Pont d'Europe and the views of the Seine, we are able to speculate on the relationship between the reality perceived by these individuals, their painted images and their own experience of these places. Finally perhaps, it will suggest that the worlds of art are not simply "there" but are constructions made by individuals at a certain time using certain techniques of representation.

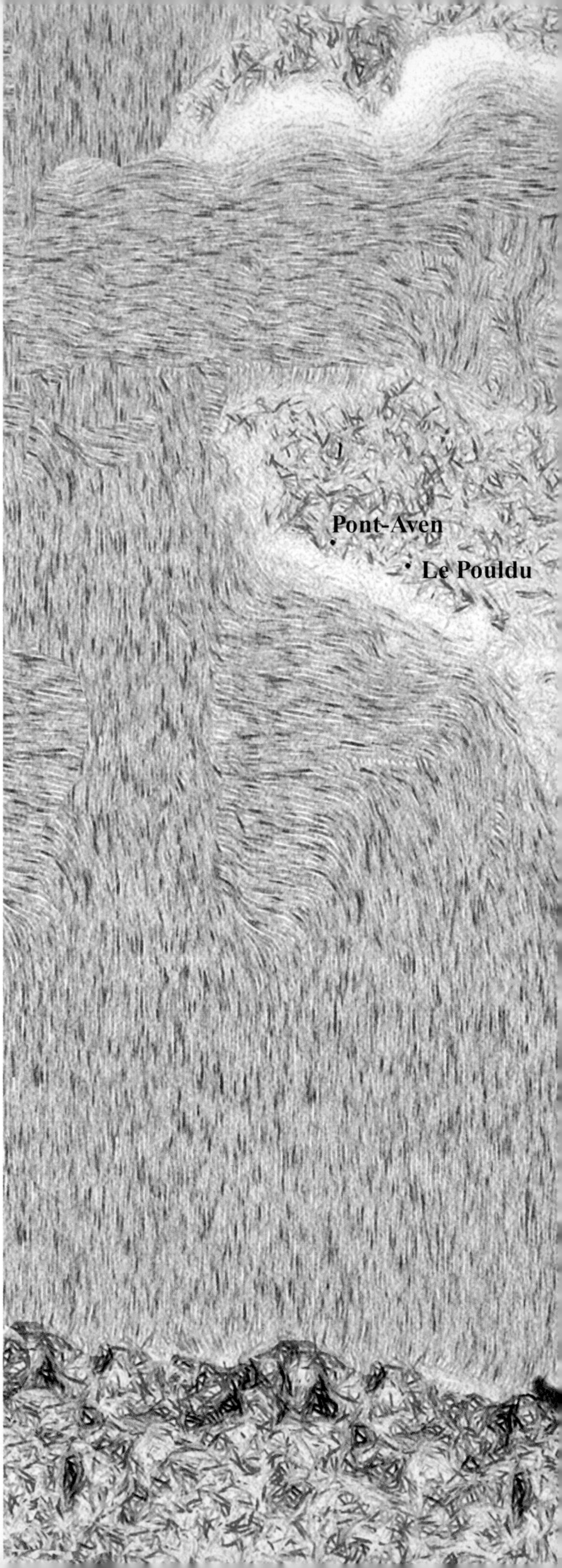

Pont-Aven

Le Pouldu

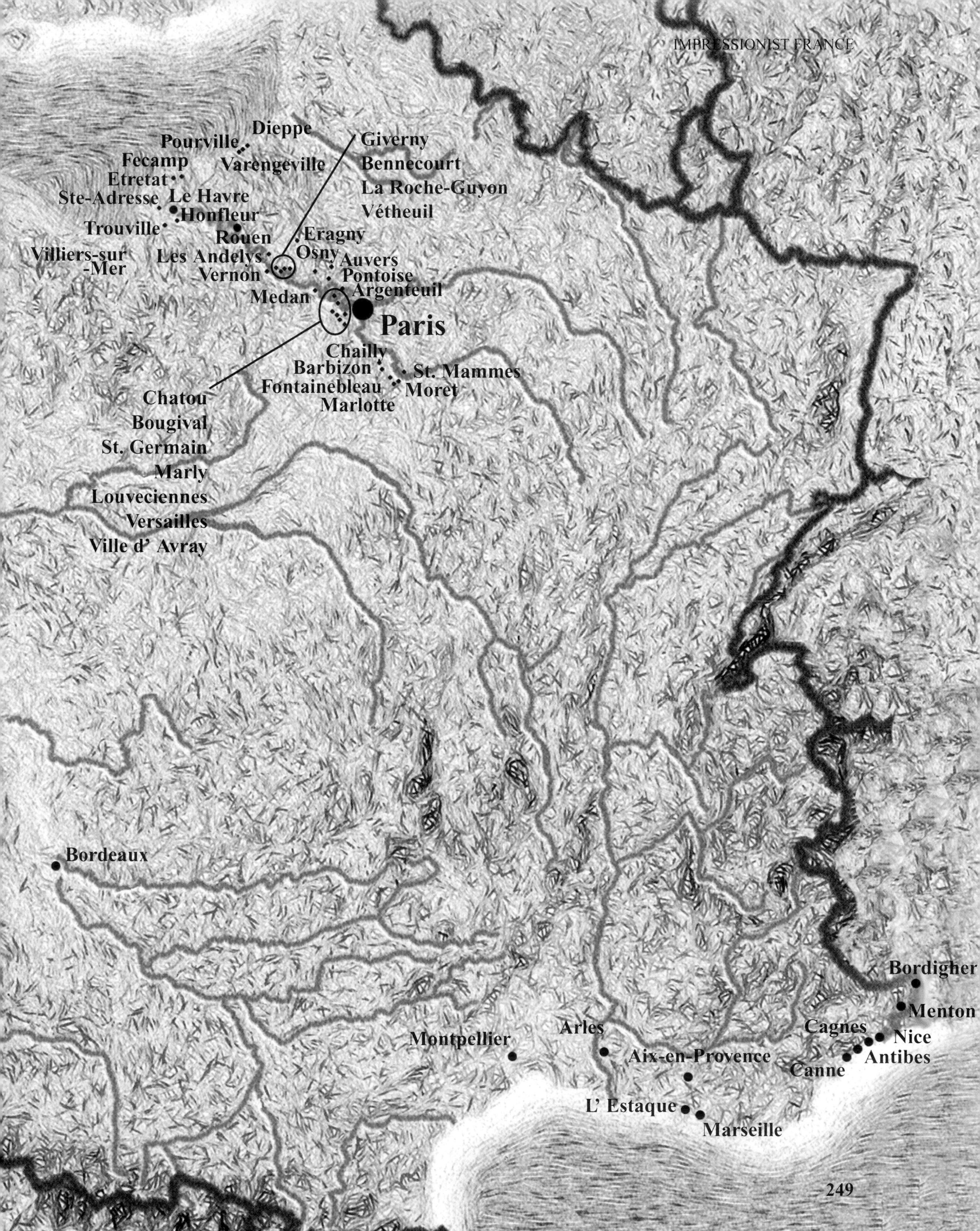
Dieppe
Pourville
Varengeville
Fecamp
Etretat
Ste-Adresse
Le Havre
Honfleur
Trouville
Rouen
Villiers-sur
-Mer
Les Andelys
Vernon
Giverny
Bennecourt
La Roche-Guyon
Vétheuil
Eragny
Osny
Auvers
Pontoise
Medan
Argenteuil
Paris
Chailly
Barbizon
St. Mammes
Fontainebleau
Moret
Marlotte
Chatou
Bougival
St. Germain
Marly
Louveciennes
Versailles
Ville d' Avray
Bordeaux
Montpellier
Arles
Aix-en-Provence
L' Estaque
Marseille
Bordigher
Menton
Cagnes
Nice
Antibes
Canne

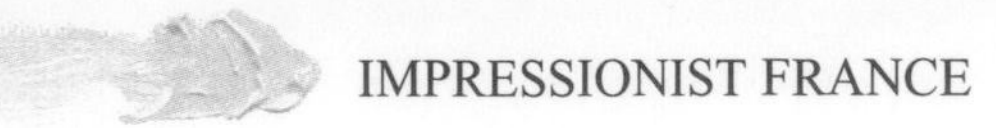

Impressionist France

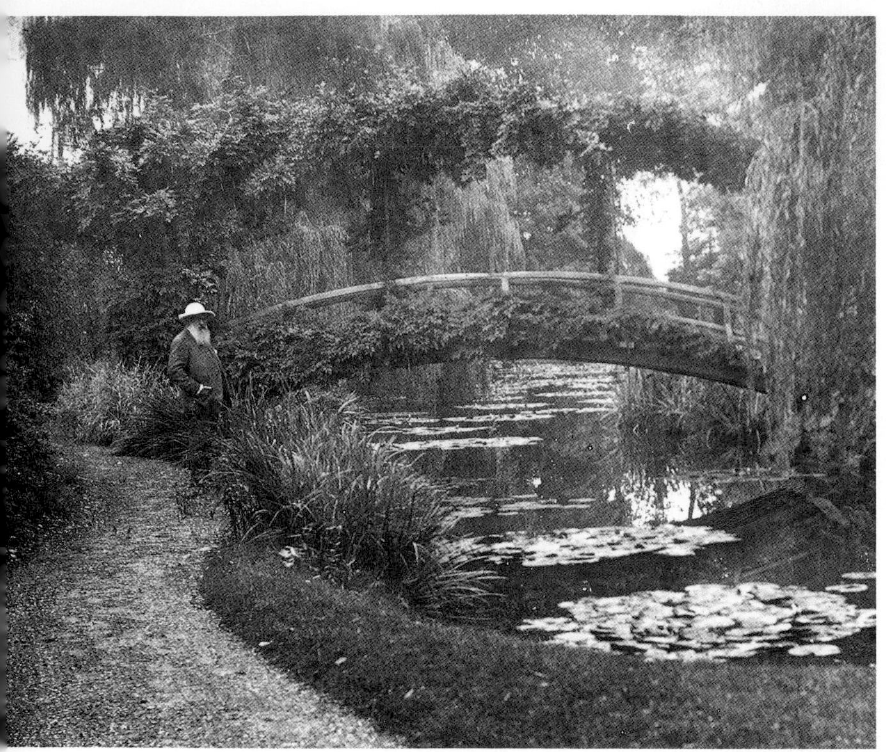

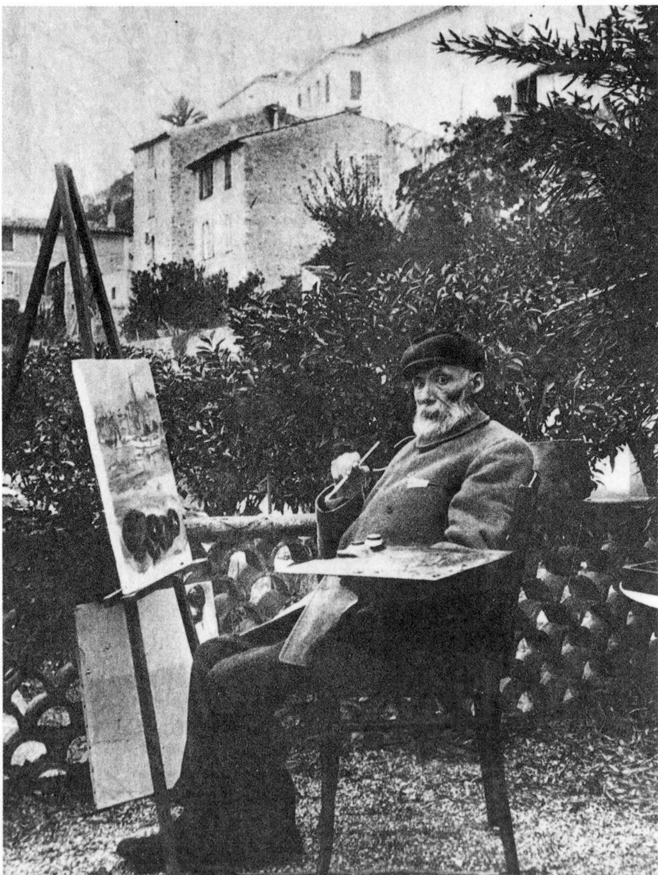

Monet

Monet traveled widely to and from Paris to the Normandy coast, but also made excursions to Belle-Ile, an island just off the coast of Brittany, the Creuse Valley, and to the south coast of France where he painted the coast and landscape around Nice and Antibes.

Renoir

Renoir essentially based himself around the Ile-de-France in the heroic early years of Impressionism, but in 1883 he made an excursion to the south of France when he painted with Monet and Cézanne and settled in Cagnes during his last years. He also, when younger, made frequent trips to the countryside of Wagremont Pas de Calais, where his friend and patron, Paul Berard had a country property.

Degas

Degas' involvement with the landscape was obscured by his own acidic references to landscape artists. However, he made early trips to the Normandy coast around Houlgate and his friends, the Valpincons had a country house in Haras-du-Pin, the horse-breeding country of Normandy. Famously, in 1888, the artist made a tour of the Burgundy region that resulted in many atmospheric and mysterious monotypes. At the end of the century he returned to the coastal region around Saint-Valéry-sur-Mer where he produced a number of large and enigmatic landscapes.

Pissarro

Based himself in the market town of Pontoise and later in the town of Eragny, which he made the center of his activities, making visits to Rouen and to the capital at various times in his career, creating images that above all bear witness to the human activities that mark the landscape.

TOP Claude Monet standing by his famous Japanese bridge in his garden at Giverny, c. 1915.

BOTTOM Pierre-Auguste Renoir, old and infirm, posing for a photograph in Cagnes in the South of France.

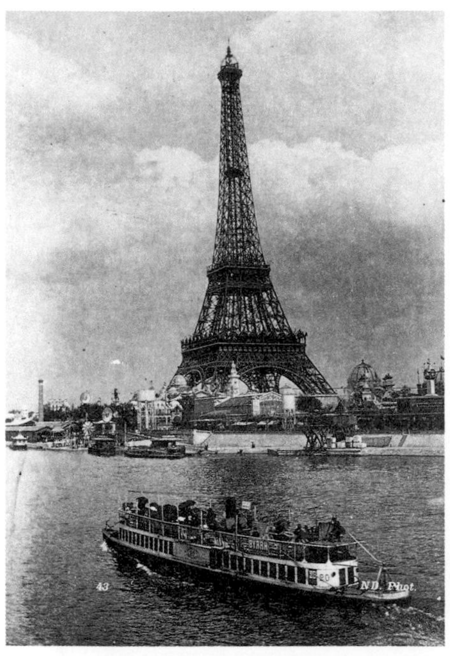

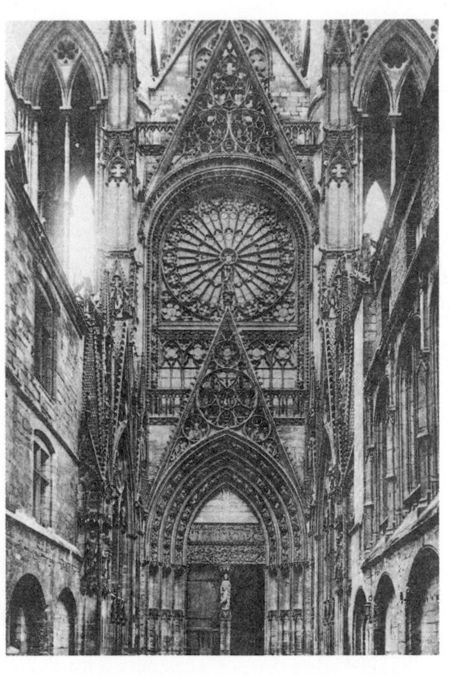

Sisley

Except for a number of visits to England, like Renoir, Sisley remained faithful to the gentle cultivated landscape of the Ile-de-France.

Morisot

Morisot, too, focused her attention on the countryside of the Ile-de-France, the gardens of her various homes and the coastal landscape of Brittany and Normandy.

Caillebotte

Like Morisot, Caillebotte's paintings reveal his love of his gardens and the rivers just outside the city. He, too, made trips to the Normandy coast.

Cézanne

Famously, Cézanne worked with Pissarro at Pontoise in the 1870s and soon after made the landscape around his home in Aix-en-Provence and the nearby coast of the Mediterrean the focus of his landscape activities.

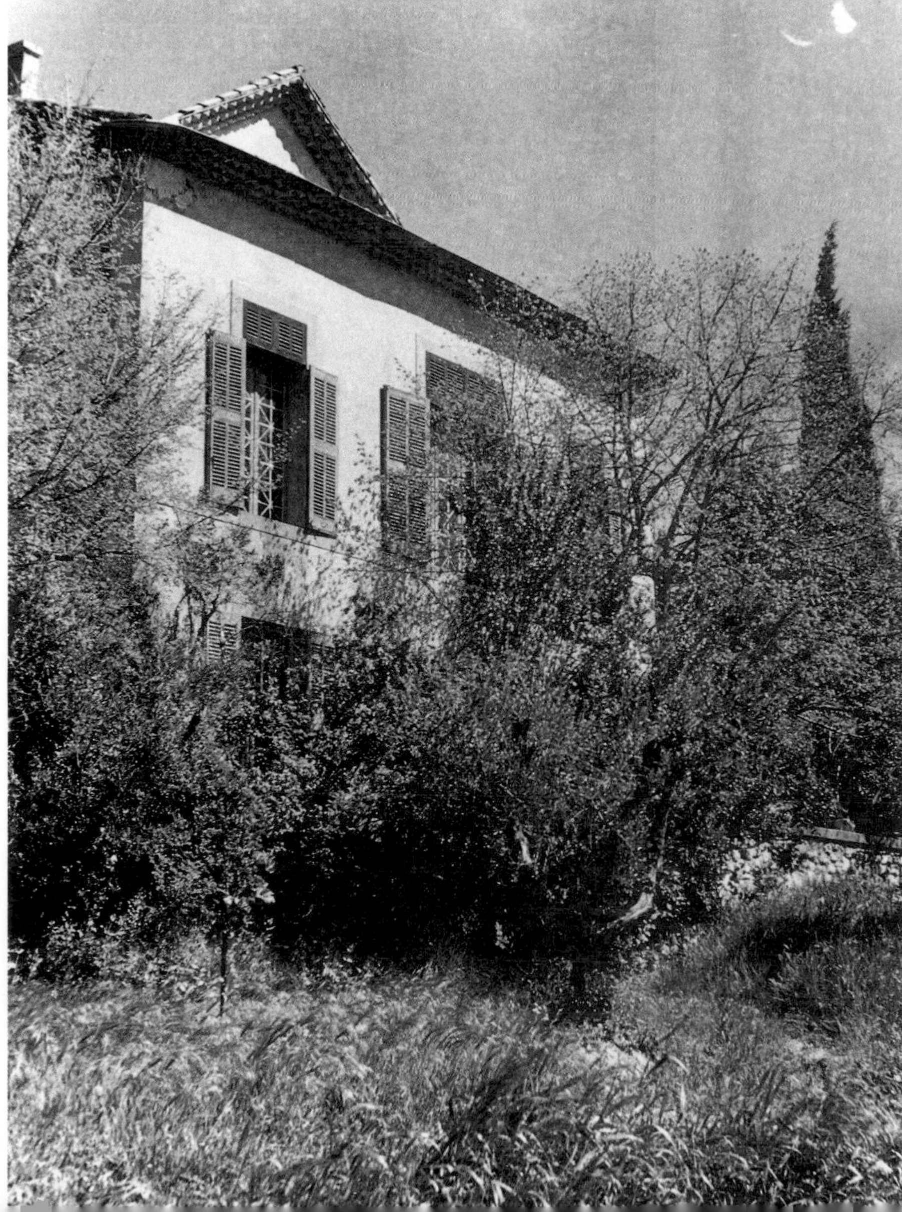

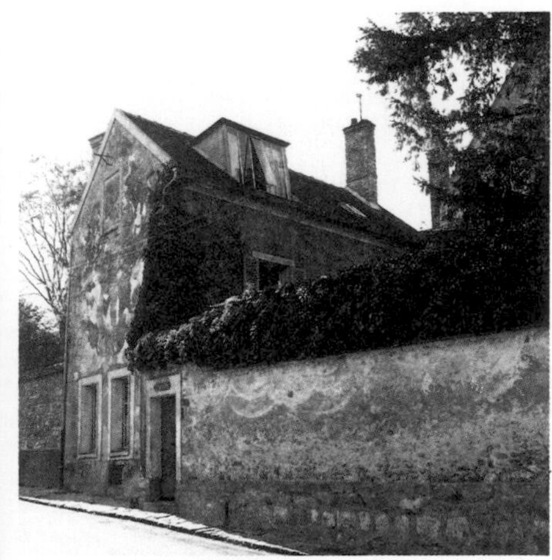

***TOP LEFT** The Eiffel Tower, which was painted by Seurat in 1889.*

***TOP RIGHT** Rouen Cathedral, 1901.*

***BOTTOM LEFT** Renoir's simple yet beautiful garden at Cagnes-sur-Mer.*

***BOTTOM RIGHT** Cézanne's famous Atelier des Lauves in Aix-en-Provence.*

Index

All page numbers in italics refer to illustrations.

Public Collections of Impressionist Art Across the World

Impressionist paintings, pastels and prints are now scattered across the surface of the globe and may be found in the art galleries of most major cities. However listed below are a number of collections which are exceptionally rich in their holdings of the art of the Impressionist era. The lack of public recognition in their home country is reflected in the relative paucity of top quality works in French public collections outside Paris.

Australia
Melbourne,
National Gallery of Art

Czech Republic,
Prague,
Náródni Galerie

France
Lyon,
Musee des Beaux-Arts
Paris,
Musee d'Orsay
Musee Marmottan
Musee de Petit Palais

Germany
Berlin,
Nationalgalerie
Frankfurt,
Stadelsches Kunstinstitut
Hamburg,
Kunsthalle
Munich,
Neue Pinakothek

Great Britain
Cambridge,
Fitzwiliam Museum
Cardiff,
National Gallery of Wales
Edinburgh,
National Gallery of Scotland
Glasgow,
Burrell Collection
London,
Courtauld Institute Galleries
National Gallery
Oxford,
The Ashmoleon Museum

Hungary
Budapest,
Szépmüvészeti Museum

Japan
Kurashiki,
Okayama, Ohara Museum of Art
Tokyo,
The National Museum of Western Art

Netherlands
Otterlo,
Rijksmuseum
Kro(umlaut)ller-Mu(umlaut)ller

Russia
Moscow,
Pushkin Museum
Saint Petersberg,
Hemitage

Scandanavia
Copenhagen,
Ny Carlsberg Glyptotek
Ordrupgaardsammlungen
Oslo,
Nasjonalgalleriet

Switzerland
Basle,
Kunstmuseum
Zurich,
E.G. Bu(a)hrle Collection
Kunsthaus

USA
Chicago,
Art Institute of Chicago
Boston,
Museum of Fine Arts
Kansas City,
The Nelson-Atkins Museum of Art
Malibu,
The J. Paul Getty Museum
New York,
Metropolitan Museum of Art
Pasadena,
Norton Simon Art Foundation
Philadelphia,
Museum of Art
Washington,
National Gallery of Art
Williamstown,
Sterling and Francine Clark Art Institute

Further Reading

Any book on this subject relies heavily upon the dedicated work of a number of inspired academics who have dedicated their professional lives to a study of the art of the Impressionists, the following list suggests some of the many texts that have informed this book. I would like to note my appreciation of their work and hope that if the reader has enjoyed this book, they will go on to read some of the following publications, which can only enrich our understanding of these fascinating works. Space precludes the inclusion of the many excellent monographs on the Impressionists.

C. Baudelaire, *The Painter of Modern Life and Other Essays* translated and edited by J. Mayne, Oxford, 1964

A Boime, *The Academy and French Painting in the Nineteenth Century*, London, 1971

D. Bomford, and others, *Art in the Making: Impressionism*, National Gallery, London, 1990

R.R. Brettell and others, *A Day in the Country: Impressionism and the French Landscape*, Los Angeles County Museum of Art, 1984

R. R. Brettell, *Pissarro and Pontoise: The Painter in a Landscape*, New Haven and London, 1990

K.S. Champa, and others, *The Rise of Landscape Painting in France: Corot to Monet*, Currier Gallery of Art, Manchester, New Hampshire, 1991

T.J. Clark, *The Painting of Modern Life: Paris in the Art of Manet and His Followers*, New York, 1984, London 1985

E. Duranty, *The New Painting*, reprinted in C. Moffett, *The New Painting*, 1986

M. Clark, *Lighting Up the Landscape: French Impressionism and Its Origins*, Scottish National Gallery of Art, Edinburgh, 1986

F. Frascina, and others, *Modernity and Painting in the Nineteenth Century*, New Haven and London, 1993

N. Green, *The Spectacle of Nature: Landscape and Bourgeois Culture in Nineteenth Century France*, Manchester, 1990

R.L. Herbert, *Impressionism: Art, Leisure and Parisian Society*, New Haven and London, 1988

J. House, and others, *Landscapes of France Impressionism and Its Rivals*, Hayward Gallery, London, 1996

J. House, *Monet: Nature into Art*, New Haven and London, 1986

M. Howard, *Impressionists by Themselves*, London, 1994

R. Kendall, *Degas Beyond Impressionism*, London and Chicago, 1996

R. Kendall and G. Pollock (eds.) *Dealing with Degas: Representation of Women and the Politics of Vison*, London, 1992

C. Moffett and others, *The New Painting: Impressionism 1874-1886*, San Francisco, Fine Arts Museum, 1986

L. Nochlin, *Realism*, London, 1971

T. Reff, *Manet and Modern Paris*, Washington, 1982

Sue Welsh Reed and Barbara Stern Shapiro, *Edgar Degas: The Painter as Printmaker*, Boston Museum of Fine Arts, 1984

J. Rewald, *The History of Impressionism*, 4th edition, New York and London, 1973 [1946]

P.H. Tucker, *Monet at Argenteuil*, New Haven and London, 1982

T. Zeldin, *France 1848-1945: Politics and Anger*, Oxford, 1979

Acknowledgments

This has been so fast and furious that there's hardly been any time to consult anyone, but thanks go to: my wife Ghislaine for her essential help, timely advice and infinite patience, Richard Kendall, Sarah Larter, Lorna Ainger and the team at Carlton Books.

Picture Credits
The publishers would like to thank the following sources for their kind permission to reproduce the pictures in this book:

AKG Photo, London: 13, 17, 19, 22, 23, 24, 29, 30, 34, 36, 41, 71, 73, 83, 91, 114, 127, 132, 140, 141, 142(detail), 143, 150, 157, 158, 160, 166-7, 182, 184, 186, 187, 196, 202, 206tl, 207tr, 208, 209, 214, 222, 223, 224, 225, 231, 237, 240, 246, 251tl,tc/Ashmolean Museum, Oxford 112/Boston Museum of Fine Arts. Anon gift in memory of Mr & Mrs Edwin S Webster 3/Christies 244/Columbus Museum of Art, Ohio 82/Musee D'Orsay 61, 146, 191/Musee Fabre 62(detail), 63/Erich Lessing 2, 4, 8, 15, 18, 27, 35, 37, 39, 40, 53, 100, 107, 109, 125, 130(detail), 131, 134, 170, 171, 173, 182, 198, 205; Art Institute of Chicago 94; Musee d'Orsay 42, 43, 47, 80, 87, 97, 120, 214, 245; Musee Marmottan 55, 78, 95/NY Carlsberg Glyptothek 121/National Gallery of Art, Washington, Gift of Eugene & Agnes E.Meyer 190/Philadelphia 72/Pushkin Museum 236/Oskar Reinhart Coll. 46/State Hermitage, St.Petersburg 96/Magyar Szepmveszeyti, Budapest 70/Tate Gallery 65, 66.
Photograph ©1997. The Art Institute of Chicago. All Rights Reserved/1922.427, Mr.&Mrs. Potter Palmer Collection 56
Ashmolean Museum, Oxford 200, 210, 219.
Bridgeman Art Library, London/Agnew & Sons Ltd. 31/Art Institute of Chicago 69/Buhrle Collection, Zurich 116/Burrell Collection, Glasgow 102, 139/Christie's Images 3-4/Courtauld Institute Galleries, University of London 129, 194/Dallas Museum of Fine Arts, Texas 99/Fitzwilliam Museum, University of Cambridge 123/Giraudon 1, 9, 28, 85, 156, 177, 178-9/Index 172/Lauros-Giraudon 168, 169(detail), 199, 220/Louvre, Paris, France 103/Musee d'Orsay, Paris, France 74, 92/Museum of Art, Rhode Island School of Design, USA 68/National Gallery, London 44, 45(detail), 122, 126, 137, 234/National Gallery of Scotland, Edinburgh 203/National Museum of Wales, Cardiff 154/National Portrait Gallery, Smithsonian Institution 163/Neue Pinakothek, Munich 174-5/Philadelphia Museum of Art, Pennsylvania 238(detail), 239, 241/Phillips Collection, Washington DC 10/Private Collection 228/Pushkin Museum, Moscow 49, 164, 165(detail), 176/Victoria &Albert Museum, London 138.
The British Museum 204.
Jean-Loup Charmet 93.
Christie's Images 81, 98.
Corbis/National Gallery 90.
Mary Evans Picture Library 33 t,b.
Fitzwilliam Museum, Cambridge 20, 212(detail), 213.
Fabbri 145, 230.
Foundation EG Burhle Collection, Zurich 104.
Hulton-Getty 64.
Leicestershire County Council 232.
Mansell Time Inc. Katz 11, 32.
The Metropolitan Museum of Art, New York/Purchased with special contributions and purchase funds given or bequethed by friends of the Museum, 1967 ©1989 (67.241) 57/Bequest of Sam A.Lewisohn, 1951. ©1990 (51.112.6) 106/Wolfe Fund, 1907. Catherine Lorillard Wolfe Collection ©1992 (07.122) 155/Bequest of Mrs H.O. Havemeyer, 1929. The H.O. Havemeyer Collection ©1989 (29.100.112) 58; ©1980 (29.100.107) 192(detail), 193.
Musee Fabre, Montpellier 60.
Museum of Fine Arts, Boston 110/Fanny P. Mason Fund in memory of Alice Thevin 188.
National Gallery, London 14, 21, 44, 45 (detail), 88.
National Gallery of Art, Washington © Board of Trustees/Auguste Renoir *Pont Neuf, Paris* Ailsa Mellon Bruce Collection 118-9/Mary Cassatt *Girl Arranging Her Hair* 162,*The Loge* 218; Berthe Morisot*In the Dining Room* 152, 153(detail); Auguste Renoir*Diana* 50 Chester Dale Collection/Claude Monet, Study for*The Luncheon on the Grass* 48, Berthe Morisot*Hanging the Laundry out to Dry* 151 Collection Mr.&Mrs.Paul Mellon/James Whistler,*The White Girl (Symphony in White, No.1)* Harris Whittemore Collection /Richard Carafelli 38.
NationalMuseum, SKM, Stockholm 51, 59.
Nelson-Atkins Museum of Art, Kansas City, Missouri/Purchase: acquired through the generosity of an anonymous donor 104/Purchase: Nelson Trust 158/Purchase: The Kenneth A. and Helen F.Spencer Foundation Acquisition Fund 77.
NY Carlsberg Glyptotek/Ole Haupt 147.
The Norton Simon Foundation, Pasadena, CA 54.
Private Collection (on extended loan to the National Gallery, London) 148
©Photo RMN 124, 144/Arnaudet 180(detail), 181/Jean 161/Herve Lewandowski 12/J.Schormans 215tr
Roger-Viollet 86, 108, 110, 233, 250t,b, 251bl,br.
Courtesy of Sotheby's, London 247.
Tate Gallery, London 217, 242, 243.
The Toledo Museum of Art, Toledo, Ohio; Camille Pissarro*The Roofs of Old Rouen, Grey Weather,* 1896, purchased with funds from the Libbey Endowment, Gift of Edward Drummond Libbey 226.
Wadsworth Atheneum, Hartford, CT. 7.
Reproduced by permission of the trustees of the Wallace Collection 26.

Every effort has been made to acknowledge correctly and contact the source and/copyright holder of each picture, and Carlton Books Limited apologises for any unintentional errors or omissions which will be corrected in future editions of this book.